Exam 70-216

MCSE

Windows® 2000
Network Infrastructure

TRAINING GUIDE

New
Riders

Dave Bixler, MCSE
Larry Chambers, MCSE, MCSD
Joseph Phillips, MCSE, MCT

MCSE Training Guide (70-216): I&A Microsoft Windows® 2000 Network Infrastructure

International Standard Book Number: 0-7357-0966-1

Library of Congress Catalog Card Number: 00-100506

Printed in the United States of America

First Printing: August, 2000

04 03 02 01   7 6 5

Interpretation of the printing code: The rightmost double-digit number is the year of the book's printing; the rightmost single-digit number is the number of the book's printing. For example, the printing code 00-1 shows that the first printing of the book occurred in 2000.

Trademarks

Warning and Disclaimer

PUBLISHER
David Dwyer

ASSOCIATE PUBLISHER
Al Valvano

EXECUTIVE EDITOR
Stephanie Wall

ACQUISITIONS EDITOR
Stacey Beheler

MANAGING EDITORS
Gina Brown
Sarah Kearns

DEVELOPMENT EDITOR
Barb Terry

PROJECT EDITOR
Caroline Wise

PRODUCT MARKETING MANAGER
Stephanie Layton

MANAGER OF PUBLICITY
Susan Nixon

COPY EDITOR
Barbara Hacha

TECHNICAL REVIEWERS
Marc Savage
Walter Glenn

SOFTWARE DEVELOPMENT SPECIALIST
Michael Hunter

INDEXER
Tim Wright

PROOFREADER/COMPOSITOR
SCAN Communications Group, Inc.

MANUFACTURING COORDINATOR
Jim Conway

COVER DESIGNER
Aren Howell

Contents at a Glance

Introduction *1*

Part I   Exam Preparation

1 Installing, Configuring, Managing, Monitoring, and Troubleshooting
   DNS in a Windows 2000 Network Infrastructure 13

2 Installing, Configuring, Managing, Monitoring, and Troubleshooting
   DHCP in a Windows 2000 Network Infrastructure 77

3 Configuring, Managing, Monitoring, and Troubleshooting Remote Access
   in a Windows 2000 Network Infrastructure 129

4 Installing, Configuring, Managing, Monitoring, and Troubleshooting
   Network Protocols in a Windows 2000 Network Infrastructure 175

5 Installing, Configuring, Managing, Monitoring, and Troubleshooting
   WINS in a Windows 2000 Network Infrastructure 241

6 Installing, Configuring, Managing, Monitoring, and Troubleshooting
   IP Routing in a Windows 2000 Network Infrastructure 283

7 Installing, Configuring, and Troubleshooting Network
   Address Translation (NAT) 353

8 Installing, Configuring, Managing, Monitoring, and
   Troubleshooting Certificate Services 379

Part II   Final Review

Fast Facts 429

Study and Exam Prep Tips 451

Practice Exam 465

Part III   Appendixes

A Glossary 487

B Overview of Certification 503

C What's on the CD-ROM 515

D Using the *ExamGear, Training Guide Edition* Software 517

Table of Contents

PART I: Exam Preparation

1 Installing, Configuring, Managing, Monitoring, and Troubleshooting DNS in a Windows 2000 Network Infrastructure   **13**

Introducing the Domain Name Service (DNS) 16
   History of DNS 16
   Installing, Configuring, and Troubleshooting DNS 28
   Installing the DNS Server Service 29
   Configuring a Root Name Server 33
   Configuring Zones 34
   Configuring a Caching-Only Server 42
   Configuring a DNS Client Computer 44
   Configuring Zones for Dynamic Updates 47
   Testing the DNS Server Service 49
   Implementing a Delegated Zone for DNS 54
   Manually Creating DNS Resource Records 55

Managing and Monitoring DNS 56
   Setting Aging/Scavenging for All Zones 57
   Scavenging Stale Resource Records Manually 58
   Setting Properties 58
   Exercises 67
   Review Questions 68
   Exam Questions 68
   Answers to Review Questions 74
   Answers to Exam Questions 75

2 Installing, Configuring, Managing, Monitoring, and Troubleshooting DHCP in a Windows 2000 Network Infrastructure   **77**

Understanding Dynamic Host Configuration Protocol 79
   The DHCP Protocol 80
   The BOOTP Protocol 82

Installing, Configuring, and Troubleshooting DHCP 82
   Installing the DHCP Server Service 83
   Understanding DHCP Scopes 88
   Understanding DHCP Superscopes 88
   Understanding Multicasting and Multicast Scopes 89
   Creating a Scope on Your DHCP Server 91
   Authorizing a DHCP Server in Active Directory 97
   Creating a Superscope 99
   Creating a Multicast Superscope 100
   Configuring DHCP for DNS Integration 102

Managing and Monitoring DHCP 104
   Exercises 117
   Review Questions 118
   Exam Questions 119
   Answers to Review Questions 124
   Answers to Exam Questions 125

3 Configuring, Managing, Monitoring, and Troubleshooting Remote Access in a Windows 2000 Network Infrastructure   129

Configuring and Troubleshooting Remote Access 132
   Understanding Remote Access Protocols 134
   Configuring Inbound Connections 135
   Creating a Remote Access Policy 139
   Configuring a Remote Access Profile 143
   Configuring a Virtual Private Network (VPN) 147
   Configuring Multilink Connections 151
   Configuring Routing and Remote Access for DHCP Integration 151

Managing and Monitoring Remote Access 152

Configuring Remote Access Security 156
   Configuring Authentication Protocols 158
   Configuring Encryption Protocols 159
   Exercises 164
   Review Questions 164
   Exam Questions 165
   Answers to Review Questions 170
   Answers to Exam Questions 172

4 Installing, Configuring, Managing, Monitoring, and Troubleshooting Network Protocols in a Windows 2000 Network Infrastructure   175

Introduction 178

Installing, Configuring, and Troubleshooting Network Protocols 178
    Understanding TCP/IP 178
    Installing TCP/IP 187
    Configuring TCP/IP 189
    Installing the NWLink Protocol 192
    Configuring NWLink 193
    Configuring Network Bindings 194

Working with TCP/IP Packet Filters 196

Configuring and Troubleshooting Network Protocol Security 199
    Network Data Security 199
    Security Hosts 200
    Kerberos V5 Authentication 201
    VPNs 202

Managing and Monitoring Traffic 203
    Understanding Network Traffic and the Network Monitor 203
    Installing Network Monitor 204
    Installing the Network Monitor Driver 206
    Using Network Monitor to Capture Data 206
    Interpreting Captured Data 209

Configuring and Troubleshooting IPSec 210
    Understanding the Architecture and Components of IPSec 212
    Enabling IPSec Through a Policy 216

Customizing IPSec 220

Managing and Monitoring IPSec 226
    Exercises 231
    Review Questions 232
    Exam Questions 233
    Answers to Review Questions 238
    Answers to Exam Questions 239

5 Installing, Configuring, Managing, Monitoring, and Troubleshooting WINS in a Windows 2000 Network Infrastructure   **241**

Installing, Configuring, and Troubleshooting WINS 244
   Introduction to WINS 244
   Installing WINS 247
   Configuring WINS 250
   Configuring WINS Replication 254

Troubleshooting WINS Issues 259

Configuring NetBIOS Name Resolution 261

Managing and Monitoring WINS 265
   Exercises 273
   Review Questions 274
   Exam Questions 274
   Answers to Review Questions 278
   Answers to Exam Questions 279

6 Installing, Configuring, Managing, Monitoring, and Troubleshooting IP Routing in a Windows 2000 Network Infrastructure   **283**

Installing, Configuring, and Troubleshooting IP Routing Protocols 286
   Introduction to IP Routing 286
   Host Routing 287
   Router Routing 289
   The Routing Process 292
   Routing Technology 295
   Routing Networks 300

Setting Up Actual Routing Protocols 302
   Working with RIP 303
   RIP Routing Metric 308
   OSPF 309
   Demand-Dial Routing 321
   Types of Demand-Dial Connections 325
   Demand-Dial Security 328

Managing and Monitoring IP Routing 331
   Using the ROUTE Command to Configure Static Routes ... 331
   Using Network Monitor 333
   Managing and Monitoring IP Routing Protocols 335
   Exercises 342

Review Questions 344
Exam Questions 344
Answers to Review Questions 348
Answers to Exam Questions 349

7 Installing, Configuring, and Troubleshooting Network Address Translation (NAT)   353

Installing Internet Connection Sharing 356
Installing NAT 361
Configuring NAT Properties 363
Configuring NAT Interfaces 366
Exercises 372
Review Questions 372
Exam Questions 373
Answers to Review Questions 376
Answers to Exam Questions 377

8 Installing, Configuring, Managing, Monitoring, and Troubleshooting Certificate Services   379

Introduction 382
Looking at Public Key Infrastructure (PKI) 382
Planning to Install a CA 386
Renewing CAs 388
Installing the CA 389
Installing and Configuring an Enterprise Subordinate CA 391
Installing and Configuring a Standalone Root CA 394
Upgrading Certificate Server 1.0 394
Renewing Certificates for CAs 397
Issuing and Revoking Certificates 399
Using the Certificates Snap-In 399
Using the Windows 2000 Certificate Services Web Page 400
Processing Requests 401
Checking on Pending Requests 401
Mapping Certificates to User Accounts 403
Viewing an Issued Certificate 405
Revoking Issued Certificates 406
Using the EFS Recovery Keys 408
Exporting EFS Keys 409
Restoring EFS Keys 411

Exercises 415
Review Questions 416
Exam Questions 416
Answers to Review Questions 423
Answers to Exam Questions 424

PART II: Final Review

Fast Facts   429

Installing, Configuring, Managing, Monitoring, and Troubleshooting
    DNS in a Windows 2000 Network Infrastructure 429

Installing, Configuring, Managing, Monitoring, and Troubleshooting
    DHCP in a Windows 2000 Network Infrastructure 433

Configuring, Managing, Monitoring, and Troubleshooting Remote Access
    in a Windows 2000 Network Infrastructure 436

Installing, Configuring, Managing, Monitoring, and Troubleshooting
    Network Protocols in a Windows 2000 Network Infrastructure 438

Installing, Configuring, Managing, Monitoring, and Troubleshooting
    WINS in a Windows 2000 Network Infrastructure 440

Installing, Configuring, Managing, Monitoring, and Troubleshooting
    IP Routing in a Windows 2000 Network Infrastructure 442

Installing, Configuring, and Troubleshooting Network Address
    Translation (NAT) 445

Installing, Configuring, Managing, Monitoring, and Troubleshooting
    Certificate Services 446

Study and Exam Prep Tips   451

Learning Styles 451

Study Tips 452
    Study Strategies 452
    Pre-Testing Yourself 453

Exam Prep Tips 453
    The MCP Exam 453
    Exam Format 454
    Question Types 456
    Putting It All Together 461

Final Considerations 464

Practice Exam   **465**

Answers to Exam Questions 479

PART III: Appendixes

A Glossary   **487**

B Overview of the Certification Process   **503**

Types of Certification 503

Certification Requirements 504

How to Become a Microsoft Certified Professional 504

How to Become a Microsoft Certified Professional+Internet 505

How to Become a Microsoft Certified Professional+Site Building 505

How to Become a Microsoft Certified Database Administrator 505

How to Become a Microsoft Certified Systems Engineer 506

How to Become a Microsoft Certified Systems Engineer+Internet 509

How to Become a Microsoft Certified Solution Developer 509

Becoming a Microsoft Certified Trainer 512

C What's on the CD-ROM   **515**

ExamGear, Training Guide Edition 515

Exclusive Electronic Version of Text 515

Copyright Information and Disclaimer 516

D Using the *ExamGear, Training Guide Edition* Software   **517**

Exam Simulation 517

Question Quality 517

Interface Design 517

Study Tools 517

Effective Learning Environment 518

Automatic Progress Tracking 518

How *ExamGear, Training Guide Edition* Works 518

Interface 518

Database 519

Installing and Registering *ExamGear, Training Guide Edition* 519

Requirements 519

Installing *ExamGear, Training Guide Edition* 519
Registering *ExamGear, Training Guide Edition* 520
Removing *ExamGear, Training Guide Edition* from Your Computer 520
Using *ExamGear, Training Guide Edition* 521
General Description of How the Software Works 521
Menu Options 522
Starting a Study Mode Session 522
Starting Practice Exams and Adaptive Exams 524
What Is an Adaptive Exam? 525
Why Do Vendors Use Adaptive Exams? 525
Studying for Adaptive Exams 525
ExamGear's Adaptive Exam 526
Question Types and How to Answer Them 526
Simulations 531
Hot Spot Questions 531
Mark Question and Time Remaining 532
Item Review 533
Examination Score Report Screen 536
Checking the Web Site 537
Obtaining Updates 537
The Catalog Web Site for Updates 537
Product Updates Dialog Box 537
Contacting New Riders Publishing 538
Technical Support 538
Customer Service 538
Product Updates 538
Product Suggestions and Comments 539
License Agreement 539
License 539
Software and Documentation 539
License Term and Charges 539
Title 539
Updates 540
Limited Warranty and Disclaimer 540
Limitation of Liability 540
Miscellaneous 541
U.S. Government Restricted Rights 541

Index   **543**

About the Authors

Dave Bixler (MCSE, MCNE, PSE, CCSE) is the Technology Services Manager for one of the largest systems integrators in the United States. He has been working in the industry for the past 13 years, working on network designs, server implementations, and network management. Lately, Dave has focused on Internet technologies, including DNS and Web servers, information security, firewalls, and his company's Windows 2000 migration. Dave has also worked on a number of Macmillan books as an author, a technical editor, or a book reviewer. Dave's industry certifications include Microsoft's MCPS and MCSE, as well as Novell's CNE for NetWare versions 3.x, 4.x and IntranetWare, ECNE, and MCNE. Dave also has IBM's PSE, Check Point Software's CCSE, and 3Com's 3 Wizard Master certifications. (He takes plenty of certification tests!)

Dave lives in Cincinnati, Ohio with his very patient wife Sarah, sons Marty and Nicholas, and two Keeshonds, Zeus and Arcus.

Larry Chambers (MCSE, MCSD, CNE) is a Network Consultant for a major systems integration firm. He has worked for the past 12 years in the computer industry, with a focus on Microsoft Technologies for the preceding 5 years. Larry lives with his wife, Denise, daughter, Courtney, and newborn son, Dylan, in Winnipeg, Manitoba, Canada.

Emmett Dulaney (MCSE, MCP+I, i-Net+, A+, Network+, CAN) is the author of over a dozen books on certification. The former Certification Corner columnist for *Windows NT Systems Magazine*, he is the cofounder of D S Technical Solutions and an instructor for Indiana University/Purdue University of Fort Wayne, Indiana.

Dale Liu (MCSE+I, MCT, MSS) is the Senior Trainer and Consultant for VanAusdall & Farrar, as well as an Adjunct Professor at Indiana Business College, teaching the Microsoft MCSE track. Dale takes a hands-on approach to teaching. Combining over 20 years of experience in programming, networking, and troubleshooting, he gives students a real-world look at technology. In addition to his Microsoft certifications, Dale has a Masters Degree in Information Technologies and also holds other various industry certifications. He combines a depth of knowledge with his sense of humor to provide an active and exciting learning experience.

Joseph Phillips (MCSE, MCT, CLP) has been a computer trainer and consultant since 1993. In tandem with his consulting practice, he has contributed to books on Lotus Notes, Windows 2000, Windows NT, Windows 98, network security, and other computer-related topics. You can visit him at http://www.josephphillips.com or in Indianapolis, Indiana.

About the Technical Reviewers

Walter Glenn (MCSE, MCT)

Walter is an independent networking consultant and freelance writer. He is experienced with most Microsoft-based operating systems, including Windows 2000 Server and Professional, Windows NT 4.0 Server and Workstation, Windows 98, and Windows 95. He also has expertise with Microsoft Exchange Server 5.5 and Exchange 2000 Server, Internet Information Server, TCP/IP-based networking, and the Microsoft Office suite. Walter lives and works in Huntsville, Alabama.

Marc Savage (MCSE, CNE, MCT, A+)

Marc is the Director of Education for PBSC Computer Training Centers—one of the biggest training centers in Canada. Marc is an experienced systems/network engineer with consulting and teaching experience in large and small client/server networks. He has also spent many years in the industry training others and developing course material.

Dedication

Dave Bixler

I would like to dedicate this book to my patient wife, Sarah, and my sons, Marty and Nick, who have been asking me to come play for far too long.

Acknowledgments

No project of this type gets done without the help and support of a lot of people.

I would like to say a heartfelt thanks to Joe Phillips, Larry Chambers, Jim Cooper, Emmett Dulaney, and Dale Liu for their outstanding contributions to the content of this book. Gentlemen, I would not have been able to get it done without you.

Thanks to Marc Savage, contributing author and Technical Editor. Marc is the man who keeps me honest project after project. Thanks, Marc . . . once again, I couldn't have done it without your expertise!

Thanks to Stacey Beheler, Acquisitions Editor. Thanks for your patience as we worked on this book. We battled illness and all sorts of other roadblocks to get this completed! I couldn't have done it without your support.

Thanks to Walter Glenn, Technical Editor. This was our first project together, Walter, but I couldn't have done it without your assistance.

Thanks to Barbara Terry, Development Editor. How you guys take these Word documents and turn them into books never ceases to amaze me. Thanks for all your help!

Also, thanks to my sisters, Susan, Laura, and Amy, whose names have now graced four of my books. You're the best sisters I ever had.

Finally, another huge thanks to my wife and sons. Sarah, Marty, and Nicholas, thanks for putting up with yet another book! I'm going to take a break now . . . honest!

—Dave Bixler

Thank you to my wife, Denise, daughter, Courtney, and baby son, Dylan, for letting me take time to do what I enjoy.

—Larry Chambers

Tell Us What You Think!

As the reader of this book, *you* are our most important critic and commentator. We value your opinion and want to know what we're doing right, what we could do better, what areas you'd like to see us publish in, and any other words of wisdom you're willing to pass our way.

As the Executive Editor for the Certification team at New Riders Publishing, I welcome your comments. You can fax, email, or write me directly to let me know what you did or didn't like about this book—as well as what we can do to make our books stronger.

Please note that I cannot help you with technical problems related to the topic of this book, and that due to the high volume of mail I receive, I might not be able to reply to every message.

When you write, please be sure to include this book's title, author, and ISBN number (found on the back cover of the book above the bar code), as well as your name and phone or fax number. I will carefully review your comments and share them with the author and editors who worked on the book.

Fax: 317-581-4663

Email: stephanie.wall@newriders.com

Mail: Stephanie Wall
      Executive Editor
      Certification
      New Riders Publishing
      201 West 103rd Street
      Indianapolis, IN 46290 USA

How to Use This Book

New Riders Publishing has made an effort in its _Training Guide_ series to make the information as accessible as possible for the purposes of learning the certification material. Here, you have an opportunity to view the many instructional features that have been incorporated into the books to achieve that goal.

CHAPTER OPENER

Each chapter begins with a set of features designed to allow you to maximize study time for that material.

List of Objectives: Each chapter begins with a list of the objectives as stated by Microsoft.

OBJECTIVES

One of the most important services for successfully implementing Active Directory Services is DHCP. In this chapter we will examine all the facets of running the DHCP service in a Windows 2000 network.

Microsoft defines the "Installing, Configuring, Managing, Monitoring, and Troubleshooting DHCP in a Windows 2000 Network Infrastructure" objectives as the following:

Install, configure, and troubleshoot DHCP.

- Install the DHCP Server service.
- Create and manage DHCP scopes, superscopes, and multicast scopes.
- Configure DHCP for DNS integration.
- Authorize a DHCP server in Active Directory.

▶ One of the first tasks when getting ready to deploy a production Windows 2000 network environment is to ensure that DHCP is installed and configured correctly. DHCP is tightly integrated with Dynamic DNS and Active Directory Services. This objective expects you to be able to install DHCP and configure it for use in an Active Directory Services network.

Manage and monitor DHCP.

▶ The final objective requires that you be able to maintain your DHCP server after it is installed, configured and authorized. The ability to manage DHCP services and monitor the DHCP server's activities is critical to the ongoing administration of a Windows 2000 network.

C H A P T E R *2*

Installing, Configuring, Managing, Monitoring, and Troubleshooting DHCP in a Windows 2000 Network Infrastructure

Objective Explanations: Immediately following each objective is an explanation of it, providing context that defines it more meaningfully in relation to the exam. Because Microsoft can sometimes be vague in its objectives list, the objective explanations are designed to clarify any vagueness by relying on the authors' test-taking experience.

Chapter Outline: Learning always gets a boost when you can see both the forest and the trees. To give you a visual image of how the topics in a chapter fit together, you will find a chapter outline at the beginning of each chapter. You will also be able to use this for easy reference when looking for a particular topic.

OUTLINE

**Installing, Configuring, and
Troubleshooting IP Routing Protocols**   XX

    Introduction to IP Routing   XX
    Host Routing   XX
    Router Routing   XX
    The Routing Process   XX
    Routing Technology   XX
      Distance-Vector Routing   XX
      Link-State Routing   XX
    Routing Networks   XX

**Installing, Configuring, and
Troubleshooting IP Routing Protocols**   XX

    Working with RIP   XX
      RIP Version 1   XX
      RIP Version 2   XX
      RIP Updates   XX
    RIP Routing Metric   XX
    Open Shortest Path First (OSPF)   XX
      Routing Hierarchies   XX
      Areas   XX
      OSPF Backbone   XX

      Area Routing   XX
      Autonomous System Routing   XX
      OSPF Operation   XX
    Demand-Dial Routing   XX
    Types of Demand-Dial Connections   XX
      Routing Considerations   XX
    Demand-Dial Security   XX

Managing and Monitoring IP Routing   XX

    Using the ROUTE Command to
      Configure Static Routes   XX
    Using Network Monitor
    Managing and Monitoring IP Routing
      Protocols   XX
      Routing and Remote Access
        Services Operation   XX
      Troubleshooting RIP Environments   XX
      Troubleshooting OSPF Environments   XX

Chapter Summary   XX

Apply Your Knowledge   XX

Study Strategies: Each topic presents its own learning challenge. To support you through this, New Riders has included strategies for how to best approach studying in order to retain the material in the chapter, particularly as it is addressed on the exam.

STUDY STRATEGIES

► You can expect a number of questions related to routing protocols and their operation. Many of these will be in scenario format, in which the implementation of a particular protocol will be based on a network topology design. Therefore, you need to have a firm understanding of the way the protocol works in small, medium, and large network designs and to understand where each protocol best fits within these network scenarios. After you have a solid understanding of the theory presented here, you should try to gain some practical experience by using Windows 2000 Advanced Server as much as possible. Implement the various protocols to see how they work, and how they are configured within a network environment.

► You should also expect scenario questions on implementing and configuring a demand-dial routing environment. Expect to have answers for where a demand-dial routing solution is best used and the special considerations that are required when implementing the various routing protocols over this type of configuration.

EXAM TIP

Know the Components and Purpose of ICS Be sure you are familiar with the components of the ICS service and remember it is geared to the small office. Microsoft has been known to give you a scenario (size of network, type of connection, and so on) and ask you to choose the correct application.

Exam Tip: Exam Tips appear in the margins to provide specific exam-related advice. Such tips may address what material is covered (or not covered) on the exam, how it is covered, mnemonic devices, or particular quirks of that exam.

INSTRUCTIONAL FEATURES WITHIN THE CHAPTER

These books include a large amount and different kinds of information. The many different elements are designed to help you identify information by its purpose and importance to the exam and also to provide you with varied ways to learn the material. You will be able to determine how much attention to devote to certain elements, depending on what your goals are. By becoming familiar with the different presentations of information, you will know what information will be important to you as a test-taker and which information will be important to you as a practitioner.

Chapter 2 INSTALLING, CONFIGURING, MANAGING, MONITORING AND TROUBLESHOOTING DHCP IN A WINDOWS 2000 NETWORK INFRASTRUCTURE   7

can receive DHCP information from any DHCP server that Windows NT worked with. However, if you want to take advantage of the features of Active Directory Services and migrate away from the legacy WINS architecture, you will need the Windows 2000 DHCP service.

The first thing we need to discuss when working with the Windows 2000 DHCP service is how to install the service.

Installing the DHCP Server Service

Install the DHCP Server service.

One of the features that is going to make Windows 2000 very popular with system administrators is its extensive use of configuration wizards. Most of the server configuration tasks have been bundled into the Configure Your Server application, allowing you to start a wizard for the most common configuration activities. We will try to highlight this new feature of Windows 2000 as much as possible because it is a major enhancement to the operating system, and could prove to be fertile ground for exam questions.

When you install Windows 2000 Server, you have the ability to install DHCP as one of the optional services. For the purposes of the exam, we will be looking at installing DHCP on a server that is already installed but that does not have DHCP loaded.

DHCP is installed as a Windows 2000 Server networking service. To install the DHCP Server service, follow these steps:

WARNING

Don't Overextend Your Partitions and Wraps It is not necessary to create an extended partition on a disk; primary partitions might be all that you need. However, if you do create one, remember that you can never have more than one extended partition on a physical disk.

NOTE

A DHCP Server Cannot Also Be a DHCP Client If you currently have your server configured as a DHCP client, the DHCP installation will prompt you to enter a static IP address for your server.

STEP BY STEP

2.1 Using the Configure Your Server Application to Install the DHCP Server Service

1. Choose Start, Programs, Administrative Tools, and Configure Your Server to go to the Configure Your Server application. You can see this utility in Figure 2.1.

continues

Objective Coverage Text: In the text before an exam objective is specifically addressed, you will notice the objective is listed to help call your attention to that particular material.

Warning: In using sophisticated information technology, there is always potential for mistakes or even catastrophes that can occur through improper application of the technology. Warnings appear in the margins to alert you to such potential problems.

Note: Notes appear in the margins and contain various kinds of useful information, such as tips on the technology or administrative practices, historical background on terms and technologies, or side commentary on industry issues.

Figure: To improve readability, the figures have been placed in the margins wherever possible so they do not interrupt the main flow of text.

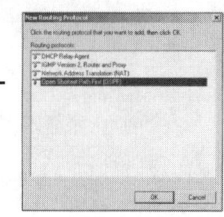

STEP BY STEP

6.6 Installing and Configuring OSPF on Windows 2000

1. Choose Start, Programs, Administrative Tools, and then click Routing and Remote Access. The Routing and Remote Access console opens.

2. Expand the console tree, and under IP Routing right-click General. From the context menu, select New Routing Protocol. The New Routing Protocol dialog box opens (see Figure 6.20).

3. Select Open Shortest Path First and click OK to install it. It now appears under IP Routing in the Routing and Remote Access console (see Figure 6.21).

FIGURE 6.20
Select the routing protocol you need to install.

Step by Step: Step by Steps are hands-on tutorial instructions that walk you through particular task or function relevant to the exam objectives.

In the Field Sidebar: These more extensive discussions cover material that perhaps is not as directly relevant to the exam, but which is useful as reference material or in everyday practice. In the Field may also provide useful background or contextual information necessary for understanding the larger topic under consideration.

Chapter 2 INSTALLING, CONFIGURING, MANAGING, MONITORING AND   13
TROUBLESHOOTING DHCP IN A WINDOWS 2000
NETWORK INFRASTRUCTURE

IN THE FIELD

WHEN TO USE SUPERNETTING

Visualize a large company that occupies five floors in a building. On each of these floors are 300 to 500 users, all on the same physical network. Traditional network design would have a routed backbone running between the floors, and each floor would be its own IP network. But there's one problem. You have too many users on these floors to be handled by a single Class C subnet. What are the alternatives?

You could place a router somewhere on each of the floors to further segment the network. This is an expensive and support-intensive solution and is generally considered to be impractical.

You could address using Class B addresses. However, that is generally very wasteful of IP addresses.

The last thing you could do is place multiple IP networks on the single routed segment. In other words, create a supernet. This capability is supported by any of the routers on the market today, including the OS-based routing services in Windows 2000, Novell NetWare and any of the UNIX flavors. So when you think about a supernet, think about a floor in a building with too many users for 254 IP addresses.

Review Break: Crucial information is summarized at various points in the book in lists or tables. You might come across a Review Break that is there just to wrap up one objective and reinforce the key points before you shift your focus to the next section.

Understanding Multicasting and Multicast Scopes

REVIEW BREAK

Before we discuss the multicast scopes, we need to look at what multicasting is. Multicasting is the act of transmitting a message to a select group of recipients. This is in contrast to the concept of a broadcast in which traffic is sent to every host on the network, or a unicast in which the connection is a one-to-one relationship, and there is only one recipient of the data.

Here's an example, using an email message. If you send an email message to your manager, it is an example of a unicast message. If you send an email message to every user on the system, it is a

CASE STUDIES

Case Studies are presented throughout the book to provide you with another, more conceptual opportunity to apply the knowledge you are developing. They also reflect the "real-world" experiences of the authors in ways that prepare you not only for the exam but for actual network administration as well. In each Case Study, you will find similar elements: a description of a Scenario, the Essence of the Case, and an extended Analysis section.

CASE STUDY: SMALL OFFICE WITH A DEDICATED CONNECTION TO THE INTERNET

ESSENCE OF THE CASE

The following points summarize the essence of the case study:

▶ There must be a dedicated connection to the Internet.

▶ The network may expand in the future, and this must be done with a minimum of configuration.

▶ Only one segment is on the network.

▶ The connection must be online at all times.

SCENARIO

You are the administrator of a small office. You have been asked by the company owner to configure a connection to the Internet. You would like to configure a dedicated connection that will allow you to assign all the workstations a TCP/IP address that will identify it on the Internet. You currently have only one segment on your company network with approximately 50 workstations. Your connection must be online at all times, and you would like to minimize the management that is necessary on your part. You believe that your network will grow within the next year, and you would like to ensure that this can be done with a minimum of configuration.

continues

Essence of the Case: A bulleted list of the key problems or issues that need to be addressed in the Scenario.

Scenario: A few paragraphs describing a situation that professional practitioners in the field might face. A Scenario will deal with an issue relating to the objectives covered in the chapter, and it includes the kinds of details that make a difference.

CASE STUDY: SMALL OFFICE WITH A DEDICATED CONNECTION TO THE INTERNET

continued

ANALYSIS

When configuring a small office network, you can connect the office to the Internet in several ways. For instance, a small office network can be connected to the Internet via a demand-dial connection, or a router can be configured with Network Address Translation. However, based on the requirements of the scenario, the most appropriate solution is to implement a dedicated connection. Because the network manager would like to minimize the configuration that is required, a configuration based on either static routes or RIP should be provided. OSPF in this type of scenario is much too complex a solution. To determine whether to use static routes or RIP you must look closely at the requirements. Because the network may expand in the future and this must be done with a minimum of configuration, it is best to pursue a dynamic routing protocol that can adapt to a change in the network topology. This would imply RIP over static routing.

Analysis: This is a lengthy description of the best way to handle the problems listed in the Essence of the Case. In this section, you might find a table summarizing the solutions, a worded example, or both.

EXTENSIVE REVIEW AND SELF-TEST OPTIONS

At the end of each chapter, along with some summary elements, you will find a section called "Apply Your Knowledge" that gives you several different methods with which to test your understanding of the material and review what you have learned.

CHAPTER SUMMARY

KEY TERMS

- Routing Information Protocol (RIP)
- Open Shortest Path First (OSPF)
- distance vector
- link state
- split horizon
- split horizon with poison reverse
- adjacency
- area

This chapter focused on routing. It covered the underlying fundamentals of routing and covered such topics as distance-vector routing and link-state routing. How a host determines whether it should deliver a packet directly to the end host or via a router was touched on. The chapter also discussed some of the problems of each type of routing and solutions to those problems, such as split horizon, split horizon with poison reverse, and triggered updates.

The next topic discussed was the Routing Information Protocol (RIP). Both version 1 and version 2 of RIP were discussed, along with specific features such as silent RIP. Features of the RIP protocol were related back to the fundamental discussion of routing covered earlier in the chapter, such as distance vector and split horizon. A

Key Terms: A list of key terms appears at the end of each chapter. These are terms that you should be sure you know and are comfortable defining and understanding when you go in to take the exam.

Chapter Summary: Before the Apply Your Knowledge section, you will find a chapter summary that wraps up the chapter and reviews what you should have learned.

APPLY YOUR KNOWLEDGE

Exercises

2.1   Installing Internet Connection Sharing

In the following exercise, you will install ICS to share a dial-up Internet connection.

Estimated time: 15 minutes

1. Open the Network and Dial-up Connections window.

2. Right-click the dial-up connection and select Properties from the context menu. Select the Sharing tab of the Connection Properties dialog box.

3. Select the Enable Internet Connection Sharing for This Connection option.

4. Click OK to close the dialog box and enable ICS.

2.2   Adding a Custom Application

The following exercise shows you how to add the Internet Relay Chat (IRC) application to a server configured to use NAT.

Estimated time: 15 minutes

1. Open the Routing and Remote Access console.

2. Expand the tree under the local server icon. Right-click the Network Address Translation (NAT) icon and select Properties.

3. Click the Translation tab of the Network Address Translation (NAT) Properties dialog box.

4. Click Applications.

5. Click Add. In the Internet Connection Sharing Application dialog box, enter the following:

    . Name of Application: Internet Relay Chat

    . Remote Server port number: 6667

    . TCP/UDP: TCP

    . Incoming Response Ports (TCP): 6668

6. Click OK to add the application.

7. Click OK to close the Properties window, and click OK again to close the Routing and Remote Access console.

Review Questions

1. You are the network administrator for a small company that wants to connect to the Internet for the first time. The company has 12 employees and you don't have a lot of experience with Windows 2000 or routing. What should you do to ensure that you connect to the Internet successfully?

2. The network administrator for a small company has grown to 50 users, and management wants to upgrade to a DSL connection. You have configured several dozen custom applications, both inbound and outbound, as part of ICS. What should you do to accommodate the DSL connections and the applications you've configured?

3. You are the Windows 2000 administrator for Fly Away Travel. Your boss has asked you to explain the difference between the NAT protocol and the ICS services. Other than manual versus automated features, what does ICS support that NAT does not?

Exercises: These activities provide an opportunity for you to master specific hands-on tasks. Our goal is to increase your proficiency with the product or technology. You must be able to conduct these tasks in order to pass the exam.

Review Questions: These open-ended, short-answer questions allow you to quickly assess your comprehension of what you just read in the chapter. Instead of asking you to choose from a list of options, these questions require you to state the correct answers in your own words. Although you will not experience these kinds of questions on the exam, these questions will indeed test your level of comprehension of key concepts.

APPLY YOUR KNOWLEDGE

Exam Questions

1. You are the network administrator for Wild Widgets Inc. You are training a new employee on the use of the DHCP service in Windows 2000 Server. She asks you how the client computer requests and receives an address from the server.

   A. The client computer broadcasts a DHCPDiscover message. The DHCP server offers an IP address. The client computer accepts the address and uses it to communicate on the network.

   B. The client computer broadcasts a DHCPDiscover message. The DHCP server offers an IP address. The client computer accepts the address and sends a request to use that address back to the DHCP server. The client computer uses the address to communicate on the network.

   C. The client computer broadcasts a DHCPDiscover message. The DHCP server offers an IP address. The client computer accepts the address and sends a request to use that address back to the DHCP server. The DHCP server acknowledges the request and grants the client computer a lease to use the address. The client computer uses the address to connect to the network.

   D. The client computer broadcasts a DHCPDiscover message. The DHCP server offers an IP address. The client computer accepts the address and sends a request to use

Answers to Review Questions

1. To successfully implement DHCP in a multinetted environment, you should consider using a superscope to ease the management of the scopes for each of the multinetted networks. For more information, see the section "Installing, Configuring, and Troubleshooting DHCP."

2. In the Performance utility, check the Declines/Sec counter for the DHCP object. The number of DHCPDecline messages received per second by the DHCP server from client computers can be used to see if the DHCP client computer has declined the IP address issued by the server. You will see this number rise when client computers start having address conflict issues. This could indicate a network issue, computers with static addresses that are also part of a scope, or potentially a "rogue" DHCP server on the network. For more information, see the section "Managing and Monitoring DHCP."

3. Check the length of the DHCP lease. If the lease has been set to a very short duration, client computers would need to request addresses frequently. For more information, see the section "Installing, Configuring, and Troubleshooting DHCP."

4. There are either a lot of DHCP requests occurring during peak hours, or the Conflict Detection Attempts parameter is set too high. If this is enabled, Windows 2000 DHCP Server will issue an address, and it will check to see if any IP address conflicts exist. This can put a lot of additional overhead on the server and drive up the DHCP Conflict Check Queue Length. For more information, see the section "Managing and Monitoring DHCP."

Answers and Explanations: For each of the Review and Exam questions, you will find thorough explanations located at the end of the section.

Exam Questions: These questions reflect the kinds of multiple-choice questions that appear on the Microsoft exams. Use them to become familiar with the exam question formats and to help you determine what you know and what you need to review or study more.

Suggested Readings and Resources

1. Droms, Ralph, and Ted Lemon. *The DHCP Handbook.* Indianapolis, IN: Macmillan Technical Publishing, 1999.

2. Siyan, Karanjit S. *Windows NT TCP/IP.* Indianapolis, IN: New Riders Publishing, 1998.

3. Kercheval, Berry. *DHCP: A Guide to Dynamic TCP/IP Network Configuration.* Upper Saddle River, NJ: Prentice Hall Computer Books, 1998.

Suggested Readings and Resources: The very last element in every chapter is a list of additional resources you can use if you want to go above and beyond certification-level material or if you need to spend more time on a particular subject that you are having trouble understanding.

Introduction

MCSE Training Guide: Windows 2000 Network Infrastructure is designed for advanced end users, network engineers, and systems administrators who are seeking to pass Exam 70-216 in pursuit of a Microsoft Windows certification. Passing the Implementing and Administering a Microsoft Windows 2000 Network Infrastructure exam qualifies you as a Microsoft Certified Professional (MCP) and counts as core credit toward the Microsoft Certified Systems Engineer (MCSE) certification. This exam measures your ability to install, manage, monitor, configure, and troubleshoot Domain Name Service (DNS), Dynamic Host Configuration Protocol (DHCP), remote access, network protocols, IP routing, and Windows Internet Naming Service (WINS) in a Windows 2000 network infrastructure. In addition, the test measures the skills required to manage, monitor, and troubleshoot Network Address Translation (NAT) and Certificate Services (CS).

WHO SHOULD READ THIS BOOK

This book is designed to help you meet your certification goals by preparing you for the Implementing and Administering a Microsoft Windows 2000 Network Infrastructure Exam (70-216). In a Windows 2000 network, the ability to install, support, and troubleshoot the various networking components and services included with Windows 2000 is critical to the success of an administrator. Windows 2000 tightly integrates services such as DHCP and DNS, and requires that they be configured correctly to function. This exam touches on all the major networking components critical to a successful Windows 2000 implementation. Although volumes of information are available on the

history, theory, and underlying applications, this book does not cover these portions of the services in detail. The purpose of this book is to acquaint you with the Windows 2000 implementations of these network services and to prepare you to take the exam.

Recognizing that a great deal of information exists on these topics that this book will not be able to cover, each chapter in this book contains a section called "Suggested Readings and Resources" that provides you with what you need to fill in the blanks. So although you may not be a virtual private networking (VPN) expert by the time you complete this book, you'll know how to configure Windows 2000's VPN service and ensure that IP Security (IPSec) is working. You'll also have a recommendation for some additional reading if you need to understand exactly what the makeup of an Authentication Header (AH) packet looks like. (Chapter 3, "Configuring, Managing, Monitoring, and Troubleshooting Remote Access in a Windows 2000 Network Infrastructure," covers IPSec.)

One of my favorite questions with any of the Microsoft certification tests is, "Do I need to take a class to pass this test?" Although the information you need to pass the exam is in this book and Microsoft has approved it as study material, one thing that is difficult for any book to provide is hands-on experience with the product. If you can set up an environment that enables you to perform the exercises outlined in this book, you're going to be in good shape. You'll be in especially good shape if you have the opportunity to work with Windows 2000 in a production environment. To pass the exam, you do not need to take a class in addition to buying this book. However, depending on your personal study habits or learning style, you may benefit from taking a class in conjunction with studying from this book.

Microsoft assumes that the typical candidate for this exam will have a minimum of one year's experience implementing and administering network operating systems in medium to very large network environments.

How This Book Helps You

This book takes you on a self-guided tour of all the areas covered by the Implementing and Administering a Microsoft Windows 2000 Network Infrastructure exam and teaches you the specific skills you need to achieve your MCSE certification. You'll also find helpful hints, tips, real-world examples, and exercises, as well as references to additional study materials. Specifically, this book is set up to help you in the following ways:

◆ **Organization**. The book is organized by individual exam objectives. Every objective you need to know for the Implementing and Administering a Microsoft Windows 2000 Network Infrastructure exam is covered in this book. We have attempted to present the objectives in an ordering that is as close as possible to that listed by Microsoft. However, we have not hesitated to reorganize where needed to make the material as easy as possible for you to learn. We have also attempted to make the information accessible in the following ways:

  • The full list of exam topics and objectives is included in this introduction.

  • Each chapter begins with a list of the objectives to be covered.

  • Each chapter also begins with an outline that provides you with an overview of the material and the page numbers where particular topics can be found.

  • The objectives are repeated where the material most directly relevant to it is covered (unless the whole chapter addresses a single objective).

  • The CD-ROM included with this book contains, in PDF format, a complete listing of the test objectives and where they are covered within the book.

◆ **Instructional Features**. This book has been designed to provide you with multiple ways to learn and reinforce the exam material. Following are some of the helpful methods:

  • *Objective Explanations*. As mentioned previously, each chapter begins with a list of the objectives covered in the chapter. In addition, immediately following each objective is an explanation in a context that defines it more meaningfully.

  • *Study Strategies*. The beginning of the chapter also includes strategies for approaching the studying and retaining of the material in the chapter, particularly as it is addressed on the exam.

  • *Exam Tips*. Exam tips appear in the margin to provide specific exam-related advice. Such tips may address what material is covered (or not covered) on the exam, how it is covered, mnemonic devices, or particular quirks of that exam.

  • *Review Breaks and Summaries*. Crucial information is summarized at various points in the book in lists or tables. Each chapter ends with a summary as well.

  • *Key Terms*. A list of key terms appears at the end of each chapter.

  • *Notes*. These appear in the margin and contain various kinds of useful information, such as tips on technology or administrative practices, historical background on terms and technologies, or side commentary on industry issues.

- *Warnings*. When you're using sophisticated information technology, the potential for mistakes always exists; catastrophes can even occur because of improper application of the technology. Warnings appear in the margin to alert you to such potential problems.

- *In the Field*. These more extensive discussions cover material that may not be directly relevant to the exam but that is useful as reference material or in everyday practice. In the Field may also provide useful background or contextual information necessary for understanding the larger topic under consideration.

- *Case Studies*. Each chapter concludes with a case study. The cases are meant to help you understand the practical applications of the information covered in the chapter.

- *Step by Steps*. These are hands-on tutorial instructions that walk you through a particular task or function relevant to the exam objectives.

- *Exercises*. Found at the end of the chapters in the "Apply Your Knowledge" section, exercises are performance-based opportunities for you to learn and assess your knowledge.

◆ **Extensive practice test options.** The book provides numerous opportunities for you to assess your knowledge and practice for the exam. The practice options include the following:

- *Review Questions*. These open-ended questions appear in the "Apply Your Knowledge" section at the end of each chapter. They enable you to quickly assess your comprehension of what you just read in the chapter. Answers to the questions are provided later in the section.

- *Exam Questions*. These questions also appear in the "Apply Your Knowledge" section. They reflect the kinds of multiple-choice questions that appear on the Microsoft exams. Use them to practice for the exam and to help you determine what you know and what you need to review or study further. Answers and explanations for them are provided.

◆ **Final Review**. This part of the book provides you with three valuable tools for preparing for the exam.

- *Fast Facts*. This condensed version of the information contained in the book is extremely useful for last-minute review.

- *Study and Exam Prep Tips*. Read this section early on to help you develop study strategies. It also provides you with valuable exam-day tips and information on exam/question formats such as adaptive tests and case study-based questions.

- *Practice Exam*. A practice test is included. Questions are written in styles similar to those used on the actual exam. Use it to assess your readiness for the real thing.

The book includes several other features, such as a section titled "Suggested Readings and Resources" at the end of each chapter that directs you toward further information that could aid you in your exam preparation or your actual work. Valuable appendixes are included as well, such as a glossary (Appendix A), an overview of the Microsoft certification program (Appendix B), a description of what is on the CD-ROM (Appendix C), and an overview of the *ExamGear* Software (Appendix D).

For more information about the exam or the certification process, contact Microsoft at:

Microsoft Education: 800-636-7544

Internet: `ftp://ftp.microsoft.com/Services/MSEdCert`

World Wide Web: `http://www.microsoft.com/train_cert`

CompuServe Forum: `GO MSEDCERT`

WHAT THE IMPLEMENTING AND ADMINISTERING A MICROSOFT WINDOWS 2000 NETWORK INFRASTRUCTURE EXAM (70-216) COVERS

The Implementing and Administering a Microsoft Windows 2000 Network Infrastructure Exam (70-216) covers the Windows 2000 networking topics represented by the conceptual groupings or units of the test objectives. The objectives reflect job skills in the following areas:

- Installing, configuring, managing, monitoring, and troubleshooting DNS in a Windows 2000 network infrastructure

- Installing, configuring, managing, monitoring, and troubleshooting DHCP in a Windows 2000 network infrastructure

- Configuring, managing, monitoring, and troubleshooting remote access in a Windows 2000 network infrastructure

- Installing, configuring, managing, monitoring, and troubleshooting network protocols in a Windows 2000 network infrastructure

- Installing, configuring, managing, monitoring, and troubleshooting WINS in a Windows 2000 network infrastructure

- Installing, configuring, managing, monitoring, and troubleshooting IP routing in a Windows 2000 network infrastructure

- Installing, configuring, and troubleshooting Network Address Translation (NAT)

- Installing, configuring, managing, monitoring, and troubleshooting Certificate Services

Before taking the exam, you should be proficient in the job skills represented by the following units, objectives, and subobjectives.

Installing, Configuring, Managing, Monitoring, and Troubleshooting DNS in a Windows 2000 Network Infrastructure

The DNS section is designed to make sure that you understand the basic concepts of installing, configuring and using DNS, as well as the Windows 2000 DNS implementation. The knowledge needed here also requires the understanding of general networking concepts such as name resolution. The objectives are as follows:

Install, configure, and troubleshoot DNS.

- Install the DNS Server service.

- Configure a root name server.

- Configure zones.

- Configure a caching-only server.

- Configure a DNS client.

- Configure zones for dynamic updates.

- Test the DNS Server service.

- Implement a delegated zone for DNS.

- Manually create DNS resource records.

Manage and monitor DNS.

Installing, Configuring, Managing, Monitoring, and Troubleshooting DHCP in a Windows 2000 Network Infrastructure

The DHCP section is designed to make sure that you understand the basic concepts of installing, configuring and using DHCP, as well as the Windows 2000 DHCP implementation. The knowledge needed here also requires the understanding of general networking concepts, such as dynamic address assignment and TCP/IP addressing. The objectives are as follows:

Install, configure, and troubleshoot DHCP.

- Install the DHCP Server service.
- Create and manage DHCP scopes, superscopes, and multicast scopes.
- Configure DHCP for DNS integration.
- Authorize a DHCP server in Active Directory.

Manage and monitor DHCP.

Configuring, Managing, Monitoring, and Troubleshooting Remote Access in a Windows 2000 Network Infrastructure

The remote access section is designed to make sure that you understand how to install, configure, and support the various remote-access methods included with Windows 2000. These include not only the more traditional dial-in remote access included with

earlier versions of the operating system, but also some of the advanced technologies included as part of Windows 2000. The objectives are as follows:

Configure and troubleshoot remote access.

- Configure inbound connections.
- Create a remote-access policy.
- Configure a remote-access profile.
- Configure a virtual private network (VPN).
- Configure multilink connections.
- Configure routing and remote access for DHCP integration.

Manage and monitor remote access.

Configure remote-access security.

- Configure authentication protocols.
- Configure encryption protocols.
- Create a remote-access policy.

Installing, Configuring, Managing, Monitoring, and Troubleshooting Network Protocols in a Windows 2000 Network Infrastructure

The network protocols section is designed to ensure that you have a basic understanding of the network protocols commonly found on networks in industry, including installing, configuring, and troubleshooting them. The objectives are as follows:

Install, configure, and troubleshoot network protocols.

- Install and configure TCP/IP.

- Install the NWLink protocol.
- Configure network bindings.

Configure TCP/IP packet filters.

Configure and troubleshoot network protocol security.

Manage and monitor network traffic.

Configure and troubleshoot IPSec.

- Enable IPSec.
- Configure IPSec for transport mode.
- Configure IPSec for tunnel mode.
- Customize IPSec policies and rules.
- Manage and monitor IPSec.

Installing, Configuring, Managing, Monitoring, and Troubleshooting WINS in a Windows 2000 Network Infrastructure

The WINS section is designed to ensure an understanding of the WINS protocol. Although not necessary in a pure Windows 2000 network, WINS is critical to the support of legacy clients and applications. The objectives are as follows:

Install, configure, and troubleshoot WINS.

Configure WINS replication.

Configure NetBIOS name resolution.

Manage and monitor WINS.

Installing, Configuring, Managing, Monitoring, and Troubleshooting IP Routing in a Windows 2000 Network Infrastructure

The IP routing section is designed to ensure a thorough understanding of the advanced TCP/IP routing features included as part of Windows 2000. Many environments are turning to the server to also function as a router, and Windows 2000 includes support for several common routing protocols. The objectives are as follows:

Install, configure, and troubleshoot IP routing protocols.

- Update a Windows 2000-based routing table by means of static routes.
- Implement Demand-Dial Routing.

Manage and monitor IP routing.

- Manage and monitor border routing.
- Manage and monitor internal routing.
- Manage and monitor IP routing protocols.

Installing, Configuring, and Troubleshooting Network Address Translation (NAT)

The Network Address Translation (NAT) section is designed to ensure an understanding of one of the more common IP address conservation mechanisms in use today. NAT is frequently used in conjunction with Internet connections and provides a measure of security by obscuring source addresses. The objectives are as follows:

Install Internet Connection Sharing.

Install NAT.

Configure NAT properties.

Configure NAT interfaces.

Installing, Configuring, Managing, Monitoring, and Troubleshooting Certificate Services

The Certificate Services section is designed to make sure that you understand the capabilities and limitations of the Windows 2000 Certificate Authority. The objectives are as follows:

Install and configure Certificate Authority (CA).

Create certificates.

Issue certificates.

Revoke certificates

Remove the Encrypting File System (EFS) recovery keys.

HARDWARE AND SOFTWARE YOU'LL NEED

As a self-paced study guide, *MCSE Training Guide: Windows 2000 Network Infrastructure* is meant to help you understand concepts that must be refined through hands-on experience. To make the most of your studying, you need to have as much background on and experience with Windows 2000 as possible. The best way to do this is to combine studying with working on real networks, using the products on

which you will be tested. This section gives you a description of the minimum computer requirements you need to enjoy a solid practice environment.

The minimum computer requirements to ensure that you can study everything on which you'll be tested are one or more workstations running Windows 98, Windows NT Workstation, or Windows 2000 Professional, and two or more servers running Windows 2000 Server—all connected by a network.

- ❖ Workstations: Windows 98, Windows NT, or Windows 2000

  - Computer on the Microsoft Hardware Compatibility List (HCL)

  - Pentium 120MHz or better (Pentium 133MHz for Windows 2000)

  - 32MB RAM (64MB for Windows 2000)

  - 750MB hard disk (2GB hard disk with a minimum of 650MB of free space for Windows 2000)

  - 3.5-inch 1.44MB floppy drive

  - VGA video adapter

  - VGA monitor

  - Mouse or equivalent pointing device

  - CD-ROM drive

  - Network Interface Card (NIC)

  - Presence on an existing network or use of a hub to create a test network

  - Microsoft Windows 98, NT Workstation 4.0, or Windows 2000

◆ Servers: Windows 2000 Server

   • Two computers on the Microsoft Hardware Compatibility List (HCL)

   • Pentium 133MHz or better

   • 128MB RAM (Microsoft minimum supported. 64MB RAM will work in a test environment, although it will probably perform poorly.)

   • 1GB free hard disk

   • 3.5-inch 1.44MB floppy drive

   • VGA video adapter

   • VGA monitor

   • Mouse or equivalent pointing device

   • CD-ROM drive

   • Network Interface Card (NIC)

   • Presence on an existing network or use of a hub to create a test network

   • Microsoft Windows 2000 Server

It is easier to obtain access to the necessary computer hardware and software in a corporate business environment. It can be difficult, however, to allocate enough time within the busy workday to complete a self-study program. Most of your study time will occur after normal working hours, away from the everyday interruptions and pressures of your regular job.

ADVICE ON TAKING THE EXAM

More extensive tips are found in the "Final Review" section titled "Study and Exam Prep Tips," but keep this advice in mind as you study:

◆ **Read all the material.** Microsoft has been known to include material not expressly specified in the objectives. This book has included additional information not reflected in the objectives in an effort to give you the best possible preparation for the examination—and for the real-world network experiences to come.

◆ **Do the Step by Steps and complete the exercises in each chapter.** They will help you gain experience using the specified methodology or approach. All Microsoft exams are task- and experienced-based and require you to have experience actually performing the tasks on which you will be tested.

◆ **Use the questions to assess your knowledge.** Don't just read the chapter content; use the questions to find out what you know and what you don't. If you are struggling at all, study some more, review, and then assess your knowledge again.

◆ **Review the exam objectives.** Develop your own questions and examples for each topic listed. If you can develop and answer several questions for each topic, you should not find it difficult to pass the exam.

> **NOTE**
>
> **Exam-Taking Advice**   Although this book is designed to prepare you to take and pass the Implementing and Administering a Microsoft Windows 2000 Network Infrastructure Exam (70-216), there are no guarantees. Read this book, work through the questions and exercises, and when you feel confident, take the Practice Exam and additional exams using the *ExamGear, Training Guide Edition* test software. This should tell you whether you are ready for the real thing.
>
> When taking the actual certification exam, make sure you answer all the questions before your time limit expires. Do not spend too much time on any one question. If you are unsure, answer it the best you can; then mark it for review when you have finished the rest of the questions. However, this advice does not apply when you are taking an adaptive exam. In that case, take your time on each question. There is no opportunity to go back to a question. Be sure to read each question carefully and read all the answers before making a selection. Questions may have an answer that is close, but one of the other answers may, in fact, be a better answer. If you select your answer before reading all the choices, you may miss the "best" answer.

Remember, the primary object of this book is not the exam; it is to ensure that you understand the material. After you understand the material, passing the exam should be simple. Knowledge is a pyramid; to build upward, you need a solid foundation. This book and the Microsoft Certified Professional programs are designed to ensure that you have that solid foundation.

Good luck!

NEW RIDERS PUBLISHING

The staff of New Riders Publishing is committed to bringing you the very best in computer reference material. Each New Riders book is the result of months of work by authors and staff who research and refine the information contained within its covers.

As part of this commitment to you, the NRP reader, New Riders invites your input. Please let us know if you enjoy this book, if you have trouble with the information or examples presented, or if you have a suggestion for the next edition.

Please note, however, that New Riders staff cannot serve as a technical resource during your preparation for the Microsoft certification exams or for questions about software- or hardware-related problems. Please refer instead to the documentation that accompanies the Microsoft products or to the applications' Help systems.

If you have a question or comment about any New Riders book, you can contact New Riders Publishing in several ways. We will respond to as many readers as we can. Your name, address, or phone number will never become part of a mailing list or be used for any purpose other than to help us continue to bring you the best books possible. You can write to us at the following address:

New Riders Publishing
Attn: Executive Editor
201 W. 103rd Street
Indianapolis, IN 46290

If you prefer, you can fax New Riders Publishing at 317-581-4663.

You also can send email to New Riders at the following Internet address:

nrfeedback@newriders.com

NRP is an imprint of Pearson Education. To obtain information or a catalog, contact us at nrmedia@newriders.com. To purchase a New Riders book, call 800-428-5331.

Thank you for selecting *MCSE Training Guide: Windows 2000 Network Infrastructure*.

EXAM PREPARATION

1 Installing, Configuring, Managing, Monitoring, and Troubleshooting DNS in a Windows 2000 Network Infrastructure

2 Installing, Configuring, Managing, Monitoring, and Troubleshooting DHCP in a Windows 2000 Network Infrastructure

3 Configuring, Managing, Monitoring, and Troubleshooting Remote Access in a Windows 2000 Network Infrastructure

4 Installing, Configuring, Managing, Monitoring, and Troubleshooting Network Protocols in a Windows 2000 Network Infrastructure

5 Installing, Configuring, Managing, Monitoring, and Troubleshooting WINS in a Windows 2000 Network Infrastructure

6 Installing, Configuring, Managing, Monitoring, and Troubleshooting IP Routing in a Windows 2000 Network Infrastructure

7 Installing, Configuring, and Troubleshooting Network Address Translation (NAT)

8 Installing, Configuring, Managing, Monitoring, and Troubleshooting Certificate Services

This chapter's discussion is about network infrastructure with Domain Name Service (DNS), the forerunner to many of the name resolution and directory services available today. Whenever you "surf the Web," you take advantage of DNS. This chapter covers the "Installing, Configuring, Managing, Monitoring, and Troubleshooting DNS in a Windows 2000 Network Infrastructure" objectives for this exam. One of the most important services in a Transmission Control Protocol/Internet Protocol (TCP/IP) infrastructure—particularly one running the Active Directory Services—is DNS. In this chapter, you examine all the facets of running the DNS Server service in a Windows 2000 network.

Microsoft defines the "Installing, Configuring, Managing, Monitoring, and Troubleshooting DNS in a Windows 2000 Network Infrastructure" objectives as follows.

Install, configure, and troubleshoot DNS.

- **Install the DNS Server service.**
- **Configure a root name server.**
- **Configure zones.**
- **Configure a caching-only server.**
- **Configure a DNS client computer.**
- **Configure zones for dynamic updates.**
- **Test the DNS Server service.**
- **Implement a delegated zone for DNS.**
- **Manually create DNS resource records.**

CHAPTER 1

Installing, Configuring, Managing, Monitoring, and Troubleshooting DNS in a Windows 2000 Network Infrastructure

▶ One of your first tasks when getting ready to deploy a production Windows 2000 network environment is to ensure that DNS is installed and configured correctly. DNS is the foundation that the Active Directory relies on, and you will need to have a thorough understanding not only of the Windows 2000 DNS Server service, but also how DNS itself functions. This objective expects you to be able to install DNS, configure it for use in an Active Directory Services network, and test it to make sure it is functioning.

Manage and monitor DNS.

▶ The final objective requires you be able to maintain your DNS server after it is installed, configured, and authorized. The ability to manage DNS Server services and monitor the DNS server's activities is critical to the ongoing administration of a Windows 2000 network, particularly a network that relies on the Active Directory.

Introducing the Domain Name Service (DNS)   **16**

History of DNS   16
    DNS Domains Defined   18
    Hierarchies   19
    Reverse Lookups   25
    DNS Record Types   26
    DNS Naming Conventions   28

Installing, Configuring, and Troubleshooting DNS   28

Installing the DNS Server Service   29

Configuring a Root Name Server   33

Configuring Zones   34

Configuring a Caching-Only Server   42

Configuring a DNS Client Computer   44

Configuring Zones for Dynamic Updates   47

Testing the DNS Server Service   49

Implementing a Delegated Zone for DNS   54

Manually Creating DNS Resource Records   55

Managing and Monitoring DNS   **56**

Setting Aging/Scavenging for All Zones   57

Scavenging Stale Resource Records Manually   58

Setting Properties   58

Chapter Summary   **65**

Apply Your Knowledge   **67**

▶ DNS provides the name resolution backbone for the Internet today. With the introduction of the Active Directory, it is now also the backbone of Microsoft's name resolution. It is very important that you understand where DNS came from, how it works, and what enhancements Microsoft made to DNS for Active Directory.

▶ Part of the power of the Microsoft DNS service is its integration with Dynamic Host Configuration Protocol (DHCP) through Dynamic DNS. Make sure you understand the relationship between the two and how Dynamic DNS works.

▶ Microsoft's Windows 2000 DNS service supports a variety of zone types and DNS server types. Be sure you understand what they are, how they work, and when you might use them in a production environment.

▶ Because of Microsoft's emphasis on practical exam questions, be sure to closely review the Step by Steps and the exercises at the end of the chapter.

INTRODUCING THE DOMAIN NAME SERVICE (DNS)

If you have ever connected to a Web site by name, you have used the Domain Name Service (DNS). The DNS is a service used on the Internet for resolving fully qualified domain names (FQDN) to their actual Internet Protocol (IP) addresses. For example, suppose you were preparing to take the latest Windows 2000 certification exam. You've asked your co-workers what the best study guide available is, and they recommend that you check out New Riders' Web site to see what is available. Your obvious question is, "Where can I find New Riders' Web site?" Before DNS, the answer would be 205.133.113.87, and if you are like most people, you'll remember that number for less than 30 seconds and will probably never find the New Riders' site (or get that study guide you were looking for). What DNS does is put a user-friendly face on that obscure numeric address. With DNS, your friend can tell you to go to www.newriders.com, and the DNS infrastructure of the Internet will translate the name to the correct address, 205.133.113.87. It's like a big phone book. You put in a name and it gives you the correct number. Fortunately for those of us with a limited ability to memorize strings of numbers, the Internet community recognized the benefits of a name resolution system as a critical part of the infrastructure that would make up the original Internet architecture. And DNS was born.

> **NOTE**
>
> **Domain Name System or Domain Name Service** You may have heard that the acronym DNS stood for Domain Name System, yet it was referred to as the Domain Name Service in the previous sections. These names are interchangeable, although Microsoft tends to use Service, whereas most Internet users use System. From here on, we will use the term Service for consistency.

History of DNS

DNS is a hierarchical database containing names and addresses for IP networks and hosts and is used almost universally to provide name resolution. This statement is now even more accurate because Microsoft is embracing DNS as its name resolution method for Windows 2000, in favor of the more proprietary, less accepted Windows Internet Naming System (WINS). (We discuss WINS and how it relates to Windows 2000 in Chapter 5, "Installing, Configuring, Managing, Monitoring, and Troubleshooting WINS in a Windows 2000 Network Infrastructure.") But before we tackle DNS in a Windows 2000 network, we should cover a little of the history and makeup of DNS in general.

Back in the early days of the Internet, when it was known as the
Advanced Research Products Agency Network (ARPAnet) and the
number of hosts on the network was less than 100, there used to be
a master list of names and IP addresses called the HOSTS.TXT file.
It was maintained by the Stanford Research Institute's Network
Information Center (known as the SRI-NIC at the time) and it
worked very well as long as the number of hosts was low and
changes were infrequent. Everyone using the network would
periodically download a copy of this file, and they would have a
local table of names and addresses to connect to computers by
name. Windows 2000 (and most TCP/IP stacks in general) still
have this functionality, although it is seldom used in conjunction
with the Internet any longer. This method of name resolution was
great for a while, but as the number of computers grew, this solution
ran into a few issues, including the following:

◆ **Traffic.** As more and more people tried to access this file, the
load on the SRI network and servers was becoming excessive.

◆ **Consistency.** As the number of hosts and the number of
changes grew larger and larger, propagation of the
HOSTS.TXT file became nearly impossible. As the file propagated to the most distant servers, new servers would have
already been added to the network, rendering the file just
distributed obsolete.

◆ **Flat-file limitations.** Windows NT Domain administrators
are familiar with these limitations. Because the HOSTS.TXT
file was a flat file (similar to the way domain objects are stored
under Windows NT 4 domains) a requirement existed that
every name be unique. No hierarchical capabilities were built
in to the naming structure. As a result, coming up with
unique names that were also intuitive was becoming more
and more difficult.

The network needed a better answer than a text file for name
resolution. In RFCs 882 and 883, Paul Mockapetris first introduced
the Domain Name System back in 1984. These have since been
superceded by RFCs 1034 and 1035, the current DNS specification.

EXAM TIP

**Be Able to Compare DNS with
HOST Files**   Be familiar with the
advantages of DNS over the flat-file
method of name resolution provided by the HOSTS file.

NOTE

A Note on RFC   Request For
Comment (RFC) documents are used
to make notes about the Internet and
Internet technologies. If an RFC can
garner enough interest, it may eventually become a standard.

DNS is a distributed database allowing local control of DNS for smaller segments of the namespace while maintaining a logical architecture to provide the local information throughout the network. Each piece of the DNS database resides on a server known as a name server. The architecture of DNS is designed so that there can be multiple name servers for redundancy, and caching of names to the local server is also supported, further enhancing DNS's robustness. In addition, with parts of the overall namespace placed on separate computers, the data storage and query loads are distributed throughout thousands of DNS servers throughout the Internet. The hierarchical nature of DNS is designed in such a way that every computer on or off the Internet can be named as part of the DNS namespace.

To effectively install, configure, and support the Windows 2000 DNS Server service, you must have some level of understanding of the underlying architecture of today's DNS. Rather than having you read the RFCs (although you are encouraged to do so to improve your further understanding of DNS) we discuss the DNS namespace architecture and how individual DNS servers support their portions of the overall namespace; then you move on to the specifics of the Windows 2000 DNS Server service.

DNS Domains Defined

As we've discussed, you probably have already used DNS, whether you were familiar with the underlying mechanism or not. Domain names are easy. Names such as www.microsoft.com, www.newriders.com, or even www.mcse.com are all easy to comprehend. All you need is the ability to read. However, this simplicity comes at a price. The DNS namespace is complex. DNS names are created as part of a hierarchical database that functions much like the directories in a file system. Hierarchies are powerful database structures because they can store tremendous amounts of data while making it easy to search for specific bits of information. Before examining the specifics of the DNS namespace hierarchy, let's review some rules about hierarchies in general.

Hierarchies

Before we get into the details of a hierarchy, we should introduce some terms:

♦ **Tree.** A type of data structure with each element attached to one or more elements directly beneath it. In the case of DNS, this structure is often called an inverted tree because it is generally drawn with the root at the top of the tree.

♦ **Top-level domain (TLD).** TLD refers to the suffix attached to Internet domain names. There are a limited number of predefined suffixes, and each one represents a top-level domain. The more popular TLDs include COM, EDU, GOV, MIL, NET, and ORG.

♦ **Node.** A point where two or more lines in the tree intersect. In the case of DNS, a node can represent a TLD, a subdomain, or an actual network node (host).

♦ **Fully qualified domain name (FQDN).** A domain name that includes all domains between the host and the root of DNS is an FQDN. For example, `www.microsoft.com` is an FQDN.

♦ **Leaf.** An item at the very bottom of a hierarchical tree structure, and it does not contain any other objects. In DNS, these are called nodes.

♦ **Zone.** A DNS zone is a logical grouping of hostnames within DNS. For example, `newriders.com` is considered the forward lookup zone for New Riders. It is where the information about the New Riders hosts is contained within DNS.

If you told typical end users that they have been working with a hierarchy since the first time they turned on a computer, many would have no idea what you were talking about. In fact, a fair number of administrators would have to think about it as well. However, it's true. MS-DOS version 2 introduced a hierarchy to PCs in the form of the file system. Why do computers need a hierarchical file system? Because storing files as an endless alphabetic listing is inefficient; they need to be stored in related groups. Now all computers use hierarchical structures for organizing file storage.

In DNS, the containers are called domains. The hierarchy starts with a root container, called the root domain. The root domain doesn't have a name, so it is typically represented by a single period (see Figure 1.1). Directly below the root domain are the TLDs. These are also sometimes called first-level domains. Lower-level domains are second-level, third-level, and so on. Every domain name has a suffix that indicates which TLD domain it belongs to. There are only a limited number of such domains. For example:

- ◆ **COM.** Originally, the COM domain was supposed to contain commercial entities, but COM has become the overwhelming favorite top-level domain, and everyone wants his personal subdomains to be in COM. Because COM has been overused and abused, it's nearly impossible to come up with a sensible new name for a COM subdomain. Crowding in COM is the main impetus behind the definition of new top-level domains. (Example of COM: mcp.com)

- ◆ **ORG.** This domain is supposed to accommodate organizations that are noncommercial in nature. Although many noncommercial organizations have registered in the COM domain, most have respected the intent of this domain. This is a good place for nonprofit organizations, professional groups, churches, and other such organizations. (Example of ORG: npr.org)

- ◆ **EDU.** This domain was originally supposed to embrace all types of educational institutions, but it began to fill up quickly as schools gained access to the Internet. Now it is primarily reserved for higher education institutions. Primary and secondary schools are supposed to register in their state domains, which are subdomains of their country domains. (Example of EDU: berkeley.edu)

FIGURE 1.1

This portion of the DNS hierarchy shows the location of www.newriders.com in the DNS database in relation to the rest of the DNS database.

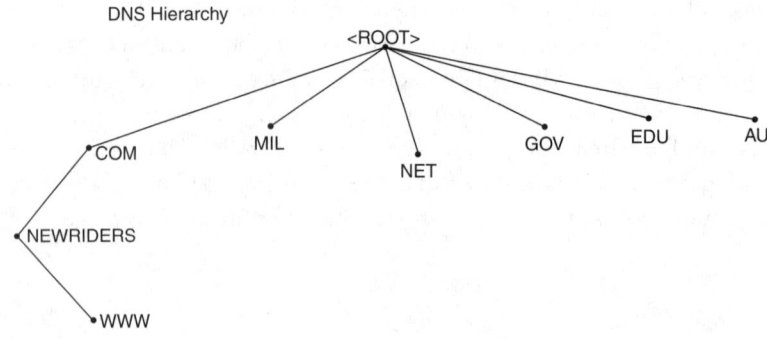

◆ **GOV.** This domain contains agencies of the United States federal government apart from the military, which has the MIL domain. (Example of GOV: whitehouse.gov)

◆ **NET.** This domain supports Internet Service Providers (ISPs) and Internet administrative computers. (Example of NET: ibm.net)

◆ **Country.** Each country is assigned a unique top-level domain. Some more common examples include the following:

  • **CA.** Canada

  • **TH.** Thailand

  • **UK.** United Kingdom

  • **AU.** Australia

  • **TO.** Tonga

◆ **CC.** This new domain was created for the same purpose as the COM domain. It is intended to extend the number of names available for commercial endeavors. (Example of CC: www.spot.cc)

Because of a shortage of domain names at the top level, the Internet Ad Hoc Committee (IAHC) proposed six new TLDs, which could start being used sometime in 2000:

◆ **STORE.** Domain name for merchants.

◆ **WEB.** Domains focused on Web activities.

◆ **ARTS.** Arts and cultural entities.

◆ **REC.** Recreation and entertainment entities.

◆ **INFO.** Information services.

◆ **NOM.** Domains registered to individuals.

The creation of these new TLDs is expected to alleviate the almost gold-rush-like fervor associated with "good" domain names. Unfortunately, the various groups ultimately in charge of implementing the new domains have been dragging their feet. Everyone wants to control the process (because that's where the money is), and they have not been able to agree on whose plan will ultimately be implemented.

EXAM TIP

Know About FQDN   For the exam, make sure you have a good understanding of what an FQDN is and how it is represented.

EXAM TIP

Know the Difference Between the Primary and the Secondary Domains   The major difference is that a secondary domain holds a read-only version of the DNS database.

NOTE

Zones in DNS   In the world of DNS, a zone is the complete information about some part of the domain namespace. In other words, it is a subset of a domain. The name server is considered to have authority for that zone, and it can respond to any requests for name resolution from that zone.

As we have discussed, DNS is used to translate a hostname to an IP address. The DNS name typically looks something like this:

```
isaac.widgets.urwrite.net
```

This is known as the host's fully qualified domain name (FQDN) because it lists the host's precise location in the DNS hierarchy. The DNS name in the example represents the host ISAAC in the subdomain WIDGETS (this is frequently a department or division in a company), which is in the subdomain URWRITE (this is frequently the name of the company or organization that has registered the domain), which is in the TLD NET.

When an organization wants to establish a domain name on the Internet, the domain name must be registered with one of the authorized registration authorities. One that many people are familiar with is Network Solutions, formerly the InterNIC. You can research new domain names and access registration forms at http://www.networksolutions.com. You can also contact your ISP for assistance. To register a domain, you will need at least two name servers. Two types of name servers are defined within the DNS specifications. They are the following:

◆ **Primary Master.** This server gets the information on the zones it is authoritative over (will resolve names for) from files on the host on which it runs. This is the server where you make additions, modifications, and deletions to the DNS zone. This is similar to the NT 4 primary domain controller. It is the only place modifications to the domain can be made.

◆ **Secondary Master.** This server gets its zone information from the master name server that is authoritative for that domain; it could either be from a primary or a secondary. When a secondary server starts, it contacts the name server it updates from (the authoritative server) and gets the latest copy of the zone data.

After you have identified the two (or more) name servers, you are ready to register your domain. To register a domain name at Network Solutions, do the following:

STEP BY STEP

1.1 Registering a DNS Domain

1. Search the Network Solutions database (www.networksolutions.com) to find a domain name that isn't already in use. This can be pretty difficult unless you are willing to use something fairly obscure. Most of the common (and even fairly uncommon) domain names have already been registered.

2. Determine the IP addresses of two domain name servers—a master and a backup (or secondary) name server that will be authoritative for your domain. If your ISP will be providing your name servers, obtain the IP addresses from your ISP.

3. Register the domain name with Network Solutions. The Web site includes online forms for registering and changing domain names.

4. Pay the registration fee, which varies depending on the options you select. The initial registration fee is for the first two years, and then you pay an annual fee to keep the name active.

NOTE

The Role of a Domain   If you ever anticipate connecting your network to the Internet, your first installation of DNS is an excellent time to do a little preparation. More important, after Active Directory has been installed, the underlying DNS domain cannot be changed without removing and re-installing Active Directory and losing all your users and permissions.

Great—now you've registered your domain, and you understand the DNS hierarchy. The next step is understanding how DNS works. In other words, after you enter the name, how does it get translated to an IP address?

The DNS name server resolves a name to an IP address using the following process:

1. The client computer makes a request to the local DNS server. This generally occurs when an application tries to make a connection using a hostname, such as when you enter www.newriders.com into your Web browser.

2. The DNS server looks in a local memory cache for names it has recently resolved. If the name is found in the local cache, the name server returns the IP address the client computer requires. Most DNS servers cache both local and remote domain names in the memory, so even a DNS request for a host on your local network may be in cache.

3. The name server looks in the DNS server's host tables to see if there is a static entry (or in the case of Dynamic DNS, a dynamic entry) for the hostname to an IP address lookup. If an entry exists, the DNS server forwards the IP address to the client computer.

4. If the request has not been resolved, the name server refers the request to a root name server. Root name servers support the root of the namespace hierarchy. At present, ten computers support the root domain.

5. The root name server refers the request to a name server for the first-level domain in the hostname. In other words, if you have requested a host address for the newriders.com domain, the root name server will forward the request to the newriders.com DNS server. The first-level domain name server refers the request to a name server for the second-level domain in the hostname, and so on, until a name server is encountered that can resolve the complete hostname.

6. The first name server that can resolve the hostname to an IP address reports the IP address to the client computer.

To ensure that this process works in your environment, you need to ensure two things. First, make sure that your network has at least one, and preferably more, DNS name servers. These name servers can include your Windows 2000 server, DNS server, older Microsoft DNS servers, third party (UNIX, Linux, OS/2, and so on) DNS servers, or even name servers provided by your ISP. Second, make sure your client computers are all configured to use these servers for DNS lookups. The rest of the process generally just works. You do not need to maintain the root name servers list or the lookup process.

NOTE

How Root Servers Work When you register your domain, you are required to provide the names and addresses of two (or more) DNS servers that will be providing DNS for the domain. The root name servers have access to these names and addresses and thus know where to send the requests.

Reverse Lookups

We have discussed how to get the most common form of DNS lookups, also known as forward lookups. These are the DNS lookups where you enter a name and the DNS server returns the IP address. There is another kind of lookup, known as a reverse lookup. A reverse lookup works very much as the name implies. You query the DNS server with an IP address, and it returns (if there is an entry) the DNS name for that host. This can be very useful if you are trying to keep track of network usage, trying to track down a host that is causing issues on the network, or trying to verify the identity of a host. Microsoft uses reverse lookups for the downloading of its 128-bit software to ensure that the user attempting to download the software is within the United States or Canada. If your host doesn't have an entry in a reverse lookup table, you will not be able to download the software. We discuss the different record types in the "DNS Record Types" section of this chapter, but it is important to know that reverse lookup tables use PTR records to resolve IP addresses to names. A PTR record is a pointer to a location (an FQDN) in the DNS domain.

IN THE FIELD

SPAM EMAILS AND REVERSE LOOKUPS

You may find that you need a reverse lookup with the sending of Internet email. One of the latest weapons in the anti-SPAM wars is the use of reverse lookups to verify the validity of the domain an email originates from. When the mail server receives an email, it checks to see whether it is from a valid domain and will reject it if it is not. A lot of SPAM used to use fictitious domains as part of the spammers' attempts to hide their real identity.

If you have not yet experienced SPAM, the electronic version of telemarketing and junk mail, not only are you very fortunate, but you are also probably due for some. SPAM is generally considered unsolicited email advertising for some product sent to an email address, mailing list, or newsgroup. In addition to being annoying for the user, it also eats up significant amounts of network bandwidth. Therefore, if you are setting up DNS on the Internet, be sure to include a reverse zone for your mail servers.

EXAM TIP

Understand the Function of the Reverse Lookup Table   Because they are used less and as a result are less understood when compared to the forward lookup table, reverse lookup tables are an excellent topic for exam questions.

The naming convention for a reverse lookup zone is

```
First Octets of the IP address.in-addr.arpa
```

Thus, the reverse table for the IP network 205.133.113.87 is 113.133.205.in-addr.arpa.

It is important to be aware that the Active Directory Installation Wizard does not automatically add a reverse lookup zone and PTR resource records. You will need to do that manually. This is because it is possible that another server may control the reverse lookup zone. You may want to add one if this is not the case. Although a reverse lookup zone is not necessary for Active Directory to work, it is useful for the reasons listed previously.

DNS Record Types

EXAM TIP

Don't Memorize the Table of DNS Record Types   Although you must understand the commonly used types, entries such as the Andrew File System Database server record will not be on the exam.

Before we continue our discussions of DNS, you should take a quick look at the different types of records you can create in a DNS domain. Table 1.1 lists the record types supported by the Windows 2000s DNS Server service—and their meaning.

TABLE 1.1

DNS RECORD TYPES

Record Type and RFC	Value and Meaning
AFSDB (RFC 1183)	Andrew File System database server record. Indicates the location of either an AFS volume location server or a Distributed Computing Environment (DCE) server.
CNAME (RFC 1035)	One of the original record types, a CNAME indicates an alias domain name for a name already specified as another resource type in this zone. CNAME is the acronym for canonical name.
ATMA	ATM address—maps a DNS name to an ATM address.
A (RFC 1035)	A host address record—maps a DNS name to an IP (version 4) address.
AAAA (RFC 1886)	Similar to the A record, the AAAA record is a host address for IPv6 hosts. It is used to map a DNS name to an IP (version 6) address.
ISDN (RFC 1183)	An Integrated Services Digital Network (ISDN) maps a DNS name to an ISDN telephone number.

Record Type and RFC	*Value and Meaning*
MX (RFC 1035)	A mail exchanger record is used to provide message routing to a specific mail exchange host for a specific DNS name.
MG (RFC 1035)	A mail group record is used to add mailbox records as members of a domain mailing group.
MB (RFC 1035)	A mailbox record maps a specified domain mailbox name to the host that hosts the mailbox.
MINFO (RFC 1035)	Mailbox or mailing list information specifies a domain mailbox name to contact. Can also specify a mailbox for error messages.
PTR (RFC 1035)	A pointer record points to a location in the domain. This is typically used for reverse lookups or IP address to DNS name lookups.
MR (RFC 1035)	A renamed mailbox record is used to specify a domain mailbox that is the proper rename of an existing mailbox record.
RP (RFC 1183)	A responsible person record specifies the domain mailbox for a responsible person for which text (TXT) records exist.
TXT (RFC 1035)	A text record is used to hold a string of characters that serve as descriptive text to be associated with a specific DNS name.
RT (RFC 1183)	A route-through record provides an intermediate-route-through binding for internal hosts that do not have their own direct wide area network (WAN) address.
SRV (RFC 2052)	A service record allows administrators to use several servers for a single DNS domain, to easily move a TCP/IP service from host to host, and to designate primary and backup services hosts.
WKS (RFC 1035)	A well-known service record is used to describe well-known TCP/IP services supported by a particular protocol (that is, TCP or UDP) on a specific IP address.
X25 (RFC 1183)	An X.25 record is used to map a DNS name to a Public Switched Telephone Network (PSTN) address.

N O T E

The Windows 2000 DNS Server Service Supports Additional Standards Microsoft has one problem with its direction of a DNS-based directory service, and it's one that has been an issue for years. Network basic input output system (NetBIOS), the legacy Microsoft naming mechanism, does not conform to the naming standards in RFC 1123. What this means is that in some environments, companies could be forced to rename all their Microsoft devices to move to a naming standard supported by Active Directory. To avoid this, Microsoft has included support for RFCs 2181 and 2044, which will allow legacy NetBIOS names to be supported under DNS.

There's a catch to Microsoft's proposed support for RFCs 2181 and 2044. If you move to a naming convention that takes advantage of the new standards, you may run into issues with non-Windows 2000 DNS servers, including Windows NT 4.0 DNS servers. Most servers do not support the standards Microsoft is proposing. The reason for this is that RFC 2044 calls for the support of the character encoding Unicode Translation Format 8 (UTF-8). UTF-8 supports characters from a variety of foreign languages, which are not supported by non-Windows 2000 versions of DNS.

DNS Naming Conventions

Before we move on to the installation portion of this chapter, we need to quickly review the parameters for creating a DNS name. Table 1.2 shows the restrictions for creating a DNS name and an FQDN.

TABLE 1.2

DNS NAME RESTRICTIONS

Restriction	Standard DNS (Including Windows NT 4.0)	DNS in Windows 2000
Characters	Supports RFC 1123, which permits A to Z, a to z, 0 to 9, and the hyphen (-).	Several different configurations are possible; RFC 1123 standard, as well as support for RFC 2181 and the character set specified in RFC 2044 (UTP-8)
FQDN length	63 bytes per label and 255 bytes for an FQDN	Domain controllers are limited to 155 bytes for an FQDN.

Now let's look at installing the Windows 2000 DNS Server service.

Installing, Configuring, and Troubleshooting DNS

Install, configure, and troubleshoot DNS.

Now that you have an understanding of how DNS in general works, we can look at installing the Windows 2000 DNS Server service. One of the first questions you will be asked is, "Do we need to upgrade to Windows 2000 DNS?" The answer is yes and no. If you don't want to take advantage of all the benefits of a Windows 2000 network and Active Directory, you don't need to upgrade. If you happen to be running a version of DNS that supports RFC 2136, covering Dynamic DNS, you can run your existing DNS and take advantage of Windows 2000's features. But let's assume you are not running an RFC 2136-compliant version of DNS. Why should you upgrade? The Windows 2000 DNS contains a number of significant improvements over standard DNS (including Windows NT's implementation), including the following:

◆ **Notification-driven zone transfers.** The standard model for DNS updates requires secondary name servers to periodically poll the master server for table updates. Under Windows 2000's DNS, the master server can notify the secondaries when an update has occurred. This immediate notification is not only more efficient than the older methods, but it also allows for much faster distribution of changes because updates are no longer dependent on polling intervals.

◆ **Integrated zone tables.** With the Windows 2000 DNS Server service, you can integrate DNS into the Active Directory, and now resource records are stored in the Active Directory and can be updated by any domain controller running DNS. This integration is a proprietary feature of the Windows 2000 DNS, but it can yield a much more secure, robust, and fault-tolerant implementation than standard DNS.

◆ **Incremental zone transfers.** The standard model for DNS zone transfers is to transfer the entire zone whenever an update is made. Transferring entire zones is very inefficient. Windows 2000 DNS allows secondary servers to request incremental updates, which contain changes only since the last transfer.

◆ **Secure DNS updates.** Windows 2000 DNS updates can be restricted to authorized secondaries.

◆ **DNS-DHCP Integration.** The power of Dynamic DNS is the integration of DHCP with the DNS table. Any Windows 2000 DHCP client computer will automatically be added to the DNS table at the time its IP address is issued.

Now that you have the justification, let's install the Windows 2000 DNS Server service.

Installing the DNS Server Service

One of the major improvements in Windows 2000 is the capability to perform tasks—installing services, for example—in various ways. In fact, there are several ways to install the DNS Server service. We

---

EXAM TIP

Be Familiar with the Advantages of the Windows 2000 Dynamic DNS Over More Traditional Servers Because Active Directory is based entirely on DNS, this is a topic that is pretty important to the success of Active Directory, which makes it a good topic for test questions.

will cover two of the most common methods. For your benefit, finding the method you are most comfortable with and sticking to it consistently is generally the best method for working with the operating system.

To install the Windows 2000 DNS Server service, do the following:

STEP BY STEP

1.2 Installing the DNS Server Service

1. Right-click the My Network Places icon on the desktop. From the context menu select Properties. The Network and Dial-up Connections window opens (see Figure 1.2).

FIGURE 1.2
From here you can add, remove, or modify your network settings and services.

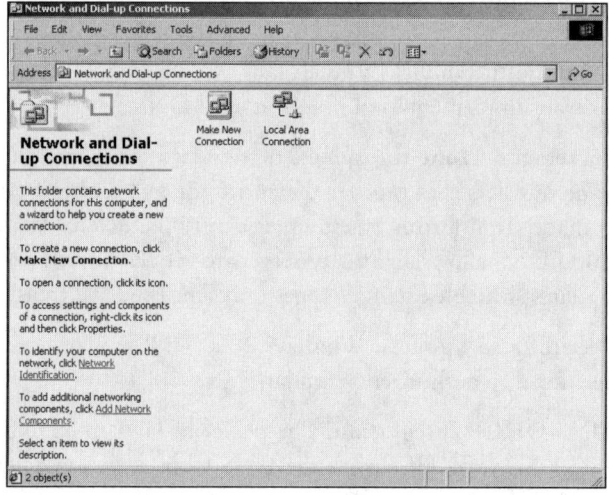

2. Click Add Network Components in the lower-left corner. (This will be visible only if you are viewing the folder as a Web page, the system default.) This hyperlink opens the Windows Components dialog box of the Windows Optional Networking Components Wizard, shown in Figure 1.3.

3. Select the Networking Services entry and click Details. This opens the Networking Services dialog box, shown in Figure 1.4. Select Domain Name System (DNS). Click the OK button. The Windows Component Wizard will prompt you for the Windows 2000 Server CD-ROM if it needs to copy files.

4. When the wizard is finished, it displays a summary window of the changes to be made. Click OK to complete the installation.

Congratulations, you just installed DNS. Now let's look at another way to do it.

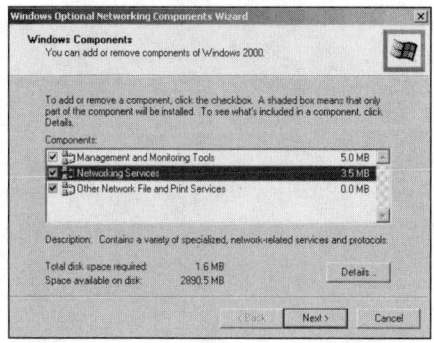

FIGURE 1.3
The Windows 2000 DNS server is part of the Networking Services components.

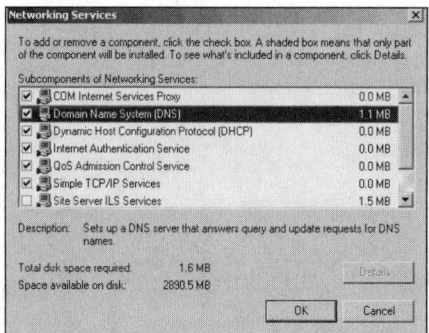

FIGURE 1.4
Selecting Domain Name System (DNS) and clicking OK installs the service.

STEP BY STEP

1.3 Using an Alternative Method to Install the Windows 2000 DNS Server

1. Open the Control Panel (see Figure 1.5) and double-click the Add/Remove Programs applet. The Add/Remove Programs dialog box opens (see Figure 1.6).

FIGURE 1.5

As in Windows NT 4, the Control Panel contains the bulk of the system applets, including Add/Remove Programs.

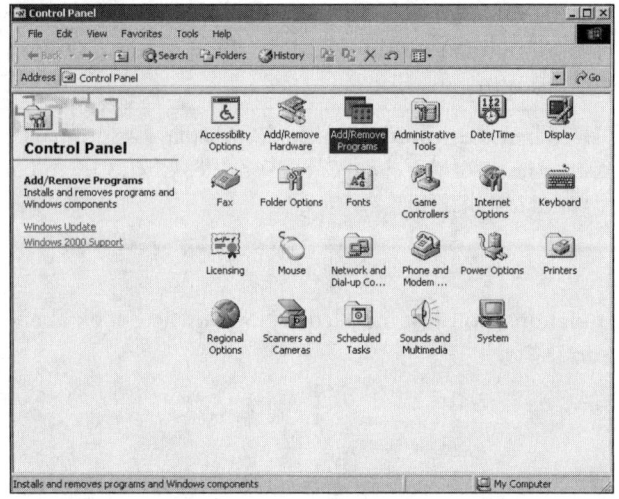

FIGURE 1.6

A major improvement over earlier versions, the Add/Remove Programs dialog box gives you more useful information about installed applications, including application size and, in some cases, the frequency of use for an installed application.

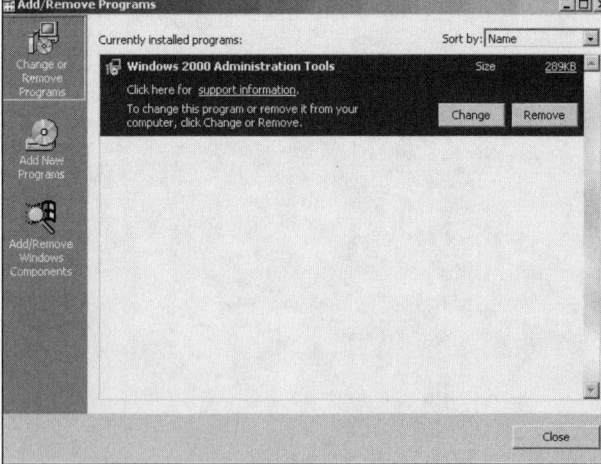

2. Click Add/Remove Windows Components. The Windows Components Wizard dialog box opens (see Figure 1.7). From here you can follow the same steps as in the previous procedure to complete the installation.

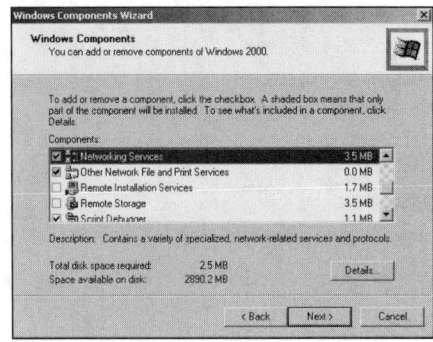

Now that DNS is installed, let's look at configuring our first DNS zone.

Configuring a Root Name Server

Let's discuss what Microsoft means when they ask you to configure a root name server. The root name server of a domain is the name server that is acting as the Start of Authority (SOA) for that zone. The SOA record is the first record in the database, and it has the following format:

```
IN SOA <source host> <contact email> <serial number>
➥<refresh time> <retry time> <expiration time>
➥<time to live>
```

◆ **Source host.** This is the DNS server that maintains this file.

◆ **Contact email.** This is the Internet email address for the person responsible for this domain's database file. See the note for important formatting information.

◆ **Serial number.** This is important. The serial number acts as the version number for the database file. This number should increase each time the database file is changed. The file with the highest serial number takes precedence during zone transfers.

◆ **Refresh time.** This is the elapsed time (in seconds) that a secondary server will wait between checks to its master server to see whether the database file has changed and a zone transfer should be requested. This is 15 minutes by default, but it can be increased in an environment where DNS doesn't change often.

◆ **Retry time.** This is the elapsed time (in seconds) that a secondary server will wait before retrying a failed zone transfer. The default for Windows 2000 is 10 minutes, and it can be increased or decreased as needed for your environment.

FIGURE 1.7
As you can see, you can reach the same Windows Components Wizard a number of ways.

N O T E   **Don't Use a Standard Email Address for the SOA**   One very important fact about the contact email in the SOA—it does not use the standard Internet email format. Instead, you replace the "@" symbol in the email name with a "."; therefore, `billg@microsoft.com` would be `billg.microsoft.com` in the zone file.

◆ **Expiration time.** This is the elapsed time (in seconds) that a secondary server will keep trying to download a zone. After this time limit expires, the old zone information is discarded. This is one day by default. It, too, can be modified as needed. You may want to increase this number for areas with intermittent connectivity where outages are common. DNS across a VPN is one example.

◆ **Time to live (TTL).** The TTL is the elapsed time (in seconds) that a DNS server is allowed to cache any resource records from this database file.

The SOA indicates the primary server for the zone. This is the root server for the domain.

Configuring Zones

DNS configuration is handled through a snap-in for the Microsoft Management Console (MMC). This may be found in the Administrative Tools program folder, under the entry DNS. It becomes available after DNS is installed. Although it is possible to manually configure the text files that DNS creates (this is discussed in the "Manually Creating DNS Resource Records" section of the chapter), the DNS console makes it much easier to manage your DNS namespace configuration. When you first install your DNS server, you will need to configure your DNS server with its first zones. We will look at how to do this using the wizard, and then take a look at how to do this if you need to add additional zones down the road.

Before we jump into the configuration of DNS zones, we need to take a moment to discuss the types of zone storage used in DNS:

◆ **Active Directory-Integrated.** This zone option stores all DNS information in the Active Directory. If your entire domain infrastructure is run on a Windows 2000 platform, this is a good selection. This is the most secure option for maintaining your DNS tables because all your DNS information is stored in the Active Directory, and all your updates pass as Active Directory updates. Unlike the text file method used by most DNS implementations, DNS tables stored in Active Directory cannot be read by a text editor such as Notepad or vi.

◆ **Standard Primary.** This zone option stores the information in a text file, like most non-Windows 2000 DNS servers, and is useful if you need to transfer information between different types of DNS servers.

◆ **Standard Secondary.** This option creates a read-only copy of an existing zone. The master copy (read/write version) is stored on a primary server. These are generally used to provide redundancy or load balancing of DNS on a network.

IN THE FIELD

USING THE MMC AND MANUALLY ADDING SNAP-INS

If you are an advanced user and would like to skip using differently configured versions of the MMC for each of the services installed on your Windows 2000 server, a very easy way exists to manage everything from a single MMC configuration. Open the MMC by going to Start, Run, MMC. This opens the MMC shell, which will be empty the first time you load it. Go to Console, Add/Remove Snap-in . . . When the Add/Remove Snap-in dialog box opens, click the Add button. In the Add Standalone Snap-in dialog box, you can select any or all of the snap-ins for Windows 2000 services.

To configure the zones on your DNS server for first time, do the following:

EXAM TIP

The Most Secure Implementation of DNS Is Active Directory-Integrated   The Active Directory is more secure than a flat file, and updates and zone transfers occur as part of Active Directory replication activities, which are encrypted.

EXAM TIP

The DNS Console Equals MMC The DNS console is really nothing more than the MMC with the DNS management snap-in installed. Microsoft creates these versions of the MMC to make managing systems easier for new users of Windows 2000. So don't be confused if you see references to the MMC in the exam. That's all the DNS console is.

FIGURE 1.8
The Configure DNS Server Wizard guides you through configuring your newly installed DNS server.

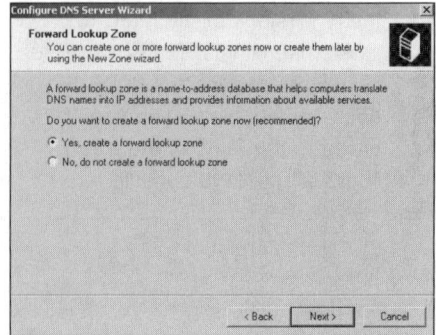

FIGURE 1.9
A forward lookup zone is used to resolve domain names to IP addresses.

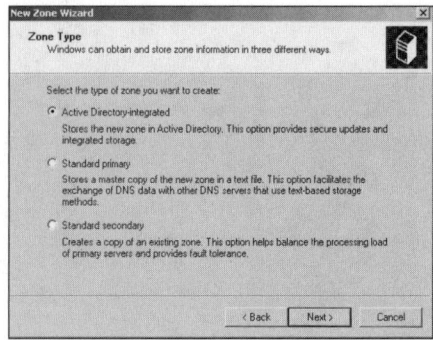

FIGURE 1.10
For the most secure implementation, store your DNS table in Active Directory.

STEP BY STEP

1.4 Configuring Zones for the First Time

1. Open the DNS console by going to Administrative Tools and selecting DNS. Right-click your new server and select Configure the Server. The Configure DNS Server Wizard (see Figure 1.8) starts. Click Next to open the Forward Lookup Zone screen (see Figure 1.9). This zone is the one that will resolve your DNS names to IP addresses.

2. Select the Yes, Create a Forward Lookup Zone option to create your first zone. The Zone Type dialog box (shown in Figure 1.10) allows you to select the type of zone to create—Active Directory-Integrated in this case. Click Next. The Zone Name dialog box (see Figure 1.11) opens.

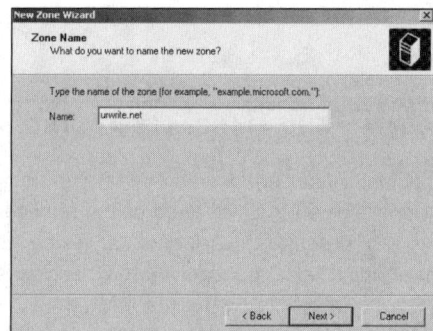

FIGURE 1.11
It is generally a good idea to use a registered domain name when creating a zone.

3. Enter the name of the domain you will be resolving names for into the Name field. If you are on a network that is not connected to the Internet and will not be resolving names for users outside your internal network, this name can be anything. Click Next to open the Reverse Lookup Zone screen (see Figure 1.12). This zone does the opposite of the forward lookup zone (as we discussed in the "Reverse Lookups" section of this chapter), and it allows users to query for the hostname associated with an IP address.

4. Select the Yes, Create a Reverse Lookup Zone option. The wizard creates a reverse lookup zone. Click Next to open the Zone Type dialog box (see Figure 1.13).

5. Select Active Directory-Integrated for the most secure implementation, and click Next. The Reverse Lookup Zone dialog box (see Figure 1.14) opens.

continues

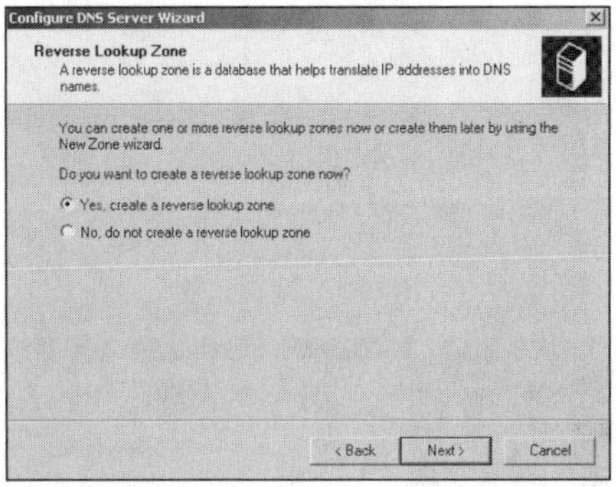

FIGURE 1.12
A reverse lookup zone allows users to resolve an IP address to a hostname.

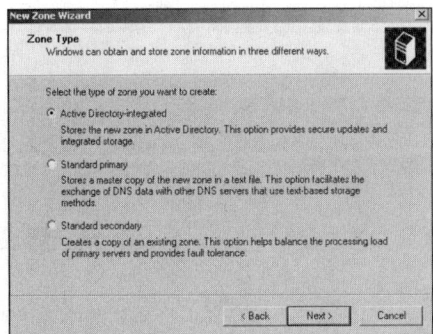

FIGURE 1.13
For the most secure implementation, store your DNS table in Active Directory.

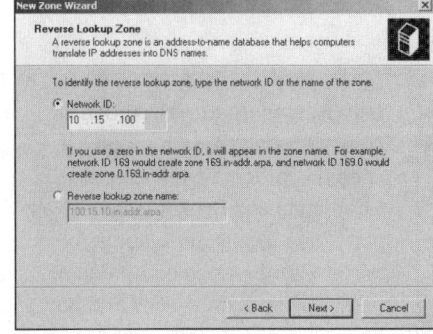

FIGURE 1.14
You can either specify a Network ID or use the standard DNS naming convention to identify the reverse lookup zone.

continued

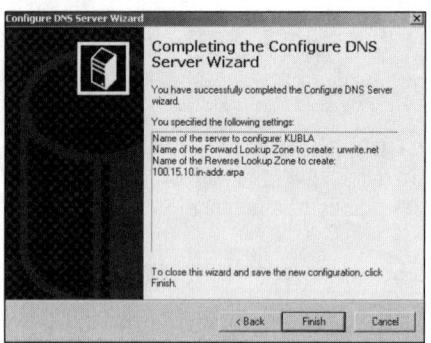

FIGURE 1.15

When you reach the final screen, you can still go back to make changes or cancel the configuration wizard without implementing the changes.

EXAM TIP

DNS Names Used with Active Directory Can't Be Changed In choosing a domain name to use when installing DNS, it is always a good idea to register a domain name with the appropriate domain name registration agency and use that even if your internal network is isolated (not connected to the Internet), because the DNS name used with Active Directory cannot be changed. That the DNS name used with the Active Directory Services cannot be changed would make an excellent exam question.

6. Identify the reverse lookup ID by the Network ID or by specifying a name. The name shown in Figure 1.14 uses the standard naming convention, which is the Network ID (in this case 10.15.100.x) in reverse order, with in-addr.arpa appended. This results in the reverse name of 100.15.10.in-addr.arpa. Notice the arpa in the name. If you were guessing that this naming convention has been around since the Internet was called the ARPAnet, you would be correct. As we discussed in the "Reverse Lookups" section of the chapter, this is the Internet-standard naming convention, and you should try to stick with it. Click Next to open the Completing the Configure DNS Server Wizard dialog box (see Figure 1.15). This screen allows you to review the configurations you selected and either go back to correct mistakes or cancel the wizard before the changes are committed.

7. Click Finish to complete the configuration. Notice in Figure 1.16 that the domains that were configured by the wizard now appear in DNS console.

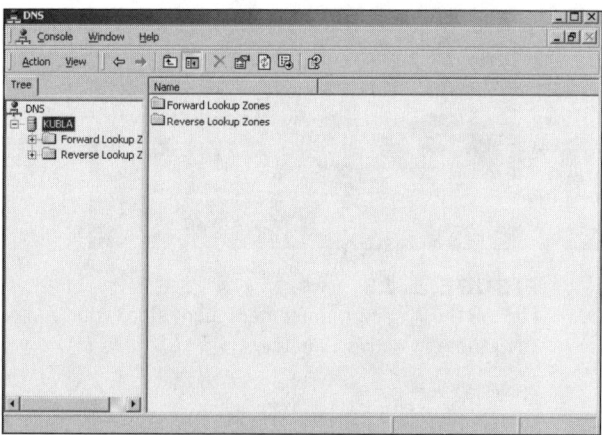

FIGURE 1.16

Your new domain(s) now appear in the DNS console application.

Now you have created a zone using the Configure DNS Server
Wizard. Let's look at creating a new zone using the DNS console
application.

To create a Standard Primary Forward Lookup zone on your DNS
server, do the following:

STEP BY STEP

1.5 Creating a Standard Primary Forward Lookup Zone

1. Open the DNS console by going to Administrative Tools
   and selecting DNS. Right-click the DNS server and
   select New Zone. The New Zone Wizard starts (see
   Figure 1.17). Click Next to open the Zone Type dialog
   box (see Figure 1.18). The Zone Type dialog box allows
   you to select the type of zone to create.

2. Select Standard Primary. If you select Active Directory-
   Integrated, you will complete the same process, but you
   will not be prompted for a zone database filename. Click
   Next. The Forward or Reverse Lookup Zone dialog box
   opens (see Figure 1.19).

continues

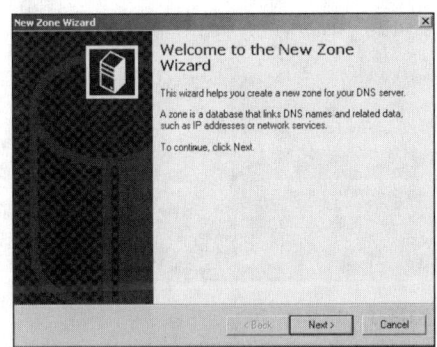

FIGURE 1.17
The New Zone Wizard guides you through
configuring a new zone on your DNS server.

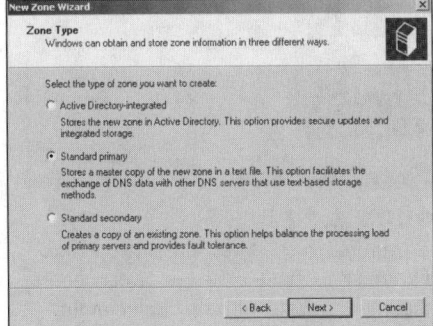

FIGURE 1.18
In this process, store your DNS table in
Standard Primary, not Active Directory.

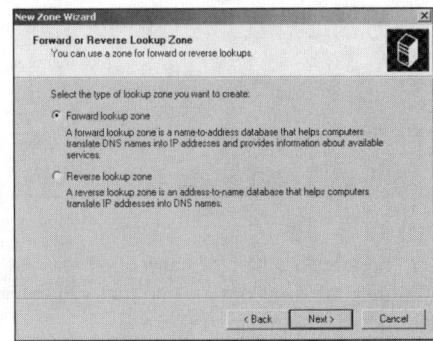

FIGURE 1.19
If you are hosting multiple domains, you will
generally create more forward lookup zones
than reverse lookup zones.

continued

3. Create either a forward (name to IP address) or a reverse (IP address to name) lookup zone.

4. Select Forward and click Next. The Zone Name dialog box opens (see Figure 1.20).

5. Enter the name of the domain you will be resolving names for into the Name field. Click Next to open the Zone File dialog box (see Figure 1.21).

6. Create a new DNS file or import an existing DNS file. Importing is particularly useful if you are replacing a non-Windows DNS server and want to import the information. Click Next to open the Completing the New Zone Wizard dialog box (see Figure 1.22). This screen allows you to review the configurations you selected and either go back to correct mistakes or cancel the wizard before the changes are committed.

7. Click Finish to complete the configuration. The new domain now appears in DNS console (see Figure 1.23).

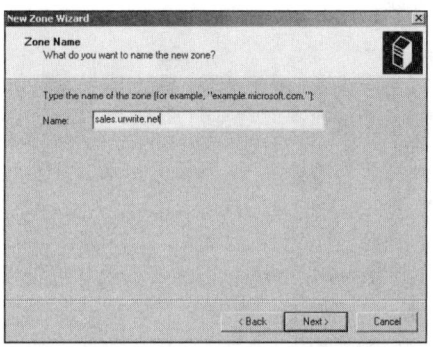

FIGURE 1.20
It is generally a good idea to use a registered domain name whenever you are creating a zone.

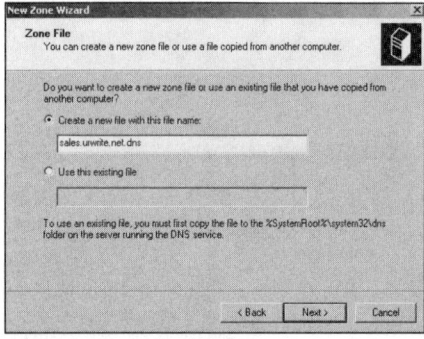

FIGURE 1.21
Using the standard naming convention for your DNS files is an excellent idea so that you can easily identify the file in the future.

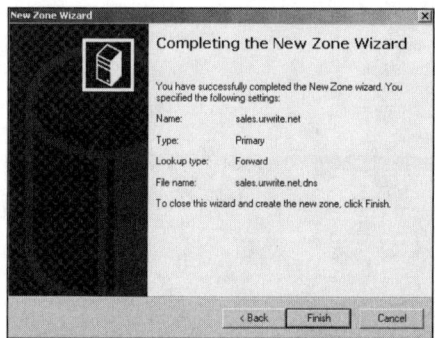

FIGURE 1.22
When you reach the final screen, you can still go back to make changes or cancel the configuration wizard without implementing the changes.

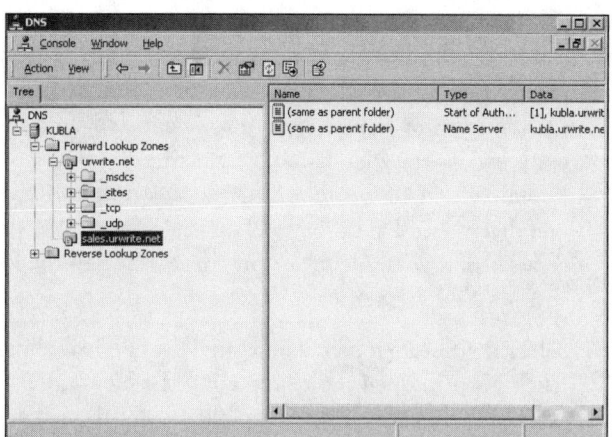

FIGURE 1.23
The DNS console immediately lists the new domain in its hierarchical order.

We created a forward lookup zone. Now let's look at creating a reverse lookup zone.

STEP BY STEP

1.6 Creating a Reverse Lookup Zone

1. Open the DNS console by choosing Administrative Tools and selecting DNS. Right-click the DNS server and select New Zone. The New Zone Wizard starts (refer to Figure 1.17). Click Next to open the Zone Type dialog box (refer to Figure 1.18). The Zone Type dialog box allows you to select the type of zone to create.

2. Select Standard Primary, and click Next. The Forward or Reverse Lookup Zone dialog box opens (refer to Figure 1.19).

3. Create either a forward (name to IP address) or a Reverse (IP address to name) lookup zone.

4. Select Reverse and click Next. The Reverse Lookup Zone dialog box opens (see Figure 1.24).

continues

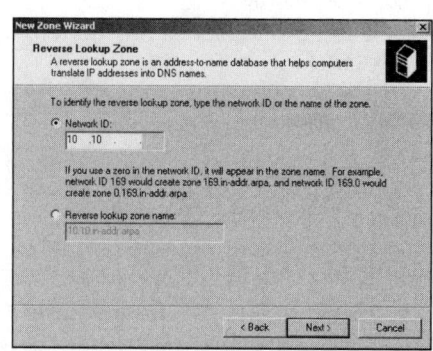

FIGURE 1.24
To be on the safe side, you should specify the network address and let the wizard create the zone name.

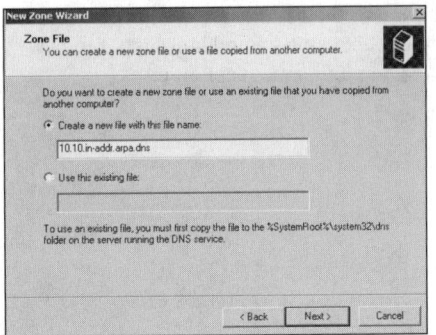

FIGURE 1.25
From the Zone File dialog box, you can create a new zone file, or you can use an existing file to populate your zone when it is created.

NOTE

Room for Cached Information All the cache entries on a caching-only server are stored in RAM. You want to be sure that your caching server has plenty of RAM; otherwise, it will not be effective.

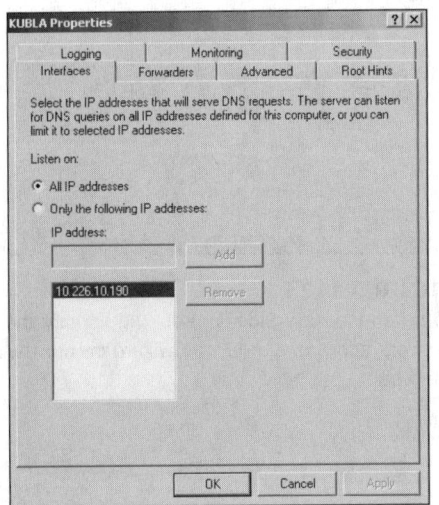

FIGURE 1.26
The DNS server Properties dialog box allows you to configure the advanced properties of the server.

continued

5. Enter the IP address of the network you want to perform reverse lookups for. If you are familiar with the naming conventions for reverse lookup zone names, you can manually specify the zone name by selecting the Reverse Lookup Zone Name option. Click Next to go to the Zone File dialog (see Figure 1.25). This dialog box allows you to create a new zone file or use an already created file from another DNS server.

6. Select the Create a New File with This File Name option. Click Next to open the Completing the New Zone Wizard dialog box. This screen allows you to review the configurations you selected and either go back to correct mistakes or cancel the wizard before the changes are committed. Click Finish to complete the configuration. The new domain appears in the DNS console.

You should have a good understanding of how zones are created. Now let's take a look at setting up a caching-only server.

Configuring a Caching-Only Server

Caching-only servers are used to speed up client computer DNS queries by gathering a large number of cached records based on client computer DNS queries. A caching-only server does not have a copy of the zone table and therefore cannot respond to queries against the zone unless they are already cached. A caching server is not authoritative on any zone.

To configure a caching-only server, install DNS as described previously in the installing DNS procedure, and then do the following:

STEP BY STEP

1.7 Creating a Caching-Only DNS Server

1. Open the DNS console by going to Administrative Tools and selecting DNS. Right-click your new server and select Properties. The DNS server Properties dialog box (see Figure 1.26) opens; the title bar reflects the name of your server.

2. Click the Root Hints tab (see Figure 1.27). If any entries exist for the root servers, delete them.

3. From the Root Hints tab, click Add to open the New Resource Record dialog box (see Figure 1.28). Add a resource record for every DNS server you want this server to cache lookups for. These name servers must already exist in your DNS hierarchy.

4. Click OK when this is completed. Notice that the name servers appear in the Root Hints window (see Figure 1.29). Click OK to return to the DNS console.

To verify that the caching function is working, ping several hosts from a workstation configured to use that server for DNS. This builds up the cache. Go to another workstation also using that server for DNS and ping the same hosts. The response should be much quicker.

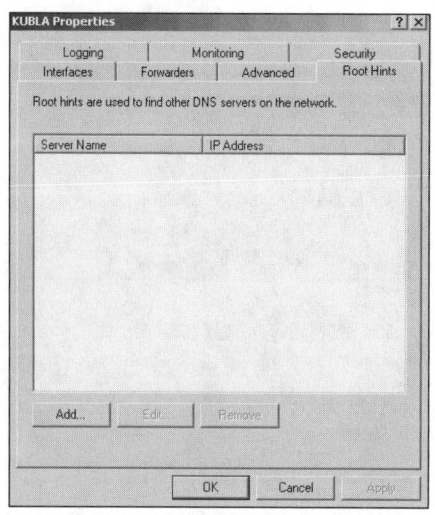

FIGURE 1.27
The root hints are used to locate other DNS servers on the network.

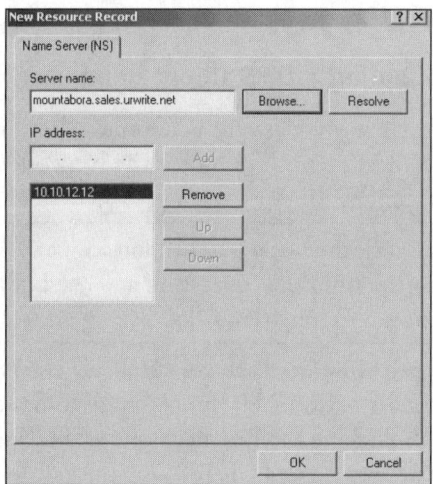

FIGURE 1.28
The New Resource Record dialog box allows you to add existing name servers to your root hints list.

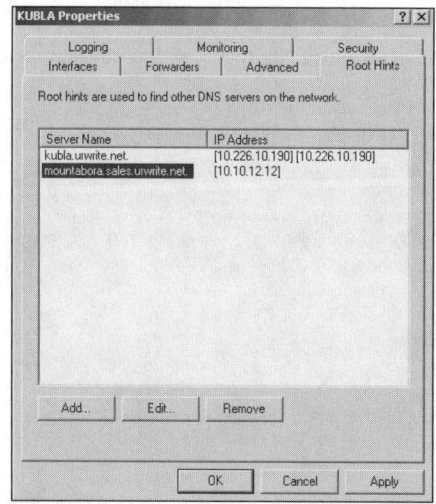

FIGURE 1.29
After you have added the name servers you will be caching, they appear in the Root Hints window.

Configuring a DNS Client Computer

Now that you have installed and configured the DNS server portion of Windows 2000 DNS, you should take a look at how to install DNS on a Windows 2000 client computer. The key to installing DNS on a Windows 2000 client computer is to keep in mind that DNS is installed in two places. First, DNS is configured as part of the TCP/IP interface. If you have ever installed DNS on a Windows NT computer, this process should be familiar.

The second place you need to install DNS under Windows 2000 is in the System Properties. The DNS information configured under System Properties is used as the DNS suffix for building FQDNs (similar to the suffix information configured under TCP/IP properties on other Windows operating systems.) It is also used as part of the process for registering the computer in Dynamic DNS, which is new with Windows 2000. Let's start by configuring the TCP/IP properties:

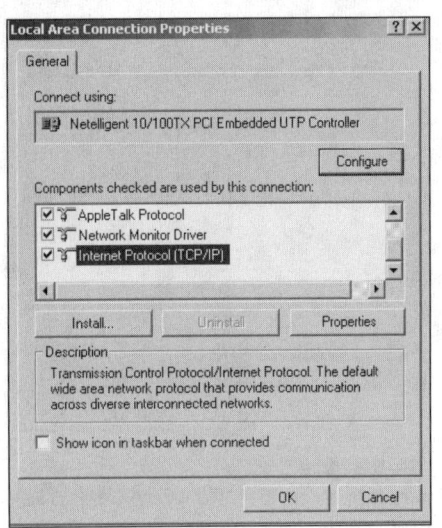

FIGURE 1.30
The Local Area Connection Properties dialog box gives you access to any of your LAN properties, including the TCP/IP settings.

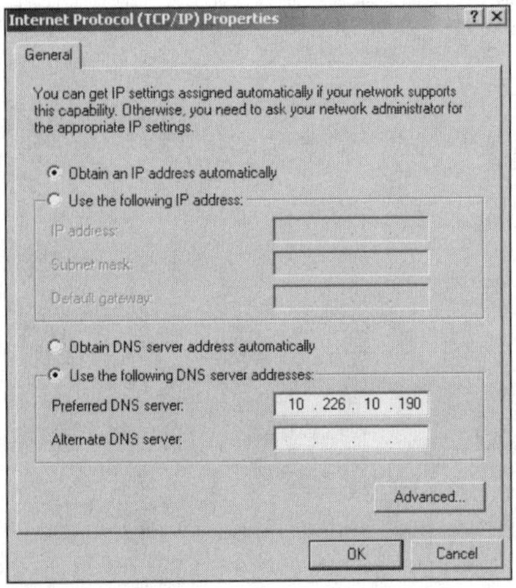

FIGURE 1.31
You can either have your DNS settings obtained automatically via DHCP or specify them manually.

STEP BY STEP

1.8 Configuring a DNS Client computer

1. Right-click My Network Places and select Properties from the context menu. This opens the Network and Dial-up Connections window.

2. Right-click the Local Connection icon and select Properties from the context menu. The Local Area Connection Properties dialog box opens (see Figure 1.30).

3. Select the Internet Protocol (TCP/IP) entry and click the Properties button. You can accomplish the same thing by double-clicking the Internet Protocol (TCP/IP) entry. The Internet Protocol (TCP/IP) Properties dialog box opens (see Figure 1.31).

4. In the DNS section of the dialog box, you can either choose to have DNS configured automatically via DHCP, or specify the Preferred and Alternate DNS servers. Click Advanced for additional DNS options. Click the DNS tab to see the DNS options shown in Figure 1.32.

5. In the Advanced TCP/IP Settings dialog box, you can configure several DNS client computer settings. For this Step by Step, leave the default settings.

6. Click OK to return to the Internet Protocol (TCP/IP) Properties dialog box. Click OK to return to the Local Area Network Properties dialog box. Click OK to close the Local Area Network Properties dialog box and put unapplied changes into effect.

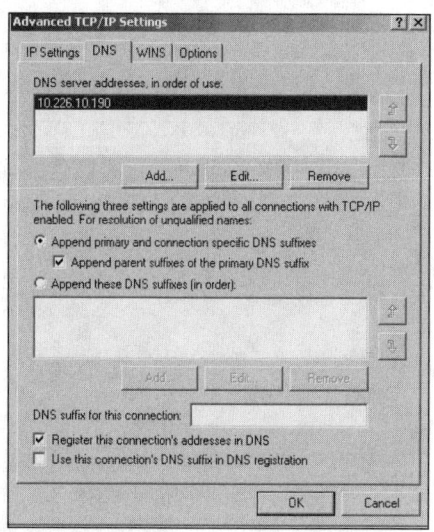

FIGURE 1.32
The Advanced TCP/IP Settings dialog box gives you additional DNS configuration options.

A number of advanced TCP/IP options can be configured in conjunction with the DNS client computer. They include the following:

◆ DNS server addresses, in order of use.

◆ Parameters for resolving unqualified domain names. The options include the following:

• **Append Primary and Connection Specific DNS Suffixes.** This option appends the domain suffixes configured in the System Properties to any unqualified domain names sent for resolution.

• **Append Parent Suffixes of the Primary DNS Suffix**. This option adds not only the specified domain suffixes, but also the suffixes of any parent domains to any unqualified domain names sent for resolution.

• **Append These DNS Suffixes (In Order).** This option allows you to specify specific DNS suffixes to be appended to any unqualified domain names sent for resolution.

• **DNS Suffix for this Connection.** This option allows you to configure a specific DNS suffix for this connection in the list of Network and Dial-up Connections. You can specify different suffixes in case you have multiple LAN Adapters loaded, or you want to use different suffixes between LAN and dial-up connections.

NOTE **The Grayed-Out Properties Button** If your computer is a domain controller, the identification information cannot be changed.

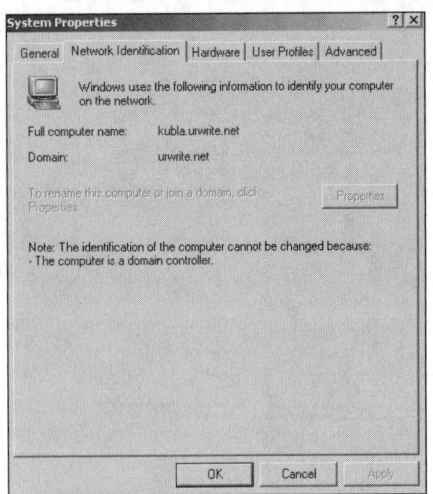

FIGURE 1.33
The Network Identification tab is where you
set the name and domain membership of
your computer.

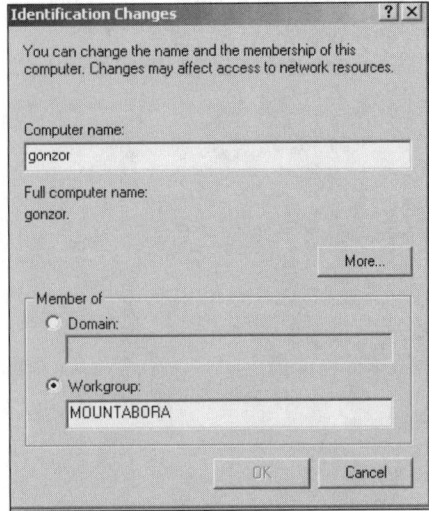

FIGURE 1.34
From this dialog box, you can set the domain
and computer name. You can also access the
domain information by clicking More.

- **Register This Connection's Addresses in DNS.** This is
  how you configure the computer to take advantage of
  Dynamic DNS.

- **Use This Connection's DNS Suffix in DNS
  Registration.** This option allows you to use the DNS suffix specified with this connection as part of the information used when the host is registered with Dynamic DNS.

To modify the DNS settings in the System Properties, do
the following:

STEP BY STEP

1.9 Modifying the DNS Settings for Active Directory Integration

1. Right-click the My Computer icon on the desktop. From
   the context menu, select Properties. The System Properties
   dialog box opens. Select the Network Identification tab
   (see Figure 1.33).

2. Click Properties. The Identification Changes dialog box
   (see Figure 1.34) opens.

3. Click More to open the DNS Suffix and NetBIOS
   Computer Name dialog box (see Figure 1.35). Fill in your
   DNS domain name. Checking the Change Primary DNS
   Suffix When Domain Membership Changes option
   ensures that the host's DNS domain matches its Active
   Directory domain.

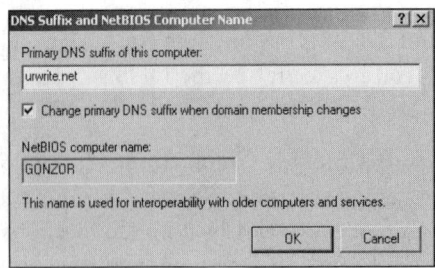

FIGURE 1.35
You set your DNS information for registration
with Dynamic DNS in this dialog box.

4. Click OK to save the changes. Click OK to return to
System Properties. Click OK twice to close the System
Properties dialog box. You will be prompted to reboot
your computer. Do so.

You have now completed configuring your Windows 2000 DNS
client computer. Now let's look at configuring the zones for
dynamic updates.

Configuring Zones for Dynamic Updates

One of the major advantages to running a Windows 2000 network
is the capability to use Dynamic DNS. Let's look at how to configure a zone for dynamic updates.

To configure your DNS zone for dynamic updates, do the following:

STEP BY STEP

1.10 Configuring Your Zone for Dynamic Updates

1. From the Administrative Tools program menu, open the
DNS console.

2. Select the zone you want to configure to receive dynamic
updates, and right-click. From the context menu, select
Properties. This opens the Properties dialog box shown in
Figure 1.36. (The title bar of the dialog box reflects the
name of the zone.)

3. Set the Allow Dynamic Updates pull-down menu to Yes.
Click OK to close the dialog box and return to the DNS
console. You have just configured the zone to accept
dynamic updates.

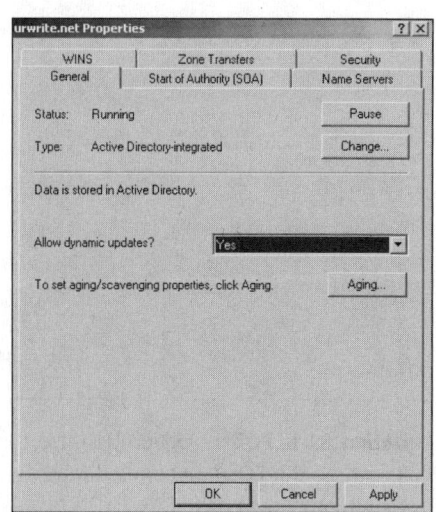

FIGURE 1.36
The zone Properties dialog box allows you to
pause the DNS Server service, change the
domain type, configure your DNS server to
accept dynamic updates, and set the
aging/scavenging options for the domain.

Before we move on to testing the DNS Server service, we should briefly discuss what Dynamic DNS is.

Dynamic DNS is specified in RFC 2136—Dynamic Updates in the Domain Name System (DNS UPDATE). It is the foundation of a successful Active Directory Services implementation. As we have discussed, DNS is used to resolve a name to an IP address, or vice versa, using a defined hierarchical naming structure to ensure uniformity. Dynamic DNS takes that architecture to the next level. This section describes the Windows 2000 implementation of dynamic update.

In Windows 2000, client computers can send dynamic updates for three types of network adapters: DHCP adapters, statically configured adapters, and remote access adapters. You looked at these configurations in the "Configuring a DNS Client Computer" section earlier in the chapter.

What Dynamic DNS does is integrates DHCP and DNS, as described in RFC 2136. Every time a computer requests a new address or renews its address, the computer sends an option 81 and its fully qualified name to the DHCP server and requests that the DHCP server register an entry in the reverse lookup DNS zone on its behalf. The DHCP client computer also requests an entry in the forward lookup zone on its own behalf. The end result is that every DHCP client computer has an entry in the DNS zones, both forward and reverse. This information can be used by other Windows 2000 computers in place of WINS for identifying the names and IP addresses of other hosts.

NOTE **Option 81 Is FQDN** Option 81 (also known as the FQDN option) allows the client computer to send its FQDN to the DHCP server when it requests an IP address.

By default, the dynamic update client computer dynamically registers its resource records whenever any of the following events occur:

◆ The TCP/IP configuration is changed.

◆ The DHCP address is renewed or a new lease is obtained.

◆ A Plug and Play event occurs.

◆ An IP address is added or removed from the computer when the user changes or adds an IP address for a static adapter.

By default, the dynamic update client computer automatically deregisters name–to–IP address mappings whenever the DHCP lease expires.

You can force a reregistration by using the command-line tool
Ipconfig. For Windows 2000–based client computers, type the
following at the command prompt:

```
ipconfig /registerdns
```

Now let's take a quick look at the dynamic update process and see
how your Windows 2000 host gets dynamically registered with
DNS. A dynamic update occurs in the following manner:

1. The DNS client computer queries its local name server to find
   the primary name server and the zone that is authoritative for
   the name it is updating. The local name server performs the
   standard name resolution process to discover the primary
   name server and returns the name of the authoritative server
   and zone.

2. The client computer sends a dynamic update request to the
   primary server. The authoritative server performs the update
   and replies to the client computer regarding the result of the
   dynamic update.

Now that DNS is installed and configured, let's look at how to
test DNS.

Testing the DNS Server Service

How can you test to make sure DNS is working? Several applications allow you to perform these tests. We'll discuss them in order of
complexity.

The first application for testing DNS is the PING.EXE utility.
What PING allows you to do is send an ICMP (Internet Control
Message Protocol) to a TCP/IP host. By using the correct flag,
PING can also perform name resolution as part of its testing proce-
dure. The correct format for this command is the following:

PING –a <destination address> where the –a flag provides hostname
resolution. A sample PING session might look like this:

```
ping -a www.newriders.com
Pinging scone.donet.com [205.133.113.87] with 32 bytes
➡of data:
Reply from 205.133.113.87: bytes=32 time=47ms TTL=241
Reply from 205.133.113.87: bytes=32 time=60ms TTL=242
Reply from 205.133.113.87: bytes=32 time=40ms TTL=242
```

```
Reply from 205.133.113.87: bytes=32 time=37ms TTL=242
Ping statistics for 205.133.113.87:
Packets: Sent = 4, Received = 4, Lost = 0 (0% loss),
Approximate round trip times in milli-seconds:
Minimum = 37ms, Maximum =  60ms, Average =  46ms
```

A number of other switches can be used with the PING utility. They are:

- **-t.** Ping the specified host until stopped. If you want to view the statistics and then continue, type Control+Break. To end the pinging, type Control+C.

- **-n count.** Ping the specified host n times.

- **-l size.** Ping the specified host with packets of l size.

- **-f.** Set the Don't Fragment flag in the packet.

- **-i TTL.** Set the time to live (TTL) to i. TTL is the equivalent of router hops.

- **-v TOS.** Set the type of service used.

- **-r count.** Record route for count hops.

- **-s count.** Time stamp for count hops.

- **-j host-list.** Loose source route along host list. This is not a frequently used flag because source routing is seldom used.

- **-k host list.** Strict source route along host list. This is also used very seldom.

- **-w timeout.** Timeout in milliseconds to wait for each reply.

> **NOTE**
>
> **An Alias for Another Server's FQDN**
> If you are familiar with the Internet's server-hosting architecture, you may surmise that this means that the server www.newriders.com is hosted by a third-party company with the domain of donet.com.

From this sample you can see several things. First, because your ping –a returned the IP address of 205.133.113.87, you know that DNS is functional. Second, because this also returned the alternate hostname of scone.donet.com, you can see that www.newriders.com is a DNS alias, or CNAME for another server's FQDN.

The rest of the information has to do with network latency and has little application for this chapter.

The next utility we need to look at is NSLOOKUP.EXE. NSLOOKUP is a standard command-line tool provided in most DNS server implementations, including Windows 2000. NSLOOKUP offers the capability to perform query testing of DNS servers and obtain detailed responses at the command prompt. This information can be useful for diagnosing and solving name resolution problems, for verifying that resource records are added or updated correctly in a zone, and for debugging other server-related problems. NSLOOKUP can be used by going to a DOS prompt and typing **NSLOOKUP** and pressing Enter. It can be run with the following options:

Commands: (Identifiers are shown in uppercase; [ ] means optional.)

◆ **NAME.** Print info about the host/domain NAME using default server.

◆ **NAME1 NAME2.** Same as the preceding, but use NAME2 as server.

◆ **help or ?.** Print info on common commands.

◆ **set OPTION.** Set an option.

- **all.** Print options, current server and host.

- **[no]debug.** Print debugging information.

- **[no]d2.** Print exhaustive debugging information.

- **[no]defname.** Append domain name to each query.

- **[no]recurse.** Ask for recursive answer to query.

- **[no]search.** Use domain search list.

- **[no]vc.** Always use a virtual circuit.

- **domain=NAME.** Set default domain name to NAME.

- **srchlist=N1[/N2/.../N6].** Set domain to N1 and search list to N1,N2, and so on.

- **root=NAME.** Set root server to NAME.

- **retry=X.** Set number of retries to X.

- **timeout=X.** Set initial timeout interval to X seconds.

- **type=X.** Set query type (for example, A, ANY, CNAME, MX, NS, PTR, SOA, SRV).

- **querytype=X.** Same as type.

- **class=X.** Set query class (for example, IN (Internet), ANY).

- **[no]msxfr.** Use MS fast zone transfer.

- **ixfrver=X.** Current version to use in IXFR transfer request.

EXAM TIP

Know NSLOOKUP Because NSLOOKUP is the standard DNS tool for troubleshooting DNS, you should be familiar with its capabilities and options for the exam.

◆ **server NAME.** Set default server to NAME, using current default server.

◆ **lserver NAME.** Set default server to NAME, using initial server.

◆ **finger [USER].** Finger the optional NAME at the current default host.

◆ **root.** Set current default server to the root.

◆ **ls [opt] DOMAIN [> FILE].** List addresses in DOMAIN (optional: output to FILE).

   • **-a.** List canonical names and aliases.

   • **-d.** List all records.

   • **-t TYPE.** List records of the given type (for example, A, CNAME, MX, NS, PTR, and so on).

◆ **view FILE.** Sort an 'ls' output file and view it with pg.

◆ **exit.** Exit the program.

Great. If you are not familiar with NSLOOKUP, those options are probably clear as mud. The best way to get a thorough understanding of the NSLOOKUP options and flags is to try them out. But for a simple test of a DNS using NSLOOKUP, select a hostname you know is in DNS and type in the following:

```
nslookup kubla.urwrite.net
```

This command returns the following:

```
Server:   kubla.urwrite.net
Address:  10.225.10.190
Name:  kubla.urwrite.net
Address:  10.225.10.190
```

In this example, you used the name of the DNS server for the test. You can use any host in the DNS table. The first name and address returned are the name and address for the DNS server you are querying. If this server does not have a PTR record in a reverse lookup zone, the server name will be returned with a message that says:

```
*** Can't find server name for address (the address
    ➡of the configured DNS server): Nonexistent domain
*** Default servers are unavailable
```

> **EXAM TIP**
>
> **Know the NSLOOKUP Modes** You should be familiar with the fact that NSLOOKUP functions in both the interactive and noninteractive modes. Noninteractive is used when you need only a single piece of information.

This does not mean anything is broken. If you still get name resolution in the Name/Address section of the response, your DNS server is working.

Another method for testing the DNS Server service is to use the monitoring capabilities built in to the DNS console application. To set up testing and monitoring, do the following:

STEP BY STEP

1.11 Testing the DNS Service

1. Open the DNS console application.

2. Right-click the DNS server and select Properties. The DNS Server Properties dialog box opens. Select the Monitoring tab. You can configure a simple query, a recursive query, and even automatic testing of the DNS service from this tab.

3. Click Test Now to perform the selected tests.

4. Click OK to return to the DNS console application.

The test we just discussed allows you to perform two types of queries. Before we move on, we should discuss exactly what those queries are and how they work:

◆ **Simple (iterative) query.** A simple (or iterative) query is one where the name server provides the best response based on what that server knows from local zone files or from caching. If a name server doesn't have any information to answer the query, it simply sends a negative response.

◆ **Recursive query.** A recursive query forces a DNS server to respond to a request with either a failure or a successful response. With a recursive query, the DNS server must contact any other DNS servers it needs to resolve the request. This is a much more resource-intensive query mechanism.

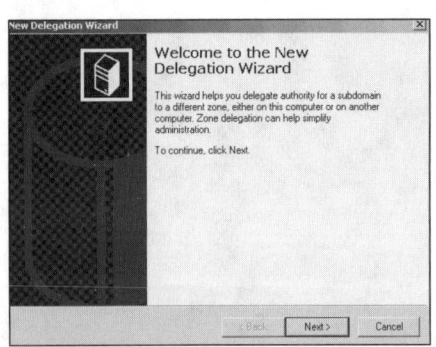

FIGURE 1.37
As with most other administrative tasks with Windows 2000, a wizard is available for creating a new delegation for a zone.

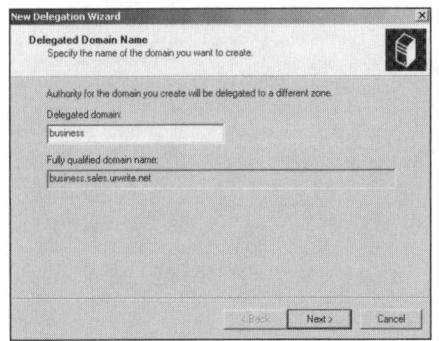

FIGURE 1.38
The Delegated Domain Name dialog box allows you to specify the domain that will be responding to delegated queries.

If the test fails, you will see an error message in the DNS console application, and an alert icon will appear on the DNS server.

A final method for testing a DNS server is to use a Web browser such as Internet Explorer. Type the FQDN you want to reach into the URL Locater box and press Enter. If DNS is working correctly, the IP address will be displayed in the lower-left corner of the application. This occurs even if the host in question is not a Web server. The browser may not connect successfully, but you should see that resolution if DNS is configured correctly.

Implementing a Delegated Zone for DNS

The next thing we need to look at is how to create a delegated zone for your DNS. Delegating a domain means that DNS queries on the existing domain will be referred to the name server in the delegated domain for resolution. You can delegate only down the hierarchy, so the delegated domain must be a subdomain of the domain doing the delegation. That may be a little confusing, but the configuration procedure should make it a little more clear.

To create a delegated zone, do the following:

STEP BY STEP

1.12 Creating a Delegated Zone

1. From the Administrative Tools program group, open the DNS console application.

2. Right-click the DNS zone you would like to delegate, and from the context menu select New Delegation. The New Delegation Wizard (see Figure 1.37) opens. Click Next to continue.

3. In the Delegated Domain Name dialog box (see Figure 1.38) enter the unqualified name for the domain you want to delegate to in the Delegated Domain field.

Click Next to continue. The Name Servers dialog box (see Figure 1.39) allows you to specify the name server that will be hosting the delegated zone.

4. Click Add and you can either browse to the name server or specify it by name or IP address. Click Next to complete the wizard. To create the delegation, click Finish.

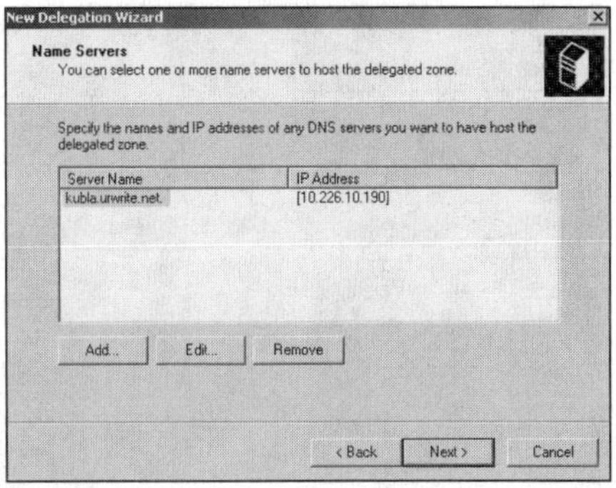

FIGURE 1.39
The Name Servers dialog box should look familiar at this point. As with the previous procedures, this dialog box is used to specify the name servers for this domain.

Manually Creating DNS Resource Records

We've spent most of the chapter looking at the dynamic methods for creating entries in the DNS table. Now let's look at how to manually create an entry. You might use this for non-Windows 2000 hosts, table entry types that are not supported by Dynamic DNS, or for hosts that you just want to configure with a static entry. When you manually create a DNS entry, you have four options on what type of entry to create:

◆ **New Host.** This creates an A record.

◆ **New Alias.** This creates a CNAME record.

◆ **New Mail Exchanger.** This creates an MX record.

◆ **Other New Records.** This allows you to select the other record types.

For this procedure, you will create a new host record. To manually create a DNS entry, do the following:

> **NOTE**
> **Names for a Record** When you create your record, you can use the FQDN name or just the hostname. If you use just the hostname, the rest of the FQDN for the domain you are creating the entry in will automatically be appended.

> **EXAM TIP**
> **Be Familiar with Table Entry Types** Prior to taking the exam, you should acquaint yourself with the other table entry types. Each needs slightly different information for its entry.

STEP BY STEP

1.13 Manually Creating a DNS Entry

1. From the Administrative Tools program group, open DNS console. Right-click the zone you want to add an entry in and select the type of entry (listed in Table 1.1) that you want to create.

continues

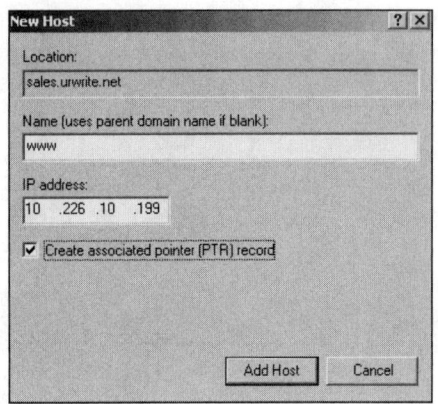

FIGURE 1.40
The New Host dialog box asks for the host-name, the IP address of the host, and whether you want to create an entry in the reverse lookup zone.

continued

2. Select New Host. The New Host dialog box (see Figure 1.40) opens. In the Name field, enter the host-name. Enter the IP address in the IP Address box. If you want to create an entry in the reverse lookup zone for that network, you can select the Create Associated Pointer (PTR) Record option. Click Add Host to create the entry.

Now you know how to install, configure, and create entries for zones. Now we need to discuss how you manage and monitor your DNS server.

MANAGING AND MONITORING DNS

Manage and monitor DNS.

We have looked at installing and configuring the Windows 2000 DNS Server service. Next we need to look at managing and monitoring the server now that it is running. If your job is typical of most, you will spend a great deal more time managing DNS servers than you will installing them.

Although the DNS server doesn't include any specific monitoring capabilities, you should be aware of a number of additional options as you manage your DNS server over the long term. One utility that is very useful for managing your DNS server is the DNS snap-in to the MMC, which is listed as DNS in the Administrative Tools menu.

For a closer look at the capabilities of the DNS console, open the DNS console application. Select the DNS server and click the Action menu to see the available actions:

◆ **Set Aging/Scavenging for All Zones.** Opens the Server Aging/Scavenging Properties dialog box.

◆ **Scavenge Stale Resource Records Manually.**

◆ **All Tasks.** Includes starting, stopping, pausing, resuming, and restarting the DNS Server service.

- ◆ **Delete.** Deletes the DNS server.

- ◆ **Refresh.** Causes all the displayed information to be refreshed with a current status.

- ◆ **Export List.** Exports the information from the DNS server to a tab- or comma-delimited text or Unicode text file.

- ◆ **Properties.** Opens the Properties dialog box for the selected DNS server.

The following sections take a closer look at several of these actions.

Setting Aging/Scavenging for All Zones

When you choose Action, Set Aging/Scavenging for All Zones, you can use the Server Aging/Scavenging Properties dialog box (see Figure 1.41) to set three options:

The Scavenge Stale Resource Records option allows the server to remove stale resource records. With Dynamic DNS updates enabled, records are automatically added to the zone when computers come on the network. In some cases, these records are not automatically deleted. For example, if a computer is disconnected from the network, its associated resource record might not be deleted. If your network has many mobile users (and whose doesn't these days?), this can happen frequently. To keep your zone table clean of inaccurate records, you should enable this option.

The No-Refresh Interval option controls the time between the most recent refresh of a record's time stamp and when the time stamp can be refreshed again. In a very dynamic network where computers come on and leave frequently, you might want to lower this from the default 7 days.

The Refresh Interval option sets the time between the earliest moment that a record time stamp can be refreshed and the earliest moment a record can be scavenged.

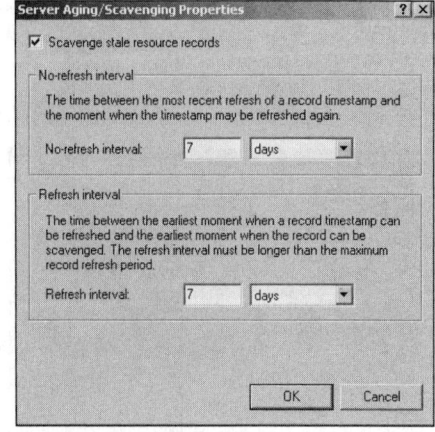

FIGURE 1.41
Setting the record scavenging parameters correctly can improve server performance and reduce problems.

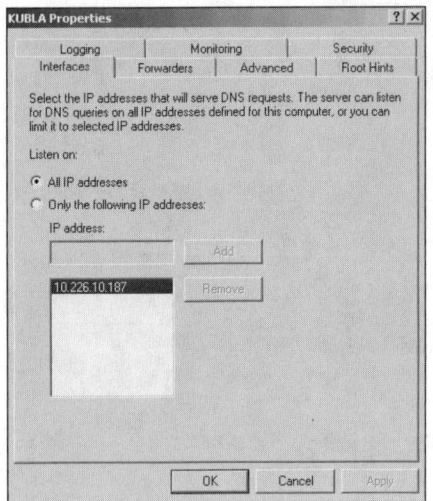

FIGURE 1.42
The Interfaces page can be used to prevent certain IP addresses from responding to DNS requests.

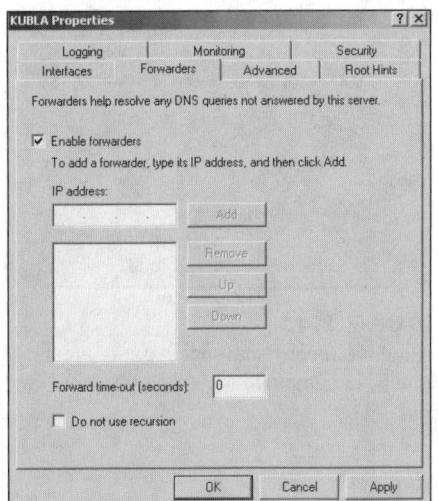

FIGURE 1.43
Forwarders can speed up domain request resolution if they are used correctly.

Scavenging Stale Resource Records Manually

The Scavenge Stale Resource Records Manually option scavenges old resource records. When you choose this command, the Update Server Data Files option writes any changes to the table that are in RAM to the server's hard drive. (To clear the server cache manually, right-click the DNS server and select Clear Cache from the context menu.)

Setting Properties

When you choose Action, Properties, the Properties dialog box opens (see Figure 1.42). In the dialog box, you access to the following tabs. (Remember that the title bar reflects the name of your server.) The Properties dialog box gives you access to the following tabs:

The Forwarders page allows you to configure a list of forwarders for the server to use (see Figure 1.43). A forwarder is sort of a shortcut to domain resolution. Ordinarily, when a DNS server receives a request for a zone that it is not authoritative on, it forwards the request to the root server for the domain and then walks the tree until it either times out or receives a resolution. By using a forwarder, you are betting that the forwarder has already cached the response to the DNS request and is able to respond much faster.

The Advanced page allows you to configure the following advanced options (see Figure 1.44):

◆ **Disable Recursion.** Allows the DNS server to make iterative queries and refer the client computer to the address of a DNS server that might have the answer. If recursion is enabled, the DNS server is forced to resolve the request itself. Iterative queries require much less overhead on the server.

◆ **BIND Secondaries.** Enables support for the BIND version of DNS.

◆ **Fail on Load If Bad Zone Data.** Prevents the server from loading if there is corrupt data in the zone file.

◆ **Enable Round Robin.** Allows you to pool servers in a DNS entry so that the response to a query for the hostname can be any of a group of addresses.

◆ **Enable Netmask Ordering.** Enabled by default; specifies that the DNS server resolves the query with the address closest to the requesting client computer's IP address and listed first in the response. If both round robin and netmask ordering are enabled, netmask ordering will be attempted first.

◆ **Secure Cache Against Pollution.** Helps ensure that bad entries are not loaded into the server's DNS cache.

◆ **Name Checking.** Allows you to specify the types of names the server will accept as part of its DNS table.

◆ **Load Zone Data on Startup.** Allows you to specify from where DNS will load its initial table when the service starts. The most secure option is From Active Directory and Registry.

◆ **Enable Automatic Scavenging of Stale Records.** Gives you the capability to automate the scavenging of stale records and also specify the scavenging period.

The Root Hints page allows you to configure other DNS servers on the network for the forwarding of DNS requests where appropriate (see Figure 1.45).

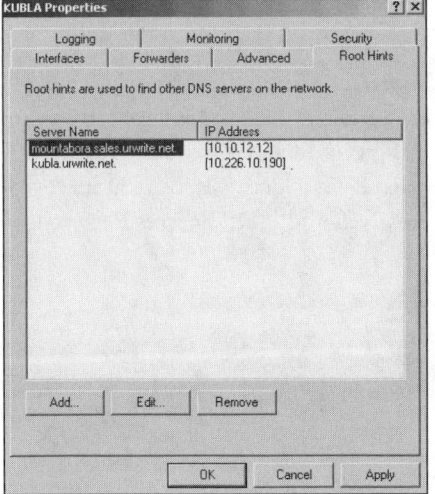

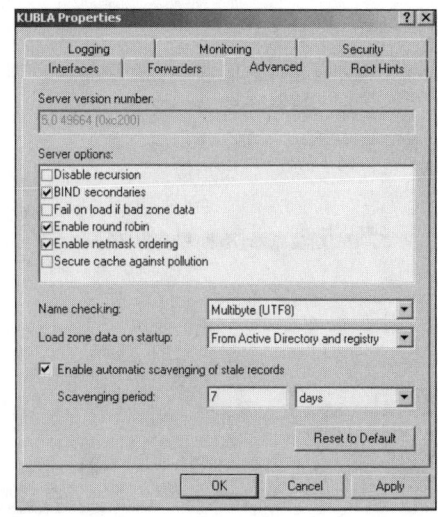

FIGURE 1.44
The Advanced page allows you to fine-tune your DNS parameters.

Know When to Use Round Robin DNS   For the exam, you should be aware that round robin DNS is also known as "Poor Man's Load Balancing." Round robin allows you to use DNS to help spread the load on a group of servers by allowing you to tie multiple IP addresses to a single DNS record. Each time a resolution is requested, DNS will return the "next" record in the list of addresses.

FIGURE 1.45
The Root Hints tab allows you to configure the addresses of additional DNS servers for lookups.

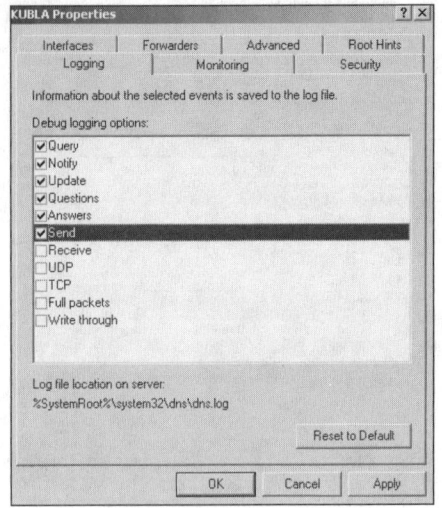

FIGURE 1.46
A number of parameters can be logged to record DNS server use.

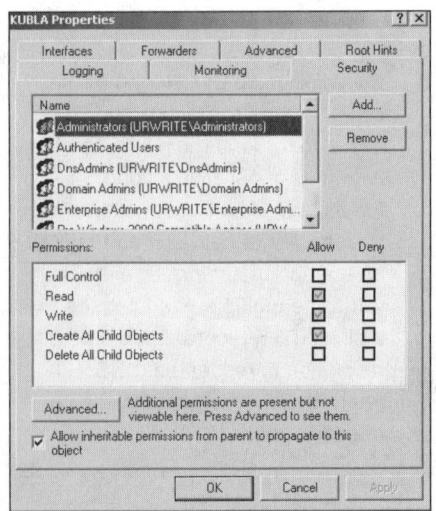

FIGURE 1.47
As with anything security related, the fewer people who have permissions on the DNS service the better.

The Logging page allows you to configure server logging (see Figure 1.46). You can specify which logging options by selecting the option to enable it. The log file can be found at %SystemRoot%\system32\dns\dns.log. %SystemRoot% is usually your Windows system file directory.

The Monitoring page automates the testing of the DNS Server service, and the Security page allows you to configure the rights to the DNS service (see Figure 1.47)

Now that you have looked at the options for managing the DNS server, let's take a look at some of the ways to monitor the service.

Before we discuss how to monitor the DNS server, we should discuss what you can monitor. The following groups of counters are available for the DNS object. Because of the large number of counters, we will discuss the types of counters instead.

◆ **AXFR Counters.** These counters are associated with the full zone transfer requests received by the master DNS server. This group includes Requests Received, Requests Sent, Response Received, Success Received, and Success Sent.

◆ **Caching Memory.** This counter tracks the amount of memory used by the DNS server.

◆ **Database Node Memory.** This counter tracks the amount of database node memory used by the DNS server.

◆ **Dynamic Update.** These counters are associated with the dynamic updating of DNS. This group includes NoOperation, NoOperation/sec, Queued, Received, Received/sec, Rejected, Timeouts, Written to Database and Written to Database/sec.

◆ **IXFR Counters.** These counters are associated with the incremental zone transfer requests received by the master DNS server. This group includes Requests Received, Requests Sent, Response Received, Success Received, Success Sent, TCP Success Received and UDP Success Received.

◆ **Nbtstat Memory.** This counter tracks the amount of Nbtstat memory in use by the server.

◆ **Notify Received/Sent.** These counters track the notifies sent and received by the secondary DNS server.

◆ **Record Flow Memory.** This counter tracks the amount of record flow memory used by the DNS server.

◆ **Recursive.** The recursive counters are associated with the recursive queries the DNS server must make. This group includes Queries, Queries/sec, Query Failure, Query Failure/sec, Send TimeOuts, and TimeOut/sec.

◆ **Secure Update.** The secure update group of counters is associated with the number of secure updates sent and received. The group includes Failure, Received, and Received/sec.

◆ **TCP/UDP.** These counters track the respective TCP and UDP queries and responses. These groups include Message Memory, Query Received, Query Received/sec, Response Sent, and Response Sent/sec.

◆ **Total.** This group of counters totals the respective categories of requests and responses. This group includes Query Received, Query Received/sec, Response Sent, and Response Sent/sec.

◆ **WINS.** Because DNS under Windows 2000 can be used for WINS lookups, the DNS counters include the following WINS-specific counters: Lookup Received, Lookup Received/sec, Response Sent, Response Sent/sec, Reverse Lookup Received, Reverse Lookup Received/sec, Reverse Response Sent, and Reverse Response Sent/sec.

◆ **Zone Transfer.** The zone transfer counters are associated with the process of transferring copies of the DNS table between DNS servers. This group includes Failure, Request Received, SOA Request Sent, and Success.

EXAM TIP

Don't Memorize All the Counters
Microsoft does not expect you to memorize all these counters. You should, however, be familiar with the different types, and know how to use the Performance console.

EXAM TIP

The VIP Counters Are AXFR and IXFR Two types of counters that are especially important are the AXFR and IXFR counters. Remember that AXFR counters are used in conjunction with full zone transfers, whereas IXFR counters are used in conjunction with incremental zone transfers.

NOTE

Identifying a Counter If you need to know what a counter means and you have left your copy of this book at home under your pillow, fear not. Microsoft has included an option that does an excellent job of defining the counters. Select the counter you want to know more about, and click the Explain button.

To configure DNS performance monitoring, do the following:

STEP BY STEP

1.14 Configure DNS Performance Monitoring

1. Open the Performance application by going to Programs, Administrative Tools, Performance (see Figure 1.48).

2. In Performance, select System Monitor (see Figure 1.49).

3. To create an entry in System Monitor, click the Add (+) icon. The Add Counters window opens. By default it opens to the Processor performance object.

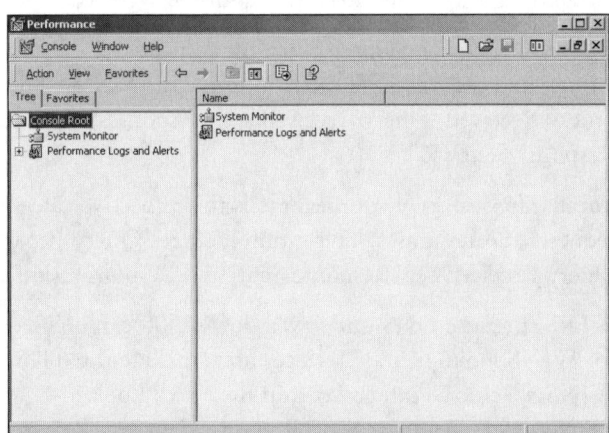

FIGURE 1.48

The Performance console allows you to monitor a variety of system and application metrics for evaluating the performance and health of the system.

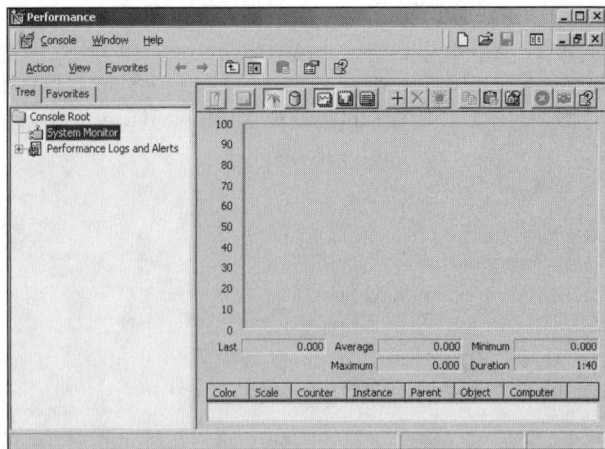

FIGURE 1.49

System Monitor allows you to monitor the performance of your server's statistics in real-time.

4. Select the DNS performance object. You will see the list of counters displayed as available for DNS (see Figure 1.50). Figure 1.51 shows the explanation function of the Performance console.

5. After you have decided on the counter you want to monitor, click Add. You can add multiple counters either by selecting each counter and clicking Add, or by using the standard Windows multiple item select method of holding down the Ctrl key while you select all the counters you wish to monitor and clicking Add. Click Close when you are done. You will see your counters being graphed, similar to those shown in Figure 1.52.

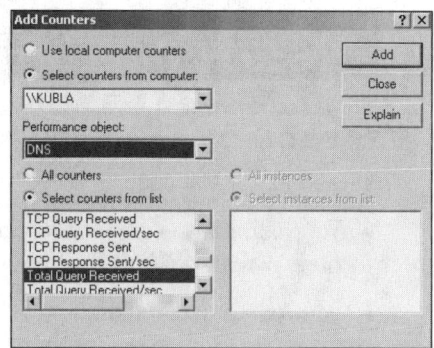

FIGURE 1.50
The counters associated with DNS allow you to comprehensively examine the DNS server's activities.

You've looked at the management options available in the DNS console application, and you've taken a look at how to monitor the performance of the different DNS counters using the Performance console. At this point you should have a good understanding of the Windows 2000 DNS Server service and DNS in general. Now let's see how you apply it in a practical situation.

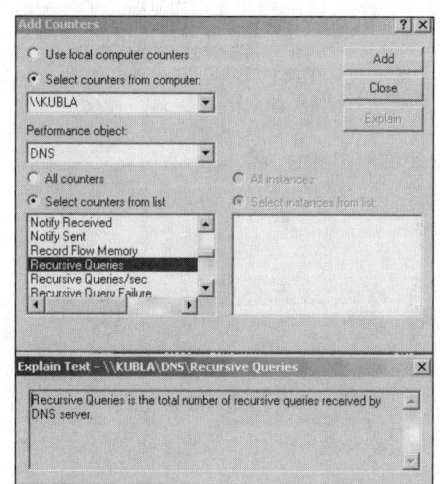

FIGURE 1.51
To find more information about a counter, select it and click the Explain button.

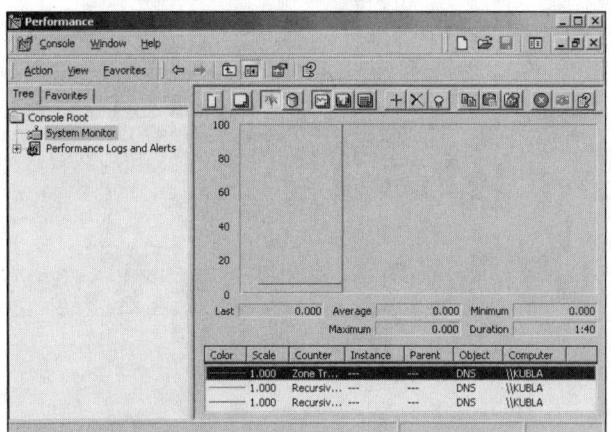

FIGURE 1.52
After the counters have been added, all that remains is successfully interpreting the data.

CASE STUDY: IMPLEMENTING DNS IN A COMPLEX ENVIRONMENT

ESSENCE OF THE CASE

The essence of the case is as follows:

▶ Your company is about to migrate to a pure Windows 2000 environment.

▶ Your company is actually made up of three companies, each needing to maintain local control of its DNS.

▶ Users for each company need to be able to resolve addresses for other company's hosts as quickly as possible.

▶ Corporate headquarters needs to resolve addresses for each of the companies but does not need to maintain a DNS domain.

SCENARIO

You are the network administrator for NR Widgets Inc., a multinational conglomerate, and you are based in the conglomerate's corporate headquarters. NR Widgets Inc. is made up of three companies: NR Manufacturing, NR Consulting, and NR Telecommunications. Each company has its own IT department and maintains its own network infrastructure. Each company also has its own DNS domain.

You have been asked to prepare the network for a complete Windows 2000 rollout, both client computers and servers, with the goal to be a pure Windows 2000 network. The first thing on your list is to implement a Windows 2000-capable DNS infrastructure. Keep in mind the following:

- Each IT department keeps control of its own domain.

- Each company's users have the fastest possible resolution for other company's hosts.

- The users in the headquarters facility need fast DNS resolution for each of the company's hosts.

- Because the headquarters is a not a computing center, you do not need to maintain any master DNS servers.

What should you do?

ANALYSIS

First, you will need to roll out Windows 2000 DNS servers. In reality, you should also have completed an Active Directory Services design, but you are concerned just with DNS services at

CASE STUDY: IMPLEMENTING DNS IN A COMPLEX ENVIRONMENT

this time. You should roll out the servers in the following manner:

- First, each company gets the primary master DNS server for its own domain. This gives it control of its DNS domain. For redundancy, each company should also have a secondary master server.

- To allow for each company to quickly resolve addresses for the other companies, each of the primary master DNS servers will also be secondary master servers for the other companies. That allows users to do local lookups.

- Corporate headquarters needs a caching-only server configured to receive cache updates from the other DNS servers on the network. An alternate possibility is to set up a DNS server acting as a secondary master to the three company domains.

- Finally, all DNS servers should be set to accept dynamic updates. This is a requirement in a pure Windows 2000 environment.

That should have been a fairly easy case study if you read the chapter carefully. Of course, after the DNS servers are set up and running, you would also want to set up some of the monitoring we discussed at the end of the chapter.

CHAPTER SUMMARY

Let's recap what we've discussed in this chapter. We have discussed all the key components of using a Windows 2000 DNS server in a Windows 2000 environment. We first covered the history and function of DNS.

We discussed reverse lookups, where an IP address can be resolved to a hostname, and the different types of records. We also looked at the naming conventions for both standard DNS and the DNS service included with Windows 2000.

KEY TERMS

- caching

- caching-only server

- domain

- Domain Name System (DNS)

- Dynamic Host Configuration Protocol (DHCP)

- DNS server

CHAPTER SUMMARY

KEY TERMS

- DNS client computer
- exclusion
- forward lookup
- reverse lookup
- record types
- lease
- Management Information Base (MIB)
- primary master
- RFC
- secondary master
- Start of Authority (SOA)
- suffix
- tree
- top-level domain (TLD)
- node
- fully qualified domain name (FQDN)
- leaf
- hierarchy
- Transmission Control Protocol/Internet Protocol (TCP/IP)
- zone

Next, we discussed installing and configuring the Windows 2000 DNS Server service. This involved all the major configuration activities from the initial installation to the manual creation of DNS records. We also covered configuring a DNS client computer and configuring a zone for dynamic updates.

We wrapped up the chapter with a discussion of managing and monitoring the DNS service. Let's take a look at some exercises and some questions.

APPLY YOUR KNOWLEDGE

Exercises

1.1   Creating a DNS Zone

In the following exercise, you will use the DNS console application to create a forward lookup zone.

Estimated Time: 10 minutes

1. Open the DNS console by going to Administrative Tools and selecting DNS. Right-click the DNS server and select New Zone.

2. Click Next to open the Zone Type dialog box. Select Standard Primary for the type of zone to create. Click Next.

3. Select Forward for the zone type, and click Next.

4. In the Name field of the Zone Name dialog box, enter the name of the domain you will be resolving names for. Click Next.

5. The Zone File dialog box opens. Accept the default to create a new zone file. Click Next.

6. The Completing the Configure DNS Server Wizard dialog box opens. Click Finish to complete the configuration. The new domain now appears in DNS console.

1.2   Manually Create a DNS Record

The following exercise shows you how to manually create a DNS record.

Estimated Time: 5 minutes

1. From the Administrative Tools program group, open DNS console. Right-click the zone you want to add an entry in and select the type of entry you want to create.

2. For this procedure, you will create a new alias (CNAME) record. Select New Alias. The New Alias dialog box opens.

3. In the Alias Name field, enter the alias name. You can use the FQDN name or just the hostname. If you use just the hostname, the rest of the FQDN for the domain you are creating the entry in will automatically be appended.

4. Enter the FQDN for the host you are aliasing in the Fully Qualified Name for Target Host box.

5. Click OK to create the entry.

1.3   Monitoring DNS Server Performance using the Performance application

This exercise will walk you through adding a counter to the Performance console so that you can baseline or troubleshoot your DNS server.

Estimated Time: 15 minutes.

1. Open the Performance application by going to Programs, Administrative Tools, Performance.

2. In Performance, select System Monitor.

3. To create an entry in System Monitor, click the Add (+) icon. The Add Counters window opens. Notice that by default it opens to the Processor performance object.

4. Select the DNS performance object.

5. Select the counter you want to monitor and click Add. You can add multiple counters either by selecting each counter and clicking Add, or by using the standard Windows multiple item select method of holding down the Ctrl key while you select all the counters you want to monitor and clicking Add. Click Close when you are done.

APPLY YOUR KNOWLEDGE

Review Questions

1. You are the network administrator for Exponent Mathematicians, and you have been asked to implement DNS for a pure Windows environment, taking full advantage of the benefits of Windows 2000. How should you do this and why?

2. You are the administrator of the Get Stuffed Taxidermists chain DNS server. You are getting complaints from several field locations that it takes a long time to resolve Internet addresses. All the sites complaining are across slow WAN links. What should you do?

3. You are the Windows 2000 administrator for Bug-B-Gone Exterminators. Your intranet is broken up into several DNS zones, each maintained by their respective departments. You are getting complaints from several field locations that it takes a long time to resolve internal addresses. All the sites complaining are across slow WAN links. What should you do?

4. You're the administrator of Little Faith Enterprise's Windows 2000 DNS server. You have an end user who is trying to download the 128-bit version of the Windows 2000 Service Pack 1. Microsoft's Web site keeps denying him access, saying that his domain cannot be resolved. What can you do to fix this?

5. You're the LAN administrator for Think About IT Consulting Services company. You are running a Windows NT 4 domain architecture and have just implemented your first Windows 2000 client computers. You have configured the client computers to perform dynamic updates to DNS, but they are not appearing in the table. Why not, and what should you do to fix the problem?

Exam Questions

1. You are the network administrator for Wild Widgets Inc. You are training a new employee on the use of the DNS service in Windows 2000 Server. She asks you how a DNS request is resolved, assuming that the name is not cached and is for someone else's domain.

   A. The client computer makes a request to the local DNS server. The DNS server looks in a local memory cache for names it has recently resolved. The name server looks in the DNS server's host tables to see if there is a static or dynamic entry for the hostname to an IP address lookup. The name server refers the request to a root name server. The root name server refers the request to a name server for the first-level domain in the hostname. The first-level domain name server refers the request to a name server for the second-level domain in the hostname, and so on, until a name server is encountered that can resolve the complete hostname.

   B. The client computer makes a request to the local DNS server. The name server looks in the DNS server's host tables to see if there is a static or dynamic entry for the hostname to an IP address lookup. The DNS server looks in a local memory cache for names it has recently resolved. The name server refers the request to a root name server. The root name server refers the request to a name server for the first-level domain in the hostname. The first-level domain name server refers the request to a name server for the second-level domain in the hostname, and so on, until a name server is encountered that can resolve the complete hostname.

APPLY YOUR KNOWLEDGE

C. The client computer makes a request to the local DNS server. The name server looks in the DNS server's host tables to see if there is a static or dynamic entry for the hostname to an IP address lookup. The name server refers the request to a root name server. The root name server refers the request to a name server for the first-level domain in the hostname. The first-level domain name server refers the request to a name server for the second-level domain in the hostname, and so on, until a name server is encountered that can resolve the complete hostname.

D. The client computer makes a request to the local DNS server. The DNS server looks in a local memory cache for names it has recently resolved. The name server looks in the DNS server's host tables to see if there is a static or dynamic entry for the hostname to an IP address lookup. The name server refers the request to a name server for the first-level domain in the hostname. The first-level domain name server refers the request to a name server for the second-level domain in the hostname, and so on, until a name server is encountered that can resolve the complete hostname.

2. You are the system administrator for Phil's Phill-up Stations, a chain of gas stations. As part of the network, you maintain a Windows 2000 DNS server to receive dynamic DNS updates. The server is installed and running but doesn't receive dynamic updates at this time. How do you set up the DNS server to receive dynamic updates?

A. Open DNS Administrator. Select the DNS server and right-click. Select Receive

Dynamic Updates. The Dynamic Updates Wizard will start. Follow the prompts to complete the configuration of dynamic updates.

B. Open the DNS console. From the Administrative Tools program menu, open the DNS console. Open the properties of the zone you want to configure to receive dynamic updates. On the General tab, set the Allow Dynamic Updates pull-down menu to Yes. Click OK.

C. Open the DNS console. From the Administrative Tools program menu, open the DNS console. Open the properties of the zone you want to configure to receive dynamic updates. From the Updates tab, click the Select to Allow Dynamic Updates option on the pull-down menu to Yes. Click OK.

D. Open the DNS console. From the Administrative Tools program menu, open the DNS console. Open the properties of the zone you want to configure to receive dynamic updates. On the Updates tab, set the Allow Dynamic Updates pull-down menu to Yes. Click OK.

3. You are the LAN administrator for the OUI Find-em detective agency. Your boss has asked you to register a DNS domain name for the company. Which of the following is not a legal second-level domain name?

A. findem.art.

B. findem.net.

C. findem.org.

D. findem.cc.

APPLY YOUR KNOWLEDGE

4. You are the LAN administrator for Little Faith Enterprises Meat Packing. You run a pure Windows 2000 network, with six Windows 2000 DNS servers for your domain. One of the secondary servers doesn't seem to be getting updates. How can you check to verify that the server is receiving updates?

   A. Open Performance Manager. Click the Add Counter icon. Select the DNS Server object and then select the Zone Transfer Success counter. Click Add to add the counter and monitor the zone transfers.

   B. Open the Performance console. Click the Add Counter icon. Select the DNS Server object and then select the AXFR Successes counter. Click Add to add the counter and monitor the zone transfers.

   C. Open the DNS console. Select the zone you are having issues with and right-click. Select Statistics from the context menu and verify that zone transfers are being received.

   D. Open Performance console. Click the Add Counter icon. Select the DNS Server object and then select the Zone Transfer Success counter. Click Add to add the counter and monitor the zone transfers.

5. You are the lead engineer for Little Faith Enterprises, and a customer has asked you to install the DNS service on her Windows 2000 server and get one zone configured and issuing addresses. What are the minimum steps you need to take to accomplish this?

   A. Go to Network and Dial-up Connections in the Control Panel and select Add Network Components to install the service. After the service is installed, authorize it in the Active Directory. Next, create the zone.

   B. Go to Network and Dial-up Connections in the Control Panel and select Add Network Components to install the service. After the service is installed, use the Configure Server Wizard to complete the setup and create the first zone.

   C. Go to Network and Dial-up Connections in the Control Panel and select Add Network Components to install the service. After the service is installed, create the zone. Create a reverse lookup zone.

   D. Go to Network and Dial-up Connections in the Control Panel and select Add Network Components to install the service. After the service is installed, create the zone.

6. You are the network administrator for the Hittem Boxing Glove Corporation. They are running a routed network with a centrally located Windows 2000 DNS server. You need to create a record in DNS to allow Internet mail to be sent to your domain. What kind of domain record do you need?

   A. A CNAME Record.

   B. An A Record

   C. A PTR Record

   D. An MX Record

APPLY YOUR KNOWLEDGE

7. You manage the Windows 2000 DNS servers for the Bang Bang Hammer Corporation. You are running in a pure Windows 2000 environment, and you need to make sure workstations are registered properly in DNS for Active Directory integration. How should you configure DNS integration?

   A. Configure the appropriate zones to accept dynamic updates.

   B. Configure the DNS server to accept dynamic updates.

   C. Configure the DHCP server to be sure to send dynamic updates.

   D. Install the Windows 2000 DNS client computer on the workstations.

8. You are the LAN administrator for UR Write Publishing, a publishing company. You are responsible for maintaining the Windows 2000 network for the company, including the Windows 2000 DNS servers. You have a remote office across a slow WAN link. What is the best way to set up DNS to resolve internal hostnames?

   A. Create a delegated zone for the remote office and have all the DNS client computers in that office resolve from that zone.

   B. Configure a caching-only server and have all the DNS client computers resolve from that server.

   C. Use a centralized DNS server and configure it for incremental updates.

   D. Configure the DNS client computers to autodiscover the closest DNS server.

9. You are the collaborative computing administrator for the Call-Me Telephone Company. You have a single DNS server resolving names for your internal domain, and you have an Internet connection. You need to configure DNS on the client computers to resolve Internet addresses. How do you do it?

   A. On each client computer, install the Microsoft DNS client. Configure the client computer to resolve to the DNS server. Configure the root hints on the server to point at the Internet root servers.

   B. On each client computer, configure the DNS settings under the TCP/IP Protocol properties to resolve to the DNS server. Configure the root hints on the server to point at the Internet root servers.

   C. Install a new DNS server to resolve Internet domain names. On each client computer, configure the DNS settings under the TCP/IP Protocol properties to resolve to the DNS server.

   D. On each client computer, configure the DNS settings under the TCP/IP Protocol properties to resolve to the DNS server.

10. Which of the following is the fully qualified domain name for the host Home in the Sales domain for the UR Write company? The company's domain is urwrite.net.

    A. HOME

    B. HOME.SALES.NET

    C. HOME.URWRITE.NET

    D. HOME.SALES.URWRITE.NET

APPLY YOUR KNOWLEDGE

11. You are the LAN administrator for Blue Sky
    Airlines. Your company has a mixed Windows
    2000 network, and you are still running a
    Windows NT 4 DNS server. You want to config-
    ure the Windows 98 computers in the sales
    department to use dynamic DNS updates for
    identification purposes. How do you do it?

    A. Upgrade your DNS server to Windows 2000.
       Configure it to accept dynamic updates.
       Configure the Windows 98 client computers
       to send dynamic updates.

    B. Upgrade your DNS server to Windows 2000.
       Configure it to accept dynamic updates.
       Upgrade your Windows 98 computers to
       Windows 98 Second Edition to get the
       dynamic DNS capability. Configure the
       Windows 98 client computers to send
       dynamic updates.

    C. Upgrade your Windows 98 computers to
       Windows 2000 Professional to get the
       dynamic DNS capability. Configure the
       Windows 2000 client computers to send
       dynamic updates.

    D. Upgrade your DNS server to Windows 2000.
       Configure it to accept dynamic updates.
       Upgrade your Windows 98 computers to
       Windows 2000 Professional to get the
       dynamic DNS capability. Configure the
       Windows 2000 client computers to send
       dynamic updates.

12. You are the network administrator for Little Big
    Men Clothiers. You have installed a Windows
    2000 DNS server, but people are unable to
    resolve names. You need to test the server. How
    do you do it?

    A. From the command prompt of a
       Windows 2000 Professional host, run the
       NSLOOKUP utility to check the function-
       ality of the DNS service.

    B. Go to File, Run, and then enter **NSLOOKUP32**.
       In the DNS Server dialog box, enter the
       address of your DNS server and click OK to
       run an NSLOOKUP test.

    C. From the Windows 2000 DNS server, type
       PING -a and the address of the DNS server.
       Examine the results to see if the server is
       working.

    D. From the Windows 2000 DNS server,
       type **PING -R** and the address of the DNS
       server. Examine the results to see if the server
       is working.

13. You are the network administrator for Big Al's
    Plumbing, and you are running a pure Windows
    2000 network. You have been having intermittent
    network outages for remote Windows 2000 users,
    and you have noticed that you are getting bad
    DNS entries for those workstations. What is the
    problem with DNS?

    A. The Dynamic DNS entry lease time is set
       too high.

    B. The DNS server is not configured to permit
       scavenging of bad DNS records.

    C. The Dynamic Update Timeout parameter
       is set too high.

    D. The Dynamic Update Timeout parameter is
       set too low.

APPLY YOUR KNOWLEDGE

14. You are the systems administrator for Round the Bend Car Parts, and you are responsible for the Windows 2000 DNS server. You are running a pure Windows 2000 network and are using dynamic updates. A new network administrator has asked you when a host dynamically updates DNS. When does an update event occur? (Select all that apply.)

    A. The TCP/IP configuration is changed.

    B. The DHCP address is renewed or a new lease is obtained.

    C. A Plug and Play event occurs.

    D. A DNS zone transfer occurs.

    E. When the DNS server cache is manually flushed.

15. You are the network administrator for Mad Hatter Top Hats Inc. You are responsible for the company's internal pure Windows 2000 network, including DNS. You have been asked to create a reverse lookup entry for each workstation on the network. How do you do it?

    A. Use DNS console to create a reverse lookup zone. Manually add each workstation to the reverse lookup zone.

    B. Use DNS console to create a reverse lookup zone. Configure the forward lookup zone to accept dynamic updates. The reverse lookup zone will be automatically updated.

    C. Use DNS console to create a reverse lookup zone. Configure the DNS server to accept dynamic updates. The reverse lookup zone will be automatically updated.

    D. Use DNS console to create a reverse lookup zone. Configure the reverse lookup zone to accept dynamic updates.

16. You are the systems administrator for Round the Bend Car Parts, and you are responsible for the Windows 2000 DNS server. You are running a pure Windows 2000 network and are using dynamic updates. You think you are experiencing issues with your zone transfers and you want to monitor the full zone transfers to see if they are the issue.

    What group of counters do you need to monitor?

    A. AXFR

    B. IXFR

    C. Dynamic Update

    D. Notify Received/Sent

17. You are the network administrator for the Hittem Boxing Glove Corporation. They are running a routed network with a centrally located Windows 2000 DNS server. You need to create a record in DNS to allow you to connect to your Web server without requiring an IP address. What kind of domain record do you need?

    A. A CNAME Record

    B. An A Record

    C. A PTR Record

    D. An MX Record

APPLY YOUR KNOWLEDGE

18. You are the system administrator for Look Out Airlines. You network consists of seven Windows 2000 servers and about 200 Windows 2000 Professional workstations. Two of the servers are running DNS for your network. You have one campus for the majority of the company, but you have a remote site with about 50 software engineers who are very technical and would like to run their own DNS for their development systems. How do you do this?

   A. Implement a secondary server at the remote location.

   B. Implement a secondary server at the central site.

   C. Implement a caching server.

   D. Implement a DNS server on the remote site and delegate a subdomain to that server.

19. When is an appropriate time to implement a delegated zone for DNS?

   A. You need to distribute the load of maintaining one large DNS database among multiple name servers.

   B. You need to host multiple DNS zones on a single DNS server.

   C. You need to host multiple DNS zones across multiple servers.

   D. You need to increase the redundancy of one small DNS zone.

20. When is an appropriate time to implement a caching server?

   A. You want a remote site to be able to make local updates to the DNS database.

   B. You want to improve the DNS performance on a network with a large number of infrequently visited hosts.

   C. You want to improve the DNS performance on a network with a small number of frequently visited hosts.

   D. You need to increase the redundancy of one small DNS zone.

21. You are the network administrator for Gone Goodbye Memorabilia. You are in the process of setting up DNS on your Windows 2000 server in preparation for a Windows 2000 rollout. Your domain name is gonegoodbye.org. By default, what is the name of your forward DNS zone file?

   A. gonegoodbye.dns

   B. gonegoodbye.txt

   C. gonegoodbye.org.dns

   D. gonegoodbye.org.txt

Answers to Review Questions

1. Placement of the DNS servers is very dependent on the network infrastructure of the company, but you will need a Windows 2000 DNS service. Windows NT 4 DNS will not support the dynamic DNS, and although other DNS servers support Dynamic DNS, the requirement for a pure Windows environment leaves them out. Although there may be benefits to some of the other platforms, a single platform solution is not uncommon in environments where the administrators are most familiar with Windows NT. See the section "Configuring Zones for Dynamic Updates."

APPLY YOUR KNOWLEDGE

2. Place a secondary master DNS server at each of the complaining sites. This will give them local DNS resolution and a local cache of commonly visited Internet addresses. See the section "Installing, Configuring and Troubleshooting DNS."

3. Place a caching only DNS server at each of the complaining sites and configure them to pull the cache information from the other DNS servers on the network. See the section "Configuring a Caching-Only Server."

4. You need to make sure he had an entry in your reverse lookup table. Microsoft's site is trying to verify his location based on your domain and needs to be able to do a reverse lookup. If you do not have a reverse lookup zone, you need to create one. See the section "Reverse Lookups."

5. Windows NT 4's DNS Server will not support dynamic DNS updates. You need to upgrade to Windows 2000 DNS or migrate to a third-party DNS that supports dynamic updates. See the section "Configuring Zones for Dynamic Updates."

Answers to Exam Questions

1. **A.** The correct order is cache, local DNS server table, root server, first-level domain server, and then any additional subdomain servers. See the section "DNS Domains Defined."

2. **B.** Dynamic updates are set using the pull-down box on the General tab of the zone properties. See the section "Configuring Zones for Dynamic Updates."

3. **A.** ART is a proposed top-level domain. ORG, NET, and CC are actual production top-level domains. See the section "History of DNS."

4. **D.** Performance Manager was the name of the Windows NT application. In Windows 2000 the Performance console runs as part of the Microsoft Management Console. There are no statistics available for the DNS server. The correct counter is Zone Transfer Success. See the section "Managing and Monitoring DNS."

5. **B.** If the task is to install it and get it resolving names, you do not need to configure a reverse lookup zone. You will need to run the Configure Server Wizard. See the section "Installing the DNS Server Service."

6. **D.** An MX (Mail Exchanger) record is used to identify the mail server(s) for a domain. A CNAME record is an alias, an A record is used for name-to-address resolution, and a PTR record is used for reverse lookups. See the section "DNS Record Types."

7. **A.** Configure the appropriate zones to accept dynamic updates. Each zone needs to be configured individually to accept dynamic updates. See the section "Configuring Zones for Dynamic Updates."

8. **B.** Configure a caching-only server and have all the remote DNS client computers resolve from that server. See the section "Configuring a Caching-Only Server."

9. **D.** You just need to configure the workstations to use the existing DNS server to resolve names. This is done under the TCP/IP properties. The server automatically forwards any requests for unknown domains to the appropriate servers. See the section "Configuring a DNS Client Computer."

APPLY YOUR KNOWLEDGE

10. **C.** HOME.URWRITE.NET is the correct answer. HOME is the server, URWRITE is the secondary domain, and NET is the top-level domain. See the section "DNS Domains Defined."

11. **D.** You need a Windows 2000 DNS server and a Windows 2000 client computer to use dynamic DNS without needing to reconfigure DHCP. Although it is possible, out of the offered answers, D is correct. See the section "Configuring Zones for Dynamic Updates."

12. **A.** Running NSLOOKUP from the command prompt is a good way to test. See the section "Testing the DNS Server Service."

13. **B.** You need to configure the DNS server to scavenge bad DNS entries. See the section "Managing and Monitoring DNS."

14. **A, B, C.** When TCP/IP is updated, when a DHCP assignment or renewal occurs, or when there is a Plug and Play event. See the section "Configuring Zones for Dynamic Updates."

15. **D.** You must create a reverse lookup zone and configure it to accept dynamic updates. See the section "Reverse Lookups."

16. **A.** AXFR counters deal with full zone transfers. IXFR is concerned with incremental transfers, and Dynamic Update and Notify Receive/Sent counters have nothing to do with zone transfers. See the section "Managing and Monitoring DNS."

17. **B.** An A record is needed to provide name-to-address resolution. See the section "DNS Record Types."

18. **D.** This is an excellent opportunity to delegate a zone. Secondary servers are read-only, and a caching server doesn't even have a DNS table, only a cache. See the section "Implementing a Delegated Zone for DNS."

19. **A.** You need to distribute the load of maintaining one large DNS database among multiple name servers. See the section "Implementing a Delegated Zone for DNS."

20. **C.** Because you are working off the DNS cache, you want to use this in an environment where all the main servers are in the cache for you to quickly retrieve. Servers that are not resolved frequently will not have their addresses cached. See the section "Configuring a Caching-Only Server."

21. **C.** By default, the name of the zone file is the name of the DNS domain with .DNS appended to it. See the section "Configuring Zones."

Suggested Readings and Resources

1. Albitz, Paul, and Cricket Liu. *DNS and Bind.* Sebastopol, CA: O'Reilly and Associates, Inc., 1998.

2. Branley, Edward. *Sams Teach Yourself DNS/Bind in 24 Hours.* Indianapolis, IN: Sams Publishing, 2000.

3. Ruth, Andy. *Concise Guide to Windows 2000 DNS.* Indianapolis, IN: Que Corporation, 2000.

4. Siyan, Karanjit S. Windows NT TCP/IP. Indianapolis, IN: New Riders Publishing, 1998.

One of the most important services for successfully implementing Active Directory Services is DHCP. In this chapter we will examine all the facets of running the DHCP service in a Windows 2000 network.

Microsoft defines the "Installing, Configuring, Managing, Monitoring, and Troubleshooting DHCP in a Windows 2000 Network Infrastructure" objectives as the following:

Install, configure, and troubleshoot DHCP.

- **Install the DHCP Server service.**

- **Create and manage DHCP scopes, super-scopes, and multicast scopes.**

- **Configure DHCP for DNS integration.**

- **Authorize a DHCP server in Active Directory.**

▶ One of the first tasks when getting ready to deploy a production Windows 2000 network environment is to ensure that DHCP is installed and configured correctly. DHCP is tightly integrated with Dynamic DNS and Active Directory Services. This objective expects you to be able to install DHCP and configure it for use in an Active Directory Services network.

Manage and monitor DHCP.

▶ The final objective requires that you be able to maintain your DHCP server after it is installed, configured and authorized. The ability to manage DHCP services and monitor the DHCP server's activities is critical to the ongoing administration of a Windows 2000 network.

CHAPTER *2*

Installing, Configuring, Managing, Monitoring, and Troubleshooting DHCP in a Windows 2000 Network Infrastructure

OUTLINE

**Understanding Dynamic Host
Configuration Protocol**   **79**

    The DHCP Protocol   80

    The BOOTP Protocol   82

**Installing, Configuring, and
Troubleshooting DHCP**   **82**

    Installing the DHCP Server Service   83

    Understanding DHCP Scopes   88

    Understanding DHCP Superscopes   88

    Understanding Multicasting and
Multicast Scopes   89

    Creating a Scope on Your DHCP Server   91

    Authorizing a DHCP Server in
Active Directory   97

    Creating a Superscope   99

    Creating a Multicast Superscope   100

    Configuring DHCP for DNS Integration   102

Managing and Monitoring DHCP   **104**

Chapter Summary   **116**

Apply Your Knowledge   **117**

STUDY STRATEGIES

▶ DHCP is a service that has been used in TCP/IP-based networks for quite a while. Microsoft has extended the functionality of DHCP as part of its Windows 2000 operating system. Be sure you understand where DHCP came from, how it works, and what enhancements Microsoft's Windows 2000 DHCP Server service add to the protocol.

▶ DHCP is used not only to dynamically allocate IP addresses, but also plays a critical part in registering hosts in the Microsoft Active Directory. Be sure you understand the role DHCP plays in a Windows 2000 network.

▶ Microsoft's Windows 2000 DHCP Server service supports several types of scopes. Be sure you understand the types, how each works, and when you would use each in a production environment.

UNDERSTANDING DYNAMIC HOST CONFIGURATION PROTOCOL

The TCP/IP protocol is the de facto standard for computer networking and appears to have no challengers in the networking protocol arena. If you are going to be working with Windows 2000, you can expect to be working with TCP/IP. One of the keys to successfully working with the TCP/IP protocol is an understanding of the concept of a TCP/IP address. The designers of the TCP/IP protocol wanted an identification scheme that was independent of any one computer or network equipment design, so they established a scheme of IP addresses.

If you've ever surfed the World Wide Web, you have almost certainly seen IP addresses (numbers such as 192.168.144.77). As you administer TCP/IP on your network, a considerable part of your time will be devoted to IP address assignment, because IP addresses don't just happen. They have to be entered manually into the configuration of each TCP/IP computer on your network. When a computer is added to your network, it needs an IP address. When it moves, it probably needs a new IP address. If you are just starting out with managing a large TCP/IP network, you may find the notion of managing all those addresses a bit daunting. Move a Domain Name Service (DNS) server, and you have to reconfigure every client computer. Move a client computer to a new subnet, and you have to update its IP address. This does not endear you to your road warriors who travel among several offices, especially if it's your regional manager. If you manually manage your IP addresses, almost any change to the network will require a visit to one or more computers to update the TCP/IP configuration. Not a happy prospect. Fortunately, the people who brought us DNS to replace the HOSTS.TXT file also came up with a solution to this dilemma.

The Dynamic Host Configuration Protocol (DHCP) was the Internet community's answer to dynamically distributing IP addresses. DHCP is open and standards based, as defined by Internet Engineering Task Force (IETF) Requests for Comments (RFCs) 2131 and 2132. (The IETF is the main standards organization for the Internet.)

Typically, IP addresses are registered with the Internet Assigned Numbers Authority (IANA) so that it can keep track of IP addresses used on the Internet. In some cases, a network will not be connected to the Internet and will not need to use registered addresses. In other cases, the network is connected to the Internet with special hardware and software that can be configured to allow the network to use unregistered addresses in conjunction with address translations. Windows 2000 includes this capability, and it is discussed in detail in Chapter 7, "Installing, Configuring, and Troubleshooting Network Address Translation (NAT)."

Quite often, network administrators use unregistered addresses on their internal network to ensure that there are addresses for all users. This model works great as long as the network is never tied directly to the Internet. However, with the shortage of Class A and Class B (and even Class C) IP addresses, there are some environments that use small pools of registered addresses to service larger numbers of DHCP clients—the idea being that not every client computer would need access simultaneously. These environments require aggressive leasing policies to ensure that everyone can get an address.

In addition to IP addresses, DHCP can also provide gateway addresses, DNS server addresses, and Windows Internet Name Service (WINS) server addresses—in essence, everything the client computer needs to participate in the network. This lets all available IP addresses be stored in a central database along with associated configuration information, such as the subnet mask, gateways, and address of DNS servers. You even get the MAC addresses of the client computers.

The DHCP Protocol

It's great to say that DHCP provides the mechanism for dynamically distributing IP addresses on a network, but there is a bit more to it than that. Here's how a client computer gets an address:

1. The client computer broadcasts a DHCPDiscover message that is forwarded to the DHCP server(s) on the network. The address of the DHCP server(s) is configured on the router, if necessary. Forwarding is done using a process called a BOOTP Forwarder. We will discuss this in more detail in the next section, "The BOOTP Protocol."

EXAM TIP

Don't Sweat the RFCs for DHCP
Although Microsoft has been known to be very detailed in its exam questions, you will not be expected to be able to recite the RFCs for each of the protocols or services in Windows 2000.

NOTE

RFCs Are Notes About the Internet
RFC documents are used to make notes about the Internet and Internet technologies. If an RFC can garner enough interest, it may eventually become a standard. Topics of RFCs range from the File Transfer Protocol (originally RFC 0114 but updated by RFC0141, RFC0172, and RFC0171) to the Hitchhikers Guide to the Internet (RFC1118). The first RFC was posted in 1969 by Steve Crocker, and the topic was Host Software. You can find listings of all the RFCs at a number of sites throughout the Internet. One place is http://www.rfc-editor.org/.

2. Each DHCP server that receives the discover message responds with a DHCP offer message. That message includes an IP address that is appropriate for the subnet where the client computer is attached. The DHCP server determines the appropriate address by looking at the source subnet for the broadcast DHCPDiscover message.

3. The client computer considers the offer message and selects one (usually the first offer it receives). It sends a request to use the address to the DHCP server that originated the offer. If there are multiple DHCP servers, great care needs to be taken in their configuration. It is very easy to inadvertently configure the servers so they conflict. It is very important if you have multiple DHCP servers on your network that they do not have the capability to offer duplicate IP addresses. Because the DHCP servers do not communicate, they have no way of telling whether an address has already been issued by another DHCP server.

4. The DHCP server acknowledges the request and grants the client computer a lease to use the address.

5. The client computer uses the IP address to bind to the network. If the IP address is associated with any configuration parameters, the parameters are incorporated into the client computer's TCP/IP configuration.

The first step of this process indicates that DHCP clients request their addresses using broadcast messages. If you are familiar with routing, particularly TCP/IP routing, you are probably familiar with the fact that one of the benefits of routing is that the router segregates broadcast domains. In other words, broadcasts do not generally cross routers. Does that mean that DHCP works only on the local segment and you need 50 DHCP servers for your 50 subnets? Not if you configure your routers to use the BOOTP protocol. BOOTP is the precursor to DHCP and was the first protocol used to assign IP addresses dynamically. The protocol was especially designed to pass across a router, and it continues to be used to allow DHCP broadcasts to propagate across routers. Thanks to BOOTP, a DHCP server can service clients on any number of subnets, and you can do something else with 48 of those DHCP servers you were planning to buy.

The BOOTP Protocol

Before we get into installing the DHCP service in Windows 2000, a brief discussion about the BOOTP protocol is necessary. A number of DHCP's features had their beginnings in BOOTP. The BOOTP (Bootstrap Protocol) protocol was originally designed in 1985 by Bill Croft and John Gilmore to automate the configuration of network devices. To use BOOTP, the network administrator must create a table with a list of client computers, their IP addresses, and network configurations. When a client computer comes onto the network, it broadcasts a request that the BOOTP server receives. The BOOTP server looks up the client computer in the table and responds with the configuration information stored in the table, allowing the client computer to communicate on the network.

Because the BOOTP protocol worked well, it was used extensively in the early 90s in conjunction with diskless workstations. (A BOOTP chip was a common option on a network interface card, and many networks thrived on BOOTP.) The downside of BOOTP was that it provided only the configuration information entered in the table. The administrator still needed to configure the table. The limitations of BOOTP effectively prevented any automation of these tasks, so it was eventually replaced with DHCP. BOOTP and DHCP packets look virtually identical, and DHCP even takes advantage of the BOOTP Forwarder functionality of many routers and switches. DHCP offers the automation features BOOTP was lacking.

Now that we've completed the history lesson, you should have a pretty good understanding of the theory of DHCP. Now let's look at how you work with DHCP in the Windows 2000 environment.

INSTALLING, CONFIGURING, AND TROUBLESHOOTING DHCP

The first thing many managers ask when presented with a request to install Windows 2000 DHCP is, "Can't we just use our existing DHCP?" The answer to this question is yes and no. If you are maintaining a legacy domain and WINS-style network, Windows 2000

can receive DHCP information from any DHCP server that
Windows NT worked with. However, if you want to take advantage
of the features of Active Directory Services and migrate away from
the legacy WINS architecture, you will need the Windows 2000
DHCP service.

The first thing we need to discuss when working with the Windows
2000 DHCP service is how to install the service.

Installing the DHCP Server Service

Install the DHCP Server service.

One of the features that is going to make Windows 2000 very popular with system administrators is its extensive use of configuration
wizards. Most of the server configuration tasks have been bundled
into the Configure Your Server application, allowing you to start a
wizard for the most common configuration activities. We will try to
highlight this new feature of Windows 2000 as much as possible
because it is a major enhancement to the operating system, and
could prove to be fertile ground for exam questions.

When you install Windows 2000 Server, you have the ability to
install DHCP as one of the optional services. For the purposes of
the exam, we will be looking at installing DHCP on a server that is
already installed but that does not have DHCP loaded.

DHCP is installed as a Windows 2000 Server networking service.
To install the DHCP Server service, follow these steps:

> **NOTE**
>
> **A DHCP Server Cannot Also Be a
> DHCP Client** If you currently have
> your server configured as a DHCP
> client, the DHCP installation will
> prompt you to enter a static IP
> address for your server.

STEP BY STEP

2.1 Using the Configure Your Server Application to Install the DHCP Server Service

1. Choose Start, Programs, Administrative Tools, and
Configure Your Server to go to the Configure Your Server
application. You can see this utility in Figure 2.1.

continues

continued

2. From the Windows 2000 Configure Your Server application, choose Networking and then select DHCP (shown in Figure 2.2).

3. Click the Start the Windows Component Wizard hyperlink. The Windows Components dialog box shown in Figure 2.3 opens.

FIGURE 2.1

The Microsoft Windows 2000 Configure Your Server application is the repository for server-configuration wizards.

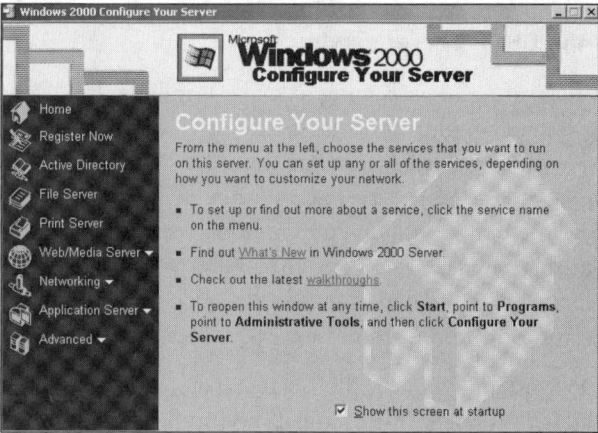

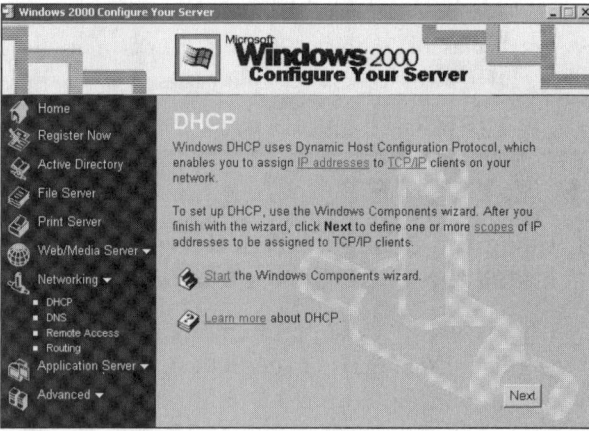

FIGURE 2.2

The DHCP configuration screen allows you to start the DHCP configuration.

4. In the Windows Component Wizard, scroll down to Networking Services (shown in Figure 2.4) and select it.

5. Click the Details button to open the list of Networking Services. From the list of Networking Services, check the box next to Dynamic Host Configuration Protocol (DHCP), shown in Figure 2.5.

6. Click the OK button to return to the Windows Components screen, and click Next to install DHCP If you selected or deselected any other services, they will be installed or removed at this time as well. When the installation is completed, the Completing the Windows Components Wizard dialog box shown in Figure 2.6 opens.

7. Click the Finish button to exit the wizard.

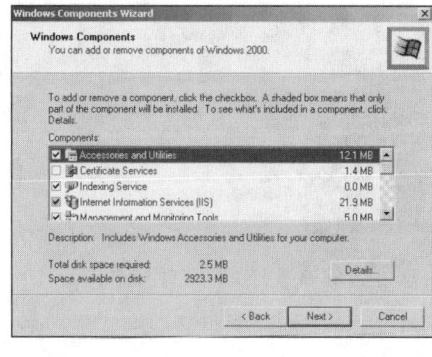

FIGURE 2.3
The Windows Components screen can be used to add or remove Windows 2000 components, including DHCP.

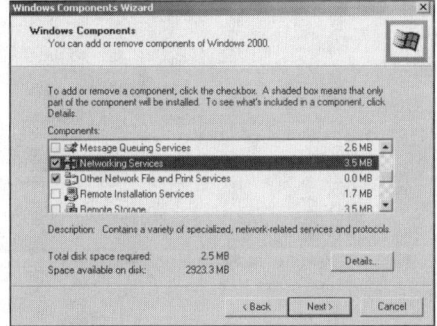

FIGURE 2.4
The Networking Services entry includes networking components such as DHCP, DNS, and WINS, among others.

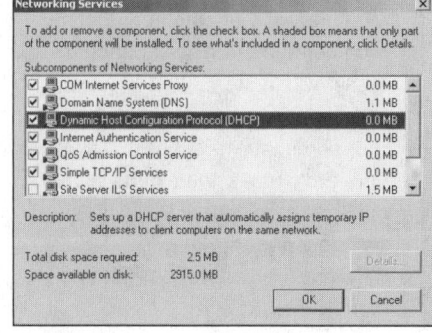

FIGURE 2.5
Selecting Dynamic Host Configuration Protocol (DHCP) starts the install process.

FIGURE 2.6
The Completing the Windows Components Wizard dialog box indicates that the service was installed correctly.

EXAM TIP

Windows 2000 Offers Many Ways to Complete Common Tasks Multiple ways of completing common configuration tasks should make administering a Windows 2000 network much easier for system administrators, but it will undoubtedly make the exams more challenging because you will probably need to know all the different methods of completing common tasks.

As we discussed, this is only one way to install the DHCP service. DHCP can also be installed in the following manner:

STEP BY STEP

2.2 Using the Control Panel to Install DHCP

1. Choose Start, Settings, Control Panel (see Figure 2.7). If you are familiar with Windows NT 4, this window should look familiar to you.

2. Double-click the Network and Dial-up Connections icon. The Network and Dial-up Connections folder (shown in Figure 2.8) opens.

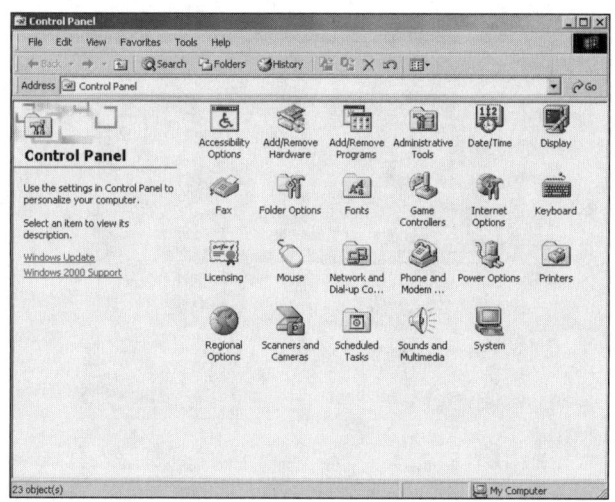

FIGURE 2.7
The Control Panel offers a manual method for installing Windows 2000 components.

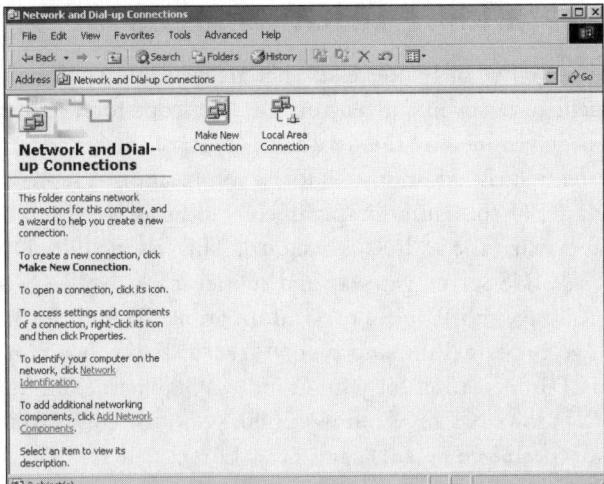

FIGURE 2.8
The Network and Dial-up Connections
folder offers another way to add or remove
network components.

3. Click the Add Network Components hyperlink at
   the lower left of the window to open the Windows
   Optional Networking Components Wizard dialog box
   (see Figure 2.9), which contains a subset of components
   that can be installed. Unlike the list of available components in the previous installation method, this list is
   limited to networking components only.

4. Select Networking Services and then click the Details
   button; the same list of Networking Services shown in
   Figure 2.5 appears. From this point, the installation
   continues exactly as the previous installation method,
   starting at step 5.

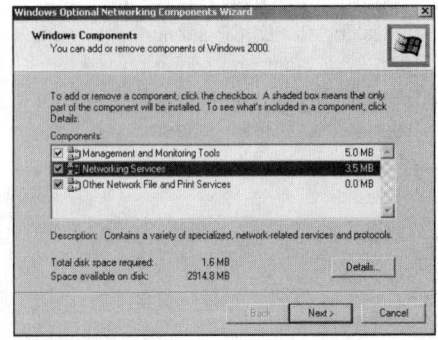

FIGURE 2.9
The Windows Optional Networking Components
Wizard dialog box presents the network com-
ponents available for installation.

Now that you have seen two of the methods for installing DHCP,
let's discuss how to configure DHCP. One of the important things
you need to understand before delving into the configuration
of your newly installed DHCP server is the concept of scopes,
including scopes, superscopes, and multicast scopes.

Understanding DHCP Scopes

A scope is a range of IP addresses that are available for dynamic assignment to hosts on a given subnet. The scope for a particular subnet is determined by the network address of the broadcast DHCP request. In addition to address information, a scope can include a set of configuration parameters to be assigned to client computers when the address is assigned. This list includes DNS servers, a WINS server, gateway and subnet mask, NetBIOS scope ID, IP routing, and WINS Proxy information. To find this information, go to Start, Run, and type **WINIPCFG**. This shows you all the DHCP information for your Windows 98 client computer. Under Windows NT or Windows 2000, go to the command prompt, type **ipconfig /all**, and press Enter.

You should make the scope as large as you can. Later in the scope-creation process, you have the ability to exclude addresses, and you can also define reservations for particular addresses that do exist within the scope.

> **NOTE**
>
> **You Need at Least One Scope**   After installing the DHCP service, you must define at least one scope on the server. Otherwise, the service will not respond to DHCP requests.

Understanding DHCP Superscopes

The next type of scope was introduced to the Windows NT product family with Service Pack 2 for Windows NT 4. What a superscope allows you to do is support a *supernetted* or *multinetted* network with a Windows 2000 DHCP Server. Great. All we need to do now is figure out what a supernetted network is. A supernetted network is a network that has multiple network addresses or subnets running on the same segment. You commonly see this configuration in network environments with more than 254 hosts on a subnet, or in an environment in which certain hosts need to be isolated from the rest of the logical network for security or routing reasons. Superscopes will support a local multinet or a multinet that is located across a router configured to use the BOOTP Forwarder service. We discuss creating a superscope in the section "Creating a Superscope."

IN THE FIELD

WHEN TO USE SUPERNETTING

Visualize a large company that occupies five floors in a building. On each of these floors are 300 to 500 users, all on the same physical network. Traditional network design would have a routed backbone running between the floors, and each floor would be its own IP network. But there's one problem. You have too many users on these floors to be handled by a single Class C subnet. What are the alternatives?

You could place a router somewhere on each of the floors to further segment the network. This is an expensive and support-intensive solution and is generally considered to be impractical.

You could address using Class B addresses. However, that is generally very wasteful of IP addresses.

The last thing you could do is place multiple IP networks on the single routed segment. In other words, create a supernet. This capability is supported by any of the routers on the market today, including the OS-based routing services in Windows 2000, Novell NetWare and any of the UNIX flavors. So when you think about a supernet, think about a floor in a building with too many users for 254 IP addresses.

Understanding Multicasting and Multicast Scopes

Before we discuss the multicast scopes, we need to look at what multicasting is. Multicasting is the act of transmitting a message to a select group of recipients. This is in contrast to the concept of a broadcast in which traffic is sent to every host on the network, or a unicast in which the connection is a one-to-one relationship, and there is only one recipient of the data.

Here's an example, using an email message. If you send an email message to your manager, it is an example of a unicast message. If you send an email message to every user on the system, it is a broadcast. Send an email message to a mailing list, and you have sent a multicast message, which falls between the previous two. Teleconferencing and videoconferencing use the concept of multicasting, as does broadcast audio, in which the connection is a one to a selected group. At this time, only a few applications take advantage of this feature, but with the growing popularity of multicast applications, you may see more multicast applications in the future.

We should discuss a few terms before discussing the Windows 2000 multicast capabilities:

◆ **Multicast DHCP (MDHCP).** An extension to the DHCP protocol standard that supports dynamic assignment and configuration of IP multicast addresses on TCP/IP-based networks.

◆ **Multicast forwarding table.** The table used by an IP router to forward IP multicast traffic. An entry in the IP multicast forwarding table consists of the multicast group address, the source IP address, a list of interfaces to which the traffic is forwarded (next hop interfaces), and the single interface on which the traffic must be received to be forwarded (the previous hop interface).

◆ **Multicast group.** A group of member TCP/IP hosts configured to listen and receive datagrams sent to a specified destination IP address. The destination address for the group is a shared IP address in the Class D address range (224.0.0.0 to 239.255.255.255).

◆ **Multicast scope.** A range of IP multicast addresses in the range of 224.0.0.0 to 239.255.255.255. Multicast addresses in this range can be prevented from propagating in either direction (send or receive) through the use of scope-based multicast boundaries.

A new feature for Windows 2000's DHCP service is the concept of a multicast scope. The Microsoft DHCP server has been extended to allow the assignment of multicast addresses in addition to unicast (single computer) addresses. A proposed IETF standard (RFC 2730), Multicast Address Dynamic Client Allocation Protocol (MADCAP) defines multicast address allocation. The proposed standard would allow administrators to dynamically allocate multicast addresses to be assigned in the same fashion as unicast addresses. The Windows 2000 DHCP multicasting capability also supports dynamic membership. Dynamic membership allows individual computers to join or leave the multicast group at any time. This is similar to registering to receive an Internet broadcast or joining and leaving an email mailing list. Group membership is not limited by size, and computers are not restricted to membership in any single group.

Now the question is, how do client computers join and leave a multicast group? The answer is the MADCAP protocol and the MADCAP API. Client computers using MADCAP must be configured to use the MADCAP API. MADCAP assists in simplifying and automating configuration of multicast groups on your network, but it is not required for the operation of multicast groups or for the DHCP service. Multicast scopes provide only address configuration and do not support or use other DHCP-assignable options. MADCAP address configuration for client computers should be done independently of how the client computers are configured to receive their primary IP address. Computers using either static or dynamic configuration through a DHCP server can also be MADCAP clients.

EXAM TIP	**Use Class D IP Addresses for the Multicast Scope** Remember that along with your primary IP address, you receive your multicast address, and it is for multicasts only and uses the Class D IP addresses specified in the multicast scope. They are not used for regular network traffic such as Web traffic or other IP-based applications.

Creating a Scope on Your DHCP Server

Now that you are familiar with the different types of scopes, let's look at creating one. To create a DHCP scope, see the following Step by Step.

STEP BY STEP

2.3 Creating a DHCP Scope

1. To open Configure Your Server, choose Start, Programs, Administrative Tools, Configure Your Server, and click the Open hyperlink (see Figure 2.10). Notice that the new DHCP server shown in Figure 2.11 appears. (You can also reach the Configure Your Server application by directly opening the DHCP manager. Just go to Programs, Administrative Tools, DHCP.)

FIGURE 2.10

Notice that different options are available for DHCP now that the service has been installed.

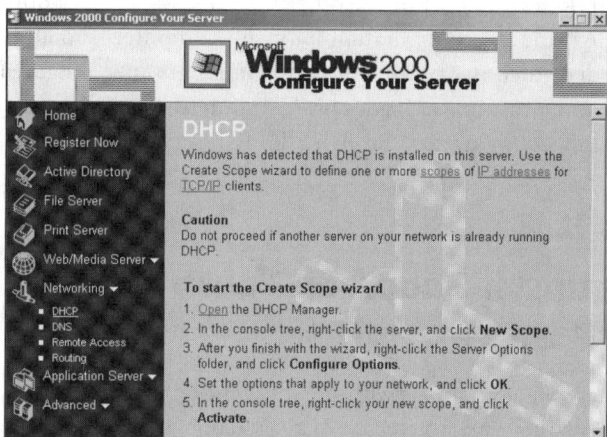

FIGURE 2.11

The DHCP manager application is used for configuring all the parameters for your DHCP server.

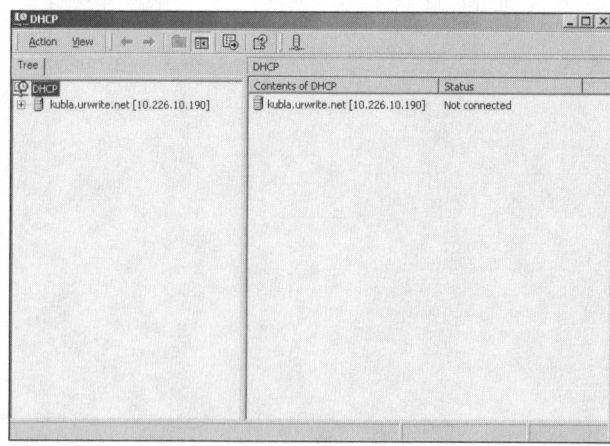

2. Select the DHCP server listed on the right in the DHCP window, choose Action, New Scope (see Figures 2.12 and 2.13). Click Next, and the Scope Name dialog box shown in Figure 2.14 opens.

3. Type a name and a description for your scope. It's a good idea to choose something descriptive for the name, so that when you need to go back after creating 35 scopes, you can tell why you created this one. Click Next, and the IP Address Range dialog box opens (see Figure 2.15).

4. Define the IP address range that your server will be using to assign addresses.

FIGURE 2.13
The New Scope Wizard walks you through creating your first (and all subsequent) scopes.

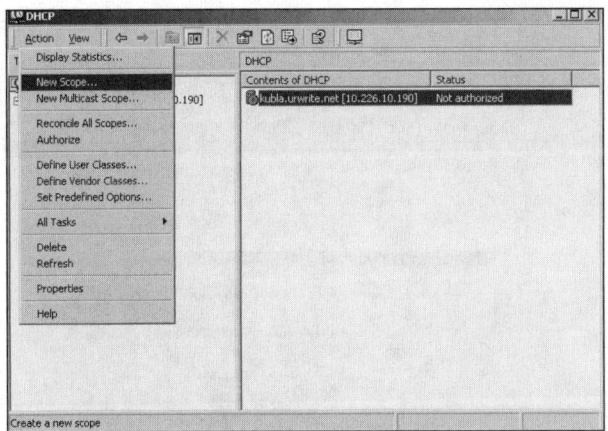

FIGURE 2.12
You can use the context menus or the Action menu to configure the DHCP server.

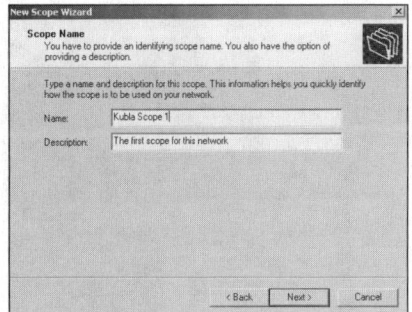

FIGURE 2.14
When you set up each scope, choose a descriptive name and a clear description to assist in identifying the scope in the future.

5. Define the subnet mask using the standard octet method (in other words, 255.255.255.248) or using the more router-centric mask length field. (This field allows you to specify the number of binary bits used to specify the subnet mask.) Click Next, and the Add Exclusions dialog box opens (Figure 2.16).

continues

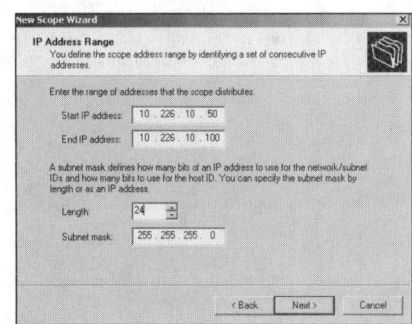

FIGURE 2.15
Make sure you are selecting a unique range of addresses. If these addresses have already been assigned or another DHCP server is servicing this subnet, you can create issues.

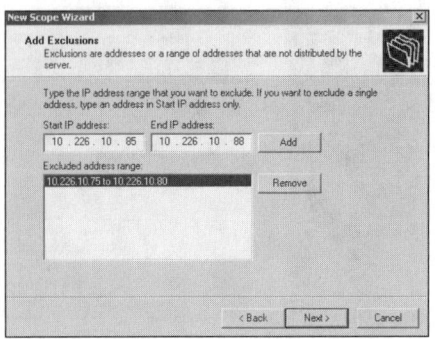

FIGURE 2.16
The Add Exclusions dialog box allows you to exclude addresses from inclusion in the pool of addresses leased to DHCP clients.

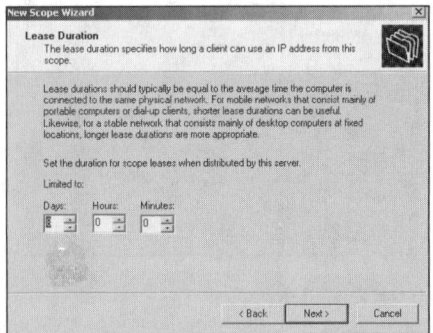

FIGURE 2.17
Be sure to set the lease duration to a length of time that matches your network environment. When in doubt, use a shorter lease and work toward a longer lease.

continued

6. Select a range of addresses that will not be leased to client computers. These are typically addresses assigned to application servers, routers, printers, or other infrastructure equipment that requires static addresses. You can have multiple excluded IP addresses or ranges for each scope. Click Next to open the Lease Duration dialog box (Figure 2.17).

7. Set the DHCP lease, the amount of time that must elapse before an IP address is automatically returned to the DHCP pool. This setting is particularly important when you have more hosts on a network than you have addresses. In that case, you want to set a very short lease. If you have more addresses than hosts, you can make the lease as high as 999 days. By default, the lease is set to eight days. This is usually sufficient for most networks. Click Next to proceed to the Configure DHCP Options dialog box (see Figure 2.18).

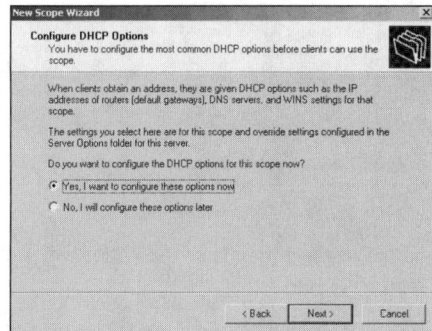

FIGURE 2.18
Unless you are running an extremely simple network, you will want to configure at least some of the additional options.

8. Configure any additional TCP/IP settings that you can assign to DHCP clients when they request an address.

9. Configure the Router, or Default Gateway (see Figure 2.19), or specify multiple gateways. You can configure an unlimited number of gateways.

10. Specify the gateway for your environment, if appropriate, and click Next. (If you are on a single network, you don't need to specify a gateway.) The Domain Name and DNS Servers dialog box opens (see Figure 2.20).

11. Specify as many DNS server addresses as you need to. You can enter only one parent domain, however. You can also use the Resolve button to get the IP address for a server by entering its name. Specify the DNS server(s) and parent domain for your environment. DNS is discussed in greater detail in Chapter 1, "Installing, Configuring, Managing, Monitoring, and Troubleshooting DNS in a Windows 2000 Network Infrastructure." Click Next, and the WINS Servers dialog box opens (Figure 2.21).

continues

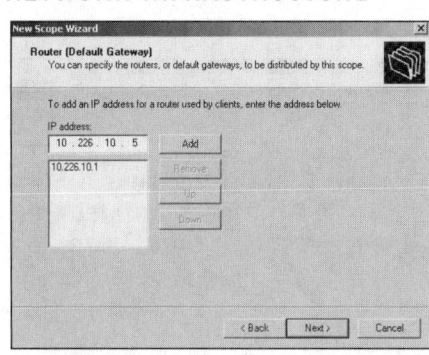

FIGURE 2.19

When you configure multiple default gateways, be sure to enter them in order of priority. The client computers will try them in the order they are issued.

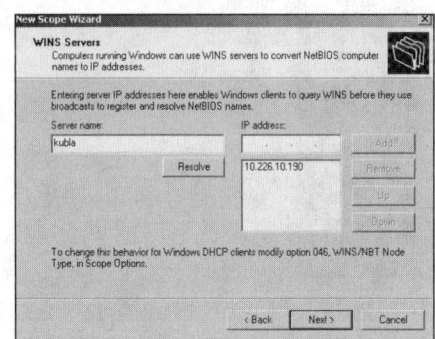

FIGURE 2.21

WINS is needed only if you are supporting legacy systems. A pure Windows 2000 network should not need a WINS server.

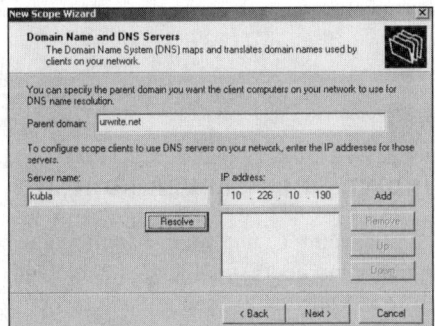

FIGURE 2.20

With Windows 2000 and Active Directory's reliance on DNS, you should have at least two DNS servers on your network and should configure at least two for your DHCP clients.

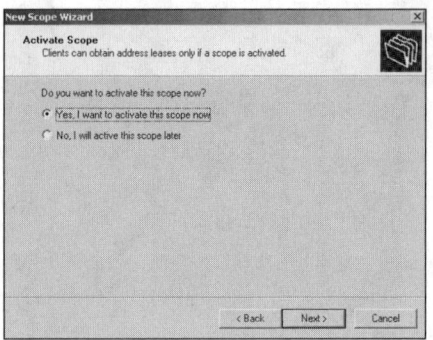

FIGURE 2.22
To make the range of addresses available to DHCP clients, the scope must be activated.

FIGURE 2.23
Each of Microsoft's wizards notifies you of the successful completion of a task.

continued

12. Provide a WINS server name and address only if you have legacy DHCP clients that still need WINS services. As in the last dialog box, the Resolve button can be used to resolve a hostname to an address. Windows 2000 is heavily reliant on DNS for name resolution, and if you are working in a pure Windows 2000 environment, a WINS server is not needed. WINS is discussed in greater detail in Chapter 5, "Installing, Configuring, Managing, Monitoring, and Troubleshooting WINS in a Windows 2000 Network Infrastructure." Click Next to complete the scope creation.

13. Specify whether to activate the scope at this time. The default on the Activate Scope dialog box (shown in Figure 2.22) is Yes, I Want to Activate This Scope Now. If you want your client computers to have immediate access to this scope, leave the default selected. If you want to activate this scope at another time, select No, I Will Activate This Scope Later.

14. Click Next and then click Finish to complete the creation of the scope (see Figure 2.23).

IN THE FIELD

FINDING DHCP SERVER CONFLICTS

If you are not careful, you may find yourself with multiple DHCP servers issuing the same address ranges. This problem is fairly easy to locate and fix. Just verify all the scopes on each of the servers.

The situation is a bit more complicated if you have someone who installs a "new" DHCP server on your network and you are not aware of it. Suddenly, your users are receiving addresses that make no sense, and they are unable to connect to anything. I inadvertently did this to my wife's PC when the Windows 2000 DHCP service used for the book conflicted with the Internet DHCP server used for our home network. She was not amused.

In my home environment, this problem was fairly easy to diagnose because I set up the new DHCP server. In your network, you can do a couple of things to find the server. First, it must be on the same segment as the workstations that are being affected. Because the

BOOTP Forwarder would need to be configured for the new server, it cannot respond to requests from other subnets. After you know the subnet the server is on, either borrow or install a Windows 2000 host on that subnet. Make sure that the Network Monitor service is installed. Load the Network Monitor service and then go to a DOS prompt and type `ipconfig /renew`, which will cause your machine to issue a DHCP request. The IP address of the DHCP server that responds will be displayed in Network Monitor.

You have successfully created a scope for your DHCP server. For it to go into production, it needs to be authorized in Active Directory. If you have been following Microsoft's objectives closely, you will notice that we are about to go out of order. That's because in the real world you would want to bring up the server and test it before creating additional scopes and/or superscopes.

Authorizing a DHCP Server in Active Directory

For security reasons, a new DHCP server must be authorized in the Active Directory before it can assign IP addresses. This prevents unauthorized DHCP servers from running on your network. One of the nastier things a troublemaker can do is to put up a "rogue" DHCP server and have it issue addresses that conflict with infrastructure devices. The nice thing about this feature is if you are running Windows 2000 client computers and they are using the Active Directory, the computers will not accept DHCP addresses from an unauthorized server. To authorize a DHCP server in the Active Directory, do the following:

STEP BY STEP

2.4 Authorizing a DHCP Server

1. Open the DHCP manager application.

2. Select the DHCP server you want to authorize and click the Action menu (Figure 2.24).

continues

WARNING

Exclude Routers from DHCP Scopes When you are configuring the gateway address for your DHCP scope, you have an excellent opportunity to ensure that your routers are excluded from your DHCP scope. You do not want to find out the hard way—when a client computer is issued the router's address and all traffic off the network stops abruptly because of an address conflict.

EXAM TIP

When to Use New Multicast Scope Option The Actions menu is creating a new scope and a new multicast scope as two different tasks. If you get a question on the exam regarding the procedure for creating a multicast scope, remember that you need to select New Multicast Scope.

EXAM TIP

DHCP Clients Automatically Attempt to Extend Leases For the exam, you should be aware of how DHCP leases work. Any DHCP client that had been assigned an address will automatically try to extend the lease when half the time of the lease has passed. If it is unable to do so, it will continue to try to do so for the duration of the lease.

continued

   3. Select the Authorize action. This starts the authorize process, which can take a few minutes to complete. When the process is complete, your scope appears in the Contents of DHCP Server (the right pane) with an Active status (see Figure 2.25). Your server is now ready to issue addresses when it receives a DHCP request.

FIGURE 2.24
In this case, the Action you want to select is Authorize.

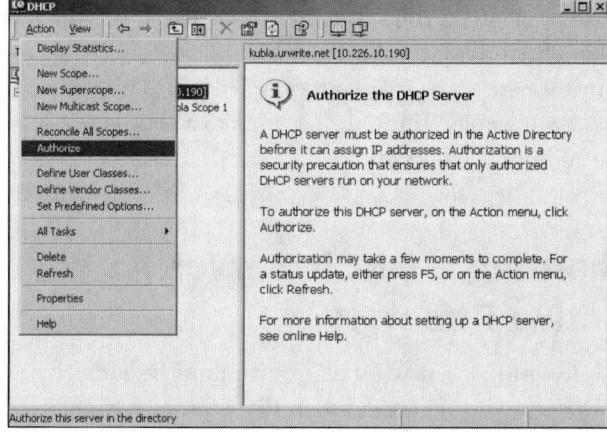

FIGURE 2.25
A server with an Active status can issue DHCP addresses.

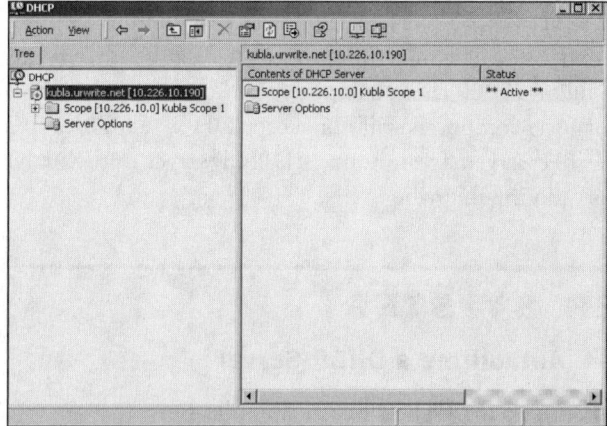

You have now installed, configured, and authorized a Windows 2000 DHCP server. Before you look at configuring your DHCP server for DNS integration, let's take a quick look at setting up a superscope.

Creating a Superscope

We've discussed how to create your first scope and how to authorize your DHCP server in the Active Directory. Now we need to look at creating a superscope. Remember a superscope is a grouping of scopes that are used to support multinetted IP subnets on the same physical network. To create a superscope, you must create more than one scope on your DHCP server. If you need to review how to do this, refer to the section "Creating a Scope on Your DHCP Server." When you have multiple scopes on the DHCP server, you can create a superscope, following the procedure in the next Step by Step.

The best reason to use superscopes is to make the scopes in a multi-netted environment easier to support. If you have an environment with a lot of multinetting, it can get very confusing identifying which scope goes with which network. However, if you create a superscope named something like 4thFloor, and you add all the multinetted addresses on the fourth floor to it, you'll know where to go when you need to modify or add a scope (or when there are issues). You can also get statistics for all the scopes within the super-scope from the superscope statistics.

STEP BY STEP

2.5 Creating a Superscope

1. Open the DHCP manager application.

2. Select the DHCP server you want to create the superscope on and choose Action, New Superscope. (You can also open the Action menu by right-clicking the DHCP server.) The New Superscope Wizard starts (see Figure 2.26). Click Next and the Superscope Name dialog box shown in Figure 2.27 opens.

---

continues

FIGURE 2.26
The New Superscope Wizard guides you through creating a superscope.

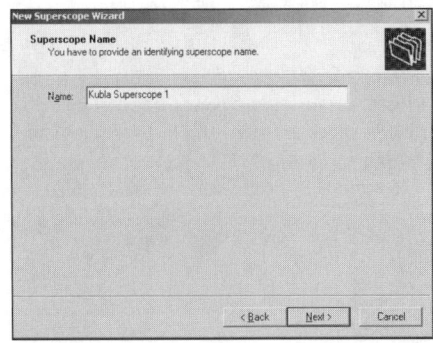

FIGURE 2.27
Using a descriptive superscope name will make it easier to identify, manage, and troubleshoot the superscope in the future.

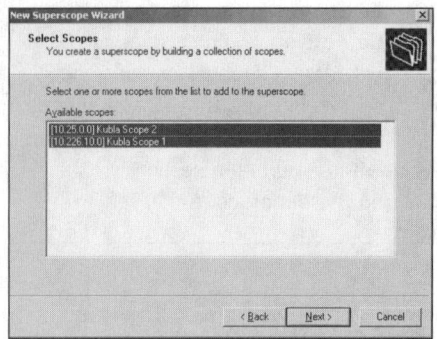

FIGURE 2.28
Select the active scopes you want included in
the superscope.

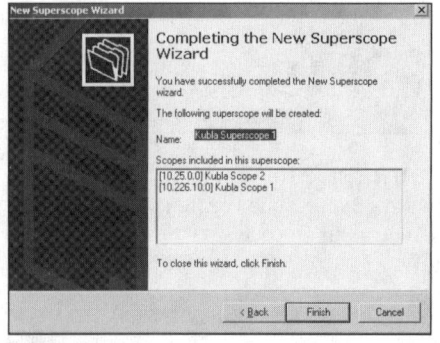

FIGURE 2.29
The final screen of the New Superscope Wizard
gives you a summary of the superscope you
are about to create.

continued

3. Type a descriptive name for the superscope and click Next to continue. The Select Scopes dialog box that appears allows you to select the active scopes to be included in the superscope (see Figure 2.28).

4. Hold down the Ctrl key, select the scopes you want to include in the superscope, and click Next to continue. The Completing the New Superscope Wizard dialog box that appears (see Figure 2.29) gives you a summary of the selections you made throughout the wizard so you can verify their accuracy.

5. If your selections are not correct, click Back to make changes, or click Cancel to exit. When everything is correct and you are ready to create the superscope, click Finish.

You have now created a superscope, which will allow you to manage multiple scopes on the same physical network.

Creating a Multicast Superscope

Now let's discuss creating a multicast scope. To create a multicast scope, do the following:

STEP BY STEP

2.6 Creating a Multicast Scope

1. Open the DHCP manager application.

2. Select the DHCP server you want to create the multicast scope on. Then choose Action, New Multicast Scope. (You can also open the Action menu by right-clicking the DHCP server.) The New Multicast Scope Wizard starts. Click Next, and the Multicast Scope Name dialog box shown in Figure 2.30 opens.

3. Type a descriptive name for the multicast scope and click Next to continue. The IP Address Range dialog opens (see Figure 2.31).

4. Select the range of addresses for the scope. They can be anywhere from 224.0.0.0 to 239.255.255.255. Enter the Time to Live amount. This is the number of routers the multicast packets can traverse before being discarded. Click Next, and the Add Exclusions dialog box opens. This is identical to the dialog box we saw earlier in the "Creating a DHCP Scope" Step by Step (see Figure 2.16).

5. Add any addresses or ranges that need to be excluded from this scope. Click Next. The Lease Duration dialog (Figure 2.32) opens.

6. Set the length of the lease for the multicast address. Because these addresses are shared between multiple computers, this lease is generally longer than leases for other types of scopes. Set the lease to the amount of time you expect the multicasting to continue.

7. Click Next, and then click Finish to complete the creation of a multicast scope.

Now let's look at integrating DHCP into DNS.

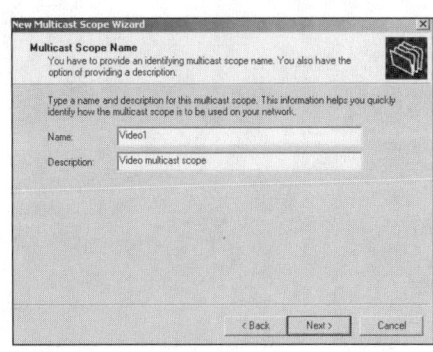

FIGURE 2.30
Using a descriptive multicast scope name will make it easier to identify, manage, and troubleshoot the scope in the future.

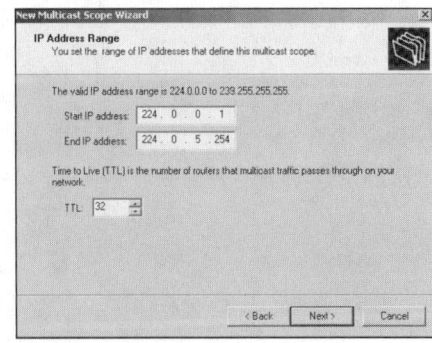

FIGURE 2.31
Enter the IP address range and TTL (Time to Live) for the scope.

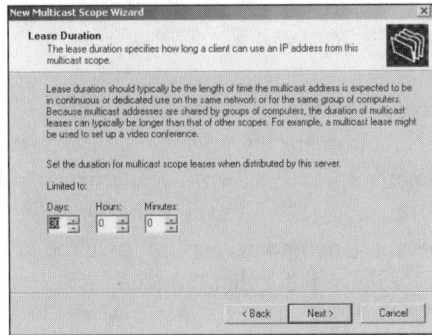

FIGURE 2.32
Multicast scopes typically have longer lease times than other types of scopes.

Configuring DHCP for DNS Integration

One of the keys to effectively implementing an Active Directory environment is the capability for Windows 2000 workstations using DHCP to be automatically registered in DNS. Three settings can be set for DNS integration:

◆ **Automatically Update DHCP Client Information in DNS.** This is enabled by default and, if selected, the DHCP server registers the DHCP client for both forward (A-type records) and reverse (PTR-type records) lookups in DNS, only when requested to by the client computer. These settings are usually adequate for a pure Windows 2000 environment because a Windows 2000 client computer updates DNS directly. If you have older Microsoft or non-Microsoft client computers on your network, you may want to change this to Always Update DNS. If the Always Update DNS option is selected, the DHCP server always registers the DHCP client for both the forward (A-type records) and reverse (PTR-type records) lookups with DNS.

◆ **Discard Forward (Name-to-Address) Lookups When Lease Expires.** This is also enabled by default and means that after the lease for an IP address expires (is no longer in use by the client computer), DHS discards any resolution requests.

◆ **Enable Updates for DNS Clients That Do Not Support Dynamic Update.** This is another parameter you may want to enable if you are using Active Directory in a mixed client computer environment.

Where do you configure the DNS server(s) to update? You don't. The DHCP server automatically updates any DNS server configured as part of the server's TCP/IP network properties. It is important to be sure that your primary DNS server is configured as one of the DNS servers, because any updates sent to it will be propagated to the rest of the DNS servers for that domain.

However, the DNS server in question must support Dynamic DNS, discussed in Chapter 1, "Installing, Configuring, Managing, Monitoring, and Troubleshooting DNS in a Windows 2000 Network Infrastructure." The Windows 2000 DNS server supports these updates, as do a number of other DNS servers.

To configure this capability, you must do the following:

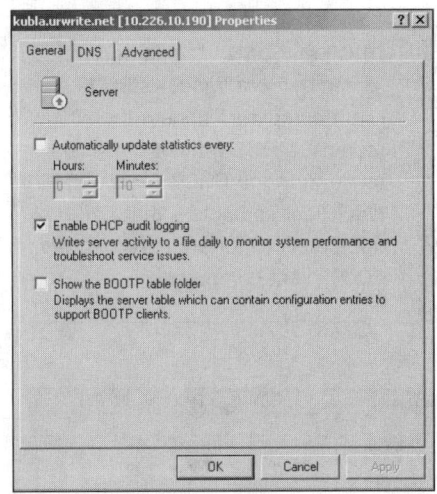

FIGURE 2.33
The General tab of the DHCP server Properties allows you to configure the server's logging and statistics parameters.

STEP BY STEP

2.7 Configuring DHCP for DNS Integration

1. Open the DHCP manager application.

2. Select the DHCP server you want to configure for DNS integration and click the Action button. (You can also open the Action menu by right-clicking the DHCP server.)

3. Select Properties. The Properties for this DHCP server open (see Figure 2.33) to the General tab.

4. To configure DNS, select the DNS tab (see Figure 2.34). You can configure three parameters in this dialog box. For this exercise, leave the settings at their default.

That takes care of the mechanics of integrating DHCP into your DNS environment. We should also discuss how the DHCP server actually makes the updates to DNS. At the writing of this book, this is still a draft standard. (The text of the proposed standard at the time of this writing can be found at `http://www.ietf.org/ internet-drafts/draft-ietf-dhc-dhcp-dns-11.txt`. This draft expires in September of 2000.) This IETF draft specifies how a DHCP server may register and update pointer (PTR) and address (A) resource records on behalf of its DHCP-enabled clients. It also specifies how to assign an additional DHCP option code (option code 81) that enables the return of a client's fully qualified domain name (FQDN) to the DHCP server. (PTR and A records, as well as FDQN, are discussed in Chapter 1.)

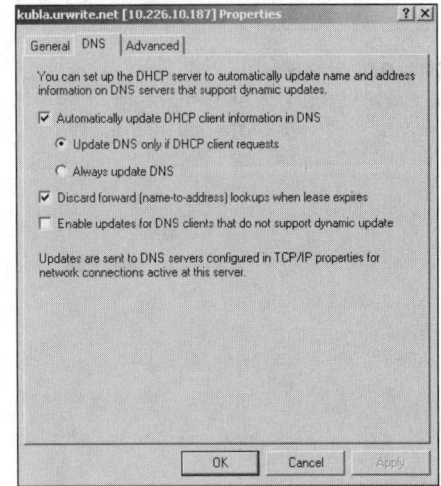

FIGURE 2.34
The DNS tab allows you to configure how the DHCP server will interact with the DNS server(s).

DHCP and DNS   It is important to remember that Windows 2000 client computers update the A records in DNS without any assistance from the DHCP server. The only client computers that DHCP updates DNS for are non-Windows 2000 client computers.

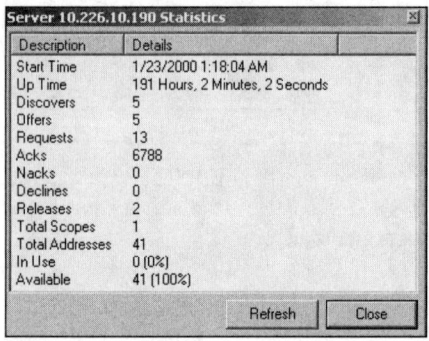

FIGURE 2.35
The Server Statistics screen gives you an excellent snapshot of the server's activities.

The capability to register both A and PTR type records lets a DHCP server register non-Windows 2000 client computers in DNS, as you just learned. The DHCP server can differentiate between Windows 2000 Professional and other client computers.

MANAGING AND MONITORING DHCP

Manage and monitor DHCP.

We have looked at installing and configuring the Windows 2000 DHCP service. The final piece of the DHCP puzzle is managing and monitoring the server after it is installed and configured. The Windows 2000 DHCP Server bundles enhanced monitoring and statistical reporting for precisely that purpose.

The DHCP manager has several additional features, found on the Action menu. The Display Statistics command opens the Server Statistics window shown in Figure 2.35. This screen displays the following statistics:

◆ **Start Time.** The date and time the service was started.

◆ **Up Time.** The total up time for the DHCP service. If you restart the service, this number resets to zero, even if the Windows 2000 server has not been restarted.

◆ **Discovers.** The number of DHCPDiscover packets the server has received.

◆ **Offers.** The number of DHCPOffer packets the server has sent.

◆ **Requests.** The number of DHCPRequest packets the server has received.

◆ **Acks.** The number of DHCP acknowledgement packets the server has sent.

◆ **Nacks.** The number of DHCP negative acknowledgement packets the server has sent.

◆ **Declines.** The number of DHCPDecline packets the server has received.

◆ **Releases.** The number of DHCPRelease messages the server has received.

◆ **Total Scopes.** The total number of scopes active on the server.

◆ **Total Addresses.** The total number of addresses available. This number includes the number of addresses for all the active scopes on the server.

◆ **In Use.** The number of addresses presently leased to DHCP client computers.

◆ **Available.** The number of addresses available for lease for the Total Address pool.

The Reconcile All Scopes command allows you to compare the information contained in the DHCP database with the information stored in the Registry. Use this option only when you are having issues with the DHCP server and need to verify the configured addresses. Clicking the Verify button shown in Figure 2.36 checks the consistency of the database and returns any errors it finds.

The Unauthorize command removes the DHCP server from the list of authorized DHCP servers in the Active Directory. You will be warned before the removal occurs (see Figure 2.37).

Define User Classes, Define Vendor Classes, and Set Predefined Options are advanced concepts that are beyond the scope of this exam. You will probably not use them in the context of a standard DHCP installation, but you should be aware of what User Classes and Vendor Classes are for the exam:

◆ **User Classes.** User classes are generally created for administrative purposes, similar to user groups. They can be used to identify all the DHCP clients in a specific department or location. User classes are used to assign DHCP options to groups of DHCP clients.

◆ **Vendor Classes.** Vendor classes are generally used to provide vendor-specific DHCP enhancements. For example, the Windows 2000 DHCP Service has the capability to disable NetBIOS over TCP/IP on its DHCP clients.

The All Tasks selection allows you to perform the following tasks for your DHCP server:

◆ **Start.** Starts the DHCP service. Available only if the service is stopped or paused.

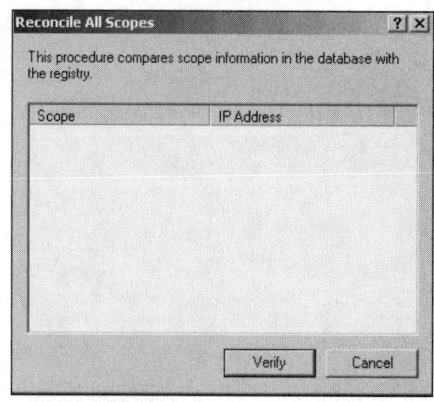

FIGURE 2.36
If you are experiencing what appears to be DHCP database corruption issues, this is the place to check the database consistency.

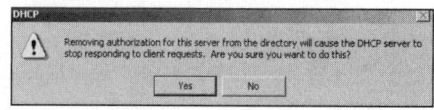

FIGURE 2.37
Only unauthorize a DHCP server when you are sure you will need it to respond to DHCP requests.

◆ **Stop.** Stops the DHCP service. Available when the service is running or paused. This option causes the server statistics to be reset.

◆ **Pause.** Pauses the DHCP service. This option does not reset the statistics.

◆ **Resume.** Resumes the DHCP service when paused. This option is available only when the service is paused.

◆ **Restart.** This option restarts the DHCP service, resetting the server statistics in the process. This option is available unless the server is stopped.

The next three commands are common ones. The Delete command deletes the DHCP server. The Refresh command causes all the displayed information to be refreshed with a current status. The Export List command allows you to export the information from the DHCP server to a tab- or comma-delimited text or Unicode text file.

The final command is Properties, which opens the Properties dialog box for the selected DHCP server. The Properties dialog box opens to the General tab, which allows you to configure the following options (see Figure 2.38):

◆ **Automatically Update Statistics Every.** This option allows you to set the automatic refresh of the statistics, as well as the interval at which they are refreshed.

◆ **Enable DHCP Audit Logging.** This option allows you to log all the DHCP activity to a file, which can be viewed in the System Log, using Event Viewer. This is an excellent option to select if you are troubleshooting a DHCP issue and want to see what activity is taking place on the server. Figure 2.39 shows a sample of the System Log with DHCP messages in it. You can also see these messages in the Audit Log, located at `C:\<%system_root%>\System32\dhcp`.

◆ **Show the BOOTP table folder**. This option deals with BOOTP backward compatibility and allows you to view the table where the BOOTP configuration entries are contained. This table appears in the Tree window of the DHCP manager (see Figure 2.40) and allows you to configure a BOOTP image file, which can be loaded to a BOOTP client from either a full server path or a TFTP file server.

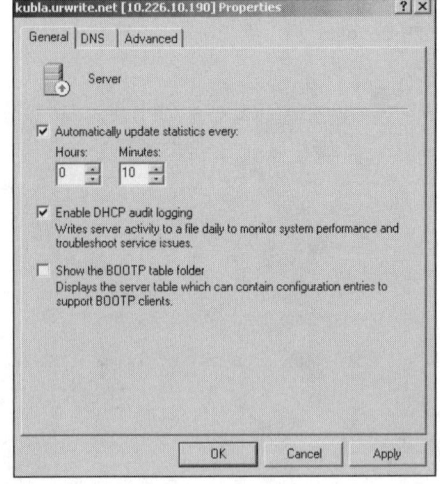

FIGURE 2.38

The General tab allows you to configure the statistics, logging, and BOOTP configuration information for your DHCP server.

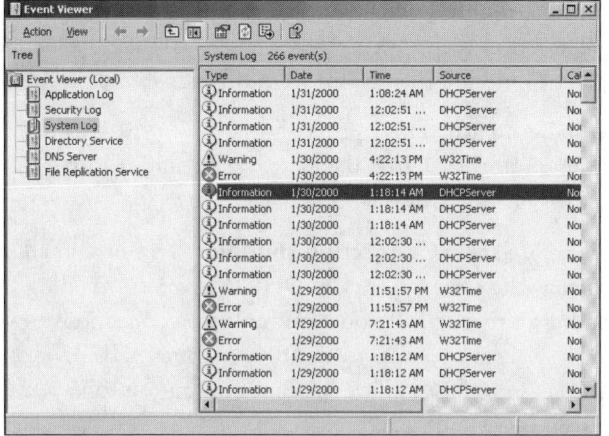

FIGURE 2.39
The System Log can be viewed using the Event
Viewer. Every DHCP action is logged in the
System Log when the Enable DHCP Audit
Logging option is selected.

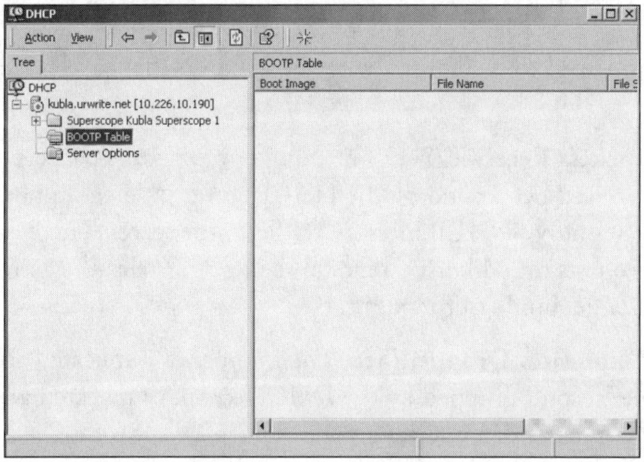

FIGURE 2.40
Use the BOOTP option only for legacy BOOTP
clients. These clients are becoming more
and more rare, and are used in few corporate
environments.

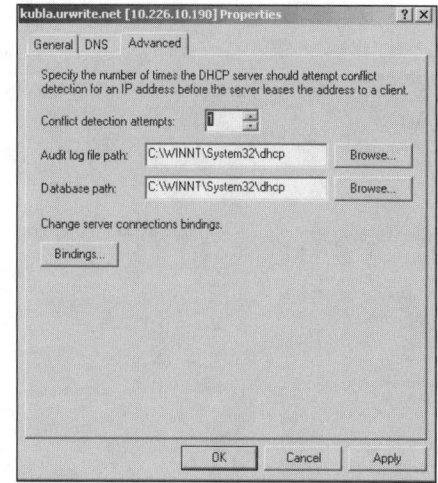

The DNS tab of the Properties dialog box was discussed in detail
in the "Configuring DHCP for DNS Integration" section earlier in
the chapter. Use the Advanced tab (shown in Figure 2.41) for the
following configuration options:

◆ **Conflict Detection Attempts.** This option will cause the
DHCP server to check for conflicting IP addresses on the network before issuing an address. Although this sounds like a
great way to make sure there are no address conflicts, this can
add significant overhead to the server and should be used only
while troubleshooting address conflict issues. By default, this
is set to 0.

FIGURE 2.41
The Advanced options shouldn't be modified
without a thorough understanding of the
options and the ramifications of the change.

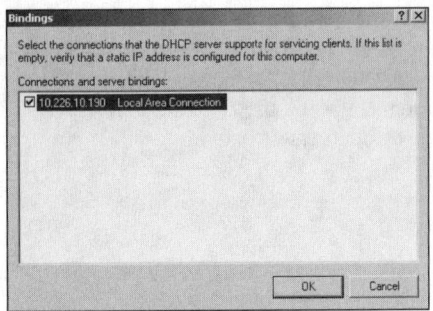

FIGURE 2.42
The Bindings section allows you to configure
the interfaces that will be used to respond to
DHCP requests.

EXAM TIP

**Know the Types of DHCP
Statistics**   Although you don't
need to memorize these counters
for the exam, you should at least
be familiar with the types of statistics that can be gathered for DHCP.

◆ **Audit Log File Path.** If Audit Logging is enabled, the log file
is located in the C:\<%system_root%>\System32\dhcp directory.
You can modify the default from this tab.

◆ **Database Path.** This option allows you to specify the
location of the DHCP database. By default, it is in
C:\<%system_root%>\System32\dhcp.

◆ **Change Server Connection Bindings.** This option allows you
to view the connections the DHCP server is providing
addresses through. If you have multiple connections to your
DHCP server, you may want to configure DHCP for only
selected interfaces. Click the Bindings button to view this
screen (see Figure 2.42).

Now that you have looked at the options for managing the DHCP
server, let's take a look at some of the ways to monitor the service.
First, you need to be familiar with the counters that can be measured for DHCP:

◆ **Packets Received/Sec.** The number of message packets
received per second by the DHCP server. A large number indicates heavy DHCP message traffic to the server. These can be
requests for addresses, renewal requests, or releases . . . not just
a large number of requests.

◆ **Duplicates Dropped/Sec.** The number of duplicate packets
per second dropped by the DHCP server. Duplicate packets
on a network are never a good sign, and in this case, it indicates DHCP clients are timing out before the server can
respond. This can be caused by client computers timing out
too fast, or the server not responding fast enough.

◆ **Packets Expired/Sec.** The number of packets per second that
expire and are dropped by the DHCP server. This is caused by
a packet remaining in the server's internal message queue for
too long. A large number here indicates that the server is either
taking too long to process some packets or causing other packets
to wait in queue, or that the traffic on the network is too high
for the DHCP server to handle. It is important to note that
high numbers here can indicate pure network traffic issues,
and not necessarily DHCP-related problems.

◆ **Milliseconds Per Packet (Avg).** The average time, in milliseconds, the DHCP server takes to process each packet it receives. This is a very subjective number because of the server configuration; therefore, a baseline for this number is a good idea. A sudden increase in this counter could indicate a disk issue or an increased load on the server.

◆ **Active Queue Length.** The current length of the internal message queue of the DHCP server. This number represents the number of unprocessed messages received by the server. A large number here could indicate an unusually high amount of network traffic or a high load on the server.

◆ **Conflict Check Queue Length.** The current length of the conflict check queue for the DHCP server. Before a Windows 2000 DHCP server will issue an address, it checks to see if any IP address conflicts exist. This queue holds the messages held in queue while the DHCP server performs address conflict detection. A large value here could indicate heavy lease traffic at the server. You may also want to check the Conflict Detection Attempts parameter, which could be set too high.

◆ **Discovers/Sec.** The number of DHCPDiscover messages received per second by the server. The DHCPDiscover message is the initial request a client computer sends when it first enters the network and is looking for a DHCP server to issue an address. A sudden increase in this counter could indicate that a large number of client computers are attempting to initialize and obtain an IP address lease from the server at the same time. You might see this first thing in the morning, when users power on their PCs, or after a power failure, when all your PCs might be powered on at about the same time.

◆ **Offers/Sec.** The number of DHCPOffer messages sent per second by the DHCP server to client computers. A DHCPOffer message is the message the server returns to the client computer after the client computer sends a DHCPDiscover message, and it indicates the server is offering to issue an address to that client computer. A sudden increase in this value could indicate heavy traffic or a heavy load on the server.

◆ **Requests/Sec.** The number of DHCPRequest messages received per second by the DHCP server from client computers. This is the request the client computer sends to request an IP address after it has found a server that can issue addresses. An increase in this number indicates that a large number of client computers are probably trying to renew their leases with the DHCP server. This could be because of a short lease time configuration, or a number of new computers could be entering the network.

◆ **Informs/Sec.** The number of DHCPInform messages received per second by the DHCP server. DHCPInform messages are used when the DHCP server queries the directory service for the enterprise root and when dynamic updates are being done on behalf of client computers by the DNS server. This is part of the Dynamic DNS integration, and an unusual increase in this number could indicate a large number of addresses being issued.

◆ **Acks/Sec.** The number of DHCPAck messages sent per second by the DHCP server to client computers. The DHCPAck message is used by the DHCP server to acknowledge requests for an address. An increase in this number indicates that a large number of client computers are probably trying to renew their leases with the DHCP server. This could be because of a short lease time configuration, or a number of new computers could be entering the network.

◆ **Nacks/Sec.** The number of DHCP negative acknowledgment messages sent per second by the DHCP server to client computers. This indicates the server is unable to fulfill the DHCP request. A very high value for this counter could indicate a network issue or misconfiguration of client computers or the server. Keep an eye out for a deactivated scope as a possible culprit.

◆ **Declines/Sec.** The number of DHCPDecline messages received per second by the DHCP server from client computers. This counter indicates that the DHCP client computer has declined the IP address issued by the server. You will see this number rise when client computers start having address conflict issues. This could indicate a network issue, computers with static addresses that are also part of a scope, or potentially a "rogue" DHCP server on the network.

◆ **Releases/Sec.** The number of DHCPRelease messages received per second by the DHCP server from client computers. A DHCPRelease message is sent only when the client computer manually releases an address, such as when the ipconfig /release command or the Release All button in the winipcfg utility is used at the client computer. Because most users do not manually release their addresses, this number should be low in all but the most unusual network environment.

To configure DHCP Performance monitoring, do the following:

STEP BY STEP

2.8 Monitoring DHCP Performance

1. Choose Start, Programs, Administrative Tools, and Performance to open the Performance application.

2. In Performance, select System Monitor (see Figure 2.43).

3. To create an entry in System Monitor, click the Add (+) icon. The Add Counters window shown in Figure 2.44 opens.

4. Select the DHCP performance object. You will see the list of counters displayed as available for DHCP (see Figure 2.45). If you need to know what a counter means, select the counter and click the Explain button. Figure 2.46 shows the explanation function of the Performance utility.

continues

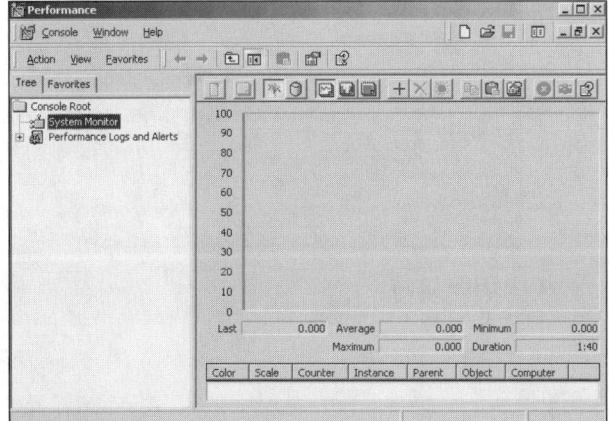

EXAM TIP

What Can You Do to Resolve Conflict Issues?   When you start seeing a high number of declines per second, you may want to enable conflict detection on the DHCP server. This will cause the server to look for conflicts before issuing an address, and it should take care of the conflict issues until you can find the problem. This should be used only until the issue is addressed. Forcing the DHCP server to detect conflicts every time it issues an address adds a lot of overhead to the server and the DHCP service and should be avoided on a long-term basis. After you have resolved the issue, be sure to turn this feature off.

FIGURE 2.43
System Monitor allows you to monitor the performance of your server's statistics in real-time.

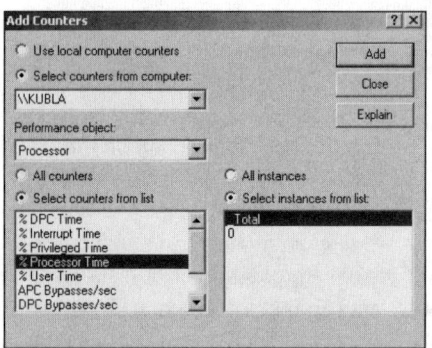

FIGURE 2.44
Counters are used to display metrics for a specific performance object. The performance object can be either hardware or software.

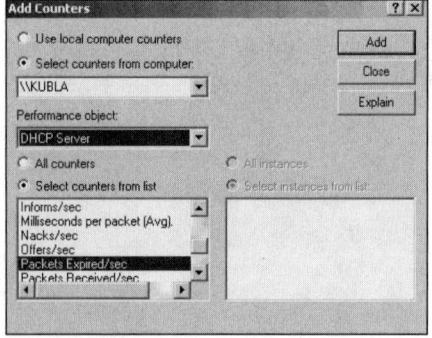

FIGURE 2.45
The counters associated with DHCP allow you to comprehensively examine the DHCP server's activities.

continued

5. When you have decided on the counter you want to monitor, click Add. You can add multiple counters either by selecting each counter and clicking Add, or by using the standard Windows multiple item select method (holding down the Ctrl key while you select all the counters you want to monitor, and then clicking Add). Click Close when you are finished. Your counters will be graphed like those shown in Figure 2.47.

You've looked at the management options available in the DHCP manager application, and you've taken a look at how to monitor the performance of the different DHCP counters using the Performance utility. One other feature of the DHCP service should be discussed.

The Simple Network Management Protocol (SNMP) and Management Information Bases (MIBs) form an industry standard set of management protocols for managing complex networks. First developed in the early 1980s, SNMP works by sending messages, called to different parts of a network. SNMP-compliant devices store statistical data about themselves in MIBs and return this data to the SNMP-compliant managers.

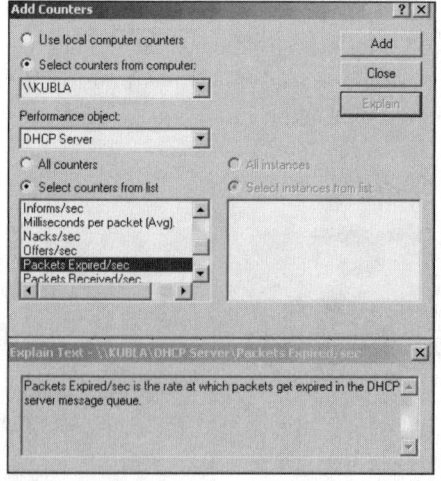

FIGURE 2.46
Click the Explain button.

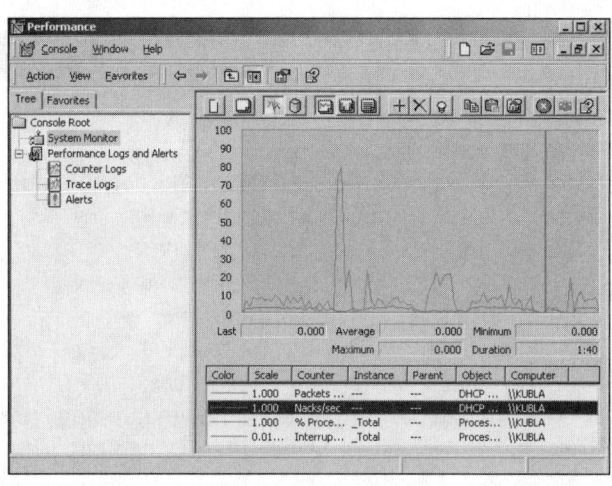

FIGURE 2.47
After the counters have been added, all that
remains is successfully interpreting the data.

The DHCP manager now supports SNMP and MIBs, which
allows the DHCP server to report statistics and send alerts to any
of a number of management platforms, including HP OpenView,
Seagate Nerve Center, and even Novell's ManageWise product.
This allows administrators to monitor DHCP information,
including the following:

◆ The number of available addresses

◆ The number of used addresses

◆ The number of leases being processed per second

◆ The number of messages and offers processed

◆ The number of requests, acknowledgements, declines, negative
status acknowledgment messages (Nacks), and releases received

◆ The total number of scopes and addresses on the server, the
number used, and the number available

If you would like to know more about SNMP and MIBS, check out
A Practical Guide to SNMPv3 and Network Management, by David
Zeltserman (Prentice Hall).

At this point, you should have a good understanding of the
Windows 2000 DHCP service. Next, you'll see how to apply it in
a practical situation.

CASE STUDY: IMPLEMENTING DHCP IN A COMPLEX ENVIRONMENT

ESSENCE OF THE CASE

The essence of the case is as follows:

▶ Your company is about to migrate to a pure Windows 2000 environment.

▶ Your company has three networks, two with users and one as a backbone. The Sales network has approximately 400 users; the Engineering network has 75 users.

▶ The three networks are connected by two routers: Router A and Router B.

▶ The Sales network has plenty of addresses because of the multinetted network. The Engineering network does not have enough addresses for its network, but the engineers are able to work because they work in shifts.

SCENARIO

You are the network administrator for NR Widgets Inc., a computer manufacturing company. NR Widgets Inc. is just about to migrate to a pure Windows 2000 environment. You have two user networks (see Figure 2.48): Sales and Engineering, and a corporate backbone network. The Sales network has more than 400 users and is multinetted to provide an adequate number of addresses for everyone. The Engineering network has only 75 users, but the network also contains a number of printers, plotters, and test equipment, so there are only 40 addresses for the users. The users work three shifts in Engineering, with 25 engineers working each shift.

Today, all the hosts use static addresses, which works okay for the Sales network, but it means that to avoid IP address resolution issues, the engineers have to be careful about which computers are left connected to the network. Yesterday your manager suggested, "While you're migrating to Windows 2000, why don't you fix the IP address problems on the network?"

Keeping in mind that the boss's "suggestions" usually mean "Have it done by the end of the week," what should you do?

CASE STUDY: IMPLEMENTING DHCP IN A COMPLEX ENVIRONMENT

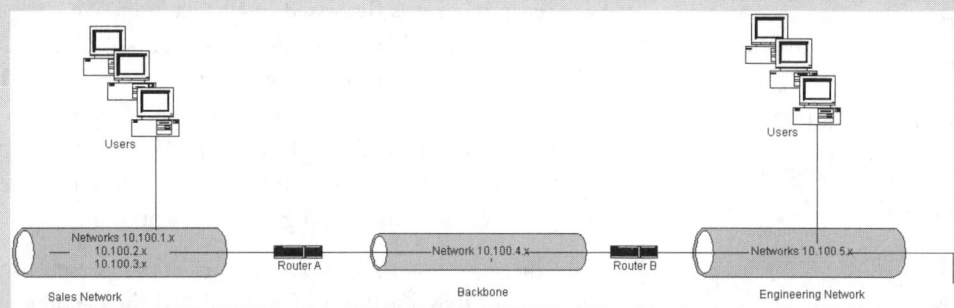

FIGURE 2.48
Case Study network diagram.

ANALYSIS

This situation provides an excellent opportunity to deploy the Windows 2000 DHCP service as part of the Windows 2000 rollout. To make it work, you need to make sure you do the following:

- Allocate the server resources to support at least one DHCP server. To avoid as much traffic traversing the router as possible, you should plan on placing the server on the network that will be generating the most DHCP requests. Because 400 users are on the Sales network, at first glance you may think that is where all the requests will be coming from. Think again. Because there are plenty of addresses for the Sales network, you can configure exceptionally long lease times, so the number of requests after the initial lease will be pretty low. On the Engineering network, however, users will be requesting a new address every time they power up the computer, because of the limited number of addresses.

- After you have identified the server and placed it on the network, you will need to install and configure DHCP. After the service is installed, you will need to authorize the server in the Active Directory.

- When you create your scopes, you should create a single scope for the Engineering network and a superscope for the Sales network. The superscope allows you to combine multiple scopes (the Sales network has three network addresses) for easier management. The lease for each of the scopes within the superscope should be at least 30 days, to ensure that a limited amount of lease traffic traverses the routers. The lease for the Engineering network should be eight hours so that addresses are available for the incoming shift as the previous shift leaves for home.

- Finally, you need to be sure that the BOOTP Forwarder service is running on the routers and is configured to point to the appropriate DHCP server for forwarding DHCP traffic.

That should have been a fairly easy case study if you read the chapter carefully. Of course, after the DHCP server is set up and running, you would also want to set up some of the monitoring discussed at the end of the chapter.

CHAPTER SUMMARY

KEY TERMS

- address pool
- Domain Name System (DNS)
- Dynamic Host Configuration Protocol (DHCP)
- DHCP server
- DHCP client
- exclusion
- lease
- Management Information Block (MIB)
- reservation
- scope
- Simple Network Management Protocol (SNMP)
- superscope
- Transmission Control Protocol/Internet Protocol (TCP/IP)
- Request For Comment (RFC) documents
- BOOTP protocol
- multicast scope
- registered IP address
- supernetted network
- unicast addresses

Let's recap what was discussed in this chapter. We have discussed all the key components of using a Windows 2000 DHCP server in a Windows 2000 environment. We first discussed what DHCP was and where it came from. We covered the different types of scopes in detail, and then went through the steps of installing DHCP, creating the first scope, and then authorizing the server in the Active Directory. That is enough to give you a working DHCP server.

From there we discussed creating superscopes and multicast scopes, integrating DNS and DHCP, and finished the chapter with a discussion of the different methods for monitoring and managing DHCP.

APPLY YOUR KNOWLEDGE

Exercises

2.1 Creating a DHCP Scope

In the following exercise, you use Report Writer to create a report on the contents of a log file.

Estimated Time: 30 minutes

1. Go to the Configure Your Server application by selecting Programs, Administrative Tools, and Configure Your Server.

2. Click the Open hyperlink to open the DHCP manager. You can also reach this screen by directly opening the DHCP manager. Just go to Programs, Administrative Tools, and DHCP.

3. Select the DHCP server listed in the DHCP windows (the one on the right) and go to Action, New Scope to start the New Scope Wizard. Click Next to start defining your scope. This opens the Scope Name dialog box.

4. Type the name **Exercise1** and a description in the fields provided and click Next. This opens the IP Address Range.

5. Enter the appropriate address range and subnet mask. For this exercise, use 10.0.0.1 to 10.0.0.100, with a subnet mask of 255.255.255.0. Click Next and the Add Exclusions dialog box opens.

6. Add addresses to be excluded as needed. For this exercise, you don't need to exclude any addresses. Click Next to open the Lease Duration dialog box.

7. For this exercise, leave the default Lease Duration. Click Next and the Configure DHCP Options dialog box opens.

8. Configure the router, or default gateway. In this exercise, use 10.0.0.254. Click Next and the Domain Name and DNS Servers dialog box opens.

9. Specify DNS server(s), as needed. For this exercise, use 10.0.1.1 and 10.0.2.1. Click Next and the WINS Servers dialog box opens.

10. Define a WINS server if you have legacy DHCP client computers that still need WINS services. For this exercise use 10.0.1.2 and 10.0.2.2.

11. Click Next and then click Finish to complete the scope creation.

2.2 Creating a Superscope

The following exercise shows you how to manage multiple scopes by creating a superscope. You will need to have completed Exercise 2.1 for this to work.

Estimated Time: 15 minutes

1. Open the DHCP manager application.

2. Select the DHCP server you want to create the superscope on, and click the Action button. You can also open this menu by right-clicking the DHCP server.

3. Select New Superscope. Click Next to continue.

4. The Superscope Name dialog box opens. Enter a name and click Next to continue. For this exercise, use the name SuperExercise1.

5. In the Select Scopes dialog box, select the scopes you want to include in the superscope and click Next to continue. You should select the Exercise1 scope created in the last exercise.

APPLY YOUR KNOWLEDGE

6. The Completing the New Superscope Wizard dialog box gives you a summary of the selections you made throughout the wizard. To create the superscope, click Finish.

2.3   Monitoring DHCP Server Performance Using the Performance Application

This exercise will walk you through adding a counter to the Performance utility, so you can baseline or troubleshoot your DHCP server.

Estimated Time: 15 minutes.

1. Open the Performance application by going to Programs, Administrative Tools, and Performance.

2. In Performance, select System Monitor.

3. To create an entry in System Monitor, click the Add (+) icon. The Add Counters windows opens. Notice that by default it opens to the Processor performance object.

4. Select the DHCP performance object.

5. Select the counter you want to monitor and click Add. You can add multiple counters either by selecting each counter and clicking Add, or by using the standard Windows multiple item select method of holding down the Ctrl key while you select all the counters you want to monitor, and then clicking Add. For this exercise, select the Offers/Sec, Requests/Sec and Releases/Sec counters. Click Close when you are done.

6. Observe the results in the monitoring window. If you have multiple workstations available, make some DHCP requests to see the effect on the counters.

Review Questions

1. You are the network administrator for Exponent Mathematicians, and you have been asked to implement DHCP on a multinetted network segment. What should you do to ensure that this is successful?

2. You are the administrator of the Get Bux pawnshop chain DHCP server. You are getting complaints from users that they keep getting address conflict messages when they turn on their computers. What DHCP counter might help you identify the issue?

3. You are the Windows 2000 administrator for Fly Away Travel. When administering Fly Away's DHCP server, you notice that the number of DHCP requests is very high for the number of users on the network. Where is the first place you should look for a server-related issue?

4. You're the administrator of Little Faith Enterprise's Windows 2000 DHCP server. You notice that the DHCP server is running sluggishly during peak hours. Checking the Performance utility, you notice the DHCP Conflict Check Queue Length option is very high. What could be causing this issue?

5. You're the administrator of Little Faith Enterprise's Windows 2000 DHCP server. You have just installed the DHCP service and created your first scope using the Scope Wizard. You are trying to provide DHCP addresses to a group of users that are two router hops away. What do you still need to do?

APPLY YOUR KNOWLEDGE

Exam Questions

1. You are the network administrator for Wild Widgets Inc. You are training a new employee on the use of the DHCP service in Windows 2000 Server. She asks you how the client computer requests and receives an address from the server.

   A. The client computer broadcasts a DHCPDiscover message. The DHCP server offers an IP address. The client computer accepts the address and uses it to communicate on the network.

   B. The client computer broadcasts a DHCPDiscover message. The DHCP server offers an IP address. The client computer accepts the address and sends a request to use that address back to the DHCP server. The client computer uses the address to communicate on the network.

   C. The client computer broadcasts a DHCPDiscover message. The DHCP server offers an IP address. The client computer accepts the address and sends a request to use that address back to the DHCP server. The DHCP server acknowledges the request and grants the client computer a lease to use the address. The client computer uses the address to connect to the network.

   D. The client computer broadcasts a DHCPDiscover message. The DHCP server offers an IP address. The client computer accepts the address and sends a request to use

that address back to the DHCP server. The DHCP server acknowledges the request and grants the client computer a lease to use the address. The client computer responds with an acknowledgement of the lease and uses the address to connect to the network.

2. You are the system administrator for Phil's Phill-up Stations, a chain of gas stations. As part of the network, you maintain a Windows 2000 DHCP server to dynamically assign addresses. You have three superscopes set up, and within each superscope are four scopes. Suddenly, you start experiencing issues with one of the scopes issuing bad addresses. You check the server and suspect that there is a database issue. How can you verify that the database is intact?

   A. Open DHCP manager. Select the scope in question and click the Action menu. Select Reconcile Scope.

   B. Open DHCP manager. Select the superscope containing the scope in question and click the Action menu. Select Reconcile All Scopes.

   C. Open DHCP manager. Select the DHCP server containing the scope in question and click the Action menu. Select Reconcile All Scopes.

   D. Open DHCP manager. Select the DHCP server containing the scope in question and click the Action menu. Select Reconcile DHCP Database.

APPLY YOUR KNOWLEDGE

3. You are the LAN administrator for Get Stuffed Taxidermy, and you are responsible for maintaining the company's Windows 2000 DHCP server. While doing your daily system checks, you notice that the number of DHCPDiscover packets spiked at 9:00 this morning. What could cause this counter to spike at 9:00 a.m.?

   A. A network issue

   B. The DHCP service being restarted

   C. A large number of computers entering the network at approximately the same time

   D. A "rogue" DHCP server issuing duplicate addresses

4. You are the LAN administrator for Get Stuffed Taxidermy, and you are responsible for maintaining the company's Windows 2000 DHCP server. While doing your daily system checks, you notice that the number of DHCPDiscover packets spiked at 9:00 this morning. How would you go about monitoring the DHCPDiscover packets?

   A. Open Performance manager. Click the Add Counter icon. Select the DHCP Server object and then select the DHCPDiscover Packets/Sec counter. Click Add to add the counter and monitor the packets.

   B. Open the Performance utility. Click the Add Counter icon. Select the DHCP Server object and then select the DHCPDiscover Packets/Sec counter. Click Add to add the counter and monitor the packets.

   C. Open Performance utility. Click the Add Counter icon. Select the DHCP Server object and then select the Discovers/Sec counter. Click Add to add the counter and monitor the packets.

   D. Open DHCP manager. Select the DHCP server you want to monitor. Right-click the server and select Display Statistics from the context menu. Observe the Discovers statistic.

5. You are the lead engineer for Little Faith Enterprises, and a customer has asked you to install the DHCP service on her Windows 2000 Server, get one scope configured and issue addresses. What minimum steps do you need to take in order to accomplish this?

   A. Go to Network and Dial-up Connections in the Control Panel and select Add Network Components to install the service. After the service is installed, authorize it in the Active Directory. Next, create the scope. Finally, configure the DNS integration.

   B. Go to Network and Dial-up Connections in the Control Panel and select Add Network Components to install the service. After the service is installed, create the scope. Configure the DNS integration.

   C. Go to Network and Dial-up Connections in the Control Panel and select Add Network Components to install the service. After the service is installed, create the scope. Create a superscope and add the scope to it. Authorize the server in the Active Directory.

   D. Go to Network and Dial-up Connections in the Control Panel and select Add Network Components to install the service. After the service is installed, create the scope. Authorize the server in the Active Directory.

APPLY YOUR KNOWLEDGE

6. You are the network administrator for the Hittem Boxing Glove Corporation. The corporation is running a routed network with a centrally located Windows 2000 DHCP server. The server is able to issue addresses to users on the local segment but cannot issue addresses to any of the sites that are across a router. What is the most probable cause of this problem?

    A. The DHCP Forwarder service is not enabled on the DHCP server.

    B. The BOOTP Forwarder service is not enabled on the DHCP server.

    C. The DHCP Forwarder service is not enabled on the routers.

    D. The BOOTP Forwarder service is not enabled on the routers.

7. You manage the Windows 2000 DHCP servers for the Really Big Screwdriver Corporation. You are running in a pure Windows 2000 environment, and you need to make sure that workstations are registered properly in DNS for Active Directory integration. How should you configure DNS integration?

    A. Set DNS integration to automatically update DHCP client information in DNS.

    B. Set DNS integration to discard forward (name-to-address) lookups when lease expires.

    C. Set DNS integration to enable updates for DNS clients that do not support dynamic update.

    D. Set DNS integration to enable DNS keep-alives.

8. You are the LAN administrator for UR Write publishing, a bookseller. Your Windows 2000 DHCP server issues a block of 40 addresses to 120 salespeople on the Sales network. These users are frequently in and out of the office, so no more than 40 users are ever on the network at one time. What do you need to do to ensure that users get addresses when needed?

    A. Set the DHCP lease to 60 minutes.

    B. Set the DHCP lease to 5 days.

    C. Configure reservations for each user.

    D. Configure an exclusion for each user.

9. You are the distributed computing administrator for Talk to Me Telephone. Your company has Windows 2000 installed with the DHCP service running. Mixed in with your DHCP client computers, you still have some old workstations on the network with BOOTP chips on their Ethernet cards. You need to add support for BOOTP for these computers. How do you ensure that support?

    A. Add the BOOTP service to the server.

    B. In the Advanced tab of the scope properties, configure the server to issue addresses to BOOTP clients.

    C. In the Advanced tab of the server properties, configure the server to issue addresses to both DHCP and BOOTP clients.

    D. In the Advanced tab of the scope properties, configure the server to issue addresses to both DHCP and BOOTP clients.

APPLY YOUR KNOWLEDGE

10. You are the network administrator for the LFE Construction Company. You have a Windows 2000 DHCP server servicing the enterprise, and you need to be alerted when the number of available addresses drops below 10. How do you set up the system to trigger the alert?

    A. Because the DHCP server supports MIBs, you need to use a MIB-compliant management application such as HP OpenView to monitor the server and alert you when there are fewer than 10 addresses.

    B. Using the Performance utility, set the Available Addresses threshold to 10. Performance will alert you when you reach the threshold.

    C. Because the DHCP server supports SNMP, you need to use a SNMP-compliant management application such as HP OpenView to monitor the server and alert you when there are fewer than 10 addresses.

    D. Open DHCP Manager. Right-click the DHCP server and select Server Statistics. Click the Alert button and select the Available Addresses metric. Set the threshold to 10 and click the Send Network Alert box.

11. You are the network administrator for BT Editing Unlimited. You have a 50-host network and are running a Windows 2000 DHCP server to assign IP addresses. You also have five IP-based printers with static IP addresses. Your assistant administrator has been working on the DHCP server and made some changes. Suddenly, your users cannot print to one of the printers. What is most likely the problem?

    A. The scope the printers were receiving their IP addresses from has been deleted.

    B. The existing scope has been modified so that it overlaps the addresses reserved for the printers.

    C. The existing scope has been modified so that it overlaps the addresses reserved for the printers and a workstation has been assigned the same address as one of the printers.

    D. The DHCP service was inadvertently stopped.

12. You are the systems administrator for the Little Faith Department Store. You are responsible for maintaining the company's Windows 2000 DHCP server. The company recently added a new router and routed a segment to the network. Now that segment must be added to the DHCP server. The address of the router port is 10.10.25.1, and it is subnetted with a Class C subnet mask. You need to provide 20 addresses, starting at 10.10.25.20. What needs to occur for you to get DHCP working on that segment?

    A. You will need to install and configure an additional DHCP server on that segment to provide DHCP services.

    B. You will need to add a scope to the DHCP server containing the addresses from 10.10.25.20 through 10.10.25.39. The scope will need a subnet mask of 255.255.255.0. You will need to configure the BOOTP Forwarder for the new segment's router, using the address of the DHCP server. You will need to activate the scope.

    C. You will need to add a scope to the DHCP server containing the addresses from 10.10.25.20 through 10.10.25.40. The scope will need a subnet mask of 255.255.255.0. You will need to configure the BOOTP

APPLY YOUR KNOWLEDGE

Forwarder for the new segment's router, using the address of the DHCP server. You will need to activate the scope.

D. You will need to add a scope to the DHCP server containing the addresses from 10.10.25.20 through 10.10.25.40. The scope will need a subnet mask of 255.255.255.0. You will need to configure the BOOTP Forwarder for the new segment's router, using the address of the DHCP server. You will not need to activate the scope, because it happens automatically when the scope is created.

13. You are the network manager for IntCo Manufacturing. You are running in a mixed Windows 2000 environment, and you are using a Windows 2000 DHCP service to support a single network segment. Your client computers consist of Windows 2000 Professional, Windows NT Workstation and Windows 98 SE workstations. What do you need to do to ensure that all your client computers can receive DHCP addresses?

A. Configure a scope for each network segment. Configure each client computer to receive IP addresses dynamically. Configure the DHCP service for backward compatibility.

B. Configure a scope for each network segment. Configure each client computer to receive IP addresses dynamically. For the Windows NT Workstation client computers, ensure that the DHCP update from Service Pack 6 has been installed.

C. Configure a scope for each network segment. Configure each client computer to receive IP addresses dynamically. Configure the DHCP service for mixed mode.

D. Configure a scope for each network segment. Configure each client computer to receive IP addresses dynamically.

14. You are a consultant from Little Faith Enterprises, a Windows 2000 consulting company. You have been asked to configure DHCP for your customer. The client is not very familiar with DHCP and wants to know what information can be assigned via DHCP.

Which of the following parameters can DHCP assign? (Choose all that apply.)

A. IP address

B. BOOTP Forwarder

C. Gateway address

D. WINS server addresses

E. Active Directory Domain Controller addresses

15. You are a consultant from Little Faith Enterprises, a Windows 2000 consulting company. You have been asked to configure DHCP for your customer. The client is not very familiar with DHCP and wants to know what information is provided to the DHCP server.

Which of the following information is provided to the DHCP server? (Choose all that apply.)

A. IP address

B. MAC address

C. Hostname

D. NetBIOS name

E. Username

APPLY YOUR KNOWLEDGE

16. You are the network administrator for BT Editing, and you are running a pure Windows 2000 network, using Active Directory and the Windows 2000 DHCP service. A user in another department has installed a DHCP server on a UNIX server. How do you prevent your client computers from receiving DHCP addresses from this server?

    A. Disable the unauthorized server in Active Directory.

    B. Make sure all your users are running Windows 2000.

    C. Reconfigure BOOTP on the router.

    D. Go to each client computer and enter the address of the production DHCP server in the TCP/IP Properties.

17. You manage the Windows 2000 DHCP servers for the Really Big Screwdriver Corporation. You are running in a mixed environment, with both Windows 2000 and non-Windows 2000 workstations. You need to make sure workstations are registered properly in DNS for Active Directory integration.

    A. Set DNS Integration to automatically update DHCP client information in DNS.

    B. Set DNS Integration to discard forward (name-to-address) lookups when lease expires.

    C. Set DNS Integration to enable updates for DNS clients that do not support dynamic update.

    D. Set DNS Integration to enable DNS keep-alives.

Answers to Review Questions

1. To successfully implement DHCP in a multinetted environment, you should consider using a superscope to ease the management of the scopes for each of the multinetted networks. For more information, see the section "Installing, Configuring, and Troubleshooting DHCP."

2. In the Performance utility, check the Declines/Sec counter for the DHCP object. The number of DHCPDecline messages received per second by the DHCP server from client computers can be used to see if the DHCP client computer has declined the IP address issued by the server. You will see this number rise when client computers start having address conflict issues. This could indicate a network issue, computers with static addresses that are also part of a scope, or potentially a "rogue" DHCP server on the network. For more information, see the section "Managing and Monitoring DHCP."

3. Check the length of the DHCP lease. If the lease has been set to a very short duration, client computers would need to request addresses frequently. For more information, see the section "Installing, Configuring, and Troubleshooting DHCP."

4. There are either a lot of DHCP requests occurring during peak hours, or the Conflict Detection Attempts parameter is set too high. If this is enabled, Windows 2000 DHCP Server will issue an address, and it will check to see if any IP address conflicts exist. This can put a lot of additional overhead on the server and drive up the DHCP Conflict Check Queue Length. For more information, see the section "Managing and Monitoring DHCP."

APPLY YOUR KNOWLEDGE

5. First, you need to activate the DHCP server in the Active Directory. It will not be able to provide addresses until that occurs. You also need to configure the BOOTP Forwarder on any routers between the DHCP server and the client workstations so that the routers know where to forward DHCP messages. For more information, see the section "Authorizing a DHCP Server in Active Directory."

Answers to Exam Questions

1. **C**. The client computer cannot use the address until the DHCP server grants the lease. After the DHCP server acknowledges the DHCP request and grants the lease, the client computer is free to use the address. No additional step is required in the process. For more information, see the section "The DHCP Protocol."

2. **C**. You need to reconcile all the scopes on the server. Answer A is almost correct because you can reconcile a single scope, but the correct command is Reconcile, not Reconcile Scope. You cannot reconcile scopes at the Superscope level, as referenced in B. The command in D does not exist. For more information, see the section "Managing and Monitoring DHCP."

3. **C**. The DHCPDiscover packet is sent when a computer first requests an address. The most likely reason for this to spike would be a large number of concurrent requests, which could happen when a large number of client workstations requested addresses at the same time. A network issue would have the opposite effect because no DHCPDiscover packets would reach the server.

The DHCP service restart or a rogue DHCP server couldn't impact the number of DHCPDiscover packets, because they are generated by client PCs. For more information, see the section "Managing and Monitoring DHCP."

4. **C**. Performance Manager was the name of the Windows NT application. In Windows 2000, the Performance utility runs as part of the Microsoft Management Console (MMC). The correct counter is Discovers/Sec. The DHCP server statistics show you only the total number of discover packets and is unable to show any spikes. For more information, see the section "Managing and Monitoring DHCP."

5. **D**. If the task is to install the DHCP service and get it issuing addresses, you do not need to configure DNS. You also need to authorize the server in the Active Directory. Even though you created a superscope in the chapter, you do not need a superscope for the server to function. For more information, see the section "Installing, Configuring, and Troubleshooting DHCP."

6. **D**. To issue addresses using DHCP across a router, the router needs to have the BOOTP Forwarder service enabled and configured. For more information, see the section "Installing, Configuring, and Troubleshooting DHCP."

7. **A**. In a pure environment, you need to configure DHCP to automatically update DNS to ensure that the client computers appear on the network correctly. Setting the DNS integration to discard lookups after a lease expires also works with a pure Windows 2000 network, but it has nothing to do with the computers registering properly. For more information, see the section "Configuring DHCP for DNS Integration."

APPLY YOUR KNOWLEDGE

8. **A**. To ensure that addresses are available, the DHCP lease needs to be set to a short interval. For more information, see the section "Installing, Configuring, and Troubleshooting DHCP."

9. **D**. You need to configure the scope to issue addresses to both DHCP and BOOTP clients. For more information, see the section "Installing, Configuring, and Troubleshooting DHCP."

10. **C**. Although the DHCP server does support MIBs, you need an SNMP-compliant management application to alert you on this type of issue. For more information, see the section "Managing and Monitoring DHCP."

11. **C**. The address from the printer has probably been issued to another computer. Because the printers use static addresses, the only change to the DHCP server that could have impacted printing would be another host with the same address. Answer B is close, but just creating an overlapping scope is not a problem until the overlapping addresses are assigned. For more information, see the section "Installing, Configuring, and Troubleshooting DHCP."

12. **B**. A single DHCP server can serve multiple segments, so you will not need an additional server. To get 20 addresses, the range must be from 10.10.25.20 to 10.10.25.39, because it is an inclusive range. Also, the last step of the Scope Wizard is authorizing the new scope. You must do this to use the scope. For more information, see the section "Installing, Configuring, and Troubleshooting DHCP."

13. **D**. You do not need to make any special configurations to the DHCP service. It can communicate with non-Windows 2000 client computers without issue. You also do not need to update any of the client computers. Windows NT and Windows 98 are capable of utilizing DHCP without needing updates applied. Just configure the appropriate scope and configure the client computers to utilize that scope. For more information see the section "Installing, Configuring, and Troubleshooting DHCP."

14. **A, C,** and **D** can all be assigned using DHCP. The list of parameters assignable includes IP addresses, gateway addresses, DNS server addresses, and WINS server addresses. For more information, see the section "The DHCP Protocol."

15. **B, C,** and **D**. MAC address, hostname, and NetBIOS name are all provided to the DHCP server by default. For more information, see the section "The DHCP Protocol."

16. **B**. Because a UNIX server cannot be enabled in Active Directory, Windows 2000 client computers will not accept DHCP addresses from the server. Answer A is not correct because you cannot put a UNIX server in Active Directory at this time. Changing the BOOTP configuration on the router might prevent remote users from receiving addresses, but local users would still be vulnerable. In answer D, there is nowhere to enter the address of the DHCP server. For more information, see the section "Authorizing a DHCP Server in Active Directory."

APPLY YOUR KNOWLEDGE

17. **C.** Because the non-Windows 2000 machines lack the capability to directly update the DNS server themselves, you need the DHCP server to make the updates to DNS. Selecting DNS integration to enable updates for DNS client computers that do not support dynamic update enables the DHCP server to perform this service. For more information, see the section "Configuring DHCP for DNS Integration."

Suggested Readings and Resources

1. Droms, Ralph, and Ted Lemon. *The DHCP Handbook.* Indianapolis, IN: Macmillan Technical Publishing, 1999.

2. Siyan, Karanjit S. *Windows NT TCP/IP.* Indianapolis, IN: New Riders Publishing, 1998.

3. Kercheval, Berry. *DHCP: A Guide to Dynamic TCP/IP Network Configuration.* Upper Saddle River, NJ: Prentice Hall Computer Books, 1998.

If you have ever used a modem to connect your Windows computer to another server or network, you have used remote access. With Windows 2000, Microsoft has introduced many new remote access capabilities to its operating system. This chapter covers the "Configuring, Managing, Monitoring, and Troubleshooting Remote Access in a Windows 2000 Network Infrastructure" objectives for this exam. As today's workforce becomes more and more diverse, the ability to provide reliable and secure remote access is becoming critical in every environment.

Microsoft defines the "Configuring, Managing, Monitoring, and Troubleshooting Remote Access in a Windows 2000 Network Infrastructure" objectives as

Configure and troubleshoot remote access.

- **Configure inbound connections.**

- **Create a remote access policy.**

- **Configure a remote access profile.**

- **Configure a virtual private network (VPN).**

- **Configure multilink connections.**

- **Configure Routing and Remote Access for DHCP Integration.**

▶ One of the functions that Windows servers have always had is as a remote access server. With Windows 2000, Microsoft enhances your remote access capabilities. This objective expects you to understand how to configure the different remote access features included with Windows 2000 Server.

Manage and monitor remote access.

▶ If you are going to use your Windows 2000 server for remote access, you need to know how to manage and monitor it. This objective tests your understanding of remote access management and monitoring.

CHAPTER 3

Configuring, Managing, Monitoring, and Troubleshooting Remote Access in a Windows 2000 Network Infrastructure

Configure remote access security.

- **Configure authentication protocols.**

- **Configure encryption protocols.**

- **Create a remote access policy.**

▶ Security is becoming more important in today's computing environment. This objective tests your understanding of the security capabilities of Windows 2000 Server and remote access.

Configuring and Troubleshooting Remote Access   **132**

   Understanding Remote Access Protocols   134

   Configuring Inbound Connections   135

   Creating a Remote Access Policy   139

   Configuring a Remote Access Profile   143

   Configuring a Virtual Private
     Network (VPN)   147

   Configuring Multilink Connections   151

   Configuring Routing and Remote
     Access for DHCP Integration   151

Managing and Monitoring Remote Access   **152**

Configuring Remote Access Security   **156**

   Configuring Authentication Protocols   158

   Configuring Encryption Protocols   159

Chapter Summary   **163**

Apply Your Knowledge   **164**

► Be sure you have a thorough understanding of the security capabilities of all the different remote access mechanisms. With the focus on security in the industry today, Microsoft considers security to be one of the cornerstones of Windows 2000.

► Review the different types of encryption available for authenticating and securing your information through remote access.

► Pay close attention to the capabilities of remote access policies. Windows 2000 includes a number of policy-based management capabilities, and understanding the policies associated with remote access is important for this exam.

► Be sure to complete the exercises at the end of the chapter. Microsoft is striving to make certification exams more rigorous. Familiarity not only with the theory, but also with the hands-on portion of the configuration and troubleshooting of remote access is important for this exam.

CONFIGURING AND TROUBLESHOOTING REMOTE ACCESS

Configure and troubleshoot remote access.

Before we begin discussing how to configure remote access with Windows 2000 Server, we should take a minute to review what exactly remote access is under Windows 2000. If you have worked with Windows NT 4, you are undoubtedly familiar with the Remote Access Service (RAS). RAS was an NT 4 add-on service, which provided the capability to receive incoming modem calls and allowed the user to connect to the network. RAS was also used for the other direction: you needed RAS to connect your Windows NT server or workstation to another host, either NT or a generic dial-in server.

This model has changed dramatically in Windows 2000. Not only is the Routing and Remote Access Service (the next generation of the Remote Access Service) installed automatically with the operating system, it also bundles a number of features that used to be distributed through other services under Windows NT. For example, not only are RAS services available with Routing and Remote Access, but the Windows 2000 VPN service is included in Routing and Remote Access, as well.

But before you jump into configuring the Routing and Remote Access Service, let's discuss some of the reasons for deploying remote access and some of the specifics surrounding the Windows 2000 Routing and Remote Access.

Microsoft has included remote access capabilities in all its operating systems since the introduction of Windows for Workgroups (a remote access client computer) and the Windows NT Advanced Server (a remote access server). If you have worked with earlier versions of Windows NT or Windows 9x, you are probably familiar with the term RAS, first used to discuss the NT Remote Access Server and later used as a generic description of most of the Windows operating system remote access applications. This changed in the midst of the Windows NT Server 4 operating system's life cycle, with the introduction of an add-on service upgrade known as the Routing and Remote Access Service, which you should note carried over to the Windows 2000 operating system. The main reason for the change is that Microsoft needed to enhance its offerings in the remote access and routing areas of networking. The Routing and Remote Access upgrade provided the first framework for integrating all network services into a single application. Routing and Remote Access introduced the following features to Windows NT networking:

- ◆ A unified service for Routing and Remote Access integrated with the operating system.

- ◆ A full set of routing protocols for IP and IPX (including the noteworthy addition of OSPF).

- ◆ APIs for third-party routing protocols, user interface, and management.

- ◆ Demand-dial routing.

- ◆ PPTP server-to-server for secure VPNs.

- ◆ Remote Authentication Dial-In User Service (RADIUS) client support.

But enough history. Let's look at what the Routing and Remote Access Service included with Windows 2000 brings to the table. Routing and Remote Access includes the following capabilities:

- ◆ Full integration into the Windows 2000 operating system. This is not an add-on or a patch, but a fully integrated service built from the ground up as part of Windows 2000.

- ◆ Consistent management interface for all routing-based activities, including remote access, VPN, and IP and IPX routing.

- ◆ Fewer reboots. If you worked with earlier versions of Windows, you are familiar with the "change any network configuration and reboot the machine" method of managing Windows networking. With Windows 2000, the number of times you need to reboot the server is dramatically lessened. Although you may still need to reboot occasionally, most activities can be done without impacting operations.

- ◆ Additional VPN services and simplified VPN management. The VPN interfaces (PPTP and L2TP) are installed and configured by default, requiring no additional configuration. There is also support for the IPSec protocol.

◆ Network Address Translation (NAT) has been added, as has Internet Connection Sharing (ICS).

◆ Additional authentication mechanisms have been added to Routing and Remote Access, including MS-CHAP v2, RADIUS, and EAP (for smart card and certificate support).

One other key point to remember when discussing Microsoft's Routing and Remote Access Service and the remote access capabilities is that in previous incarnations, the term RAS, or Remote Access Service, was used interchangeably to refer to the dial-in connections and the service that ran the dial-up server. With the new Routing and Remote Access Service, Microsoft is striving to clarify its use of terminology. So in Windows 2000 parlance, Routing and Remote Access refers only to the Routing and Remote Access application. The server is called either a dial-in or dial-up server, or in the case of VPN, a VPN server. The client computers are called dial-in or dial-up clients.

It is important to keep in mind that Microsoft's Routing and Remote Access Service considers all connections to be LAN connections. What this means from a functionality perspective is that all the services that are available via LAN connection are also available via a modem connection.

Understanding Remote Access Protocols

Microsoft's Routing and Remote Access Service supports two data link control protocols for asynchronous connections:

◆ **Serial Line Interface Protocol (SLIP).** The granddaddy of serial line protocols, SLIP is supported for legacy applications and is almost never used.

◆ **Point-to-Point Protocol (PPP).** PPP is the protocol most of us use when connecting via modem. PPP can automatically establish and re-establish connections; it uses error correction, and it can support multiple protocols. The Windows 2000 implementation for PPP is fully RFC 1661 "Point-to-Point Protocol" compliant.

Windows 2000 can connect to any other RFC 1661-compliant dial-up server and can accept connections from any compliant client computers. The real strength of this protocol is the support for multiple network protocols, such as IPX, IP, and AppleTalk. SLIP was restricted to IP only. PPP also uses a number of authentication protocols, discussed later in the chapter.

We will discuss many of these features as we move through this chapter. For now, let's take a look at the simplest use for the Routing and Remote Access Service.

Configuring Inbound Connections

If you have mobile users, it is a safe bet that you have dealt with requests for access to the network. This could be for access to mail, the company intranet, or even to file shares or applications. Windows 2000 includes as part of Routing and Remote Access the capability to permit inbound connections via attached modems.

EXAM TIP	**Support for Inbound Dial-In Connections** Windows 2000 Server supports 256 inbound dial-in connections. Windows 2000 Professional supports 1.

IN THE FIELD

ISSUES TO CONSIDER IN CONFIGURING SYSTEMS FOR MOBILE USERS

If you deploy Windows 2000 as your remote access solution for mobile users, you will need to keep a couple of things in mind. First, because any server has only a limited number of communication ports, you will probably need a multiport modem card. Various manufacturers offer these types of products, but be sure to check the Microsoft Hardware Compatibility List before making any purchases.

You should also avoid installing this capability on any domain controllers or application servers. Although the overhead associated with supporting dial-in users is fairly low, the security ramifications of connecting a modem or modems to a production application server, or even worse—a domain controller, are significant. You should try to avoid that architecture if at all possible.

In the latest version of Routing and Remote Access, Microsoft has added some new features as part of the management. One of the features that has the most impact on the discussion of remote access is the addition of remote access policies. Remote access

continues

continued

policies are a radical departure from the Windows NT 3.5x and 4 models, in which user authorization was based on a simple Grant Dial-In Permission to User option in User Manager or the Remote Access Admin console. Callback options were also configured on a per-user basis. In Windows 2000, authorization is granted based on the dial-in properties of a user account and remote access policies.

Remote access policies are a set of conditions and connection settings that give network administrators more flexibility in authorizing connection attempts. The Windows 2000 Routing and Remote Access Service uses remote access policies to determine whether to accept or reject connection attempts. With remote access policies, you can grant remote access by individual user account or through the configuration of specific remote access policies. We look at setting up a policy in the "Creating a Remote Access Policy" section later in the chapter.

Windows 2000 uses three types of policies to control remote access:

◆ **Local Internet Authentication Services policies**. These local policies are derived from RADIUS and can be used to define access permissions based on a number of client attributes.

◆ **Central Internet Authentication Services policies**. A dial-up server can be configured to use a central IAS RADIUS server to provide its policies. This allows multiple Routing and Remote Access dial-up servers to use the same policies without requiring the manual replication of policies and settings.

◆ **Group Policies.** More in line with the older versions of remote access. Access can be controlled by group policies.

Now let's look at how to configure a Windows 2000 server to support an inbound connection.

EXAM TIP

Be Familiar with IAS   Internet Authentication Services (IAS) are the new RADIUS authentication capabilities included with Windows 2000. They are used heavily in conjunction with Routing and Remote Access policies.

EXAM TIP

Know Where Remote Access Group Policies Are Stored   They're stored in the file system in the default WINNT\SYSVOL\SYSVOL\ <domain name> directory.

EXAM TIP

Remember to Use the Snap-in   If you are configuring Routing and Remote Access for dial-up access on a domain controller, you must use the Routing and Remote Access snap-in.

STEP BY STEP

3.1 Configuring Remote Access Inbound Connections

1. Right-click the My Network Places icon on the desktop. From the Context menu, select Properties. The Network and Dial-up Connections window opens. (You can also open this window by going to Start, Settings, Network and Dial-up Connections).

2. Double-click the Make New Connection icon. The Network Connection Wizard starts. If you have not already configured your dialing location information (see Figure 3.1) you will be prompted to do so before continuing with the wizard. Fill in the information and click OK. You will see the new location entry in the Phone and Modem Options window. Click OK to close it and return to the wizard.

3. Click Next to start the wizard process. The Network Connection Type dialog box opens (see Figure 3.2). Select the Accept Incoming Connections option and click Next. The Devices for Incoming Connections dialog box (see Figure 3.3) opens.

continues

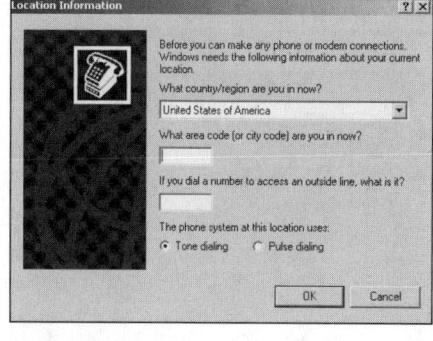

FIGURE 3.1
The Location Information is needed so that the server knows whether a call is local or long distance. In the case of a dial-in server, this is needed for callbacks.

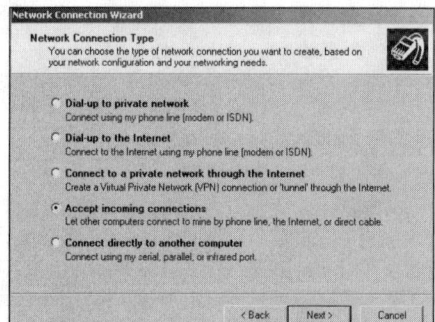

FIGURE 3.2
The Network Connection Type dialog box allows you to select from a variety of Routing and Remote Access connection options.

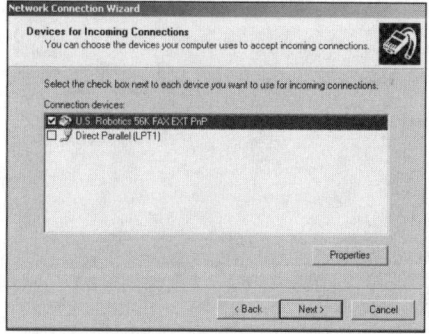

FIGURE 3.3
This dialog box allows you to selectively enable the devices that will be accepting incoming calls.

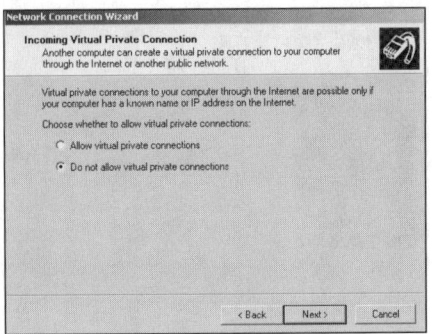

FIGURE 3.4

In addition to supporting inbound modem connections, Windows 2000 also has the capability to accept inbound virtual private connections.

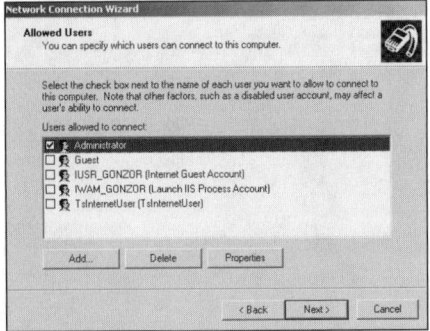

FIGURE 3.5

You can select the users who should be able to connect. However, if their account is disabled or locked, they will not be able to connect.

continued

4. Select the device(s) that you want to receive the incoming calls and click Next. The Incoming Virtual Private Connection dialog box opens (see Figure 3.4).

5. Because we will discuss creating a virtual private network (VPN) connection in the "Configuring a Virtual Private Network (VPN)" section of this chapter, select Do Not Allow Virtual Private Connections and click Next. The Allowed Users dialog box opens (see Figure 3.5).

6. Select the users you want to have dial-in access. Click Properties to open the user properties. This allows you to configure callback, if necessary.

7. Click the Callback tab (see Figure 3.6). For the most secure access, select Always Use the Following Callback Number and enter the user's phone number. Click OK to return to the wizard, and click Next to continue. The Networking Components dialog box opens (see Figure 3.7).

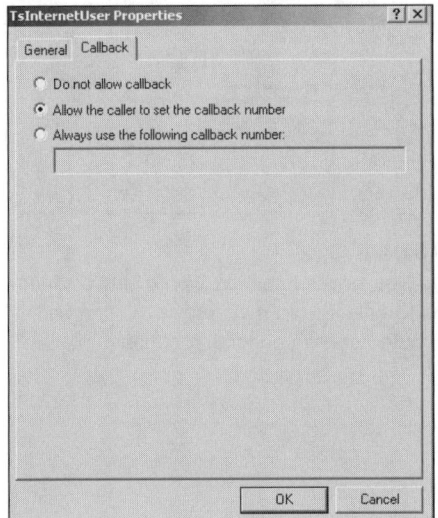

FIGURE 3.6

In a highly secure environment, use of the callback options included with Windows 2000 is a necessity.

8. Select the components you want the dial-in user to have access to after they connect. By default, all components are selected. Click Next to continue. The Completing the Network Connection Wizard dialog box opens (see Figure 3.8).

9. Enter an intuitive name for the new connection and click Finish to complete the installation.

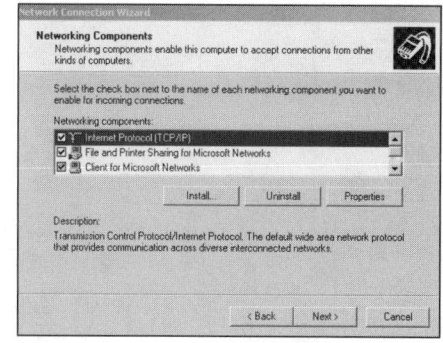

FIGURE 3.7
The Networking Connections dialog box determines which services are available to dial-in users.

Now that you have a dial-up connection, let's take a look at creating a remote access policy to define what can be done with the new connections.

Creating a Remote Access Policy

A remote access policy is a set of actions that can be applied to a group of users that meet a specified set of requirements. The example Microsoft uses to illustrate this point is to think about email rules. In many email packages, you can configure a rule that allows you to delete all messages from a specific user or group of users. A remote access policy is similar in that you can specify actions based on a number of criteria. To illustrate how this works, let's run through creating a remote access policy.

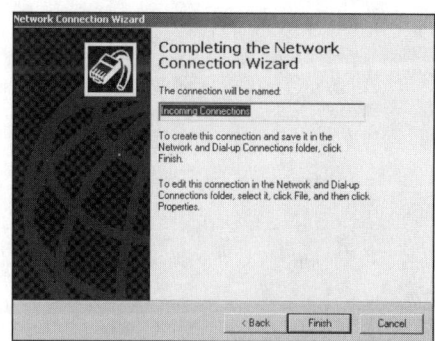

FIGURE 3.8
This dialog box allows you to enter a descriptive name for the new connection.

STEP BY STEP

3.2 Creating a Remote Access Policy

1. Open the Routing and Remote Access console by going to Start, Programs, Administrative Tools, Routing and Remote Access (see Figure 3.9).

2. Expand the application tree in the left pane by double-clicking the server. Right-click Remote Access Policies and select New Remote Access Policy. The Add Remote Access Policy window opens (see Figure 3.10).

FIGURE 3.9

The Routing and Remote Access console allows you to manage your remote access server, including creating remote access policies.

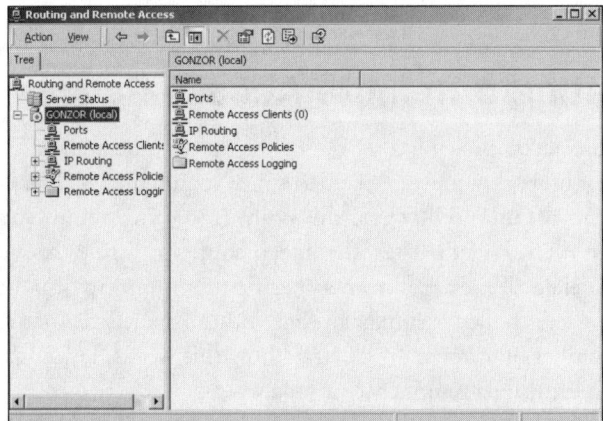

FIGURE 3.10

This dialog box allows you to give your policy a user-friendly name.

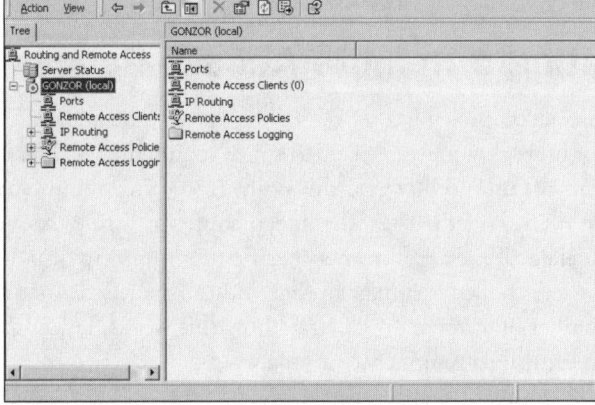

3. Enter a user friendly name and click Next to continue. The Add Remote Access Policy Conditions dialog box opens (see Figure 3.11).

4. Click Add to add a condition. Select one attribute from the list of attributes (shown in Figure 3.12). Each attribute will create a slightly different process, and you will need to configure the attribute appropriately. For this example, select Windows-Groups. Using the Windows-Groups attribute allows you to enable remote access by user groups, as defined in the Users and Groups console.

5. Click Add to go to the Groups dialog box (see Figure 3.13). Then click Add to open the Select Groups dialog box

continues

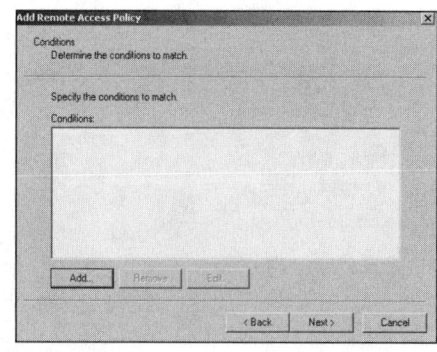

FIGURE 3.11
The first step in creating a remote access policy is to set the conditions.

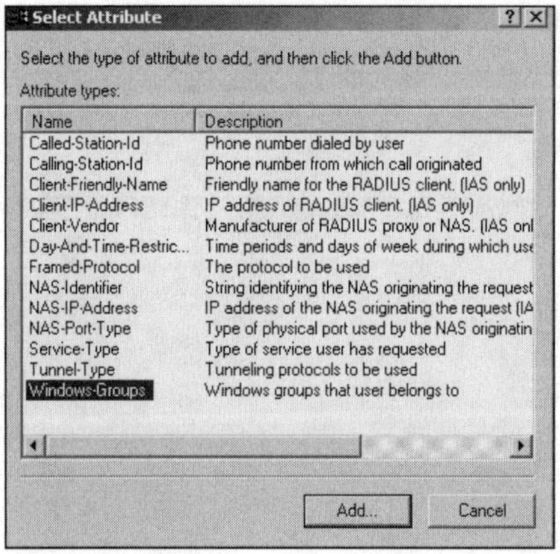

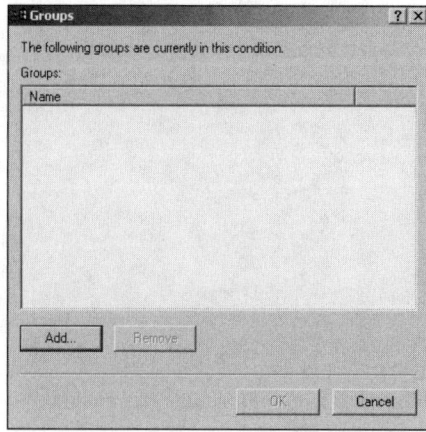

FIGURE 3.12
Select the appropriate attributes for the policy you are trying to create.

FIGURE 3.13
As a general rule, Windows-Groups is an attribute that is used frequently with remote access policies because it allows you to intuitively group users by department, function, or access rights.

continued

shown in Figure 3.14 and select the appropriate group(s) for the rule. Click OK to return to the Groups dialog box. Click OK to add the Windows-Groups condition to the policy. If you were to add an additional condition, users would need to meet both conditions to have the policy applied (a logical AND operation).

6. Click Next to open the Add Remote Access Policy permissions dialog box shown in Figure 3.15. You can either Grant or Deny Remote Access Permission by selecting the appropriate option. Select the Deny Remote Access Permission option and click Next. The Edit Dial-in Profile dialog box that opens allows you to access the dial-in

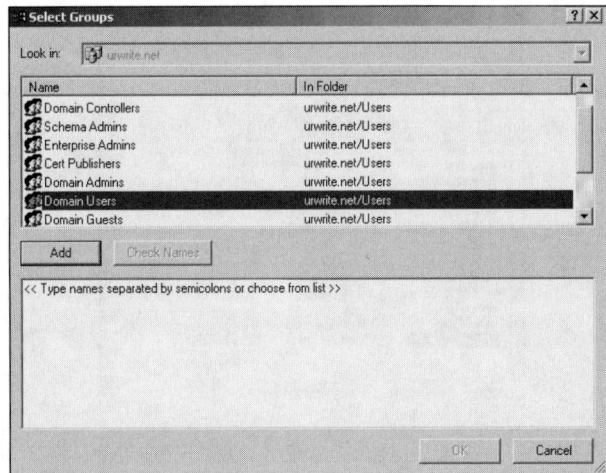

FIGURE 3.14
Select the appropriate groups for remote access permissions.

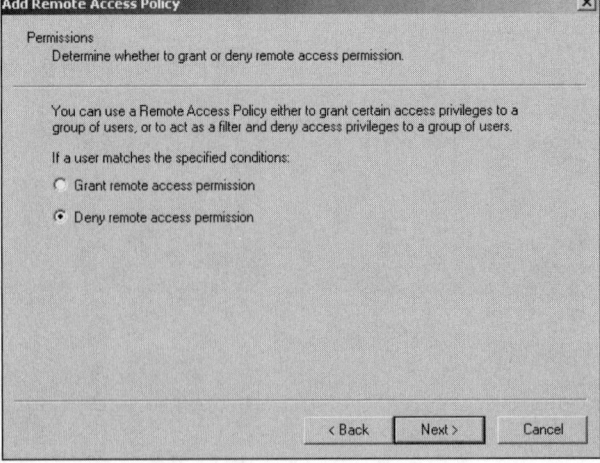

FIGURE 3.15
You can grant or deny permissions from this screen.

profile for the users affected by this policy (see Figure
3.16). You can restrict a number of access parameters,
which we discuss at the end of the section.

7. Click OK to return to the User Profile screen.

8. Click Finish to complete the creation of the profile.

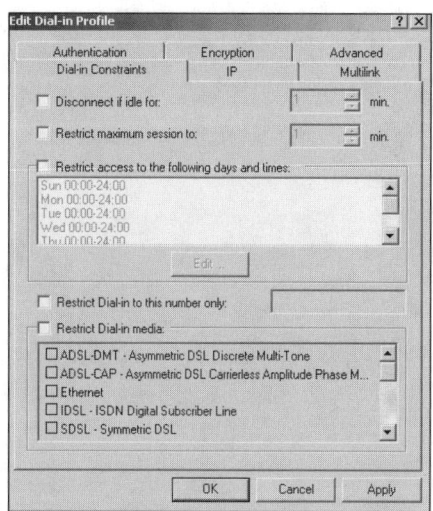

FIGURE 3.16
The Edit Dial-in Profile dialog box allows
you access to the granular settings for the
dial-in users.

IN THE FIELD

DESIGN YOUR POLICIES WITH CARE

One thing you will find if you work in a large remote access environment is the uses for group-based policies. A couple of places
these types of groups can be very useful include creating a group
for contractors who work for your company intermittently. You can
create an allow access and a deny access group, and then
depending on the status of any projects, you can control their
access to remote access just by moving their account from one
group to another. People on a leave of absence might be placed in
an LOA group to block them from remote access until they come
back on the job. The variations are endless. The trick is to really
put some thought into the policy design before you start creating
users. If you just start creating users with the thought of going
back and organizing later, you have probably created three times
as much work for yourself.

Configuring a Remote Access Profile

Now that you understand how to create a remote access policy, we
need to discuss the next phase of the process—configuring a remote
access profile. To configure a remote access profile, follow the steps
in Step by Step 3.3.

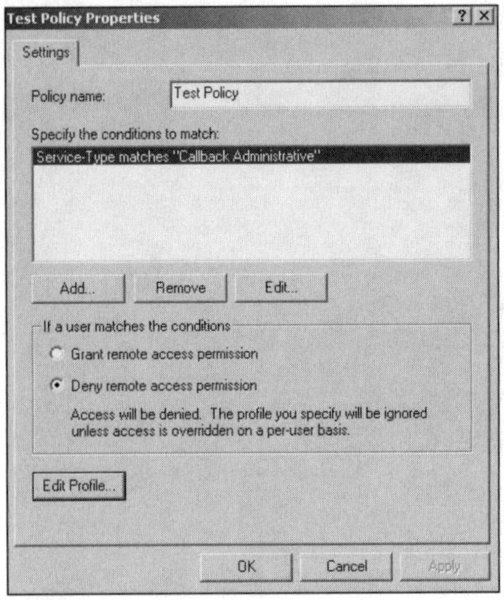

FIGURE 3.17
The Policy Properties dialog box contains all the information regarding the policy.

STEP BY STEP

3.3 Configuring a Remote Access Profile

1. Open the Routing and Remote Access console by going to Start, Programs, Administrative Tools, Routing and Remote Access.
2. Right-click the remote access policy you want to configure the remote access profile for. Select Properties from the Context menu. The Policy Properties dialog box opens (see Figure 3.17). The name in the title bar reflects the name of the policy.
3. Click the Edit Profile button. The Edit Dial-in Profile dialog box opens (refer to Figure 3.16).
4. Make any modifications necessary and click OK to return to the Properties dialog box. Click OK again to commit the changes and return to the OS.

That's how you get to the parameters for the profile. Now let's take a look at some of the parameters you can configure before we move on to VPNs in the next section.

The dial-in profile contains the following settings:

- **Dial-in Constraints.** This tab (refer to Figure 3.16) allows you to configure the restrictions on the dial-in users, including the idle disconnect timer, the maximum length of the session, the time and day access is permitted, the dial-in number allowed, and the dial-in media allowed.

NOTE

What Is Dial-in Media? This is more applicable with a VPN connection than a dial-in connection, but you have the ability to disallow specific network media from connecting to the server. For example, if you didn't want ADSL users to be able to connect, you can specifically deny it.

◆ **IP.** This tab (shown in Figure 3.18) is used to determine the IP Address Assignment Policy, if necessary. The following are three possible settings for the IP Address Assignment Policy:

- **Server Must Supply an IP Address.** For this to work, the server must have a DHCP range configured for remote access. The client computer cannot connect without requesting an address.

- **Client May Request an IP Address.** This setting leaves the determination on whether to use a DHCP address to the client computer. If the client computer has a statically configured address, it will still be able to connect.

- **Server Settings Define Policy.** This setting defers the decision on IP address policy to the Routing and Remote Access Server's global policy.

You can also apply IP Packet Filters from the IP tab. Packet filters can be configured for traffic sent to the client computer or traffic received from the client computer. These filters are applied by network and can be used to filter a variety of IP-based protocols, including Any, Other, ICMP, UDP, TCP, and TCP [established].

◆ **Multilink.** This tab (see Figure 3.19) allows you to configure Windows 2000's capability to aggregate multiple analog phone lines connected to multiple modems to provide greater bandwidth. The Multilink Settings section allows you to configure the following:

- **Default to Server Settings.** Defers the configuration to the Routing and Remote Access global settings.

- **Disable Multilink (Restrict Client to a Single Port).** This setting is self-explanatory.

- **Allow Multilink.** This configuration allows a client computer to connect using multiple ports, and you can configure the number of ports they can use.

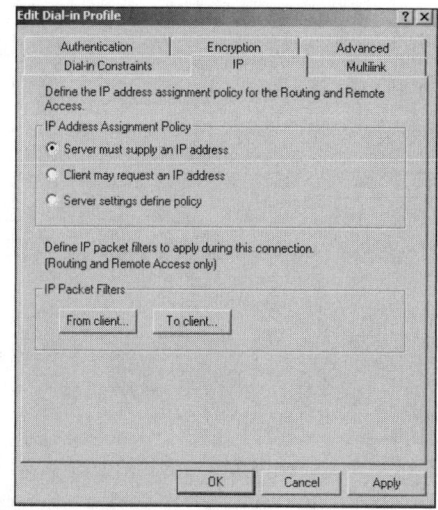

FIGURE 3.18
The IP tab can be used to set IP filters on a policy.

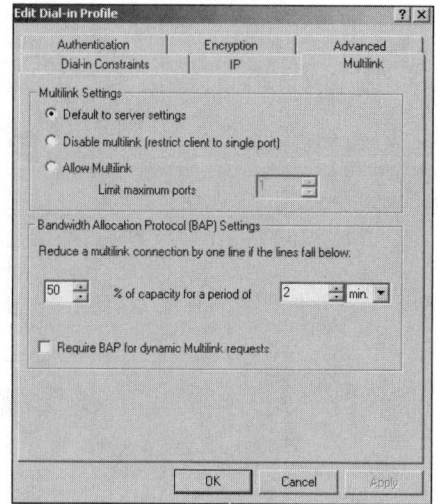

FIGURE 3.19
The multilink capabilities of Windows 2000 allow you to maximize bandwidth across multiple analog phone systems.

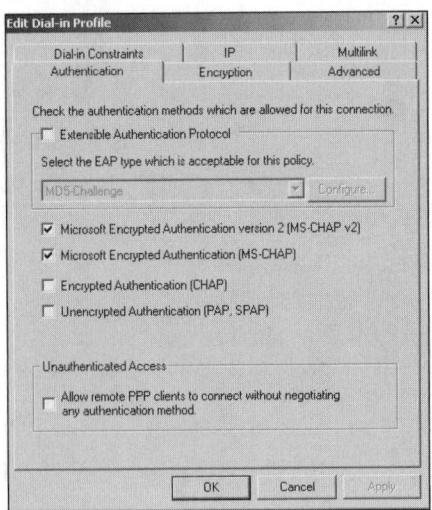

FIGURE 3.20

To take advantage of the multilink capabilities of Windows 2000, you need to enable it here for the appropriate group.

The Bandwidth Allocation Protocol (BAP) Settings can be used to configure when to drop one of the multilink lines, based on usage. If the usage drops below a configurable amount of bandwidth (50% is the default) for a specified amount of time (2 minutes is the default), one of the multilink lines is dropped. You can also enable the Require BAP for Dynamic Multilink Requests.

◆ **Authentication.** This tab (see Figure 3.20) allows you to configure the authentication methods supported by Windows 2000. (The protocols listed in the figure are discussed later in this chapter.)

◆ **Encryption.** This tab (see Figure 3.21) allows you to set the level of encryption required with Routing and Remote Access authentication. You can set it to No Encryption, Basic, or Strong, or allow any combination of the three.

◆ **Advanced.** The Advanced tab (see Figure 3.22) allows you to add connection attributes to be returned to the Remote Access Server. This is usually used in conjunction with RADIUS.

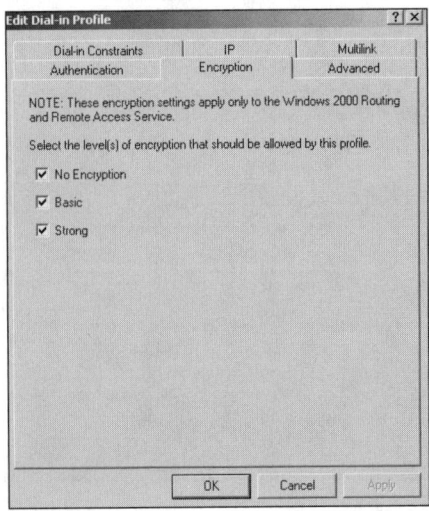

FIGURE 3.21

Routing and Remote Access supports three levels of encryption.

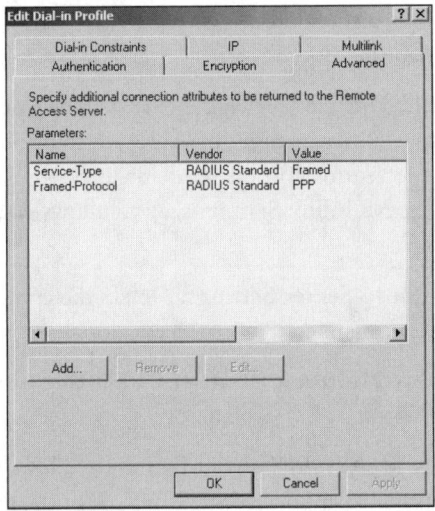

FIGURE 3.22

If you need to configure RADIUS attributes, use this tab.

IN THE FIELD

PUTTING RADIUS TO WORK

If you have worked in a large remote access environment, you might have run across RADIUS already. But for those of you who haven't, we will discuss it a bit here. RADIUS (Remote Authentication Dial-in User Service) is an authentication and accounting system used by many Internet Service Providers (ISPs) and enterprise networks. When you dial in to the ISP, you must enter your username and password. This information is passed to a RADIUS server, which checks that the information is correct and then authorizes access to the ISP system. Though not an official standard, the RADIUS specification is maintained by a working group of the IETF.

Another place you see RADIUS used is to leverage the account information in a Windows 2000 domain. The built-in RADIUS server can be used not only to authenticate Routing and Remote Access client computers, but it can also be used by third-party dial-in servers as an authentication method. In fact, some ISPs authenticate users for an enterprise account by passing RADIUS authentication requests to a local RADIUS server, allowing the company to control who gets access to the Internet.

Configuring a Virtual Private Network (VPN)

Before we delve into configuring the Windows 2000 VPN, let's look at VPNs in general and some of the factors that led to the creation of them. If you have been around the industry for a while, you are probably aware that one of the most misused terms in the computer industry today is VPN. It seems as though every vendor has a VPN to sell you, and many times one vendor's VPN can seem to be the exact opposite of another's. For example, not too long ago, one of the major telecommunications vendors offered a VPN service that consisted of a private frame-relay network that users could dial in to, and then utilizing the frame relay network, connect to the business's network. This service involved no encryption, and the only true security provided by the solution was whatever mechanism the customer provided at the frame relay's point of entry to the corporate network. Another VPN vendor will try to sell you a dedicated hardware platform designed to provide strictly VPN services. Firewall vendors will try to sell you VPN in their firewall platform, and router vendors will try to convince you that the VPN services bundled with your router are the solution for you. Finally, there are the solutions that run on a network operating system, such as the VPN bundled with Windows 2000. For the sake of our discussion, a VPN is a private network that is constructed using a public network (such as the Internet) to connect its nodes.

The first thing you need to be aware of when discussing the Windows 2000 VPN is the encryption protocols available. Windows 2000 has two main encryption protocols that are used in the VPN. They include

◆ **Point-to-Point Tunneling Protocol (PPTP).** PPTP is Microsoft's legacy protocol for supporting VPNs. Developed jointly by Microsoft Corporation, U.S. Robotics, and several remote access vendor companies, known collectively as the PPTP Forum, PPTP encountered some security issues in its original form. It has been revised by Microsoft but has never been widely accepted by the security community. Although still supported on a variety of vendors' VPN servers, PPTP is rapidly being overtaken by the more widely adopted IPSec protocol.

◆ **IP Security Protocol (IPSec).** IPSec is a suite of cryptography-based protection services and security protocols that are used for the first standards-based VPN protocol. In Windows 2000, IPSec is used to provide machine-level authentication, as well as data encryption, for L2TP-based (Layer 2 Tunneling Protocol) VPN connections. Unlike some other IPSec-based VPNs, Microsoft's implementation uses the L2TP protocol for encrypting the usernames, passwords, and data, whereas IPSec is used to negotiate the secure connection between your computer and its remote tunnel server.

TABLE 3.1	
THE DIFFERENCES BETWEEN L2TP/IPSEC AND PPTP	
L2TP/IPSec	*PPTP*
Standards-based	Microsoft proprietary
Windows, Linux, Macintosh, Solaris, and other platforms	Windows OS and Linux platforms
DES / 3DES encryption	Microsoft proprietary encryption
Requires only that the tunnel media provide packet-oriented point-to-point connectivity	Requires an IP-based transit internetwork
Supports header compression	No header compression

EXAM TIP

Know the Differences Between L2TP and PPTP   Because Microsoft uses a custom protocol configuration for its IPSec VPN implementation, you should be sure that you understand the differences between IPSec and PPTP, as well as how Microsoft implemented its version of IPSec. Table 3.1 can help you keep them straight.

Now that you know what a VPN is and how it works, let's set up one. The good news is that installing Routing and Remote Access automatically makes a VPN connection available. What you need to understand at this point is how to configure the VPN that is installed. To configure the VPN service, do the following:

STEP BY STEP

3.4 Configuring a Virtual Private Network

1. Open the Routing and Remote Access by going to Start, Programs, Administrative Tools, Routing and Remote Access.

2. Click the Ports entry under the server. Notice that the sample configuration in Figure 3.23 shows five PPTP ports and five L2TP/IPSec ports. This is because the server had five user licenses configured when the Routing and Remote Access Service was installed.

continues

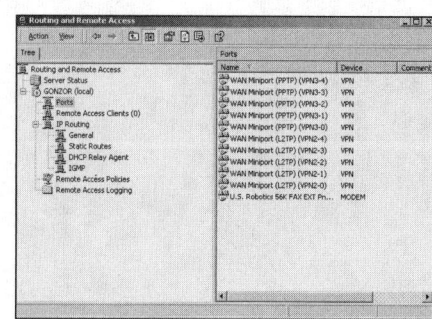

FIGURE 3.23
All the configured VPN ports will be displayed in the right window.

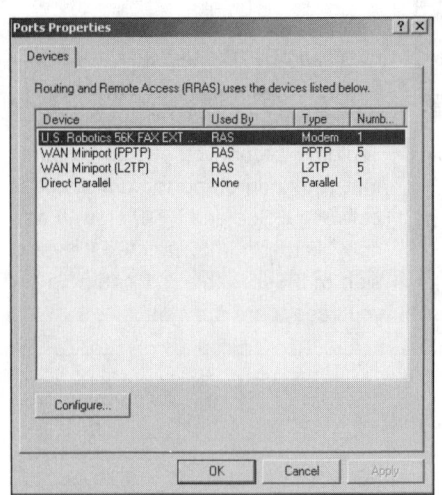

FIGURE 3.24
All the configured remote access connections appear here after they are installed.

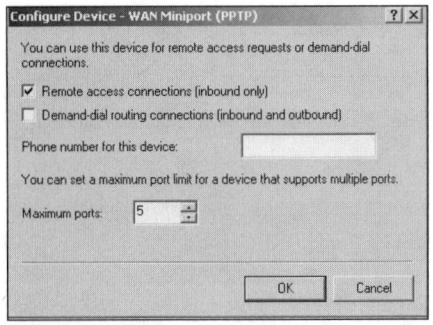

FIGURE 3.25
The Configure Device dialog box allows you to fine-tune the properties for the device, including the number of ports available.

continued

3. To configure the ports, select Ports in the left pane and right-click. From the Context menu select Properties. The Ports Properties dialog box opens (see Figure 3.24). You can see each of the protocols listed.

4. Select the protocol you want to modify and click Configure. The Configure Device dialog box (see Figure 3.25) opens. This screen allows you to set the direction of the interface (Inbound Only or Inbound and Outbound) as well as the number of ports. You can also set the phone number of the device, although this is of limited use with a VPN implementation.

That is all there is to configuring the VPN server bundled with Windows 2000.

IN THE FIELD

YOUR VPN IS ONLY AS GOOD AS YOUR INTERNET CONNECTION

Although VPNs are being used frequently to replace more traditional remote access methods, such as dial-in, people overlook a couple of things when putting together a VPN. First, the assumption is that a VPN will be faster than dialing a remote access server. This is not necessarily true. You can have a bottleneck at your ISP connection, congestion issues on the Internet, or even server capacity issues on the VPN server itself. Make sure you set realistic expectations for your users regarding the capabilities of your new VPN. Second, just putting up a VPN does not mean that all your remote access problems are solved. You'll find that a host of new issues can quickly arise. How end users get access to the Internet, the size and capacity of the VPN server, even the available Internet bandwidth can place a quick bottleneck on the performance of your VPN.

Configuring Multilink Connections

First introduced as part of Windows 98, Windows 2000 includes the capability of aggregating multiple modem lines to form a single, higher-bandwidth connection to a remote access server. This is usually an Internet Service Provider connection, but it could also be to another Windows 2000 Server, perhaps at a different location. As part of this capability, you also have the ability to leverage the Bandwidth Allocation Protocol (BAP). BAP is a PPP control protocol that is used to dynamically add or remove additional links to a multilink connection.

To set up a multilink connection, you just need to open the Network and Dial-up Connections window, right-click the Incoming Connections icon, select Properties (see Figure 3.26), and then select Enable Multilink.

Multilink is now configured. If a user dials in with two modems, the server will now aggregate the connections and allow the user to use the additional bandwidth as needed.

Configuring Routing and Remote Access for DHCP Integration

If you have users that are connecting to your Routing and Remote Access server, you will probably want to dynamically assign them a TCP/IP address on the network. The best way to do this is with DHCP, which will need to be configured.

DHCP and the Routing and Remote Access Service have an important relationship that you need to understand. When the remote access server is configured to use DHCP, the Routing and Remote Access Server uses the DHCP client component to obtain 10 IP addresses from a DHCP server. This could be on the network or on the same server as Routing and Remote Access Server. The remote access server uses the first IP address obtained from DHCP for the RAS interface, and subsequent addresses are allocated to TCP/IP-based remote access client computers as they connect. IP addresses freed because of remote access client computers disconnecting are reused. When all 10 addresses have been allocated, the process starts again with the DHCP client computer requesting an additional 10 addresses.

> **NOTE**
>
> **Before You Begin Configuring Multilink** If you want to configure multilink, there are a couple of prerequisites. First, you must have at least two modems installed on the system. After all, it's tough to multilink a single modem. Second, you need to have an incoming remote access connection created. Use Step by Step 3.1 to complete this activity.

> **EXAM TIP**
>
> **Know Where Multilink Is Enabled** More important, you should understand what is needed for a multilink connection and what benefits multilink provides.

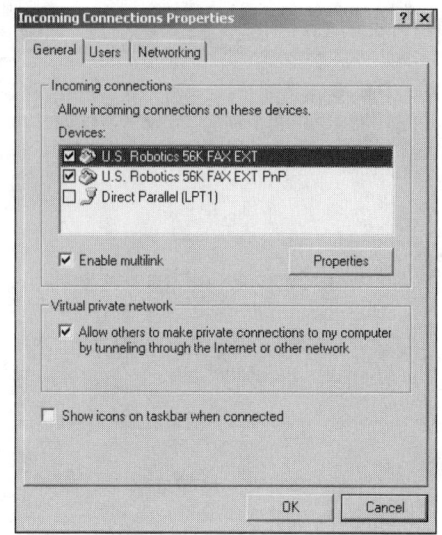

FIGURE 3.26
The Incoming Connections Properties dialog box allows you to configure all the parameters for dialing in, including the multilink configuration.

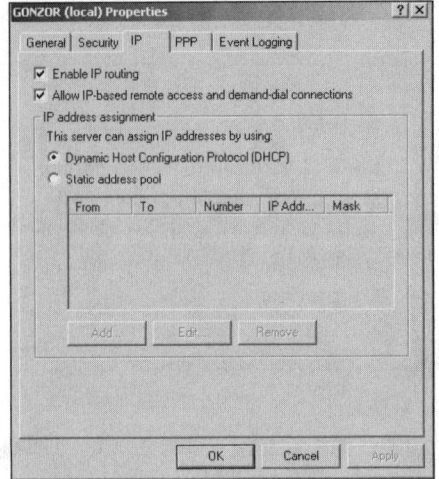

FIGURE 3.27
Configuring Routing and Remote Access to use DHCP is as easy as clicking an option.

To configure Routing and Remote Access for DHCP integration, do the following:

STEP BY STEP

3.5 Configure Routing and Remote Access for DHCP Integration

1. Open the Routing and Remote Access console by going to Start, Programs, Administrative Tools, Routing and Remote Access.

2. From the tree, right-click the server and select Properties from the Context menu. Click the IP tab (see Figure 3.27).

3. In the IP address assignment section, click the Dynamic Host Configuration Protocol (DHCP).

Your Routing and Remote Access will now issue DHCP addresses for users connecting via dial-in or VPN.

MANAGING AND MONITORING REMOTE ACCESS

Manage and monitor remote access.

Now you have a functional Routing and Remote Access server up and running. How do you manage and monitor it? Let's start by taking a look at what kinds of information the Performance console can provide. It is generally the best tool for monitoring specifics about Windows 2000 services. The Performance console offers the following counters for the RAS object:

◆ **Alignment Errors.** The size of the packet received is different from the size expected.

◆ **Buffer Overrun Errors.** The software is unable to handle the rate that data is being received.

◆ **Bytes Received.** Total amount of bytes received by the service.

◆ **Bytes Received/Sec.** Number of bytes received by the service in a second.

◆ **Bytes Transmitted.** Total amount of bytes transmitted by the service.

◆ **Bytes Transmitted/Sec.** Number of bytes transmitted by the service in a second.

◆ **CRC Errors.** A frame received contains erroneous data and the packet did not pass the Cyclic Redundancy Check (CRC).

◆ **Frames Received.** Total number of frames received by the service.

◆ **Frames Received/Sec.** Number of frames received by the service per second.

◆ **Frames Transmitted.** Total number of frames transmitted by the service.

◆ **Frames Transmitted/Sec.** Number of frames transmitted by the service per second.

◆ **Percent Compression In.** Tells how well inbound traffic is being compressed.

◆ **Percent Compression Out.** Tells how well outbound traffic is being compressed.

◆ **Errors—Serial Overrun Errors, Timeout Errors, Total Errors, and Total Errors/Sec.** These objects handle all the error information for the Routing and Remote Access Service.

> **EXAM TIP**
>
> **What Are We Measuring— Aggregate or Port Level?** The Performance console allows you to monitor these counters on either a port–by–port or an entire server level. Select RAS Ports to look at a single port or RAS Total to see the stats for the entire server.

Now that we have looked at the counters for the service, let's take a look at some of the ways to monitor the service.

To configure Routing and Remote Access Performance monitoring, do the following:

STEP BY STEP

3.6 Monitor Routing and Remote Access

1. Open the Performance console by going to Programs, Administrative Tools, Performance (see Figure 3.28).

2. In Performance, select System Monitor.

3. To create an entry in System Monitor, click the Add (+) icon. The Add Counters window opens. By default, it opens to the Processor performance object.

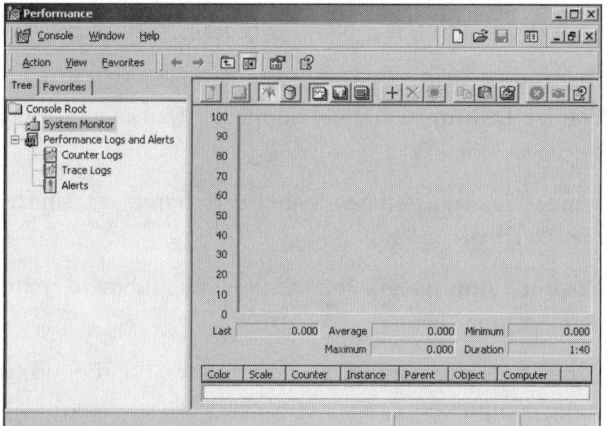

FIGURE 3.28
The Performance console allows you to monitor various system and application metrics for evaluating the performance and health of the system.

4. Select the RAS Port performance object. You will see the list of counters available for RAS displayed on the left and a list of RAS devices in the right pane (see Figure 3.29).

5. Select the port you want to monitor. After you have decided on the counter you want to monitor, click Add. You can add multiple counters either by selecting each counter and clicking Add, or by using the standard Windows multiple item select method of holding down the Ctrl key while you select all the counters you want to monitor, and clicking Add.

6. Click Close when you are done. You will see your counters being graphed similar to those shown in Figure 3.30.

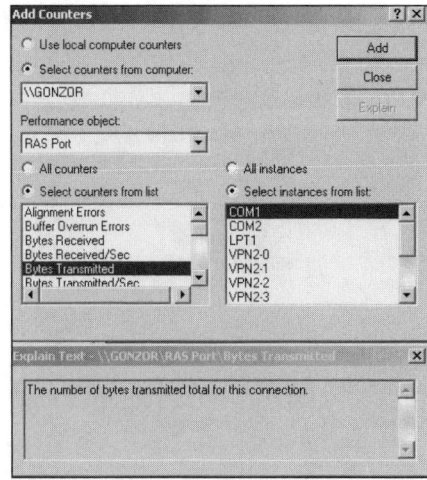

FIGURE 3.29
The counters associated with RAS are very similar to the errors offered for most LAN connections, including Ethernet.

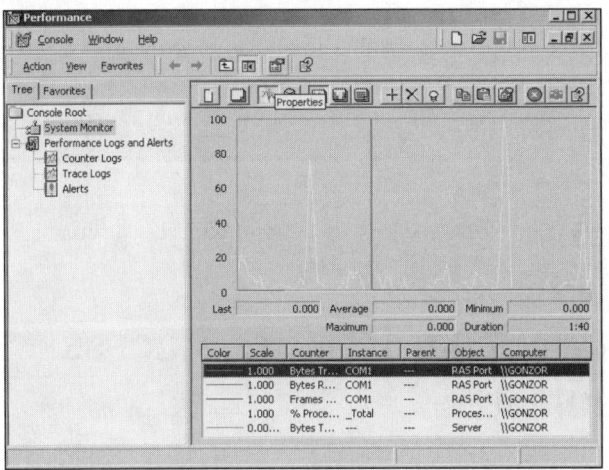

FIGURE 3.30
To find out what kinds of errors you may be experiencing in the field, keep an eye out for sudden jumps, either up or down. The graph in this figure shows that no RAS errors exist at this time.

If you want to see statistics on a VPN connection, do the following:

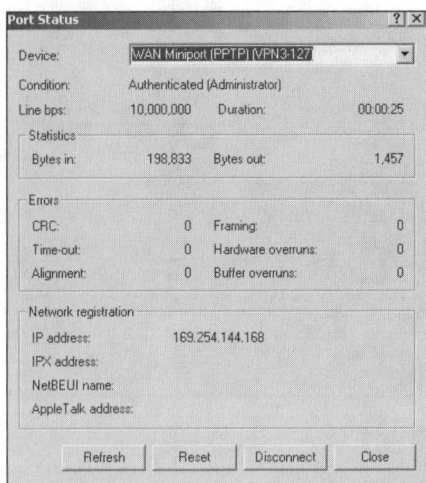

FIGURE 3.31
You can get a fairly complete port status here.

STEP BY STEP

3.7 Checking the Status of a Port

1. Open the Routing and Remote Access utility.

2. Select Ports in the left pane. A list of available ports appears in the right pane. Select the port you want to gather statistics from and right-click. From the Context menu, select Status. The Port Status dialog box opens (see Figure 3.31). You can see the port condition, the line speed, the call duration, network statistics, errors, and the network protocols being used, with addresses for the port.

3. You can reset or refresh the statistics by clicking the appropriate button at the bottom of the dialog box, and in the event someone is connected to the port, you can disconnect that connection by clicking Disconnect.

Now let's take a look at configuring remote access security.

CONFIGURING REMOTE ACCESS SECURITY

Configure remote access security.

The name of this section of the chapter is a bit of a misnomer. Most of what we have discussed in this chapter so far has to do with remote access security. But Microsoft has used the term Remote

Access Security for one specific group of settings. To configure this group of settings, do the following:

STEP BY STEP

3.8 Configuring Remote Access Security

1. Open the Routing and Remote Access console.

2. Right-click the server and select Properties. This opens the server properties.

3. Select the Security tab (see Figure 3.32). By default, the Authentication provider is Windows Authentication. You can also set it for RADIUS authentication. Select RADIUS from the pull-down menu.

4. Click Configure to configure the RADIUS server. The Edit RADIUS Server dialog box opens (see Figure 3.33). From here you can set the Name/Address of the RADIUS server, the shared secret, Timeout, Initial Score and RADIUS Port. You can also require the use of digital signatures.

5. Click OK to add the RADIUS server. Click OK to close the RADIUS Authentication dialog box. You will need to restart Routing and Remote Access to take advantage of the RADIUS authentication. Click OK to close the window.

Now that you have looked at how to do the RADIUS and Windows authentication, let's look at the authentication protocols Windows 2000 uses.

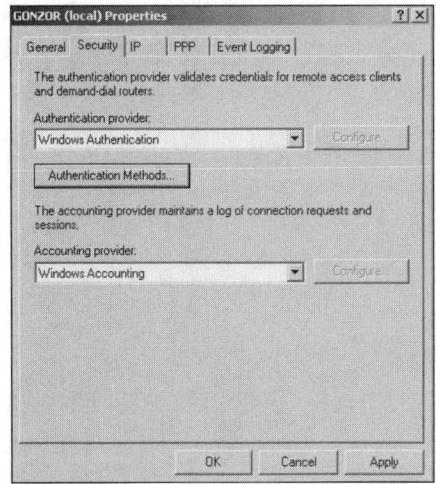

FIGURE 3.32
Remote Access security is controlled from this dialog box.

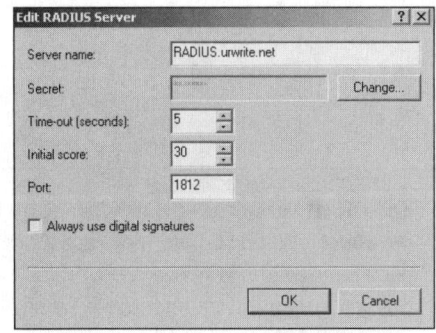

FIGURE 3.33
Adding a RADIUS server looks pretty easy, but you need to be sure your information matches the RADIUS server configuration.

Configuring Authentication Protocols

Windows 2000 supports a number of authentication protocols; therefore, almost any connection configuration is supported. The protocols include the following:

◆ **Extensible Authentication Protocol (EAP).** EAP-TLS is an extension to the PPTP. EAP provides a standard mechanism for support of additional authentication methods within PPP, such as smart cards, one-time passwords, and certificates. EAP is critical for secure Windows 2000 VPNs because it offers stronger authentication methods (such as X.509 certificates) instead of relying on the user ID and password schemes used traditionally.

◆ **Challenge Handshake Authentication Protocol (CHAP).** CHAP negotiates an encrypted authentication using MD5 (Message Digest 5), an industry-standard hashing scheme. CHAP uses challenge-response with one-way MD5 hashing on the response. This allows you to authenticate to the server without actually sending your password over the network. Because this is an industry standard authentication method, it allows Windows 2000 to securely connect to almost all third-party PPP servers.

◆ **Microsoft-Created Microsoft Challenge Handshake Authentication Protocol (MS-CHAP).** Microsoft created MS-CHAP, an extension of CHAP, to authenticate remote Windows workstations, increasing the protocol's functionality by integrating the encryption and hashing algorithms used on Windows networks. Like CHAP, MS-CHAP uses a challenge-response mechanism with one-way encryption on the response. Although MS-CHAP is consistent with standard CHAP as much as possible, the MS-CHAP response packet is in a format specifically designed for computers running a Windows operating system. A new version of the Microsoft Challenge Handshake Authentication Protocol (MS-CHAP v2) is also available. This new protocol provides mutual authentication, stronger initial data-encryption keys, and different encryption keys for sending and receiving.

> **NOTE**
>
> **MS-CHAP Versus MS-CHAP v2 Protocol** When you are making a VPN connection, Windows 2000 Server attempts to authenticate using the MS-CHAP v2 protocol before offering the MS-CHAP protocol. If you are using an updated Windows client computer, you should be able to authenticate with the MS-CHAP v2 protocol. Windows NT 4 and Windows 98-based computers can use only MS-CHAP v2 authentication for VPN connections.

◆ **SPAP.** Shiva Password Authentication Protocol (SPAP) is used specifically to allow Shiva client computers to connect to a Windows 2000 Server and to allow Windows 2000 client computers to connect to Shiva servers.

◆ **PAP.** Password Authentication Protocol (PAP) uses unencrypted (plain text) passwords for authenticating users and is considered the least secure authentication protocol available. PAP is usually used as the authentication of last resort—used when a more secure form of authentication is not available. You might need to use this protocol when you are connecting to a non-Windows-based server.

To configure these protocols, do the following:

STEP BY STEP

3.9 Configuring Authentication Protocols

1. Open the Routing and Remote Access console.

2. Right-click the server and select Properties. This opens the server properties.

3. Select the Security tab and click Authentication Methods (refer to Figure 3.32). The Authentication Methods dialog box opens (see Figure 3.34).

4. Select the appropriate protocol for a connection and click OK. Click OK to return to the Routing and Remote Access console.

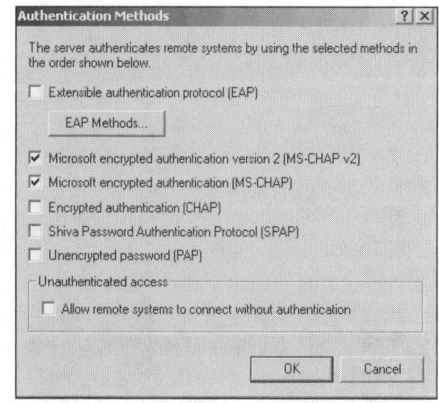

FIGURE 3.34
Remote Access security is controlled from this dialog box.

Configuring Encryption Protocols

The first thing you need to be aware of when discussing the encryption protocols available with Windows 2000 is that two main encryption protocols are used in a Windows 2000 VPN. We discussed PPTP and IPSec earlier in the chapter, but a couple of encryption protocols are used in conjunction with IPSec that we need to cover.

Under the Microsoft model, IPSec encryption does not rely on any authentication methods for its initial encryption keys. The encryption method is determined by the IPSec SA (Security Association). An SA is a combination of a destination address, a security protocol, and a unique identification value, called an SPI (Security Parameters Index). The available encryptions for IPSec include the following:

◆ **Data Encryption Standard (DES).** DES uses a 56-bit encryption key. This is considered barely adequate encryption for business use, and this level of encryption has been broken using specialized hardware.

◆ **Triple DES (3DES).** Like DES, 3DES uses a 56-bit key. But as the name implies, it encrypts the data using three 56-bit encryption keys. This is considered to be a 168-bit encryption key ($3 \times 56 = 168$) and is used in high-security environments. Until recently, the U.S. government tightly controlled the export of applications using 3DES encryption. Although these restrictions have been relaxed, exporting 3DES applications still requires government approval.

These are the encryption protocols available for remote access in Windows 2000. Windows 2000 does use other encryption, such as Kerberos, for logging on to a domain, but it is not applicable to remote access. To configure these protocols, do the following:

STEP BY STEP

3.10 Configuring Encryption Protocols

1. Open the Routing and Remote Access console and select Remote Access Policies from the tree view. In the right pane, right-click the policy you want to set the encryption level for and select Properties.

2. From the Policy Properties dialog box, click Edit Profile. The Edit Dial-in Profile dialog box opens.

3. Click the Encryption tab shown in Figure 3.35. You can set the encryption levels to No Encryption, Basic, Strong, or any combination of the three. Select the appropriate level, and then click OK twice and you are back to the Routing and Remote Access console.

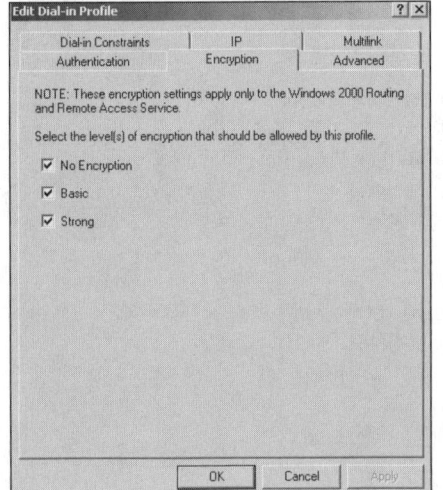

FIGURE 3.35
Windows 2000 supports three levels of encryption.

CASE STUDY: IMPLEMENTING ROUTING AND REMOTE ACCESS IN A COMPLEX ENVIRONMENT

ESSENCE OF THE CASE

The essence of the case is as follows:

▶ The management of your company is reluctant to make a major investment in toll charges for a dial-based remote access solution.

▶ Your company has three main populations of users, each with different remote access requirements.

▶ Each team has the requisite level of security.

SCENARIO

You are the network administrator for NR Widgets Inc., a multinational conglomerate, and you are based in the conglomerate's corporate headquarters. NR Widgets Inc. has a mobile population of about 200 people who need access to the network for submitting expense reports.

About 100 of the users live and work within your local area code, and the rest are scattered throughout the country. Your management does not want to pay for long-distance calls for remote access.

Your mobile users consist of three groups. The first group is the highly technical telecommuters, who need access to everything. They are also very security conscious and want to make sure their information is as secure as possible. The second group is the local users who need access, but are not too concerned about the security of the connection. The third group consists of about 35 users who work from home and have high-speed Internet connections.

What is the best way to do this so that you can accomplish the following:

- Each group has access to the network.

- Each group of users has the information security it needs.

- Long-distance or toll-free numbers are not allowed.

What should you do?

continues

CASE STUDY: IMPLEMENTING ROUTING AND REMOTE ACCESS IN A COMPLEX ENVIRONMENT

continued

ANALYSIS

As you have discovered in this chapter, you can meet these requirements by installing the Windows 2000 Routing and Remote Access Service. But by now you probably realize that it is a bit more complicated than just running the configuration wizard. First you need to take a close look at each population of users. The technical telecommuters, who have access to confidential information, will need to have a configuration that leverages the robust security and encryption mechanisms of the Windows 2000 Routing and Remote Access Service. You may need their profile configure dial-back, and may also need to use smart cards for authentication. For the second group of users, you will probably need to limit their access to sensitive information on the network, since they are using a less secure, more user-friendly authentication policy. Finally, while it is easy to configure a network—for example, an Internet-based VPN, you still need to make decisions. You need to examine the amount of bandwidth you have to the Internet to support these users. You need to consider where the server is placed. Should it be behind a firewall or directly on the Internet? You need to consider which VPN protocol is best suited for your environment. You may even find that your remote users who are not in the local area code want to utilize a local ISP in conjunction with the VPN solution, allowing you to further save on toll charges. All this is very dependent on the environment and the circumstances and requires effective planning. You need to install the following:

- One server running Windows 2000 Server and the Routing and Remote Access Service.

- The server needs to have modems installed and configured for dial-in users.

- Users who do not have the ability to dial locally to the server need to leverage the Windows 2000 VPN service; therefore, the server needs an Internet connection.

- The server needs remote access profiles to control the session security for each group.

This should be fairly straightforward after you have read the chapter. Let's do a quick chapter recap and then move on to some exercises.

CHAPTER SUMMARY

In this chapter we have covered in detail how to use the Windows 2000 Routing and Remote Access Service to provide remote access services. We started the chapter discussing how to configure Routing and Remote Access to support inbound connections, DHCP, VPNs, multilink connections, and we also discussed the creation and use of a remote access policy. We have examined how to use and configure a remote access profile as well.

We then discussed monitoring and managing the Routing and Remote Access Service and wrapped up the chapter by discussing the different security aspects of the service, including configuring remote access security, authentication protocols, and encryption.

And that wraps up the chapter summary. Let's take a look at some exercises and questions.

KEY TERMS
- virtual private network (VPN)
- modem
- multilink
- encryption
- Dynamic Host Configuration Protocol (DHCP)
- authentication
- Remote Access Service (RAS)
- callback

APPLY YOUR KNOWLEDGE

Exercises

3.1 Creating a Remote Access Policy

In the following exercise, you will use the Routing and Remote Access console to create a remote access policy. For this exercise you will create a policy for users connecting with PPP.

Estimated Time: 10 minutes

1. Open the Routing and Remote Access console.

2. Expand the application tree in the left pane by double-clicking the server. Right-click Remote Access Policies and select New Remote Access Policy.

3. Enter the name **Exercise 1** and click Next to continue.

4. Click Add to add a condition. Select the Framed Protocol attribute from the list of attributes and click Add.

5. Select PPP from the list of protocols. Click Add.

6. Click OK to add the condition. Click Next.

7. Select the Grant Remote Access Permission option. Click Next.

8. Click Finish to complete the creation of the profile.

3.2 Configuring an Idle Timeout for Routing and Remote Access Server

This exercise will walk you through modifying a profile to add an idle timeout for a remote access policy.

Estimated Time: 15 minutes

1. Open the Routing and Remote Access console.

2. Right-click the Exercise 1 remote access policy created in the last exercise. Select Properties from the Context menu.

3. Click the Edit Profile button.

4. Go to the Dial-Constraints tab. Select the Disconnect If Idle option and set the timeout value to 30 minutes.

5. Click OK to commit the changes. Click OK to return to the Routing and Remote Access console.

3.3 Monitoring Routing and Remote Access Using the Performance Console

This exercise will walk you through adding a counter to the Performance console so that you can see how many errors the Routing and Remote Access ports are experiencing.

Estimated Time: 15 minutes.

1. Open the Performance console.

2. In Performance, select System Monitor.

3. Click the Add (+) icon to add the counter.

4. Select the RAS Total performance object.

5. Select the Total Errors counter and click Add.

6. Click Close to complete the exercise.

Review Questions

1. You are the network administrator for Exponent Mathematicians and you have been asked to review the authentication protocols being used by your Routing and Remote Access server. What are the available protocols, and how do they work?

APPLY YOUR KNOWLEDGE

2. You are the administrator of the Get Stuffed Taxidermists chain Routing and Remote Access server. You have users who are utilizing the Windows 2000 VPN, both with IPSec and PPTP protocols. What are those protocols, and which is the industry standard?

3. You are the Windows 2000 administrator for Bug-B-Gone Exterminators. Your users are all connecting to your network using 56K modems, and they are complaining about performance. You are using the Routing and Remote Access Service with a modem bank for providing access, and they are running Windows 2000 Professional. You have used the performance monitoring capabilities of Windows 2000 to determine that no issues exist with Routing and Remote Access, so the issue appears to be bandwidth limitations. What should you do?

4. You have just installed Routing and Remote Access for providing VPN services to 100 of your end users. You are able to get the first five users connected, but then the server denies access. What is the problem and how do you fix it?

5. You're the LAN administrator for Think About IT Consulting Services company. You have just installed your first Routing and Remote Access server and your users are connecting without a problem. You want to see how much traffic is being added to the network by the additional users. How can you check?

Exam Questions

1. What portion of the Routing and Remote Access Service can be used to aggregate bandwidth across multiple modem connections?

   A. Multinet

   B. Multilink

   C. X.25

   D. VPN

2. You are the system administrator for Phil's Phill-up Stations, a chain of gas stations. As part of the network, you maintain a Windows 2000 Routing and Remote Access server to provide remote access services as part of a VPN. What VPN protocols will the server support?

   A. PPTP

   B. IPSec

   C. PPP

   D. EAP

   E. L2TP

3. You are the LAN Administrator for the OUI Find-em detective agency. You have people connecting to your Windows 2000 Routing and Remote Access from all over the country, most working from home. How can you minimize the users toll charges using Routing and Remote Access?

   A. Configure the user's RAS client computer for Connect as Needed mode.

   B. Use IPSec to tunnel to the RAS server through the public phone network, bypassing the toll charges.

   C. Get each user a personal 800 number.

   D. Set the Routing and Remote Access server security to use callback.

APPLY YOUR KNOWLEDGE

4. You are the LAN Administrator for Little Faith Enterprises Meat Packing. As part of the troubleshooting of a support issue, you need to check to see whether a user is connected to the Routing and Remote Access server.

   How can you check to see if the user is logged on?

   A. Open Performance Manager. Click the Add Counter icon. Select the RAS object and choose the Connected Users counter. Click OK and check the resulting statistic.

   B. Open the Performance console. Click the Add Counter icon. Select the RAS object and choose the Connected Users counter. Click OK and check the resulting statistic.

   C. Open the Routing and Remote Access console. Right-click the RAS server and choose Connected Users. Check for the user in the Connected Users dialog box.

   D. Open the Routing and Remote Access console. Under the server in the tree view, select Remote Access Clients. Check for the user in the Remote Access Clients.

5. You need to configure strong authentication for your Windows 2000 Routing and Remote Access server. Which protocol(s) should you use?

   A. IPSec

   B. PAP

   C. EAP

   D. CHAP

   E. MS-CHAP

6. You manage a Windows 2000 Routing and Remote Access server used for remote dial-in access. You have an end user who is trying to connect to the Routing and Remote Access server, but he keeps getting the message that he is not an authorized user. He is able to connect to the network and log in from his office across the LAN.

   What might be causing the problem?

   A. The user is not using the correct password.

   B. The user is not using an ID that is authorized to use the dial-in server.

   C. He is trying to use his LAN account instead of his dial-in account.

   D. One of the modems on the server is probably down.

7. You manage a Windows 2000 Routing and Remote Access server used for remote dial-in access. You have an end user who is trying to connect to the Routing and Remote Access server, but keeps getting the message that he is not an authorized user. He is able to connect to the network and login from his office across the LAN. After doing some research you find that the user ID was not authorized for remote access. How would you fix this situation?

   A. Using the Routing and Remote Access console, open the user's ID and under the Remote Access tab, grant him access.

   B. Using the Routing and Remote Access console, create a remote access policy. Use the Windows-Groups criteria and add the user to an authorized group.

   C. Using the Routing and Remote Access, create a remote access profile. Use the Windows-Groups criteria and add the user to an authorized group.

APPLY YOUR KNOWLEDGE

D. Using the Routing and Remote Access, create a remote access profile. Configure that profile to Grant Remote Access Permission.

8. You are the network administrator for Runaway Travel and you have just installed a new Windows 2000 Routing and Remote Access server to replace a hardware RAS server. Your users are using a third-party PPP dialer that was used for the old system.

What is the most secure authentication protocol that can be used for this connection?

A. PAP

B. EAP

C. CHAP

D. IPSec

9. You are the network administrator for Runaway Travel and you have just installed a new Windows 2000 Routing and Remote Access server to replace a hardware RAS server. Your users are using the Windows 2000 Professional dialer.

What is the most secure authentication protocol available?

A. CHAP

B. MS-CHAP

C. PPP

D. IPSec

10. You are the network administrator for Runaway Travel and you have just installed a new Windows 2000 Routing and Remote Access server to replace a hardware RAS server. Your

users are using a variety of client computer operating systems and PPP dialers.

What is the most secure way to ensure that all your users have access?

A. In the dial-in profile for those users, select Microsoft Encrypted Authentication (MS-CHAP) and Microsoft Encrypted Authentication version 2 (MS-CHAP v2).

B. In the dial-in profile for those users, select Encrypted Authentication (CHAP).

C. Use IPSec in conjunction with RAS.

D. Allow remote PPP client computers, as well as all the other protocols, to connect without negotiating any authentication method.

11. You are the network administrator for Go to Philly bus company and you have a requirement for a Windows 2000 Routing and Remote Access server to replace a hardware solution.

How do you install and configure the service?

A. Using the Networking and Dial-up Connections Wizard, install the Routing and Remote Access Service.

B. Using the Networking and Dial-up Connections Wizard, install the Remote Access Service.

C. Use the Routing and Remote Access Service to configure the service. Configure it with Windows 2000 Administration.

D. Use the Add/Remove Programs to add the Routing and Remote Access Service to the server. Configure the application using the Routing and Remote Access Service.

APPLY YOUR KNOWLEDGE

12. You are the system administrator for Blue Cap Haberdashery, and you have a Windows 2000 Routing and Remote Access server acting as a dial-in server. You have 15 modems on the server for users to dial in. Ten users have connected and are able to connect to the network. The eleventh user is able to connect, but cannot reach anything on the network.

    What could the problem be?

    A. The server is licensed for only 10 dial-in users.

    B. The DHCP server was down when the eleventh user tried to connect.

    C. The user has an incompatible modem.

    D. The user's IPSec password is incorrect.

13. You are the system administrator for Blue Cap Haberdashery, and you have a Windows 2000 Routing and Remote Access server acting as a dial-in server. You have 15 modems on the server for users to dial in. Users are able to connect without any problems, but they cannot reach any systems by DNS name. They are able to connect using the IP address of the system.

    What could the problem be?

    A. The Routing and Remote Access server is not running the DNS service.

    B. The Routing and Remote Access server is not running the WINS service.

    C. The network DHCP server has a bad DNS configuration.

    D. The network WINS server has a bad DNS configuration.

14. You are the security administrator for Barb's House of Pancakes. You have been asked to implement smart cards for remote access authentication using the Windows 2000 Routing and Remote Access Service.

    What protocol do you need?

    A. IPSec

    B. PPTP

    C. MS-CHAP v2

    D. EAP

15. You are the network administrator for Phil 'Em Up gas stations. You have installed a Windows 2000 Routing and Remote Access server to provide access to the corporate network remotely. You want to see what kind of utilization the server is experiencing.

    What is the easiest way to find out?

    A. Use Performance Manager to log the utilization. Check the performance logs for the information.

    B. Use the Performance console to log the utilization. Check the performance logs for the information.

    C. Go into the Registry and enable logging. Check the log file for the information.

    D. Go to the Event Logging tab in the Routing and Remote Access Server properties. Check the application log using the Event Viewer application to view the statistics.

16. You are the network administrator for Ye of Little Faith advertising, and you are running a Windows 2000 network made up of six Windows 2000

APPLY YOUR KNOWLEDGE

servers and 300 Windows 2000 Professional client computers. You have added 30 modems to the backup domain controller and need to install and configure the server for inbound connections. A secondary objective would be to install and configure VPN services.

You do the following:

Open the Networking and Dial-up Properties and double-click the Make New Connection icon. You follow the wizard to complete the installation, selecting Allow Virtual Private Connections to ensure that your VPN works.

This solution:

A. Is functional and meets the primary and secondary objectives.

B. Is functional but meets only the primary objective.

C. Is functional but meets only the secondary objective.

D. Is not functional.

17. You are the system administrator for Run to the Hills Travel. You have a Windows 2000 Routing and Remote Access server configured to use multilink. You would like to configure the server to automatically drop a connection when the lines are not being used.

What protocol can you use to accomplish this?

A. PPP

B. BAP

C. PPTP

D. EAP

18. You are the Internet administrator and you are using Windows 2000 Server as a VPN server. You need to configure additional IPSec VPN ports.

How do you accomplish this?

A. Run the VPN wizard and configure the additional ports.

B. Go to the Networking and Dial-up Connections window and double-click New Connection. When the New Connection wizard starts, select New Inbound VPN and follow the prompts.

C. In the Routing and Remote Access console, edit the properties of the L2TP ports and add the additional connections.

D. In the Routing and Remote Access console, edit the properties of the IPSec ports and add the additional connections.

19. You are the security administrator for a small police force. Your network is based on Windows 2000 Server, and you have just purchased smart cards for the entire force. You would like to take advantage of these for remote access, but you are unsure how to configure Routing and Remote Access. You know you need the EAP protocol.

Where do you configure this protocol?

A. In the remote access policy.

B. In the modem pool properties.

C. Under the Security tab of the Routing and Remote Access server properties.

D. In the dial-in profile for the pertinent policy.

APPLY YOUR KNOWLEDGE

20. What is the strongest encryption protocol supported by Windows 2000?

    A. DES

    B. IPSec

    C. MS-CHAP v2

    D. 3DES

21. You are the security administrator for Jolly Snowmen Ice Cream. You have been asked by your manager to explain the use of encryption on your Windows 2000 server. You know you are running DES.

    What service does DES provide to your installation?

    A. DES encrypts dial-in traffic over the phone lines.

    B. DES encrypts L2TP VPN traffic.

    C. DES provides encrypted authentication.

    D. DES provides encrypted address information in conjunction with PPTP.

Answers to Review Questions

1. The authentication protocols available include the following:

    • **EAP-TLS.** The Extensible Authentication Protocol (EAP) is an extension to the Point-to-Point Protocol (PPP). EAP provides a standard mechanism for support of additional authentication methods within PPP, such as smart cards, one-time passwords, and certifi-

    cates. EAP is critical for secure Windows 2000 VPNs because it offers stronger authentication methods (such as X.509 certificates) instead of relying on the user ID and password schemes used traditionally.

    • **CHAP.** The Challenge Handshake Authentication Protocol (CHAP) negotiates an encrypted authentication using MD5 (Message Digest 5), an industry-standard hashing scheme. CHAP uses challenge-response with one-way MD5 hashing on the response. This allows you to authenticate to the server without actually sending your password over the network. Because this is an industry-standard authentication method, it allows Windows 2000 to securely connect to almost all third-party PPP servers.

    • **MS-CHAP.** Microsoft created Microsoft Challenge Handshake Authentication Protocol (MS-CHAP), an extension of CHAP, to authenticate remote Windows workstations, increasing the protocol's functionality by integrating the encryption and hashing algorithms used on Windows networks. Like CHAP, MS-CHAP uses a challenge-response mechanism with one-way encryption on the response. Although MS-CHAP is consistent with standard CHAP as much as possible, the MS-CHAP response packet is in a format specifically designed for computers running a Windows operating system. A new version of the Microsoft Challenge Handshake Authentication Protocol (MS-CHAP v2) is also available. This new protocol provides mutual authentication, stronger initial data encryption keys, and different encryption keys for sending and receiving.

APPLY YOUR KNOWLEDGE

- **SPAP.** Shiva Password Authentication Protocol (SPAP) is used specifically to allow Shiva client computers to connect to a Windows 2000 Server and to allow Windows 2000 client computers to connect to Shiva servers.

- **PAP.** Password Authentication Protocol (PAP) uses unencrypted (plain text) passwords for authenticating users and is considered the least secure authentication protocol available. PAP is usually used as the authentication of last resort—used when a more secure form of authentication is not available. You might need to use this protocol when you are connecting to a non-Windows-based server.

2. Understanding the differences between IPSec and PPTP is important. These points should help you distinguish between the two:

- **IPSec (IP Security Protocol).** IPSec is a suite of cryptography-based protection services and security protocols used to provide a secure VPN connection. IPSec provides machine-level authentication, as well as data encryption, for L2TP-based (Layer 2 Tunneling Protocol) VPN connections. Unlike some other IPSec-based VPNs, Microsoft's implementation uses the L2TP protocol for encrypting the usernames, passwords, and data, whereas IPSec is used to negotiate the secure connection between your computer and its remote tunnel server. All authentication under the Microsoft IPSec VPN occurs through L2TP connections. These use all standard PPP-based

authentication protocols to authenticate the user after the secure IPSec communication is established.

- **PPTP (Point-to-Point Tunneling Protocol).** PPTP is Microsoft's legacy protocol for supporting VPNs. Developed jointly by Microsoft Corporation, U.S. Robotics, and several remote access vendor companies, known collectively as the PPTP Forum, PPTP encountered some security issues in its original form. It has been revised by Microsoft, but it has never been widely accepted by the security community. Although still supported on a variety of vendors' VPN servers, PPTP is rapidly being overtaken by the more widely adopted IPSec protocol.

3. The only way to provide additional bandwidth short of a different access media is to enable multilink and have the users add an additional modem and modem line on the remote end. This will allow the users to aggregate their bandwidth across two separate connections.

4. By default, Routing and Remote Access is configured with five connections for the VPN. You need to open the Routing and Remote Access application and go into the Port properties. Add additional ports as needed.

5. To find out the raw numbers on bandwidth through the server, you need to use the Performance console. Go to the RAS Total object and add the Total Bytes Received and Total Bytes Transmitted counters. Add the two counters to get the total additional traffic.

APPLY YOUR KNOWLEDGE

Answers to Exam Questions

1. **B.** The correct term for this feature is multilink. See "Configuring Multilink Connections."

2. **A, B, E.** The Windows 2000 Routing and Remote Access will support the following VPN protocols: IPSec, PPTP, and L2TP. See "Configuring a Virtual Private Network (VPN)."

3. **D.** If you configure the Routing and Remote Access server to use callback, all the toll charges following the initial connection will be on the company's bill, not the end user's. This is an old trick for reducing costs by leveraging the company's generally more favorable long distance rates. See "Configuring a Remote Access Profile."

4. **D.** You can see this information in the right pane of the Routing and Remote Access console by clicking the Remote Access Clients entry. See "Configuring Authentication Protocols."

5. **C, D, E.** IPSec is not an authentication protocol. PAP sends the authentication information as clear text. EAP, CHAP, and MS-CHAP are all secure authentication protocols. See "Creating a Remote Access Policy."

6. **B.** The user is not using an ID that is authorized to use the dial-in server. You must be authorized in a remote access policy before you can connect via dial-in. See "Creating a Remote Access Policy."

7. **B.** Using the Routing and Remote Access console, create a remote access policy. Use the Windows-Groups criteria and add the user to an authorized group. See "Creating a Remote Access Policy."

8. **C.** With a third-party dialer, the best you will be able to manage for authentication is the CHAP protocol. CHAP is an industry-standard protocol supported by virtually all PPP dialers. PAP would also work, but offers no security whatsoever. IPSec is not an authentication protocol. EAP is a protocol used for devices such as smart cards. See "Configuring Authentication Protocols."

9. **B.** When you are communicating between Windows PPP client computers, MS-CHAP is the most secure protocol listed. See "Configuring Authentication Protocols."

10. **D.** The trick here is to understand that the "connect without negotiating any authentication method" configuration is the lowest common denominator for connections. That's the only way to ensure that all your users can get to the network using your RAS solution. Users can still connect using greater security. See "Configuring Authentication Protocols."

11. **C.** The Routing and Remote Access Service is installed with the operating system. You will need the Routing and Remote Access console to make sure everything is configured correctly. See "Configuring Inbound Connections."

12. **B.** The Routing and Remote Access Service will request 10 addresses from the network DHCP server when it starts. When those 10 have been issued, RRAS will request an additional 10 addresses. If the DHCP server has gone down since the original 10 addresses were issued, the user would be able to connect but would not be able to get on the network because the Routing and Remote Access Service couldn't get additional IP addresses from the DHCP server. See "Configuring Routing and Remote Access for DHCP Integration."

APPLY YOUR KNOWLEDGE

13. **C.** Because the Routing and Remote Access server gets its DHCP information from the network DHCP server, a bad DNS configuration on the DHCP server could cause the issue described. See "Configuring Routing and Remote Access for DHCP Integration."

14. **D.** EAP is the protocol needed to support smart cards. See "Configuring Authentication Protocols."

15. **D.** In the latest version of Routing and Remote Access, logging is enabled in the server properties. The results of the logging can be found in the Event Viewer. See "Managing and Monitoring Remote Access."

16. **D.** This solution will not work because you must use the Routing and Remote Access console to configure remote access on a domain controller. See "Configuring Inbound Connections."

17. **B.** BAP (Bandwidth Access Protocol) is used to accomplish this function in conjunction with multilink. See "Configuring Multilink Connections."

18. **C.** You can just edit the properties of the L2TP ports, which are installed and configured when Routing and Remote Access is installed. Because by default IPSec used L2TP as a transport under Windows 2000, the ports are L2TP ports, not IPSec ports. See "Configuring a Virtual Private Network (VPN)."

19. **D.** The authentication protocols are configured in the dial-in profile. Although A is almost right, this is not configured as part of the policy, but is instead part of the profile. See "Configuring a Remote Access Profile."

20. **D.** 3DES or Triple DES is the strongest encryption protocol used by Windows 2000. See "Configuring Encryption Protocols."

21. **B.** DES is used in conjunction with IPSec. Because IPSec is used with L2TP, B is the correct answer. See "Configuring Encryption Protocols."

Suggested Readings and Resources

1. Boswell, William. *Inside Windows 2000 Server.* Indianapolis, IN: New Riders Publishing, 2000.

2. Siyan, Karanjit S. *Windows NT TCP/IP.* Indianapolis, IN: New Riders Publishing, 1998.

Microsoft defines the objectives for "Installing, Configuring, Managing, Monitoring, and Troubleshooting Network Protocols in a Windows 2000 Network Infrastructure" as:

Install, configure, and troubleshoot network protocols.

- **Install and configure TCP/IP.**

- **Install the NWLink protocol.**

- **Configure network bindings.**

. A Windows 2000 server obviously requires connectivity with other computers and devices on a network to be effective. You'll need to be knowledgeable in the fundamentals of Transmission Control Protocol/Internet Protocol (TCP/IP) and NWLink for this exam. In addition, a complete understanding of network bindings is essential. Network bindings are a method of "linking" a protocol to a network card or service in a particular, defined order.

Configure TCP/IP packet filters.

▶ As a Windows 2000 administrator, you'll want control of how packets are allowed to enter and leave your network. Proper network design, coupled with TCP/IP packet filters, will ensure both a good foundation for network security.

Configure and troubleshoot network protocol security.

▶ As networks become more sophisticated, more connected to the outside world, and reliant on the Wide Area Network (WAN) connectivity, more back doors are created and, therefore, more doors to lock. We'll examine how Windows 2000 provides basic protocol security and how you can implement and troubleshoot your security plan.

CHAPTER 4

Installing, Configuring, Managing, Monitoring, and Troubleshooting Network Protocols in a Windows 2000 Network Infrastructure

Manage and monitor network traffic.

▶ Windows 2000 includes some wonderful tools to monitor, manage, and troubleshoot network traffic. For this exam, you'll need a working knowledge of these tools. We'll examine the productivity of these tools and how you can implement plans to reduce overall network traffic while increasing reliability.

Configure and troubleshoot Internet Protocol Security (IPSec).

• **Enable IPSec.**

• **Configure IPSec for transport mode.**

• **Configure IPSec for tunnel mode.**

• **Customize IPSec policies and rules.**

• **Manage and monitor IPSec.**

▶ As a Windows 2000 administrator, you should be familiar with IPSec to secure data from network to network. We'll examine, configure, and troubleshoot IPSec for different network environments. You'll need a firm understanding of IPSec policies and rules, configuring IPSec transport and tunneling modes, and monitoring IPSec.

OUTLINE

Introduction	**178**
Installing, Configuring, and Troubleshooting Network Protocols	**178**
Understanding TCP/IP	178
Mechanics of IP	179
IP Addresses	181
Subnets and Subnet Masks	184
Variable Length Subnet Masks	185
Default Gateway	187
Installing TCP/IP	187
Configuring TCP/IP	189
Installing the NWLink Protocol	192
Configuring NWLink	193
Configuring Network Bindings	194
Working with TCP/IP Packet Filters	**196**
Configuring and Troubleshooting Network Protocol Security	**199**
Network Data Security	199
Security Hosts	200
Kerberos V5 Authentication	201
Windows 2000 Domain Controllers	201
Kerberos V5 Interoperability	202
VPNs	202

Managing and Monitoring Traffic	**203**
Understanding Network Traffic and the Network Monitor	203
Installing Network Monitor	204
Installing the Network Monitor Driver	206
Using Network Monitor to Capture Data	206
Interpreting Captured Data	209
Configuring and Troubleshooting IPSec	**210**
Understanding the Architecture and Components of IPSec	212
Authentication Header (AH)	212
ESP	213
Internet Security Key Association Key Management Protocol (ISAKMP/Oakley)	215
L2TP and IPSec	215
Enabling IPSec Through a Policy	216
Customizing IPSec	**220**
Managing and Monitoring IPSec	**226**
Chapter Summary	**229**
Apply Your Knowledge	**231**

OUTLINE

STUDY STRATEGIES

▶ Windows 2000 networking encompasses many areas. As you study network protocol security, break down the issue modularly. Examine and learn a chunk at a time, and then begin to combine those chunks to fit into different network solutions. The Step by Steps not only offer you the essential hands-on experience, but also offer a second learning channel.

▶ Make sure that you understand the basics of TCP/IP. Windows 2000 is very reliant on TCP/IP; no doubt, this exam will focus heavily on the more complex issues of TCP/IP and how it works with Windows 2000. Take some time to review the basics of IP and then build from there.

▶ Get your hands dirty. The Step by Steps throughout this book provide plenty of directions and exercises, but go beyond these examples and create some of your own. If you can, experiment with each of the objectives to see how they work and why you would use each one.

INTRODUCTION

The way you design your network should take into account the geographical locations of your servers, the topology of your network—including Ethernet, token ring, Fiber Distributed Data Interface (FDDI), and so on—and, of course, the protocols your network will use to communicate with servers, workstations, and printers. In this chapter, we discuss the TCP/IP and NWLink Internetwork Packet Exchange/Sequenced Packet Exchange (IPX/SPX)-compatible protocols.

TCP/IP is becoming the protocol of choice as our networks grow and interact with other networks around the world. NWLink is a necessity when you migrate legacy NetWare servers to or integrate them with Windows 2000.

As our network grows, we must also examine the security measures and threats that protocols allow. This chapter focuses on protocol security, management, and monitoring.

INSTALLING, CONFIGURING, AND TROUBLESHOOTING NETWORK PROTOCOLS

First, let's examine the security measurements needed for TCP/IP and NWLink in a Windows 2000 environment. To get started, we need a brief understanding of these protocols and how to install and configure them with Windows 2000.

Understanding TCP/IP

Install, configure, and troubleshoot network protocols.

What is TCP/IP? TCP/IP is a suite of protocols that allows host, networks, and operating systems to communicate with each other. As you may know, TCP/IP was originally intended for the Department of Defense (DOD) to allow its mainframes and servers to chat with each other locally and remotely.

As mentioned in Chapter 1, "Installing, Configuring, Managing, Monitoring, and Troubleshooting Domain Name Service (DNS) in a Windows 2000 Network Infrastructure," TCP/IP actually evolved from a network created by a vast research agency—the Advanced Research Projects Agency (ARPA)—which performed advanced technical research for the DOD. This collection of networks, called ARPAnet, connected research centers, such as universities, to each other and with DOD sites, such as the Pentagon.

ARPAnet ran on top of the original routing protocol, Network Core Protocol (NCP). NCP was composed of the TCP and IP protocols. Yes, they're actually two separate components—which we'll examine in a moment.

The basic design on TCP/IP is simple, fault tolerant, routable, and (thankfully) vendor neutral.

Originally, TCP/IP was to connect the mainframes. However, the '80s saw the evolution of UNIX and personal computers (PCs). UNIX led the way, at the University of California, Berkley (with some resistance), in integrating TCP/IP to connect these PCs. The Macintosh world used the AppleTalk protocol, and much of the Windows world stuck with either NetBios Extended User Interface (NetBEUI) or NWLink IPX/SPX-compatible for connectivity with NetWare.

And then this thing called the World Wide Web happened; everyone needed TCP/IP and needed it now.

Mechanics of IP

IP allows data to travel from one computer to another either on a local network or through a router to a remote network. How does this work?

If you have eight computers in Chicago connected on the same Ethernet network, you've got a Local Area Network (LAN). There's no routing—and no need for it. In an Ethernet network, each computer receives every packet, regardless of whether the packet is intended for it or not. Recall that it's the physical address (Media Access Control [MAC] address) of the network card that determines whether the packet is to be accepted or discarded.

When Computer A needs to send a packet to Computer B on the same Ethernet network via TCP/IP, the packets don't have to pass through a router. What has to happen, however, is Computer A needs to know the IP address of Computer B. Then IP resolves that IP address to the MAC address of the network adapter card in Computer B. That MAC address is in the header of the packets sent out onto the network, and only Computer B will accept those headers because only Computer B has that exact MAC address on its network card.

But what about when Computer A in Chicago needs to talk to Computer Z in Atlanta (see Figure 4.1)? Now we have a WAN, so we need a router. A router is a device that routes packets from network to network to network and eventually to the host. Now when Computer A needs to chat with Computer Z, the packets are forwarded onto the router because the destination is not on the local network.

The router then forwards the packet, based on its routing table, to the next router, and onward until eventually the packet ends up at the final network and onto the target computer.

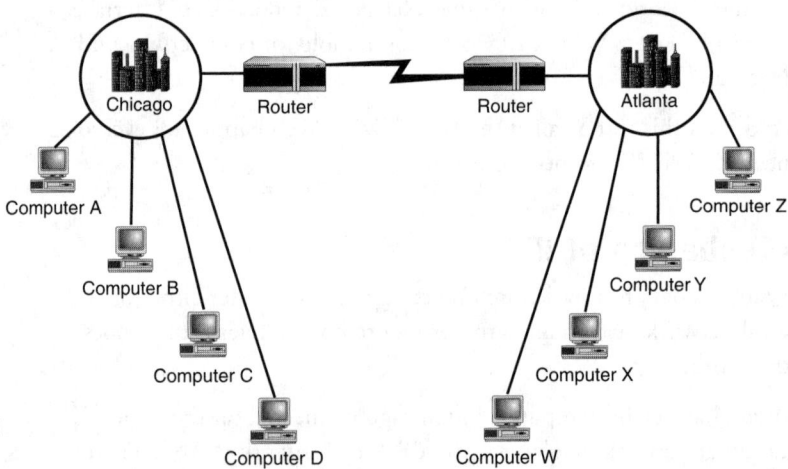

FIGURE 4.1
A WAN with computers located in Chicago and Atlanta connected via routers.

IP Addresses

For routing to happen, a network design must be based on specific rules. The first rule of TCP/IP is that you use a valid IP address. An IP address is a series of numbers that represents your computer—for example, 131.108.116.55. Each of the numbers in this IP address is an octet, made up of 8 bits; the whole IP address is 32 bits.

If you were to look at 131.108.116.55 in binary, as the computer sees it, you would see 10000011 1101100 1110100 00110111.

IP addresses are typically displayed in decimal format, called dotted decimal notation. Each host that requires connectivity on a TCP/IP network requires its own unique IP address. A network address in dotted decimal notation is easier for humans to read than an address in binary form. However, having the address in dotted decimal notation is not convenient for the computer, which uses binary form. It is sometimes helpful to understand what the computer is doing when it works with network addresses, especially in such things as identifying which route may be used for a particular address, determining the binary representation of a subnet mask, or in general, troubleshooting the TCP/IP protocol.

You can convert a dotted decimal address to its binary representation using a very simple technique. Each decimal value separated by a dot is converted by repeatedly dividing the number by 2 and recording the quotient and remainder. The remainder (a series of zeroes and ones) forms the binary equivalent. Table 4.1 shows how to convert the address 127.0.0.1 to its binary equivalent.

TABLE 4.1

DECIMAL TO BINARY CONVERSION

(1) *Action*	*(2)* *Quotient*	*(3)* *Remainder*	*(4)* *Notes*
Divide the four parts of the dotted decimal notation into separate values. Start with the last part of the dotted decimal notation, 1.	0	1	Four parts of the address are 127, 0, 0, and 1. The last part is 1.
Divide decimal number 1 by 2, record quotient and remainder in next row.			

continues

TABLE 4.1	*continued*

DECIMAL TO BINARY CONVERSION

(1) Action	(2) Quotient	(3) Remainder	(4) Notes
Stop! Quotient = 0	0	1	1/2 = 0 remainder 1
Proceed with the third part of the dotted decimal notation, 0. Because the quotient is 0 to begin with, there is nothing to proceed with.	0		Quotient is 0 already.
Proceed with the second part of the dotted decimal notation, 0. Because the quotient is 0 to begin with, there is nothing to proceed with.	0		Quotient is 0 already.
Proceed with the first part of the dotted decimal notation, 127			
Divide decimal number 127 by 2, record quotient and remainder in next row.	127		
Repeat the procedure. Divide by 2, record quotient and remainder in the next row.	63	1	127/2 = 63 remainder 1
Repeat the procedure again.	31	1	63/2 = 31 remainder 1
Repeat the procedure again.	15	1	31/2 = 15 remainder 1
Repeat the procedure again.	7	1	15/2 = 7 remainder 1
Repeat the procedure again.	3	1	7/3 = 1 remainder 1
Repeat the procedure again.	1	1	3/2 = 1 remainder 1
Stop! Quotient = 0	0	1	1/2 = 0 remainder 1

We have now completed the conversion of all four octets. You can determine the resulting binary format of the dotted decimal notation by the digits in the remainder column (column 3). Starting with the bottom (last) remainder digit in the column, write the binary number from left to right, using a dot to separate each octet. If eight digits are not present, pad the binary value on the left with zeros until there are eight digits. In this example, the binary equivalent of 127.0.0.1 is

```
127.0.0.1 =  01111111.00000000.00000000.00000001
```

In addition to knowing how to convert from decimal to binary, you will also want to know how to convert from binary to decimal. To convert from binary to decimal, you use a place value system. If a binary value is 1, the place it represents within the string of 1's and 0's represents the decimal value. If you add these place values, you come up with the decimal equivalent of the binary string. The position of the place value is calculated from the right and starts at 0, which represents decimal 1. Each increment in position value doubles the previous position's decimal place value.

For example, if we take the value 10110111, the following represents a binary string, its place values, and their decimal equivalents.

2^7	2^6	2^5	2^4	2^3	2^2	2^1	2^0	Place
128	64	32	16	8	4	2	1	Decimal Place Value
1	0	1	1	0	1	1	1	Binary Value

The total of 128 + 32 + 16 + 4 + 2 + 1 is 183. Each power of 2 position value doubles the previous one. Each place value represents a power of 2 result for the binary value. The position −1 indicates what the power should be.

IP addresses are organized by classes: Class A, Class B, and Class C. Table 4.2 defines the range and amount of hosts included with each network.

TABLE 4.2

DETAILS OF IP ADDRESSES

Class	From	To	Net IDs	Host IDs
A	1	126	126	16,777,214
B	128	191	16,384	65,534
C	192	223	2,097,152	254

The subnet masks for these class addresses are defined in Table 4.3.

TABLE 4.3

CLASS SUBNET MASKS

Address Class	Bits for Subnet Mask	Subnet Mask
Class A	11111111 00000000 00000000 00000000	255.0.0.0
Class B	11111111 11111111 00000000 00000000	255.255.0.0
Class C	1111111 11111111 11111111 00000000	255.255.255.0

Subnets and Subnet Masks

If we assume that an IP address identifies your computer, it's fair to say that a subnet identifies where your computer is. The component of an IP address that determines whether packets are to be sent locally or through a router is the subnet mask. The subnet mask tells the protocol whether the local host and the destination host are on the same subnet.

Basically, when the subnet bits match, the host and destination host are on the same subnet and no routing is needed. When the subnet bits don't match, the destination host is on a remote network and the packets are sent to the router.

The Internet community has standardized some predefined subnet masks. These subnet masks break the total defined address space on the Internet into various classes, called as Class A, Class B, and Class C. Refer to Table 4.2 for the range and amount of hosts included with each network.

Variable Length Subnet Masks

When you're working with TCP/IP, one of the most difficult topics to understand is the concept of variable length subnet masks. As the use of TCP/IP has grown more widespread, it has become obvious that sometimes assigning even a full Class C address with 254 available hosts is a waste of address space—in a branch office with five employees, a file server, and a printer, for example. An IP address range must be broken into smaller pieces to allow for more efficient use of the address space. Variable length subnet masks (also known as subnet addressing) is the method for "borrowing" bits from the host ID portion of an IP address and applying them to the network ID.

Suppose that you have been assigned the Class B address 172.18.0.0. You need to create four separate networks from your one IP address range. The technique is to borrow three bits from the host ID field. These three bits let you configure six separate subnets. If you do the math, it should be eight subnets, as discussed later in this chapter.

To see how subnet addressing works, let's first convert the IP address 172.18.0.0 to binary form:

```
10101100 00010010 00000000 00000000
```

Remember, in a Class B address, the first 16 bits are the net ID and the last 16 bits are the host ID.

To indicate that bits are being borrowed from the host ID, you make use of a subnet mask, which is also a 32-bit binary number. To make the purpose of the subnet mask clear, you need to examine it beside the binary IP address, like this:

```
10101100 00010010 00000000 00000000
11111111 11111111 11100000 00000000
```

In dotted decimal, this is 255.255.224.0 for the subnet mask. The rules of subnet masking are simple:

◆ 1 in the network mask indicates that a bit in the IP address is part of the net ID.

◆ 0 in the network mask indicates that a bit in the IP address is part of the host ID.

This example has 19 bits in the network mask, so within the net ID are 19 bits for addressing. This subnet mask allows the following subnetworks (subnet IDs) to be used within the Class B address range:

```
10101100 00010010 00100000 00000000
10101100 00010010 01000000 00000000
10101100 00010010 01100000 00000000
10101100 00010010 10000000 00000000
10101100 00010010 10100000 00000000
10101100 00010010 11000000 00000000
```

Why only six subnets? We have to avoid two "forbidden" subnets (000 and 111), which are not available because of TCP/IP conventions. A subnet ID cannot consist entirely of 1s because all-1s addresses are used to address broadcast messages. Notice that the last range of addresses below includes 255 in the network range and is not addressable.

A second restriction is that the subnet ID should not be entirely of 0s. This is less clear because there are no addressing restrictions regarding the use of decimal 0 in a network ID. Windows 2000 will allow you to use the 0 network, although by convention, it should be excluded.

If you do the math to convert the binary addresses to decimals, you find that the subnet mask 255.255.224.0 lets you construct six valid subnets and two "illegal" subnets, with the following address ranges:

◆ 172.18.0.1 to 172.18.31.254

◆ 172.18.32.1 to 172.18.63.254

◆ 172.18.64.1 to 172.18.95.254

◆ 172.18.96.1 to 172.18.127.254

◆ 172.18.128.1 to 172.18.159.254

◆ 172.18.160.1 to 172.18.191.254

- 172.18.192.1 to 172.18.223.254

- 172.18.224.1 to 172.18.255.254

The subnet mask actually becomes part of the configuration of each host on the network, enabling the hosts to discriminate net ID, subnet ID, and host ID.

Default Gateway

A default gateway is the IP address of the router that the packets from a host should use to leave this subnet. The typical process of how a packet leaves a host and gets to a destination is as follows:

1. Computer A resolves Computer Z to an IP address.

2. The IP address of Computer Z is determined to be local or remote.

3. If the address is remote, Computer A sends the packets to the default gateway's MAC Address.

4. The default gateway then forwards the packets onto the next router according to its routing table.

5. If Computer Z's IP address is on the same subnet, the IP address of Computer Z is resolved to the MAC address through Address Resolution Protocol (ARP).

6. Computer A and Computer Z communicate and there is no need for routing.

This section briefly explained the basics of TCP/IP, its evolution, mechanics, and components. Now you can install TCP/IP.

Installing TCP/IP

Install, configure, and troubleshoot network protocols.

To begin using TCP/IP on your network, you need a list of valid IP addresses, the IP address of your gateway (router), and the subnet mask for your network. More than likely, your Windows 2000 computer already has TCP/IP installed as its default protocol. Step by Step 4.1 walks you through the process of adding TCP/IP, in case you chose not to install it during Windows 2000 installation.

STEP BY STEP

4.1 Adding TCP/IP

1. To add TCP/IP, open Control Panel and then open Network and Dial-up Connections, shown in Figure 4.2.

2. Double-click the Local Area Connection icon to bring up the Local Area Connection Status dialog box (see Figure 4.3).

3. Click the Properties button. The Properties dialog box for the Local Area Connection opens (see Figure 4.4). By default, when you install Windows 2000, the TCP/IP protocol is also installed.

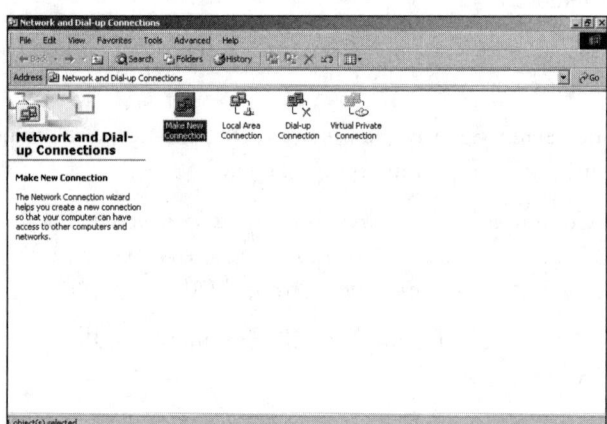

FIGURE 4.2
The Network and Dial-up Connections window shows all the configured connections on your computer.

4. If you don't see TCP/IP in the list, click Install. The Select Network Component Type dialog box opens (see Figure 4.5).

5. Choose Protocol, Add; then select IP (TCP/IP) and click OK. You're returned to the General tab of the Local Area Connection Properties. Click OK to exit.

Configuring TCP/IP

Now that you've installed the TCP/IP protocol, you'll need to configure the protocol with the necessary TCP/IP information. You can configure your Windows 2000 computer with an IP address in two ways. The first is through Dynamic Host Configuration Protocol (DHCP). A DHCP server maintains a database, also known as a scope, of valid IP addresses for a subnet. When a computer configured for DHCP requires an IP address, the computer searches the network for a DHCP server. The DHCP server or servers respond with a valid IP address for the subnet the host is located on.

Using DHCP has many advantages, including the following:

◆ Centralized management

◆ Changes made at the server rather than on each computer

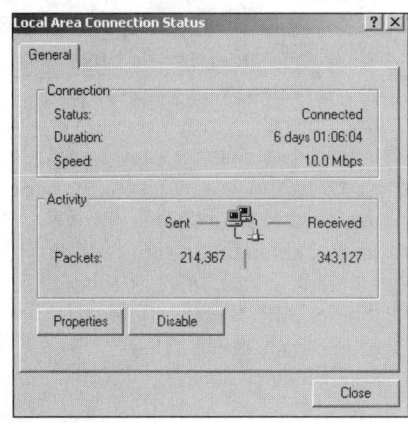

FIGURE 4.3
The Local Area Connection Status dialog box shows whether the connection is active and how much information is being sent and received.

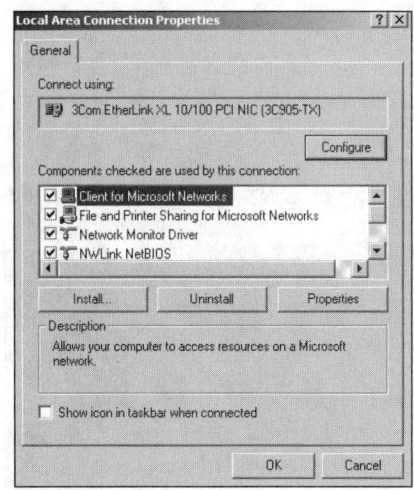

FIGURE 4.4
The Local Area Connection Properties box displays the adapter type and shows which protocols are installed.

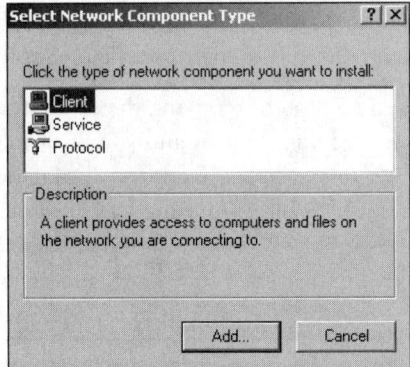

FIGURE 4.5
Use this box to select the type of component you want to install.

What IP Address Should I Use?   If you're working within a large network, there's probably a group of folks responsible for adding and removing the IP addresses assigned to the network. You'll want to check with these gurus before arbitrarily adding an IP address to the network. A wrong IP address on your end could mean big headaches on theirs.

If you're isolated from a production environment, you can use whatever IP address you want.

◆ Resolves conflicts of IP addresses

◆ Resolves problems when hosts move from subnet to subnet

◆ Saves time from visiting each computer to set the IP properties

The second choice, which is waning in popularity, is to manually set the IP address on each computer. Although this option may not be popular for workstations, it may be realistic for servers. Most services that manipulate TCP/IP, such as Windows Internet Name Service (WINS), DNS, DHCP, and others, require the server to have a static IP address.

Step by Step 4.2 guides you through the process of using DHCP on this host or assigning a manual IP address.

STEP BY STEP

4.2 Configuring TCP/IP

1. Open Control Panel and then open Network and Dial-up Connections (refer to Figure 4.2).

2. Double-click the Local Area Connection icon to bring up the Local Area Connection Status dialog box (refer to Figure 4.3). Click the Properties button.

3. On the General tab of the Local Area Connection Properties dialog box (refer to Figure 4.4), select IP (TCP/IP), and then click Properties. The IP (TCP/IP) Properties dialog box opens (see Figure 4.6).

4. Choose a method of receiving the IP address. If your network uses a DHCP server and you want to configure this computer to receive its IP address automatically, select the Obtain an IP Address Automatically option. All IP information will be pulled from the DHCP server. (Notice, however, that you may edit the IP address of the DNS server or obtain this info through DHCP as well.)

5. To assign an IP address, select the Use the Following IP Address option.

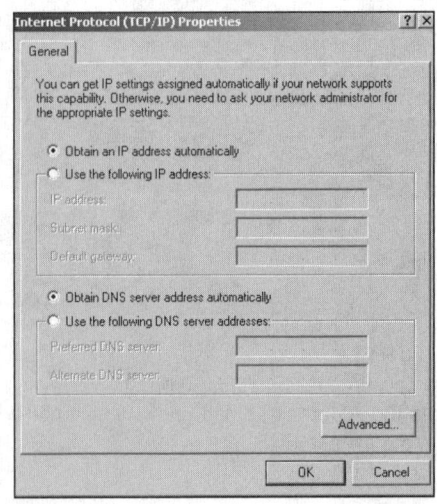

FIGURE 4.6
IP (TCP/IP) properties.

6. In the IP address field, enter a valid IP address for your network. Enter the subnet mask for your network. Enter the IP address of the router or gateway for your network. Enter the IP address of the preferred DNS server and, if applicable, the secondary DNS server. Figure 4.7 shows how the dialog box should look when completed.

7. To accept these settings, click OK and then click OK again.

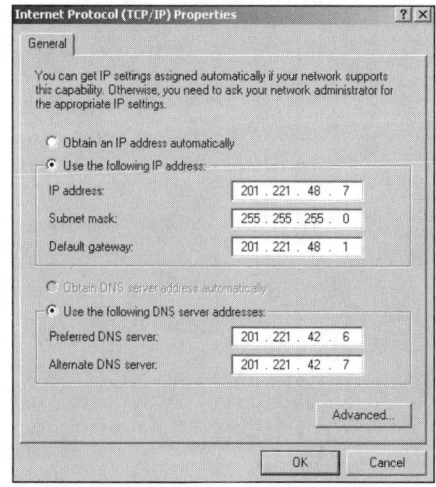

FIGURE 4.7
When entering an IP address either manually or through DHCP, you can still specify what the DNS servers should be.

After you've added and configured TCP/IP, you may still have to set some additional settings on the protocol. On the TCP/IP Properties dialog box, click the Advanced button to access these settings. The following is a listing and explanation of these additional settings:

◆ **IP Settings.** This tab reveals the currently configured IP address assigned to the network card. In addition, it allows you to add additional IP addresses to a network card. This option may rarely be used; however, it is used if this computer is hosting a Web site. You could assign two IP addresses to one card. Each IP address would represent a different domain name hosted on this server. In addition, this tab allows you to specify additional default gateways.

◆ **DNS.** This tab reveals the DNS servers used to query fully qualified domain names (FQDNs) and hostnames. In addition, you can specify that Windows 2000 should search for hostnames within this domain first. To connect to a computer whose FQDN is server5.publishing.Midwest.newriders.com, for example, you enter **http://server5** rather than the entire FQDN. You can also specify that Windows 2000 search other specified domains for computer names.

◆ **WINS.** WINS is a service that resolved NetBIOS names to IP addresses. It's still around in Windows 2000 to support network basic input output system (NetBIOS) names in older operating systems. If you're using WINS (and you probably will be if your network includes operating systems such as Windows 98, Windows 95, and possibly Windows NT 4), you'll need to enter the IP address of the WINS server.

◆ **Options.** The Options tab allows you to access IP Security settings and the TCP/IP filtering settings. These settings are covered in more detail later in this chapter.

Installing the NWLink Protocol

NWLink is Microsoft's 32-bit implementation of IPX/SPX. NWLink, like its Novell counterpart, is a routable, reliable protocol. Older versions of NetWare, such as NetWare 3, were reliant on IPX/SPX, but newer versions of NetWare can use TCP/IP.

Before installing NWLink on your Windows 2000 computers, you need to gather some information. Following are some common questions you'll need to answer before installing NWLink:

◆ Will you be migrating your NetWare server to Windows 2000? Or will you be integrating NetWare and Windows 2000?

◆ What version of NetWare are you integrating with Windows 2000? Can that version use TCP/IP in lieu of IPX/SPX?

◆ What is the internal network number for your NetWare server(s) that is being integrated?

◆ What is the frame type in place with your NetWare servers?

The actual process of adding NWLink is fairly straightforward. When you have the answers to the preceding questions, you're ready to add the protocol and begin the conversion from NetWare or the integration with NetWare. Step by Step 4.3 guides you through the installation process.

STEP BY STEP

4.3 Adding NWLink to Windows 2000

1. Open Control Panel and then open the Network and Dial-up Connections window.

2. Open the Local Area Connection Properties (or the appropriate connection you'll be using to connect to your NetWare servers).

3. Click the Install button to access the Network Component Type dialog box. Choose Protocol and then click the Add button. The Select Network Protocol dialog box opens (see Figure 4.8).

4. Choose NWLink IPX/SPX/NetBIOS Compatible Transport Protocol and then click OK. Windows 2000 will install the protocol and return to the Local Area Connection Properties window. Click OK to close.

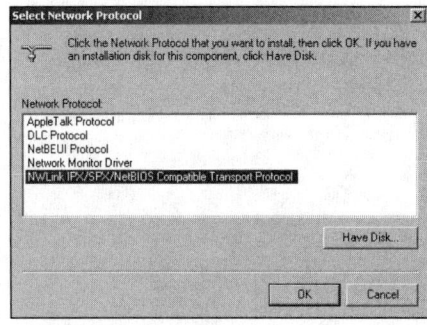

FIGURE 4.8
Select the protocol you want to install from the list.

Configuring NWLink

After adding NWLink, you can then further configure the protocol with the necessary information to lay the foundation to communicate with NetWare servers and client computers. Remember, this is only the protocol to connect to NetWare servers; typically, additional software, such as Client Services for NetWare (CSNW), Gateway Services for NetWare (GSNW), or File and Print Services for NetWare (FPNW) are required to complete connectivity with NetWare servers and client computers.

CSNW allows a Windows 2000 client computer to connect to NetWare server shares. GSNW allows Windows 2000 servers to connect to NetWare shares and then act as a gateway by providing Windows network shares linking to the NetWare share points. FPNW allows Windows 2000 servers to provide network share points that can be accessed by NetWare computers.

To configure the NWLink protocol, follow these steps:

STEP BY STEP

4.4 Configuring the NWLink Protocol

1. Open Control Panel and then open the Network and Dial-up Connections (refer to Figure 4.2).

2. Right-click the connection you'll use to connect to your NetWare server and then choose Properties (see Figure 4.4).

continues

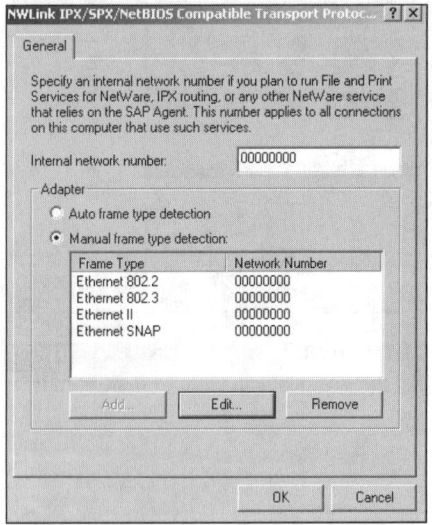

FIGURE 4.9
You can enter the internal network numbers here.

---

continued

3. Click the General tab, select the NWLink IPX/SPX/NetBIOS Compatible Transport Protocol, and then click the Properties button.

4. To use services that require Service Advertising Protocol (SAP), such as FPNW or IPX routing, you need to supply the internal network number for your NetWare network (see Figure 4.9).

5. Choose to use either the Auto Frame Type Detection option, or you can specify all frame types in use by your NetWare servers. Figure 4.9 shows the manual frame type entries for a Windows 2000 and NetWare environment.

6. Click OK and then click Close to approve the changes.

EXAM TIP

Know Network Bindings On the exam, you'll be tested on your knowledge of what network bindings are and how to configure and edit them.

Configuring Network Bindings

Network bindings are configurations indicating which protocol Windows 2000 will use first on a network connection for a network service. For example, if your network is locally configured to connect both to NetWare servers via IPX/SPX and to Microsoft networks via TCP/IP, you can specify which protocol should be referenced, or used first, when attempting to connect to resources.

In dealing with network bindings in the past, a specific protocol was associated with a network card. Although that description still holds some truth, Windows 2000 has added a layer of functionality: allowing you to first determine the provider order.

A provider is the component that allows you to connect to network resources. The default provider in Windows 2000 is the Microsoft Windows Network. As you add additional providers, such as GSNW, you need to determine which provider should be used first.

Network providers aren't the only components involved in bindings. You also get to choose print providers. Like its counterpart, a print provider helps you get to a different type of resource—a printer.

To set up a binding, position the provider you use most often, (for example, the Microsoft Windows Network) first in the list of providers, followed by FPNW. Position TCP/IP as the first in the list of protocols and NWLink as the second. You establish these priorities by modifying the bindings order.

Changing the bindings sounds easy, but it does take a little planning. As your network grows, you'll probably find that you add more and more services; when adding these services, you're also automatically binding the installed protocols to each service. Most likely, your binding order will change as your network changes.

Why should you even worry about bindings? A simple, tiny change in the configuration of your bindings can make a great impact on the speed of your server-to-server and server-to-client relationships. Later in this chapter, you examine networks and monitor the impact the bindings order change has had on your overall network performance.

Step by Step 4.5 walks you through the actions required to configure network and print providers. This example presumes that you have a second provider, such as GSNW, installed.

STEP BY STEP

4.5 Arranging the Provider Order

1. Choose Start, Settings, Control Panel, and Network and Dial-up Connections, and then choose the network connection (typically the local area connection).

2. From the Advanced menu, click Advanced Settings.

3. In the Advanced Settings dialog box, click the Provider Order tab, in which you can see the providers installed on this computer (see Figure 4.10).

4. Select the provider you want to change. If, for example, you've added GSNW and want to place it first in the list of Network Providers, click GSNW and then click the up arrow to move it up in the list.

5. Arrange the Print Providers in the order in which you want them to be accessed with this network connection.

6. Click OK to approve your settings.

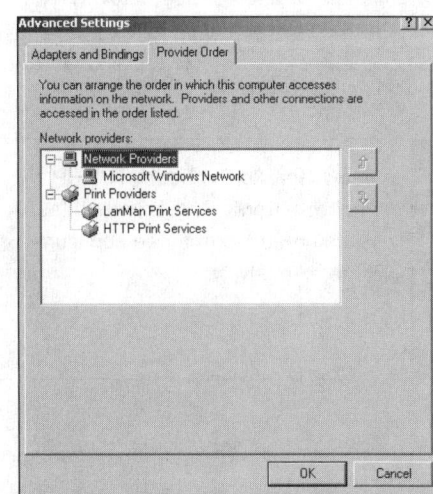

FIGURE 4.10

You can use the Advanced Settings dialog box to modify the binding order.

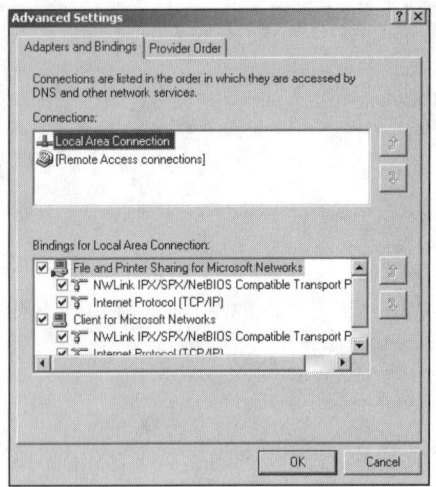

FIGURE 4.11
Bindings are a way of associating a protocol with a network card, service, and connection.

You can also arrange the order of the protocols on the installed services. What you are actually doing here is telling Windows 2000 which protocol to expect to use first. This improves performance—the service will connect and be connected to faster. Figure 4.11 shows the binding order of a typical Windows 2000 server.

WORKING WITH TCP/IP PACKET FILTERS

Configure TCP/IP packet filters.

Now that you know how to add and configure protocols, arrange the bindings for your connections services, and prioritize providers, let's look at controlling TCP/IP packets. This section guides you through defining and modifying packet filters.

Windows 2000 allows you to control the type of TCP/IP information that is sent to your computer. You can configure a universal rule for the type of data that reaches all network cards in your server, or you can configure each card individually.

TCP provides guaranteed packet delivery. Table 4.4 lists the common TCP ports that you can allow or deny access to:

TABLE 4.4

COMMON TCP PORT NUMBERS

TCP Port Number	Description
20	FTP Server data channel
21	FTP Server control channel
23	Telnet
80	Web Server – specifically hypertext transport protocol (HTTP)
139	NetBIOS Session service

User Datagram Protocol (UDP) does not provide guaranteed packet delivery; rather, it makes a best-effort attempt for delivery. Table 4.5 lists common UDP ports that you can allow or deny access to:

TABLE 4.5

COMMON UDP PORT NUMBERS

UDP Port Number	Description
53	DNS name queries
69	Trivial File Transfer Protocol (TFTP)
137	NetBIOS Name Server (NBNS)
161	Simple Network Management Protocol (SNMP)
520	Routing Information Protocol (RIP)

IP is composed of different protocols. Table 4.6 lists common IP protocol numbers that you can allow or deny access to:

TABLE 4.6

COMMON IP PROTOCOL NUMBERS

Protocol Number	Protocol
1	Internet Control Message (ICMP)
2	Internet Group Management (IGMP)
3	Gateway-to-Gateway (GGP)
4	IP in IP (encapsulation)
5	ST Stream
6	TCP
7	Computer-base training (CBT)
8	Exterior Gateway Protocol (EGP)

TCP/IP packet filtering allows you to determine the type of TCP ports that can be accessed, the UDP ports that are accessed, and more directly, which IP protocols can access this computer. For example, you can filter port 80, which is used by the HTTP protocol. By filtering this port, you deny access to all Web servers.

To create a TCP/IP packet filter, assign the appropriate port or IP protocol number in the Advanced properties of TCP/IP. Step by Step 4.6 guides you through the process of creating an IP packet filter.

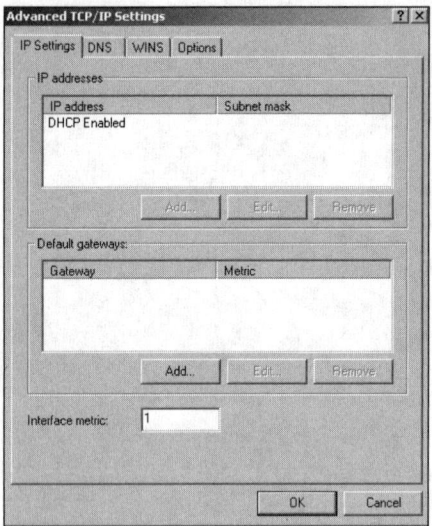

FIGURE 4.12
The Advanced TCP/IP Settings dialog box provides further configuration options for the Internet Protocol.

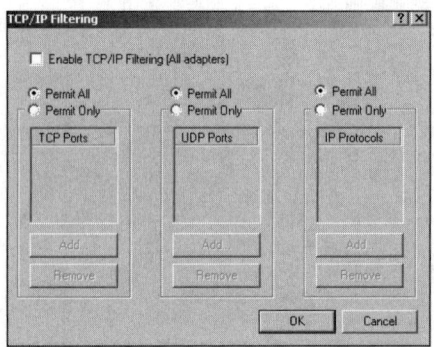

FIGURE 4.13
TCP/IP filtering can be set on all adapter cards or on one card at a time.

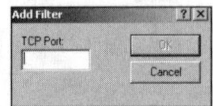

FIGURE 4.14
Enter the TCP/IP port number that you want to permit access.

STEP BY STEP

4.6 Establishing IP Filtering

1. Open Control Panel and then open the Network and Dial-up Connections dialog box.

2. Right-click the connection you'd like to configure and then choose Properties. The Local Area Connection Status dialog box opens. Click the Properties button to open the connection properties.

3. From the General tab, choose IP, and then choose Properties.

4. From this General tab of IP Properties, click the Advanced button. The Advanced TCP/IP Settings dialog box opens (see Figure 4.12).

5. In the Advanced TCP/IP Settings, click the Options tab, choose TCP/IP Filtering, and then choose Properties. The TCP/IP Filtering window opens (see Figure 4.13).

6. Make sure that the Enable TCP/IP Filtering (All Adapters) option is unchecked for now.

7. Above TCP Ports, select the Permit Only option and then click the Add button. The Add Filter dialog box opens (see Figure 4.14).

8. Specify Port Number 23 for Telnet sessions, and then click OK.

9. Click Add again and enter Port Number 80 for Web Access, and then click OK.

10. Select the Permit Only option for UDP Ports and then click the Add button.

11. Enter Port Number 69 for TFTP sessions, and then click OK.

12. Click Add again and enter Port Number 161 for SNMP, and then click OK.

13. Click OK to approve these settings. These settings allow only TCP ports 23 and 80 and UDP ports 69 and 161 to be accessed on the server.

After you've established a packet filter, you may find it necessary to revise the existing filter. To change a filter, open the TCP/IP properties and choose Advanced. On the Options tab, make changes as needed. Approve your changes to enforce the setting.

Configuring and Troubleshooting Network Protocol Security

Configure and troubleshoot network protocol security.

As networks grow and interact with other networks, data becomes more vulnerable to attack, interception, and eavesdropping. You must secure your networks to secure your data. This section looks at configuring and troubleshooting your protocols, including the following topics:

◆ Network data security

◆ Using security hosts

◆ Understanding Kerberos

◆ Virtual private networks (VPNs) and tunneling security features

Network Data Security

Windows 2000 has many facets of network protocol security. The most well known is the IPSec. We'll examine IPSec in detail in a moment. For now, know that IPSec is used to secure IP packets between hosts on a LAN or WAN environment. IPSec provides private communications over the Internet.

The Windows 2000 Router Service provides data security in both LAN and WAN environments. You implement VPNs where you see the router service and security working in tandem, which we'll discuss in more detail later. VPNs and the router service are grounded on either point-to-point tunneling protocol (PPTP) or Layer-2 Tunneling Protocol (L2TP).

A proxy server, although not a standard component of Windows 2000, is a valuable feature to secure client computers on a network. A proxy server accepts outbound network requests and completes the request as a "proxy" for the originating host. Typically, a proxy server acts as a firewall defense to block incoming packets from ever reaching the internal network.

Security Hosts

Security hosts are intermediary devices between remote dial-up client computers and your network. These devices intercept the dial-up request and require additional information to access and be authenticated on your network. You can use two types of security hosts with Windows 2000:

◆ **Authentication at the time of the call.** These intermediary devices typically require an additional piece of information to access the server. A prime example is a security manager and security card. The security manager is the software located at the dial-up server. The security card is a business card-sized device and looks like a pocket calculator. The security card has a liquid crystal display (LCD) that changes numbers every minute or so. The numbers in the display are in sync with the security manager software. When a user calls in to the server, she must provide the number on the security card before she enters her Windows 2000 credentials.

◆ **Authentication in tandem with the logon process.** These components can be hardware and/or software based. A common example is the Remote Authentication Dial-In User Service (RADIUS) server, which authenticates client computers on behalf of Routing and Remote Access. Other examples include software programs that could communicate and verify remote smart cards to allow the users to provide network credentials.

Kerberos V5 Authentication

Kerberos V5 is the authentication protocol used within a Windows 2000 domain. You don't have to do anything to implement Kerberos—it's already there. Kerberos authenticates Windows 2000 client computers logging in to a Windows 2000 domain and is the foundation of Windows 2000 network security.

Windows 2000 is not the first operating system to use Kerberos—it's been around for a while. It was developed by MIT in the '80s. Different operating systems (OSs) using Kerberos can be configured to interact with one another to access objects in the Active Directory.

A user must complete several steps to log in to a Windows 2000 domain and access network resources. The steps are as follows:

1. A user enters a valid username and password. A Key Distribution Center (KDC) approves the logon request.

2. At logon, the KDC generates a ticket, which will allow the user to request a network service. This ticket is called a ticket-granting ticket, or (TGT).

3. The client computer presents the TGT to the ticket-granting service (TGS). The TGS issues a service ticket to the requestor.

4. The user attempts to access a resource or, more specifically, a network service. The service ticket allows the client computer to have a level of access to the network service by providing the user's identification to the service.

Windows 2000 Domain Controllers

Every domain controller that authenticates users also serves as a KDC. As client computers log on to the domain, they are assigned their ticket-granting ticket.

Recall that in Windows 2000, Domain Name Service (DNS) is used to locate the nearest domain controller for the client computer. Should the nearest domain controller be unavailable, DNS will look up the next available domain controller, or KDC, for authentication of the user account.

Kerberos V5 Interoperability

As mentioned earlier, Microsoft Windows 2000 is not the first OS to use Kerberos. Because other OSs already use this authentication protocol, you can configure your domains to interact with these systems so that client computers using other OSs (such as UNIX), that use Kerberos-based security, may access resources on Windows 2000 servers.

Windows 2000 supports two types of interoperability:

◆ A trust relationship between a Windows 2000 domain and a MIT-based realm.

◆ UNIX workstations and servers can have accounts within the Active Directory and will obtain authentication from the KDC.

VPNs

A VPN consists of two or more locations linked via a shared or public network, such as the Internet. Through a VPN, users can connect to remote servers and resources as if the resources were on a LAN. The following process creates a VPN connection:

1. Data is encapsulated. The header provides routing information to the destination network or host ID.

2. The data travels through the public network to the remote host. These packets are encrypted.

3. As packets reach the destination, the packets are de-encrypted and the information is read as if the packet came through a secure, private network.

Windows 2000 supports two types of VPNs:

◆ PPTP. This protocol uses point-to-point protocol (PPP) authentication and Microsoft Point-to-Point encryption (MPPE) for data.

◆ L2TP with IPSec.

The L2TP allows you to access your Windows 2000 domain over the Internet as if the entire routable path were on a private network. L2TP is an industry-standard protocol that has similar features to PPTP.

A primary difference between PPTP and L2TP is that PPTP will not support tunneling over X.25, frame relay, or asynchonous transfer mode (ATM) networks. It's designed for Internet tunneling only.

As with PPTP, L2TP encapsulates packets and then sends them on to the remote network. This feature allows client computers and servers to use protocols independent of TCP/IP. This capability is useful should an application require a specific protocol to operate properly, such as Appletalk 6.07. L2TP also provides support for header compression and tunnel authentication, whereas PPTP does not.

PPTP uses PPP encryption for authentication, whereas L2TP uses the IPSec encryption standard. L2TP combined with IPSec ensures a secure transfer of data between two host IDs. We'll discuss the IPSec encryption standard further in a moment.

MANAGING AND MONITORING TRAFFIC

As a network administrator, you will find that network traffic can directly influence your productivity and design of a network. You'll want to implement a solid plan to monitor existing traffic, and then deduce how to manage that traffic. Your constant battle will be that when you add new service, you lose a percentage of bandwidth. Through planning, tweaking, and design, you can keep those lost percentages small. This section covers the following:

◆ Network traffic basics

◆ Network Monitor

◆ Configuring Network Monitor

◆ How to reduce network traffic

Understanding Network Traffic and the Network Monitor

Network traffic is any activity to and from a host on your network. Any packet that leaves a network card is contributing to network traffic. The more hosts you have on a network, the more services you add to a network, and the more network you fail to segment properly—the more network traffic you'll have.

Why is the issue of network traffic so important? A crowded network, like rush-hour traffic, clogs the speed of the network, causes the network to become a bottleneck, and ultimately, can cause your network to fail.

As a rule, the more network services, shares, and resources you add to a network, the more network traffic you are generating. Think of this situation: you've got 100 Windows 2000 Professional workstations and four Windows 2000 servers in a domain. You've added DHCP, WINS, DNS, GSNW, TCP/IP, NetBEUI, AppleTalk, and NWLink on every server. This contributes to network traffic in a major way—especially if your only client computers are Windows 2000 Workstations running TCP/IP. This is definitely a time when less is more.

Windows 2000 has lots of tools and third-party add-ons to monitor your network's activity. However, one tool is more powerful than any piece of software: your brain! Plan your networks before you implement them and you'll be happier in the long run. Following are a few tips for designing a network with traffic in mind:

◆ Less is more.

◆ Get rid of unneeded protocols.

◆ Get rid of unneeded services.

◆ Organize your shares to create a swift, easy-to-navigate structure.

◆ Don't be afraid to segment your network. The more users you have in an environment, the more chatter—and contention—you'll experience.

◆ Use Network Monitor to create a baseline of network activity. Use this baseline to compare how your network is evolving.

> **WARNING**
>
> **Limited Network Monitor**
> Windows 2000 includes a limited version of Network Monitor. This limited version of Network Monitor captures only frames between the host and other computers. The full version of Network Monitor, included with Systems Management Server (SMS), can capture frames sent to and from all computers in a network segment.

Installing Network Monitor

You'll use Network Monitor to capture packets on your network. From these packets you can troubleshoot network problems, discern how busy a network load is, and predict how your network will grow.

Network Monitor comprises two primary components:

◆ **Network Monitor**. Network Monitor is the tool you'll use to capture packets sent to and from this server. This version of Network Monitor records only packets sent to and from this server and the LAN.

◆ **Network Monitor Driver**. The Network Monitor Driver is
installed automatically when you install Network Monitor on a
server. However, you may want to install just the Network
Monitor Driver for remote computers to be monitored through
the full version of Network Monitor included with SMS.

Network Monitor is not installed by default, but it's easy enough to
add. Step by Step 4.7 walks you through the steps to add this software:

STEP BY STEP

4.7 Adding Network Monitor

1. Choose Start, Settings, Control Panel, Add/Remove
Programs.

2. Click the Add/Remove Windows Components icon.
The Windows Components dialog box opens (see
Figure 4.15).

3. Within the Components list, select Management and
Monitoring Tools. The Management and Monitoring
Tools dialog box shown in Figure 4.16 opens.

4. Select the Network Monitor Tools option in the subcom-
ponents list, click OK, and then click Next. (You can also
select Connection Manager Components and SNMP.)

5. You may be asked to provide your Windows 2000 CD or
the path to where the source files are located.

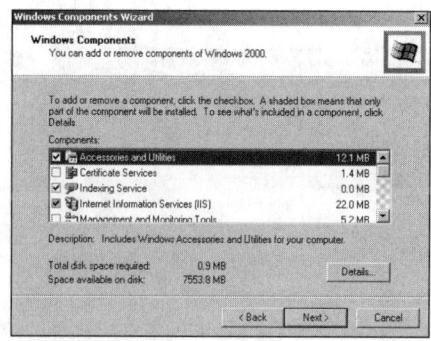

FIGURE 4.15
Use Add/Remove Windows Components to add
the Network Monitor.

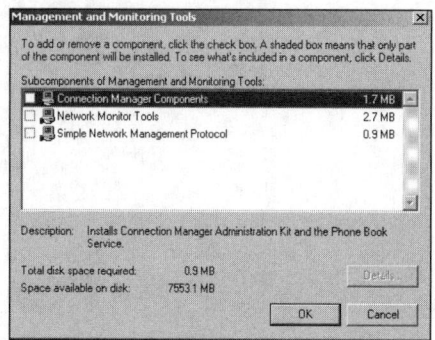

FIGURE 4.16
If you need more information about a subcom-
ponent of the Management and Monitoring
Tools, click Details.

> **Installing the Network Monitor Driver.** This is only required if the computer you want to monitor is on a different subnet than the computer you are using to monitor. If they are on the same subnet, the full version of Network Monitor will be able to capture and analyze the traffic.

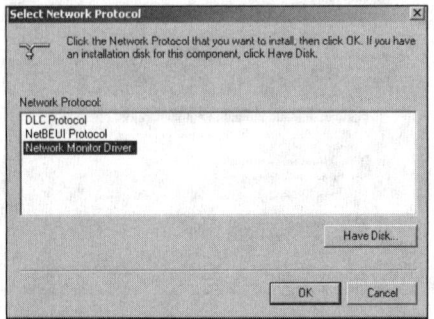

FIGURE 4.17
The Network Monitor Driver is required so that the SMS Network Monitor can retrieve the packets sent to and from this network adapter.

Installing the Network Monitor Driver

If you'll be using the SMS Network Monitor from another computer on this network, you'll need to add the Network Monitor Driver. Step by Step 4.8 guides you through the process of adding only the driver.

STEP BY STEP

4.8 Adding the Network Monitor Driver

1. Click Start, Settings, Control Panel. From Control Panel, open the Network and Dial-up Connections dialog box.

2. Right-click the Local Area Connection, and choose Properties. The Local Area Connection Properties dialog box opens.

3. Click the Install button.

4. Choose Protocol from the list of available components, and then click Add. The Select Network Protocol dialog box opens (see Figure 4.17).

5. Select Network Monitor Driver and click OK. The necessary files are added.

6. If necessary, you may need to provide your Windows 2000 CD or type a path to access the setup files.

Using Network Monitor to Capture Data

Network Monitor, shown in Figure 4.18, captures frames, or packets, to and from the local computer and the network. This section walks you through the process of using Network Monitor and creating a simple capture. Later, we will go into greater detail on creating a capture filter through Network Monitor.

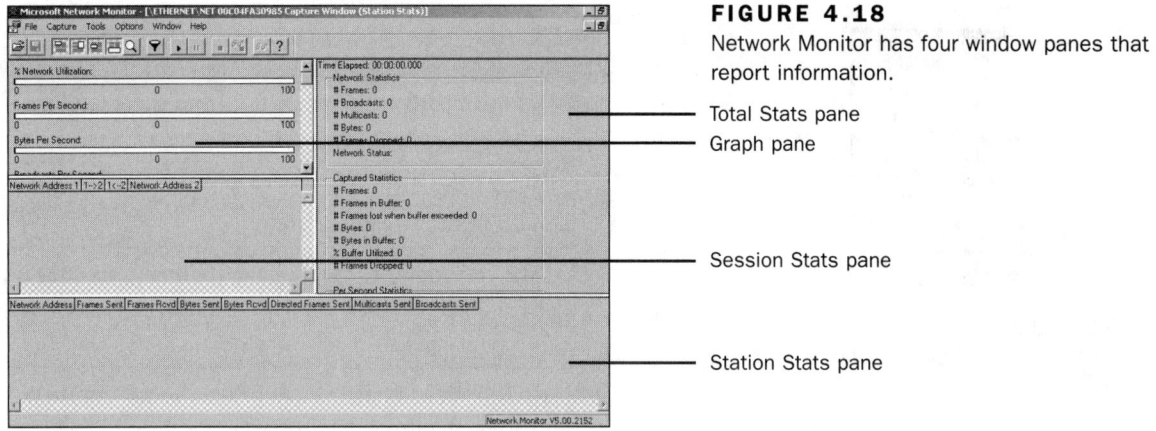

FIGURE 4.18
Network Monitor has four window panes that report information.

Total Stats pane
Graph pane

Session Stats pane

Station Stats pane

Four panes with Network Monitor report information about your current activity, or captured file:

◆ The Graph pane reports back percentages of activity in a bar chart format.

◆ The Session Stats pane reports back individual statistics of client-to-server activity during the capture or live activity.

◆ The Station Stats pane reports information on each workstation's activity on a network. Keep in mind that this is actually activity between that workstation and this server with this version of Network Monitor.

◆ The Total Stats pane reports the totals of the stats for all the other panes.

STEP BY STEP

4.9 Creating a Network Capture

1. Choose Start, Programs, Administrative Tools, Network Monitor. The Network Monitor window opens.

continues

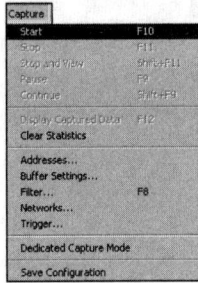

FIGURE 4.19
Select Start from the Capture menu to begin recording activity.

continued

2. Choose Capture, Start (see Figure 4.19). Network Monitor records activity to and from this computer. You can generate some activity by sending a PING command.

3. Choose Start, Run; then type CMD and press Enter to launch the command prompt.

4. At the command prompt, ping another computer on this network—or even an Internet address. For example, you can type ping www.newriders.com.

5. Switch back to Network Monitor, choose Capture, Stop and View. Figure 4.20 displays the captured packets in the detail pane. The captured data is displayed.

6. To see the results of your PING command, find ICMP in the Protocol column, and select that line..

7. Close the Display window to return to the Network Statistics window.

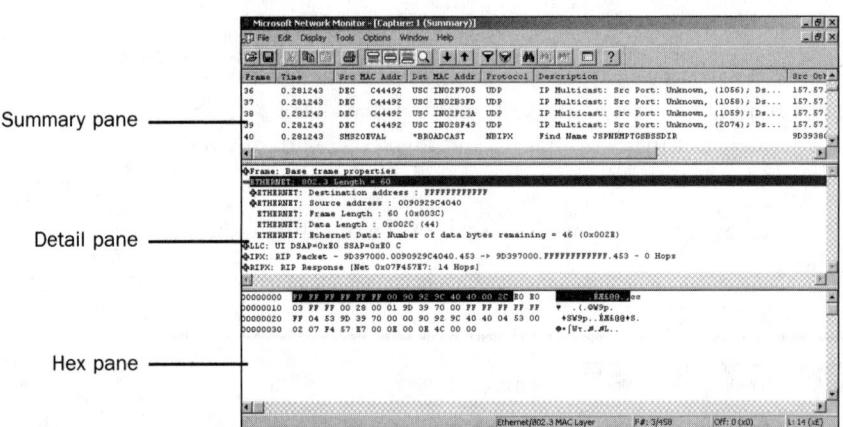

FIGURE 4.20
The Detail view allows you to check out the details of each packet captured.

Interpreting Captured Data

Interpreting captured data depends on the type of server you're working with. What is this server's role in the domain? Is it a domain controller? An application server? A file server? Each of these roles will have different traffic patterns. What we need to get an accurate picture of the activity for this server is a filter.

Filters allow us to strip away packets that may not be relevant to the server, capture, or type of packets we're looking for. Within Network Monitor, choose Filter from the Capture menu. The Capture menu dialog box will allow you to do the following:

- **Specify capture filter protocols.** You can designate which protocols you'd like displayed in your capture. Complete the SAP/ETYPE= field by designating the protocol(s) you'd like displayed.

- **Specify address pairs.** This option allows you to pick up to three pairs of addresses that have sent and received packets from each other.

- **Specify frame data patterns to capture.** This setting includes many options to build your own variables to display the captured data. You can display frames that contain a designated pattern.

Before you implement changes to your network, always create a baseline. A baseline is a snapshot of how your network is operating under normal conditions.

After creating the baseline, make the desired changes and run the test again. After running the test, ask yourself the following questions:

- Did the changes help or hinder performance?

- If the changes hindered performance, have I configured all the options for this change properly? For example, have I configured bindings again?

- Has one area of network performance improved, such as logon times, but other areas of network performance worsened, such as communication between domain controllers?

- Is this network capacity more than 75%? If so, should I add a switch or router to break up the network?

After you've added and configured the changes to your network, create another baseline as a snapshot of how the system is after these changes. Over the next few days, weeks, and months, periodically run the same test again and compare these results to this baseline. This will help you predict how your network will be growing and what resources are using your bandwidth.

CONFIGURING AND TROUBLESHOOTING IPSEC

IPSec is a framework of open standards for ensuring private, secure communications over IP networks. This protocol is rapidly becoming the underlying framework for secure communications using VPNs and will likely replace PPTP as Microsoft's VPN protocol of choice. IPSec takes advantage of many of the most popular encryption protocols in use today. For more information on encryption protocols, see the section "Configuring Encryption Protocols" in Chapter 3, "Configuring, Managing, Monitoring, and Troubleshooting Remote Access in a Windows 2000 Network Infrastructure." IPSec is based on an end-to-end security model, which means that the only computers that must know about IPSec are the sending and receiving computers. The packets will travel the network without being affected by any of the intervening network devices. Each IPSec device handles its own security and functions with the assumption that the transport medium is not secure. The Internet is an excellent example of a transport medium that is not secure.

The Microsoft Windows 2000 implementation of IPSec is based on standards developed by the Internet Engineering Task Force (IETF) IPSec working group. An IPSec VPN configured to use transport mode secures an existing IP packet from source to destination, using the encryption and authentication methods discussed later in this section. Tunnel mode puts an existing IP packet inside a new IP packet that is sent to a tunnel end point in the IPSec format. Both transport and tunnel mode can be encapsulated in Encapsulating Security Payload (ESP) or AH headers. The IETF Request for

Comments (RFC) IPSec tunnel protocol specifications did not include mechanisms suitable for remote access VPN clients, instead focusing on site-to-site VPN implementations. For that reason, Microsoft's implementation of tunnel mode relies on the use of the L2TP protocol developed jointly with Cisco to provide this additional packet format. (An introduction to the components of IPSec comes later in this chapter.)

The Windows 2000 IPSec VPN implementation includes the following features:

◆ IPSec on Windows 2000 is policy based. It cannot be configured without an IPSec policy being in place, allowing an administrator to more easily apply settings to groups of objects such as computers or users.

◆ IPSec on Windows 2000 can use Kerberos V5 for user authentication.

◆ IPSec mutually authenticates computers prior to any data being exchanged.

◆ IPSec establishes a security association (SA) between the two host computers involved in the data transfer. An SA is the collection of a policy and keys, which define the rules for security settings.

◆ IPSec encrypts data using Data Encryption Standard (DES), Triple DES (3DES), or 40-bit DES.

◆ IPSec can use public key certificates to trusted hosts from non-Windows 2000 domains.

◆ IPSec permits preshared key support. If Kerberos authentication is not available, a shared key, such as a password, may be configured to set the IPSec session.

◆ IPSec is invisible to users. IPSec operates at the network level of the Open System Interface (OSI) model; therefore, users and applications do not directly interact with the protocol. After an IPSec tunnel has been created, users can connect to applications and services as if they were on the local network and not on the other side of a public network.

EXAM TIP

Protecting VPN Connections By default, client remote access VPN connections are protected using an automatically generated IPSec policy that uses IPSec transport mode (not tunnel mode) when the L2TP tunnel type is selected. You will probably see this configuration in almost every production implementation of a Windows 2000 IPSec implementation. To enable this configuration, install Routing and Remote Access and configure it for L2TP VPN connectivity, as described in the section "Configure a Virtual Private Network (VPN)" in Chapter 3.

EXAM TIP

Understand IPSec The exam includes questions and scenarios on IPSec. Although you don't need to memorize the minutiae surrounding the encryption protocols used by IPSec, you should be familiar with what the components of IPSec are, how to implement an IPSec tunnel, and especially how to work with IPSec policies.

IPSec operates at the network layer; therefore, it is invisible to applications and computers. An understanding of the following features, however, will help you troubleshoot problems that may arise in connectivity.

◆ IPSec policies are part of the local (and/or) group policies within Active Directory. This built-in feature allows changes and management to be centralized. Settings for IPSec are enforced on the computer as the policy is enforced.

◆ The Internet Security Key Association Key Management Protocol (ISAKMP) monitor the negotiations between the hosts and provides the keys to use with security algorithms.

◆ The installed IPSec driver secures traffic between the two hosts.

Understanding the Architecture and Components of IPSec

Let's take a look at the underlying architecture and components of the IPSec protocol. IPSec provides data and identity protection services for each IP packet by adding a security protocol header to each IP packet. This header is made up of several components, each with its own function.

Authentication Header (AH)

The IPSec AH provides three services as part of the IPSec protocol. First (as its name might suggest), AH authenticates the entire packet. Second, it ensures data integrity. Third, it prevents any replaying of the packet by a third party who might be trying to penetrate the IPSec tunnel. One service AH doesn't provide is payload encryption. AH will protect your data from modification, but an attacker who is snooping the network would still be able to read the data. To prevent the modification of the data, AH uses two hashing algorithms to "sign" the packet for integrity.

◆ Message Digest 5 (MD5) applies the hashing function to the data in four passes.

◆ Secure Hash Algorithm (SHA) process is closely modeled after MD5. SHA uses 79 32-bit constants during the computation of the hash value, which results in a 160-bit key. Because SHA has a longer key length, it is considered more secure than MD5.

AH uses an IP protocol decimal ID of 51 to identify itself in the IP header. The AH header contains the following fields:

◆ **Next Header.** Identifies the next header that uses the IP protocol ID.

◆ **Length.** Indicates the length of the AH header.

◆ **Security Parameters Index (SPI).** Used in combination with the destination address and the security protocol (AH or ESP), the SPI is used by the receiver to identify the cryptographic keys and procedures to be used to decode the packet.

◆ **Sequence Number.** Provides the anti-replay functionality of AH. The sequence number is an incrementally increasing number (starting from 0) that is never allowed to cycle and that indicates the packet number. The machine receiving the packet checks this field to verify that the packet has not been received already. If a packet with this number has already been received, the packet is rejected.

◆ **Authentication Data.** Contains the Integrity Check Value (ICV) used to verify the integrity of the message. (This is the hash value mentioned previously.) The receiver calculates the hash value and checks it against the ICV to verify packet integrity.

AH can be used alone or in combination with the ESP protocol.

ESP

ESP provides confidentiality in addition to authentication, integrity, and anti-replay. This is the portion of the IPSec protocol that encrypts the data contents of the packet. The format of the ESP varies, depending on the type and mode of encryption being utilized. ESP can be used alone, in combination with AH, or using Microsoft's implementation, nested within the L2TP.

ESP appears in the IP header with an IP protocol decimal ID of 50. The ESP header contains the following fields:

◆ **SPI.** Used in combination with the destination address and the security protocol (AH or ESP), the SPI is used by the receiver to identify the cryptographic keys and procedures to be used to decode the packet.

◆ **Sequence Number.** Provides the anti-replay functionality of ESP. The sequence number is an incrementally increasing number (starting from 0) that is never allowed to cycle and indicates the packet number. The machine receiving the packet checks this field to verify that the packet has not been received already. If a packet with this number has already been received, the packet is rejected.

The ESP trailer contains the following fields:

◆ **Padding.** 0 to 255 bytes used for 32-bit alignment and with the block size of the block cipher.

◆ **Padding Length.** Indicates the length of the Padding field in bytes.

◆ **Next Header.** Identifies the makeup of the payload, such as TCP or UDP.

The ESP Authentication Trailer contains one field: Authentication Data. This field contains the ICV and a MAC used to verify the sender's identity and ensure message integrity.

ESP is inserted after the IP header and before an upper layer protocol, such as TCP, UDP, or ICMP, or before any other IPSec headers (such as AH) that have already been inserted. Everything following ESP (the upper layer protocol, the data, and the ESP trailer) is encrypted. The IP header is not signed, and therefore, not necessarily protected from modification unless tunneling mode is active.

The final piece of the IPSec protocol is the authentication and key exchange mechanism. This is accomplished using a pair of protocols.

NOTE

Replaying——Why Is It Bad? You may have noticed that replaying has been included several times as part of the discussion of IPSec. Replaying is a somewhat obscure method for obtaining access to a system. A replay attack becomes an issue because TCP/IP protocols such as Network File System (NFS) have no mechanisms to determine whether a packet is being replayed—even after several hours. Fortunately, the anti-replay mechanisms in IPSec make a replay attack a virtual impossibility.

Internet Security Key Association Key Management Protocol (ISAKMP/Oakley)

ISAKMP/Oakley (also known as ISAKMP/IKE, for Internet Key Exchange) provides the mechanism that allows disparate VPN servers to share encryption key information and make the IPSec protocol practical in today's environment. Before secured data can be exchanged between VPN servers, a contract between the two computers must be established. In this contract, called SA, both computers agree on how to exchange and protect information. In other words, the two servers (or the server and client computer) need to agree on how to encrypt and decrypt the data to be sent.

To enable this process, the IPSec protocol uses a standard process to build this contract between the two computers. This process combines the ISAKMP and the Oakley key generation protocol. ISAKMP provides the centralized security association management while Oakley actually generates and manages the encryption keys used to secure the information.

The final piece of this puzzle that needs to be covered is Microsoft's IPSec/L2TP implementation, which adds an additional tunneling protocol to the IPSec implementation.

L2TP and IPSec

The major difference between the ESP tunnel and the L2TP is that the L2TP tunnel performs at Layer 2 of the OSI Model, the data link layer. This allows L2TP to tunnel additional protocols, such as IPX or NetBEUI. IPSec's ESP tunneling protocol will tunnel only the TCP/IP protocol, based on the standard. When L2TP and IPSec are used in combination to provide a secured tunnel, the original packet header is used to carry the packet's source and final destination, whereas the tunnel packet's IP header might contain the address of an IPSec gateway. The L2TP header carries the information needed to route the packet over the network. The PPP header within the encapsulated packet identifies the protocol of the original packet. In other words, when using L2TP to transfer data, IPSec is used to secure the tunnel. L2TP encapsulates the packet in a PPP frame. The PPP frame is then added to a UDP-type frame assigned to port 1701. UDP, which is part of the TCP/IP suite, qualifies for IPSec to secure the contents; thus, the contents of L2TP are secure regardless of the originating protocol and/or data type.

One additional benefit of the L2TP method is that you do have a choice of additional encryption algorithms for securing the data.

Now that you have a basic introduction to the benefits and background of the IPSec protocol, you are ready to look at working with IPSec.

Enabling IPSec Through a Policy

Before enabling IPSec on your local computer or domain, you'll want to configure IPSec through policies. An IPSec policy is a set of rules that define how and when communication is secured between two end points. This is done through the configuration of various rules. Each rule contains a collection of actions and filters that begin when they encounter end points that match.

Policies allow you to quickly and easily configure IPSec based on the settings required within your organization. Step by Step 4.10 shows how to configure your first IPSec policy.

NOTE

L2TP Tunneling——Part of the Standard? If you've read the RFP for IPSec, you may have noticed that L2TP is not mentioned anywhere in the document. L2TP is Microsoft's addition to IPSec. At the writing of this book, Microsoft was petitioning the IPSec working group to include its L2TP variant in the next revision of the specification. At this time, there is no indication whether Microsoft will be successful in its efforts. However, L2TP is a joint venture between Microsoft and Cisco, and Cisco has been heavily involved in the development of the IPSec specification. Time will tell whether Microsoft is successful.

STEP BY STEP

4.10 Creating an IPSec Policy

1. Choose Start, Run; then type MMC and press Enter. The Console menu opens (see Figure 4.21).

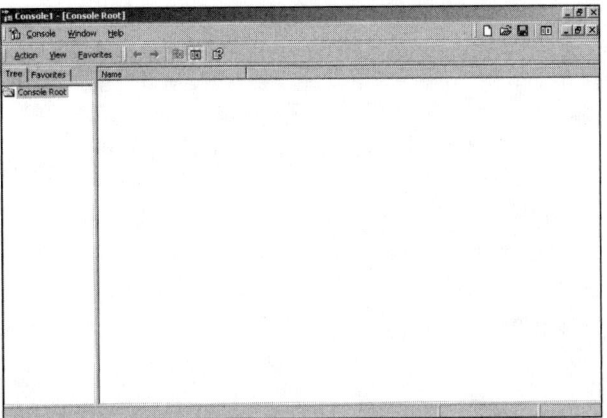

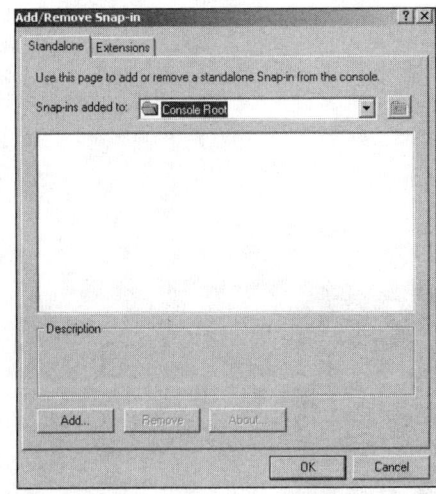

FIGURE 4.21
Running MMC /s from the Run prompt will bring up a blank Microsoft Management Console (MMC).

2. From the Console menu, choose Add/Remove Snap-in. The Add/Remove Snap-in dialog box appears (see Figure 4.22). Click the Add button (see Figure 4.23).

3. From the list of components, choose the IP Security Policy Management and then click Add.

4. Choose Local Computer. Notice that the other options include Domain Policy, Manage a Domain Policy for Another Domain, or another computer. Click Finish, Close, and OK to return to MMC. You can also access the IP Security Policies by opening the Local Security Policy console by going to Start, Programs, Administrative Tools, Local Security Policy. This console is shown in Figure 4.24.

continues

FIGURE 4.22
You can use the Add/Remove snap-in dialog box to create your own customized MMC.

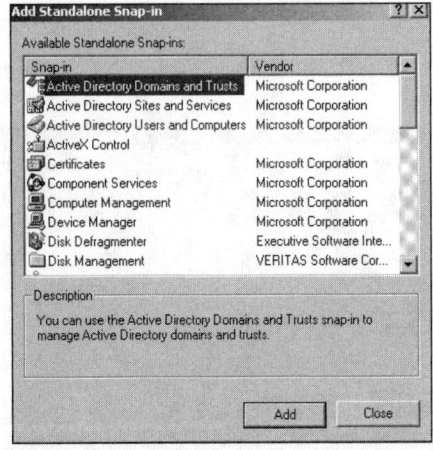

FIGURE 4.23
Select the components you want to add to the MMC.

continued

FIGURE 4.24
The Local Security Policy console gives you
access to all the Windows 2000 security policies, including the IP Security policies.

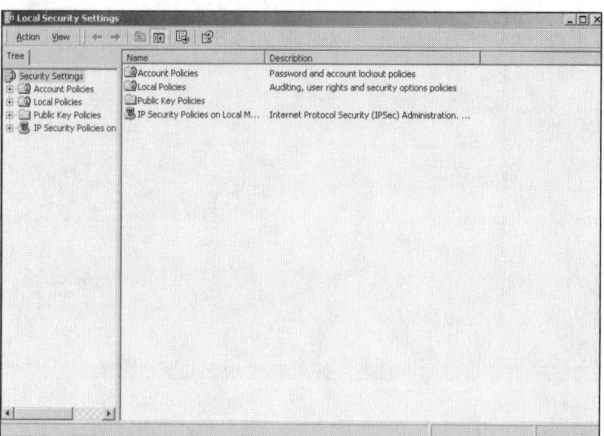

5. From the console tree, right-click the IP Security Policies
and select Create IP Security Policy. The IP Security
Policy Wizard opens (see Figure 4.25).

6. Click Next to open the IP Security Policy Name dialog
box (see Figure 4.26). Enter a descriptive name and a
description of the policy. This aids in managing policies as
the number gets greater.

7. Click Next to open the Requests for Secure Communication
dialog box (see Figure 4.27). This allows you to set the new
policy as the default policy for any secure communications
requests. The Activate the Default Response Rule option will
always be selected by default.

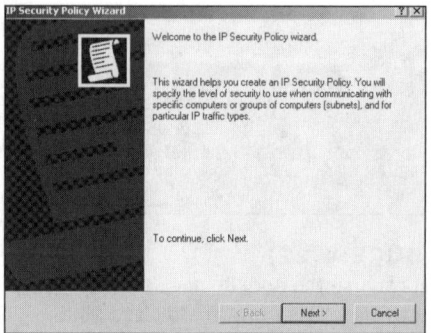

FIGURE 4.25
The IP Security Policy Wizard guides you
through creating IP Security Policies.

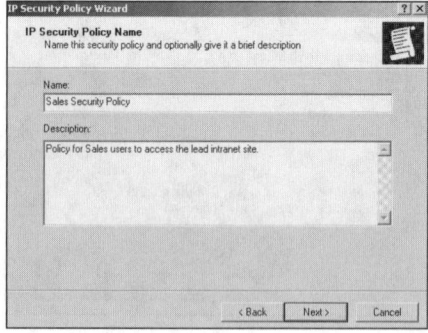

FIGURE 4.26
The IP Security Policy Name dialog box
allows you to give each policy a name and
a description.

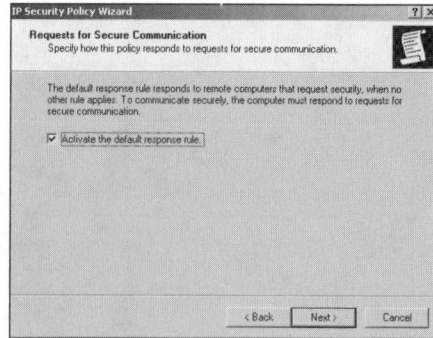

FIGURE 4.27
The Requests for Secure Communication
dialog box allows you to configure whether
the policy will be the default for secure
communications requests.

8. Click Next to open the Default Response Rule Authentication Method dialog box (see Figure 4.28). This dialog allows you to configure the default authentication method for secure communications requests. Leave the Windows 2000 default (Kerberos V5 Protocol) selected. You can also use a certificate or configure a string to be used to protect the IPSec key exchange.

9. Click Next to go to the Completing the IP Security Policy Wizard dialog box (see Figure 4.29). You will be offered the opportunity to edit the policy properties after the wizard is completed.

10. Leaving the Edit Properties option selected, click Finish to complete the wizard and go to the Security Policy Properties dialog box (see Figure 4.30.) Note that all IP traffic requires security to be accepted. Take a moment to view the other settings for the client computer and server settings as well.

11. Click OK to close the properties and return to the Local Security Policy console. Notice that your new policy is now listed in the right pane. To activate the policy, right-click the policy and select Assign. The Policy Assigned entry will go from No to Yes, and the policy will be active.

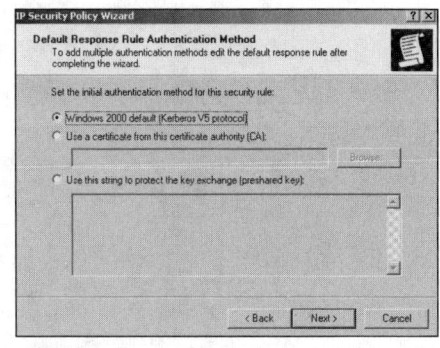

FIGURE 4.28
The Default Response Rule Authentication Method dialog box allows you to configure how secure communications requests will need to authenticate using the default rule.

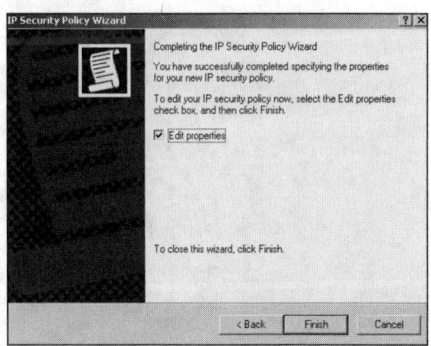

FIGURE 4.29
After the IP Security Policy Wizard is complete, you will need to edit the policy properties to customize it further.

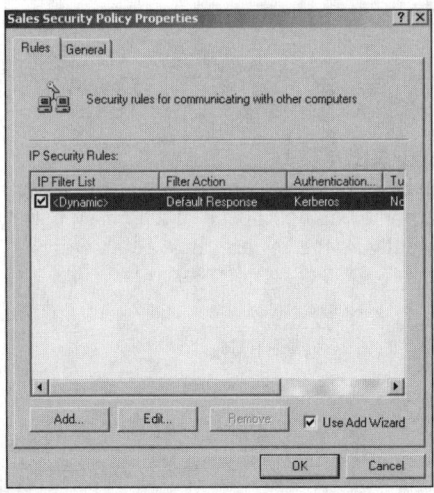

FIGURE 4.30
The Security Policy Properties allows you to fine-tune the configuration of your IPSec security policy.

CUSTOMIZING IPSEC

The next piece of the IPSec puzzle is how to customize the IPSec configuration once you have it installed and configured. To that end, let's look at the IP Security Policy Properties, which is used to manage all IPSec connections to the Windows 2000 server. The IP Security Policy Properties are broken into two tabs, the Rules tab (refer to Figure 4.30) and the General tab (see Figure 4.31).

Let's look at the Rules tab first. The IP Security Rules window lists all the IP Security Rules that are active for that policy. Editing a rule opens the Edit Rule Properties dialog box, shown in Figure 4.32. There are three tabs for this section:

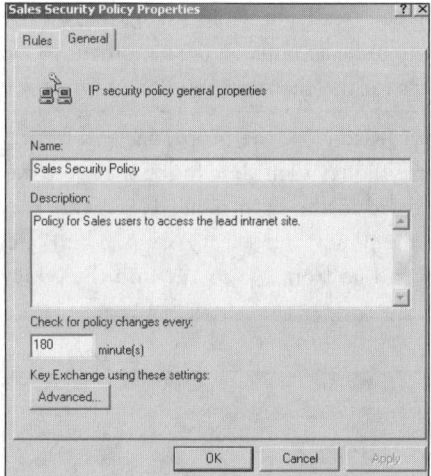

FIGURE 4.31
The General tab not only allows you to change the name and description of the policy, but also to configure the key exchange parameters.

◆ **Security Methods.** The Security Methods tab allows you to configure what security methods can be used when negotiating with another computer to create an IPSec tunnel. You can not only configure the security methods to be used, but you can also customize the order of precedence for the security methods.

◆ **Authentication Methods.** The Authentication Methods tab (see Figure 4.33) allows you to determine whether Kerberos, a certificate, or a string will be used to protect the key exchange. You can also have multiple methods and configure the order of precedence.

◆ **Connection Type.** The Connection Type tab (see Figure 4.34) determines for what types of connections the rule will be applied: LAN, Remote Access, or All Network Connections.

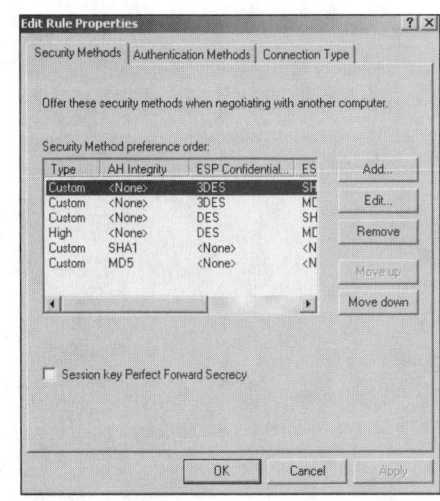

FIGURE 4.32
The Edit Rule Properties dialog box allows you to customize an active IP Security Rule.

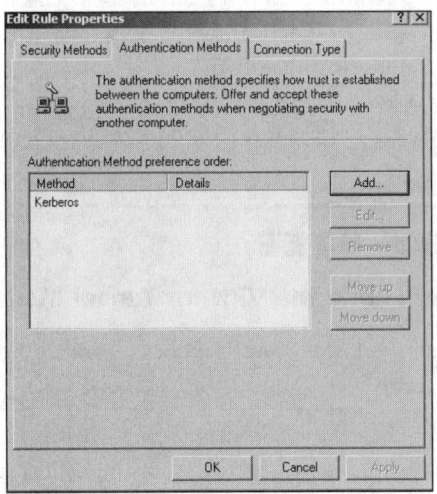

FIGURE 4.33
Configuring the Authentication Methods is a key piece of a secure IPSec implementation.

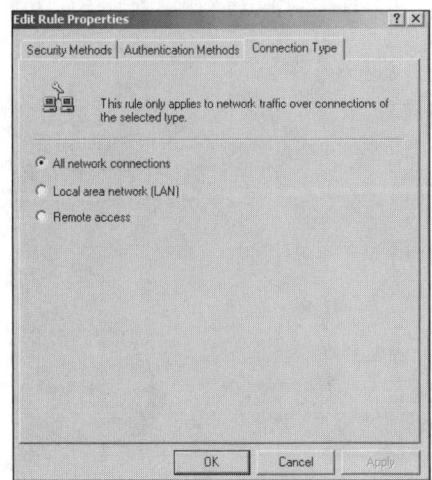

FIGURE 4.34
The Connection Type tab allows you to decide on what network interfaces this policy will be active.

You have seen the two types of IPSec implementation (transport mode and tunnel mode) and learned how to create an IPSec security policy. As discussed earlier, configuring a Windows 2000 server to use transport mode for IPSec is as simple as installing Routing and Remote Access and enabling the VPN. L2TP/IPSec (transport mode) is enabled by default. In cases in which the Windows 2000 server must interoperate with third-party routers or gateways that do not support L2TP/IPSec, you need to do some customizing to use tunnel mode.

Before we get into the specific steps, we should look at the general steps required for this to work.

1. You must have an IPSec policy, such as the one you created in Step by Step 4.10.

2. You must build two filters: one to match packets going from the local network to the remote network (tunnel 1), and one to match packets from the remote network to the local network.

3. You need to configure a filter action to specify how the tunnel should be secured. Each tunnel is represented by a rule, so you need two rules for this to work.

To configure your VPN for tunnel mode, do the following steps.

STEP BY STEP

4.11 Configuring the VPN for Tunnel Mode

1. Open the Local Security Policy console by going to Start, Program Files, Administrative Tools, Local Security Policy.

2. Right-click the IP Security Policy created in Step by Step 4.10 and select Properties from the context menu. The New IP Security Policy Properties dialog box opens (see Figure 4.35).

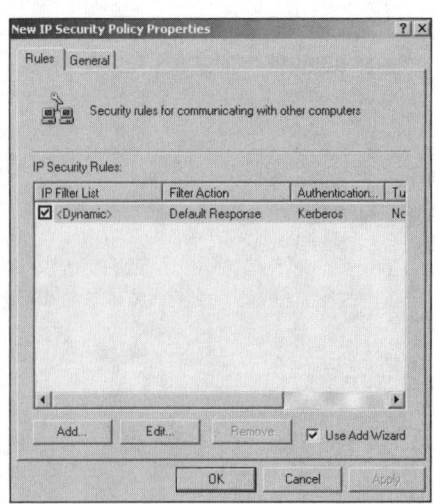

FIGURE 4.35
IPSec policy rules are added, modified, and deleted from the Rules tab.

3. Deselect the Use Add Wizard option, if necessary, and then click Add to create a new rule. The New Rule Properties dialog box shown in Figure 4.36 opens.

4. On the IP Filter List tab, click Add. The IP Filter List dialog box shown in Figure 4.37 opens.

5. Type an appropriate name and description for the filter list. Deselect the Use Add Wizard option, if necessary, and then click Add. The Filter Properties dialog box shown in Figure 4.38 opens.

6. In the Source Address pull-down list, select a specific IP subnet and then fill in the IP Address and Subnet Mask boxes to reflect the local network. In the Destination Address pull-down list, do the same but use the IP address and subnet mask of the remote network. Deselect the Mirrored option.

continues

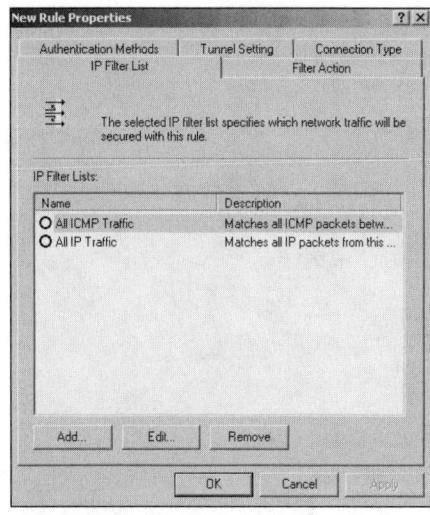

FIGURE 4.36
You will need to manually configure the rules to configure a tunnel mode VPN connection.

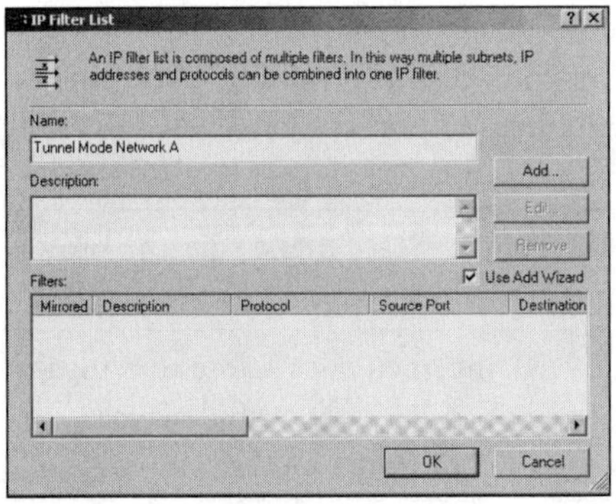

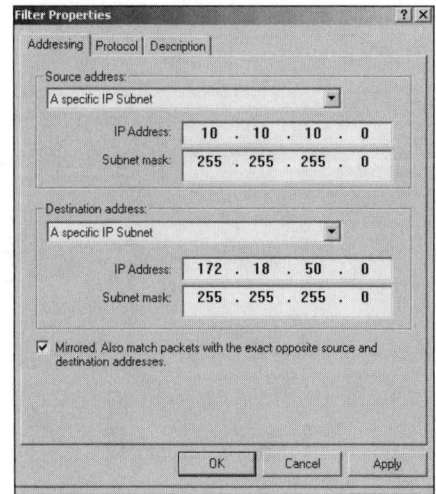

FIGURE 4.37
The IP Filter List dialog box enables you to group a list of filters into a single IP filter.

FIGURE 4.38
You will need to configure the addressing and protocol(s) and provide a description for each filter you add.

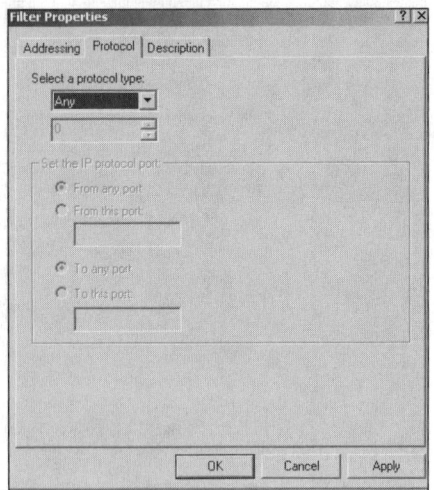

FIGURE 4.39
Be sure that the protocol type Any is selected. IPSec tunnels won't support protocol-specific filters.

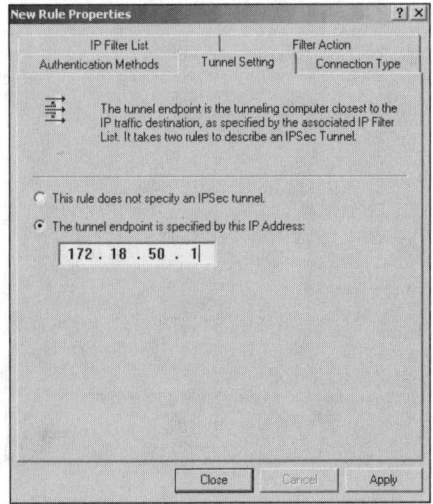

FIGURE 4.40
You will need to specify the endpoint address of the remote gateway.

continued

7. On the Protocol tab shown in Figure 4.39, make sure the protocol type is set to Any.

8. Click OK, and then click Close to return to the New Rule Properties dialog box. You have successfully created the filter from the local network to the remote network.

9. In the New IP Security Policy Properties dialog box, deselect the Use Add Wizard option, and then click Add to create a new rule. The New Rule Properties dialog box opens (refer to Figure 4.35).

10. On the IP Filter List tab, click Add. The IP Filter List dialog box opens.

11. Type an appropriate name and description for the filter list. Deselect the Use Add Wizard option and then click Add. The Filter Properties dialog box opens.

12. In the Source Address pull-down list, select a specific IP subnet, and then fill in the IP Address and Subnet Mask boxes to reflect the remote network. In the Destination Address pull-down list, do the same but use the IP address and Subnet mask of the local network. Deselect the Mirrored option.

13. On the Protocol tab, make sure the protocol type is set to Any.

14. Click OK, and then click Close to return to the New Rule Properties. You have successfully created the filter from the remote network to the local network.

15. On the IP Filter List tab, click the filter list you created. Select the Tunnel Setting tab shown in Figure 4.40, select The Tunnel Endpoint Is Specified By This IP Address option, and then type the IP address assigned to the third-party gateway external network adapter (the other endpoint).

16. On the Connection Type tab (refer to Figure 4.34), select the All Network Connections option.

17. On the Filter Action tab (shown in Figure 4.41), deselect the Use Add Wizard option, if necessary, and then click Add to create a new filter action. The New Filter Action Properties dialog box opens (see Figure 4.42).

18. Make sure that the Negotiate Security option is selected, and deselect the Accept Unsecured Communication, But Always Respond Using IPSec option. Click Add, and keep the default High (ESP) option selected on the New Security Method dialog box. Click OK.

19. On the General tab, type a name for the new filter action, and then click OK.

20. Select the filter action you just created. On the Authentication Methods tab, click Add and configure the authentication method to Preshared Key, and then click Close.

21. In the IPSec Policy Properties dialog box, click Add to create a new rule, and on the IP Filter List tab, click the filter list you created.

22. On the Tunnel Setting tab (refer to Figure 4.40), select the Tunnel Endpoint Is Specified by This IP Address option, and then enter the IP address assigned to the Windows 2000 gateway external network adapter.

23. On the Connection Type tab, select the All Network Connections option, and then on the Filter Action tab, select the filter action you created.

24. On the Authentication Methods tab, configure the same method used in the first rule (the same method must be used in both rules).

25. Click OK, make sure both rules you created are enabled in your policy, and then click OK again to return to the Local Security Policy console.

Congratulations. You just customized the rules and filter actions you need to create a tunnel mode Windows 2000 VPN connection.

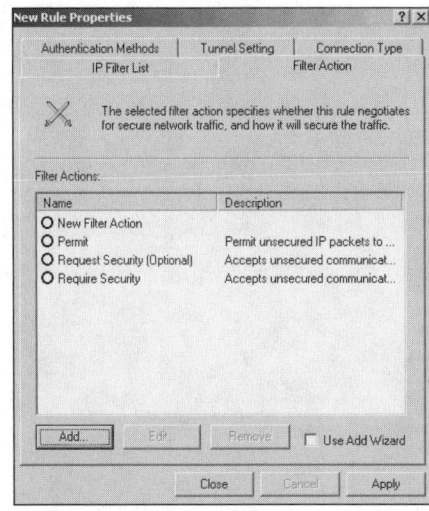

FIGURE 4.41
If you do not create a new filter action, all data will pass without any security.

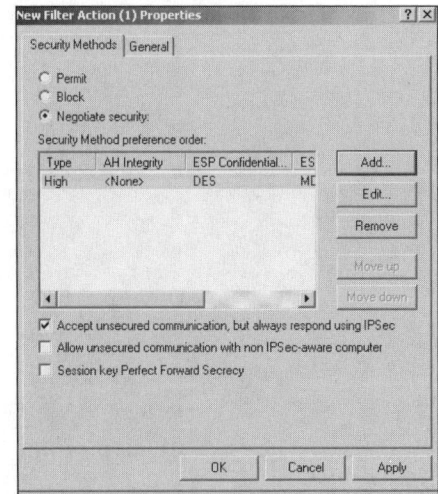

FIGURE 4.42
From the New Filter Action Properties dialog box, you can configure the Security Preference order and specify the types of connections that will be accepted by the server.

Managing and Monitoring IPSec

The last piece of the puzzle is managing and monitoring IPSec. The nice thing about Microsoft's implementation of IPSec is that it is implemented as a remote access technology. A lot of the information you need to manage and monitor your IPSec connections can be found in the Routing and Remote Access console.

Step by Step 4.12 shows how to see who is connected to an IPSec port.

STEP BY STEP

4.12 Monitoring IPSec Connections

1. Go to Start, Programs, Administrative Tools, Routing and Remote Access. The Routing and Remote Access console opens (see Figure 4.43).

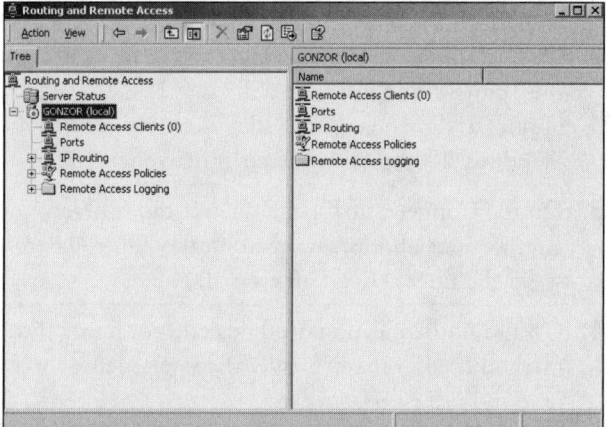

FIGURE 4.43
The Routing and Remote Access console is used to manage all remote access connectivity.

2. From the Tree pane, select the Ports entry. All the PPTP and L2TP ports will be listed in the right pane. The L2TP ports will show any IPSec connections. Double-click the port you want to get a status from, and you will get information similar to the information displayed in Figure 4.44.

The other method of monitoring IPSec is to ensure that the log file is configured correctly. Step by Step 4.13 shows how to set the log file parameters.

STEP BY STEP

4.13 Configuring Remote Access Logging

1. Go to Start, Programs, Administrative Tools, Routing and Remote Access. The Routing and Remote Access console opens.

2. From the Tree pane, select the Remote Access Logging entry. Right-click and from the context menu, select Properties. The Local File Properties dialog box opens (see Figure 4.45).

continues

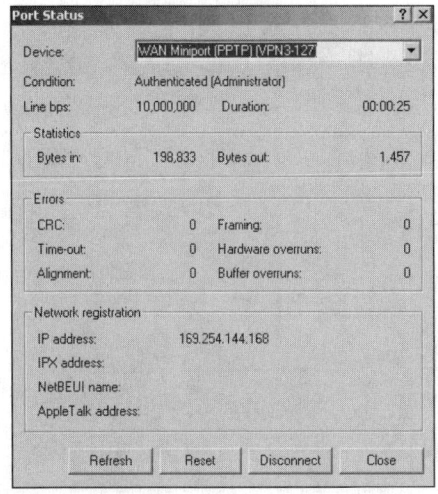

FIGURE 4.44
The PPTP and L2TP ports show the status of any VPN connections.

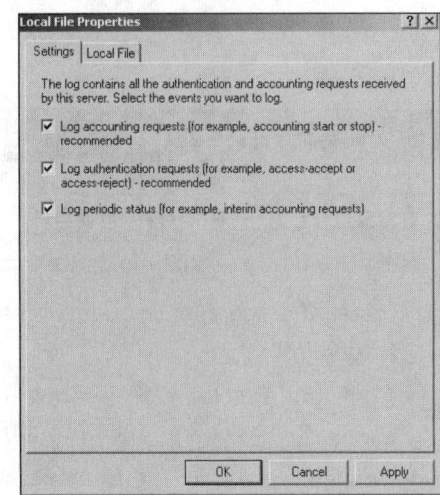

FIGURE 4.45
The Local File Properties dialog box allows you to configure the remote access logging.

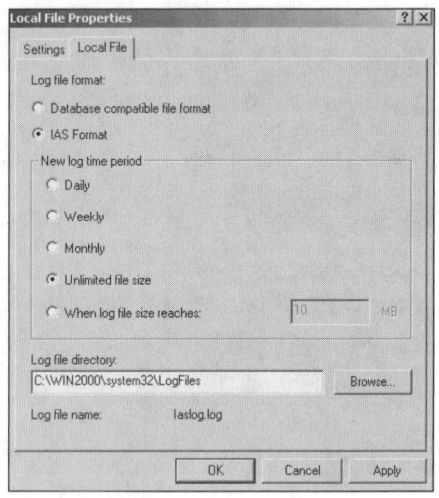

FIGURE 4.46
Depending on the number of connections, you may want to log everything to a single file (small number of connections), or you may want a new log file every day (larger environments).

continued

3. Under the Settings tab, select Log Accounting Requests, Log Authentication Requests, and Log Periodic Status to receive the maximum amount of information.

4. Under the Local File tab (see Figure 4.46), you can configure the format for the log file, the frequency a new log file is created, and the path to the log file.

Now that you know how to manage and monitor IPSec, let's look at the Case Study.

CASE STUDY: MORGAN ENTERPRISES

ESSENCE OF THE CASE

Here are the essential elements in this case:

▶ Install the appropriate protocol for the environment.

▶ Configure a method for securing the data between the sites on their network.

▶ Configure a way for the NetWare servers to remain active in this domain.

▶ Configure a method for the dial-up client computers to be securely authenticated.

SCENARIO

Morgan Enterprises is a conglomerate of companies consisting of publications, commercial printers, investment companies, insurance brokerages, and distribution centers. The network is being upgraded from Windows NT, where each division has its own domain.

The conglomerate already has a plan in place to flatten the domains and make one domain through Windows 2000. The system administrators are somewhat concerned, however, because they've never connected all the networks to each other in Windows NT 4. They need a protocol for connectivity, but the data must remain secure and reliable.

CASE STUDY: MORGAN ENTERPRISES

Many sales people from all divisions travel with laptops and need to dial in to the office and access resources. The authentication between the dial-up client computers and the server must be secured to prevent unauthorized users from entering the network.

In addition, two NetWare 3 servers are in the Texas office that must remain available to users from the Dallas office.

All client computers will be using Windows 2000 Professional, and all servers, except the NetWare servers, will be using Windows 2000 Advanced Server.

ANALYSIS

The first step is to install a reliable, routable protocol for Morgan Enterprises. At first glance, IPX may be tempting because it is routable, it can be secured over the Internet, and it is needed by the users in Dallas for connectivity to the NetWare

servers. However, a network of this magnitude in a Windows 2000 environment is more suited for TCP/IP.

To secure the data between sites, IPSec should be implemented. The protocol L2TP will be used to compress and encrypt the data between the sites, using the Internet as the backbone.

In the Dallas office, you can use NWLink for the servers that need to connect to the NetWare servers. The recommendation is that Morgan Enterprises upgrade these servers to Windows 2000—or use a connection tool such as GSNW at the very least.

Finally, for the dial-up client computers, implement a security host, such as the security card, which has a changing number in sync with the software on the server. As users dial in to the server, they'll be required to enter the number on the secure card before being able to provide their Windows 2000 authentication information.

CHAPTER SUMMARY

To have a secure, reliable, routable network, effective planning should be the first thing you implement.

Within Windows 2000, TCP/IP is installed by default. We've seen that so many features of Windows 2000 rely on TCP/IP. TCP/IP requires a valid IP address, subnet mask, default gateway, and DNS servers. This information may be entered manually at each client computer and server or, preferably, through DHCP. DHCP assigns the host an IP address as it's needed by the client computer.

KEY TERMS

- TCP/IP
- IP address
- subnet mask
- DNS server
- NWLink
- frame type

CHAPTER SUMMARY

KEY TERMS

- network binding
- provider connections
- TCP/IP filter
- Kerberos V5
- L2TP
- Network Monitor
- baseline
- IPSec
- tunneling

If you're mixing Windows 2000 with older NetBIOS-reliant OSs, chances are that you'll be using WINS as well. WINS resolves NetBIOS names, such as Computer5, to an IP address. You can access the WINS properties through the Advanced tab of TCP/IP Properties.

When integrating with NetWare, you need information about the network number and frame type that the NetWare servers will require.

Network Bindings are a way of ordering network providers, protocols, and connections in the order in which they will most likely be used by the OS.

Kerberos V5 Authentication is the protocol Windows 2000 uses by default. No configuration is required to use this security protocol with Windows 2000. Computers in a trusted MIT-realm can be allowed to access resources in the local Kerberos (Windows 2000) domain.

VPNs are a way of connecting networks while, most likely, using the existing structure of the Internet as their backbone. IPSec can be coupled with VPNs to ensure quality and guarantee delivery of packets.

As a network grows, so does the amount of traffic created. Administrators need to monitor this traffic through Network Monitor. Network Monitor allows you to capture real-time activity, create filters on the type of protocols you would like to view, and then save that information to a file.

Keep in mind that the Network Monitor included with Windows 2000 is not the full Network Monitor. The full Network Monitor is included with SMS.

APPLY YOUR KNOWLEDGE

Exercises

4.1 Testing TCP/IP

This exercise guides you through the process of retrieving IP address information. Then you use a few command-line entries to test the configuration and connectivity of the IP address.

Estimated Time: 5 minutes

1. Click Start, Run, enter CMD, and then press Enter.

2. At the command prompt, enter the command **IPCONFIG** and press Enter.

3. What is your IP address?

4. What is your subnet mask?

5. Can you see the IP address of the DNS server?

6. Enter **Ipconfig /all**. What additional information can you now see?

7. Enter **PING 127.0.0.1/**. This is the special loopback test that tells you whether your modem is dead, just playing sick, or hopefully, just fine.

8. Enter **PING XX**, where *XX* is your favorite Web site.

9. If you have another computer on this network, ping the IP address of that computer.

10. Finally, ping the name of the computer.

4.2 Creating a TCP/IP Packet Filter

This exercise walks you through the process of creating a TCP/IP filter on your computer.

Estimated Time: 20 minutes

1. Open Control Panel and then open the Network and Dial-up Connections dialog box.

2. Right-click the Local Area Connection and choose Properties.

3. Click IP and then choose Properties.

4. Click the Advanced tab.

5. In the Advanced TCP/IP Settings, click the Options tab.

6. Choose TCP/IP Filtering and then choose Properties.

7. Click the option button next to Permit Only for TCP Ports, and then click the Add button.

8. Enter **port 23** for Telnet and **port 80** for Web Server.

9. Click the option button next to Permit Only for UDP Ports, and then click the Add button.

10. Enter **port 53** for DNS and **port 161** for SNMP.

11. Click the option button next to Permit Only for IP Protocols, and then click the Add button.

12. Enter **2** for IGMP and then choose OK.

13. Choose OK throughout the dialog boxes to approve your changes. You'll need to restart your computer to test the changes.

14. After your computer has restarted, go to another computer on the network. Open a command prompt and ping the IP address of the server that has the IP filtering configured.

15. Were you able to ping the computer?

16. Open TCP/IP Filtering on the original computer again. In the Permit Only IP Protocol section, add **1** for ICMP. Approve these settings and restart.

17. Go to another computer on the network. Are you able to ping the computer now?

APPLY YOUR KNOWLEDGE

18. Return once more to the original computer and remove all the IP packet filters. Approve your changes, reboot, and test the PING command now.

4.3 Capturing and Filtering Network Traffic

This exercise walks you through the mechanics of capturing network traffic through Network Monitor. Then you'll create a filter to extract only the packets you want to examine. This exercise presumes you have at least two computers on a local network.

Estimated Time: 20 minutes

1. Click Start, Programs, Administrative Tools, and choose Network Monitor.

2. From the Capture menu, choose Start. Packets sent to and from this computer will then be captured.

3. Switch to another computer and browse the resources on this computer.

4. From the computer running Network Monitor, browse the resources on another computer in the network.

5. Ping the computer running Network Monitor.

6. From the Capture menu, choose Stop and View to display the contents of the capture.

7. Scroll through the list of packets captured. You should see Broadcasts, ICMP, ARP, and other protocols.

8. To set a filter on the captured packets, click the button on the toolbar that looks like a funnel, or choose Filter from the Display menu.

9. The Display Filter window appears. Double-click the value Protocol=Any. This setting means to capture all protocols. The Expression window appears.

10. On the Protocol tab, click the button to Disable All.

11. From the list of disabled protocols, find and select ICMP, and then choose Enable. Click OK to approve this single protocol.

12. Choose OK again to set the filter into play.

13. The list of ICMP packets is displayed. Double-click an ICMP packet to see the details on the packet.

14. What are the ICMP packets sending? HINT: Look at the ICMP:Echo and notice the binary contents.

15. What is this ICMP packet responsible for? If you said PING, you're correct!

16. Take a moment to create some other filters and examine the details and the contents of the binary information.

Review Questions

1. What are three requirements for a valid IP address in a Windows 2000 environment?

2. How does TCP/IP know if the packets are local to this network or need to be forwarded to another network?

3. Why should a company choose to use DHCP over manually assigning IP addresses?

4. Why is it important to have a DNS server's IP address for a client computer in a Windows 2000 network?

5. What is NWLink used for?

APPLY YOUR KNOWLEDGE

6. Why is a matching frame type important for NWLink?

7. Why should a network administrator be concerned about bindings?

8. What must an administrator do to enable Kerberos Authentication in a Windows 2000 domain?

9. What is a VPN?

10. What is a baseline and why is it important to create one?

11. Why is IPSec so important in a routed environment?

12. What is tunneling?

Exam Questions

1. You are the network consultant for New Riders Distributors. This company is currently composed of one Windows 2000 domain consisting of two domain controllers and 139 Windows 2000 Professional workstations. All 139 workstations are connected to the two servers through a LAN in the office building in Santa Fe. Your client connects to the Internet through a T1 line in the building. New Riders Distributors has just acquired another distribution firm, which has an office in San Antonio. The San Antonio firm is using both NetWare servers and a Windows 2000 domain, and currently connects to the Internet through a fractional T1 connection. Your task is to connect the Windows 2000 domains and

NetWare resources between the two locations. Data security and price are issues. Of the following, choose the best solution for your client:

A. Connect the two domains with a private leased line.

B. Connect the two domains with a private leased line. Add NWLink to the office in Santa Fe.

C. Connect the two domains through a VPN. Implement IPSec and L2TP to encrypt network protocols on both ends. Add NWLink at the Santa Fe office.

D. Connect the two domains through a VPN. Implement IPSec and L2TP to encrypt network protocols on both ends. You do not need to add NWLink at the Santa Fe office because IPSec will convert all packets to TCP/IP.

2. Maria is a LAN administrator at a manufacturing company and is planning her network configuration for a Windows 2000 domain she will be implementing. The domain will consist of 8 locations, 16 Windows 2000 servers (10 of which will be domain controllers), and 862 Windows 2000 Professional Workstations. She will be using TCP/IP in this routed environment, and has decided to use four DHCP servers for fault tolerance across the network. Her supervisor, Paulo, is upset that Maria wants to use DHCP. He insists that it's too hard to configure, causes downtime, and won't allow an administrator to know who has what IP address the way that a simple spreadsheet

APPLY YOUR KNOWLEDGE

of computer names and IP addresses would. What are some arguments Maria could offer to squelch his claims? Of the following, choose all that apply:

A. DHCP can show you what computer is assigned a given IP address.

B. DHCP actually saves time as computers move from segment to segment.

C. DHCP is complex and somewhat hard to configure.

D. In Maria's plan, downtime would be at a minimum because she's distributed the available scopes across four DHCP servers.

3. You are a LAN administrator for your company. Your task is to configure the IP addresses of your network. You decide to implement DHCP to automate the process and ensure less downtime. You have decided, however, to manually enter the IP address of certain hosts in your network. Of the following, which would be good candidates to enter the IP address of a computer manually? Choose all that apply:

A. A laptop that moves from segment to segment through the week

B. A DNS server

C. An Exchange server

D. A print server located on the largest subnet

4. Janice, a user from the accounting department, calls you, the LAN administrator, to report that she's having a tough time connecting to resources on your Windows 2000 domain. You ask for more information and Janice reveals that she is trying to connect to a server in Washington. Other users can connect to the server, but she

cannot. She can ping the IP address of other hosts on her segment, her default gateway, and even the IP address of the server in Washington, but when she uses the server's host name to enter the name of the server, she cannot connect. What do you suspect is the problem?

A. Janice has a blank or invalid DNS server IP address.

B. Janice has a blank or invalid subnet mask.

C. Janice has a faulty network adapter card.

D. Janice needs to renew her IP address by running the command `ipconfig /release` and then `ipconfig .renew`.

5. You are the network administrator for Wright Brothers Shipping. Your Windows 2000 domain consists of three domain controllers, 567 Windows 2000 Professional workstations, and three NetWare servers you'll be integrating with. You've added the NWLink protocol to one of your domain controllers and have successfully configured GSNW with two of three NetWare servers. One server, however, cannot be found. Of the following, which is the most likely explanation of why the NetWare 3 server cannot be found, but the two NetWare 4 servers were?

A. NetWare 3 servers will not work with GSNW.

B. NetWare 3 servers use a frame type 802.3. Manually enter the frame types.

C. NetWare 3 servers use a frame type 802.2. Manually enter the frame types.

D. Enable SAP on the GSNW server before adding the NetWare 3 server.

APPLY YOUR KNOWLEDGE

6. You are the consultant for Best Importers. Its TCP/IP network consists of eight domain controllers in three locations, four NetWare servers (accessed through NWLINK and GSNW; these are all located in Boston), and 431 Windows 2000 Professional workstations. Pierre, the owner of Best Importers, has reported to you that the network seems slower than it should be—especially after Alice added NWLink and GSNW on all the servers. He's asked you to inspect the Windows 2000 servers to see if they're configured properly. He wants you to make recommendations on how to speed up the network without spending any additional monies. Of the following, which choice would be most beneficial to this company?

   A. Configure the provider binding order to use the Microsoft Windows Network first and NetWare Network second on all servers.

   B. Configure the Provider Order to use the Microsoft Windows Network first, and then NetWare Network second on all servers. Configure NWLink to be used only with GSNW and not with each network component.

   C. Remove GSNW and NWLink from all servers except for one. Access the NetWare resources through this one server with GSNW and NWLink. Configure the network provider to be Microsoft Network first and then NetWare Networks.

   D. Remove GSNW and NWLink from all servers except for one. Access the NetWare resources through this one server with GSNW and NWLink. Configure the network provider to be Microsoft Network first and then NetWare Networks. Disable NWLink from all network components except for GSNW.

7. You've been hired as a network administrator by the Freedom Bell Agency. Your Windows 2000 domain consists of two domain controllers, 18 Windows 2000 Professional workstations on the LAN, and 223 Windows 2000 Professional laptops that the sales reps use to dial in to the LAN. A major concern with management is to resolve a way to guarantee that users who dial in to the server are who they say they are. Management is worried that should a sales rep lose a laptop, an unauthorized user could dial in to the network. Of the following choices, which would resolve the problem of unauthorized users dialing in to the network?

   A. Issue strong passwords.

   B. Make users change their passwords often.

   C. Issue users a security card that displays a new code every minute. The code must match the code on the server software for the user to be able to authenticate.

   D. Issue users a mobile phone. All dial-up connections would be configured through the mobile phone.

8. You are the network administrator for Office Products USA. Your domain consists of two domain controllers and 176 Windows 2000 Professional workstations. You've decided to implement Kerberos V5 in your network. What steps must you complete to implement the security authentication protocol?

   A. Add the Protocol through the Network and Dial-up Connections applet.

   B. Add the Protocol through the Local Area Connection in the Network and Dial-up Connections applet.

C. Add the Kerberos service through the Local Area Connection in the Network and Dial-up Connections applet.

D. Do nothing; it's installed when a Windows 2000 domain is created.

9. Maria is the network administrator for Fielding Gloves. Her Windows 2000 domain consists of two sites, four domain controllers, and 762 Windows 2000 Professional workstations. Most of her domain members are in Boston, but about 200 are in Woburn. She would like to connect these two in a more cost-effective, but secure, solution than the private leased line between the sites she is using now. What Windows 2000 solution would be best for her situation?

A. Add IPSec and create a dial-on-demand router.

B. Create a VPN using the Internet as a backbone.

C. Create a VPN and implement IP filtering on the routers.

D. Create a VPN and implement L2TP using the Internet as the backbone.

10. You are the network consultant for a military subcontractor. Its network consists of two domains: one in Chicago and the other in Knoxville. Each domain has two domain controllers and close to 75 Windows 2000 Professional workstations each. You've been hired to help create a VPN between the company's office in Chicago and its office in Knoxville. The office in Chicago is located in a military base and uses ATM for remote access with the Knoxville office. Lamont, the team leader for the subcontractors, would like to use the security features of L2TP with his current network. You inform him that, unfortunately, he cannot. Why?

A. L2TP requires IPSec. IPSec is not available on ATM.

B. L2TP is not available for ATM, but Internet tunneling only.

C. Military domains (.mil) are excluded from IPSec.

D. Military domains are excluded from L2TP because of federal restrictions on encryption of data.

11. You are a consultant for Albatross International. Its Windows 2000 domain consists of four domain controllers, 872 Windows 2000 Professional workstations, and a few Macintosh client computers that connect to one server occasionally. The company hired you to inspect its TCP/IP network to improve performance. Upon inspecting the network, you discover they've added these protocols to each server: services for Macintosh, NWLink, GSNW, DHCP (although only two are functional), NetBEUI and TCP/IP. Of the following recommendations, which would be the best solution for improving network performance?

A. Arrange the bindings to use the network providers from Microsoft Network and then Novell. Arrange the protocols on each component to be TCP/IP, NWLink, and then NetBEUI. Unbind NWLink and NetBEUI from the DHCP service.

B. Remove the GSNW and NWLink from all servers. Arrange the bindings for each component to use TCP/IP first and then NetBEUI.

C. Remove the following from all servers: GSNW, NWLink, and NetBEUI. Remove Services for Macintosh from all servers except for the server the Macs actually connect to.

APPLY YOUR KNOWLEDGE

D. Remove the following from all servers: GSNW, NWLink, and NetBEUI. Remove Services for Macintosh from all servers except for the server the Macs actually connect to. Remove the DHCP Server service from the two servers that are not currently functioning as DHCP servers.

12. Ralph is the network administrator for a Windows 2000 domain. His domain consists of three domain controllers and 87 Windows 2000 Professional workstations. He still has 75 Microsoft Windows NT 4 Workstations. All his computers are using TCP/IP. He would like to configure Network Monitor to track the activity of the NT 4 Workstations to see what impact they are having on his network, and then to predict what his network performance will be like after he gets approval to upgrade them. For some reason, Ralph is having difficulty configuring Network Monitor to capture frames to and from these NT 4 Workstations. What do you suspect is the problem?

   A. Ralph's network card is not in promiscuous mode.

   B. Ralph's Network Monitor is the Windows 2000 version that captures only the frames to and from this server.

   C. Ralph must create a filter to capture NT LanManager (NTLM) packets only from the specific IP addresses.

   D. Ralph is using IPSec with his Windows 2000 server, but not with his Microsoft Windows NT 4 Workstations. The unsecure packets are being discarded.

13. You are the administrator for a Windows 2000 domain. Your network consists of three domain controllers and 192 Windows 2000 Professional workstations spread across 4 subnets. You've added an SMS server to your environment and plan on using the Network Monitor included with SMS. What must you add to each of the Windows 2000 computers for the SMS monitor to be able to track their network activity?

   A. You must add IPSec with L2TP.

   B. You must add file and printer sharing for each workstation and create an SMS account in the Domain Administrators local group.

   C. You must add the Network Monitor driver on one PC per subnet.

   D. You must add the Network Monitor protocol.

14. You've just been hired as the network administrator for a large insurance brokerage in Atlanta. Its Windows 2000 network consists of eight domain controllers and 694 Microsoft Windows 2000 Professional workstations. In addition, nearly 400 Windows NT 4 Workstation computers are in the network. You've also discovered that three NetWare servers are being used for file and printer servers. All computers and servers are using TCP/IP. What should you do first in this environment before making any changes?

   A. Migrate the NetWare servers to Windows 2000.

   B. Implement IPSec.

   C. Create a network baseline.

   D. Upgrade the Windows NT 4 Workstation client computers to Windows 2000 Professional.

APPLY YOUR KNOWLEDGE

15. You are a security consultant for a financial agency. Its network uses TCP/IP and Windows 2000. Its domain consists of 18 domain controllers and 982 Windows 2000 Professional workstations. Many of the users use dial-up connections and leased lines to connect to their offices. Sal, the manager of security, has asked you to develop a plan that will allow for data to be secure on shared lines and between locales. What do you recommend?

   A. Implement smart cards to ensure authenticated users who are logging on from any location.

   B. Implement PPTP to use packet encapsulation.

   C. Implement IPSec and L2TP for all computers, including dial-up computers.

   D. Implement Kerberos V5 Authentication.

Answers to Review Questions

1. IP address, subnet mask, and default gateway.

2. The subnet mask defines the network ID portion of the IP address. If the destination of the packet has a different network ID, it is forwarded to the gateway.

3. DHCP allows the dynamic assignment of IP addresses and provides greater flexibility in address management. For example, a client computer using DHCP does not have a hard-coded IP address and can be moved to another network without having to modify the TCP/IP configuration.

4. A DNS server provides the capability of resolving hostnames to IP addresses. Without a DNS server, you would need to know the actual IP address of the target computer. Also, with Windows 2000 Active Directory and DHCP, DNS can be dynamically updated.

5. NWLink is the IPX/SPX compatible protocol used to communicate to NetWare servers.

6. NWLink must use a matching frame type to communicate with NetWare servers. If NWLink is configured with an incorrect frame type for the IPX network it is trying to access, it will not be able to communicate.

7. A network administrator should review what bindings are installed and modify the order in which the bindings are accessed so that the most frequently used one is accessed first. For example, if you primarily communicate with a NetWare network and only rarely access the Internet, you would want to move the NWLink protocol above the IP.

8. Nothing. Kerberos is implemented automatically with Windows 2000.

9. A VPN consists of two or more locations linked via a shared or public network, such as the Internet.

10. A baseline is a set of performance readings taken at a specific time and used to reference future readings to identify changes in performance.

11. IPSec provides data integrity between two host IDs. The data and identity is safe and kept from being changed or read by other users through intermediary software.

12. Tunneling is the process of encapsulating packets inside other packets for secure, private transmissions on LANs and WANs.

APPLY YOUR KNOWLEDGE

Answers to Exam Questions

1. **C.** Connect the two domains with a VPN. By implementing IPSec and L2TP, data is encrypted and encapsulated between the two networks. Only the Santa Fe office requires NWLink. You will then add GSNW to a server in Santa Fe, and users from both domains will access the resources through GSNW. For more information, see the section "VPNs."

2. **A, B, D.** DHCP can reveal what IP address any computer has been assigned. DHCP does save time as computers move from segment to segment. Downtime will be minimal, should a DHCP server go down, because Maria's plan has the scopes distributed across four servers. For more information, see the section "Configuring TCP/IP."

3. **B, C, D.** DNS servers require static IP addresses; typically, mail servers require static IP addresses. For more information, see the section "Configuring TCP/IP."

4. **A.** If Janice can successfully ping local and remote hosts, including the server she is trying to connect to, most likely she has either a missing DNS IP address or a DNS IP address that has been configured incorrectly. For more information, see the section "Configuring TCP/IP."

5. **B.** When you are having difficulty connecting to a NetWare server of any version, with NWLink always check the frame types. A frame type that does not match the NetWare server will keep communication from initializing. For more information, see the section "Installing the NWLink Protocol."

6. **D.** GSNW and NWLink do not need to be installed on all servers throughout the domain— only on the server that will connect to the NetWare server to complete the gateway. Configure the network provider to be the Microsoft Windows Network first and then Novell on this server. Unbind NWLink from all network components except for GSNW. For more information, see the section "Configuring Network Bindings."

7. **C.** By issuing clients a secure card, you'll have a more reliable method of protecting data through dial-up connections. The risk involved with secure card sessions, however, is that should a user lose both the laptop and secure card together, a window of opportunity may exist for the unauthorized user to gain access. Most secure card software has means to disable or ignore logon requests from a lost or stolen secure card. In addition, the administrator would want to change the user's identification and password on the network to cover the logon authentication. For more information, see the section "Security Hosts."

8. **D.** Kerberos V5 is installed with Windows 2000 domains when you install a domain controller. For more information, see the section "Kerberos V5 Authentication."

9. **D.** Maria should create a VPN between the two sites. By implementing IPSec and L2TP, she can be assured that data is safe between the two locations and that only authorized IP packets will be allowed to enter either network. For more information, see the section "VPNs."

APPLY YOUR KNOWLEDGE

10. **B**. L2TP with IPSec is not available on ATM networks. L2TP is designed for Internet tunneling only. For more information, see the section "L2TP and IPSec."

11. **D**. You should remove GSNW, NWLINK, and NetBEUI from all servers. Remove Services for Macintosh from all servers except for the server where it's actually being used. Remove DHCP from the two servers that are not actually being used as DHCP. Just by removing these extra configurations from the servers, network performance will increase because fewer network services and resources are contending for network time. For more information, see the section "Managing and Monitoring Traffic."

12. **B**. Windows 2000's Network Monitor does not allow for capturing packets throughout the entire network, only between the local network and the computer it is run from. For more information, see the section "Using Network Monitor to Capture Data."

13. **C**. Before using SMS's Network Monitor, each subnet that is to be monitored must have one computer with the Network Monitor Driver installed. For more information, see the section "Installing the Network Monitor Driver."

14. **C**. Whenever you step into a new environment, when you are about to make major changes to a network, or when you have made major changes to a network, always create a baseline first. A baseline will help you see before and after results of your network. In addition, it will help you gather information about how and when your network is being utilized. For more information, see the section "Interpreting Captured Data."

15. **C**. Implementing IPSec and L2TP for all computers, including dial-up computers, will secure data and ensure that only authorized packets may access the network resources. For more information, see the section "Configuring and Troubleshooting IPSec."

Suggested Readings and Resources

1. Minasi, Mark, Christa Anderson, Brian M. Smith, and Doug Toombs. *Mastering Windows 2000 Server*. Alameda, CA: Sybex Press, 2000.

2. Morimoto, Rand. *Windows 2000 Design and Migration*.

3. Shields, Paul, Ralph Crump, and Martin Weiss. *Windows 2000 Server System Administration Handbook*. Rockland, MA: Syngress Media, 1999.

4. Web sites
   - www.isi.edu

You may be aware that if you implement the Microsoft Active Directory with the required Domain Name Service (DNS) infrastructure, you can do away with your legacy Windows Internet Naming Service (WINS) servers. However, because most environments require support for legacy servers, domains, and applications, it is important that Windows 2000 support WINS and that administrators understand how to install, maintain, and troubleshoot a Windows 2000 WINS implementation.

Microsoft defines the "Installing, Configuring, Managing, Monitoring, and Troubleshooting WINS in a Windows 2000 Network Infrastructure" objectives as:

Install, configure, and troubleshoot WINS.

▶ As with any of the Windows 2000 services, it is critical that you understand how to install, configure, and troubleshoot WINS. Although WINS is not strictly required by Windows 2000, having been replaced by DNS and Active Directory Services, WINS is an absolute requirement in mixed environments that contain Windows NT servers and workstations. WINS is the foundation that the legacy domain infrastructure relies on in an IP environment. You need to have a thorough understanding not only of the Windows 2000 WINS service, but also how WINS itself functions. This objective expects you to be able to install WINS, configure it for use in conjunction with legacy hosts, and be able to determine the issue if it is not working.

Configure WINS replication.

▶ One of the key features of WINS is the WINS database that can be replicated between WINS servers. In a distributed NT domain environment, this capability is critical for providing WINS resolution for all IP segments. You need to understand how WINS replication works and how to install the service.

C H A P T E R 5

Installing, Configuring, Managing, Monitoring, and Troubleshooting WINS in a Windows 2000 Network Infrastructure

Configure NetBIOS name resolution.

▶ The key to legacy Microsoft networking is the use of NetBIOS name resolution for locating hosts and services on the network. For this objective, you need to understand how NetBIOS name resolution works, as well as how to configure it on a Windows 2000 server.

Manage and monitor WINS.

▶ The final objective requires that you be able to manage and monitor the WINS service. As with any other service provided by Windows 2000, you absolutely must be able to maintain WINS after installation. The majority of work on any Windows 2000 implementation will be the long-term maintenance of the server and services, particularly given the number of installation and configuration wizards included with Windows 2000.

Installing, Configuring, and Troubleshooting WINS   **244**

   Introduction to WINS   244

   Installing WINS   247

   Configuring WINS   250

      General Settings   252

      Intervals Settings   252

      Database Verification Settings   253

      Advanced Settings   254

   Configuring WINS Replication   254

Troubleshooting WINS Issues   **259**

Configuring NetBIOS Name Resolution   **261**

Managing and Monitoring WINS   **265**

Chapter Summary   **271**

Apply Your Knowledge   **273**

▶ Be sure that you have a thorough understanding of the WINS service and NetBIOS name resolution. Although this is a legacy Microsoft protocol, it will still be required in most environments, and Microsoft wants to be absolutely sure you understand how it works.

▶ Review the use of the monitoring tools and the different parameters of WINS that can be monitored. In its exams, Microsoft has focused a great deal of attention on the monitoring and troubleshooting of the different services, including the WINS service.

▶ Be sure to complete the exercises at the end of the chapter. As Microsoft strives to make its exams more rigorous, a familiarity with not only the theory, but also the hands-on portion of the installation, configuration, and troubleshooting of the WINS service will be of importance.

INSTALLING, CONFIGURING, AND TROUBLESHOOTING WINS

Install, configure, and troubleshoot WINS.

If you are at all familiar with Windows NT 4 networks, you are undoubtedly familiar with the intricacies of a WINS infrastructure. You may also be wondering why Microsoft didn't get rid of WINS with Windows 2000. Well, the good news is that with Windows 2000, WINS is for backward compatibility only. Windows 2000 Server running in native mode does not use WINS at all. The Active Directory and DNS are used to provide the functionality of WINS—resolving names into addresses.

So that means we don't need to talk about WINS, right? Sorry, but you don't get off that easily. Until your network is 100% Windows 2000, you will still need WINS to provide backward compatibility for legacy Windows operating systems, particularly with your NT domains. With that in mind, let's talk about what WINS is and how it works.

> **EXAM TIP**
>
> **I Don't Need WINS** That is an accurate statement only if the client computer is running DNS. Don't make the mistake of assuming that DNS is implied when you get WINS questions.

Introduction to WINS

In the Internet-centric environment that most companies are designing and maintaining, Transmission Control Protocol/Internet Protocol (TCP/IP) has become the ubiquitous networking protocol. For old time UNIX users, using TCP/IP is a good thing. TCP/IP came out of the UNIX arena and has been the native protocol for UNIX systems since the late 1980s.

Microsoft, on the other hand, started with a different protocol as its LAN Manager operating system's native protocol—NetBIOS Extended Use Interface (NetBEUI). NetBEUI was a pretty good protocol for small networks; it required no configuration and didn't require complex addressing like TCP/IP does. However, NetBEUI cannot handle routing and does not perform well in large environments. Microsoft needed to add TCP/IP support.

When Microsoft began to add TCP/IP support to its LAN server products, the company ran into a little problem. The naming system used on Microsoft networks at that time would not function on routed TCP/IP networks. Microsoft LAN Manager computers used the computer's NetBIOS names for identification. Although this makes maintaining the network very simple for an administrator because servers are automatically advertised on the network by name, this naming system was a problem with the TCP/IP protocol.

NetBIOS has a design limitation that shows up in routed networks because NetBIOS relies heavily on broadcast messages to advertise servers and their shared resources. Broadcast messages are messages that are received by every computer on a network segment, rather than by a specific computer. This paradigm is usable on smaller networks but can add overwhelming amounts of broadcast traffic on an enterprise network. If you have ever suffered from a broadcast storm on your network, you are familiar with the issue. To confine the impact of broadcast messages on a TCP/IP network, IP routers will not forward broadcast messages. Unlike the Microsoft NWLink protocol for IPX compatibility, which was written by Microsoft to support broadcasts, TCP/IP conforms to very strict standards. To function in a TCP/IP environment, Microsoft's TCP/IP implementation had to conform to the standard. Therefore, Microsoft had to find a way to make NetBIOS naming work in a standard TCP/IP network.

IN THE FIELD

THE NWLINK PROTOCOL

Most of the Windows 2000 documentation and most of the chapters in this book discuss the TCP/IP protocol and TCP/IP services. However, it is important to recall that a significant population of companies still run Windows operating systems in conjunction with a Novell NetWare server.

The NWLink protocol was originally written to allow Windows to communicate using the IPX/SPX protocol used by Novell NetWare servers, back in the days when Novell was the dominant Intel-based network operating system. Although Novell has also embraced TCP/IP as its primary protocol, you still stand a pretty good chance of running into IPX, and you may find that you need to run the NWLink protocol. So be sure you understand all the TCP/IP information contained in this chapter and in this book, but don't be surprised if you find yourself loading NWLink on your Windows 2000 server one of these days.

Microsoft's first solution, introduced in its older LAN Manager server, was to use a LAN Manager HOSTS (LMHOSTS) file on each computer on the network. Similar to the HOSTS file used before DNS was available, an LMHOSTS consists of records matching NetBIOS names to IP addresses. When a computer couldn't find a particular NetBIOS computer on the local network, it would consult its LMHOSTS file to see if the computer could be found elsewhere.

An LMHOSTS file is a text file that must be edited manually. After creating a master LMHOSTS file, an administrator must copy the file to every computer on the network. Every time a computer was installed or removed, the master LMHOSTS file had to be updated and redistributed. Doesn't that sound like fun? (If you have read Chapter 1, "Installing, Configuring, Managing, Monitoring, and Troubleshooting DNS in a Windows 2000 Network Infrastructure," this should sound familiar. The architects of TCP/IP faced a similar issue with HOSTS files before the DNS specification was written.)

Microsoft also needed a dynamic name service that would keep itself current on computers on the network—a name service that could work in routed TCP/IP environments. Microsoft's answer was the WINS. Four elements can be found in a WINS network:

◆ **WINS servers.** When WINS client computers enter the network, they contact a WINS server using a directed message. The client computer registers its name with the WINS server and uses the WINS server to resolve NetBIOS names to IP addresses.

◆ **WINS client computers.** WINS client computers use directed (P-node) messages to communicate with WINS servers and are typically configured to use H-node communication. Windows 2000, Windows NT, Windows 95 and 98, and Windows for Workgroups computers can be WINS client computers.

◆ **Non-WINS client computers.** Older Microsoft network client computers that can't use P-node can still benefit from WINS. Their broadcast messages are intercepted by WINS proxy computers that act as intermediaries between the B-node

client computers and WINS servers. MS-DOS and Windows
3.1 client computers function as non-WINS clients.

◆ **WINS proxies.** Windows NT, Windows 95 and 98, and
Windows for Workgroups client computers can function as
WINS proxies. They intercept B-node broadcasts on their
local subnet and communicate with a WINS server on behalf
of the B-node client computer.

As we discuss in the "Configuring WINS Replication" section of this
chapter, WINS servers can replicate their databases so that each
WINS server can provide name resolution for the entire network.
Whenever possible, it is desirable to have at least two WINS servers.
This lets name resolution take place when one name server is down.
It also lets administrators distribute WINS activity across multiple
servers to balance the processing loads. WINS server addresses are
one of the configuration settings that can be issued with Dynamic
Host Configuration Protocol (DHCP).

Installing WINS

As discussed in earlier chapters, Windows 2000 allows you to perform tasks such as installing services in a number of ways. This section covers two of the more common methods for installing WINS.
Finding the method you are most comfortable with and sticking to
it consistently is generally the best method for working with the
operating system.

To install the Windows 2000 WINS service, do the following:

STEP BY STEP

5.1 Using the Network and Dial-Up Connections Properties to Install the Windows Internet Naming Service

1. Right-click the My Network Places icon on the desktop.
From the context menu, select Properties. The Network
and Dial-up Connections window opens (see Figure 5.1).

continues

EXAM TIP

Managing Windows 2000 Services
The Step by Step examples use a
utility called the WINS manager.
It is important to note that this
manager is nothing more than the
Microsoft Management Console
(MMC) with the WINS management
snap-in installed. Microsoft creates
these versions of the MMC to make
it easier for new users of Windows
2000 to manage their systems. So
don't be confused if you see references to the MMC in the exam.
That's all the WINS manager is.

continued

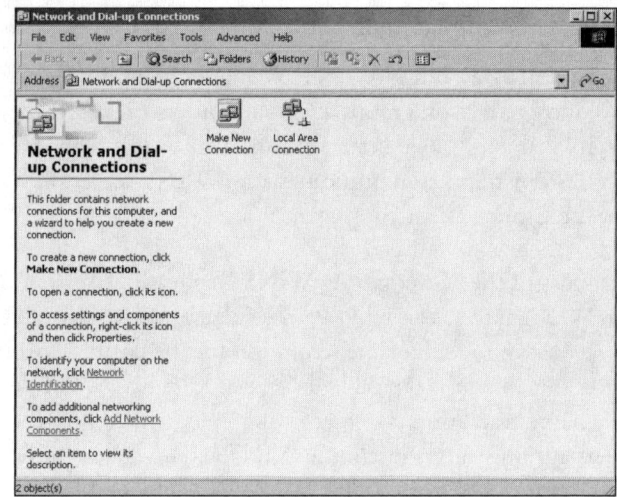

FIGURE 5.1
From here you can add, remove, or modify your
network settings and services.

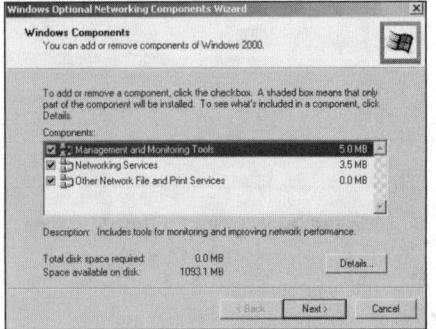

FIGURE 5.2
The Windows 2000 WINS service is part of the
Networking Services components.

2. Click Add Network Components in the lower-left corner.
   (This icon is visible only if you are viewing the folder as a
   Web page, the system default.) This hyperlink opens the
   Windows Components dialog box of the Windows
   Optional Networking Components Wizard, shown in
   Figure 5.2.

3. Select the Networking Services entry and click Details. This
   opens the Networking Services window, shown in Figure
   5.3. Select WINS.

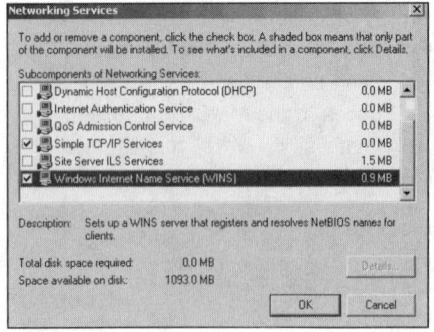

FIGURE 5.3
Selecting WINS and clicking OK installs
the service.

4. Click the OK button. This returns you to the Windows
   Optional Networking Components Wizard dialog. Click
   Next to start the installation. The Windows Component
   Wizard will prompt you for the Windows 2000 Server
   CD-ROM if it needs to copy files. When the wizard is
   finished, it displays a summary window of the changes to
   be made. Click OK to complete the installation.

Congratulations, you just installed WINS. Keep in mind that you
still need to configure your client computers to use the new server,
but the server portion of the install is complete. Now let's look at
another way to do it.

STEP BY STEP

5.2 Using the Add/Remove Programs Applet to Install the Windows Internet Naming Service

1. Open the Control Panel (see Figure 5.4) and double-click
   the Add/Remove Programs applet. The Add/Remove
   Programs dialog box opens (see Figure 5.5).

continues

> **NOTE**
>
> **DHCP and the WINS Service**
> If for some reason you have your
> Windows 2000 server configured
> to use DHCP addressing, you will
> receive a message from the installa-
> tion process indicating that the WINS
> service should be installed only on a
> server with a static address. The
> Local Area Connection Properties dia-
> log box will open to allow you to cor-
> rect the issue. Microsoft included this
> message because it is actually a very
> bad idea to put WINS on a
> dynamically addressed server.
>
> You don't want your WINS server
> to use a dynamic address, because
> the address might change one day. If
> that occurs, all your users will lose
> access to the server because the
> addresses used to point at
> the WINS server are configured
> statically. The same is true for a DNS
> server.

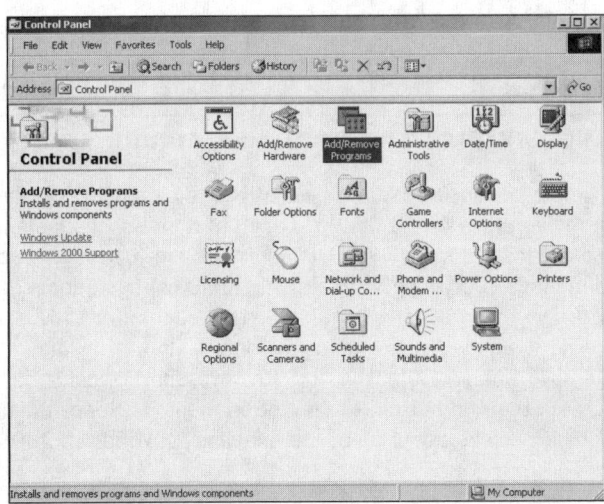

FIGURE 5.4
The Control Panel contains the system applets,
including the Add/Remove Programs applet used
to install WINS in this example.

continued

FIGURE 5.5

A major improvement over earlier versions, the Add/Remove Programs dialog box gives you more useful information about installed applications, including application size and, in some cases, the frequency of use for an installed application.

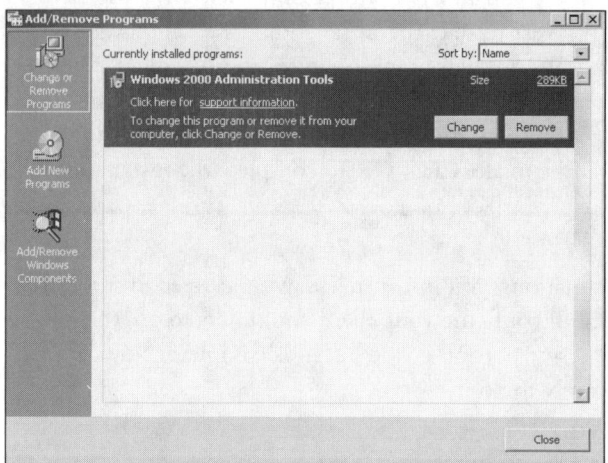

2. Select Add/Remove Windows Components. The Windows Components dialog box opens (see Figure 5.6).

3. From here you can follow the same steps as the previous procedure to complete the installation.

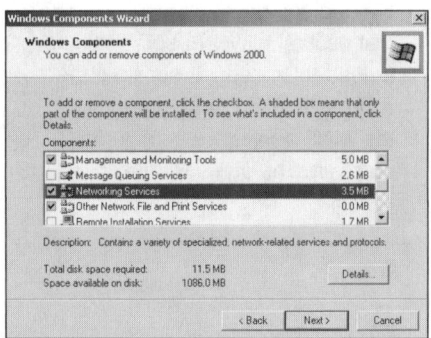

FIGURE 5.6

You can reach the same Windows Components Wizard a number of ways.

Now that WINS is installed, let's look at configuring it.

Configuring WINS

IN THE FIELD

USING THE MMC AND MANUALLY ADDING SNAP-INS

If you are an advanced user and would like to skip using differently configured versions of the MMC for each of the services installed on your Windows 2000 server, Microsoft has provided a very easy way to manage everything from a single MMC configuration. Open the MMC by going to Start, Run, MMC. This opens the MMC shell, which will be empty the first time you load it. Go to Console, Add/Remove Snap-in. After the Add/Remove Snap-in dialog box opens, click the Add button. In the Add Standalone Snap-in dialog box, you can select any or all of the snap-ins for Windows 2000 services. The list of snap-ins includes:

- Active Directory Domains and Trusts

- Active Directory Sites and Services

- Active Directory Users and Computers

- ActiveX Control

- Certificates

- Component Services

- Computer Management

- Device Manager

- DHCP

- Disk Defragmenter

- Disk Management

- Distributed File System

- DNS

- Event Viewer

- Fax Service Management

- Group Policy

- Indexing Service

- Internet Information Services

- IP Security Policy Management

- Local Users and Groups

- Performance Logs and Alerts

- Routing and Remote Access

- Services

- System Information

- WINS

This is not a comprehensive list. You should see several services
that we have discussed already in this book and others that you
will be seeing in the following chapters. The MMC is a very flexible
tool, and you shouldn't limit yourself to the preconfigured Microsoft
versions loaded with each service.

N O T E **To Back Up or Not to Back Up?**
You should always configure the default database path and the automatic backup of the database on shutdown to removable media whenever possible. This configuration ensures the maximum fault tolerance for the WINS database in case the server doesn't come back up.

A number of properties can be configured in the WINS. They can be accessed by opening WINS console (Start, Programs, Administrative Tools, WINS) and selecting the server you want to configure (see Figure 5.7). Right-click the server and select Properties. The sections that follow describe the property options.

General Settings

The General tab (shown in Figure 5.8) is used to configure statistics and backups. You can use this tab to configure the automatic update of WINS statistics and the interval that they update from this tab. You also can configure the default backup path for the WINS database, and you can enable the automatic backup of the database when the server is shut down.

FIGURE 5.7
The WINS manager is used for all configurations for the WINS service.

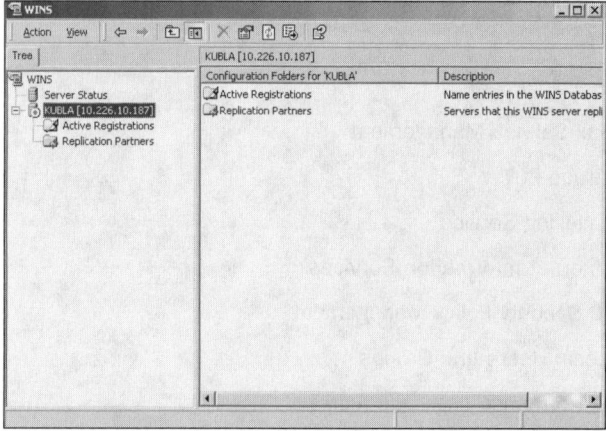

Intervals Settings

The Intervals tab (shown in Figure 5.9) is used to set the WINS database records renewal, deletion, and verification intervals. You can set the following intervals:

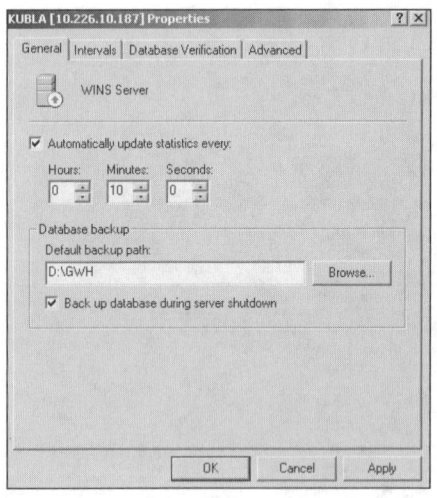

FIGURE 5.8
The General tab is used for configuring statistics and backups for the WINS database.

◆ **Renew Interval.** Determines the frequency of record renewal. The default is six days and is good for all but the most dynamic environments. If you have a very dynamic environment with computers entering and exiting the network frequently, you may want to reduce this interval.

◆ **Extinction Interval.** Determines the length of time before a record is considered extinct and is removed from the database. Again, in all but the most dynamic environments, the four-day default is usually adequate.

◆ **Extinction Timeout.** Determines the length of time a record is checked before it is declared extinct. When this occurs, the record is deleted after the Extinction Interval is met.

◆ **Verification Interval.** Determines the frequency that database records are verified for accuracy.

Database Verification Settings

The Database Verification tab (shown in Figure 5.10) allows you to configure the parameters associated with the WINS database. You can enable database verification for a specific interval. The default interval is 24 hours; thus, if enabled, the database consistency will be verified once a day. You also specify the time to begin the consistency check, the number of database records to check for each period, as well as the source to verify the database against. You can verify database consistency against owner servers (these are the servers that the record being verified was replicated from) or randomly selected partner servers.

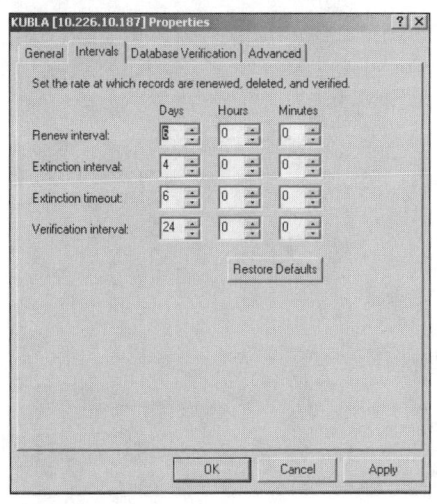

FIGURE 5.9
In most networks, the default intervals are usually adequate for a stable WINS environment.

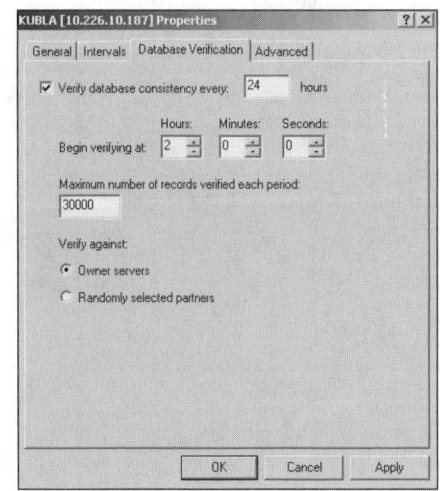

FIGURE 5.10
Ensuring the consistency of the WINS database is critical to a stable WINS environment.

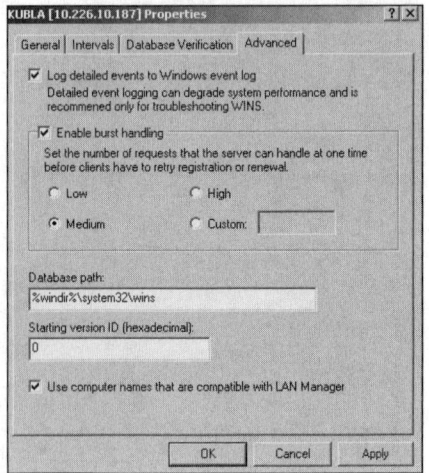

FIGURE 5.11

The Advanced tab functions as the catchall for the remaining WINS parameters and contains some important parameters for troubleshooting and load regulating.

Advanced Settings

The Advanced tab (shown in Figure 5.11) is used to configure the remaining WINS parameters, including

◆ **Logging.** You can enable detailed event logging for troubleshooting WINS when there are problems.

◆ **Burst handling.** You can configure the load that can be put on the server by specifying the number of WINS requests that the server will accept before returning a retry message. This can be set to Low, Medium, High, or Custom, which allows you to specify a number of connections.

◆ **Database path.** This is the path for the WINS database. If you have fault-tolerant drives in your server, make sure that the WINS database is located on one of them.

◆ **Database version number.** You should not need to modify this parameter, but the starting version number is used for consistency purposes. By giving each version of the database an incrementing version number, Windows 2000 is able to compare two WINS databases and tell which is the most recent. DNS uses a similar mechanism for synchronizing its tables.

◆ **LAN Manager compatibility.** You can also set WINS to use LAN Manager-compatible computer names so that any legacy LAN Manager installations can still use WINS for name resolution.

That covers the configuration of a WINS server. Let's look at configuring WINS replication between two WINS servers.

Configuring WINS Replication

Configure WINS replication.

In most environments that rely on WINS for name resolution for legacy systems, it is important to ensure that more than one WINS server exists so that you provide redundancy and availability. To ensure that each server has a current copy of the database, it is important to configure replication between your WINS servers. Let's take a quick look at the different types of replication you can configure for the WINS service:

◆ **Pull replication.** In pull replication, your server pulls the database from the replication partner. A pull replication is time based and occurs at the time you have configured. You can decide whether to establish a persistent connection for replication, and you can set the start time and interval for replication.

◆ **Push replication.** In push replication, your server pushes its database to the replication partner. A push replication is event driven, and the number of database updates determines when the event occurs. You can decide whether to use a persistent connection for push activities, and you can set the number of changes in version ID before replication.

◆ **Replication partner type.** The partner type can be push, pull, or push/pull, depending on your requirements. (In push/pull replication, database replication can occur using either method: push or pull.)

To configure WINS replication, do the following:

STEP BY STEP

5.3 Configuring WINS Replication

1. Open the WINS manager by choosing Start, Programs, Administrative Tools, WINS.

2. In the right pane, right-click Replication Partners and select New Replication Partner. The New Replication Partner dialog box opens (see Figure 5.12) and asks you to enter the address of another WINS server. This can be either the server name or IP address. If the server name cannot be resolved, you will be prompted to enter the address of the server.

continues

EXAM TIP

WINS Replication One new feature of the Windows 2000 WINS servers is the capability to maintain a persistent connection with one or more of the replication partners, enabling real-time replication. Because this is one of the new features of the WINS service, you will probably find it on the test. Microsoft is more likely to test your familiarity with new features of the service than your understanding of the general WINS functionality because WINS has been part of the Windows server operating systems since its inception.

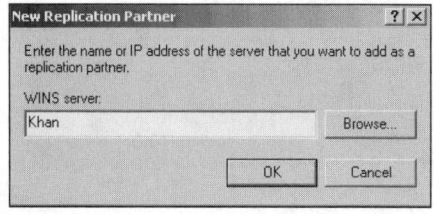

FIGURE 5.12
The replication partner can be listed by name or address.

continued

3. Enter the name of the server and click OK.

4. Click Replication Partners in the left pane. You should see your new replication partner in the right pane (see Figure 5.13).

5. Right-click the newly created replication partner and select Properties. This opens the Replication Partner Properties dialog box, which shows only the name and address of the replication partner.

6. Click the Advanced tab (see Figure 5.14). On this tab, you can configure the replication properties for the replication partner. Select the appropriate type for your environment.

7. Click OK when the settings meet your requirements.

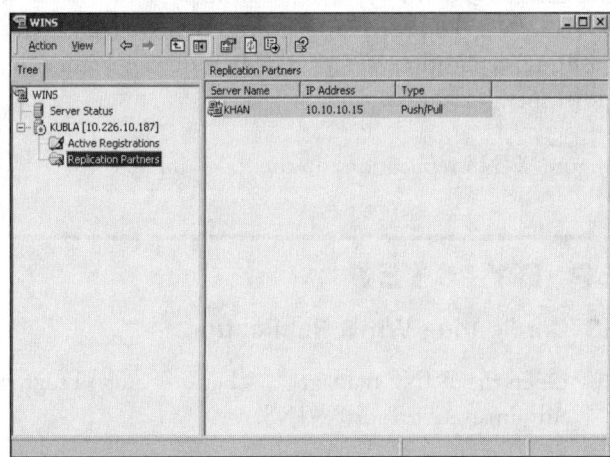

FIGURE 5.13

After the replication partner has been created, it will be listed in the Replication Partners pane of WINS manager.

You have now configured replication with a WINS replication partner. Now let's look at the global replication properties. To review the
global replication properties, open the WINS manager application as
described in the Step by Step and select the Replication Partners
folder in the left pane. Right-click and select Properties from the
context menu. This opens the Replication Partners Properties. This
opens to the General tab. Replication partners configurations can be
set on the following tabs:

◆ **General.** The General tab allows you to restrict replication to
replication partners as well as configuring the server to allow
the overwriting of static mappings on the server.

◆ **Push Replication.** As you can see in Figure 5.15, you can use
this tab to establish whether replication will start at system
startup. You also can use this tab to establish when an address
changes (and you can configure the number of changes
required to trigger the push replication) and whether to
use persistent connections for the push replication.

◆ **Pull Replication.** As you can see in Figure 5.16, you can
use this tab to establish whether pull replication starts at system startup, when the replication should start, the interval
between replications, the number of retries, and whether to
use persistent connections.

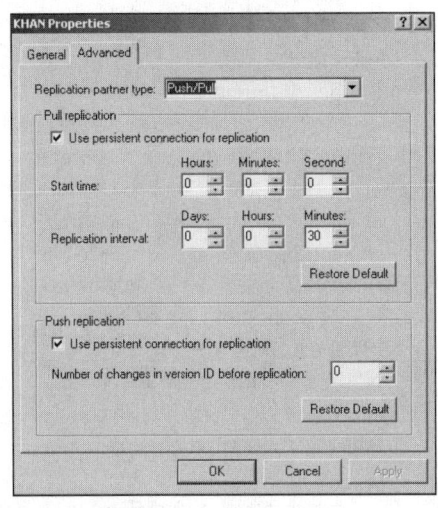

FIGURE 5.14
The Advanced tab allows you to customize
the WINS replication setting to meet your
network's requirements.

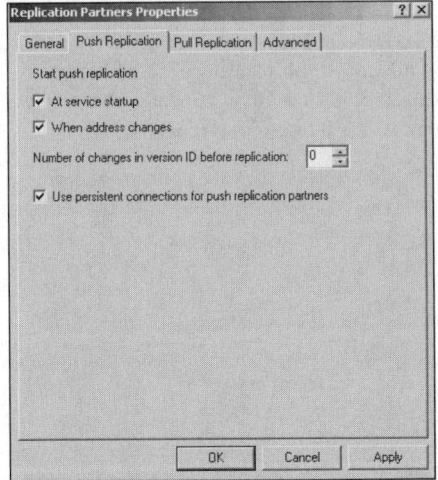

FIGURE 5.15
The Push Replication tab allows you to set the
thresholds for triggering a push replication.

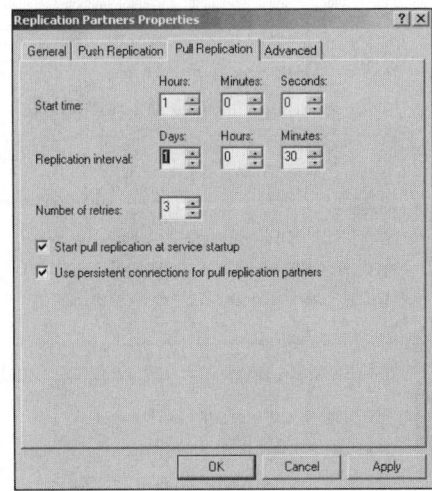

FIGURE 5.16
The Pull Replication tab allows you to configure
the timing for a pull replication.

N O T E

What's Multicasting? Multicasting is the act of transmitting a message to a select group of recipients. This is in contrast to the concept of a broadcast, where traffic is sent to every host on the network, or a unicast, where the connection is a one-to-one relationship, and there is only one recipient of the data. Think about sending an email message. If you send an email message to your manager, it is an example of a unicast message. If you send an email message to every user on the system, it is a broadcast. Send to an email message to a mailing list and you have sent a multicast message, which falls between the previous two. Teleconferencing and videoconferencing use the concept of multicasting, as does broadcast audio, where the connection is a one to a selected group. At this time, only a few applications take advantage of this feature, but with the growing popularity of multicast applications, you may see more multicast applications in the future. WINS is one that you can keep on the list, but only for small networks.

E X A M   T I P

Global Replication Settings Because we just finished discussing configuring replication partners, these parameters should look familiar. However, in this section the changes apply to any replication partners created after the modifications are made. They will not be applied to existing replication partners.

♦ **Advanced.** The tab shown in Figure 5.17 allows you to block servers from being able to replicate, as well as to configure the autodiscovery and autoconfiguration of WINS partners. Because this uses multicasts (or multicasting) to find and configure the servers, enable this for small networks only.

You have now successfully configured all the possible Windows replication partner parameters. Let's take a quick look at identifying WINS issues.

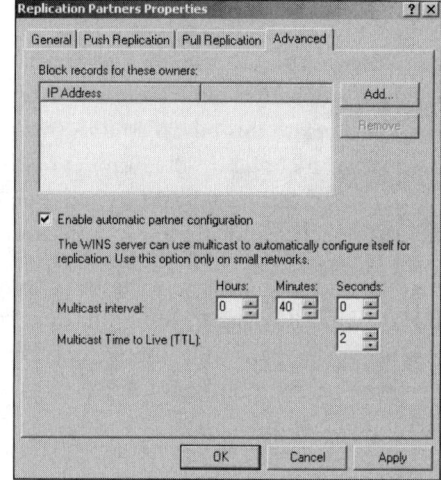

FIGURE 5.17
The Advanced tab allows you to set up your WINS server for a small network, as well as to block WINS servers from replicating.

TROUBLESHOOTING WINS ISSUES

The majority of WINS issues you will encounter will be related to connectivity, so the first thing we need to take a look at is testing TCP/IP connectivity. The first application for testing IP connectivity is the PING.EXE utility. What PING allows you to do is send an Internet Control Message Protocol (ICMP) to a TCP/IP host. By using the correct flag, PING can also perform name resolution as part of its testing procedure. The correct format for this command is

```
PING -a <destination address>
```

where the -a flag provides hostname resolution. A sample PING session might look like this:

```
ping -a wins1.newriders.com
Pinging wins1.newriders.com [205.123.113.87] with 32 bytes
➥of data:
Reply from 205.123.113.87: bytes=32 time=47ms TTL=241
Reply from 205.123.113.87: bytes=32 time=60ms TTL=242
Reply from 205.123.113.87: bytes=32 time=40ms TTL=242
Reply from 205.123.113.87: bytes=32 time=37ms TTL=242
Ping statistics for 205.123.113.87:
Packets: Sent = 4, Received = 4, Lost = 0 (0% loss),
Approximate round trip times in milliseconds:
Minimum = 37ms, Maximum = 60ms, Average = 46ms
```

Because the number of sent packets equals the number of receive packets, the connection between the workstation and the WINS server is good. If you do not get any packets returned, you should investigate the network issues further.

The next piece of the WINS puzzle is the client computer WINS configuration. To check to see whether the WINS configuration of your Windows 2000 client computers is correct, do the following:

STEP BY STEP

5.4 Checking the WINS Settings in a Client Computer

1. Open a command prompt by choosing Start, Programs, Accessories, Command Prompt.

2. At the command prompt, type `ipconfig /all`. You will get a result similar to the one shown in Figure 5.18.

3. Check for the entry Primary WINS Server, toward the end of the list of parameters. Verify that a WINS server is configured and that it is the correct server. If there is no server or if the server is incorrect, you will need to set the correct server in one of two places. If you use DHCP, you will need to update your DHCP settings. If you are using static addresses, the WINS server can be configured by using the Network applet in the Control Panel and setting the correct server in the TCP/IP Properties.

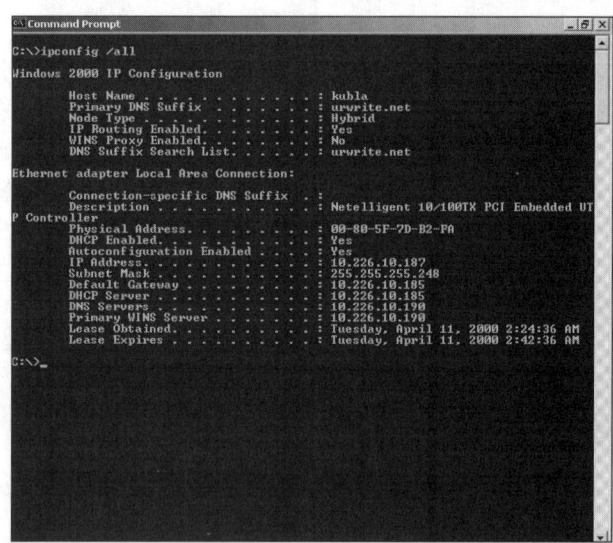

FIGURE 5.18
The IPConfig utility gives you all the information on the IP configuration of any of your adapters.

The final piece of the WINS puzzle is verifying that the server is functioning. You should check several things:

◆ **Is the WINS service running?** You can determine this by opening the Task Manager (press Ctrl+Alt+Del and select Task Manager) and on the Processes tab (see Figure 5.19), verify that the WINS service (WINS.EXE) is running. If the service is not running, you should probably reboot the server to ensure that there are not other issues.

◆ **Is the WINS service responding to requests?** The best way to discover this is to check the server statistics. (You can also use the Performance console to get some of this information. That will be discussed in depth in the "Managing and Monitoring WINS" section of this chapter.) To check the server statistics, right-click the server in the WINS manager and select WINS Server Statistics (see Figure 5.20). If you check these statistics over a 15-minute period of time and they don't increment, you probably have a WINS issue somewhere.

We have covered the basic steps in troubleshooting WINS. As with any equipment-down situation, your steps may vary. Every situation is unique and may require unique troubleshooting steps.

Configuring NetBIOS Name Resolution

Configure NetBIOS name resolution.

Microsoft TCP/IP uses NetBIOS over TCP/IP (NetBT) as specified in Request for Comment (RFC) 1001 and 1002 to support the NetBIOS client and server programs in the LAN and WAN environments. Before we look at the specifics of NetBIOS name resolution, let's briefly review how computers communicate on the network. This should help in understanding how the different NetBIOS modes work, and why some are preferable to others.

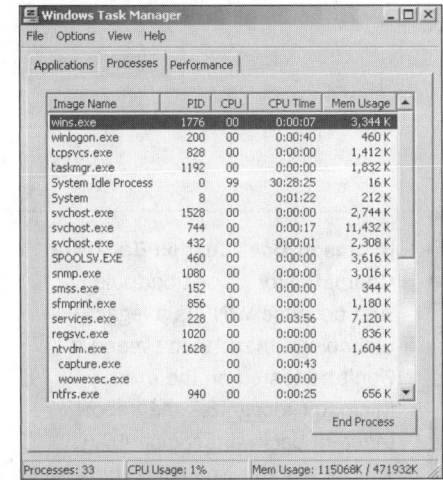

FIGURE 5.19
Task Manager is one of the fastest ways to verify that a service is running.

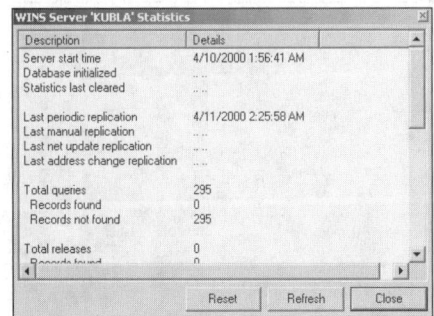

FIGURE 5.20
The WINS Server Statistics provide an excellent snapshot of the WINS service.

Computers can use two ways to communicate on a network:

◆ Through broadcast messages, which every computer receives

◆ Through directed messages, which are sent to a specific computer

EXAM TIP

Microsoft Does Test on Backward Compatibility Don't be fooled. Just because WINS is a legacy technology, that doesn't mean it won't be tested on the exam. Microsoft recognizes the importance of backward compatibility, and as a result, you can expect to see questions on WINS for this exam. If you have not worked with it in a legacy environment, make sure you understand how WINS works.

Whenever possible, it is preferable to communicate through directed messages. This cuts down on the amount of network traffic and ensures that only the affected hosts receive the message. This also ensures that the messages will propagate across routers. So, Microsoft needed to make sure that WINS communicated primarily with directed messages. The company accomplished this by allowing several types of NetBIOS naming methods. These naming methods are commonly called node types. A node is simply a device on a network. Every computer on a Microsoft computer is configured as one of four node types. The node type determines whether the computer will learn names through broadcast messages, directed messages, or some combination of broadcast and directed messages. Before you can work with WINS, you need to know what the node types are and when they are used:

◆ **B-node (broadcast node).** Relies exclusively on broadcast messages and is the oldest NetBIOS name resolution mode. A host needing to resolve a name request sends a message to every host within earshot, requesting the address associated with a hostname. B-node has two shortcomings: broadcast traffic is undesirable and becomes a significant user of network bandwidths, and TCP/IP routers don't forward broadcast messages, which restricts B-node operation to a single network segment.

◆ **P-node (point-to-point node).** Relies on WINS servers for NetBIOS name resolution. Client computers register themselves with a WINS server when they come on the network. They then contact the WINS server with NetBIOS name resolution requests. WINS servers communicate using directed messages, which can cross routers, so P-node can operate on large networks. Unfortunately, if the WINS server is unavailable, or if a node isn't configured to contact a WINS server, P-node name resolution fails.

◆ **M-node (modified node).** A hybrid mode that first attempts to resolve NetBIOS names using the B-node mechanism. If that fails, an attempt is made to use P-node name resolution.

M-node was the first hybrid mode put into operation, but it
has the disadvantage of favoring B-node operation, which is
associated with high levels of broadcast traffic.

◆ **H-node (hybrid node).** A hybrid mode that favors the use of
WINS for NetBIOS name resolution. When a computer needs
to resolve a NetBIOS name, it first attempts to use P-node
resolution to resolve a name via WINS. Only if WINS resolution fails does the host resort to B-node to resolve the name
via broadcasts. Because it typically results in the best network
utilization, H-node is the default mode of operation for
Microsoft TCP/IP client computers configured to use WINS
for name resolution. Microsoft recommends leaving TCP/IP
client computers in the default H-node configuration.

IN THE FIELD

THE METHOD WINS USES TO RESOLVE A NAME

The time may come when you need to understand exactly how
WINS resolves a name. (Because H-node is not only the default but
is also the recommended configuration, we will restrict our discussion to the H-node name resolution.) When a WINS client computer
configured for Hybrid mode needs to resolve a hostname, it goes
through the following series of steps:

1. Checks its NetBIOS name cache. If the name is found, returns it.

2. Queries the WINS server. If the name is found, returns it.

3. Issues a broadcast to find the host on the local network. If the
   name is found, returns it.

4. Looks for the LMHOSTS file to check for an entry. If the name is
   found, returns it.

5. Looks for the host file to check for an entry. If the name is
   found, returns it.

6. Queries the DNS server for the entry. If the name is found,
   returns it.

7. If all these methods fail, the WINS client computer issues an
   error message saying that it cannot communicate with the host.

Although networks can be organized using a mixture of node types,
Microsoft recommends against it. B-node client computers ignore

P-node directed messages, and P-node client computers ignore B-node broadcasts. Therefore, it is conceivable that two client computers could separately be established with the same NetBIOS name. If WINS is enabled on a Windows 2000 Professional computer, the system uses H-node by default. Without WINS, the system uses B-node by default. Non-WINS client computers can access WINS through a WINS proxy, which is a WINS-enabled computer that listens to name query broadcasts and then queries the WINS server on behalf of the requesting client computer.

To see which node type is configured on a Windows 2000 computer, do the following:

EXAM TIP

Registering with WINS When your Windows client computer enters the network, it registers with WINS so that other Microsoft client computers can resolve its name to an address. For the exam, you should be aware that although a WINS proxy server can be used to resolve names for hosts that have registered with WINS, it cannot be used to register with WINS. You need access to the WINS server to successfully register.

STEP BY STEP

5.5 Identifying the NetBIOS Node Type

1. Open a command prompt by going to Start, Programs, Accessories, Command Prompt.

2. At the command prompt, type **ipconfig /all**. You will get a result similar to the one shown in Figure 5.21. The node type is indicated to the right of the heading Node Type. In this example, the machine is running in Hybrid mode, the default for Windows 2000.

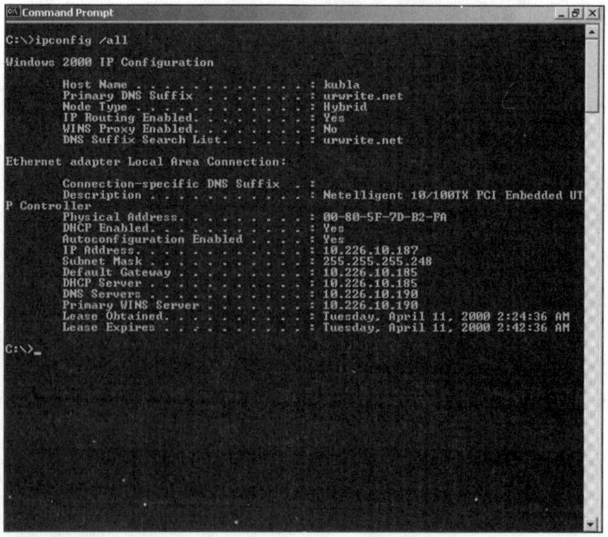

FIGURE 5.21

The IPConfig utility gives you all the information on the IP configuration of any of your adapters, including the node type.

Let's wrap up the chapter by looking at the best way to manage and monitor WINS and manage your new WINS server.

MANAGING AND MONITORING WINS

Manage and monitor WINS.

We have looked at installing and configuring the Windows 2000 WINS Server service. Next, we need to look at managing and monitoring the server now that it is running. If your job is typical of most, you will spend a great deal more time managing WINS servers than installing them.

Although the WINS server includes limited monitoring capabilities, you do have access to the WINS statistics referenced in the "Troubleshooting WINS Issues" section of the chapter. To get the server statistics, just open WINS manager and right-click the server in question. From the context menu select Display Server Statistics, and a snapshot of the server statistics (see Figure 5.22) will be displayed.

The WINS manager application has additional capabilities. From the open WINS manager application, you can select the WINS server and then use the Action menu to access these available actions:

◆ The Display Server Statistics option displays statistics discussed in a preceding section.

◆ The Scavenge Database option allows you to manually clean unused entries from the WINS database.

◆ The Verify Database Consistency option causes the server to go out to the network hosts and verify the entries in the WINS database. This process can be very processor and network intensive, so be sure to run it after hours.

◆ The Verify Version ID Consistency option forces the WINS server to go to all the other WINS servers on the network and has them check the database version numbers to ensure that they are consistent. This is potentially another long operation, so it should be run after hours—or at least not when everyone in the office is trying to read email.

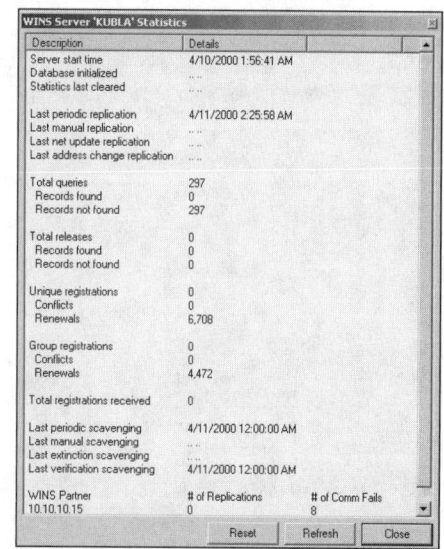

FIGURE 5.22

The WINS Server Statistics provide a good snapshot of WINS activity.

◆ The Start Push Replication option manually performs a push replication.

◆ Start Pull Replication option manually performs a pull replication.

◆ The Back Up Database option allows you to make a backup copy of the WINS database. Always make sure you have a copy of this database, just in case. If you specify the backup directory, the server will automatically back up the database every 24 hours.

◆ The Restore the Database option allows you to restore a backup copy of the database.

◆ The Tasks option leads to a menu consisting of the following commands:

  • **Start.** Starts the WINS Server service. This option is available only if the service is stopped or paused.

  • **Stop.** Stops the WINS Server service. Available when the service is running or paused. This option causes the server statistics to be reset.

  • **Pause.** Pauses the WINS Server service. This option does not reset the statistics.

  • **Resume.** Resumes the WINS Server service when paused. This option is available only when the service is paused.

  • **Restart.** Restarts the WINS Server service. This option is available unless the server is stopped.

◆ The Delete option deletes a WINS server from the WINS manager.

◆ The Refresh option causes all the displayed information to be refreshed with a current status.

◆ The Export List option allows you to export the information from the DNS server to a tab- or comma-delimited text or Unicode text file.

◆ The Properties option opens the server properties, as discussed in a preceding section.

The Windows 2000 WINS service also includes some new functionality for managing the WINS database. If you open the WINS manager and click the Active Registrations, you will see a list of all the
dynamically added entries in the WINS database. Although this is useful, it would be nice to be able to search for a specific entry, or even to
filter on specific record types. The good news is that you can. If you
right-click the Active Registration folder and select Find by Name or
Find by Owner, you can search the WINS database for specific entries.
And under Find by Owner, you can even filter what WINS record
types should be shown. If you are working in a large environment
(500 computers or greater), you will find these capabilities invaluable,
because computers can often enter 10 to 12 entries each into the
WINS database. I don't know about you, but I don't relish reading
through 5000 to 6000 WINS records looking for a specific machine.

Windows 2000's WINS service also allows you to delete not only
static records, but also dynamic records. This is a major improvement over previous versions of WINS, in which you couldn't delete
dynamic entries.

Now that you have looked at the options for managing the WINS
server, let's take a look at some of the ways to monitor the service.
Before you get into the Step by Step, you should look at what
counters you can use to monitor WINS. The WINS object has the
following counters associated with it.

- **Failed Queries/Sec.** Gives you the number of failed WINS
  queries per second. If this number is very high or suddenly
  spikes, you may have an issue with WINS resolution.

- **Failed Releases/Sec.** Gives you the number of failed WINS
  releases per second. If this number is very high or suddenly
  spikes, you may have an issue with WINS resolution.

- **Group Conflicts/Sec.** The rate at which group registrations by
  the WINS server resulted in conflicts with the database.

- **Group Registrations/Sec.** The rate at which group registrations are being received.

- **Group Renewals/Sec.** The rate at which group renewals are
  being received.

- **Queries/Sec.** The rate at which queries are being received.

- **Releases/Sec.** The rate at which releases are being received.

◆ **Successful Queries/Sec.** The number of successful queries per second. This is useful if you are trending your WINS usage.

◆ **Successful Releases/Sec.** The number of successful releases per second. This is useful if you are trending your WINS usage.

◆ **Total Number of Conflicts/Sec.** This is the sum of the unique and group conflicts per second.

◆ **Total Number of Registrations/Sec.** This is the sum of the unique and group registrations per second.

◆ **Total Number of Renewals/Sec.** This is the sum of the unique and group renewals per second.

◆ **Unique Conflicts/Sec.** The rate at which unique registrations/renewals caused conflicts with the database.

◆ **Unique Registrations/Sec.** The rate at which unique registrations are received by the server.

◆ **Unique Renewals/Sec.** The rate at which unique renewals are received by the server.

To configure WINS performance monitoring, do the following:

STEP BY STEP

5.6 Monitoring WINS Performance

1. Open the Performance application by choosing Programs, Administrative Tools, Performance (see Figure 5.23).

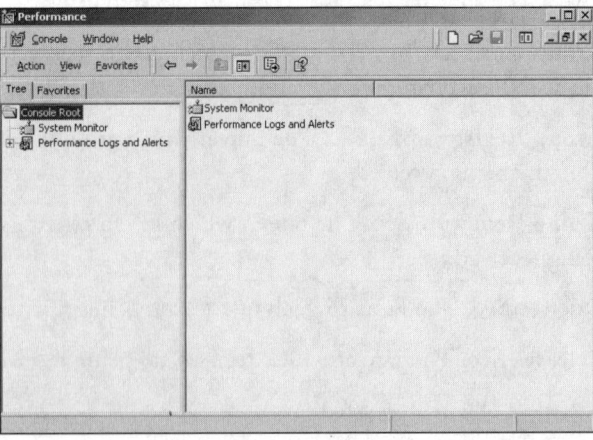

FIGURE 5.23
The Performance console allows you to monitor a variety of system and application metrics for evaluating the performance and health of the system.

2. In Performance, select System Monitor (see Figure 5.24).

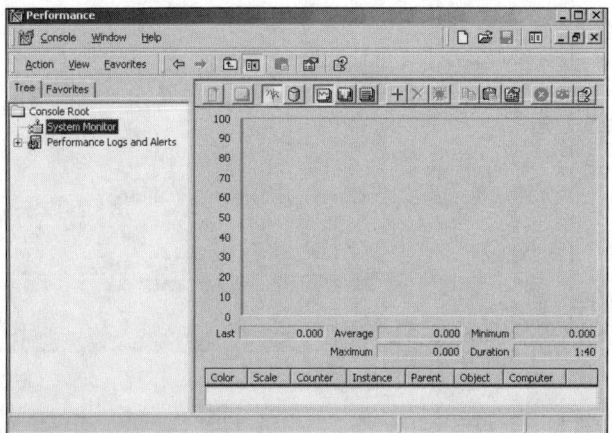

FIGURE 5.24
System Monitor allows you to monitor the performance of your
server's statistics in real-time.

3. To create an entry in System Monitor, click the Add (+)
icon. The Add Counters window opens. By default, it
opens to the Processor performance object.

4. Select the WINS Server performance object. You will see
the list of counters displayed as available for the WINS
service. Figure 5.25 shows the explanation function of the
Performance console.

5. After you have decided on the counter you want to monitor, click Add. You can add multiple counters either by
selecting each counter and clicking Add, or by using the
standard Windows multiple item select method of holding
down the Ctrl key while you select all the counters you
wish to monitor, and clicking Add. Click Close when you
are done. You will see your counters being graphed similar
to those shown in Figure 5.26.

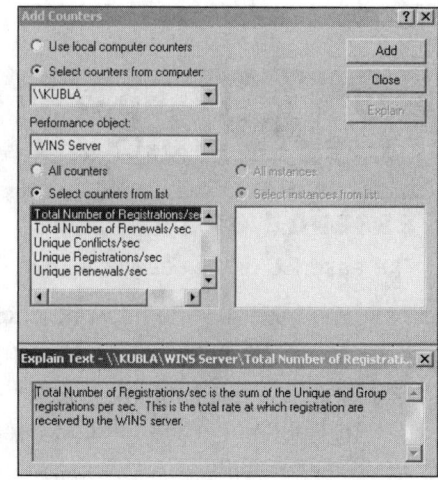

FIGURE 5.25
Clicking the Explain button.

FIGURE 5.26
After the counters have been added, all that
remains is successfully interpreting the data.

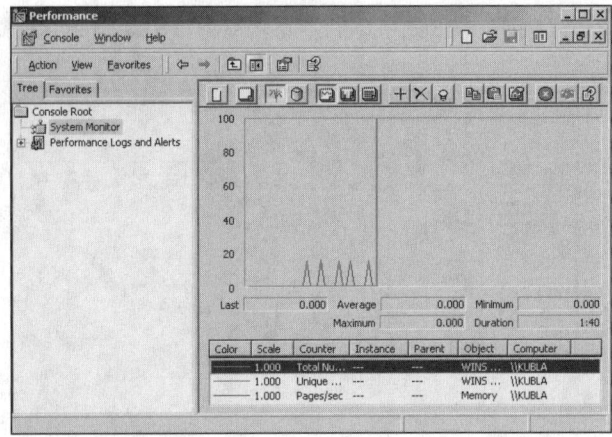

We've looked at the management options available in the WINS
manager application, and we've taken a look at how to monitor the
performance of the different WINS counters using the Performance
console. At this point you should have a good understanding of the
Windows 2000 WINS Server service and WINS in general. Now
let's see how you do applying it in a practical situation.

CASE STUDY: CONFIGURING NETWORK ADDRESS TRANSLATION (NAT) IN A 100-USER NETWORK

ESSENCE OF THE CASE

The essence of the case is as follows:

▶ You have a 5-site network, each site with
its own IP subnet.

▶ You need a centralized NetBIOS name
resolution service to allow users to
resolve names.

▶ You want to deploy this to all users, and
it must resolve for all Microsoft servers.

SCENARIO

You are the network administrator for LFE
Incorporated. LFE Inc. is a lawn furniture manufacturing company. You have a 5-site network, and
each site has its own IP subnet. You are presently
running a lot of Windows NT Workstations and
Servers and are in the process of upgrading to
Windows 2000 servers right now.

You have been using LMHOSTS files for NetBIOS
name resolution thus far, but you would like to
move to a centralized name resolution solution
as part of the Windows 2000 migration to support legacy applications. You need to make sure

CASE STUDY: CONFIGURING NETWORK ADDRESS TRANSLATION IN A 100-USER NETWORK

name resolution is available for all computers on all subnets, and that they resolve all hosts on the network.

What do you need to do?

ANALYSIS

This is an excellent example of a small Microsoft network desperately in need of a WINS infrastructure. A good WINS design requires that there be a WINS server at each location for both local and remote resolution. To make it work, you need to make sure you do the following:

- Install the Windows 2000 WINS service on at least one Windows 2000 Server in each location.

- Configure the WINS Servers as replication partners and make sure they replicate their databases appropriately.

- Configure each of the client computers to use WINS resolution with the local WINS server as the primary server.

- If you are using DHCP, make sure to update the DHCP setting to reflect the new WINS servers.

If you are migrating to a Windows 2000 network and you do not have a WINS infrastructure for your existing Microsoft client computers, this might be a good model to deploy for interim support until you have completed your Windows 2000 migration.

CHAPTER SUMMARY

Let's recap what we've discussed in this chapter. We started with a discussion of what WINS is, and what services it provides. In a Windows 2000 environment, it provides name resolution for non-Windows 2000 client computers.

Then we moved on to the installation, configuration, and troubleshooting of WINS. The installation is wizard driven and configuration consists mainly of setting parameters for your environment. We also discussed the different areas to check if you are having issues with WINS.

KEY TERMS

- Domain Name System (DNS)

- Dynamic Host Configuration Protocol (DHCP)

- Windows Internet Naming Service (WINS)

- replication partner

CHAPTER SUMMARY

KEY TERMS

- Transmission Control Protocol/Internet Protocol (TCP/IP)

- Request For Comment (RFC) documents

- NetBIOS

- push replication

- pull replication

- push/pull replication

- Active Directory

- NWLink protocol for IPX

- LAN Manager HOSTS (LMHOSTS)

- Internet Control Message Protocol (ICMP)

- H-node

- B-node

- P-node

- M-node

We discussed how to configure NetBIOS, as well as configuring WINS replication partners. We wrapped up the chapter with a discussion of the different mechanisms available for managing and monitoring your WINS servers.

In the next chapter we discuss "Installing, Configuring, Managing, Monitoring, and Troubleshooting IP Routing in a Windows 2000 Network Infrastructure."

APPLY YOUR KNOWLEDGE

Exercises

5.1   Installing WINS on a Windows 2000 Server

In the following exercise, you will install WINS on your Windows 2000 server.

Estimated Time: 15 minutes

1. Open the Network and Dial-up Connections window.

2. Click the Add Network Components link.

3. Select the Networking Services entry and click Details.

4. Select Windows Internet Name Service (WINS).

5. Click the OK button.

6. Click Next to start the installation.

7. If you have not already done so, insert the Windows 2000 Server installation media in the drive, or point the application to the appropriate directory or share for the installation files.

8. When the summary window appears, click OK to complete the installation.

5.2   Configuring a Replication Partner

In this exercise you will configure a replication partner.

Estimated Time: 10 minutes

1. Open the WINS manager by choosing Start, Programs, Administrative Tools, WINS.

2. Right-click Replication Partners and select New Replication Partner from the context menu.

3. Enter the server name WINSTEST. You will be prompted to enter the address of the server.

4. Enter 10.10.10.254 and click OK. You will be returned to the WINS manager.

5. Click Replication Partners in the left pane. You should see your new replication partner in the right pane.

5.3   Performing a Manual Push Replication

In this exercise you will manually perform a push replication.

Estimated Time: 10 minutes

1. Open the WINS manager by choosing Start, Programs, Administrative Tools, WINS.

2. Right-click WINS server and select Start Push Replication.

3. Enter the server name or IP address of the other WINS server and click OK.

4. Select Start for This Partner Only as the replication method. You can select Propagate to All Partners as the other method. Click OK. You will receive a message that the replication request has been queued.

5. Check the event log for a status of the request, and to see when it is completed.

5.4   Performing a Manual Pull Replication

In this exercise you will manually perform a pull replication.

Estimated Time: 10 minutes

1. Open the WINS manager by choosing Start, Programs, Administrative Tools, WINS.

2. Right-click the WINS server and select Start Pull Replication.

APPLY YOUR KNOWLEDGE

3. Enter the server name or IP address of the other WINS server and click OK.

4. When asked to confirm the request, click Yes. You will receive a message stating that the replication request has been queued.

5. Check the event log for a status of the request, and to see when it is completed.

Review Questions

1. You are the network administrator for a small company with several sites, each with host computers. You are in the process of migrating to Windows 2000, but you want to be sure that all your legacy Windows NT 4 computers can browse the network. What should you do?

2. You have successfully deployed WINS in your environment, and it is working. Your users can browse the network. How does the WINS database get populated to make this possible?

3. After the WINS is fully implemented and the database is populated, how are entries deleted from the database?

4. What is the major difference between push replication and pull replication?

5. You're the administrator of Little Faith Enterprise's Windows 2000 server, and you are considering setting up WINS. You feel you need a better understanding of how NetBIOS works and how the different node types work. What are the four NetBIOS node types, and how do they work?

Exam Questions

1. You are the WINS administrator for LFE Incorporated. You want to be sure to have a reliable backup of your WINS database available in case of problems, but you don't want to manually back up the database every day. What is the best way to automatically back up your WINS database?

   A. Purchase a third-party backup utility and schedule nightly backups of the entire server.

   B. Use the Windows scheduler service and configure a WINS Database Backup task.

   C. In the WINS manager, specify the backup directory and the backup interval.

   D. In the WINS manager, specify the backup directory.

2. You are the network administrator for Lost in the Woods Guide Service. You have a Windows 2000 server running WINS in your corporate headquarters and another in a branch office. You want the server in the branch office to get a replica of the corporate server's database every two hours.

   How do you do it?

   A. Configure the branch WINS server as a push replication partner with a two-hour interval.

   B. Configure the branch WINS server as a pull replication server with a two-hour interval.

   C. Configure the corporate WINS server as a push replication partner with a two-hour interval.

   D. Configure the corporate WINS server as a pull replication server with a two-hour interval.

APPLY YOUR KNOWLEDGE

3. You are the network administrator for a five-location pet food manufacturer. You have WINS servers at all five locations, and you would like them to replicate with each other automatically.

   How do you do it?

   A. Configure each WINS server as a replication partner. In Replication Partner properties, select Replicate with all Partners.

   B. Configure each WINS server as a replication partner. In Replication Partner properties, select Replicate Only with Partners.

   C. In Replication Partner properties, deselect Replicate Only with Partners. The server will automatically replicate with any WINS servers.

   D. Install WINS. Any WINS servers on the network will automatically replicate.

4. You are the network administrator for LFE Inc., a novelty manufacturing company. You have a large population of Windows NT 4 Workstation client computers on your Windows 2000 network. You have a new administrator who is trying to learn how WINS works. You want to explain. By default, which WINS server will a client computer use for resolution?

   A. The WINS server that responds to the broadcast request first

   B. The default WINS server it receives from DHCP or that is configured in TCP/IP properties

   C. The primary WINS server it receives from DHCP or that is configured in TCP/IP properties

   D. The WINS server that is the least number of network hops away

5. You are the network administrator for BT Machines, a heavy equipment manufacturing company. You have a large population of Windows NT 4 Workstation client computers on your Windows 2000 network. You are concerned that there are computers coming on the network that have the same NetBIOS name. What WINS statistic should you check to see if this is the case?

   A. Unique Conflicts/Sec

   B. Total Number of Conflicts/Sec

   C. Group Conflicts/Sec

   D. Failed Releases/Sec

6. You are the network administrator for BT Machines, a heavy equipment manufacturing company. You have a large population of Windows NT 4 Workstation client computers on your Windows 2000 network. You want to quickly check the total number of client computers adding updates to the WINS database.

   What parameter should you check?

   A. Unique Registrations/Sec

   B. Total Number of Registrations/Sec

   C. Total Number of Renewals/Sec

   D. Total Number of Registrations/Sec and Total Number of Renewals/Sec

APPLY YOUR KNOWLEDGE

7. You are the network administrator for Blue Sky Air, and you are training another administrator to assist with maintaining the network. She is having a hard time understanding the different NetBIOS node types, especially what type the new Windows 2000 Professional computers use.

   What is the default node type for Windows 2000?

   A. H-node

   B. M-node

   C. P-node

   D. B-node

8. Now that your new assistant understands the node type used by Windows 2000 Professional by default, she would like you to help her differentiate the different node types.

   Which of the following statements about node types is accurate?

   A. H-node and M-node favor WINS servers, but M-node does not have the capability to use broadcast if the WINS server is down.

   B. H-node and B-node favor WINS servers, but B-node does not have the capability to use broadcast if the WINS server is down.

   C. B-node and M-node both favor broadcast resolution first, but B-node can resolve using a WINS server if the host is on another subnet.

   D. H-node and P-node both favor WINS servers, but H-node can use a broadcast for name resolution if the WINS server is not available.

9. You are the LAN administrator for Little Faith Enterprises, a publishing company. You have a Windows 2000 server for corporate headquarters, but have a mix of Windows 2000 and Windows NT 4 client computers on the network. You have deployed WINS for backward compatibility, but you are unsure whether WINS is working.

   What is the best way to find out?

   A. Using the Performance console, select the WINS server object and the Successful Resolutions/Sec counter. Verify that the counter value is greater than 0.

   B. Using the Performance console, select the WINS server object and the Queries/Sec counter. Verify that the counter value is greater than 0.

   C. Open the WINS manager, select the server in question, and from the Action menu choose Server Statistics. Verify that the number of Total Queries is increasing. Click Refresh to update the statistics.

   D. Open the WINS manager, select the server in question, and from the Action menu choose Server Statistics. Verify that the number of Records Found Under Total Queries is increasing. Click Refresh to update the statistics.

10. You are the system administrator for New Riders Harley Davidson, and you are installing a WINS server on your Windows 2000 server. Your end users are all using DHCP.

    What is the best way to configure the workstations to utilize the WINS server?

APPLY YOUR KNOWLEDGE

A. Make sure the WINS server is installed on a Domain Controller. WINS resolution will happen automatically.

B. Modify the DHCP scope options for the WINS server to include the address of the new WINS server.

C. Open the Network applet and open the TCP/IP properties. On the WINS tab, modify the TCP/IP properties to point at the WINS server. Repeat this for each machine.

D. Update the LMHOSTS file to include the address of the new WINS server.

11. You are the administrator for a three-location car dealership. One location is headquarters and the other two are dealerships. You are migrating from a workgroup-based Windows NT 4 network to a Windows 2000 network. Each site is connected to the other two using a frame relay connection and a bridge. As part of the migration, you have decided to deploy WINS for the legacy client computers. Because money is a main component of this as a temporary service for the migration only, management would like to spend as little as possible.

What is the least expensive way to roll out WINS in this environment?

A. Install one WINS server on the headquarters network.

B. Install one WINS server on each network.

C. Install a WINS server at headquarters and another for redundancy in one of the dealerships.

D. Install one server on each dealership network, and two in the headquarters network for redundancy.

12. The WINS service was created to replace what?

A. The Domain Name Service

B. The HOSTS file

C. The LMHOSTS file

D. The WINS file

13. You are the administrator for a single-site direct-marketing company. You have two network segments in your building, with servers on both networks, and a Windows 2000 server is being used to route between segments. You have a mixture of DOS, Windows 95/98, and Windows NT Workstations as client computers in this network. You install WINS on the server, and your DOS client computers are unable to see the servers on the other side of the router.

Why can't the DOS client computers see computers across the router?

A. DOS does not use a dynamic routing protocol, so it can't see across the router.

B. DOS cannot interpret WINS names for resolution.

C. DOS requires a WINS client computer before being able to interface with the WINS server.

D. DOS uses B-node resolution of NetBIOS names.

APPLY YOUR KNOWLEDGE

14. You are the manager of a small consulting company. This company has a single network segment of 225 computers and has two WINS servers installed on Windows 2000 servers. You suspect that you have two computers with the same name on the network, but you have been unable to find the culprits.

    How can you tell if you have two computers with the same name?

    A. Open the WINS utility and from the Action menu, choose Statistics. Check to see whether the Duplicate Names statistic is incrementing.

    B. Open the WINS utility and from the Action menu, choose Statistics. Check to see whether the Conflicts statistics are incrementing.

    C. Open the Performance console and add the Duplicate Names counter for the WINS server object. Check the trend for the statistic.

    D. Open the Performance console and add the Names Conflicts counter for the WINS server object. Check the trend for the statistic.

15. You are the WAN administrator for the Women's Place clothing store. You have six satellite locations all connected with low-bandwidth WAN links. Each location has its own WINS server for name resolution and will need to be replicated to.

    What is the best configuration for the WINS replication from the corporate WINS server to those in the field?

    A. Configure a pull replication from the remote servers to the central server and schedule it to occur whenever 100 entries have been added to the table.

    B. Configure a push replication from the remote servers to the central server and schedule it to occur whenever 100 entries have been added to the table.

    C. Configure a pull replication from the central server to the remote servers and schedule it to occur whenever 100 entries have been added to the table.

    D. Configure a push replication from the central server to the remote servers and schedule it to occur whenever 100 entries have been added to the table.

Answers to Review Questions

1. You need to deploy WINS in your environment. Depending on your environment, you may be able to deploy redundant WINS servers in your central site, or you may need to deploy WINS servers to each location. In either event you will need to configure replication between the servers. For more information, see the section "Installing WINS."

2. The WINS database is populated by the WINS client computer. When the WINS client computer comes on the network, it registers its name and address with the WINS server automatically. After the client computer is registered, it receives a time to live for its registration. For more information, see the section "Configuring WINS."

3. There are two automated mechanisms for removing entries. When a client computer shuts down gracefully, it will send a release request to the WINS server. The entries are also removed when the time to live for that client computer's registration expires. For more information, see the section "Configuring WINS Replication."

APPLY YOUR KNOWLEDGE

4. The main difference between push and pull replication (besides the direction the database is replicated) is the trigger for the event. In the case of a push replication, the trigger is event based. When a specified number of changes are made to the database, the replication is triggered. A pull replication is triggered by the time configured for the replication. This is user configured. For more information, see the section "Configuring WINS Replication."

5. There are four node types, and the main differentiator between the types is the methods they use for name resolution (broadcast versus direct connection) They are:

   B-node (broadcast node), which relies exclusively on broadcast messages and is the oldest NetBIOS name resolution mode. A host needing to resolve a name request sends a message to every host within earshot, requesting the address associated with a hostname. B-node has two shortcomings: broadcast traffic is undesirable and becomes a significant user of network bandwidths, and TCP/IP routers don't forward broadcast messages, which restricts B-node operation to a single network segment.

   P-node (point-to-point node), which relies on WINS servers for NetBIOS name resolution. Client computers register themselves with a WINS server when they come on the network. They then contact the WINS server with NetBIOS name resolution requests. WINS servers communicate using directed messages, which can cross routers, so P-node can operate on large networks. Unfortunately, if the WINS server is unavailable or if a node isn't configured to contact a WINS server, P-node name resolution fails.

M-node (modified node) is a hybrid mode that first attempts to resolve NetBIOS names using the B-node mechanism. If that fails, an attempt is made to use P-node name resolution. M-node was the first hybrid mode put into operation, but it has the disadvantage of favoring B-node operation, which is associated with high levels of broadcast traffic.

H-node (hybrid node) is also a hybrid mode that favors the use of WINS for NetBIOS name resolution. When a computer needs to resolve a NetBIOS name, it first attempts to use P-node resolution to resolve a name via WINS. Only if WINS resolution fails does the host resort to B-node to resolve the name via broadcasts. Because it typically results in the best network utilization, H-node is the default mode of operation for Microsoft TCP/IPs configured to use WINS for name resolution. Microsoft recommends leaving TCP/IP client computers in the default H-node configuration. For more information, see the section "Configuring NetBIOS Name Resolution."

Answers to Exam Questions

1. **D.** If you specify the backup directory, the server will automatically back up the WINS database every 24 hours. For more information, see the section "Managing and Monitoring WINS."

2. **B.** Pull replications are triggered by a time interval. For the branch WINS server to get a replica of the corporate WINS database, it would need to be scheduled to pull the information at a two-hour interval. For more information, see the section "Configuring WINS Replication."

APPLY YOUR KNOWLEDGE

3. **B.** After the WINS servers have been configured as replication partners, they will replicate with each other based on the replication configuration. For more information, see the section "Configuring WINS Replication."

4. **C.** Because there is no default WINS server (don't confuse it with the default gateway) the answer is C, the primary WINS server. For more information, see the section "Configuring NetBIOS Name Resolution."

5. **A.** The conflicts per second would show you if you have computers that have name conflicts. For more information, see the section "Managing and Monitoring WINS."

6. **D.** If you want to capture all the client computers that are registering with the server and not just new registrations, you need to look at the total for both the Total Number of Registrations/Sec and Total Number of Renewals/Sec. For more information, see the section "Managing and Monitoring WINS."

7. **A.** Windows 2000 Professional computers use H-node (hybrid) for NetBIOS name resolution. This node type favors the WINS server for name resolution, but will attempt to resolve the name by broadcast if the WINS server is unavailable. For more information, see the section "Configuring NetBIOS Name Resolution."

8. **D.** H-node (Hybrid) is the preferred method because it relies on the WINS server before resorting to a broadcast. P-node (point-to-point) will use a WINS server but cannot use broadcasts for NetBIOS name resolution. For more information, see the section "Configuring NetBIOS Name Resolution."

9. **D.** Although C is almost a correct answer, the Total Queries includes records not found. If all the queries are returning a Records Not Found result, the server probably has a problem. You should make sure that the number of Records Found (successful queries) is increasing. For more information, see the section "Managing and Monitoring WINS."

10. **B.** Because this is a DHCP environment, just add/update the WINS option for the DHCP scope. C might work, but it is much more labor intensive than the one-time scope update. For more information, see the section "Configuring WINS."

11. **A.** Because this is a bridged network, you need just a single server to provide WINS for each location. In a bridged network, there is only one logical segment. This means that broadcasts will propagate across the WAN connections. Although this is not a typical configuration, it does still exist on smaller legacy networks. For more information, see the section "Configuring WINS."

12. **C.** WINS is a dynamic replacement for the LMHOSTS file. For more information, see the section "Introduction to WINS."

13. **D.** DOS cannot use WINS because it is limited to a B-node resolution. B-node is a broadcast-only resolution method, and the broadcasts cannot cross the router. For more information, see the section "Configuring NetBIOS Name Resolution."

14. **B.** If you have frequently incrementing conflict statistics, you probably have a duplicate name. For more information, see the section "Managing and Monitoring WINS."

APPLY YOUR KNOWLEDGE

15. **D.** For this question, keep two components in mind: the trigger—when a certain number of entries are added (this is the least bandwidth-intensive mechanism—and the direction the information must travel. Answer D is the only one with the right combination of these factors. For more information, see the section "Configuring WINS Replication."

Suggested Readings and Resources

1. Boswell, William. *Inside Windows 2000 Server.* Indianapolis, IN: New Riders Publishing, 2000.

2. Heywood, Drew. *Networking with Microsoft TCP/IP, Third Edition.* Indianapolis, IN: New Riders Publishing, 1998.

3. Microsoft Corporation, *Microsoft Windows 2000 Server Resource Kit.* Redmond, WA: Microsoft Press, 2000.

This chapter helps you prepare for the MCSE Windows 2000 Network Infrastructure exam by covering the following objectives:

Install, configure, and troubleshoot IP routing protocols.

- **Update a Windows 2000-based routing table by means of static routes.**

- **Implement demand-dial routing.**

▶ To understand how to install, configure, and troubleshoot IP routing protocols, it is necessary to have an understanding of how they function. Then the procedures for properly configuring and implementing the protocols can be understood.

▶ Network environments that try to minimize communication costs between remote locations and a central office can make use of demand-dial routing. This feature of Windows 2000 also provides the capability to build fault tolerance into a network design.

▶ In some types of network environments, it is easier to implement routing by manually configuring the routing tables rather than incurring the overhead of a dynamic routing protocol. To do this, the network administrator will need to be familiar with the ROUTE command.

Manage and monitor IP routing.

- **Manage and monitor border routing.**

- **Manage and monitor internal routing.**

- **Manage and monitor IP routing protocols.**

▶ One of the tasks in implementing computer software and hardware is that of managing and monitoring its ongoing operation and troubleshooting issues that may arise. To help with this task, it is necessary to understand how to use the tools to monitor its operation and manage changes in the configuration.

CHAPTER 6

Installing, Configuring, Managing, Monitoring, and Troubleshooting IP Routing in a Windows 2000 Network Infrastructure

OUTLINE

**Installing, Configuring, and
Troubleshooting IP Routing Protocols**   **286**

   Introduction to IP Routing   286

   Host Routing   287

   Router Routing   289

   The Routing Process   292

   Routing Technology   295

      Distance-Vector Routing   296

      Link-State Routing   299

   Routing Networks   300

Setting Up Actual Routing Protocols   **302**

   Working with RIP   303

      RIP Version 1   303

      RIP Version 2   306

      RIP Updates   307

   RIP Routing Metric   308

   OSPF   309

      Routing Hierarchies   311

      OSPF Operation   318

   Demand-Dial Routing   321

   Types of Demand-Dial Connections   325

   Demand-Dial Security   328

Managing and Monitoring IP Routing   **331**

   Using the ROUTE Command to
     Configure Static Routes   331

   Using Network Monitor   333

   Managing and Monitoring IP Routing
    Protocols   335

      Routing and Remote Access
       Services Operation   335

      Troubleshooting RIP Environments   336

      Troubleshooting OSPF Environments   338

Chapter Summary   **340**

Apply Your Knowledge   **342**

▶ You can expect a number of questions related to routing protocols and their operation. Many of these will be in scenario format, in which the implementation of a particular protocol will be based on a network topology design. Therefore, you need to have a firm understanding of the way the protocol works in small, medium, and large network designs and to understand where each protocol best fits within these network scenarios. After you have a solid understanding of the theory presented here, you should try to gain some practical experience by using Windows 2000 Advanced Server as much as possible. Implement the various protocols to see how they work and how they are configured within a network environment.

▶ You should also expect scenario questions on implementing and configuring a demand-dial routing environment. Expect to have answers for where a demand-dial routing solution is best used and the special considerations that are required when implementing the various routing protocols over this type of configuration.

Installing, Configuring, and Troubleshooting IP Routing Protocols

Install, configure, and troubleshoot IP routing protocols.

This chapter's main purpose is to explain how the routing protocols within Windows 2000 work and how to implement and configure them on a Windows 2000 network. The underlying theory of routing is discussed so that you have a firm foundation for the later discussion on routing protocols, such as Open Shortest Path First (OSPF) and Routing Information Protocol (RIP).

The chapter also explains demand-dial routing, including how demand-dial routing works and the special considerations that must be taken into account when implementing a demand-dial routing configuration into your network environment. Step by Steps for implementing, managing, and monitoring a demand-dial configuration are included.

Finally, this chapter gives a brief overview of some of the problems you may encounter within a routing environment, and it discusses tools that can be used to help diagnose problems and issues.

Introduction to IP Routing

Routing is the process of forwarding a packet based on the destination IP address. Routing occurs at a sending TCP/IP host, which is known as host routing, and at an IP router, which is known as router routing. In both cases—at a sending host and at a router—a decision has to be made about where the packet is to be forwarded.

To make these decisions, the IP layer consults a routing table stored in memory. Routing table entries are created by default when TCP/IP initializes and additional entries are added either manually by a system administrator or automatically through communication with routers.

Host Routing

For a host to communicate with a destination computer, it must first identify where that host exists. End users prefer to communicate with a destination host using the name of the host, which is much easier to remember than a network address that consists of numbers. For the computers to communicate however, they must know the network address of the destination host. To obtain this destination address, the sending host uses an address resolution mechanism such as the Domain Name System (DNS) or Windows Internet Naming System (WINS) to obtain the address. (See Chapter 1, "Installing, Configuring, Managing, Monitoring, and Troubleshooting DNS in a Windows 2000 Network Infrastructure," and Chapter 5, "Installing, Configuring, Managing, Monitoring, and Troubleshooting WINS in a Windows 2000 Network Infrastructure," for more information.)

After the address has been obtained, the sending host must then determine whether it can send directly to the destination or whether it will need to forward it to a router to send on its behalf. To determine this, the sending host compares the network address of the source with the network address of the destination. If the two network addresses are the same, the sending host knows that the destination is on the same segment and addresses the packet to the destination's physical address.

If the two network addresses do not match, the host must forward the message on to a router so that it can try to send the packet to the destination on the sending host's behalf. Based on the destination address, the router then uses its table of routes to determine the best interface to send the packet out to reach its destination. Each router along the path repeats this process until the destination host finally receives the packet. If routers determine that the destination host is unreachable, a destination unreachable packet is sent back to the host.

For the host to send the packet to its destination via the router, it must first determine the address of the router to send the packet to. This can be accomplished using one of the following processes:

◆ The default gateway address is determined and the local Address Resolution Protocol (ARP) cache is queried to identify the physical address to be used to reach the desired router.

◆ An Internet Control Message Protocol (ICMP) redirect message is sent by an IP router to the sending host, informing it of a better route to a destination host. The better route becomes a host route in the routing table.

◆ A TCP/IP host can "listen" to the routing protocol traffic used by routers. This is known as eavesdropping or wiretapping. Eavesdropping hosts have the same routing information as the routers. Windows 2000 implements eavesdropping through a feature called silent RIP.

STEP BY STEP

6.1 Enabling RIP "Listening" on a Windows 2000 Professional Workstation

1. Choose Start, Settings, and Control Panel, as shown in Figure 6.1, and then double-click Add/Remove Programs.

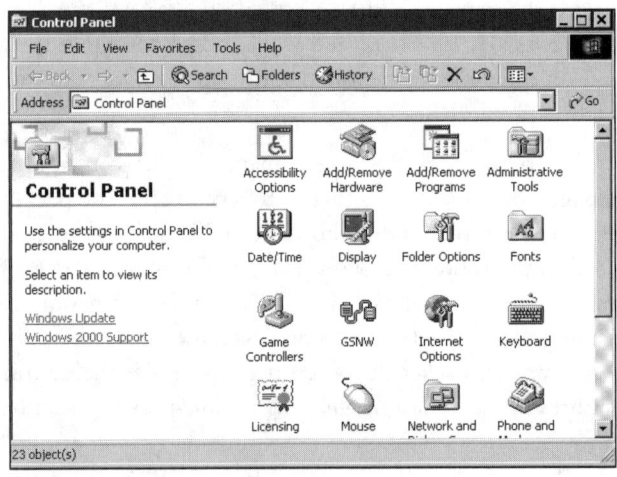

FIGURE 6.1
Use Add/Remove Programs in the Windows 2000 Control Panel to access the Windows Components.

2. Click Add/Remove Windows Components. The Windows Components dialog box opens (see Figure 6.2).

3. In Components, highlight Networking Services (but do not select the option), and then click Details. The Networking Services dialog box (shown in Figure 6.3) opens.

4. Select the RIP Listener option, and then click OK.

5. Click Next, and then follow the instructions in the wizard.

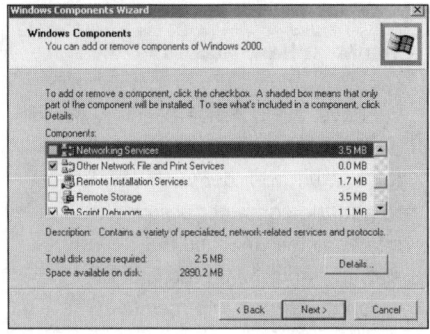

FIGURE 6.2
The Windows Components Wizard gives you access to the Networking Services option.

Router Routing

When a router receives a packet that must be forwarded to a destination host, the router must either deliver it to the destination host or to another router that will, in turn, continue on the process of forwarding it to the destination host. To determine whether to forward to a host or to forward to a router, the router examines the destination network address and determines whether it is attached to that network. If so, the router forwards the packet to the destination host on that network.

If the router is not attached to the destination network directly, it uses the information in its routing tables to choose the best interface to forward the packet out. It does this by addressing the packet to the physical address of another router along the path to the destination host that is connected to a network segment that the current router is connected to. The decision as to which router to forward the packet to is determined by a number of variables about each of the network paths to the destination host, including the number of hops, the cost of each hop, and so on.

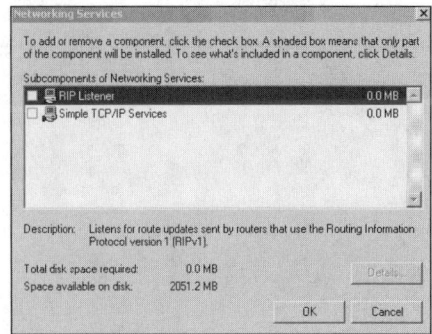

FIGURE 6.3
To enable the RIP Listener, you must use the Details button when the Networking Services option is highlighted but not selected.

NOTE **You Must Have Access**   If the server you are working with is a member of a Windows 2000 Active Directory domain and you are not a domain administrator, instruct your domain administrator to add the computer account of this server to the RAS and IAS Servers security group in the domain of which the server is a member. The domain administrator can add the computer account to the RAS and IAS Servers security group by using Active Directory Users and Computers or with the netsh ras add registered server command.

Windows 2000 Advanced Server provides router routing using Routing and Remote Access Services (RRAS). To enable RRAS within Windows 2000 Advanced Server, complete the following Step by Step.

STEP BY STEP

6.2 Enabling Routing and Remote Access Services

1. Choose Start, Programs, Administrative Tools, Routing and Remote Access. By default, the local computer is listed as a server (see Figure 6.4).

2. In the console tree, right-click the server you want to enable, and then click Configure and Enable Routing and Remote Access. The Routing and Remote Access Server Setup Wizard starts.

3. Click Next to start configuring Routing and Remote Access. The Common Configurations dialog box opens (see Figure 6.5).

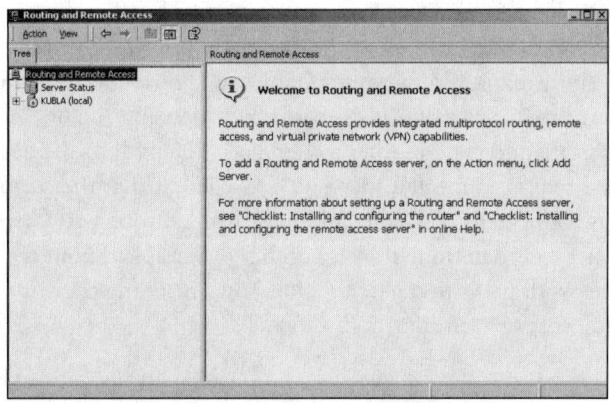

FIGURE 6.4
The Routing and Remote Access console is used to configure all routing for Windows 2000.

4. Select Network Router and click Next to continue. The Routed Protocols dialog box opens (see Figure 6.6).

5. On the Routed Protocols dialog box, ensure that the protocols you will be routing are available on the server. For this chapter, you will need TCP/IP installed. Click Next to continue. The Demand-Dial Connections dialog box opens (see Figure 6.7).

6. On the Demand-Dial Connections dialog box, select whether you would like to enable demand-dial connections to access remote networks. Select No and click Next to continue. The Completing the Routing and Remote Access Server Setup Wizard summary dialog box opens (see Figure 6.8).

7. On the summary page, click Finish to complete the enabling of routing services.

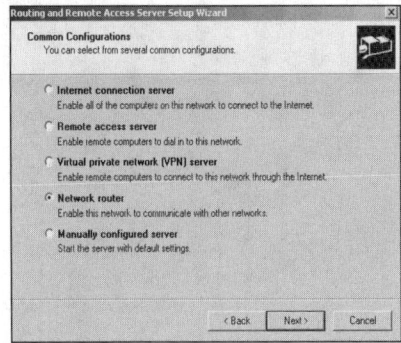

FIGURE 6.5
The Common Configurations dialog box allows you to customize the wizard to configure the server for your specific purpose.

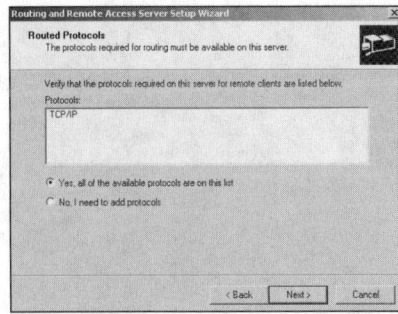

FIGURE 6.6
The Routed Protocols dialog box shows you the installed protocols and allows you to add additional protocols as needed.

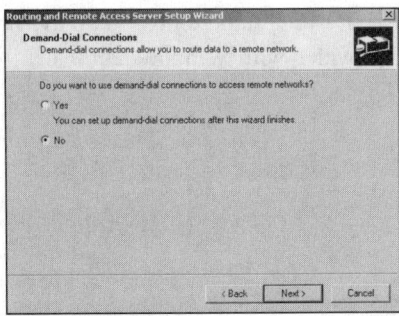

FIGURE 6.7
The Demand-Dial Connections can be configured after the wizard finishes.

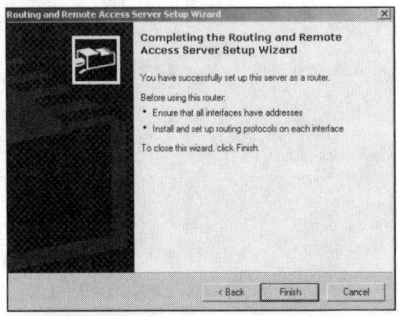

FIGURE 6.8
The Completing the Routing and Remote Access Server Setup Wizard dialog box is your last chance to cancel the Routing and Remote Access installation.

The Routing Process

When a packet is received by a router or is forwarded by a host, they both must make decisions about how to send the packet. To do this, the router and host consult a database of information known as the routing table. This database is stored in RAM so that the lookup process is optimized. As the packet is forwarded through various routers toward its destination, each router makes a decision as to how to proceed by consulting its routing table. When a destination host replies to a packet, it is possible that the same path may not be used to reach the original sender. This depends on the metrics of each path along the route.

The information in the routing table can be generated in one of two ways. The first method is to manually configure the routing table with the routes for each destination network. This is known as static routing. Static routing is more suited to small environments where the amount of information to configure is small, and the overhead of generating the routing information is unacceptable. Static routers do not scale well to large or dynamically changing internetworks because of their manual administration.

The second method for generating routing table information is to make use of a dynamic routing protocol. A dynamic routing protocol consists of routing tables that are built and maintained automatically through an ongoing communication between routers. Periodically or on demand, messages are exchanged between routers for the purpose of updating information kept in their routing tables. Dynamic routers generally require little maintenance after they have been configured. This allows them to be used in much larger environments where it would not be practical to use static routers. Two dynamic routing protocols that are provided with Windows 2000 are

◆ Routing Information Protocol (RIP)

◆ Open Shortest Path First (OSPF)

Dynamic routers can detect information from other routers, making dynamic routing fault tolerant. If a router or link goes down, the routers sense the change in the internetwork topology through the expiration of the route information in the routing table. The router can then rebuild its links based on the new network topology and forward the routing information to other routers so that all the routers on the internetwork become aware of the new internetwork topology. This capability is not available with static routers. After a router is configured in a static router, it remains until it is manually changed, making it unable to adapt to changes in the internetwork.

IN THE FIELD

DISCERNING WHEN A ROUTER IS DOWN

Assume that you have a network that has three Routers: Router 1 connects to Router 2 over Network A, and Router 2 connects to Router 3 over Network B (see Figure 6.9). If Router 1 goes down, Router 2 will be unable to reach Router 1 over Network A as indicated by the route in its routing table. After a period of time, Router 2 expires the route information in its routing table and requests an update, at which time it will determine that it can no longer reach Router 1. This will then be reflected in its routing tables. Router 2 will eventually broadcast its routing information to Router 3, at which time Router 3 will update its tables with the information that Router 1 is not available.

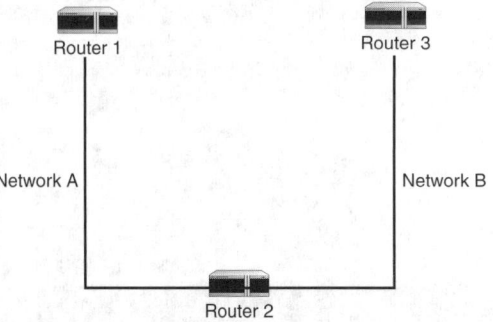

FIGURE 6.9
This diagram shows the networks and routers involved in discerning when a router is down.

STEP BY STEP

6.3 Adding the RIP

1. Open the Routing and Remote Access console by choosing Start, Programs, Administrative Tools, Routing and Remote Access (see Figure 6.10).

2. In the left pane, expand the list under IP Routing and right-click General. From the context menu, select New Routing Protocol. The New Routing Protocol dialog box (see Figure 6.11) opens.

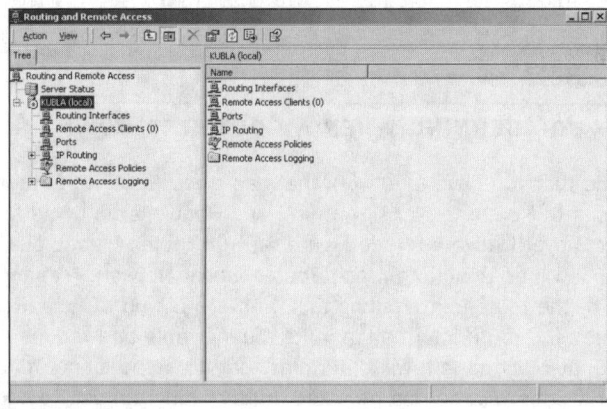

FIGURE 6.10
The Routing and Remote Access console is used to configure the routing protocols under Windows 2000.

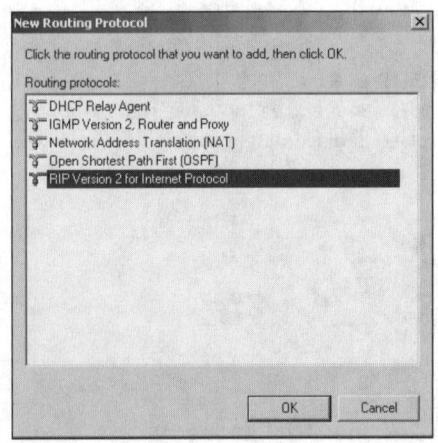

FIGURE 6.11
Five routing protocols are available for installation.

3. Select RIP Version 2 for Internet Protocol and click OK.
You will see RIP appear under the IP Routing entry
(see Figure 6.12). RIP is now installed on your
Windows 2000 server.

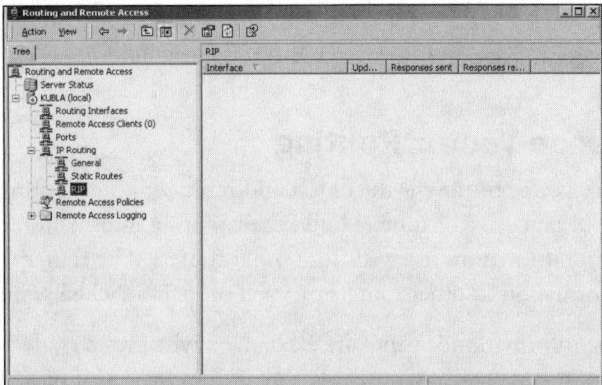

FIGURE 6.12
Installed routing protocols are listed under the
IP Routing section of the tree.

The capability to scale and recover from internetwork faults makes
dynamic routing, rather than static routing, the better choice for
medium, large, and very large internetworks.

Routing Technology

Routing protocols are based either on a distance-vector or link-state
technology. The main differences between distance-vector and link-
state routing protocols are the following:

◆ **What routing information is exchanged.** When a link
or router fails, the internetwork must reconfigure itself to
reflect the new topology. Information in routing tables must
be updated.

◆ **How the information is exchanged.** The time it takes for the internetwork to reconverge is known as the convergence time. The convergence time varies based on the routing protocol and the type of failure (downed link or downed router).

◆ **How quickly the internetwork can recover from a downed link or a downed router.** How quickly it can recover is determined by the type of fault, how it is sensed, and how the routing information is propagated through the internetwork.

Distance-Vector Routing

Distance-vector routing is the oldest and most common routing algorithm. Distance-vector routers build their routing information tables based on information received from other routers. The routers pass this information to other routers on each of their attached segments.

Routing information is generally exchanged when routers are started, when routes change, and at regular intervals. On receipt of new routing information, routers update their routing information tables and broadcast the new routing information onto all attached networks. If, however, a router cannot communicate at all (that is, the router is not available), a route-aging algorithm must come into play to remove the route information from a router's tables.

The time required to update all routers on routing information changes is called convergence. One of the negative attributes of distance-vector-based routing is slow convergence. Using distance-vector-based routing methods, each router receives route change information, updates its tables, calculates the hop counts to existing routes, and broadcasts new routing information.

The count-to-infinity problem is one of the major disadvantages of distance-vector routing. This condition is caused when a router (or a link to a router) becomes unavailable. The convergence time is slow and, therefore, incorrect routing information can propagate through the system.

IN THE FIELD

THE EXCHANGE OF INFORMATION

Assume that you have two routers: 1 and 2 (see Figure 6.13). Router 1's connection to Network A has been destroyed. Router 1 knows it cannot reach Network A itself, but Router 2 advertises that Network A is two hops away. Router 1, therefore, assumes that it is now three hops from Network A and Router 2 is the way to access Network A. Router 2 still believes that Router 1, however, is the way to Network A, and it resets its routing information tables to reflect that Network A is now four hops away, using Router 1 as the best route. Again, Router 2 broadcasts this information, and Router 1 resets its tables again to reflect that it is now five hops away, using Router 2 as the best way to Network A.

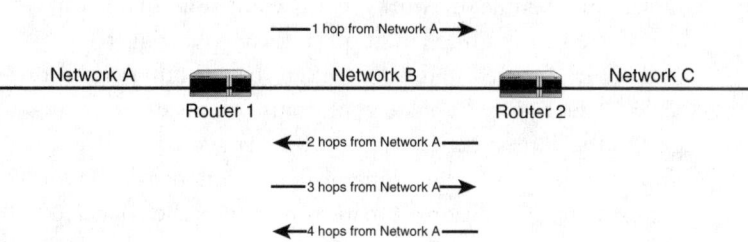

FIGURE 6.13
This diagram shows the way the routers calculate the hops in transferring data.

The routers continue to reset their routing information tables and increase the hop count value until "infinity" is reached. Infinity usually means the maximum number of hop counts a routing protocol can accept before a routing information packet is discarded.

Routing protocols can take various steps to avoid the count-to-infinity problem. Three avoidance mechanisms that can be implemented are

◆ **Split horizon.** This mechanism relies on not sending routing information back in the direction it was received from. Basically, the router says, "I learned about network xx from you, so you can't get to network xx through me." Split horizon eliminates count-to-infinity and routing loops during convergence in single-path internetworks and reduces the chances of count to infinity in multipath internetworks.

◆ **Split horizon with poison reverse.** This mechanism differs from split horizon because it announces all networks. However, those networks learned in a given direction are announced with a hop count of 16, indicating that the network is unreachable. In a single-path internetwork, split horizon with poison reverse has no benefit beyond split horizon. However, in a multipath internetwork, split horizon with poison reverse greatly reduces count-to-infinity and routing loops. Count to infinity can still occur in a multipath internetwork because routes to networks can be learned from multiple sources.

◆ **Triggered updates.** This mechanism allows a router to announce changes in metric values almost immediately, rather than waiting for the next periodic announcement. The trigger is a change to a metric in an entry in the routing table. For example, networks that become unavailable can be announced with a hop count of 16 through a triggered update. If triggered updates were sent by all routers immediately, each triggered update could cause a cascade of broadcast traffic across the IP internetwork. Triggered updates improve the convergence time of RIP internetworks but at the expense of additional broadcast traffic as the triggered updates are propagated.

Other disadvantages of distance-vector routing are slow convergence and high overhead. In distance-vector routing, when a change is made, the changes must be propagated to each router. This propagation causes all routing tables affected by this change to be recalculated. Distance-vector routing can be very slow converging after a change in topology occurs. In addition, should there be a large number of routes within the network, it can lead to very large routing tables, which requires additional resources on each router and can cause significant traffic on the network during updates of routing information.

The advantages of distance-vector routing are that it requires low maintenance and is easy to configure, making it popular in small network environments.

Link-State Routing

As previously discussed, distance-vector-based routing protocols periodically broadcast route information to each other, whether or not the information has changed. Link-state-routing protocols, on the other hand, exchange information only about the specific routes that have changed.

Routers using link-state routing protocols learn about their network environment by "meeting" their neighboring routers. This is done through a "hello" packet. This network information is then sent to each of the neighboring routers using a link-state advertisement. The neighboring routers copy the contents of the packet and forward the link-state advertisement to each attached network, except for the one the link-state advertisement was received on. This is known as flooding.

Routers using a link-state routing protocol build a tree, or "map," of shortest paths with itself as the root. The tree is based on all the link-state advertisements seen. The tree contains the route to each destination in the network. Figure 6.14 depicts a network that is using a link-state routing protocol.

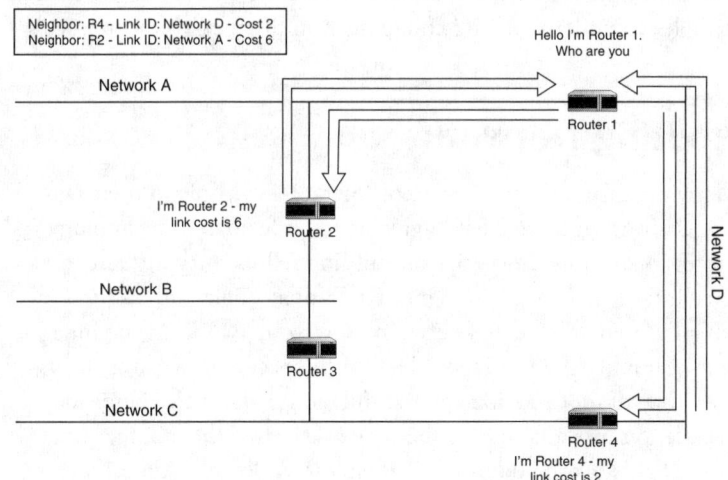

FIGURE 6.14

The network in this diagram uses link-state communication.

Router 1 transmits a "hello" packet to learn about its neighboring routers. Each neighbor replies with information regarding the link it is attached to and the route cost. Router 1 builds its routing database directly from the information received in response to the "hello" packets.

The next step in link-state routing is to transmit link-state advertisements to its neighbors. The link-state advertisements that will be transmitted contain information about router 1's neighbors and their associated costs. This packet is copied by each neighbor, and the link-state advertisement is forwarded to each of their neighbors. Because the routers maintain the original link-state advertisement, whenever another router needs link-state advertisement information, it requests a copy of the original from its neighbor. Because the link-state advertisement is never altered by a router, it is considered to be first-hand information.

Because link-state advertisements contain information only about the neighbors of a particular router, this leads to smaller routing tables. In addition, because link-state information is not exchanged after the network has converged, it does not have the impact on the network that distance-vector routing does, making it more efficient.

The disadvantages of link-state-based protocols are that they are more complex to understand and configure than distance-vector protocols.

Routing Networks

Many organizations today cannot tolerate downtime in their networks. To meet service-level agreements, information technology professionals must find ways of building redundancy or fault tolerance into their network designs. Traditional single-path designs, in which a single path exists between any two networks in the internetwork, simplify the routing tables and the packet flow paths; however, they do not provide any redundancy. A dynamic router may be able to sense a fault, but the networks across the failure are unreachable for the duration of the fault. A downed link or a downed router must be brought back up before packets can be delivered successfully across the downed link or router.

In a multipath routing infrastructure, multiple paths exist between networks in the internetwork. Multipath internetworks provide redundancy when dynamic routing is used, and some routing protocols, such as OSPF, can balance the load of network traffic across multiple paths with the same metric value. Multipath internetworks, however, can be more complex to configure and can have a higher probability of routing loops during convergence when using distance-vector-based routing protocols.

In small networks, information about each network ID is maintained in the routing table. This allows every host to connect to every other host on the network by referring to the network on which the host is located. The routers within such a network maintain information about every route to a particular network ID so that routing of network/host address pairs can be accomplished. Each network is not classified into smaller networks using net/subnet information, only network and host information. This type of network is considered to have a flat routing infrastructure.

This type of infrastructure does not scale to very large networks. One such large network is the Internet. The Internet has evolved into a collection of Internet Service Providers (ISP). Providers are interconnected among themselves to provide Internetwide connectivity among all their subscribers.

Initially, IP routing on the Internet was designed using a flat model approach consisting of network/host address information. Each host on the Internet is represented by an address that identifies both the network that the host is located on, as well as the address of the individual host. Routing entries for each network address are maintained within a routing table and are used to route information between hosts.

As the Internet grew, address utilization became inefficient and routing suffered scalability issues (there are 2,097,152 Class C networks; a routing table entry for each network would result in large and inefficient routing tables).

To accommodate scalability issues, routing between multiple interconnected providers who each may have a significant number of networks, subnets, and hosts, the IP routing architecture modeled each Internet provider as a collection of interconnected autonomous

---

NOTE

The Class System Within the Internet Internet addresses are segmented into different classes. There are five classes of addresses, Class A through Class E. Generally, the most popular of the classes are Classes A, B, and C. The class is determined by the high order bits of the address. Class A has the high order bit of the address set to 0. The next 7 bits form the network number part, and the remaining 24 bits form the host number part. Class B has the high order 2 bits set to 10 (binary). The next 14 bits form the network number part, and the remaining 16 bits form the host number part. Finally, Class C has the high order 3 bits set to 110 (binary). The next 21 bits form the network number part, and the remaining 8 bits form the host number part.

Address utilization with this type of structure is very inefficient. For example, a Class A network can have 16,777,216 hosts per network. It is unlikely that any one organization will have this number of hosts on one network. As a result, the concept of subnetting was introduced. See Chapter 4, "Installing, Configuring, Managing, Monitoring, and Troubleshooting Network Protocols in a Windows 2000 Network Infrastructure," for more information on subnetting.

systems. Routing within each autonomous system is provided by means of intradomain (interior) routing protocols, such as RIP, OSPF, or Interior Gateway Protocol (IGP). Routing among autonomous systems is provided by means of interdomain (exterior) routing protocols, such as Exterior Gateway Protocol (EGP) and Border Gateway Protocol (BGP). Interdomain (exterior) routing protocols, summarize IP routes and help to remove the scalability issues that interior gateway protocols can have.

Autonomous systems may be further divided into routing domains (also known as regions or areas) that define a hierarchy within the autonomous system. This type of network infrastructure is called a hierarchical internetwork. The network IDs in a hierarchical internetwork have a network/subnet/sub-subnet structure. A routing table entry for the highest level (the network) is also the route used for the subnets and sub-subnets of the network. When routing between routing domains, groups of network IDs can be represented as a single routing table entry through route summarization.

Hierarchical routing infrastructures simplify routing tables and lower the amount of routing information that is exchanged, but they require more planning.

SETTING UP ACTUAL ROUTING PROTOCOLS

Up to this point, this chapter discussed the theory behind different routing protocols, how they work, and some of the mechanisms that are used to resolve issues that arise with the different types of routing protocols. Next, this discussion focuses on the actual routing protocols, beginning with the RIP, followed by the OSPF protocol.

Working with RIP

RIP is a distance-vector protocol that uses hop count as its metric for measuring the number of routers that must be crossed to reach the desired network. RIP is widely used for routing traffic in the global Internet and is an IGP, which means that it performs routing within a single autonomous system. There are two versions of RIP, version 1 and version 2.

RIP Version 1

In RIP Version 1, all route announcements are addressed to the IP subnet (all host bits are set to 1) and a MAC-level broadcast is initiated. As a result, non-RIP hosts and RIP hosts receive RIP announcements. For large or very large RIP internetworks, the amount of broadcast traffic on each subnet can become significant.

To configure RIP on a Routing and Remote Access Server, proceed with the following Step by Step.

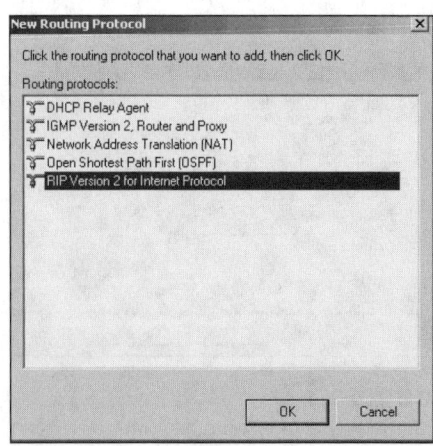

FIGURE 6.15
Select RIP Version 2 for Internet Protocol.

STEP BY STEP

6.4 Configuring RIP on Windows 2000

1. Choose Start, Programs, Administrative Tools, Routing and Remote Access. The Routing and Remote Access console opens.

2. Expand the console tree and select IP Routing. Right-click the General interface and from the context menu select New Routing Protocol. The New Routing Protocol dialog box opens (see Figure 6.15).

3. Select RIP Version 2 for Internet Protocol and click OK. You will return to the Routing and Remote Access console and RIP now appears under the IP Routing entry.

4. Select the newly created RIP icon and right-click to choose New Interface. The New Interface for RIP Version 2 for Internet Protocol dialog box opens (see Figure 6.16).

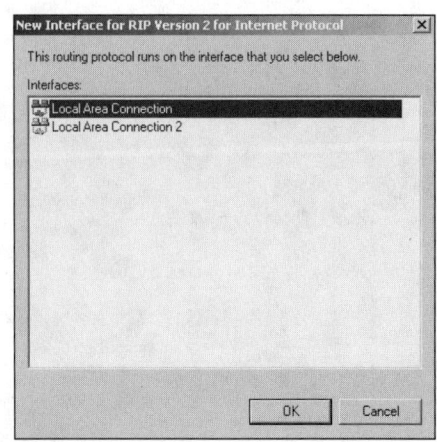

FIGURE 6.16
You need to select an interface on which to run RIP. In many cases, you will need to do this multiple times; once on each local area network connection.

continues

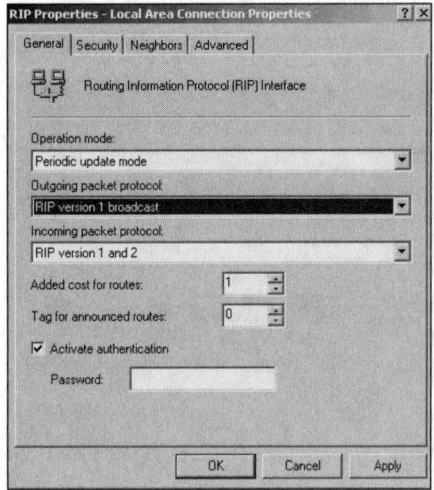

FIGURE 6.17
RIP is a fairly complex protocol with many configuration options.

continued

5. Select the appropriate Local Area Connection and click OK. The RIP Properties dialog box opens (see Figure 6.17).

6. On the General tab, in Outgoing Packet Protocol, select RIP Version 1 Broadcast. In Incoming Packet Protocol, select RIP Version 1 and 2. Click OK to return to the Routing and Remote Access console and activate the changes.

While the RIP routing protocol produces additional broadcast traffic, the broadcast nature of RIP Version 1 enables the use of silent RIP. A silent RIP router processes RIP announcements but does not announce its own routes. Silent RIP could be enabled on nonrouter hosts to produce a routing table with as much detail as the RIP routers. With more detailed routes in the routing table, a silent RIP host can make better routing decisions. To enable silent RIP on your router, complete the following:

STEP BY STEP

6.5 Enabling Silent RIP on Windows 2000

1. Choose Start, Programs, Administrative Tools, Routing and Remote Access. The Routing and Remote Access console opens.

2. Expand the console tree and select RIP. The list of available interfaces running RIP will appear in the right pane of the console (see Figure 6.18).

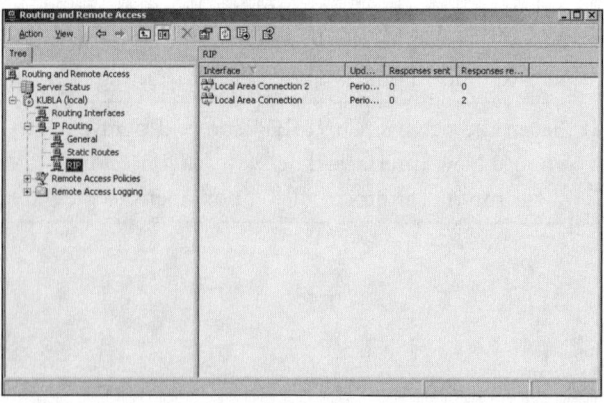

FIGURE 6.18
You can have multiple interfaces running RIP. Each has to be configured individually.

3. Right-click the interface that you want to configure for silent RIP mode, and from the context menu select Properties. The Local Area Connection Properties opens (see Figure 6.19).

4. On the General tab, in Outgoing Packet Protocol, select Silent RIP from the pull-down menu. Click OK to return to the Routing and Remote Access console and apply the changes.

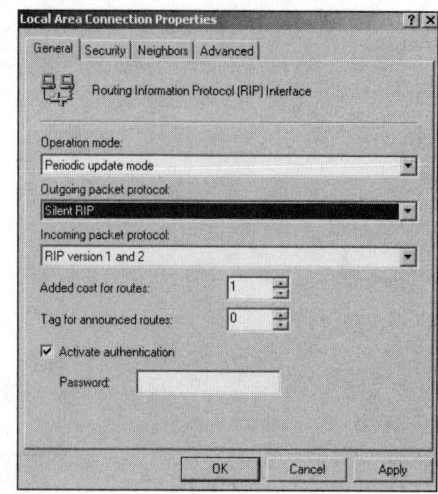

FIGURE 6.19
The Local Area Connection Properties dialog box includes the RIP configuration.

RIP Version 1 was designed for class-based IP internetworks in which the network ID can be determined from the values of the first 3 bits of the IP address in the RIP route. Because the subnet mask is not included or announced with the route, the RIP router must determine the network ID based on a limited set of information. For each route in a RIP Version 1 message, the RIP Version 1 router performs the following process:

◆ If the network ID fits the address classes (Class A, Class B, or Class C), the default class-based subnet mask is assumed.

◆ If the network ID does not fit the address class and the network ID fits the subnet mask of the interface on which it is received, the subnet mask of the interface on which it was received is assumed. If the network ID does not fit the subnet mask of the interface on which it is received, the network ID is assumed to be a host route with the subnet mask 255.255.255.255.

As a result of the assumptions listed previously, supernetted routes might be interpreted as a single network ID rather than as the range of network IDs that they are designed to represent, and subnet routes advertised outside of the network ID being subnetted might be interpreted as host routes.

As mechanisms for supporting subnetted environments, RIP Version 1 routers do not advertise the subnets of a subnetted class-based network ID outside the subnetted region of the IP internetwork. However, because only the class-based network ID is being advertised outside the subnetted environment, subnets of a network ID in a RIP Version 1 environment must be contiguous. If subnets of an IP network ID are noncontiguous, known as disjointed subnets, the class-based network ID is announced by separate RIP Version 1 routers in different parts of the internetwork. As a result, IP traffic can be forwarded to the wrong network.

Finally, RIP Version 1 does not provide any protection from a rogue RIP router starting up on a network and announcing false or inaccurate routes. RIP Version 1 announcements are processed regardless of their source. A malicious user could use this lack of protection to overwhelm RIP routers with hundreds or thousands of false or inaccurate routes.

RIP Version 2

RIP Version 2 seeks to address some of the problems associated with RIP Version 1. The design goals of RIP Version 2 were to minimize broadcast traffic, use variable length subnetting to conserve IP addresses, and secure routing environments from misconfigured or malicious routers. To help resolve these issues, several key features were added:

◆ Rather than broadcasting RIP announcements, RIP Version 2 supports sending RIP announcements to the IP multicast address of 224.0.0.9. Non-RIP nodes are not disturbed by RIP router announcement traffic. The disadvantage of this new feature is that silent RIP nodes must also be listening for multicast traffic sent to 224.0.0.9. If you are using silent RIP, verify that your silent RIP nodes can listen for multicasted RIP Version 2 announcements before deploying multicast RIP Version 2. The use of multicasted announcements is optional. The broadcasting of RIP v2 announcements is also supported.

◆ RIP Version 2 announcements send the subnet mask (also known as a network mask) along with the network ID. RIP Version 2 can be used in subnetted, supernetted, and variable-length subnet mask environments. Subnets of a network ID do not have to be contiguous (they can be disjointed subnets).

◆ RIP Version 2 supports the use of authentication mechanisms to verify the origin of incoming RIP announcements. Simple password authentication was defined in RFC 1723, but newer authentication mechanisms, such as Message Digest 5 (MD5), are available.

RIP Updates

RIP sends routing update messages at regular intervals and when the network topology changes. When a router receives a routing update that includes changes to an entry, it updates its routing table to reflect the new route. The metric value for the path is increased by one, and the sender is indicated as to the next hop. RIP routers maintain only the best route (the route with the lowest metric value) to a destination. After updating its routing table, the router immediately begins transmitting routing updates to inform other network routers of the change. These updates are sent independently of the regularly scheduled updates that RIP routers send.

If the RIP router is storing a complete list of all the networks and all the possible ways to reach each network, the routing table can have hundreds or even thousands of entries in a large IP internetwork with multiple paths. Because only 25 routes can be sent in a single RIP packet, large routing tables have to be sent as multiple RIP packets.

RIP routers advertise the contents of their routing tables every 30 seconds on all attached networks through an IP subnet and a MAC-level broadcast. (RIP Version 2 routers can be configured to multicast RIP announcements.) Large IP internetworks carry the broadcasted RIP overhead of large routing tables. This can be especially problematic on WAN links in which significant portions of the WAN link bandwidth are devoted to the passing of RIP traffic. As a result, RIP-based routing does not scale well to large internetworks or WAN implementations.

RIP Routing Metric

RIP uses a single routing metric (hop count) to measure the distance between the source and a destination network. Each hop in a path from source to destination is assigned a hop count value, which is typically 1. When a router receives a routing update that contains a new or changed destination network entry, the router adds one to the metric value indicated in the update and enters the network in the routing table. The IP address of the sender is used as the next hop.

RIP prevents routing loops from continuing indefinitely by implementing a limit on the number of hops allowed in a path from the source to a destination. The maximum number of hops in a path is 15; therefore, there can only be 15 routers between any two hosts. If a router receives a routing update that contains a new or a changed entry, and if increasing the metric value by one causes the metric to be infinity (that is, 16), the network destination is considered unreachable.

NOTE

RIP Stability   To adjust for rapid network topology changes, RIP specifies a number of stability features that are common to many routing protocols. RIP, for example, implements the split horizon, the split horizon with poison reverse, and the trigger update mechanisms to prevent incorrect routing information from being propagated. In addition, the RIP hop count limit prevents routing loops from continuing indefinitely.

OSPF

OSPF is a link-state routing protocol. It functions by sending link-state advertisements (LSAs) to all other routers within the same hierarchical area. Don't worry if you don't understand what is meant by hierarchical area. This will be discussed in a later section, "Routing Hierarchies." LSAs for routers consist of a router, its attached networks, and their configured costs. As OSPF routers accumulate link-state information into a database called the link-state database, they use the Shortest Path First (SPF) algorithm to calculate the shortest path to each node. OSPF has the following features:

◆ OSPF has better convergence than RIP because routing changes are propagated instantaneously and not periodically.

◆ OSPF calculated routes are always loop free. There is no possibility of loops occurring.

◆ OSPF sends updates only when routing changes rather than sending routing updates periodically. This ensures better use of bandwidth.

◆ OSPF allows for logical definition of networks where routers can be divided into areas. This provides a mechanism for aggregating routes and cutting down on the unnecessary propagation of subnet information.

◆ OSPF was designed to advertise the subnet mask with the network. OSPF supports variable-length subnet masks (VLSM), disjointed subnets, and supernetting.

◆ OSPF allows for routing authentication using different methods of password authentication.

◆ Routes outside of the OSPF autonomous system are advertised within the autonomous system so that OSPF routers can calculate the least cost route to external networks. This keeps track of external routes injected by exterior protocols.

To configure OSPF on a Routing and Remote Access server, proceed with the following Step by Step.

NOTE

Subnetting and Supernetting
Variable-length subnetting is a technique of allocating subnetted network IDs that use subnet masks of different sizes. However, all subnetted network IDs are unique and can be distinguished from each other by their corresponding subnet mask.

Supernetting is the process of concatenating pieces of the Class C address space. Supernetting can be used to consolidate several Class C network addresses into one logical network. To use supernetting, the IP network addresses that are to be combined must share the same high order bits, and the subnet mask is shortened to take bits away from the network portion of the address and add them to the host portion.

Disjointed subnets are subnets of an IP Network ID that are noncontiguous.

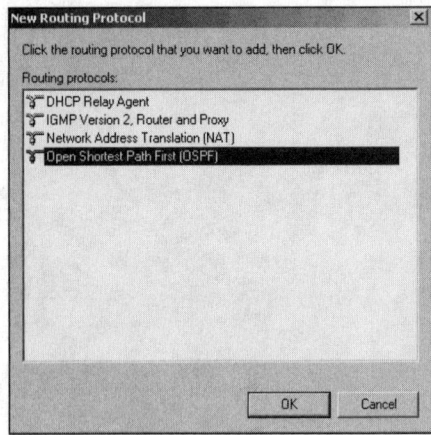

FIGURE 6.20
Select the routing protocol you need to install.

STEP BY STEP

6.6 Installing and Configuring OSPF on Windows 2000

1. Choose Start, Programs, Administrative Tools, and then click Routing and Remote Access. The Routing and Remote Access console opens.

2. Expand the console tree, and under IP Routing right-click General. From the context menu, select New Routing Protocol. The New Routing Protocol dialog box opens (see Figure 6.20).

3. Select Open Shortest Path First and click OK to install it. It now appears under IP Routing in the Routing and Remote Access console (see Figure 6.21).

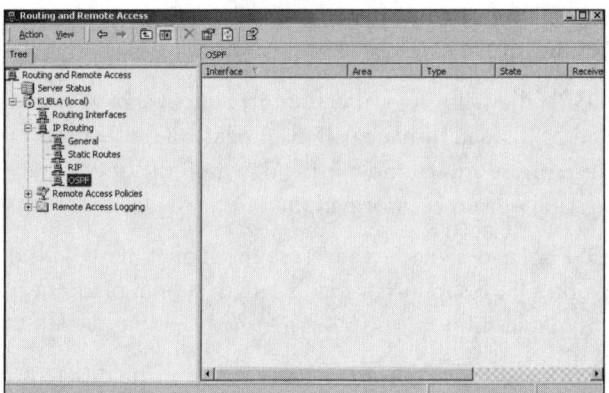

FIGURE 6.21
All the TCP/IP routing protocols are listed in the console tree under IP Routing.

4. Select the newly installed OSPF protocol and right-click. From the context menu, select New Interface. The New Interface for Open Shortest Path First (OSPF) dialog box opens (see Figure 6.22).

5. Select Local Area Connection and click OK. The OSPF Properties dialog box opens (see Figure 6.23).

6. On the General tab, select the Enable OSPF for This Address option. In Area ID, click the ID of the area to which the interface belongs. In Router Priority, click the arrows to set the priority of the router over the interface. In Cost, click the scroll arrows to set the cost of sending a packet over the interface. If the area to which the interface belongs is enabled for passwords, in Password, type a password. Under Network Type, set the type of OSPF interface as broadcast. Click OK to complete the installation of the interface and return to the Routing and Remote Access console.

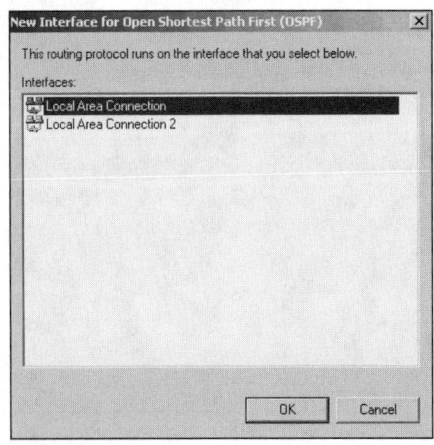

FIGURE 6.22
You need to select the interface to run OSPF across. This may be on multiple interfaces in some environments.

Routing Hierarchies

Unlike RIP, OSPF can operate within a hierarchy. The basic structure to this hierarchy includes areas, autonomous systems, and the backbone. The largest entity within the hierarchy is the autonomous system. An autonomous system is a collection of networks under common administration, sharing a common routing strategy. Each autonomous system can be further divided into areas, with areas linked by an OSPF backbone, which, in itself, is also an area.

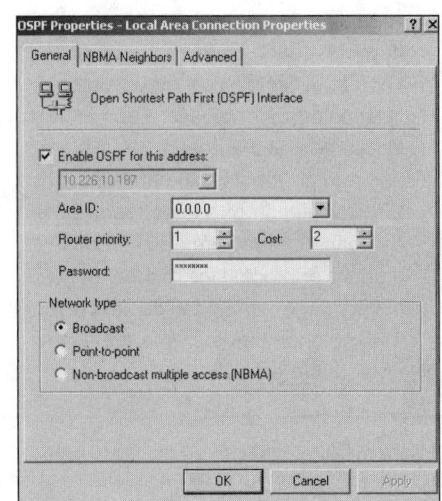

FIGURE 6.23
You can modify the default OSPF settings while installing the first interface.

Areas

An autonomous system can be divided into a number of continuous groups of networks called areas. Each area is identified by an area ID. This identifier has no relation to an IP address or IP network ID. Area IDs are not used to reflect routing data. However, if all the networks within an area correspond to a single subnetted network ID, the area ID can be set to reflect the network ID for administrative convenience. For example, if an area contains all the subnets of the IP network 10.1.0.0, the area ID can be set to 10.1.0.0. The purpose of defining areas within an autonomous system is to reduce the size of a topological database.

To keep the size of topological databases for each router to a minimum, LSAs for an area's networks and routers are flooded within the area, but not to routers outside of the area. Each area becomes its own link-state domain with its own topological database.

Routers with multiple interfaces can participate in multiple areas. These routers, which are called area border routers, maintain separate topological databases for each area. The routing tables within these routers are a combination of the routing table entries of all the SPF trees for each topological database, as well as static routes, Simple Network Management Protocol (SNMP) configured routes, and routes learned from other routing protocols. To reduce the number of entries in the routing table, the networks inside of the area can be advertised outside the area using summary route advertisements. By keeping area topologies separate, OSPF passes less routing traffic than it would if the autonomous system were not partitioned.

OSPF Backbone

An OSPF backbone is responsible for distributing routing information between areas. There is at least one backbone per OSPF internetwork. A backbone has a reserved area ID of 0.0.0.0. It consists of all area border routers, networks not in any one area, and their attached routers. The backbone has to be at the center of all areas within the autonomous system. That is, all areas have to be physi-

> **NOTE**
>
> **Topological Databases** A topological database is essentially an overall picture of networks in relationship to routers. The topological database contains the collection of LSAs received from all routers in the same area. In a very large AS with a large number of networks, each OSPF router must keep the LSA of every other router in its topological database. Each router in a large OSPF autonomous system has a large topological database. The SPF calculation of a large topological database can require a substantial amount of processing and can result in very large routing tables. To prevent this, autonomous systems are further divided into areas.

cally connected to the backbone. The reasoning behind this is that
OSPF expects all areas to inject routing information into the backbone and, in turn, the backbone will disseminate that information
into other areas. Figure 6.24 shows an example of an internetwork
with several areas and a backbone.

In this example, Routers 4, 5, 6, 10, 12, and 14 make up the backbone. If Host 1 in Area 3 wants to send a packet to Host 2 in Area
2, the packet is sent to Router 13, which forwards the packet to
Router 12, which sends the packet to Router 14. Router 14 forwards the packet along the backbone to area border router Router
10, which sends the packet through two intra-area routers (Router 9
and Router 7) to be forwarded to Host 2.

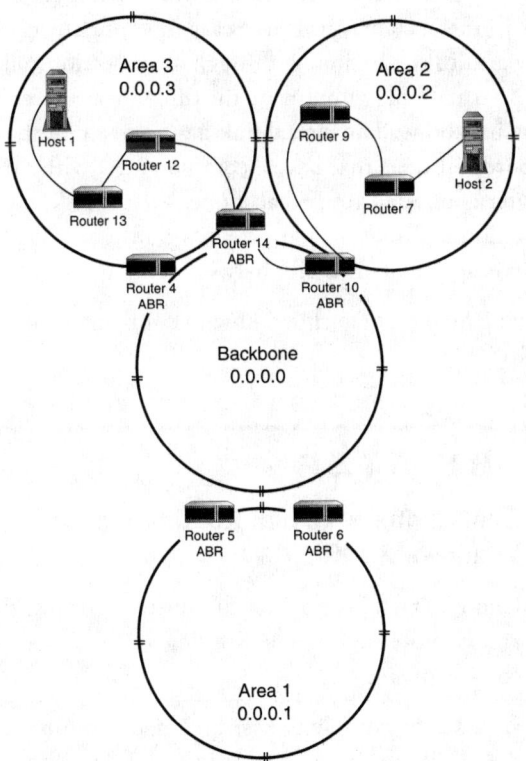

FIGURE 6.24
This OSPF network has several areas and a
backbone.

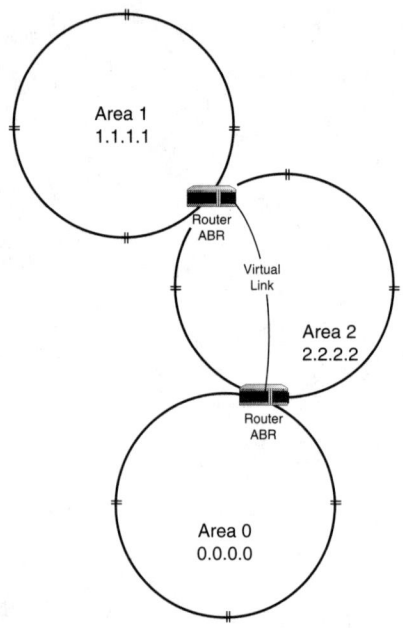

FIGURE 6.25
This OSPF network has a virtual link, which is
configured over a transit area.

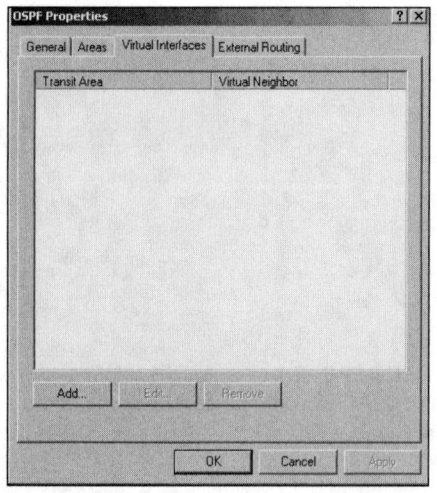

FIGURE 6.26
You can modify the OSPF settings by opening
the OSPF Properties.

Because the backbone itself is an OSPF area, all backbone routers
can use the same procedures and algorithms to maintain routing
information within the backbone that any area router would. This
allows backbone routers not only to route host traffic between areas,
but also to disseminate summary routes within areas to other routers
on the backbone that can then propagate the information within
their own areas to area routers. This ensures that any host within an
area can reach any host in another area. To minimize the size of
routing tables, OSPF ensures that the backbone topology is invisible
to all intra-area routers in the same way that individual area topologies are invisible to the backbone.

In rare cases it is possible that a new area is introduced to the
autonomous system that cannot have direct physical access to the
backbone. In this instance, it is necessary to configure a connection
of the new area to the backbone through a connection called a virtual link. A virtual link will provide the disconnected area a logical
path to the backbone. The virtual link has to be established between
two area border routers that have a common area, with one area
border router connected to the backbone. Virtual links are configured over a nonbackbone area known as a transit area. Figure 6.25
provides an example of an OSPF network with a virtual link.

The following Step by Step shows how to configure a virtual link
within RRAS.

STEP BY STEP

6.7 Configuring a Virtual Routing Link for Windows 2000

1. Choose Start, Programs, Administrative Tools, Routing
   and Remote Access. The Routing and Remote Access
   console opens.

   ---

2. Expand the console tree and select IP Routing. Right-click
   the OSPF interface you want to configure and select
   Properties from the context menu. The OSPF Properties
   dialog box opens (see Figure 6.26).

   ---

3. On the Virtual Interfaces tab, click Add. The OSPF
   Virtual Interface Configuration dialog box opens (see
   Figure 6.27). In Transit Area ID, click the transit area over
   which you are connecting the virtual link.

4. In Virtual Neighbor Router ID, type the OSPF router ID
   of the router at the other endpoint of the virtual link. In
   Transit Delay (Seconds), click the arrows to set the transit
   delay in seconds. In Retransmit Interval (Seconds), click
   the arrows to set the retransmit interval in seconds. In
   Hello Interval (Seconds), click the arrows to set the hello
   interval in seconds. In Dead Interval (Seconds), click the
   arrows to set the dead interval in seconds. Click OK to
   add the virtual interface, and click OK again to return to
   the Routing and Remote Access console.

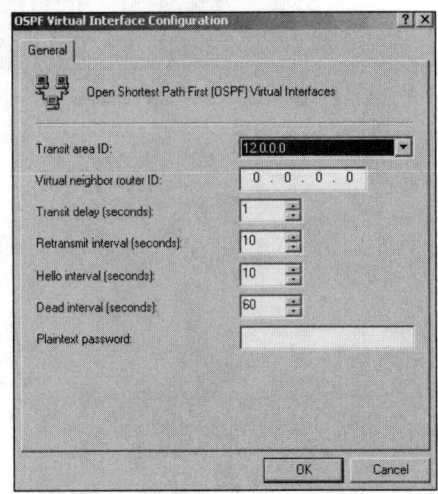

FIGURE 6.27
Be sure you have a thorough understanding
of OSPF and your network before configuring a
virtual interface.

Area Routing

Area partitioning creates two types of OSPF routing, depending
on whether the source and destination are in the same or in
different areas.

◆ Intra-area routing occurs when the source and destination are
  in the same area. With intra-area routing, the source routes
  the packet to its default gateway (an internal area router).
  The internal area router then makes use of the explicit routes
  (as calculated by the SPF algorithm) maintained in the area
  routers and routes the packet through the appropriate interface to the destination internal area router. The destination
  internal area router then forwards the packet to the destination host.

◆ Inter-area routing occurs when the source and destination are
  in different areas. When routing between areas, the source
  routes the packet to its default gateway (an internal area
  router), the area router then forwards the packet to an area
  border router using the shortest path. The area border router

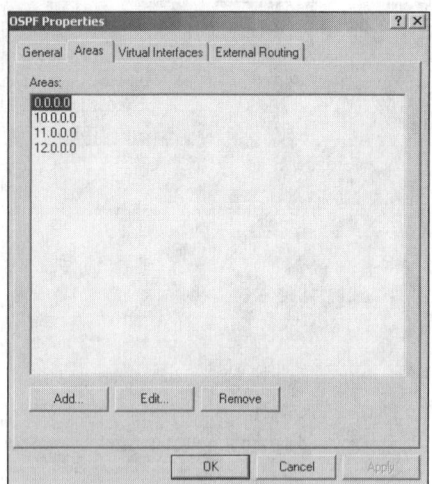

FIGURE 6.28
The Areas tab is used to add, modify, and delete the OSPF areas configured on the server.

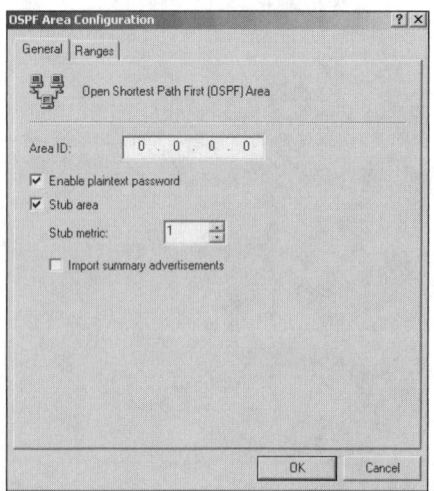

FIGURE 6.29
The General tab allows you to set the Area ID, a password, and determine whether the area is a stub area.

then forwards the packets through backbone routers using the shortest path to the area border router for the destination host. The area border router for the destination host then forwards the packets through internal area routers using the shortest path, until the packets reach their destination.

One other important concept when discussing areas is the stub area. A stub area is any area configured with a default route.

The following Step by Step allows you to create additional OSPF areas.

STEP BY STEP

6.8 Creating an OSPF Area with Windows 2000 Routing and Remote Access

1. Choose Start, Programs, Administrative Tools, Routing and Remote Access. The Routing and Remote Access console opens.

2. Expand the console tree and select IP Routing. In the details pane, right-click the OSPF interface you want to configure and select Properties from the context menu. The OSPF Properties dialog box opens.

3. Select the Areas tab (see Figure 6.28).

4. Click Add to open the OSPF Area Configuration dialog box (see Figure 6.29).

5. On the General tab, type a dotted decimal number that identifies the area. To use a plaintext password, verify that the Enable Plaintext Password option is selected. To mark the area as a stub, select the Stub Area option. In Stub Metric, click the arrows to set the stub metric. To import routes of other areas into the stub area, select the Import Summary Advertisements option. Click OK twice to apply the changes and return to the Routing and Remote Access console.

Autonomous System Routing

Routing does not occur only within areas using OSPF. When internetworks are connected to other internetworks that are under different
administrative control, routing must be established. This type of routing between autonomous systems is established using external routes.
Autonomous system border routers running OSPF learn about exterior routes through other routing protocols, such as Internet Group
Recommended Practice (IGRP), RIP, or BGP. Autonomous system
border routers are similar to area border routers, except that they route
between different autonomous systems.

By default, autonomous system border routers advertise all external
routes within its autonomous system. This allows all areas and networks within areas to reach destination networks that may lie outside the autonomous system. As a network manager, you may find it
necessary to restrict the external routes that are advertised within the
autonomous system. Using Windows 2000 Router and Remote
Access Services, you can configure the autonomous system border
router to accept or ignore the routes of certain external sources, such
as routing protocols (RIP v2) or other sources (static routes or
SNMP). You can also configure the autonomous system border
router to accept or discard specific routes by configuring one or
multiple [Destination, Network Mask] pairs. To enable autonomous
system border routing, do the following:

STEP BY STEP

6.9 Configuring Autonomous System Border Routing
in Windows 2000 Routing and Remote Access

1. Choose Start, Programs, Administrative Tools, Routing
and Remote Access. The Routing and Remote Access
console opens.

2. Expand the console tree and select IP Routing. In the
details pane, right-click the OSPF interface you want to
configure and select Properties from the context menu.
The OSPF Properties dialog box opens.

3. On the General tab (see Figure 6.30), click Enable
Autonomous System Boundary Router.

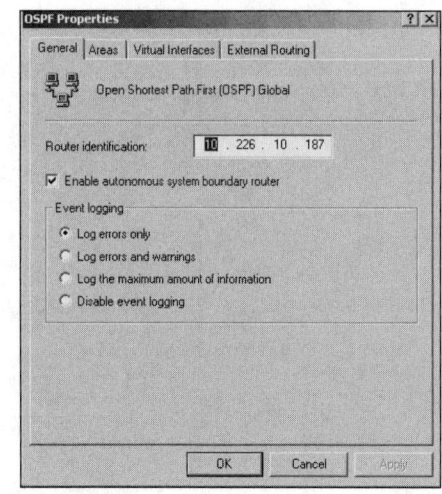

FIGURE 6.30
Autonomous system boundary routing can be
enabled by selecting the Enable Autonomous
System Boundary Router option.

continues

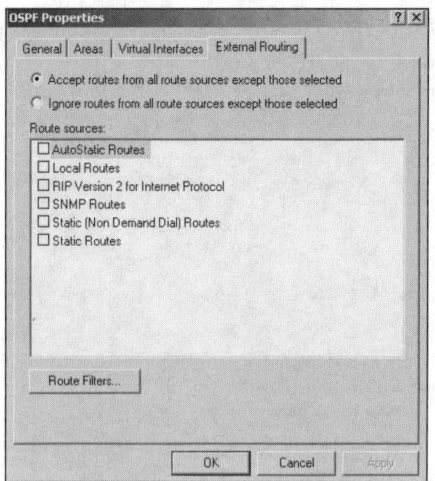

FIGURE 6.31
The External Routing tab allows you to configure the OSPF routing sources for Windows 2000.

continued

4. Select the External Routing tab (see Figure 6.31) and click Accept Routes from All Route Sources Except Those Selected. If you want to exclude a specific route source, select it in the window below. You can also select Ignore Routes from All Route Sources Except Those Selected.

5. Click OK to return to the Routing and Remote Access console and enable the OSPF boundary routing.

As a network manager, you will want to tune your routing protocols for the best efficiency that you can obtain. If external routes are allowed to be flooded into areas within your autonomous system, this will consume routing resources. To avoid using additional resources on your routers, you can configure area border routers to advertise a default route into the area. The default route is then flooded to all routers within the area. This default route will then be used by all routers within the area for any destination addresses that are not reachable within the autonomous system. Areas configured with a default route are known as stub areas.

OSPF Operation

The SPF routing algorithm is the basis for OSPF operations. When an SPF router is powered up, it initializes its routing protocol data structures and then waits for indications from lower-layer protocols that its interfaces are functional.

After a router is assured that its interfaces are functioning, it uses the OSPF Hello protocol to acquire neighbors. Neighbors are routers with interfaces to a common network. The router sends hello packets to its neighbors and receives their hello packets. In addition to helping acquire neighbors, hello packets also act as keep-alives to let routers know that other routers are still functional.

Designated Routers

On multiaccess networks (networks supporting more than two routers), the Hello protocol elects a designated router and a backup designated router. Because the designated router is adjacent to all other routers, it acts as a hub for the distribution of link-state information, maintaining the synchronization of the topological database

and for controlling adjacencies between routers within the network.
(The relationship between neighboring routers for the purposes of
synchronizing the topological database is called an adjacency; this
will be discussed in more detail in the section, "Adjacencies.")

As an example of why a designated router is required, consider a
broadcast network with six OSPF routers. Without controlling the
adjacency behavior, each router could establish an adjacency with
each of the other routers for a total of 15 adjacency relationships.
On a broadcast network with n routers, a total of $n*(n\text{-}1)/2$ adjacencies would be formed. This can result in unneeded flooding traffic as
routers attempt to synchronize with all their adjacent routers.
Designated routers allow a reduction in network traffic and in the
size of the topological database.

The designated router is elected via the Hello protocol. Hello packets are exchanged via IP multicast packets on each segment. The
router with the highest OSPF priority on a segment will become
the designated router for that segment. In the case of a tie, the
router with the highest router ID will win. The default for the interface OSPF priority is 1. A Router Priority of 0 means that the router
does not become a designated router.

In addition to electing a designated router, a backup designated
router is also elected for each multiaccess network to prevent the
loss in connectivity associated with the loss of a designated router.
Like the designated router, the backup designated router is adjacent
to all routers on the network. When the designated router fails, the
backup designated router immediately becomes the designated
router by sending LSAs to all its adjacent routers, announcing its
new role. There is a very short period of time when transit traffic
could be impaired as the backup designated router takes over the
role of the designated router.

Like the designated router, the backup designated router is elected
by the exchange of hello packets. Each hello packet contains a field
for the backup designated router of the network. If the backup designated router is not specified, the router with the highest router
priority that is not already the designated router becomes the
backup designated router. If multiple routers are with the highest
router priority, the router with the highest router ID is elected the
backup designated router.

Adjacencies

When the topological databases of two neighboring routers are synchronized, the routers are said to be adjacent. On multiaccess networks, the designated router determines which routers should become adjacent. Topological databases are synchronized between pairs of adjacent routers. Adjacencies control the distribution of routing protocol packets. These packets are sent and received only on adjacencies.

Adjacencies are first developed when an OSPF router initializes; it sends out a periodic OSPF hello packet. The OSPF hello packet contains configuration information such as the router's Router ID and the list of neighboring routers for which the router has received a hello packet. Initially, the neighbor list in the OSPF hello packet does not contain any neighbors.

The initializing OSPF router also listens for neighboring routers' hello packets. From the incoming hello packets, the initializing router determines the specific router or routers with which an adjacency is to be established. Adjacencies are formed with the designated router and backup designated router, which are identified in the incoming hello packets.

To begin the adjacency, the routers forming the adjacency describe the contents of their topological databases through a sequence of database description packets. This is known as the database exchange process, during which the two neighboring routers form a master/slave relationship. The contents of each router's topological database is acknowledged by its neighboring router.

Each router compares its LSAs with the LSAs of its neighbor and notes which LSAs need to be requested from the neighbor to synchronize the topological database. The missing or more recent LSAs are then requested through link-state request packets. Link-state update packets are sent in response to the link-state request packets and their receipt is acknowledged. When all link-state requests of both routers have been satisfied, the topological databases of the neighboring routers are fully synchronized and an adjacency is formed.

After the adjacency has formed, each neighboring router sends a periodic hello packet to inform its neighbor that the router is still active on the network. The lack of hello packets from a neighbor is used to detect a downed router.

If an event occurs, such as a downed link or router or the addition of new network that changes the topological database of one router, the topological database of adjacent routers are no longer synchronized. The router whose topological database has changed sends link-state update packets to its adjacent neighbor. The receipt of the link-state update packets is acknowledged. After the exchange, the topological databases of the adjacent routers are again synchronized.

Demand-Dial Routing

In some network environments, a network manager may require that redundancy be built in to the network design so that if the permanent network connection between sites goes down, an alternate route via a demand-dial link is in place as a backup route. In other locations a permanent connection is required, but the cost of establishing the connection or the technologies available to implement the connection may be limited. In such cases, a technology called demand-dial routing can be put in place that will allow packets to be routed across a dial-up link.

A demand-dial network consists of a calling router and an answering router. Both the calling and receiving routers have Routing and Remote Access Services installed. To enable demand-dial routing on an existing RRAS server, complete the following Step by Step.

STEP BY STEP

6.10 Enabling Demand-Dial Routing

1. Choose Start, Programs, Administrative Tools, Routing and Remote Access. The Routing and Remote Access console opens.

2. Expand the console tree and right-click the server. Select Properties from the context menu. The server (local) Properties dialog box (see Figure 6.32) opens.

3. On the General tab, select LAN and Demand-Dial Routing. Click OK to return to the Routing and Remote Access console.

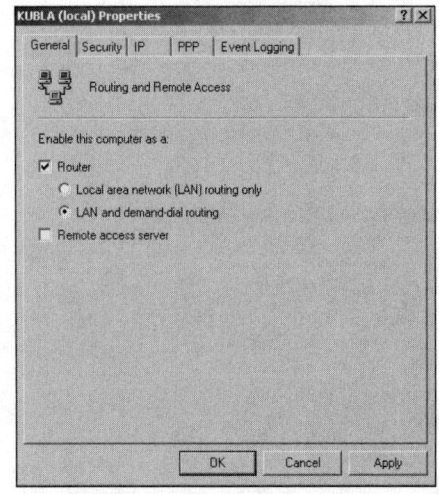

FIGURE 6.32

The Windows 2000 router can be either a dedicated LAN router, or a LAN and demand-dial router.

continues

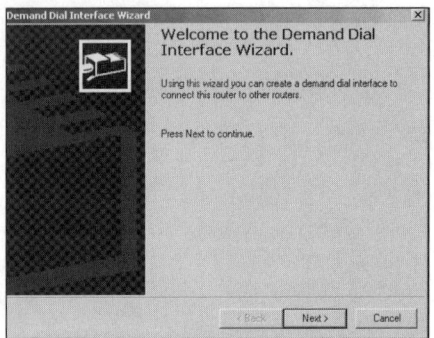

FIGURE 6.33
As with most Windows 2000 tasks, a wizard is available for configuring a demand-dial interface.

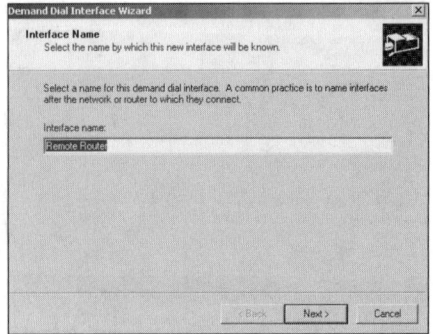

FIGURE 6.34
You need to name each demand-dial interface.

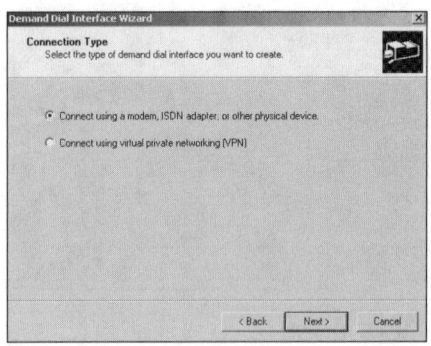

FIGURE 6.35
You can connect using a physical device such as a modem, an ISDN adapter, or by using VPN.

continued

4. Right-click the Routing Interfaces within the console tree and select New Demand-Dial Interface from the context menu. This will bring up the Demand-Dial Interface Wizard (see Figure 6.33).

5. Click Next to proceed. The Interface Name dialog box opens (see Figure 6.34).

6. On the Interface Name field, type a name for this connection interface. Click Next to continue. The Connection Type dialog box opens (see Figure 6.35).

7. On the Connection Type dialog box, select Connect Using a Modem, ISDN Adapter, or Other Physical Device and click Next to continue. The Select a Device dialog box opens (see Figure 6.36).

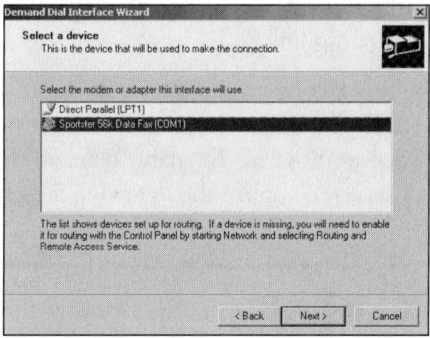

FIGURE 6.36
You need to select the device that will be dialing. This is usually a modem or ISDN card.

8. Select the serial device you want to use for your connection interface (a modem, for example) and click Next. The Phone Number dialog box opens (see Figure 6.37).

9. Enter the phone number of the answering router in the space provided. Click Next to continue. The Protocols and Security dialog box opens (see Figure 6.38).

10. From this dialog box, you can select the protocols you want to route over this connection. Select Route IP Packets on This Interface. Click Next to continue. The Dial Out Credentials dialog box opens (see Figure 6.39).

11. Enter in the security credential information that will allow you to connect to the answering router. This includes User Name, Domain, and Password. Click Next to continue.

12. Click Finish on the completion dialog box to return to the Routing and Remote Access console.

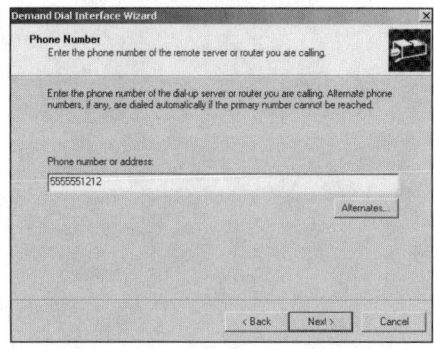

FIGURE 6.37
To use a demand-dial router, you need the phone number of the router you will be dialing.

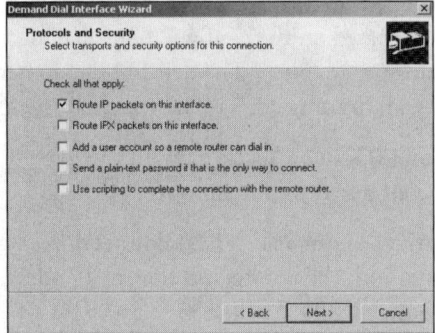

FIGURE 6.38
You can configure the protocols to be routed and the security for the demand-dial connection from here.

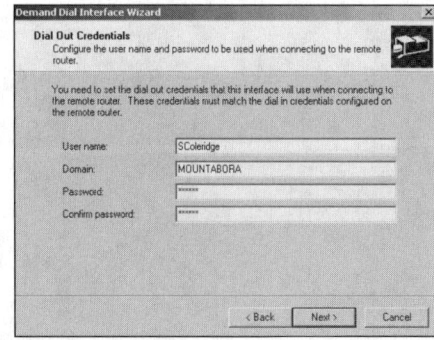

FIGURE 6.39
To successfully connect to the remote router, you need to configure the login credentials.

When a calling router receives a packet over the network, the router determines the best route to forward the packet. If the route chosen is a demand-dial route, a connection is initiated with the other side. The type of connection that is established is a Point-to-Point Protocol (PPP) connection that is initiated over either a physical connection such as an analog or ISDN line or over a logical connection known as a tunnel. The tunnels are established using either Point-to-Point Tunneling Protocol (PPTP) or Layer 2 Tunneling Protocol (L2TP).

After the demand-dial router determines that a connection needs to be established, the demand-dial router determines whether one currently exists. If the status is connected, the packet is forwarded to the destination host. If no connection is in place, the calling router must establish a connection.

To establish a connection from the calling router to the answering router, the calling router checks the dial-out hours and demand-dial filters configured on the interface. If dial-out hours or demand-dial filters prohibit establishing a connection, the connection attempt fails and the host that originated the packets is notified that the destination host is unreachable. If after checking, the connection is able to proceed, the router retrieves the configuration of the demand-dial interface and then, based on the configuration, a connection is established with the answering router. The demand-dial router must accommodate several types of connections. These include the following:

- **Modem or ISDN connection.** With this type of configuration, the configured phone number is dialed.

- **Virtual private network (VPN) connection.** With this type of configuration, the configured host or IP address is used to establish either a PPTP or IPSec connection.

- **Direct serial or direct parallel port connection.** With this type of configuration, a direct connection is made between the calling router and the answering router over the serial port or parallel port.

After the connection has been made, it is then necessary for the calling router to negotiate a PPP connection with the answering router. Part of the negotiation is to send the credentials of the calling router. The answering router then checks the credentials against a local accounts database and/or remote policies or forwards the connection attributes to a RADIUS server where the credentials will be checked.

In addition to authenticating the users' credentials, PPP negotiates
parameters for the connection, such as the IP addresses of both
routers and the name servers to be used and any static routes that
may have been put in place by the user.

Finally, the answering router looks up the user initiating the connection for a matching interface. If a matching demand-dial interface is
located, the connection state is changed to a connected state and the
routing connection is established. If a matching interface is not
found, the calling entity is then identified as a remote access client
computer, and a routing connection will not be established.

Types of Demand-Dial Connections

Two types of connections are available with demand-dial routing:
on-demand connection and persistent connection. An on-demand
connection is initiated when a packet is received by the calling
router. When the calling router receives information for the
answering router, it initiates the connection. After the information
has been transmitted to the answering router and the connection
has remained idle for a period of time, the connection is dropped.
You can configure the demand-dial timeout on the Options tab of
the Demand-Dial Interface properties.

In a demand-dial environment, one router can be configured to initiate the connection, or both routers can be configured to initiate connections. If only one router is configured to initiate the connection,
this is known as a one-way connection. If both routers are configured
to initiate connections, this is known as a two-way connection.

In a one-way initiated connection, the calling router is configured
with a username that is used to connect to the answering router.
Associated with this user account are static routes that define which
packets are to be routed to the other side. When the connection is
initiated and the username is authenticated by the answering router,
the static routes associated with the username are added to the routing table of the answering router.

A two-way initiated connection is very similar to a one-way initiated
connection, except that both routers must now be configured with the
necessary information to allow each to establish the connection. In
addition, the calling and answering routers must both be configured.

In both a one-way initiated connection and a two-way initiated connection, the router initiating the call must be configured with a username that matches the demand-dial interface on the answering router.

An on-demand connection can introduce problems for time-sensitive applications because the application must be able to tolerate a delay while the calling router initiates the connection with the answering router, and the static routes configured on both routers are propagated throughout the internetworks on both sides. The length of this delay varies for the type of physical or logical connection being established.

The second type of connection that is available within a demand-dial routing environment is a persistent connection. With this type of connection, there is no delay while the calling router initiates a connection with the answering router. The connection is available on a permanent basis. This type of connection is generally found in WAN environments where the connection is over a leased line, X.25 connection or ISDN connection. With a persistent connection, if the connection is lost, the calling router can be configured to reestablish the connection automatically.

The choice of connection will provide insight into the type of routing that should be configured over the connection. If the connection is persistent, one of the dynamic routing protocols, such as RIP or OSPF, may be used with special configuration to take into consideration the use of a demand-dial connection.

In an on-demand connection scenario, the choice of a dynamic routing protocol may not be the most appropriate. Dynamic protocols need to periodically exchange information between routers to keep their routing tables up to date. This is a function of how dynamic routing protocols work. This requirement to periodically exchange information with other routers in the environment can cause a connection to be made each time the update process takes place, or in some cases, it can keep the connection up permanently depending on how often the update process takes place. This may not be what is desired in an environment where you are trying to minimize costs.

In an on-demand connection, the preferred way of enabling routing is to use either static routes or autostatic updates.

An autostatic update is a request from a router for all known routes or services from the router on the other side of the connection. After the request is received, the router adds the requested routes to its routing table. An autostatic update is a one-time, one-way exchange of routing information. Autostatic updates do not occur automatically on initiation of a demand-dial connection. Rather, the autostatic update must be manually initiated, or a schedule must be put in place to update routes. After the routes have been sent, the two routers do not exchange updates of routing information unless a manual request to update is made or a scheduled request occurs, depending on how autostatic updates are configured within your environment. Autostatic updates are useful for environments where you require routes to be added once across a connection, but there are too many to make adding them using static routes unpractical.

Configuring static routes within a demand-dial network is different from configuring static routes using the ROUTE command. Step by Step 6.11 outlines how to configure static routes for a demand-dial interface.

One consideration when configuring static routes is to consider the default IP route (0.0.0.0) carefully. The default IP route is used to specify what should be done with network traffic when none of the existing routes provide a path for it. If no route exists, the router will forward the traffic through the default route.

This is fine for Internet traffic, because the probability is that the destination address is a host on the Internet. Within an intranet, this may not be the case. This can have an impact on a demand-dial router. For instance, if the default route is specified through the demand-dial router, every time an invalid address is specified, it will be routed through the demand-dial router. This will initiate a connection and the traffic will be forwarded, only to determine that the host does not exist on the other side. Therefore, you have incurred a cost for routing traffic to an unreachable host.

In this type of situation, you will want to ensure that your demand-dial router is configured with routes that are specific to the destination network and that do not specify the demand-dial router as the default route.

Demand-Dial Security

Security concerns for most companies are a by-product of today's interconnected world. As companies have become connected to the Internet, companies have needed to take measures to ensure that their networks are protected against malicious attacks and unauthorized access. Demand-dial security provides a number of security features to ensure that the appropriate calling router is initiating the connection and that the proper answering router is answering the connection. These features include the following:

◆ Remote access permission

◆ Authentication

◆ Encryption

◆ Callback

◆ Caller ID

◆ Remote access account lockout

In a demand-dial routing environment, the primary mechanism for enabling security between a calling router and an answering router is to associate a user account with the router that is initiating the connection. This provides the answering router with a mechanism to ensure that the router initiating the connection is authorized and has the appropriate permissions to access the router via a remote dial-in connection. To enable an account with the appropriate permissions, an administrator can either explicitly enable the account through the Dial-in Properties tab of the user account within either Computer Management or Active Directory Users and Computer, or the account can have permissions enabled for it by being associated with a remote access policy that is configured within a RADIUS/Internet Authentication service server.

In addition to ensuring that the account has appropriate permissions, the answering router must authenticate the user account to ensure that the initiator can verify authenticity. This authentication can occur in one direction from the calling router to the answering router, or in both directions. If the authentication is one way, it does not protect against masquerading routers.

Windows 2000 includes support for PPP authentication protocols at both the end-user level and the computer level. The protocols supported are the following:

◆ Password Authentication Protocol (PAP)

◆ Shiva Password Authentication Protocol (SPAP)

◆ Challenge Handshake Authentication Protocol (CHAP)

◆ Microsoft Challenge Handshake Authentication Protocol version 1 (MS-CHAP v1)

◆ Microsoft Challenge Handshake Authentication Protocol version 2 (MS-CHAP v2)

◆ Extensible Authentication Protocol-Message Digest 5 CHAP (EAP-MD5)

Each of these protocols provides a set of rules to ensure that the end users are actually who they claim to be.

Each of the preceding protocols involves the transfer of a username, a domain name, and a password so that they can be authenticated. If passing credential information for authentication is not preferred, authentication can occur using certificates that represent the end user or the computer initiating the connection. Certificate-based authentication is provided through the following mechanisms:

◆ Extensible Authentication Protocol-Transport Layer Security (EAP-TLS). Using this protocol, the answering router authenticates itself to the calling router by sending its certificate to the calling router, where it can be verified.

◆ If IPSec is used for a L2TP over an IPSec demand-dial connection, no user authentication can be done. Rather, two computers must authenticate themselves to each other. This type of computer-level authentication is performed through the exchange of certificates (also known as machine certificates) during the establishment of the IPSec security association.

After the connection has been authenticated, it still may be necessary to further secure the connection. To prevent unauthorized access to information being transferred over the connection, one of the encryption technologies available to demand-dial routing can be used. Two types of encryption are

◆ Microsoft Point-to-Point Encryption protocol (MPPE)

◆ Internet Protocol Security (IPSec)

Each of these types of encryption schemes can be used to ensure that unauthorized access to information is not obtained while it is being transferred over the connection.

Callback is a feature that is available to the network manager to further secure the connection between the calling router and the answering router. With callback, the calling router makes the initial connection to the answering server. The answering server is then configured to call the calling router back at a predefined number.

Another security feature that the network manager can use is caller ID. This feature allows the answering router to ensure that the incoming call is coming from a specified phone number. This feature requires significant configuration with respect to other security features. With caller ID, the caller's phone line, the phone system, the remote access server's phone line, and the Windows 2000 driver for the dial-up equipment must all be configured to support caller ID.

A final security feature available in a demand-dial routing environment is remote access account lockout. This feature works similar to user account lockout. That is, the network manager specifies as part of the configuration the number of times a remote access authentication fails against a valid user account before the user is denied remote access. This type of feature is useful against malicious attacks that involve a dictionary attack. A dictionary attack is a brute force type of attack that has the attacker repeatedly trying the connection with username/password combinations until the proper username/password pair are guessed.

MANAGING AND MONITORING IP ROUTING

Manage and monitor IP routing.

Up to this point, this chapter discussed the theory behind routing protocols and further explored the individual routing protocols. This section focuses on some of the other tools that can be used within a network environment to help configure routing and to troubleshoot routing issues. The section finishes with a discussion of some troubleshooting options for each of the routing protocols.

Using the ROUTE Command to Configure Static Routes

The ROUTE command is primarily used to configure static routes within a network. It can also be used to troubleshoot by listing all the routes that this computer knows about.

The syntax of the ROUTE command is as follows:

```
route [-f] [-p] [command [destination] [mask subnetmask]
➡[gateway] [metric costmetric]]
```

The –f parameter is used to clear the routing tables of all entries. The –p parameter is used to make the route persistent. When a route is added to the router, by default the entry is not kept across reboots of the system. The –p parameter ensures that the entry is maintained in the routing table across reboots of the system.

The following commands are used to specify what can be done with the ROUTE command:

◆ **Print.** Prints the existing entries in the routing table.

◆ **Add.** Adds a new route to the routing table.

◆ **Delete.** Deletes an existing route from the routing table.

◆ **Change.** Modifies an existing route in the routing table.

The destination parameter specifies the destination that you want to reach. The destination parameter can contain the following:

◆ Host address

◆ Subnet address

◆ Network address

◆ Default gateway

The mask parameter defines what portion of the destination address must match for that route to be used. When the mask is written in binary, a 1 is significant (must match) and a 0 need not match. For example, a 255.255.255.255 mask is used for a host entry. The mask of all 255s (all 1s) means that the destination address of the packet to be routed must exactly match the network address for this route to be used. For another example, the network address 157.57.8.0 has a netmask of 255.255.248.0. This netmask means the first two octets must match exactly, the first 5 bits of the third octet must match (248=11111000), and the last octet does not matter. Thus, any address of 157.57 and the third octet of 8 through 15 (15=00001111) will use this route.

The gateway parameter specifies where the packet needs to be sent. This can be the local network card or a router on the local subnet.

The metric parameter specifies a cost that is to be associated with that route. This cost is used in the decision on how packets should be routed. Packets are routed through the route that has the lowest cost.

Step by Step 6.11 shows how to configure a static route for the network 10.100.10.0.

STEP BY STEP

6.11 Adding a Static Route to Windows 2000

1. Open the command prompt by going to Start, Programs, Accessories, and selecting Command Prompt. The Command Prompt window opens.

2. Within the Command Prompt window, type the following command and press Enter. A successful entry returns you to the command prompt, with no message. If the entry addition is unsuccessful, you will receive an error message.

```
Route Add 10.100.10.0 mask 255.255.255.0
➥10.100.5.1 metric 2
```

3. To display the newly added route, type **Route print** and press Enter. This will display the following information (Note that this will change depending on the configuration of your computer).

```
=========================================================
Interface List
0x1 ....................... MS TCP Loopback interface
0x2 ...00 10 a4 e3 4b c0 ... Xircom CardBus Ethernet 10/100 Adapter
                          (Microsoft's Packet Scheduler)
=========================================================
=========================================================
Active Routes:
Network Destination      Netmask          Gateway       Interface  Metric
        127.0.0.0        255.0.0.0        127.0.0.1     127.0.0.1     1
     10.100.10.0     255.255.255.0     10.100.5.1          2          2
  255.255.255.255  255.255.255.255  255.255.255.255        2          1
=========================================================
Persistent Routes:
  None
```

Using Network Monitor

Network Monitor is a tool for capturing network traffic. It can be used to diagnose problems when two computers do not communicate or when a computer has trouble functioning within a network environment. For instance, a computer may have issues resolving names or finding a path to another computer (routing issues).

Network Monitor can be configured to capture network traffic in several ways. It can be configured to capture all network traffic that it receives, configured to respond to events on the network, configured to monitor only a subset of the traffic (for instance, a particular protocol, such as HTTP traffic only). After the network data has been captured, Network Monitor will analyze the data and translate it into its logical frame structure to make the protocol information readable to the person capturing the information. Each frame contains the following:

◆ The source address of the computer that is sending the frame

◆ The destination address of the computer that received the frame

◆ Headers from each protocol used to send the frame

◆ The data or a portion of the information being sent

After the data has been translated, the information is presented through the graphical display provided by Network Monitor. Figure 6.40 shows an example of what the data looks like after it has been captured. Chapter 4, "Installing, Configuring, Managing, Monitoring, and Troubleshooting Network Protocols in a Windows 2000 Network Infrastructure," discusses using Network Monitor to monitor network traffic.

EXAM TIP

Network Analysis Is Not on the Exam Teaching you how to analyze the traffic you see in Network Monitor is not only well beyond the scope of this book, it is also not testable. Network analysis is a science that takes a good deal of training and experience to master. For the exam, just be aware that Network Monitor gives you the capability to capture and analyze packets.

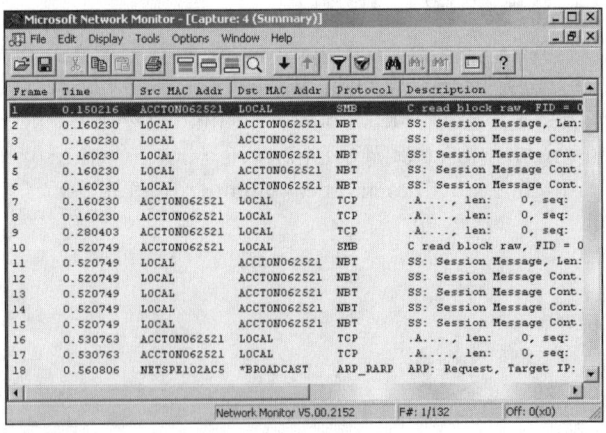

FIGURE 6.40
Use Network Monitor to capture data on network traffic.

Managing and Monitoring IP Routing Protocols

As a network administrator, you will have the task of configuring and installing Routing and Remote Access Services. After these services are configured and installed, you will then be responsible for managing additional changes to the existing configuration, monitoring the installed configuration for problems, and troubleshooting problems when they arise. This chapter provides an overview of some of the steps for accomplishing these tasks.

Routing and Remote Access Services Operation

After you have installed RRAS you can perform several tasks to manage its ongoing operation. Some of the items you will be required to manage and monitor include the following:

◆ Administer a remote router.

◆ Check the status of existing interfaces.

◆ View existing routing tables and verify that routes are being received from routing protocols.

◆ Determine the status of RRAS services and reset the services, if required.

In a number of organizations today, users are distributed throughout various locations. The information services department is generally centralized to minimize costs. This presents an issue for managing remote installations. With RRAS, it is possible to remotely manage RRAS routers from a central location.

After you can manage the local server and remote servers, you will want to use this tool to quickly determine whether the existing interfaces are active. In addition to monitoring the event logs for possible messages indicating a problem, you can also check the individual interfaces to see what their operational state is.

You may have determined that the interfaces for a particular server are operational. But it's still possible that the existing interfaces are not receiving routes to update its routing tables. You, as an administrator, would like to determine whether the router is indeed receiving updates. Again, the management tool provided with Windows 2000 Advanced Server will allow you to do this. To view the routing tables of a particular protocol, within the Routing and Remote Access tool, select and expand the server and IP Routing, and then select Static Routes. Right-click Static Routes and select the Show IP Routing Table option. You can then verify if the router is receiving updates to its routing table from other routers within the network.

Finally, you may want to check the overall status of the services to determine if they are running. If they are not running, then you would need to start them by choosing Computer Management, selecting Services and Applications, and then selecting Services. In the Details pane for Routing and Remote Access, verify that the Status column displays Started. If the service is not started, right-click Routing and Remote Access, and then click Start. If the router does not start, check the system event log for error messages.

Troubleshooting RIP Environments

After RIP is configured within your environment, you may be called on from time to time to troubleshoot issues that arise with routing. Although every problem is unique, the following outlines some of the items that may help when you're responding to issues within a RIP environment.

TABLE 6.1

RIP ISSUES AND RESOLUTION

Problem	*Solution*
Routing tables have improper routing information within a mixed RIP Version 1 and 2 network.	RIP Version 2 routers are configured to multicast announcements. Multicast announcements are never received by RIP Version 1 routers.
	If you have a mixed environment of RIP Version 1 and RIP Version 2, ensure that the routers configured with RIP Version 2 are using broadcast instead of multicast.

Problem	*Solution*
Silent RIP hosts are not receiving routes.	RIP Version 2 routers are configured to multicast announcements. Multicast announcements are never received by silent RIP hosts.
	If silent RIP hosts on a network are not receiving routes from the local RIP router, verify the version of RIP supported by the silent RIP hosts. If it is the listening service in Windows NT 4 Service Pack 4 or Windows 2000, you must configure the RIP routers for RIP Version 1 or RIP Version 2 broadcasting.
RIP routers are not being updated properly with valid routes.	You are deploying variable-length subnetting, disjointed subnets, or supernetting in a RIP Version 1 or mixed RIP Version 1 and RIP Version 2 environment.
	Do not deploy variable length subnetting, disjointed subnets, or supernetting in a RIP Version 1 or mixed RIP Version 1 and RIP Version 2 environment because it is not supported.
RIP routers are not being updated properly with valid routes.	You are using autostatic RIP and you did not do an initial manual update.
	When you use autostatic RIP on a demand-dial interface, the first time you make a connection, you must manually update routes.
	You must also update routes manually on the router for the corresponding interface. The routes then appear in the IP routing table.
Host or default routes are not being propagated.	RIP by default is not configured to propagate host or default routes. If these need to be propagated, change the default settings on the Advanced tab of the properties of a RIP interface.

These are only some of the issues that can arise within a RIP environment. For further troubleshooting information, refer to Microsoft Technet or the Windows 2000 Advanced Server documentation.

Troubleshooting OSPF Environments

OSPF is a more complex protocol to understand than RIP. As such, there is more risk of issues arising because of the complexity of the protocol. Because OSPF is more hierarchical than other protocols, this offers an opportunity to help troubleshoot issues that may arise; it becomes easier to isolate issues to a particular area or the interconnectivity between areas. Considerations include the following:

TABLE 6.2

OSPF ISSUES AND RESOLUTION

Problem	Solution
OSPF adjacency is not forming between two neighbors.	OSPF is not enabled on the interface. Verify that OSPF is enabled on the interface on the network segment where an adjacency should form. By default, when you add an interface to the OSPF routing protocol, OSPF is disabled for the interface and must be manually enabled.
OSPF adjacency is not forming between two neighbors.	PING the neighboring router to ensure basic IP and network connectivity. Use the TRACERT command to trace the route to the neighboring router. There should not be any routers between the neighboring routers.
A virtual link is not forming between two areas.	Mismatched configuration of password, hello interval, or dead interval. Verify that the virtual link neighbor routers are configured for the same password, hello interval, and dead interval.
A virtual link is not forming between two areas.	Virtual link neighbors are configured for the incorrect transit area ID. Verify that both virtual link neighbors are configured for the same correct transit area ID.
Routing tables are not being updated with OSPF routes or improper OSPF routes.	Not receiving summarized routes. If you are not receiving summarized OSPF routes for an area, verify that the area border routers (ABRs) for the area are configured with the proper {Destination, Network mask} pairs summarizing that area's routes.

Problem	*Solution*
Routing tables are not being updated with OSPF routes or improper OSPF routes.	All ABRs are not connected to the backbone. Verify that all ABRs are either physically connected to the backbone or logically connected to the backbone by using door routers, which are routers that connect two areas without going through the backbone.

These are only some of the issues that can arise within a OSPF environment. For further troubleshooting information, refer to Microsoft Technet or the Windows 2000 Advanced Server documentation.

CASE STUDY: SMALL OFFICE WITH A DEDICATED CONNECTION TO THE INTERNET

ESSENCE OF THE CASE

The following points summarize the essence of the case study:

▶ There must be a dedicated connection to the Internet.

▶ The network may expand in the future, and this must be done with a minimum of configuration.

▶ Only one segment is on the network.

▶ The connection must be online at all times.

SCENARIO

You are the administrator of a small office. You have been asked by the company owner to configure a connection to the Internet. You would like to configure a dedicated connection that will allow you to assign all the workstations a TCP/IP address that will identify it on the Internet. You currently have only one segment on your company network with approximately 50 workstations. Your connection must be online at all times, and you would like to minimize the management that is necessary on your part. You believe that your network will grow within the next year, and you would like to ensure that this can be done with a minimum of configuration.

continues

CASE STUDY: SMALL OFFICE WITH A DEDICATED CONNECTION TO THE INTERNET

continued

ANALYSIS

When configuring a small office network, you can connect the office to the Internet in several ways. For instance, a small office network can be connected to the Internet via a demand-dial connection, or a router can be configured with Network Address Translation. However, based on the requirements of the scenario, the most appropriate solution is to implement a dedicated connection. Because the network manager would like to minimize the configuration that is required, a configuration based on either static routes or RIP should be provided. OSPF in this type of scenario is much too complex a solution. To determine whether to use static routes or RIP, you must look closely at the requirements. Because the network may expand in the future and this must be done with a minimum of configuration, it is best to pursue a dynamic routing protocol that can adapt to a change in the network topology. This would imply RIP over static routing.

CHAPTER SUMMARY

KEY TERMS

- Routing Information Protocol (RIP)
- Open Shortest Path First (OSPF)
- distance vector
- link state
- split horizon
- split horizon with poison reverse
- adjacency
- area
- autonomous system
- Interior Gateway Protocol (IGP)
- Exterior Gateway Protocol (EGP)

This chapter focused on routing. It covered the underlying fundamentals of routing and covered such topics as distance-vector routing and link-state routing. How a host determines whether it should deliver a packet directly to the end host or via a router was touched on. The chapter also discussed some of the problems of each type of routing and solutions to those problems, such as split horizon, split horizon with poison reverse, and triggered updates.

The next topic discussed was the RIP. Both version 1 and version 2 of RIP were discussed, along with specific features such as silent RIP. Features of the RIP protocol were related back to the fundamental discussion of routing covered earlier in the chapter, such as distance vector and split horizon. A discussion of how RIP functions within a network environment was provided along with a Step by Step for implementing RIP using the RRAS features of Windows 2000 Advanced Server.

CHAPTER SUMMARY

The second routing protocol to be discussed was the OSPF protocol. The features of OSPF and how they differ from RIP were presented. The discussion then looked at the components and processes that make up the OSPF routing protocol. A discussion of how OSPF functions within a network environment was provided along with a Step by Step for implementing OSPF using the RRAS features of Windows 2000 Advanced Server.

Demand-dial routing provides a facility for connecting remote locations into corporate networks or for providing redundancy when building fault-tolerant networks. The chapter began with a discussion of how demand-dial routing works and then provided insight into some of the routing issues that you must consider when implementing a demand-dial solution. Security is an issue that every network manager must consider in any solution. As such, a discussion of the security features available for demand-dial routing was provided.

Lastly, an overview of some of the tools for working with routing and diagnosing problems with routing was provided. A discussion of the ROUTE command and an overview of network monitor was provided. These are the tools that will help you to diagnose problems. In addition to an overview of the tools used, a brief discussion of problems that may arise with the different protocols and what can be done to resolve these problems was provided. By no means are they comprehensive, but they do provide insight into some of the different things to check should problems arise.

APPLY YOUR KNOWLEDGE

Exercises

6.1 Add a Static Route to the Existing Routing Table

This exercise explores using the ROUTE command to add a static route to an existing routing table on a RRAS. This method provides a way for you to add static routes to routing configurations.

Estimated Time: 10 minutes

1. Click Start.

2. Select Start, Programs, Accessories.

3. Select Command Prompt

4. Within the Command Prompt window, type

   ```
   route ADD 157.0.0.0 MASK 255.0.0.0
   157.55.80.1 METRIC 3 IF 2
   ```

5. Type **Route Print** at the Command Prompt window.

6. Type **exit** to leave the Command Prompt window.

6.2 Add a Demand-Dial Interface to a RRAS Server

This exercise explores using the Routing and Remote Access Services tool to add a demand-dial interface to an existing router. The Routing and Remote Access Services tool is an important tool for configuring routing in a Windows 2000 environment.

Estimated Time: 15 minutes

1. Start Routing and Remote Access by clicking Start, Programs, Administrative Tools, and then click Routing and Remote Access.

2. In the console tree, click Routing Interfaces by using the plus (+) button to expand the Routing and Remote Access option and select the server you want to work with.

3. Right-click the routing interfaces and then select New Demand-Dial Interface.

4. Follow the instructions in the Demand-Dial Interface Wizard and enter information for the following:

   - **Interface Name.** The name of the interface.
   - **Connection Type.** Either modem, ISDN adapter, or other physical device.
   - **Select a Device.** The device being used to create the connection.
   - **Phone Number or Address.** Phone number or address of the answering router.
   - **Protocols and Security.** The protocols to route and a user account that a remote router can use to dial in.
   - **Dial-in Credentials.** The domain and password for the account that will be used to authenticate the answering router.
   - **Dial-out Credentials.** The credentials used to authenticate the calling router when it initiates a connection with the answering router.

6.3 Configure an Autonomous System Border Router

This exercise explores using the Routing and Remote Access Services tool to configure a border router for an autonomous system within an OSPF network.

Estimated Time: 15 minutes

APPLY YOUR KNOWLEDGE

1. Start Routing and Remote Access by clicking Start, Programs, Administrative Tools, and then click Routing and Remote Access.

2. In the console tree, click OSPF by using the plus (+) button to expand the Routing and Remote Access option, select the server and highlight the IP Routing option.

3. Right-click OSPF and click Properties.

4. On the General tab, click Enable Autonomous System Boundary Router.

5. On the External Routing tab, click either Accept routes from all route sources except those selected or Ignore routes from all route sources except those selected.

6. Select or clear the appropriate options next to the route sources.

6.4   Configure an Interface of a Virtual Link

This exercise explores using the Routing and Remote Access Services tool to configure a virtual interface for one side of an OSPF virtual link.

Estimated Time: 15 minutes

1. Start Routing and Remote Access by clicking Start, Programs, Administrative Tools, and then click Routing and Remote Access.

2. In the console tree, click OSPF by using the plus (+) button to expand Routing and Remote Access option, select the server, and highlight the IP routing option.

3. Right-click OSPF and then click Properties.

4. On the Virtual Interfaces tab, click Add.

5. In the Transit Area ID, click the transit area over which you are connecting the virtual link.

6. In the Virtual Neighbor Router ID, type the OSPF router ID of the router at the other end-point of the virtual link.

7. In the Transit Delay (Seconds), click the arrows to set the transit delay in seconds.

8. In Retransmit Interval (Seconds), click the arrows to set the retransmit interval in seconds.

9. In Hello Interval (Seconds), click the arrows to set the hello interval in seconds.

10. In Dead Interval (Seconds), click the arrows to set the dead interval in seconds.

11. If the backbone area is configured to have a password, in Plaintext Password, type a password.

6.5   Add an IP Routing Protocol to an RRAS Server

This exercise explores using the Routing and Remote Access Services tool to configure a virtual interface for one side of an OSPF virtual link.

Estimated Time: 15 minutes

1. Start Routing and Remote Access by clicking Start, Programs, Administrative Tools, and then click Routing and Remote Access.

2. In the console tree, click General by using the plus (+) button to expand Routing and Remote access option, select the server, and then highlight the IP routing option.

3. Right-click General and click New Routing Protocol.

4. In the Routing Protocols, click the IP protocol and click Add.

APPLY YOUR KNOWLEDGE

Review Questions

1. What is a topological database?

2. Provide one reason why link-state protocols are more efficient than distance-vector algorithms.

3. What is split horizon?

4. If you use autostatic updates, what must you do the first time you connect to a remote router?

5. Which parameter of the ROUTE command will clear all existing routing table entries?

6. What is the ID reserved for the OSPF backbone?

7. What is one of the major problems of distance-vector routing?

8. What is an autonomous system?

Exam Questions

1. You are the network administrator of a medium-sized network. The network spans three floors and is interconnected using a Windows 2000 server. You have decided to configure routing using static routes. The segments are all configured with Class C addresses. What is the route command needed to configure the network segment that contains the workstation with address 199.199.42.2?

   A. Route –f add 199.199.42.0 mask 255.255.255.0 199.199.40.1 metric 2

   B. Route add 199.199.42.0 mask 255.255.0.0 199.199.40.1 metric 2

   C. Route –f add 199.199.42.0 mask 255.255.0.0 199.199.40.1 metric 2

   D. Route add 199.199.42.0 mask 255.255.255.0 199.199.40.1 metric 2

2. You have configured a Windows 2000 server as a router to replace your existing Novell server that was acting as a router. You have three segments configured that are connected to the server. Each segment has a Class C address associated with it, and you have configured the appropriate ROUTE commands to add the network entries to the static routing table. You have set the subnet mask as 255.255.255.0, and you have not configured a default gateway for the router. What will happen when a packet arrives for a route that has not been configured on the router?

   A. The packet will be routed through the first segment that was configured on the router.

   B. The packet will be routed through all segments configured on the router.

   C. The router will use an ARP to resolve the address so that it knows how to route it.

   D. The packet will be dropped by the router.

3. You are the network administrator of a medium-sized organization. You are receiving calls from the Help desk indicating that they cannot get access to the server. You check into it and determine that you cannot ping the server across the router. You check the router and the services seem as though they are started and running fine. You would now like to check the routing tables. Which utilities can you use to determine what the routing tables contain?

APPLY YOUR KNOWLEDGE

    A. The routing and remote access services administration tool

    B. The ROUTE command

    C. The TRACERT command

    D. The ARP command

4. You have a campus network that is very large and growing. You are undergoing an expansion on the network. Your network makes use of the RIP protocol to route information throughout the infrastructure. As you add routers to the network, users indicate that they cannot reach some segments on the network. When you added the routers, you did some preliminary testing to determine whether routing was occurring. You look further into the issue and determine that some of the routers do not have any information about other routers in the network. What could the problem be?

    A. The RIP protocol is not propagating information.

    B. The RIP protocol cannot support more than 15 hops.

    C. The RIP protocol is suffering from a count-to-infinity problem.

    D. The routers that are not reachable are not functioning properly.

5. You have a campus network that is very large and growing. You are undergoing reconfiguration on the network and you remove some segments from the overall network topology. Your network makes use of the RIP protocol to route information

throughout the infrastructure. Users indicate that they cannot reach some segments on the network. When you added the routers, you did some preliminary testing to determine whether routing was occurring. You look further into the issue and determine that some of the routers do not have any information about other routers in the network. What could the problem be?

    A. The RIP protocol is not propagating information.

    B. The RIP protocol cannot support more than 15 hops.

    C. The RIP protocol is suffering from a count-to-infinity problem.

    D. The routers that are not reachable are not functioning properly.

6. You have a local network with several segments. You have a host on one segment that needs to send data to a host on the same segment. What method or methods will the host use to reach the other host?

    A. The host will query the DNS for the address of the host and will use this address to reach the host.

    B. The host will use ARP to determine how to send to the other host on the network.

    C. The host will send the information to the router who will, in turn, send it to the host.

    D. The routers will broadcast the information on the local segment to the destination host.

APPLY YOUR KNOWLEDGE

7. You receive a call from a user who is trying to transfer information from the user's computer via a custom-built application to another computer. You check into the issue and determine that the two hosts are on separate segments. You check both configurations on each computer and find that each seems fine. You do some basic checks as to whether you can ping the IP address, and you determine that you can. You are unsure what the problem is. You need to investigate further. What tool can you use to further investigate what the problem may be?

   A. Network Monitor

   B. Performance Monitor

   C. System Monitor

   D. SNMP

8. You have a network with 4 locations: one in Toronto, one in New York, and two in Los Angeles. The central IS department is located in Toronto, and your network is configured with high speed T3 segments from Toronto to all locations. The Los Angeles location also has a router set up with a connection to Toronto and another ISDN connection to the other Los Angeles location. Your users in Los Angeles communicate with application servers in the other Los Angeles location on a regular basis. The company uses the RIP protocol. When routing traffic, which route will the traffic take, based on the information provided?

   A. The traffic will be routed through Toronto to the other Los Angeles location.

   B. The traffic will be routed directly to the other Los Angeles location.

   C. The traffic will be load balanced both through Toronto and directly to the Los Angeles location.

   D. The traffic will take the least congested route toward the Los Angeles location.

9. You are the administrator of a large corporate network. You have a number of Windows 2000 servers acting as routers. You have started to replace these Windows 2000 servers with Cisco routers. All your Windows 2000 Server routers use RIP Version 1. You implement one of the Cisco routers but find that after the router has been implemented, there is improper routing information within the routing tables. What could the problem be?

   A. The RIP Version 2 router is not broadcasting all its routes within its routing table.

   B. The RIP Version 2 router is propagating incompatible information to RIP Version 1 routers.

   C. The RIP Version 2 router calculates costing information differently than RIP Version 1 routers.

   D. The RIP Version 2 routers are configured to use multicast announcements, whereas the RIP Version 1 routers are configured to listen for broadcasts.

10. You have a demand-dial routing connection between your head office and a remote office. Your company is quite concerned about cost; therefore, you have implemented an on-demand connection. During operation, however, you notice that the connection is coming up fairly regularly, even during the evening when you

APPLY YOUR KNOWLEDGE

know that there is no communication occurring between the offices. What could the problem be?

A. This is normal, and it is an indication that your demand-dial routing solution is functioning normally.

B. Legitimate data is being transferred during the connection.

C. A default route has been configured on the calling router, and anytime that a packet is received, it is forwarded to the destination demand-dial router.

D. A default route has been configured on the answering router, and anytime that a packet is received, it is forwarded to the destination demand-dial router.

11. You have a large corporate network that is using OSPF as the routing protocol within your environment. Your company has just merged with another company that is also using OSPF to route within their network. You are charged with bringing the two networks together, and you establish a virtual link with their network. However, the virtual link is not forming. What could the problem be?

A. The router on the other side has been set up to filter routes, and therefore the virtual link will take time to be established.

B. The password is different between the two routers.

C. The router interfaces on each router are set to different connection speeds.

D. The router is configured with a hello interval that is different from the other router's.

12. You have a large corporate network that is using OSPF as the routing protocol within your environment. You have partitioned your network into several areas, with each area having a single router connected to the backbone. You are tuning performance and would like to ensure that as little routing traffic as possible is broadcast onto the network. What is the best method of doing this?

A. Configure each area as a stub area and have each area router specify a default route.

B. Configure each area router to distribute external routes only upon startup.

C. Configure each area as a transit area and have each area router specify a default route.

D. Configure each area router to implement external route filters.

13. You have configured a demand-dial routing connection between your corporate office and your regional office. You have configured RIP as the routing protocol and you have set it up as a persistent connection. However, when you try to contact a host workstation on the other end, you cannot reach it. You check everything and it seems fine. What can the problem be?

A. The host on the other end is not functioning properly.

B. The connection is too slow and the workstation being used to reach the destination station is timing out.

C. The router has not been manually updated with routes yet.

D. The router has not been set up with a default protocol.

APPLY YOUR KNOWLEDGE

14. You have configured a demand-dial routing connection between your corporate office and your regional office. The connection is persistent and uses RIP to maintain the routes to the remote location. The regional office has a router that the calling router receives updates from on a scheduled basis. You bring the router in the remote location down for routine maintenance and then bring it back up a little while later. However, when you bring the router up, you start to receive calls from the Help desk indicating that the users on the calling router side of the demand-dial connection cannot reach the hosts on the answering router side. What can the problem be?

    A. The router that was brought back up after maintenance was not configured properly.

    B. The router that was brought back up after maintenance has not received routing updates from the calling side of the connection.

    C. The calling router's connection to the regional office has been dropped.

    D. The calling router's routing entries have been dropped.

15. You have configured a demand-dial routing connection between your corporate office and your regional office. You have configured the connection as an on-demand connection, and it uses the RIP protocol to maintain the routes to the remote location. You begin to test the connection and when you send information to the remote router, the on-demand connection will not be initiated. What can the problem be?

    A. The RIP protocol cannot be configured for on-demand connections.

    B. The answering router was configured with a username, but the calling router does not specify the password during the initiation of the call.

    C. The router has not been configured with the proper protocol to allow traffic to be forwarded to the remote location.

    D. The IP routing protocol has not been enabled on the calling router.

Answers to Review Questions

1. A topological database is essentially an overall picture of networks in relationship to routers. The topological database contains the collection of LSAs received from all routers in the same area. In a very large AS with a large number of networks, each OSPF router must keep the LSA of every other router in its topological database. Each router in a large OSPF autonomous system has a large topological database. The shortest path first calculation of a large topological database can require a substantial amount of processing and can result in very large routing tables. To prevent this, autonomous systems are further divided into areas. See the section "OSPF."

2. A link-state routing protocol is generally more efficient than a distance-vector protocol. Because link-state advertisements contain only information about the neighbors of a particular router, this leads to smaller routing tables. For large networks, the link-state advertisements contain only neighbor information, and therefore the impact on the network is much less than on a network using a distance-vector routing protocol. With a

APPLY YOUR KNOWLEDGE

distance-vector routing protocol, all the routes in a routing table are propagated resulting in more usage of bandwidth than link-state protocols. In addition, because link-state information is not exchanged after the network has converged, it does not have the impact on the network that distance-vector routing does. Distance-vector routing, by default, broadcasts its information on a periodic basis whether required or not. See the section "Routing Technology."

3. Split horizon is a mechanism that prevents routing information from being sent back in the direction it was received from. Basically, the router says, "I learned about network xx from you, so you can't get to network xx through me." Split horizon eliminates count-to-infinity and routing loops during convergence in single-path internetworks and reduces the chances of count to infinity in multipath internetworks. See the section "Routing Technology."

4. Autostatic updates do not occur automatically on initiation of a demand-dial connection. Rather, the autostatic update must be manually initiated or a schedule must be put in place to update routes. After the routes have been sent, the two routers do not exchange updates of routing information unless a manual request to update is made or a scheduled request occurs, depending on how autostatic updates are configured within your environment. Therefore, the first time a connection is made, an autostatic update must be manually initiated to configure the router with proper routes to the destination network. See the section "Demand-Dial Routing."

5. The –f parameter is used to clear the routing tables of all entries. See the section "Using the ROUTE Command to Configure Static Routes."

6. An OSPF backbone has a reserved area ID of 0.0.0.0. An OSPF backbone is responsible for distributing routing information between areas. There is at least one backbone per OSPF internetwork. It consists of all area border routers, networks not in any one area, and their attached routers. The backbone has to be at the center of all areas within the autonomous system. That is, all areas have to be physically connected to the backbone. The reasoning behind this is that OSPF expects all areas to inject routing information into the backbone and in turn, the backbone will disseminate that information into other areas. See the section "OSPF."

7. The count-to-infinity problem is one of the major disadvantages of distance-vector routing. This condition is caused when a router (or link to a router) becomes unavailable. The convergence time is slow and, therefore, incorrect routing information is propagated through the system. See the section "Routing Technology."

8. An autonomous system is a collection of networks under common administration, sharing a common routing strategy. Each autonomous system can be further divided into areas with areas being linked by a OSPF backbone, which is also an area. See the section "OSPF."

Answers to Exam Questions

1. **D.** This command adds a route for a Class C address to the routing table. The –f will remove existing routes from the routing table. Because the address being configured is a Class C address, you will need to configure the proper subnet

APPLY YOUR KNOWLEDGE

mask. B does not provide the proper subnet mask. See the section "Using the ROUTE Command to Configure Static Routes."

2. **D.** By default, if a default gateway is not configured, the router drops the packet and sends an ICMP message back to the host indicating that the destination host is unreachable. See the section "Managing and Monitoring IP Routing Protocols."

3. **A, B.** The two utilities that can be used to check routing tables are the RRAS administration tool and the ROUTE command. Use the print qualifier to display the existing routes. The TRACERT command is used to determine reachability through the network. The ARP command is used to display the IP to Physical Address table. See the section "Using the ROUTE Command to Configure Static Routes."

4. **B.** By default, the maximum number of hops between routers is 15. Given the scenario presented, this is the most likely cause of the problem because you tested the routers when you installed them. The count-to-infinity problem occurs only when a segment is removed from the network. See the section "Routing Technology."

5. **B and C.** In this particular scenario, segments are being removed from the overall network; nothing is indicated about routers or segments being added. This indicates that the problem could indeed be a count-to-infinity problem. Because infinity is 15 hops, this leads to answer B also being correct. See the section "Routing Technology."

6. **A, B.** To send to a destination host on the local segment, the sending host must first determine the network address from the hostname. To do this, it queries the DNS to resolve the name to

an IP address. The host then queries its local ARP table to see if it has a MAC address for the IP address. The host then sends a directed broadcast of the information to the destination host. See the section "Host Routing."

7. **A.** To further check what might be going on between the two machines, you need to use Network Monitor. Performance Monitor is used for gathering statistics about the performance of your machine. System Monitor is a tool that is available on Windows 95/98 that provides similar information for monitoring performance. SNMP is used for managing and configuring network devices. See the section "Using Network Monitor."

8. **B.** The traffic will be routed directly to the Los Angeles location. RIP routes traffic on a least-cost basis. Because there was no mention of costs being assigned to each of the segments, the cost will default to 1 for each segment. To route through the Toronto location would incur a total cost of two hops, even though this is probably the fastest path to the other Los Angeles location, given the line speed. See the section "Working with RIP."

9. **D.** RIP Version 2 routers are configured to multicast announcements. Multicast announcements are never received by RIP Version 1 routers. If you have a mixed environment of RIP Version 1 and RIP Version 2, ensure that the routers configured with RIP Version 2 are using broadcast instead of multicast. See the section "RIP Version 2."

10. **C.** Although the default route can be used to simplify configuration of static routing over on-demand connections, you must consider its implications. The default IP route effectively summarizes all IP destinations and becomes the

APPLY YOUR KNOWLEDGE

route used to forward IP packets when another more specific route is not found. This can cause traffic to be routed across the on-demand connection. See the section "Demand-Dial Routing."

11. **B, D.** To establish a virtual link between the two organizations, it is necessary to ensure that the password, the hello interval, and the dead interval are configured to be the same. If not, the virtual link will have trouble being established. See the section "OSPF."

12. **A.** A stub area contains a single entry and exit point. Routing to all autonomous system external networks in a stub area is done through a default route (destination 0.0.0.0 with network mask 0.0.0.0). To create the default route, the area border router of the stub area advertises a default route into the stub area. The default route is flooded to all the routers within the stub area but not outside the stub area. The routers within the area use the default route to route any addresses that are not reachable within the autonomous system. See the section "OSPF."

13. **C.** In this particular scenario, an autostatic update has not occurred. As such, no routing information is available to allow the source station to reach the destination station. The default

operation mode for demand-dial interfaces for RIP is autostatic update mode. Autostatic updates do not occur automatically when the demand-dial connection is made. As such, they must be manually requested or a scheduled request must be set up. See the section "Demand-Dial Routing."

14. **D.** Based on the information outlined in the scenario, the correct answer is that the routing table entries have been lost from the calling router side. This probably occurred during the scheduled autostatic update. When an autostatic update is requested, the existing routes that were obtained through a previous autostatic update are deleted before the request for routes is sent, clearing out the routing table entries. If there is no response to the request, the router cannot replace the routes it has deleted. See the section "Demand-Dial Routing."

15. **B, D.** In both a one-way initiated connection and a two-way initiated connection, the router initiating the call must be configured with a username that matches the demand-dial interface on the answering router. If IP is not enabled on the demand-dial interface, a connection will not be initiated. See the section "Demand-Dial Routing."

Suggested Readings and Resources

Marcus, Scott J. *Designing Wide Area Networks and Internetworks: A Practical Guide.* Upper Saddle River, NJ: Addison Wesley, 1999

Microsoft Corporation Staff. *Microsoft Windows NT 4.0 Network Administration Training Kit.* Redmond, WA: Microsoft Press, 1998.

Thomas, Thomas M. *OSPF Network Design Solutions.* Indianapolis, IN: Cisco Press, 1998.

With the release of the Windows 2000 operating system, Microsoft included the Internet Connection Sharing (ICS) and Network Address Translation (NAT) features as part of the Network and Dial-up Connections. This feature enables you to use your Windows 2000 server to connect your office network to the Internet. ICS provides a simple configuration for NAT, IP address allocation, and name resolution services.

Microsoft defines the "Installing, Configuring, and Troubleshooting Network Address Translation (NAT)" objectives as follows:

Install Internet Connection Sharing.

▶ ICS provides an automated method for configuring Demand-Dial Routing, Network Address Translation, DHCP, and a DNS Proxy service to an ISP's DNS server. Because it is well suited for small offices, Microsoft expects you to know how to install this service.

Install NAT.

▶ NAT is used in conjunction with an Internet connection and is for offices that want to use the security and address-preservation features of NAT. Microsoft expects you to understand the installation process for NAT.

Configure NAT properties.

▶ After NAT is installed, you need to understand the properties associated with it. Understanding NAT properties is critical not only to the functioning of NAT, but also to the security of your network. Improper configuration could potentially result in security holes. Microsoft expects you to have a thorough understanding of these properties for this objective.

CHAPTER 7

Installing, Configuring, and Troubleshooting Network Address Translation (NAT)

Configure NAT interfaces.

▶ The final objective requires you to be able to configure the interface within NAT. Much like the properties discussed in the previous objective, understanding how to configure the interfaces is critical not only to the functioning of NAT, but also to the security of your network. Improper configuration could potentially result in security holes. Microsoft expects you to have a thorough understanding of the interface configuration for this objective.

Installing Internet Connection Sharing   **356**

Installing NAT   **361**

Configuring NAT Properties   **363**

Configuring NAT Interfaces   **366**

Chapter Summary   **371**

Apply Your Knowledge   **372**

▶ Internet Connection Services provide a wizard-driven mechanism for configuring all the services you need to connect a small office to the Internet. Be sure you understand the features of this service, as well as how it differs from manually configuring NAT.

▶ Make sure you understand the function of NAT and how to properly configure both the interfaces and properties. Although installing NAT is relatively easy, Microsoft recognizes that the configuration is the key to NAT.

▶ Review the TCP/IP section of Chapter 4, "Installing, Configuring, Managing, Monitoring, and Troubleshooting Network Protocols in a Windows 2000 Network Infrastructure," to be sure you are familiar with how TCP/IP works. Understanding TCP/IP is critical to understanding how NAT works.

INSTALLING INTERNET CONNECTION SHARING

Install Internet Connection Sharing

In the first section of this chapter, the ICS services are discussed. The ICS services provide an automated demand-dial installation process for the following services:

◆ Network Address Translation (NAT)

◆ Dynamic Host Configuration Protocol (DHCP)

◆ DNS Proxy

These services make ICS a great solution for a small office looking for a quick and easy way to connect to the Internet via dial-up.

ICS has a few features that are not available in the NAT implementation. Microsoft will probably add them in a Windows 2000 service pack. These features include the following:

◆ **H.323 Proxy.** This feature permits users to make and receive Microsoft NetMeeting calls.

◆ **Lightweight Directory Access Protocol (LDAP) Proxy.** The capability to proxy LDAP requests enables users to register with an Internet Locater Service (ILS) server as part of a NetMeeting directory.

◆ **Directplay Proxy.** This allows users to play Directplay games across the NAT router. This feature is more suited for home use than for a small office; it is also offered in the Windows 98 version of ICS.

Now you know what ICS does for you. Before you jump right into installing ICS, you should learn exactly what this automated process is going to install and configure. Keep in mind that a server running ICS must have a LAN and a modem connection. Otherwise you will not be able to install the service. ICS does the following at installation:

◆ ICS sets the IP address of the LAN interface to 192.168.0.1, a private IP address. Because you are working with the internal interface for the ICS server (that is the internal NIC in the Windows 2000 server), it is set to a private address for security reasons. You can reset this address, although it is a good idea to use a private network address on the internal network whenever possible. Private addresses cannot be routed over the Internet, so using them adds an additional layer of security.

◆ The WAN interface (usually a modem) is set to be a Demand-Dial Router pointed at the Internet Service Provider (ISP).

◆ A DNS Proxy service is installed to provide DNS services to the office. This service passes client computer DNS requests to the DNS server configured in the ICS server's DHCP settings.

◆ The AutoDHCP service is installed. This service provides a subset of the services included with a full DHCP installation, but AutoDHCP is configured to issue addresses on the new 198.168.0.0 network.

Now let's look at the process of installing ICS.

EXAM TIP

The DDL That Controls DNS Proxy and AutoDHCP Service The dynamic link library used to control both the DNS Proxy and the AutoDHCP service is IPNATHLPR.DLL.

EXAM TIP

The AutoDHCP Service Uses a Private Network Although it is unlikely that Microsoft will expect you to memorize the exact network that the AutoDHCP service uses, you should be aware that it is a private network.

STEP BY STEP

7.1 Installing the Internet Connection Sharing Service.

1. Open Network and Dial-up Connections by right-clicking the My Network Places icon on the desktop and clicking Properties. (You can also open Properties by opening the Control Panel and clicking Network and Dial-up Connections.) For the installation to continue, you need a LAN and an ISP connection (see Figure 7.1).

continues

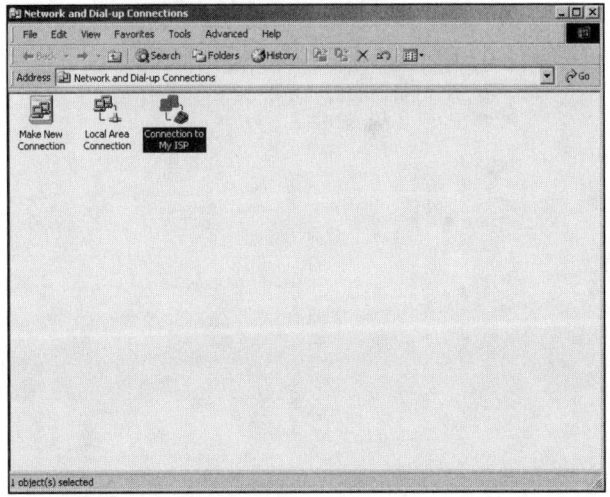

FIGURE 7.1
Network and Dial-up Connections allows you to install ICS only if you have already installed a LAN and a dial-up network connection.

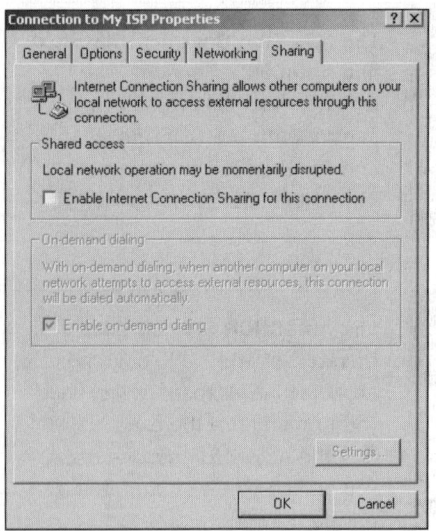

FIGURE 7.2
The Sharing tab of the Connection Properties
dialog box allows you to enable Internet
Connection Sharing as well as on-demand
dialing.

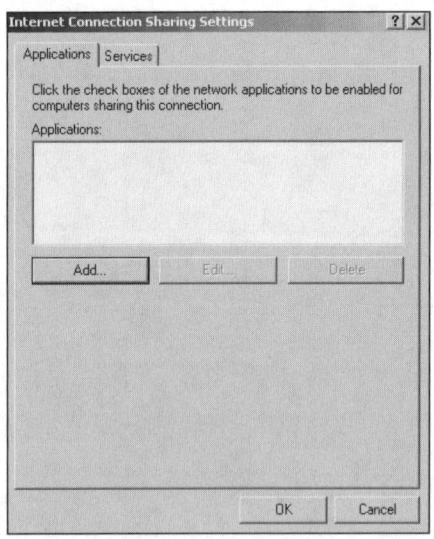

FIGURE 7.3
After you have enabled ICS, you need to
configure the applications that can be used.

continued

2. Right-click the dial-up connection and select Properties
   from the context menu. The Connection Properties dialog
   box opens. Click the Sharing tab (see Figure 7.2).

3. Select the Enable Internet Connection Sharing for This
   Connection option. The Enable On-Demand Dialing
   option is enabled by default.

4. Click the Settings button to open Internet Connection
   Sharing Settings (see Figure 7.3). The Applications tab
   allows you to configure custom applications so that you
   can connect across the NAT connection.

5. Click the Add button to add a custom application.
   Figure 7.4 shows the addition of the Internet Relay Chat
   application. Click OK to return to the Settings window.

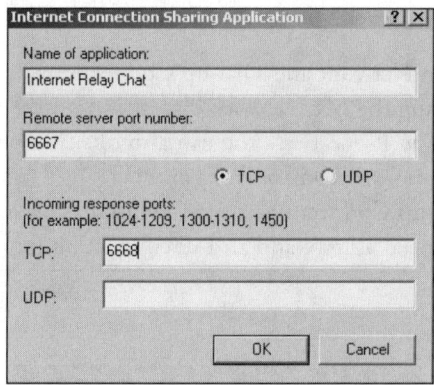

FIGURE 7.4
To add an application, you need to know what
TCP/IP ports it uses.

6. Click the Services tab (see Figure 7.5). This tab enables you to configure services to be accessed from the Internet. For example, if you want to set up an FTP server on the internal network, this is where you enable it. To complete the configuration, you need to know the private address of that server. Just select the option for that application and fill in the DNS name or address of the server (see Figure 7.6). The Name of the Service and Service Port is filled in for you and cannot be changed. Click OK to return to Services.

7. Click Add to add a custom application for inbound access. You need the name of the service, the service port, and the server DNS name or IP address for the new service (see Figure 7.7). Enter the information and click OK to add the service. Click OK to enable ICS.

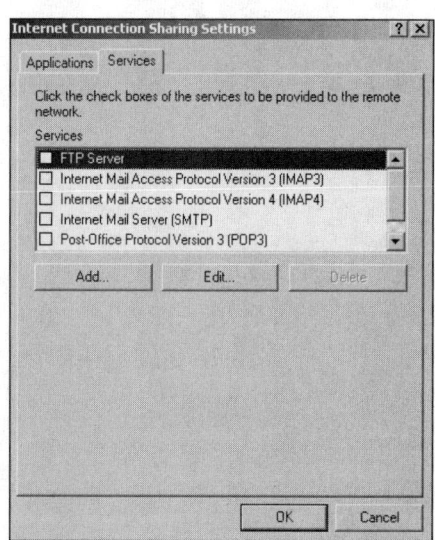

FIGURE 7.5
If you want users on the Internet to be able to access servers on your private network for activities such as Mail, FTP, or Telnet, select the Services tab to configure them.

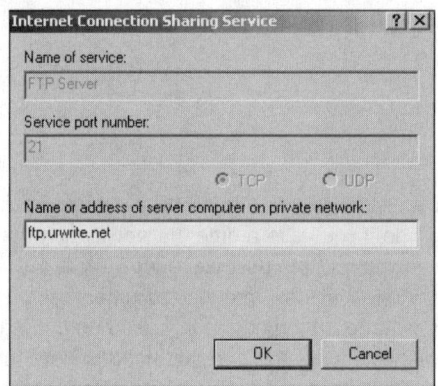

FIGURE 7.6
To make a server accessible from the Internet, you need the server address or DNS name. If you are adding a custom application, you also need the port of the application you want to use.

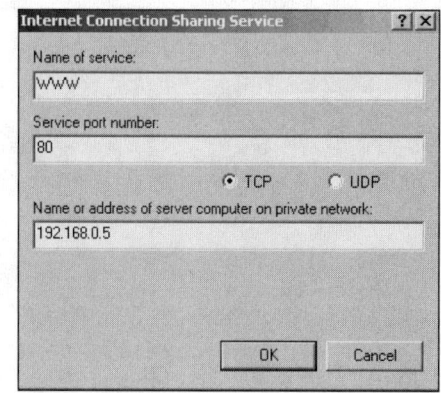

FIGURE 7.7
You can add any service for inbound access as long as you know the TCP/IP port required.

IN THE FIELD

HOW DO YOU DETERMINE THE PORT NUMBER AN APPLICATION USES?

If you are working with ICS, you have the ports of common applications predefined in the application. These are shown in Table 7.1.

TABLE 7.1

PREDEFINED PORTS OF COMMON APPLICATIONS

Application	Port
FTP Server	21
Internet Mail Access Protocol Version 3 (IMAP3)	220
Internet Mail Access Protocol Version 4 (IMAP4)	143
Internet Mail Server (SMTP)	25
Post-Office Protocol Version 3 (POP3)	110
Telnet Server	23
WWW	80

This is great if you want to use one of the predefined applications. But what do you do if you have a different application that you want to enable? How can you find the port you need? There are four methods generally used. First, check the product documentation and Help files. If you are using an application commonly used on the Internet, the vendor generally documents the port you need to have open to use the application. If you cannot find the information in the product documentation, you can look to the Internet, or more specifically the Internet Assigned Numbers Authority (http://www.iana.net). This authority provides registration services for vendors who want to reserve a TCP/IP port for their application. If you cannot find your application listed, there's a good chance the vendor is using an unregistered port. The next step in tracking down the port is network analysis. You can use network analysis tools to analyze the traffic the application uses. If you are running the application on a Windows NT or a Windows 2000 server, you can use the Network Monitor tool included with the operating system to provide this information. When all else fails, find a comfortable chair and a speakerphone and call the vendor. You may have to wait on hold for a while, but the vendor can almost always tell you what port its application uses.

That is about all there is to the ICS service. It is an easy, quick service perfect for a small office environment. Now let's see what to do if you are in a larger environment or need more flexibility in your connection.

INSTALLING NAT

Install NAT.

Suppose you have a larger network than the one described in the ICS section, but you still want to use Windows 2000 to connect to the Internet. You will find the NAT capabilities of Windows 2000 to be very useful. But just in case you are not familiar with NAT, take a quick look at how NAT works and what it does before you jump right into installing it.

NAT does pretty much what the name describes. It takes an IP address entering on one interface of the Windows 2000 Server and translates it to a different address exiting a different (usually the Internet-connected) interface. For example, suppose that your PC has an IP address of 10.10.10.10. This is an address in the reserved network of 10.0.0.0, which is not routable on the Internet. You want to be able to connect to the Internet, so you need to have an Internet-routable (registered) IP address. A server running NAT takes each packet from your workstation, strips the 10.10.10.10 address from it, and resends the packet with a registered address. The original address and the registered address are stored in a table so that the server knows what translation was used. The packet is routed to the appropriate destination. If the destination responds with a packet, the NAT server looks up the address in its NAT table and reverses the original process, placing 10.10.10.10 into the destination address and resending the packet.

There are basically two reasons for doing this:

◆ **Security.** If you are connecting your network to the Internet, you really don't want uninvited users connecting to your private hosts. By translating the addresses of those hosts, you provide a level of security for that host.

> **EXAM TIP**
>
> **Know NAT** For the exam, you need to understand what NAT is and how it works. The key features are the replacing of the "internal" addresses and the NAT table for maintaining the translation.

◆ **IP Address Conservation**. As hard as it is to believe, the Internet is running out of addresses. In the mid-1990s, some enterprising people recognized that this problem was coming and came up with NAT as a mechanism for conserving addresses. Although clearly a stop-gap mechanism until the next version of IP is widely adopted, NAT allows a company to use private addresses on its internal network and translate those addresses to a single address or to multiple registered addresses. This many-to-few address-conservation mechanism has contributed in large part to the Internet's capability to continue to grow.

NAT can handle the address translation in two ways. If the translating device has only a single registered IP address available, it translates the address in the IP packet to the registered address and then sets the source port to a random port number.

For example, if the NAT device handles a request for an HTTP connection, it connects to the server on port 80, but listens for the response on the random port it assigned during the translation. It substitutes its address in the source address field and the random port number in place of the client's computer original port. It then uses this information to create an address mapping in the NAT table that tells it where to send the HTTP responses.

Now if you have multiple registered IP addresses, the NAT device performs a one-to-one translation of the address and skips any port translations.

One final point before we look at the installation: Like the ICS service, NAT is a two-way street. You can configure NAT not only for outbound private-to-public translations, but also for public-to-private translations for inbound requests. If you want to put a Web server on your internal network, NAT allows you to do that.

Now that you know what NAT is, let's install it.

> **NOTE**
>
> **I Wish There Were an RFC for This**
> You're in luck. The RFC defining the private addresses usually used in conjunction with NAT is RFC 1597. It sets aside the address ranges 10.0.0.0 to 10.255.255.255, 172.16.0.0 to 172.31.255.255, and 192.168.0.0 to 192.168.255.255. RFC 1631 defines the method for NAT.

STEP BY STEP

7.2 Installing Network Address Translation.

1. Go to Start, Programs, Administrative Tools, Routing and Remote Access console. The Routing and Remote Access window opens.

2. Expand the tree under the local server icon. Under the IP Routing icon, you will find the General icon. Right-click it and select New Routing Protocol from the context menu. The New Routing Protocol sheet opens (see Figure 7.8).

3. Select Network Address Translation and click OK. You should see Network Address Translation show up as an additional icon under IP routing.

Now that you have installed NAT, take a look at configuring it.

CONFIGURING NAT PROPERTIES

Configure NAT properties.

A number of properties can be configured in conjunction with NAT. They can all be accessed by opening the Routing and Remote Access window (as described in Step by Step 7.2), right-clicking the Network Address Translation icon, and selecting Properties from the context menu. You will see the following tabs: General, Translation, Address Assignment, and Name Resolution.

The General tab shown in Figure 7.9 is used to configure Event Logging. Any logging enabled in this section appears in the System Event Log. You can configure Event Logging for the following levels:

◆ **Log Errors Only.** Logging errors is a useful setting when you want to restrict your logging to critical messages. In a busy environment, it is frequently difficult to review logs filled with warnings that are not in fact real issues. By keeping the logging to errors only, you increase the chances that you will see serious errors in the log.

◆ **Log Errors and Warnings.** The default setting, logging errors and warnings, is a good idea in smaller networks. If you find that the warnings are filling the log, it may be time to log only errors.

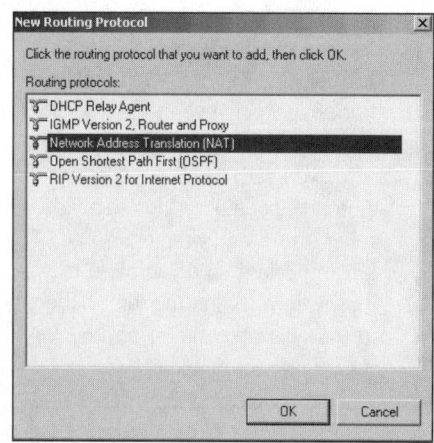

FIGURE 7.8
NAT is considered a routing protocol and is added like any other routing protocol.

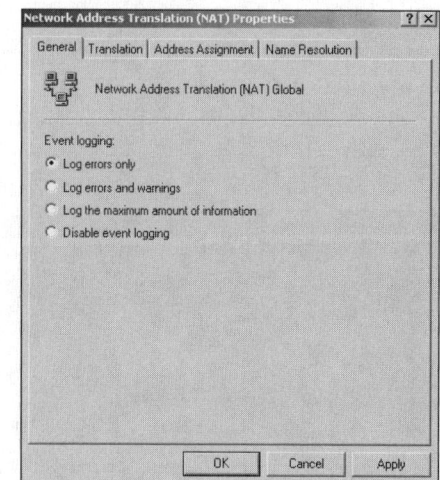

FIGURE 7.9
If you want to configure logging for the NAT protocol, do it from the General screen.

Use the Event Viewer to Check Out Logging Events Remember that any logging events are logged in the System Event Log and can be viewed with the Event Viewer. Microsoft considers the capability to log errors and warnings to be very important, and you need to know where to find the information so that you can answer any logging questions surrounding NAT.

To Log or Not to Log? Keep in mind that logging uses resources. If you have resources to burn (CPU, RAM, hard drive), feel free to leave the Log the Maximum Amount of Information option enabled. Otherwise, you may want to restrict your logging to Errors and Warnings, the default setting.

◆ **Log the Maximum Amount of Information.** When you first set up your NAT, you may want to log the maximum amount of information to get a good understanding of what is going on with NAT. Keep in mind that the information logged at this level is extremely detailed and sometimes decipherable only by Microsoft support. It's great to use if you are troubleshooting an issue with Microsoft; otherwise, this is probably not a setting you will need to use.

◆ **Disable Event Logging.** Unless you are extremely resource bound on this server, you should never disable logging.

The Translation tab shown in Figure 7.10 is used to set the timeout values for the translations. You also have the capability to add inbound applications exactly the way you could in ICS. In fact, any applications configured in ICS (if you were to switch to NAT) are automatically added to the NAT translations.

IN THE FIELD

WHAT SETTINGS WORK BEST IN REAL LIFE?

As a general rule (and this is true with many Microsoft applications), the defaults will usually work for your network. However, you might want to reset these timeout values in the case of a special application that requires higher timeouts to function. For example, if you have a UDP-based application that needs to maintain connections for a long period of time, you might want to set the UDP mapping timer to 60. However, I am not aware of any UDP-based applications that have that requirement, because of the connectionless nature of UDP. In the TCP field, you might want to lower the TCP mapping timer if you have a large number of users connecting across the server for limited periods of time, and if you are resource constrained. Making this parameter shorter causes resources to become available more quickly. Remember that if you are using this for NAT, you probably don't want to be resource constrained. You should consider an upgrade if the situation is that severe.

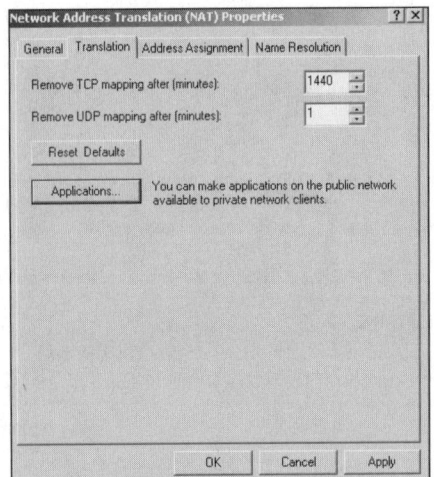

FIGURE 7.10
Use the Translation tab to set the timeouts and to add inbound application translations for the NAT protocol.

The Address Assignment tab allows you to configure the private IP addresses and configure the DHCP service used in conjunction with NAT (see Figure 7.11). To enable the NAT DHCP, just check the box marked Automatically Assign IP Addresses by Using DHCP. This DHCP service can be used in place of the Windows 2000 DHCP service discussed in Chapter 2, "Installing, Configuring, Managing, Monitoring, and Troubleshooting DHCP in a Windows 2000 Network Infrastructure." If you are using the Windows 2000 DHCP service, do not select the NAT DHCP option.

The Name Resolution tab (see Figure 7.12) is used to configure DNS for the NAT protocol. From this tab you can configure who should receive DNS resolution services and how to handle resolution of nonlocal names. You can even configure the server to automatically dial the Internet if it needs to resolve a name.

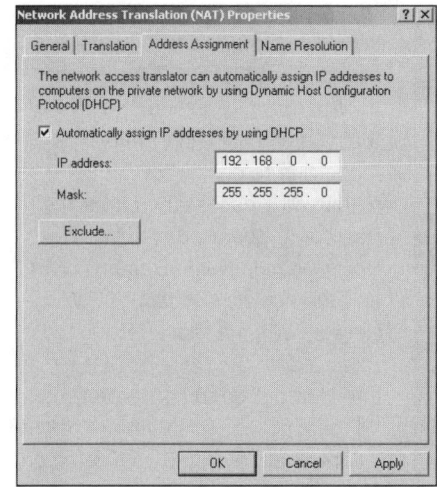

FIGURE 7.11
The Address Assignment tab allows you to configure the DHCP service for the NAT protocol.

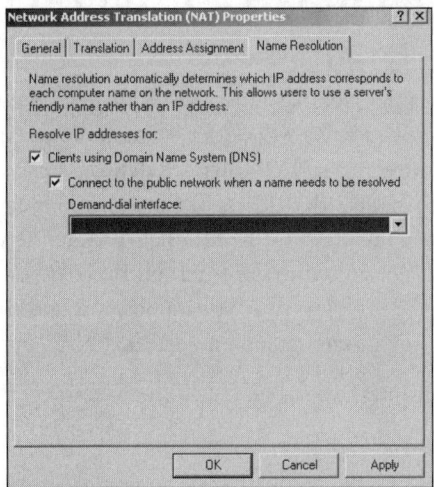

FIGURE 7.12
Use the Name Resolution tab to set the DNS resolution parameters for the NAT protocol.

Use the NAT DHCP Service to Enable Client's Computer If you are planning to use NAT, the easiest way to enable the client's computer is through the NAT DHCP service. This will configure the client with the correct information to use the NAT gateway when they are assigned their IP address via DHCP. If you are using the NAT DHCP, you will not need the Windows 2000 DHCP service.

EXAM TIP

You Can Configure NAT Properties to Dial an ISP for DNS Resolution For the exam, you should be aware that you can configure NAT Properties to dial an ISP for DNS resolution if necessary. Just select Resolve IP Addresses for Clients Using Domain Name System (DNS) and then select Connect to Public Network When a Name Needs to Be Resolved. In the Demand-Dial Interface pull-down box, select your ISP connection. This will work only if you have a dial-up ISP configured on the system.

EXAM TIP

Know the Difference Between the Public and Private Interfaces Be sure to know the difference between the public and private interfaces for the exam. The public interface is your connection to the Internet, and the private interface is your internal network. All interface configuration occurs on the public interface.

You should have noticed that although ICS and NAT are different services, the capabilities are in large part the same. The configuration does differ fairly significantly, however. To recap, both ICS and the NAT service provide Network Address Translation, Dynamic Host Configuration Protocol (DHCP), and DNS Proxy capabilities. ICS automates the installation and configuration of these services, whereas the NAT interface requires some configuration by the administrator. In addition, ICS supports features not included in NAT, such as H.323 Proxy, Lightweight Directory Access Protocol (LDAP) Proxy, and Directplay Proxy.

Now let's look at the final part of configuring NAT—configuring the interfaces.

CONFIGURING NAT INTERFACES

Configure NAT interfaces.

So far in this chapter, you have installed NAT and configured the properties. What you haven't done yet is configure the interface that NAT will run through. A NAT Interface defines the Connection Properties for the Network Address Translation. This can be either the private interface, connected to the internal (private) network, or the public interface, connected to the Internet. Because your NAT server will most likely be bridging your private network and the Internet, you need to set up an internal and an external NAT interface.

To configure an interface for NAT, do the following:

STEP BY STEP

7.3 Configuring a NAT Interface

1. Open the Routing and Remote Access window and right-click the Network Address Translation (NAT) icon. From the context menu, select New Interface. New Interface for Network Address Translation (NAT) shown in Figure 7.13 opens.

2. Select the LAN interface to be added and click OK. The Local Area Connection Properties dialog box for that connection opens (see Figure 7.14). This allows you to set the interface as a private (internal) or public (Internet) interface. If you have a LAN connection to the Internet, you need to configure a public and a private interface. Select the appropriate type and click OK. If you select the public interface, you need to do some additional configuration.

3. Select the Address Pool tab (see Figure 7.15) to configure the public addresses for the server. These are supplied by your ISP; it is these addresses that your internal addresses are translated to for routing over the Internet.

continues

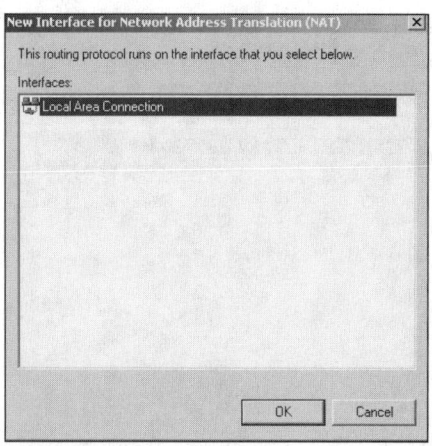

FIGURE 7.13
New Interface for Network Address Translation (NAT) enables you to configure the interface(s) that will be supported by NAT. You will see only LAN connections in this dialog box because WAN connections are assumed to be connected to the public network.

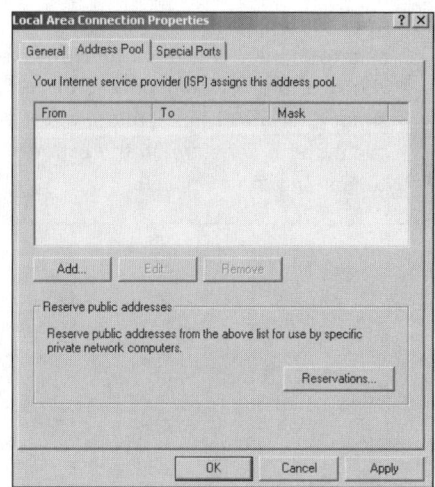

FIGURE 7.15
You need to configure registered addresses for the public interface.

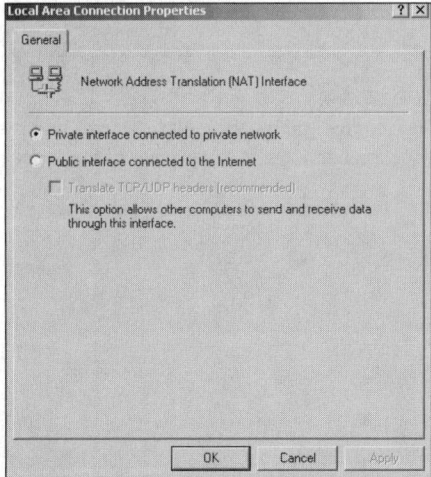

FIGURE 7.14
You need to identify whether the interface is connected to a public or private network so that Windows 2000 knows how to translate the addresses.

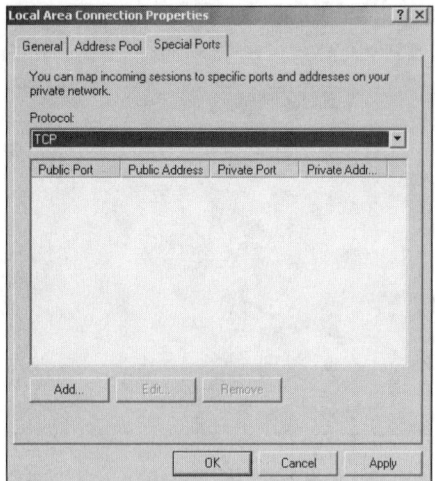

FIGURE 7.16
The Special Ports tab is used to configure custom inbound connections.

continued

4. Select the Special Ports tab (see Figure 7.16) to configure any special port/address mappings you might need.

5. In the Routing and Remote Access window, you should see the interface (see Figure 7.17). You can also see the statistics for mappings and their direction when the service is being used.

That completes the installation, configuration, and interfaces for the NAT protocol. Let's see how well you can apply what was covered with this case study.

> **Remember Where the Mappings Are Located**   Because being able to monitor these mappings is one of the key components to supporting a NAT installation, you might see a question on the exam concerning the mappings.

EXAM TIP

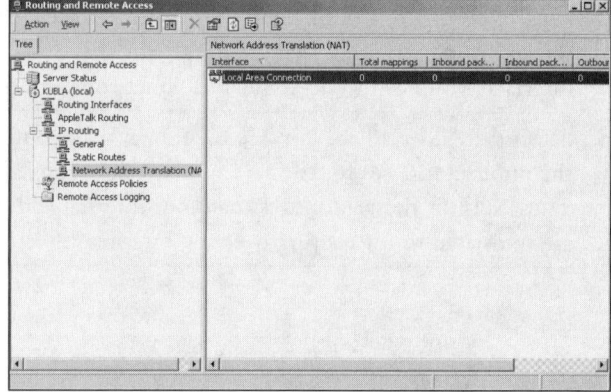

FIGURE 7.17
After the interface has been added, you can use the Routing and Remote Access console to keep track of the mappings being used.

CASE STUDY: CONFIGURING NETWORK ADDRESS TRANSLATION IN A 100 USER NETWORK

ESSENCE OF THE CASE

The essence of the case is as follows:

▶ Your company is implementing an Internet connection using a T1 and Windows 2000 server. The T1 will connect to the server using a LAN interface.

▶ You need to connect 100 users to the Internet for Web browsing.

▶ You need to set up a Web server on the internal network, but it needs to be accessible from the Internet for customers.

▶ You have no existing DNS or DHCP services on the network.

SCENARIO

You are the Security Administrator for LFE Incorporated. LFE Inc. is a lawn furniture manufacturing company. You have just decided to get your first connection to the Internet. You are getting a T1 connection that will be up all the time. This will connect to your Windows 2000 server, providing routing services as an Ethernet connection. The T1 will be used for Web browsing by the 100 employees, and your manager has also asked you to bring up a Web server on the internal network so that customers can look at your lawn furniture.

At this time you have not implemented any DNS or DHCP services on the network. Everyone uses static IP addresses and connects to other hosts by address. You planned ahead and are using 10.0.1.x addresses for all your machines.

What do you need to do?

ANALYSIS

This situation provides an excellent opportunity to deploy the Windows 2000 NAT protocol as part of the Windows 2000 Routing and Remote Access Service. Because of the size of the network and the fact that you will not be using a demand-dial connection to the Internet, the Internet Connection Sharing service is not an option. To make the NAT protocol work, you need to make sure you do the following:

• Install the NAT protocol using the Routing and Remote Access console.

continues

CASE STUDY: CONFIGURING NETWORK ADDRESS TRANSLATION IN A 100 USER NETWORK

continued

- Add the internal and external interfaces. Be careful not to confuse the two interfaces.

- Configure the DHCP properties to reflect the 10.0.1.x network addressing. You should also be sure to exclude any hosts that will retain a static address, such as servers and printers.

- Convert your users to DHCP. Not only will it make managing the IP addresses easier, but it will also provide the client configuration information needed to use the NAT gateway to the Internet.

- Configure the DNS service to connect to the Internet to provide name resolution. Your users will need to be able to resolve names so that they can surf the Internet effectively.

- Finally, you need to go to the Translation tab of the Network Address Translation (NAT) Properties and configure the translation for the Web server. You will use port 80 for HTTP and will need the internal address of the server to complete the configuration.

This is a particularly good case study if you are working on a smaller company, because more and more companies are using NAT capabilities to connect to the Internet. Although the basic mechanism is the same no matter what device you use to provide the translation, the interface provided by Windows 2000 is very clean and easy to configure and use.

CHAPTER SUMMARY

Let's recap what was discussed in this chapter. You started looking at the ICS service, which is an automated installation for a suite of services designed to get a small office up and connected to the Internet quickly.

Then you moved on to the manually installed and configured NAT protocol. You learned about installing, configuring, and adding interfaces for NAT.

In the next chapter, I discuss "Installing, Configuring, Managing, Monitoring, and Troubleshooting Certificate Services," the final chapter in the book.

KEY TERMS

- Domain Name System (DNS)
- Dynamic Host Configuration Protocol (DHCP)
- Network Address Translation (NAT)
- Internet Connection Sharing (ICS)
- Routing and Remote Access
- Transmission Control Protocol/Internet Protocol (TCP/IP)
- Request For Comment (RFC) document
- registered IP address
- private IP address
- Internet Service Provider (ISP)

APPLY YOUR KNOWLEDGE

Exercises

2.1   Installing Internet Connection Sharing

In the following exercise, you will install ICS to share a dial-up Internet connection.

Estimated Time: 15 minutes

1. Open the Network and Dial-up Connections window.

2. Right-click the dial-up connection and select Properties from the context menu. Select the Sharing tab of the Connection Properties dialog box.

3. Select the Enable Internet Connection Sharing for This Connection option.

4. Click OK to close the dialog box and enable ICS.

2.2   Adding a Custom Application

The following exercise shows you how to add the Internet Relay Chat (IRC) application to a server configured to use NAT.

Estimated Time: 15 minutes

1. Open the Routing and Remote Access console.

2. Expand the tree under the local server icon. Right-click the Network Address Translation (NAT) icon and select Properties.

3. Click the Translation tab of the Network Address Translation (NAT) Properties dialog box.

4. Click Applications.

5. Click Add. In the Internet Connection Sharing Application dialog box, enter the following:

   . Name of Application: Internet Relay Chat

   . Remote Server port number: 6667

   . TCP/UDP: TCP

   . Incoming Response Ports (TCP): 6668

6. Click OK to add the application.

7. Click OK to close the Properties window, and click OK again to close the Routing and Remote Access console.

Review Questions

1. You are the network administrator for a small company that wants to connect to the Internet for the first time. The company has 12 employees and you don't have a lot of experience with Windows 2000 or routing. What should you do to ensure that you connect to the Internet successfully?

2. The network administrator for a small company has grown to 50 users, and management wants to upgrade to a DSL connection. You have configured several dozen custom applications, both inbound and outbound, as part of ICS. What should you do to accommodate the DSL connections and the applications you've configured?

3. You are the Windows 2000 administrator for Fly Away Travel. Your boss has asked you to explain the difference between the NAT protocol and the ICS services. Other than manual versus automated features, what does ICS support that NAT does not?

APPLY YOUR KNOWLEDGE

4. That was a good start, but now she wants to know what services are included as part of ICS.

5. You're the administrator of Little Faith Enterprise's Windows 2000 server, and you are considering setting up NAT. Why would you want to set up NAT?

Exam Questions

1. You are the Internet administrator for Lost in the Woods Guide Service. You have a Windows 2000 server connected to the Internet and you have ICS running on it. You have been asked to configure a custom outbound application. How do you do it?

   A. Open the Internet Connection Sharing console. Select the Network Address Translation entry and right-click to open NAT Properties. On the Sharing tab, use the Add button to add the application.

   B. Open the Routing and Remote Access console. Select the Network Address Translation entry and right-click to open NAT Properties. On the Sharing tab, use the Add button to add the application.

   C. Open the properties for the dial-up entry in the Network and Dial-up Connections window. Under the Sharing tab, add the application using the Add button.

   D. Open the properties for the dial-up entry in the Network and Dial-up Connections window. Under the Sharing tab, select Settings, and on the Applications tab add the application using the Add button.

2. You are the Internet administrator for Lost in the Woods Guide Service. You have a Windows 2000 server connected to the Internet and you have Network Address Translation running on it. You have been asked to configure a custom outbound application. How do you do it?

   A. Open the Routing and Remote Access console. Select the Network Address Translation entry and right-click to open NAT Properties. On the Sharing tab, use the Add button to add the application.

   B. Open the Routing and Remote Access console. Select the Network Address Translation entry and right-click to open NAT Properties. On the Translation tab, use the Applications button to access the Add button to add the application.

   C. Open the properties for the dial-up entry in the Network and Dial-up Connections window. Under the Sharing tab, add the application using the Add button.

   D. Open the properties for the dial-up entry in the Network and Dial-up Connections window. Under the Sharing tab, select Settings, and on the Applications tab add the application using the Add button.

3. Which of the following are modifications made by ICS? (Select all that apply.)

   A. Installs DNS

   B. Installs DHCP

   C. Installs NAT

   D. Sets the address of the internal interface to 198.168.0.1.

APPLY YOUR KNOWLEDGE

E. Sets the external interface to get its address dynamically.

4. You have installed and configured NAT on your Windows 2000 server. How can you most easily monitor the usage?

   A. Open Performance Manager. Click the Add Counter icon. Select the NAT object.

   B. Use the Routing and Remote Access console and select the Network Address Translation icon. Right-click and select Statistics.

   C. Use the Routing and Remote Access console and select the Network Address Translation icon. The statistics will appear in the right pane of the application.

   D. Open the Routing and Remote Access console, set logging to All Events and use the Event Viewer to view usage.

5. You are the lead engineer for Little Faith Enterprises. You have been asked to configure Windows 2000 to connect to the Internet using a DSL connection. What should you do?

   A. Open the Routing and Remote Access console and install the NAT protocol. Configure the properties appropriately and add the internal interface to the protocol.

   B. Open the Routing and Remote Access console and install the NAT protocol. Configure the properties appropriately and add the internal interface to the protocol. Then add the external interface to the protocol.

   C. Open the Network Connection console and install the NAT protocol. Configure the properties appropriately and add the internal interface to the protocol. Then add the external interface to the protocol.

   D. Install ICS and enable the demand-dial connection.

6. You are the network administrator for the Blue Sky Corporation. The corporation is running a T1 Internet connection with a NAT installed. One user has just downloaded a new chat application to allow him to start chats with his friends, in German. The application doesn't work. What's the most likely reason?

   A. The English language version of NAT was installed.

   B. You can't use chat applications with NAT; you need ICS.

   C. The application needs to be added as an outbound application.

   D. The application needs to be added as an inbound application.

7. Your corporation is running a T1 Internet connection with NAT installed. As the network administrator, you have tried to add a game to the outbound NAT applications, but it still doesn't work. Why not?

   A. NAT was not designed to support games.

   B. NAT cannot support Directplay games.

   C. You did not add the application correctly. Most games require inbound access to the host.

APPLY YOUR KNOWLEDGE

D. You added the application to the
wrong interface.

8. You just upgraded your Internet connection to
DSL from a dial-up connection, and your
Windows 2000 server's NAT from the ICS ser-
vice to the NAT protocol. NetMeeting over the
Internet has stopped working since the upgrade.

Why?

A. NetMeeting requires a dial-up connection to
function.

B. You did not add the NetMeeting application
to the application list.

C. The NAT protocol cannot support
NetMeeting, whereas the ICS service can.

D. You need to reconfigure your DNS server to
connect to the Internet for name resolution.

9. What are two reasons for implementing NAT?

A. Add security to your Internet connection.

B. So you can host an Internet NetMeeting
server on your local network.

C. Conserve IP addresses.

D. Control users' access to Internet Web sites.

10. You are the network administrator for the LFE
Construction Company. You have a Windows
2000 server running NAT for your Internet connection. You need to add an additional segment
and give it access to the Internet.

How do you add an additional segment to NAT?

A. After the segment has been configured on the
server, load the Routing and Remote Access
console. Run the Add Interface Wizard to add
the interface.

B. After the segment has been configured on the
server, open the Connection Properties for
the new segment. Under the Sharing tab,
enable NAT.

C. After the segment has been configured on the
server, load the Routing and Remote Access
console. Go to the Network Address
Translation protocol and right-click. Select
Add Interface and select the new interface.

D. After the segment has been configured on the
server, load the Routing and Remote Access
console. Go to the Network Address
Translation protocol and right-click. Select
New Interface and select the new interface.

11. You are the network administrator for NR
Publishing Unlimited. You have a 100-user
network and you just installed a Windows 2000
server to connect the network to the Internet.
None of your users are able to connect to the
Internet, even though the server connects fine.
What is the likely problem?

A. The users are have not gotten addresses from
the DHCP server installed with NAT.

B. IP forwarding needs to be enabled.

C. You need to add an application to NAT
before anyone will be able to connect.

D. You didn't install NAT or ICS.

APPLY YOUR KNOWLEDGE

12. You are the lead consultant for Zoom Package Delivery Services. You have configured a Windows 2000 server with NAT for your 30 users. Some of your users have complained that they have been experiencing intermittent connection issues with the Internet. You want to check the log to find out what the issue might be. Where should you look?

    A. The `<system directory>\SYSTEM32\ETC\NAT\ logddmmyy.log` file

    B. The Application Event Log

    C. The System Event Log

    D. The Security Event Log

13. You are the network administrator for Gollywillikers Candy, and you are in the process of setting up your first Internet connection using Windows 2000 and the NAT protocol. Your ISP has given you a range of registered IP addresses for your NAT. Where do you configure these?

    A. In the Networking properties, under TCP/IP protocol

    B. On a private interface for the NAT protocol

    C. On the public interface for the NAT protocol

    D. Under the Network tab of NAT Properties

14. You are network administrator of Little Faith Enterprises, a booming retail garden center. You are trying to determine whether to use the Windows 2000 server's ICS service or NAT, but you cannot decide. Your manager has asked you what the difference is. You respond that NAT doesn't support all the protocols that ICS does. Which protocol does NAT not support that ICS does?

    A. TCP/IP

    B. DNS

    C. LDAP Proxy

    D. HTTP

15. You are the system administrator for Barb's House of Cheese, a leading cheese manufacturing company. You have decided to make a Web site available on the Internet. This site resides on your internal network, and you have the Windows 2000 NAT protocol running on the server that connects you to the Internet. In the interests of security, your Web server does not use the standard port 80 for HTTP traffic, but instead uses port 333. Now you have to figure out how to configure the translation. Where do you do it?

    A. The internal NAT interface

    B. The public NAT interface

    C. The Network Applications Settings in the Network Address Translation Properties

    D. The TCP Mapping dialog in the Network Address Translation Properties

Answers to Review Questions

1. You should implement Internet Connection Sharing in conjunction with a dial-up ISP connection. ICS is easy to install and maintain, and it bundles the services you need to make this connection work.

APPLY YOUR KNOWLEDGE

2. Just migrate to the NAT protocol. This will accommodate the DSL connection without a problem (although you will need to manually configure both the internal and external interfaces), and the applications you configured will still appear in the NAT list of custom applications.

3. ICS supports the following standards: H.323 Proxy, LDAP Proxy, and Directplay Proxy.

4. ICS installs a DNS and DHCP service. It also sets the IP address of the LAN interface to 192.168.0.1 and sets the WAN interface to be a Demand-Dial Router pointed at the (ISP).

5. Two reasons exist for using NAT. The first is to provide a level of security for your network when it is connected to the Internet. Not only does NAT hide your internal addresses, but it also restricts the services that can access the internal network. You will also need to conserve public IP addresses. Unless you are fortunate to have enough registered addresses for your users, you will need NAT.

Answers to Exam Questions

1. **D.** All ICS settings are configured through the dial-up connection properties. To set up or modify the applications, you need to get into the Sharing Settings and add them on the Applications tab. See "Installing Internet Connection Sharing."

2. **B.** To add an application through NAT, you need to use the Routing and Remote Access console. The Translation tab is where the applications are

configured for outbound use. See "Configuring NAT Properties."

3. **A, B, D.** The Internet Connection Sharing service does install versions of DNS and DHCP, but does not install NAT. It provides that functionality as part of its services, but does not install the actual protocol. Although it does set the address of the internal interface, the external interface is configured as part of the dial-up configuration. See "Installing Internet Connection Sharing."

4. **C.** The usage statistics will automatically appear next to the appropriate interface in the right pane of the application. See "Configuring NAT Interfaces ."

5. **B.** Because DSL connects as a LAN interface, you need to use the NAT protocol for this connection. You also need to be sure to add both interfaces. See "Configuring NAT Interfaces."

6. **C.** For a new application to communicate across the NAT server, it needs to be added to the list of outbound applications. See "Configuring NAT Properties."

7. **B.** NAT cannot support Directplay applications at this time. See "Configuring NAT Properties."

8. **C.** NetMeeting is one of the applications that ICS will support, but NAT will not. See "Installing Internet Connection Sharing."

9. **A, C.** NAT is good for security and address conservation. See "Installing NAT."

10. **D.** You need to use the Routing and Remote Access console to add the new interface. The correct command is "New Interface," not "Add Interface." See "Configuring NAT Interfaces."

APPLY YOUR KNOWLEDGE

11. **D.** You need to install NAT for the connection to work. See "Installing NAT."

12. **C.** All NAT logging is done to the System Event Log and can be viewed with the Event Viewer. See "Configuring NAT Properties."

13. **C.** You will need to configure the registered IP addresses on the NAT public interface. So that the packets are routed correctly, they need to be translated from private addresses to registered addresses. The registered addresses must be configured on the public interface for this routing to occur. See "Configuring NAT Interfaces."

14. **C.** ICS supports LDAP Proxy, and NAT does not. See "Installing Internet Connection Sharing."

15. **B.** This kind of custom port mapping is done on the public interface of the NAT interfaces. See "Configuring NAT Interfaces."

Suggested Readings and Resources

1. Boswell, William. *Inside Windows 2000 Server.* Indianapolis, IN: New Riders Publishing, 2000.

2. Atkins, Derek. *Internet Security: Professional Reference.* Indianapolis, IN: New Riders Publishing, 1997.

This chapter details the Microsoft-specified objectives for the Certificate Services section of the 70-216 exam objectives. The exam objectives for Certificate Services are as follows:

Install and configure Certificate Authority (CA).

▶ Windows 2000 includes Certificate Services for intranet and Internet security. This chapter examines the planning and implementation of CA.

Issue and revoke certificates.

▶ As part of a successful implementation of Certificate Services, you'll need to set guidelines for issuing and revoking certificates. We will implement and explore these guidelines.

Remove the Encrypting File Systems (EFS) recovery keys.

▶ Part of Certificate Services is the implementation of EFS. We will examine the attributes of EFS and how the recovery keys work in tandem with CA.

CHAPTER 8

Installing, Configuring, Managing, Monitoring, and Troubleshooting Certificate Services

Introduction 382

  Looking at Public Key Infrastructure (PKI) 382
    Certificates 383
    CAs 384
    Windows 2000 Enterprise CA 384
    Standalone CAs 385
  Planning to Install a CA 386
    Planning the PKI 387
    Planning the CA Hierarchies 387
  Renewing CAs 388

Installing the CA 389

  Installing and Configuring an Enterprise
    Subordinate CA 391
  Installing and Configuring a
    Standalone Root CA 394
  Upgrading Certificate Server 1.0 394
  Renewing Certificates for CAs 397

Issuing and Revoking Certificates 399

Using the Certificates Snap-In 399
Using the Windows 2000 Certificate
  Services Web Page 400
Processing Requests 401
Checking on Pending Requests 401
Mapping Certificates to User Accounts 403
  User Principal Name Mapping 404
  One-to-One Mapping 404
  Many-to-One Mapping 404
Viewing an Issued Certificate 405
Revoking Issued Certificates 406
  Revoking an Issued Certificate 406
  Working with the Revocation List 407

Using the EFS Recovery Keys 408

  Exporting EFS Keys 409
  Restoring EFS Keys 411

Chapter Summary 414

Apply Your Knowledge 415

▶ Certificates are a new feature for Windows 2000. To fully prepare for the exam objectives, you'll require a working knowledge of what certificates are, where they are derived from, and how they are configured.

▶ Complete the Step by Steps. Hands-on experience will behoove your study process. Be familiar with CA and the fundamentals of why an entity would want to use certificates.

▶ Invest time in experimenting with CA and EFS. This book covers all the exam objective details, but it's up to you to take the information presented here and transform it to knowledge.

INTRODUCTION

As you may realize, networks today keep growing and intermingling with other networks. This growth presents a challenge for Microsoft Certified Systems Engineers (MCSEs) in that it increases network exposure to less-than-honest users. What makes it possible for all these networks to be vulnerable to attack? They share a common protocol.

The common protocol used in the exchange of data is Transmission Control Protocol/Internet Protocol (TCP/IP). Data sent via TCP/IP is broken up and sent over various routes to the final destination. Because of the very design of TCP/IP, data can be intercepted easily without the sender or the receiver knowing that the data may have been intercepted. Certainly, as data passes through networks around the globe, it is susceptible to interception or forgery, and users are often the recipients of data whose content may jeopardize their own data.

We need a way to protect our outgoing data and ensure that our incoming data has not been compromised. Enter certificates. This chapter introduces the fundamentals of certificates and then discusses installing and configuring CA Services.

Looking at Public Key Infrastructure (PKI)

To combat the openness of TCP/IP without losing the functionality of the protocol, PKI has been developed in tandem with TCP/IP as a means of offering security for data sent between hosts—on an intranet or on the Internet.

Using encryption, network administrators and security experts can ensure that the data is read only by the intended recipient, and that data received has not been tampered with. The analogy of physical signature and envelopes sealed with wax is an excellent parallel to how PKI is used today. In lieu of your "John Hancock" and sealing wax, you use a digital signature.

A digital signature ensures that the message is from the source it says it's from and that the message hasn't been digitally "steamed open." In addition to digital signatures, you can implement digital identifications; thus, the digital certificate.

Certificates

What exactly is a digital certificate? Essentially, it's your electronic version of your password or employee identification. It proves that you are who you say you are. This certificate is what ultimately allows you to access resources and data.

Certificates are issued not only to individuals, but also to organizations, businesses, routers, and other entities as a way of controlling and securing data. A digital certificate contains the following information:

◆ The user's name

◆ The user's public key

◆ Serial number

◆ Expiration date

◆ Information on the certificate itself

◆ Information on the organization (called a CA) that issued the certificate

When transferring secure data, an electronic seal is inserted into the data through cryptography. When the recipient opens the data, the electronic seal is verified to exist and that it has not been tampered with. In addition, the recipient can be assured that the sender of the data is accurate.

Traditionally, when you want to send encrypted data to other users, you use your key to encrypt and secure the data. When the recipients want to open the encrypted data, they use their copy of the key to unlock the data. Should others without the key intercept the packets, they will not be able to decrypt the information. This method of security is not really all that secure. The problem is that when unauthorized users gain access to the key, they gain access to the data—not unlike discovering your house keys in the outside lock of your door.

Digital certificates, however, use a slightly different method of locking and unlocking the data. With digital certificates, you no longer have to make copies of keys for others to unlock your data. Digital certificates use a private key to lock the data and then a different key, the public key, to unlock the data. No longer is the same key used to lock and unlock data.

With this two-key technology, your key remains private. No one but the rightful owner should ever have access to it. However, by means of the digital certificate, you can disperse the public key to whomever may need it.

When Margo wants to send a private message to Alice, for example, Margo uses Alice's public key to encrypt the message. No one other than Alice can decrypt the message, but now the private key, Alice's key, is required to unlock the contents. When Alice responds to Margo, she can use Margo's public key to encrypt the response. Margo then uses her own private key to unlock the message.

CAs

All certificates are issued by a CA, such as VeriSign. The CA verifies that the owner of the certificate is who he says he is. A CA is a trusted third party that is responsible for physically verifying the legitimacy of the identity of an individual or organization before issuing a digital certificate. A CA is also responsible for issuing certificates, revoking certificates, and publishing a list of revoked certificates.

With Windows 2000, you can use a third-party CA, or you can create your own CA through Microsoft's Windows 2000 Certificate Services, which offers these types of CAs: Enterprise Root CA, Enterprise Subordinate CA, Standalone Root CA, and Standalone Subordinate CA. We take a closer look at these types of CAs throughout the chapter.

If you elect to create an internal CA for your organization, you'll want to establish some rules and guidelines to verify that users are employees. You can use social security numbers, employee badges, or an even more secure method—smart cards, which are physical, portable devices that allow users to log in and access and send data, such as email and data on a network.

NOTE

A Leading CA Clearly, the leading Internet CA is VeriSign. VeriSign has dispersed its CA certificates in the majority of Web browsers, servers, and other network hardware devices. VeriSign also insures the security and validity of its service to $100,000 of coverage against theft, loss, or forgery.

Windows 2000 Enterprise CA

A Windows 2000 Enterprise CA provides certificates for the internal security of an entire organization, whereas an external CA provides security for external security needs. Microsoft provides support for both, and you may mix and match to fit your business needs.

If users request a certificate in a Windows 2000 environment, the Windows 2000 user account acts as the credentials for the users because they are logged on and recognized in the Active Directory.

A Windows 2000 Enterprise CA has five characteristics:

- ◆ The CA server may run on any Windows 2000 server. Plan for activity, network load, and physical placement of the server for best implementation.

- ◆ Because the CA name is integrated into the certificates it assigns, the name of the server should be determined before implementing CA services.

- ◆ The Enterprise CA Authority is integrated into the Active Directory.

- ◆ When you've installed an Enterprise CA, a policy module is created. An administrator may edit the policy.

- ◆ Because the CA is crucial for the successful implementation of the PKI, it must have a fault-tolerance scheme and a schedule of regular secure backups.

Standalone CAs

Another type of CA that Windows 2000 allows you to install is a Standalone CA. The Standalone CA doesn't require the interaction of an Active Directory, but it can use one if it's available.

A Standalone CA is useful in issuing certificates and digital signatures and supports secure email (S/MIME) and secure sockets layer (SSL) or Transport Layer Security (TLS).

A typical Standalone CA has these characteristics:

- ◆ It doesn't require Active Directory interaction.

- ◆ It can be used with extranets.

- ◆ It doesn't verify the requests for certificates. (All requests are pending until an administrator approves them.)

◆ Users requesting a certificate from a Standalone CA must supply all user account information. This is not required within an Enterprise CA because the user is recognized by the logon account in the Active Directory.

◆ No certificate templates are used.

◆ Windows 2000 logon credential certificates are not stored on smart cards. Other certificates can be, however.

◆ An administrator must distribute the Standalone CA certificate to the Trusted Root Certificate Store.

If an Active Directory exists and a Standalone CA can access it, additional options are available:

◆ If a domain administrator with write access to the Active Directory installs the Standalone CA, the standalone is added to the Trusted Root Certification Authorities Certificate Store. In this situation, make certain that the default action of pending requests isn't changed to allow the Standalone CA to automatically approve all requests for certificates. Do not change the default action of pending certificate requests on a Standalone CA.

◆ If a domain administrator group member of the parent domain (or an administrator with write access to the Active Directory) installs the Standalone CA, the Standalone CA will publish the certificate and the Certificate Revocation list to the Active Directory.

Planning to Install a CA

After you've decided that you want to install a CA, some planning must take place. Before your installation of the CA, you need to have a plan that addresses these questions:

◆ Who will manage the security?

◆ Will administrative duties be delegated?

◆ How will the CA be monitored? Who will monitor it?

◆ What kind of auditing should be in place for the CA?

◆ Where will the CA be located?

After you've answered these questions and have documented your answers to formulate a plan, you're ready to move into the final stages of planning.

Planning the PKI

When you are preparing to install a CA, you should start by planning how to configure your PKI. As we've discussed, certificates and CAs are a means to prove an identity. But what if a user discovers Bob's password and logs on to the domain as Bob? As far as the system is concerned, the unauthorized user must be Bob because, after all, it is Bob's username and password.

The most popular solution to securing a network is, of course, physical security. Next is the implementation of a strong policy: strong passwords that change frequently. Finally, another secure choice is the implementation of smart cards because they allow users to carry their digital credentials with them from home to office or anywhere they need to go.

Windows 2000's group policy can allow you to publish and revoke certificates directly to user accounts. This feature can allow you to change a user's digital information and enforce it for accessing and retrieving data. Finally, your PKI scheme should include measures for your enterprise to secure email using S/MIME and SSL and/or TLS.

Planning the CA Hierarchies

Windows 2000 PKI allows for and encourages a dispersed hierarchy of CAs. Building a tree of CAs allows for scalability with other organizations, internal and external resources, and compatibility with third-party CA implementations.

Ideally, an enterprise would have one CA; this is not usually a reality, however. Each CA hierarchy begins with the Root CA, and multiple CAs branch from this Root CA in a parent-child relationship. The child CAs are certified by the parent CA all the way back to the Root CA. The parent CAs bind a CA public key to the child CA's identity.

In this parent-child relationship, child CAs are trusted by the parent. That parent is, in turn, trusted by its parent CA, all the way back to the originating Root CA. Also in this model, when an organization trusts a CA by adding its certificate in the Trusted Root Certification Authorities Certificate Store, the organization therefore trusts every Subordinate CA in the hierarchy. Should a Subordinate CA have its certificate revoked by the issuing CA, the revoked CA is no longer trustworthy.

Hierarchies serve many purposes. Some of the reasons for creating a CA hierarchy include

◆ **Varying usages.** Certificates can be issued for a number of purposes, such as secure email, SSL, and TSL. Different CAs can be responsible for different areas of security.

◆ **Politics.** A hierarchy allows for various departments within an enterprise to use unique policies.

◆ **Geography.** In a wide area network (WAN) environment, a different CA may be needed in each physical location to save network resources.

◆ **Security.** The Root CA requires a very secure environment with fault-tolerant devices. Subordinate CAs do not require the same amount and type of security as the root.

◆ **Revoking.** Most organizations need to have the capability to revoke individual CAs rather than be forced to revoke an entire enterprise.

As you're planning your hierarchy, remember that a Root CA is a CA from which all Subordinate CAs branch. This CA should be the most secure and should probably be taken offline after the installation to ensure the security of the originating certificate and keys.

Renewing CAs

When a Root or Subordinate CA issues a certificate, the certificate includes a validity period. A validity period is the length of time the certificate is good for—not unlike a digital expiration date.

At the end of the validity period, the certificate is disabled, assuming that the certificate has not been revoked prior to this expiration date.

When the certificate expires, a new certification must be renewed.

In a parent-child relationship between CAs, the parent CA issues a certificate as part of the relationship to designate the child CA. Just like the certificate to a client, the certificate to a Subordinate CA includes a validity period.

When the validity period expires for a CA, its own certificate must be renewed before it can grant any certification requests from client computers. When organizing your PKI, take into account the time a certification in a parent-child relationship should last.

As a safety and security measure, the program is set up so that a CA cannot issue certificates to requestors that will last beyond its own certificate's expiration date. This is handy because it ensures, for example, that a CA scheduled to expire this October cannot issue a certificate that may expire later than October.

Even the Root CAs own certificate will eventually expire. Because of this, certificates that it issues to subordinates will be staggered from its own expiration date. In other words, when the Root CA expires, all Subordinate CAs will have expired as well. No Subordinate CAs are valid beyond the date of the originating CA.

INSTALLING THE CA

Install and configure Certification Authority (CA).

When you understand Certificate Services and have a plan for installing the service and a plan for renewing certificates for users, servers, and CAs, you are ready to install a CA.

You can choose from four options for installing a CA:

◆ **After Windows 2000 has been installed.** Use Add/Remove Programs in Control Panel to add the Certificate Services to the current installation.

◆ **As part of the Windows 2000 installation.** During the installation of Windows 2000, you can choose from the optional components. After Windows 2000 is installed, you will complete the installation of the service according to your PKI plans.

◆ **Upgrading from Certificate Server 1.0.** When you install Windows 2000 on a server that is running Certificate Server 1.0, the Windows 2000 installation program automatically upgrades the service.

◆ **Through an unattended installation.** If you are using an unattended installation to install Windows 2000, you can include the installation of a CA through the setup file.

Whichever method you choose to install Certificate Services, you'll be required to supply the following information:

◆ **CA type.** What type of CA will this be?

• **Enterprise Root CA.** The Enterprise Root CA is the root of all CAs in your hierarchy. Typically, there is only one of these per enterprise. Requires Active Directory. Intermediate Subordinate CAs branch off of this server. The Enterprise Root CA can only be a parent.

• **Enterprise Subordinate CA.** A Subordinate CA must obtain its certificate from a CA higher in the hierarchy. Requires Active Directory. This is the child of another CA. It is possible that this CA could also be a parent to another CA.

• **Standalone Root CA.** A Standalone Root CA is like an Enterprise Root CA, except that it does not require Active Directory but can use it if it exists. Often this CA is offline to protect the validity of the originating certificates and keys.

• **Standalone Subordinate CA.** This CA does not require Active Directory but may use it if Active Directory is available. The Subordinate CA must obtain its certificate from another CA. This is the child in the relationship but may become a parent if it supplies a certificate to another CA.

◆ **Advanced options.** If you enable advanced options during the install of your CA, you'll have to provide the following:

• **The Cryptographic Service Provider (CSP).** To generate the public and private keys.

- **Key length.** The longer the key, the more secure the key.

- **Hash algorithm.** A computation to produce a hash value of some piece of data. The default is Secure Hash Algorithm (SHA)-1, which is a 160-bit hash value.

◆ **CA Name.** You can use just about any character you want. The name you assign the CA will also be the common name (CN) of the CA's distinguished name in Active Directory. Special characters (non-American Code for Information Interchange ASCII and ASCII punctuation) are stripped out in a sanitized name. Also remember Active Directory is limited to 64 characters before it truncates names.

◆ **Organization.** The name of your organization as it is known throughout its community.

◆ **Organizational Unit.** The division this CA manages.

◆ **Locality.** City.

◆ **State or Province.**

◆ **Country.** The X.500 two character code for your country.

◆ **Location of the database.** By default, it's stored in \systemroot\system32\certlog.

◆ **Shared folder.** You can create a shared folder for CA information if the CA is not participating in an Active Directory (such as a standalone server).

Installing and Configuring an Enterprise Subordinate CA

After you've installed a Root CA, you'll most likely want to install additional CAs. These are Subordinate CAs. The relationship between the Root CA and each immediate Subordinate CA is parent-child. The child CA can then form a relationship to another CA and become the parent in that relationship. There can be a long line of parent-child CA chains, or these can branch out to cover different organizational units, divisions, geographical locations, and so on.

To install and configure an Enterprise Subordinate CA:

STEP BY STEP

8.1 Installing and Configuring a CA

1. Log on to the prospective Subordinate CA as domain administrator and choose Start, Settings, Control Panel (shown in Figure 8.1).

FIGURE 8.1
To install a CA, use Add/Remove Programs in the Control Panel of Windows 2000.

2. Double-click Add/Remove Programs and then double-click Add/Remove Windows Components. The Windows Components Wizard opens and a list of components to add or remove displays (see Figure 8.2).

3. Select the Certificate Services option and click Next. You're warned that the computer cannot be named, added, or removed from the domain after you add this service (see Figure 8.3).

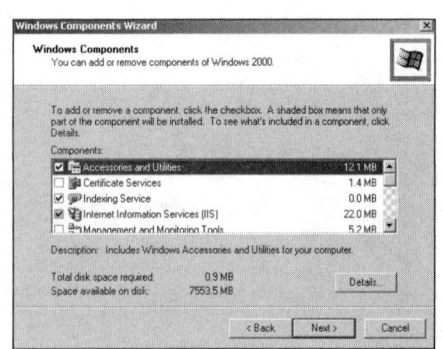

FIGURE 8.2
You can use the Windows Components Wizard to selectively add components to your computer.

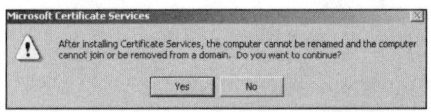

FIGURE 8.3
Installing Certification Services is serious business and cannot be revoked.

4. Click Yes to close the warning dialog box, select the CA option you want to set up (shown in Figure 8.4), select Advanced Options, and click Next to continue. The Public and Private Key Pair dialog box then opens (see Figure 8.5).

5. Select the CSP, the Hash Algorithm, the Use Existing Keys, the Key Length, and then click Next. The CA Identifying Information dialog box opens (see Figure 8.6).

6. Enter the details about this CA and then click Next. The Data Storage Location dialog box opens (see Figure 8.7).

continues

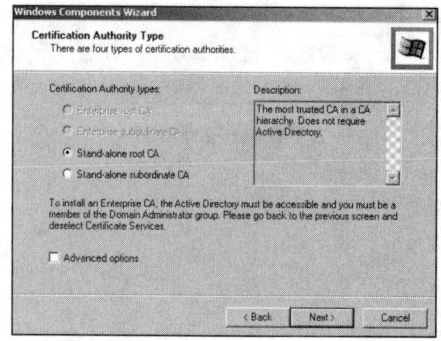

FIGURE 8.4
Select the type of CA you want to install.

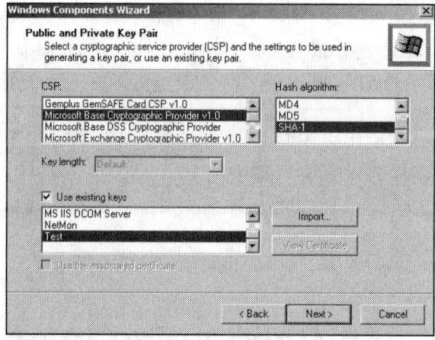

FIGURE 8.5
Entering the specific settings in the Public and Private Key Pair dialog box generates a key pair or selects an existing key pair.

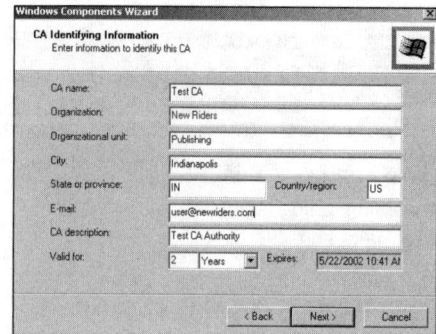

FIGURE 8.6
Enter the identifying information for the CA that you want to install.

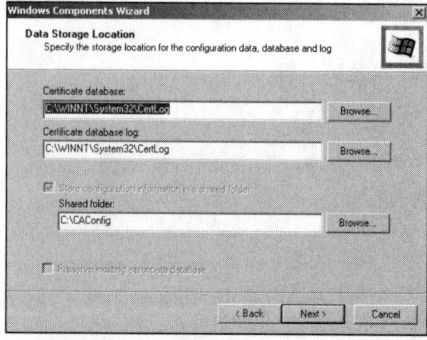

FIGURE 8.7
Enter the path to the Certificate Database and the Certificate Database Log.

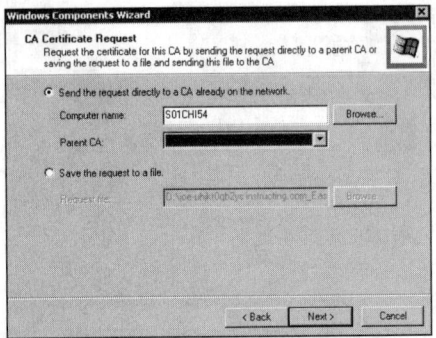

FIGURE 8.8
You can either directly request a certificate or save the request to a file.

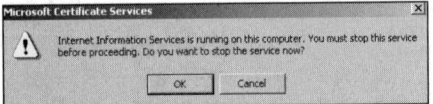

FIGURE 8.9
The warning dialog box gives you the opportunity to make sure the service is ready to stop.

continued

7. Enter the location of the Certificate Database or accept the default and then click Next. The CA Certificate Request dialog box opens (see Figure 8.8).

8. If the parent CA is online, select the Send the Request Directly to a CA Already on the Network option and ensure that the correct computer name and parent CA are displayed. If the parent CA is offline, select the Save the Request to a File option and make sure that the correct request filename is displayed. When you are sure that the contents of the CA Certificate Request dialog box are accurate, click Next.

9. If you have a World Wide Web (WWW) service running, the warning dialog box shown in Figure 8.9 appears, asking whether you want to stop the service. Click OK.

10. Click OK to install the service with the supplied parameters, and then click Finish to exit the wizard.

Installing and Configuring a Standalone Root CA

Installing a Standalone CA server is similar to installing an Enterprise CA server. The main difference in installing a Standalone CA server is that you will not need to request a certificate from an existing CA server, since a Standalone CA server generates its own originating certificate.

Upgrading Certificate Server 1.0

When you upgrade to Windows 2000 from a Windows NT 4 server that is also running Certificate Server 1.0, Windows 2000 automatically upgrades Certificate Server 1.0 with the CA services.

When Certificate Server 1.0 is using its own policy before the upgrade, Windows 2000 will allow the server to continue to its policy instead of the default policy included with Windows 2000's Certificate Services. This original policy will be referred to as a "legacy policy module."

When Certificate Server 1.0 is using the default policy included with that software, Windows 2000 upgrades the policy to the default security policy it uses for certification services.

Remember that Certificate Server 1.0 is not automatically upgraded as part of the installation. The new certification services are installed, but the configuration is blank. You'll have to finish the configuration. To import the old database into the upgraded CA, follow these steps:

STEP BY STEP

8.2 Importing an Old Database into the Newly Upgraded CA

1. Open the Microsoft Management Console (MMC) and expand the Services and Applications tree; then click Services. On the right side of the MMC, which should list all services on the computer, right-click Certificate Services and choose Stop from the pop-up menu (see Figure 8.10).

2. Choose Start, Run, type **cmd**, and press Enter to open the command prompt.

continues

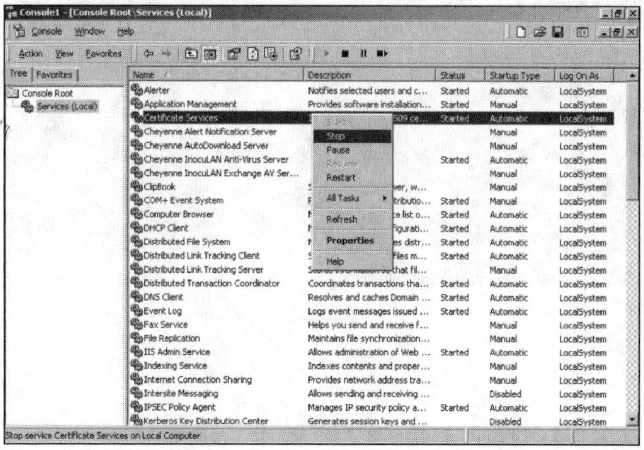

FIGURE 8.10

When you right-click a name in the Console tree, a pop-up menu appears.

continued

3. At the command prompt, type `certutil ConvertMDB`, as shown in Figure 8.11.

4. Choose Start, Programs, Administrative Tools, and select CA (see Figure 8.12). Right-click the CA server, and from the context menu select All Tasks, Start Server (see Figure 8.13). The CA server will start.

FIGURE 8.11

To import an old database, you must use the MS-DOS command prompt.

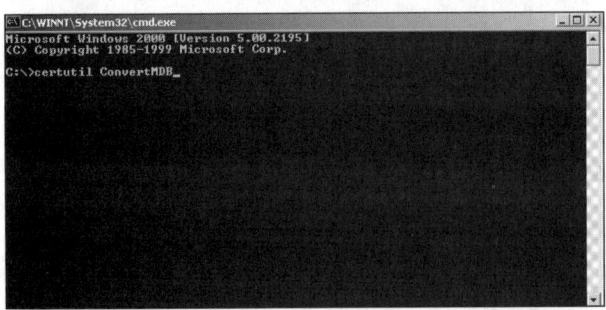

FIGURE 8.12

The CA is added to the Administrative Tools menu when the CA service is installed.

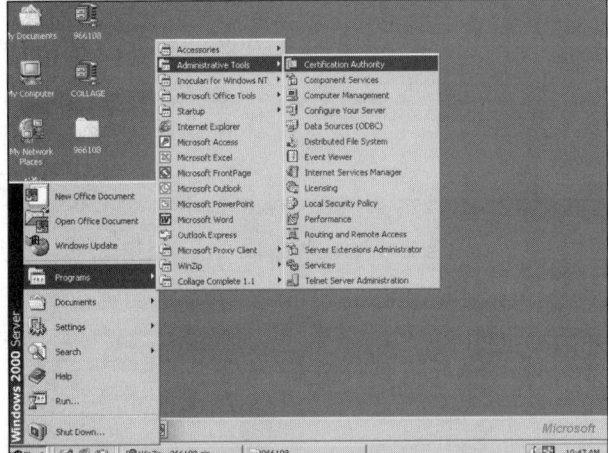

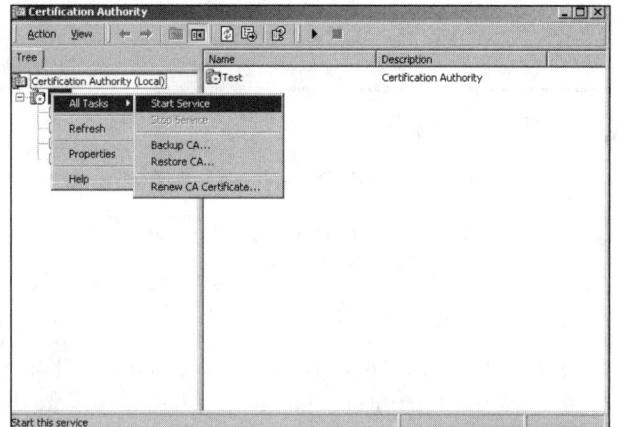

FIGURE 8.13
You can also start and stop the CA service from the CA administration tool.

Renewing Certificates for CAs

Part of your role will be to renew the certificates for each type of CA in your environment. The Root CA is the most important CA in the hierarchy. Often for security it's in a physically secure environment, with hardware fault tolerance, and possibly is even offline to prevent any tampering. Because of the demands placed on a Root CA, plan to configure the Root CA's certificate so that it doesn't expire for a long time.

IN THE FIELD

THE KEY TO SECURITY

When creating the Root CA, you also need to ensure a long lifetime for the public and private key of this CA by using a long key length as a deterrent to hackers who make brute force attacks. The longer the key, the longer you may use the private and public keys with confidence that the keys have not been compromised.

Microsoft recommends creating a 4096-bit RSA key during Certification Service setup. A brute force attack against a key of this size may last for 15–20 years. In addition, the 4096-bit key could be configured during setup to expire in five years. When the CA needs to be renewed, technology may have surpassed the 4096-bit key length and a different algorithm could be used.

Follow these steps to renew a Root CA:

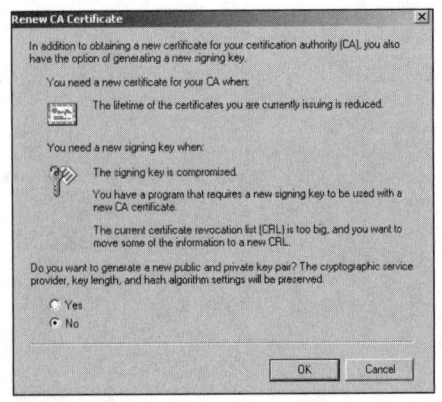

FIGURE 8.14
Use the Renew CA Certificate dialog box to review the reasons for creating a new CA in contrast to renewing an existing one.

Be Aware of Expiration Dates
When you choose to renew a CA certificate from a subordinate, keep in mind that the expiration date on a Subordinate CA is slightly shorter than the expiration date on a parent CA. In other words, renew the parent CA's certificate before renewing the child CA's certificate. Otherwise, you'll renew a new certificate but the expiration date will be influenced by the expiration date on the parent CA.

STEP BY STEP

8.3 Renewing a Root Certification Authority

1. Log on to the system as an administrator.

2. Choose Start, Programs, Administrative Tools, CA to open the CA window (refer to Figure 8.12).

3. Select the Root CA and then choose Action, All Tasks, Renew CA Certificate. The Renew CA Certificate dialog box shown in Figure 8.14 opens.

4. Select Yes to generate a new public and private key or select No to continue using the existing public and private key pair. Then click OK.

Microsoft recommends issuing Subordinate CAs a new certificate 6 to 12 months before their certificates are actually scheduled to expire. Within your hierarchy, you may have created Intermediate CAs that do not issue certificates to users but only to other subordinates below them. This delegation of certificate issuance is acceptable because these Intermediary CAs are the only CAs that would communicate with the Root CAs.

The planning involved, however, is when will the certificates issued by the Root CA expire on these Intermediary CAs? Recall that the Root CA staggers the validity date for its subordinates. An Intermediary Subordinate, then, will also stagger its issuance of certificate validity. The guideline is that you will need to monitor when certificates are due to expire and from that allow plenty of time (6 to 12 months) to create and issue a new certificate to all subordinates.

ISSUING AND REVOKING CERTIFICATES

Issue and revoke certificates.

Before a CA can issue a certificate, a request must be made. Requests for certificates can be made from users, computers, or even services—such as other CAs.

Based on how the CAs are installed and configured, requests for certificates can happen automatically. An example of this is using a smart card to log on to a domain. As part of the smart card logon, a certificate request can be issued automatically.

Using the Certificates Snap-In

With the Certificates snap-in, users can use the Certificate Request Wizard to request a new certificate from the Windows 2000 Enterprise CA.

As an administrator, you can add the snap-in to your MMC and manage your user account, the computer account, and local services. As a regular user, you can manage only your own user account certificates.

To add the Certificate snap-in to the MMC, follow these steps:

STEP BY STEP

8.4 Starting the Certificate Snap-In

1. Choose Start, Run, type MMC and press Enter or click OK. The MMC opens (see Figure 8.15).

continues

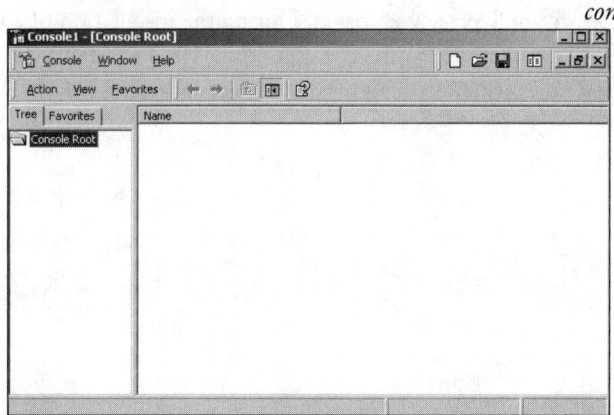

FIGURE 8.15
The MMC allows you the capability to administer many functions of a Windows 2000 server from one interface.

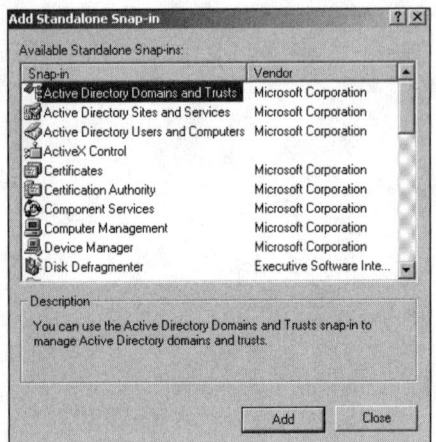

FIGURE 8.16
To use the MMC in managing your CA, you need to add the CA snap-in.

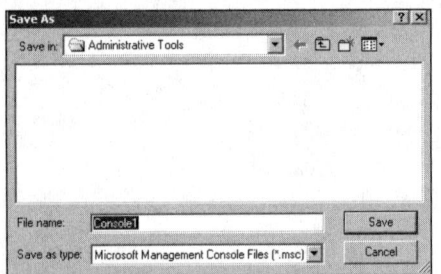

FIGURE 8.17
The MMC will allow you to save different configurations of the console.

continued

2. Choose Console, Add/Remove Snap-In, and then click Add. The Add Standalone Snap-In dialog box opens (see Figure 8.16).

3. Double-click Certificates. An administrator can choose User, Computer, or Services. A nonadministrator receives only the Certificate option for managing his or her own account.

4. Click Close to close the Add Snap-In dialog box, and then click OK.

5. Choose Console, Save. The Save As dialog box opens (see Figure 8.17).

6. Name the console **Certificates** and click Save.

When you've added the Certificates snap-in, you can query the CA for a certificate. Within the Certificate console, select the CA from which you will be requesting the certificate.

You'll also need to choose the appropriate certificate template for the new certificate. A certificate template is a predefined set of rules for the certificate to be issued. Through the Advanced Options, you can choose CSP for the keys to be assigned from the CA.

Using the Windows 2000 Certificate Services Web Page

The second way a certificate can be requested is through the Windows 2000 Certificate Servers Web pages. During the installation of a CA, Web pages are installed on the corresponding IIS. By default, users can access these pages through http://servername/certsrv.

To request certificates from a standalone server, you must use the Windows 2000 Certification Services Web page because standalone servers are not reliant on Active Directory to disperse their certificates. In addition, if you do not mark your keys as exportable, you have to use these Web pages to export the keys; the Certificate Request Wizard does not offer that option.

Processing Requests

So what happens when the requests issued by any method arrive at the CA?

The request is immediately processed whether or not the CA is an Enterprise CA. The results of the processed request will be either failed or granted. When a certificate is granted, it is issued to the requestor and a prompt to install the certificate is issued.

If, however, your request has been issued to a standalone server, the standalone server marks all certificate requests by default as pending. They remain in pending mode until an administrator approves or denies the request.

Checking on Pending Requests

When you've submitted a request to a standalone server, the request is marked as pending. To check the status of the pending request, use Internet Explorer and follow these steps:

STEP BY STEP

8.5 Checking on a Pending Certificate Request

1. Open Internet Explorer if it is not open already, and type `http://servername/certsrv`, replacing the word *server-name* with the actual name of the CA server, as shown in Figure 8.18.

2. When the page loads, select the Check On a Pending Certificate option, and then click Next.

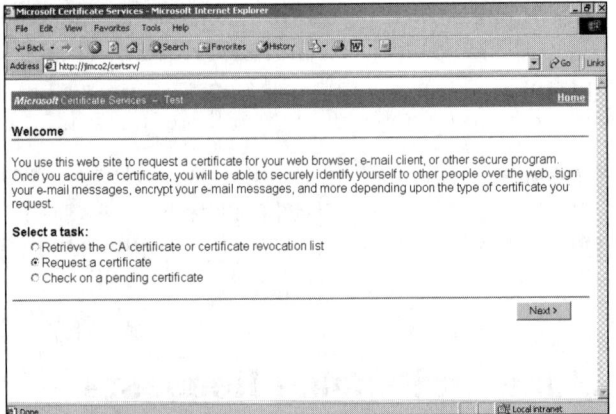

FIGURE 8.18
You must access the Web site of the Certificate Services server to acquire certificates.

3. If no certificate requests are pending, Microsoft informs you of that, as shown in Figure 8.19. Otherwise, select the request you want to check and then click Next. The pending requests are reported back as still pending, issued, or denied.

4. If you'd like to cancel the request for a certificate that is pending, select the request and then click Remove.

5. When you are finished reviewing the certificate requests, close Internet Explorer.

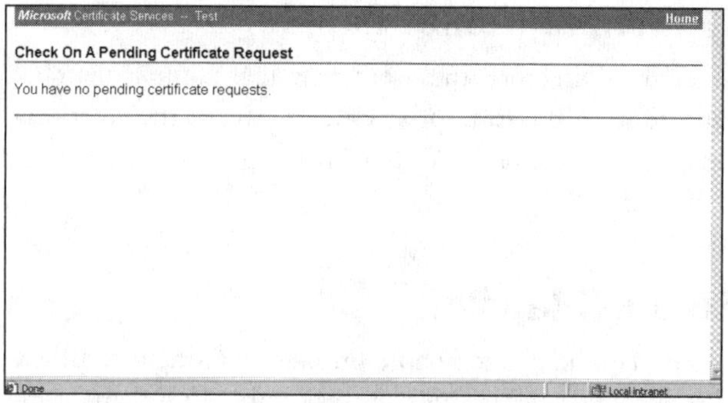

FIGURE 8.19
The Certificate Services server can provide reports on pending certificate requests.

Mapping Certificates to User Accounts

Thus far, we've discussed the request for a certificate and the response of a CA. But what about preparing the certificates and then mapping them out to users? We can do that, too.

With the standard (without the use of a smart card) logon to a Windows 2000 domain, logon requests are forwarded to a domain controller. The user's valid logon identifier (ID) and password are verified, and then the user is allowed to log on.

This model of a client/server relationship through a named pipe is reliable and guarantees user authentication. What if our networks continue to grow and intermingle with other networks and eventually our database could contain, or need to contain, millions of user accounts? A new solution will be required. The solution? A mapped certificate to a user account.

A mapped certificate to a user's account would replace the need for a centralized database of usernames and passwords at logon time. In its place, a public key is mapped to each user account so that at logon time, the certificate can be examined to verify or deny the user logon.

The user presents the system its certificate, and then the system examines the key and determines which user account should be allowed to log on.

Mapping is accomplished either through Active Directory or through IIS. One certificate is typically mapped to only one user account: one-to-one mapping. You can choose, however, to map many certificates to one user account: many-to-one mapping.

User Principal Name Mapping

Through Active Directory, the user's principal name is matched with the certificate from the Enterprise CA. As part of the creation of certification on an Enterprise CA, users' principal names are included in the certificate.

One-to-One Mapping

One-to-one mapping, as the name implies, is a single certificate mapped to a single user account. An example of implementing one-to-one mapping is through an extranet. If a company had created a Web site that allows sales reps to update and submit sales reports, check on commissions, status of orders, and other related sales information, you would no doubt want the site secure.

By issuing your users certificates that are mapped to Windows 2000 accounts, the users can access the site over the Internet, supply their credentials, and then access the information on the page as if they were right on the local area network (LAN) in your office.

Many-to-One Mapping

A bit more rare, but occasionally needed, is many-to-one mapping. Just as its names implies, this option allows you to map many certificates, from different CAs to one individual Windows 2000 account.

IN THE FIELD

MANY-TO-ONE MAPPING AIDS IN ACQUISITIONS

An example of many-to-one mappings could be if your company acquires another company. The existing CAs of the acquired company provide one-to-one mapping for its resources, but you want the employees of the acquired firm to use the resources on the net that your company provides. For the time being, users will need resources from both sites. Configure your domain so that users will have accounts in your domain, map your certificates to their accounts, and then map the certificates from the acquired company CA to their accounts, as well. You can add the acquired company's CA by installing it as a Trusted Root in your enterprise.

Viewing an Issued Certificate

After a certificate has been issued, you can then view the information that has been included in the certificate. To view the information about a certificate, open the appropriate MMC, choose Certificates, Logical Store, Certificates, and double-click the certificate in the details pane. The dialog box that opens displays pages that provide the following information:

◆ An overview of certificates.

◆ Uses of the certificate.

◆ To whom the certificate was issued.

◆ Validity period of the issued certificate.

◆ The Trusted Root CA.

◆ The Subordinate CA certificate.

◆ The status of trust.

◆ The certification status.

◆ The version of the certificate.

◆ The serial number.

◆ The algorithm.

◆ The issuer.

◆ The subject—that is, the name of the CA (or individual issuing the certificate).

◆ The public key.

◆ The thumbprint algorithm.

◆ The thumbprint.

◆ The friendly name.

◆ The Enhance Key Usage option, which defines how this certificate may be used.

Revoking Issued Certificates

There are times when you'll find it necessary to revoke an issued certificate. Reasons include, but are not limited to, the following:

- ◆ A user with an issued certificate leaves the entity.

- ◆ A user with an issued certificate can no longer be trusted by the entity.

- ◆ Suspicion that the user's private key has become jeopardized.

- ◆ A user obtained the certificate when they truly were not to have rights to it.

When you revoke an issued certification, the certificate is added, and then published, to the certificate revocation list (CRL). Like a commercial CA, these CRLs are available for client computers to access so that they can verify valid certificates.

Revoking an Issued Certificate

You can use the Certificates snap-in to revoke certifications. This activity should be performed as soon as the certificate becomes suspect. After the certificate has been revoked, it's scheduled to be published on the CRL.

To revoke a certificate, follow these steps:

STEP BY STEP

8.6 Revoking a Certificate

1. Log on as Administrator and open the CA snap-in in an MMC console.

2. From the Console tree, shown in Figure 8.20, click Issued Certificates.

3. In the details pane, click on the certificate that needs to be revoked.

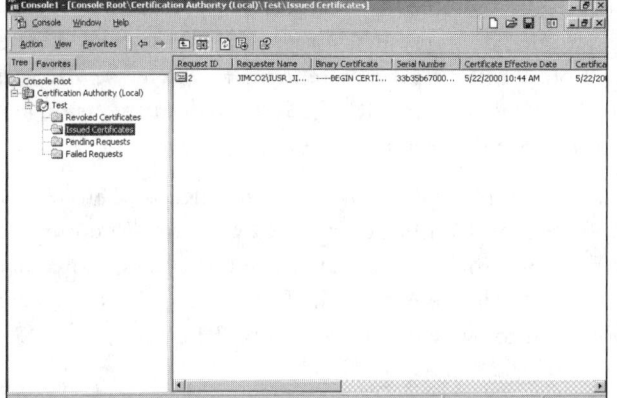

FIGURE 8.20
To revoke a certificate, you need to access it from the CA snap-in.

4. Choose Action, All Tasks, Revoke Certification. The Certificate Revocation dialog box opens, asking that you specify the reason for revoking the certificate (see Figure 8.21).

5. Choose one of the following reasons to revoke the certificate: Unspecified, Key Compromise, CA Compromise, Change of Affiliation, Superseded, Cease of Operation, or Certificate Hold. Then click Yes. This revokes the certificate.

6. To view the certificates that you revoked, go to the Console tree, select Revoked Certificates, choose Action, Properties. Select the View Current CRL option, and then click the Revocation Lists tab.

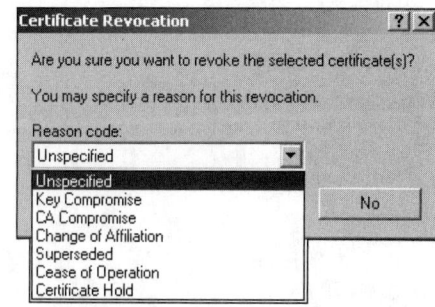

FIGURE 8.21
In the Certification Revocation dialog box, you specify a reason for revoking the certificate.

Working with the Revocation List

After you've revoked a certificate, the certificate is slated to be published in the CRL. As an administrator, you can set the timings for publishing the CRL or choose to force an early publication date.

Each certificate has CRL distribution points included within itself as a way to update the system if the certificate is deleted. The distribution points are actually pointers to where the CRL can be retrieved. By default, the CRL file is located on the issuing CA's systemroot\system32\certsrv\certenroll.

You can set the timings for how often the CRL is published by selecting Revoked Certificates in the Console tree, choosing Action, Properties, and providing the required information. To manually publish a CRL, choose Action, All Tasks, Publish, and then confirm that you want to overwrite the previous CRL.

USING THE EFS RECOVERY KEYS

Remove the EFS recovery keys.

Have you ever seen someone work hard to select a great user ID and password to secure an Windows operating system, only to have someone else walk up to the computer, put a floppy disk in the drive, boot to DOS, and read all the computer files anyway? This method is common for illegally accessing data on PCs. With the correct tools, someone with physical access to a system can bypass even the built-in security features of the Windows 2000 operating system file system access control by reading the files in Windows NT file system (NTFS).

So, what can you do? Removing alternate boot methods is an alternative, albeit a stop gap at best. If people really want your data, they can take your hard drive. To effectively secure your data, you need to look to data encryption technologies. Microsoft Windows 2000 includes a new EFS. EFS is built on the same security principles that are involved in certificates. EFS works by encrypting data files on a computer's hard drive using EFS keys, much the same way information is encrypted using certificates. EFS encrypts data in NTFS files on the disk. If a user attempting to access an encrypted NTFS file has the private key to that file, the user can open the file and work with it transparently as a normal document. A user without the private key to the file is denied access. The EFS keys can then be stored on media separate from the computer.

EFS is an ideal data security tool, especially for laptop users. For example, an employee leaves on a business trip with a laptop containing company secrets. You may think that you are safe because the company secrets are encrypted. But what if the laptop is stolen and the thief is able to guess the logon name and password? What if the smart card was in the briefcase along with the laptop?

Exporting EFS Keys

To protect your data from theft, you can remove the EFS keys from all vulnerable computers and store the keys on the network, a floppy, or some other type of media.

By removing the EFS keys, you prevent an intruder from gaining access to the data simply by logging on to the computer. The keys for the data are stored elsewhere. Again, think physical security. Where will we keep these floppies?

To remove the EFS keys, follow these steps:

STEP BY STEP

8.7 Exporting the EFS Keys

1. Open the Certificates snap-in, access the Personal folder shown in Figure 8.22, and open the Certificates subfolder. The User certificates on this computer are displayed in the details pane.

continues

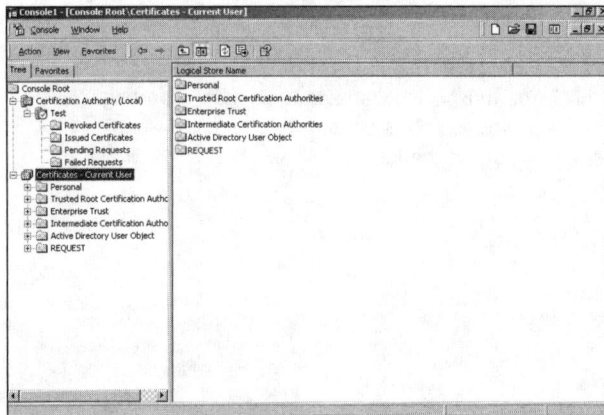

FIGURE 8.22
You use the Certificates MMC snap-in to view User certificates.

FIGURE 8.23
You can use the Certificate Export Wizard to export certificates.

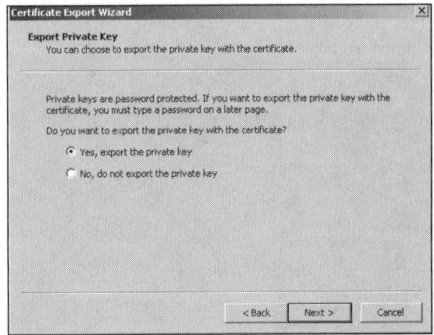

FIGURE 8.24
The Certificate Export Wizard warns you that exporting keys requires a password when you begin the process.

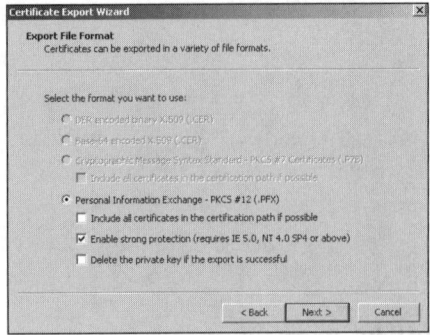

FIGURE 8.25
You can choose to include all user certificates, enable strong protection, and delete the private key after export.

continued

2. Right-click the certificate, choose All Tasks, Export from the drop-down menu that appears. The Certificate Export Wizard dialog box opens (see Figure 8.23).

3. Navigate to the Export Private Key dialog box shown in Figure 8.24 and select the Yes, Export the Private Key option. Click Next and the Export File Format dialog box opens (see Figure 8.25).

4. Select the Personal Information Exchange—Public-Key Cryptography Standards (PKCS) #12 (PFX) option. The Enable Strong Protection option is selected by default. Select the Delete the Private Key if the Export Is Successful option and click Next. Because you chose to export the private key, you are prompted to supply a password you can use when you want to import the key later (see Figure 8.26).

FIGURE 8.26
You must supply a password when exporting a private key. This password is required when importing the key.

5. Enter an appropriate password and click Next. The File to Export dialog box opens (see Figure 8.27).

6. Save the filename to a network location or to a floppy, click Next, check your work in the window that displays the settings you chose, and click Finish to close the Certificate Export Wizard.

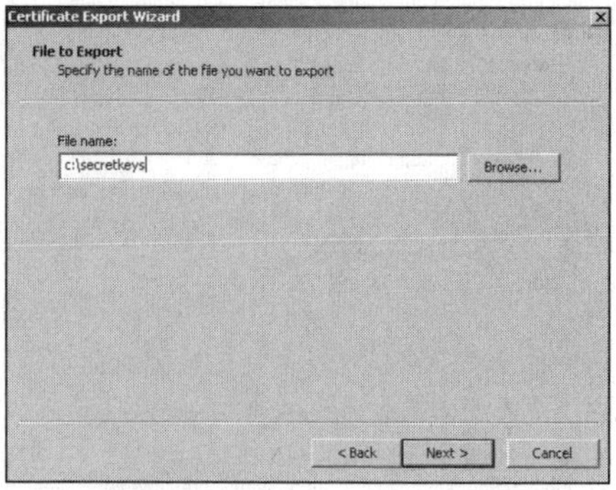

Restoring EFS Keys

After you've exported the EFS keys and made backups of them, you will need to import the keys back into the system when you want to access files using EFS. The importing process is very similar to exporting, as you can see in the following steps:

STEP BY STEP

8.8 Importing EFS Keys

1. Open the Certificates snap-in, access the Personal folder, and open the Certificates subfolder. The User certificates on this computer are displayed in the details pane.

2. Right-click the certificate, choose All Tasks, Import from the drop-down menu that appears. The Certificate Import Wizard dialog box opens (see Figure 8.28).

continues

FIGURE 8.27
You must specify the filename and location where you want to export the private key.

WARNING

Password Alert Choose your password for all EFS operations wisely. If you forget this password, your data will be inaccessible.

FIGURE 8.28
You can use the Certificate Import Wizard to import certificates.

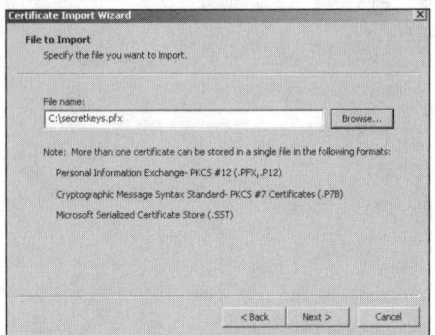

FIGURE 8.29
Use the File to Import dialog box to specify the file to be imported.

continued

3. Click Next to locate the exported keys. The File to Import dialog box opens (see Figure 8.29)

4. Enter the path to where the file is stored and click Next. The Password dialog box opens (see Figure 8.30).

5. Supply the password for the private key and click Next. The Certificate Store dialog box opens (see Figure 8.31).

6. Designate where the keys are kept, and click Next.

7. Review the Import Wizard details to start the process, and then click Finish.

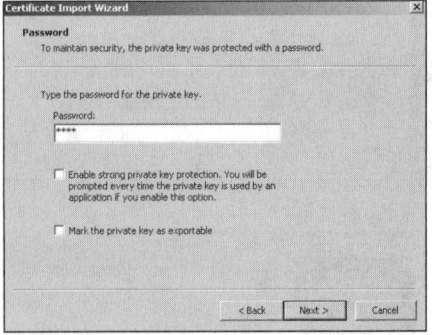

FIGURE 8.30
Supplying the correct password is critical to the success of importing a key.

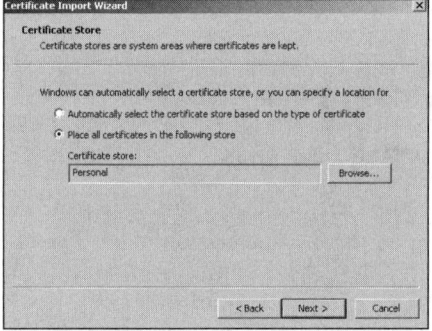

FIGURE 8.31
Use the Certificate Store dialog box to specify where to store the imported EFS keys on the system.

CASE STUDY: ROCKWELL FINANCIAL SERVICES

ESSENCE OF THE CASE

Here are the essential elements in this case:

▶ Upload sensitive data over the Internet.

▶ Allow clients to securely access their own data over the Web.

▶ Secure data from start to finish.

SCENARIO

Rockwell Financial Services is a company that deals in all aspects of financial management and investments. It has agents throughout North America that represent various firms for insurance and investments.

These agents use Windows 2000 Professional on their laptops. From the client's site, agents use the laptop to enter the investment information, and then they commute back to the their respective networks and transfer the data to their local Structured Query Language (SQL) server, which is then transferred to a centralized SQL server in Chicago.

The company realizes the need for the security of this data, and this is why the agents currently must return to the office to transfer their information. However, the agents are complaining that they are losing valuable time that could be used to visit other clients, and in some cases, sales are lost because the market may fluctuate and opportunities are missed.

Rockwell Financial Services would like to implement a plan that would allow its agents to use the Internet to connect to the central SQL server and upload the data through a Web interface—while securing data. In addition, they'd like to offer services to their clients that would allow their clients to access their account information online.

continues

CASE STUDY: ROCKWELL FINANCIAL SERVICES

continued

ANALYSIS

Rockwell Financial should install Certificate Services. A hierarchy of CA could start in the central office of Chicago and then be dispersed to a child CA in each geographical location.

Sales reps would be issued a certificate from the local CA. A Web presence with a sales front and a SQL interface would be created that would support secure uploads of clients' data over the Internet. In addition, a plan could be developed to secure any data saved on the laptops by the sales reps through smart cards or through EFS implementation.

A Web presence would be created for clients accessing their personal data. A certificate would be issued by a CA that would verify that the clients have access to only their data.

CHAPTER SUMMARY

KEY TERMS

- certificate
- CA
- Standalone Certification Authorities
- validity period
- Enterprise Root CA
- Intermediate CA
- User Principal Name mapping
- one-to-one mapping
- many-to-one mapping
- revoked certificate
- revocation list
- EFS

Certificates are a mechanism for ensuring that data is secure between users, computers, and services. Certificates may be issued through a third-party CA, such as VeriSign, or through Microsoft's CA Services.

A CA scheme needs to be developed to determine the amount of CAs to be created, the location of CAs, and the role of each CA. An Enterprise Root CA is the foundation of a typical CA schema. The Enterprise Root CA would issue certificates to Intermediary CAs. The intermediates would then issue certificates to Subordinate CAs.

As servers and services are removed from the network, and more likely, users leave the company, it becomes necessary to revoke certificates.

The EFS is a component that allows your data to be kept secure, especially on a laptop, should the physical security of the computer become jeopardized. By encrypting the data on the laptop and then removing the public and private keys, the data is secure even if the computer is vandalized or stolen. To access the data, the private key would be required.

APPLY YOUR KNOWLEDGE

Exercises

8.1 Installing and Configuring an Enterprise Root CA

This exercise guides you through the installation of a Root CA for your environment. This exercise presumes you've not installed the CA services onto your server. For the exam, a working knowledge of the mechanics of adding and configuring this service is required.

Estimated Time: 15–20 minutes

1. Log on to your server as administrator.

2. Click Start, Settings, Control Panel, and then open the Add/Remove Programs applet.

3. Click the Add/Remove Windows Components icon. The Add/Remove Windows Components Wizard opens.

4. Click the option to add the Certificate Services. After the warning about the computer name and Certificate Services, click Next.

5. Choose the option to install an Enterprise Root CA. Click the option for Advanced Options, and then click Next.

6. You can choose an alternate CSP, hash algorithm, key length, and the choice to use existing keys. For now, choose the key length to be 4096. Click Next to continue.

7. Enter the details about this CA. In the Valid for Years option, enter **4** and then click Next.

8. The cryptographic keys are built and the service is installed. This step may take several minutes, depending on the speed of your processor.

9. You'll be prompted to stop the IIS services. Do so, and then the Certificate Services will be installed.

8.2 Requesting a Certificate

This exercise guides you through requesting a certificate from the CA you created in Exercise 8.1.

Estimated Time: 5–10 minutes

1. If the MMC is not open, open it now.

2. From the Console menu choose Add/Remove Snap-In. Click Add in the Add/Remove Snap-In window.

3. Choose Certificates, and then choose Current User and click OK. The Certificates Snap-In is added.

4. From the Certificates Snap-In tree, choose Personal and then Certificates.

5. Right-click Certificates and from the pop-up menu choose All Tasks and then choose Request New Certificate.

6. The Certificate Request Wizard appears. Read the intro and then click Next to start the process of adding a certificate.

7. From the Certificate Template choice window, choose User and then click Next. Assign this certificate the friendly Name of My User Certificate. In the description, you can enter a brief description of the certificate if you want. Click Next to continue.

8. The wizard reports the completion of the certificate. Click Finish to complete the wizard.

APPLY YOUR KNOWLEDGE

9. A dialog box appears, informing you that the certificate was successful. Click View Certificate to view details on what this certificate can do for your account.

10. Click OK and then click Install Certificate. A message appears, telling you that the installation was successful. Click OK and then exit the console.

Review Questions

1. What is a certificate?

2. What is a CA?

3. What is an Enterprise CA?

4. What is the role of an Intermediary CA?

5. Why would an organization have a Standalone CA?

6. Why would an issued certificate need to be revoked?

7. Why would a CA need to renew its certificate?

8. How are certificate requests handled at a Standalone CA server?

9. What is many-to-one mapping?

10. How can EFS be effective when planning for the worst, such as on a lost or stolen laptop?

Exam Questions

1. You are the administrator for a Windows 2000 network. Your network consists of eight domain controllers, two member servers, and 874 Windows 2000 Professional workstations. Your network spans three cities: Redmond, Atlanta, and Chicago. You would like to implement certificates as an additional step for security. Your boss, Maria, wants to know why you'd like to implement certificates. Of the following, which are valid reasons for implementing certificates in your environment?

    A. Certificates ensure that incoming and outgoing data has not been compromised.

    B. Certificates speed up network traffic because all data is encrypted.

    C. Certificates can be issued through Microsoft's CA Services.

    D. Certificates can be created only through a third-party vendor, such as VeriSign.

2. You are the network administrator for Flagston Enterprises. Their Windows 2000 network consists of eight domain controllers, four member servers, and 592 Windows 2000 Professional workstations. You have created a plan to implement CA. You report to your supervisor that the first CA will be a Root CA. Your plans then call for an Intermediary CA. Your supervisors want to know why an additional CA is required. Of the following, which is a valid reason for adding an Intermediary CA?

    A. All Enterprise CAs require Intermediary CAs to communicate with other CAs.

    B. Enterprise CAs require Active Directory and the Intermediary CAs do not. Intermediary CAs are used to function with CAs outside of this domain.

    C. The Root CA would be secured and taken offline while the Intermediary CA would remain online to issue certificates to certificate requestors.

APPLY YOUR KNOWLEDGE

D. The Intermediary CA would handle all communication between the Subordinate CAs and the Root CA.

3. Johnson Chemicals and Supply has a Windows 2000 domain that spans four states. They have seven Windows 2000 domain controllers, five member servers, and nearly 1,000 Windows 2000 Professional workstations. 346 Windows 2000 Professional workstations are installed onto laptops. Larry Johnson, the owner, is concerned about using laptops with sensitive data. His primary concern is that the laptops could be stolen or lost and the data on the laptop could be jeopardized. You're hired to resolve a solution for Larry Johnson.

Required result:

The solution you offer must have a plan for securing data should the laptop be stolen or lost.

Optional desired results:

The solution must not incur any new expenses to the company.

The solution must be easy for the sales reps to use and understand.

Proposed solution:

Implement a certificate for each user of a laptop. The successful logon of a user would guarantee that the user is a valid user account. After the user has logged on, he or she can access the necessary data securely and efficiently.

Evaluation of proposed solution:

Which result(s) does the proposed solution produce?

A. The proposed solution produces the required result but neither of the optional results.

B. The proposed solution produces the required result and one of the optional results.

C. The proposed solution produces the required result and both of the optional results.

D. The proposed solution does not produce the required result.

4. Johnson Chemicals and Supply has a Windows 2000 domain that spans four states. They have seven Windows 2000 domain controllers, five member servers, and nearly 1,000 Windows 2000 Professional workstations. 346 Windows 2000 Professional workstations are installed onto laptops. Larry Johnson, the owner, is concerned about using laptops with sensitive data. His primary concern is that the laptops could be stolen or lost and the data on the laptop could be jeopardized. You're hired to resolve a solution for Larry Johnson.

Required result:

The solution you offer must have a plan for securing data should the laptop be stolen or lost.

Optional desired results:

The solution must not incur any new expenses to the company.

The solution must be easy for the sales reps to use and understand.

Proposed solution:

Implement smart cards on each of the laptops. Without the smart card, the laptop cannot be accessed.

APPLY YOUR KNOWLEDGE

Evaluation of proposed solution:

Which result(s) does the proposed solution produce?

A. The proposed solution produces the required result but neither of the optional results.

B. The proposed solution produces the required result and one of the optional results.

C. The proposed solution produces the required result and both of the optional results.

D. The proposed solution does not produce the required result.

5. Johnson Chemicals and Supply has a Windows 2000 domain that spans four states. The company has seven Windows 2000 domain controllers, five member servers, and nearly 1,000 Windows 2000 Professional workstations. 346 Windows 2000 Professional workstations are installed onto laptops. Larry Johnson, the owner, is concerned about using laptops with sensitive data. His primary concern is that the laptops could be stolen or lost and the data on the laptop could be jeopardized. You're hired to resolve a solution for Larry Johnson.

Required result:

The solution you offer must have a plan for securing data should the laptop be stolen or lost.

Optional desired results:

The solution must not incur any new expenses to the company.

The solution must be easy for the sales reps to use and understand.

Proposed solution:

Implement EFS for each laptop user. Export the private key to a network location and then copy it to a floppy; delete the local key. Instruct the sales force to keep the floppy separate from the laptop unless they are importing the key to access data.

Evaluation of proposed solution:

Which result(s) does the proposed solution produce?

A. The proposed solution produces the required result but neither of the optional results.

B. The proposed solution produces the required result and one of the optional results.

C. The proposed solution produces the required result and both of the optional results.

D. The proposed solution does not produce the required result.

6. You are the network administrator for Queens Agricultural Services. Your Windows 2000 network consists of four domain controllers, two member servers, and 462 Windows 2000 Professional workstations. 143 of these workstations are on laptops throughout the Midwest. You've been given the task of creating a way to ensure that the data on these laptops and internal workstations is secure. The solution must be easy for users and must take into account the laptops in the Midwest. In addition, the plan must allow for growth and future technologies. Of the following, which is the best plan for securing data on this network?

A. Implement smart cards for all users—remote and local.

APPLY YOUR KNOWLEDGE

B. Implement a Standalone CA. Users will be mapped a certificate that will be downloaded each time they log on to the network.

C. Implement smart cards for all users—remote and local. Create a Root CA. Certificate will be downloaded to users at each logon.

D. Implement smart cards for all users—remote and local. Create a CA. For each user, issue certificates that will be stored in the smart card.

7. You are the network administrator for a large accounting firm in Illinois. Your headquarters are located in downtown Chicago. In addition, you have seven offices around Chicago, one in Springfield, one in Peoria, and one in Urbana. Your Windows 2000 network consists of 12 domain controllers, seven member servers, and 1,300 Windows 2000 Professional workstations throughout the network. You connect to each of these networks through a virtual private network (VPN). Your supervisor has asked you to create a plan to secure data between each geographical site so that data is secure. Of the following, which is a valid plan for implementing security in this network?

A. Install EFS on each workstation and server, remove the private key, and then delete the local key.

B. Install an Enterprise Root CA at the headquarters. From this secured Root CA, add an Intermediary CA. Branched from this Intermediary CA, install a subsidiary CA in each geographical location.

C. Install an Enterprise Root CA in the headquarters, and then install a Standalone CA in each geographical location.

D. Install an Enterprise Root CA at the headquarters. From this secured Root CA, add an Intermediary CA. Branched from this Intermediary CA, install a subsidiary CA in each geographical location. Take the Root CA offline.

8. You are a network consultant for Primary Colors, Ltd. Their Windows 2000 domain consists of eight domain controllers, six member servers, and 1,322 Windows 2000 Professional workstations. Recently, they've acquired a company named AllPaints. Their network is located forty miles away from the company headquarters, and management has agreed to keep and operate both domains for the present time.

Both networks have vendors and subcontractors that need to access internal resources. You have been hired to create an appropriate security scheme for this network.

Required result:

Users from both domains must be able to easily access Internet and intranet resources.

Optional results:

Users from both domains must only have to log on to their respective domains.

Vendors and subcontractors must be allowed to access intranet resources.

Proposed solution:

Create a CA within the Primary Colors domain. Issue certificates for all users from both domains. Create accounts for subcontractors and vendors to use to access resources on the intranet.

APPLY YOUR KNOWLEDGE

Evaluation of proposed solution:

Which result(s) does the proposed solution produce?

A. The proposed solution produces the required result but neither of the optional results.

B. The proposed solution produces the required result and one of the optional results.

C. The proposed solution produces the required result and both of the optional results.

D. The proposed solution does not produce the required result.

9. You are a network consultant for Primary Colors, Ltd. Their Windows 2000 domain consists of eight domain controllers, six member servers, and 1,322 Windows 2000 Professional workstations. Recently, they've acquired a company named AllPaints. Their network is located forty miles away from the company headquarters, and management has agreed to keep and operate both domains for the present time.

Both networks have vendors and subcontractors that need to access internal resources. You have been hired to create an appropriate security scheme for this network.

Required result:

Users from both domains must be able to easily access Internet and intranet resources.

Optional results:

Users from both domains must only have to log on to their respective domains.

Vendors and subcontractors must be allowed to access intranet resources.

Proposed solution:

Create a CA within the Primary Colors and within the AllPaints domain. Issue certificates for all users from both domains.

Evaluation of proposed solution:

Which result(s) does the proposed solution produce?

A. The proposed solution produces the required result but neither of the optional results.

B. The proposed solution produces the required result and one of the optional results.

C. The proposed solution produces the required result and both of the optional results.

D. The proposed solution does not produce the required result.

10. You are a network consultant for Primary Colors, Ltd. Their Windows 2000 domain consists of eight domain controllers, six member servers, and 1,322 Windows 2000 Professional workstations. Recently, they've acquired a company named AllPaints. Their network is located forty miles away from the company headquarters, and management has agreed to keep and operate both domains for the present time.

Both networks have vendors and subcontractors that need to access internal resources. You have been hired to create an appropriate security scheme for this network.

Required result:

Users from both domains must be able to easily access Internet and intranet resources.

APPLY YOUR KNOWLEDGE

Optional results:

Users from both domains must only have to log on to their respective domains.

Vendors and subcontractors must be allowed to access intranet resources.

Proposed solution:

Create a CA within the Primary Colors domain and a CA within the AllPaints domain. Add both CAs as a Trusted Root in each CA. Issue certificates for all users from both domains. Create accounts for subcontractors and vendors to use to access resources on the intranet.

Evaluation of proposed solution:

Which result(s) does the proposed solution produce?

A. The proposed solution produces the required result but neither of the optional results.

B. The proposed solution produces the required result and one of the optional results.

C. The proposed solution produces the required result and both of the optional results.

D. The proposed solution does not produce the required result.

11. You are the network administrator for Nebuchadnezzar Furnaces. Their Windows 2000 domain consists of domain controllers, two members servers, and 765 Windows 2000 Professional workstations. Daniel, your supervisor, reports to you that he suspects that Sam is still accessing the network through the Internet, although he has been fired from the company twelve days ago. He asks you to resolve the matter so that Sam cannot

access the network remotely. Of the following, which remedy would ensure that Sam cannot access the network?

A. Delete Sam's previously assigned certificate.

B. Revoke Sam's previously assigned certificate.

C. Force Sam's certificate to expire early.

D. Publish the RCL.

12. You are the network administrator for BrightLight Enterprises. Your network consists of four domain controllers, four member servers, and 320 Microsoft Windows 2000 Professional workstations. 120 Workstations are located at a manufacturing plant in Phoenix. Users from the Santa Fe office are complaining that when they send messages to the plant location in Phoenix, messages are arriving changed, with missing text, or not at all. You've been assigned to create a method to secure data from both networks when the data travels over the Internet. Of the following, which is the best method to implement this security?

A. Create a Root CA in Phoenix and in Santa Fe. Assign users certificates from each CA.

B. Create one CA server. From this CA create a Subordinate CA in each network. Assign users certificates to send secure data over this network.

C. Install EFS on each workstation. Create one CA server. From this CA create a Subordinate CA in each network. Assign users certificates to send secure data over this network.

D. Install EFS on each workstation. Remove the private keys and delete the local key. Create one CA in Santa Fe and assign users certificates to send secure data over this network.

APPLY YOUR KNOWLEDGE

13. You have been hired as a Windows 2000 consultant for Khunle Distributors Corporation. The company's network consists of two domain controllers, one member server, and 432 Microsoft Windows 2000 Professional workstations. Of the 432 workstations, 398 of the workstations are used in tractor trailers throughout the country. The drivers of the trucks currently dial in to the Kansas City headquarters via an 800 number to check email and fill out reports through an Internet site. Bethany, the office manager, is concerned that competition may attempt to access the Web site to view sensitive material about the company's distribution plans. You've been assigned to secure this network.

    Required results:

    Only the employed truck drivers must be able to access the Web site.

    Optional results:

    Data, such as email, must be secure between the truckers and the headquarters.

    Data on the laptop must be secure should the laptop be lost or stolen.

    Proposed solution:

    Install a CA on the Khunle network. Issue each remote user a certificate for accessing the Internet site. Install and use EFS to secure data on the local laptop and when transmitting data over the Internet.

    Which result(s) does the proposed solution produce?

    A. The proposed solution produces the required result but neither of the optional results.

    B. The proposed solution produces the required result and one of the optional results.

    C. The proposed solution produces the required result and both of the optional results.

    D. The proposed solution does not produce the required result.

14. You have been hired as a Windows 2000 consultant for Khunle Distributors Corporation. Their network consists of two domain controllers, one member server, and 432 Microsoft Windows 2000 Professional workstations. Of the 432 workstations, 398 of the workstations are used in semitrailers throughout the country. The drivers of the trucks currently dial in to the Kansas City headquarters via an 800 number to check email and fill out reports through an Internet site. Bethany, the office manager, is concerned that competition may attempt to access the Web site to view sensitive material about the company's distribution plans. You've been assigned to secure this network.

    Required results:

    Only the employed truck drivers must be able to access the Web site.

    Optional results:

    Data, such as email, must be secure between the truckers and the headquarters.

    Data on the laptop must be secure should the laptop be lost or stolen.

    Proposed Solution:

    Install a CA on the Khunle network. Issue each remote user a certificate for accessing the Internet site. Issue a certificate for transmitting secure email for each of the remote users. Install EFS on each remote machine to secure the local data.

    Which result(s) does the proposed solution produce?

APPLY YOUR KNOWLEDGE

A. The proposed solution produces the required result but neither of the optional results.

B. The proposed solution produces the required result and one of the optional results.

C. The proposed solution produces the required result and both of the optional results.

D. The proposed solution does not produce the required result.

15. You have been hired as a Windows 2000 consultant for Khunle Distributors Corporation. Their network consists of two domain controllers, one member server, and 432 Microsoft Windows 2000 Professional workstations. Of the 432 workstations, 398 of the workstations are used in semi-trailers throughout the country. The drivers of the trucks currently dial in to the Kansas City headquarters via an 800 number to check email and fill out reports through an Internet site. Bethany, the office manager, is concerned that competition may attempt to access the Web site to view sensitive material about the company's distribution plans. You've been assigned to secure this network.

Required results:

Only the employed truck drivers must be able to access the Web site.

Optional results:

Data, such as email, must be secure between the truckers and the headquarters.

Data on the laptop must be secure should the laptop be lost or stolen.

Proposed solution:

Install a CA on the Khunle network. Install smart cards on each of the remote users' laptops. The smart cards will carry all certificate information for accessing the secured Web site and sending data over unsecured lines. Install EFS on each machine. Remove the private key and delete the local key. Configure the smart cards to contain the key. Instruct the truckers to keep the smart cards separate from the laptops unless the laptop is in use.

Which result(s) does the proposed solution produce?

A. The proposed solution produces the required result but neither of the optional results.

B. The proposed solution produces the required result and one of the optional results.

C. The proposed solution produces the required result and both of the optional results.

D. The proposed solution does not produce the required result.

Answers to Review Questions

1. A certificate is a component that allows you to send and receive secure data over a network. It assures the recipient that you are whom you claim to be, and it assures the sender that the data will reach the recipient without being jeopardized. For more information, see the section titled "Certificates."

2. A CA is an entity that is responsible for verifying the credentials of a certificate requestor before giving the requestor a certificate. You may use a third-party CA or use Microsoft's Certificate Services. For more information, see the section titled "CAs."

APPLY YOUR KNOWLEDGE

3. An Enterprise CA is the Root CA in an organization. Typically, as additional CAs are added, they are issued certificates from the Root CA. For more information, see the section titled "Windows 2000 Enterprise CA."

4. An Intermediary CA is responsible for issuing certificates to child CAs. The Enterprise Root CA issues a certificate to the Intermediary CA. The Intermediary CA then issues certificates to all child CAs rather than the Root CA issuing the certificates directly. For more information, see the section titled "CAs."

5. A Standalone CA is an excellent choice when Active Directory is not present or when you want to manually approve certificate requests. For more information, see the section titled "Standalone CAs."

6. An issued certificate would be revoked for a number of reasons: the user has left the organization; the keys may have been jeopardized; a certification was assigned under false pretenses. For more information, see the section titled "Revoking Issued Certificates."

7. When a CA is created, it is assigned a certificate. This certificate, like all certificates, is set to expire. When a certificate has or is about to expire, an administrator can choose to renew the certificate. For more information, see the section titled "Renewing Certificates for CAs."

8. Standalone CAs mark all requests as pending. An administrator must manually approve or deny each certificate request. For more information, see the section titled "Standalone CAs."

9. Many-to-one mapping is the process of assigning multiple certificates to one Windows 2000 user account. For more information, see the section titled "Many-to-One Mapping."

10. When using EFS on a laptop, you need to export the private keys and delete the local keys. This secures the data should the laptop be lost or stolen. For more information, see the section titled "Exporting EFS Keys."

Answers to Exam Questions

1. **A, C**. Certificates ensure that incoming and outgoing data is secure. You can add Certificate servers as part of Windows 2000. For more information, see the section titled "Certificates."

2. **C**. The creation of an Intermediary CA will allow the Root CA to be taken offline and secured. The Intermediary server would then issue certificates to other CAs. For more information, see the section titled "CAs."

3. **D**. The proposed solution does not produce the required results. The required result calls for a way to secure data should the laptop be lost or stolen. The offered solution does not ensure that the data on the laptop will remain secure. For more information, see the section titled "Exporting EFS Keys."

4. **B**. The proposed solution meets the required result, but only one of the optional results. The required result calls for a way to secure data should the laptop be lost or stolen. The offered solution does solve the accessing of data, but smart cards are an additional expense. For more information, see the section titled "Exporting EFS Keys."

APPLY YOUR KNOWLEDGE

5. **C**. The proposed solution meets the required result and both of the optional results. By implementing EFS and exporting the private key (and deleting the local key), access to the data on the laptop is not accessible should someone gain entry. For more information, see the section titled "Exporting EFS Keys."

6. **D**. By creating a CA and issuing users a certificate to be stored within the smart card, only users with valid smart cards will be able to log on to the network. For more information, see the section titled "Certificates."

7. **D**. Create an Enterprise Root CA. Off of the Root CA, create an Intermediary CA responsible for all CAs directly below it. For security, take the Root CA offline. For more information, see the section titled "Installing and Configuring an Enterprise Subordinate CA."

8. **D**. The proposed solution does not produce the required result. For users from both domains to access resources in both domains, users will require a certificate to access resources in each domain. For more information, see the section titled, "Installing and Configuring an Enterprise Subordinate CA."

9. **B**. The proposed solution does produce the required result, but only one of the optional results. By creating two independent CAs and issuing users from each domain a certificate, they can access resources in each domain. Users will only have to log on to their respective domains. This solution, however, does not provide for vendors and subcontractors. For more information, see the section titled "Installing and Configuring an Enterprise Subordinate CA."

10. **C**. The proposed solution does produce the required result and the optional results. By creating a CA in each domain and then trusting each Root CA, users can access resources in each domain because their certificate is trusted by the other domain. By creating accounts for vendors and subcontractors, you can assign and control access to intranet and Internet resources. For more information, see the section titled "Installing and Configuring an Enterprise Subordinate CA."

11. **B**. You should revoke Sam's certificate to prevent him from accessing any network resources. For more information, see the section titled "Revoking Issued Certificates."

12. **B**. Because this is one organization, no need exists to create a Root CA in each geographical location. Instead, create one CA and Subordinate CAs in each location. Assign users from each location a certificate from their respective CA. For more information, see the section titled "Installing and Configuring an Enterprise Subordinate CA."

13. **A**. The proposed solution does meet the required result but neither of the optional results. By assigning certificates to the drivers from your CA, only these drivers will be able to be authenticated to access the Web servers. The solution, however, does not broach the optional results. For more information, see the section titled "Installing and Configuring an Enterprise Subordinate CA."

14. **B**. The proposed solution does meet the required result but only one of the optional results. By assigning certificates to the drivers to access the secure Web servers, only these drivers will be able

APPLY YOUR KNOWLEDGE

to access the Web site. Assigning a certificate to send and receive secure email resolves one of the optional results. Simply installing EFS is not enough to secure the data on the laptop. For more information, see the section titled "Installing and Configuring an Enterprise Subordinate CA."

15. **C.** The proposed solution does meet the required result and both of the optional results. By assigning certificates to the drivers to access the secure Web servers, only these drivers will be able to

access Web site. Assigning a certificate to send and receive secure email resolves one of the optional results. Simply installing EFS is not enough to secure the data on the laptop; you must remove the private keys from the laptop to ensure that the data is safe. By implementing smart cards, the experience for the truckers can be very easy because the cards can be programmed to dial, send and receive mail, and secure the local data. For more information, see the section titled "Installing and Configuring an Enterprise Subordinate CA."

Suggested Readings and Resources

1. Marcus, Scott J. *Designing Wide Area Networks and Internetworks: A Practical Guide.* Upper Saddle River, NJ: Addison Wesley, 1999.

2. Thomas, Thomas M. *OSPF Network Design Solutions.* Indianapolis, IN: Cisco Press, 1998.

FINAL REVIEW

Fast Facts

Study and Exam Prep Tips

Practice Exam

Now that you have finished reading this book and working through the exercises, you're ready for the exam. This final chapter is intended to be the "final cram in the parking lot."

Organized by chapter, this section is not only a summary, but it is a concentrated review of the most important points. If you know and are comfortable with the content and concepts presented here, the odds are good that you are truly prepared for the certification exam.

INSTALLING, CONFIGURING, MANAGING, MONITORING, AND TROUBLESHOOTING DNS IN A WINDOWS 2000 NETWORK INFRASTRUCTURE

HOSTS files can do name resolution, and this was the original method employed on the predecessor to the Internet. As the number of computers grew, this solution ran into problems because it was a flat-file solution, and propagation of the file became nearly impossible.

Domain Name System (DNS) replaced HOSTS files. DNS is a distributed, hierarchical database residing on servers known as a name servers. It is designed so that there can be multiple name servers for redundancy, and caching of names to the local server is also supported.

Fast Facts

IMPLEMENTING AND ADMINISTERING A MICROSOFT WINDOWS 2000 NETWORK INFRASTRUCTURE

DNS terminology includes the following:

◆ **Tree.** A data structure with each element attached to one or more elements directly beneath it. DNS is often called an inverted tree because it is generally drawn with the root at the top of the tree.

◆ **Top-level domain (TLD).** The suffix attached to Internet domain names. The number of predefined suffixes is limited, and each one represents a top-level domain. Examples include com, edu, org, net, and country identifiers.

◆ **Node.** The point at which two or more lines in the tree intersect, also known as a leaf.

◆ **Fully qualified domain name (FQDN).** A domain name that includes all domains between the host and the root. The DNS information configured under System Properties is used as the DNS suffix for building FQDNs.

◆ **Zone.** A logical grouping of hostnames within DNS. A zone is the complete information about some part of the domain namespace.

Two types of name servers are defined within the DNS specifications:

◆ **Primary master.** The server where you make additions, modifications, and deletions to the DNS zone.

◆ **Secondary master.** This server gets its zone information from another domain name server that is authoritative for that domain.

The DNS name server resolves a name to an Internet Protocol (IP) address using the following process:

1. The client computer makes a request to the local DNS server.

2. The DNS server looks in a local memory cache for names it has recently resolved. If the name is found in the local cache, the name server returns the IP address that the client computer requires.

3. The name server looks in the DNS server's host tables to see if a static entry exists (or in the case of Dynamic DNS, a dynamic entry) for the hostname to an IP address lookup. If an entry exists, the DNS server forwards the IP address to the client computer.

4. The name server refers the request to a root name server. Root name servers support the root of the namespace hierarchy. At present, ten computers support the root domain.

5. The root name server refers the request to a name server for the first-level domain in the hostname.

6. The first name server that can resolve the hostname to an IP address reports the IP address to the client computer.

With a reverse lookup, you query the DNS server with an IP address and it returns (if an entry exists) the DNS name for that host.

Summary Table 1 lists the main record types supported by Windows 2000's DNS Server service, along with their meaning.

SUMMARY TABLE 1
DNS RECORD TYPES

Record Type	Value and Meaning
CNAME	One of the original record types, a CNAME indicates an alias domain name for a name already specified as another resource type in this zone. CNAME is the acronym for canonical name.
A	One HOST address record—maps a DNS name to an IP (version 4) address.
MX	A mail exchanger record is used to provide message routing to a specific mail exchange host for a specific DNS name.
MG	A mail group record is used to add mailbox (MB) records as members of a domain mailing group.
MB	An MB record maps a specified domain mailbox name to the host that hosts the mailbox.
MINFO	Mailbox or mailing list information specifies a domain mailbox name to contact. Can also specify a mailbox for error messages.
PTR	A pointer record points to a location in the domain. This is typically used for reverse lookups or IP address to DNS name lookups.
TXT	A text record is used to hold a string of characters that serve as descriptive text to be associated with a specific DNS name.
RT	A route-through record provides an intermediate-route-through binding for internal hosts that do not have their own direct wide area network (WAN) address.
SRV	A service record allows administrators to use several servers for a single DNS domain to easily move a TCP/IP service from host to host, and to designate primary and backup services hosts.
WKS	A well-known service record is used to describe well-known TCP/IP services supported by a particular protocol (that is, Transmission Control Protocol (TCP) or User Datagram Protocol (UDP)) on a specific IP address.

Summary Table 2 shows the restrictions for creating a DNS name and an FQDN.

SUMMARY TABLE 2
DNS NAME RESTRICTIONS

Restriction	Standard DNS (Including Windows NT 4)	DNS in Windows 2000
Characters	Supports Request for Comments (RFC) which permits "A" to "Z", "a" to "z", "0" to "9", and the hyphen (-).	Several configurations are possible: RFC 1123 standard, as well as support for RFCs 2181 and the character set specified in RFC 2044 (UTP-8)
FQDN length	63 bytes per label and 255 bytes for an FQDN.	Domain controllers are limited to 155 bytes for FQDN.

Windows 2000 DNS contains a number of significant improvements over standard DNS, including the following:

◆ Notification-driven zone transfers

◆ Integrated zone tables

◆ Incremental zone transfers

◆ Secure DNS updates

◆ DNS—Dynamic Host Configuration Protocol (DHCP) integration

The root name server of a domain is the name server that is acting as the Start of Authority (SOA) for that zone. The SOA record is the first record in the database, and it contains the following fields:

◆ Source Host

◆ Contact Email

◆ Serial Number

◆ Refresh Time

◆ Retry Time

◆ Expiration Time

◆ Time to Live (TTL)

Dynamic DNS integrates DHCP and DNS and is necessary for Active Directory. Every time a computer requests a new address or renews its address, the computer sends its fully qualified name to the DHCP server and requests that the DHCP server register an entry in the reverse lookup DNS zone on its behalf. The DHCP client computer also requests an entry in the forward lookup zone on its own behalf.

Configuring a zone for dynamic updates allows Windows 2000 client computers to register as part of DNS. In Windows 2000, client computers can send dynamic updates for three types of network adapters: DHCP adapters, statically configured adapters, and remote access adapters. By default, the dynamic update client computer dynamically registers its A resource records whenever any of the following events occur:

◆ The TCP/IP configuration is changed.

◆ The DHCP address is renewed or a new lease is obtained.

◆ A Plug and Play event occurs.

◆ An IP address is added or removed from the computer when the user changes or adds an IP address for a static adapter.

You can also force a reregistration by using the command ipconfig /registerdns.

To go from no DNS service to a functional DNS server, you will need to complete the following steps:

1. Installation can be accomplished through the use of the Configure Your Server application and is completely wizard driven. You can also install it via the Network and Dial-up Connections section of the Control Panel.

2. After the service is installed, you will need to configure it. This is done by opening the DNS console. The first thing to do in this application is to start the Configure DNS Server Wizard. This guides you through configuring the server with its first zone(s).

3. After the wizard completes the process, you are ready to resolve names.

The three types of zones supported by Windows 2000 DNS are

◆ Active Directory integrated

◆ Standard primary

◆ Standard secondary

For the most secure implementation, you should choose Active Directory integrated. Caching-only servers are used to speed up client DNS queries by gathering a large number of cached records based on client DNS queries. A caching-only server does not have a copy of the zone table and therefore cannot respond to queries against the zone unless they are already cached. A caching server is not authoritative on any zone.

Delegating a domain means that DNS queries on the existing domain will be referred to the name server in the delegated domain for resolution. You can only delegate down the hierarchy, so the delegated domain must be a subdomain of the domain doing the delegation.

Parameters configured in the Networking Properties section are used for resolving names, whereas the System Properties parameters are used while registering the system with the Active Directory.

The following are four methods of testing the DNS resolution:

- ◆ Use the PING utility with the a flag.
- ◆ Use the NSLOOKUP utility.
- ◆ Use the built-in monitoring in the DNS console.
- ◆ Use the Internet Explorer browser.

In managing DNS, you can configure a number of optional parameters, including the following:

- ◆ **Set Aging/Scavenging for All Zones.** This controls how the server handles stale resource records.
- ◆ **Scavenge Stale Resource.** This allows you to manually scavenge the record.
- ◆ **Update Server Data Files.** This option writes any changes to the table that are in random access memory (RAM) to the server's hard drive.
- ◆ **Clear Cache.** This option allows you to flush the server's cache.
- ◆ **All Tasks.** This allows you to start, stop, pause, resume, or restart the service.
- ◆ **Delete.** Deletes the DNS server.
- ◆ **Properties.** Opens the Properties dialog box.

The Performance application can be used to monitor the available and extensive DNS counters. Different categories of counters available for DNS include

- ◆ AXFR counters
- ◆ Caching memory
- ◆ Database node memory
- ◆ Dynamic update
- ◆ IXFR counters
- ◆ NBTSTAT memory
- ◆ Notify received/sent

- ◆ Record flow memory
- ◆ Recursive
- ◆ Secure update
- ◆ TCP/UDP
- ◆ Total
- ◆ Windows Internet Name Service (WINS)
- ◆ Zone transfer

INSTALLING, CONFIGURING, MANAGING, MONITORING, AND TROUBLESHOOTING DHCP IN A WINDOWS 2000 NETWORK INFRASTRUCTURE

The DHCP is open and standards based. It is the Internet community's answer to dynamically distributing IP addresses. In addition to IP addresses, DHCP can also provide gateway addresses, DNS server addresses, WINS server addresses—in essence, everything the client computer needs to participate in the network.

Often network administrators use unregistered addresses (not registered with IANA) on their internal network to ensure that there are addresses for all users. This model works great as long as the network is never tied directly to the Internet.

When using DHCP, a client computer gets an address through the following steps:

1. The client computer broadcasts a DHCPDiscover message that is forwarded to the DHCP server(s) on the network. The address of the DHCP server(s) is configured on the router, if necessary. Forwarding is done using a process called a bootstrap (BOOTP) Forwarder.

2. Each DHCP server that receives the discover message responds with a DHCP offer message that includes an IP address appropriate for the subnet where the client computer is attached. The DHCP server determines the appropriate address by looking at the source subnet for the broadcast DHCPDiscover message.

3. The client computer considers the offer message and selects one (usually the first offer it receives). It sends a request to use that address to the DHCP server that originated the offer. If multiple DHCP servers exist, great care needs to be taken in their configuration.

4. The DHCP server acknowledges the request and grants the client computer a lease to use the address.

5. The client computer uses the IP address to bind to the network. If the IP address is associated with any configuration parameters, the parameters are incorporated into the client computer's TCP/IP configuration.

Any DHCP client computer that had been assigned an address will automatically try to extend the lease when half the time of the lease has passed. If it is unable to do so, it will continue to try to do so for the duration of the lease.

If you are maintaining a legacy domain and a WINS-style network, Windows 2000 can receive DHCP information from any DHCP server that Windows NT worked with. However, if you want to take advantage of the features of Active Directory Services and migrate away from the legacy WINS architecture, you will need the Windows 2000 DHCP Service.

A DHCP server cannot be a DHCP client computer. If you currently have your server configured as a DHCP client computer, the DHCP installation will prompt you to enter a static IP address for your server.

A scope is a range of IP addresses that are available for dynamic assignment to client computers on a given subnet. The scope for a particular subnet is determined by the network address of the broadcast DHCP request. After installing the DHCP service, you must define at least one scope on the server. Otherwise, the service will not respond to DHCP requests.

A superscope allows you to support a supernetted or multinetted network with a Windows 2000 DHCP server. A supernetted network is a network that has multiple network addresses or subnets running on the same segment. You can select only active scopes for inclusion in the superscope.

Multicasting is the act of transmitting a message to a select group of recipients. This is in contrast to the concept of a broadcast, in which traffic is sent to every host on the network, or a unicast, in which the connection is a one-to-one relationship and only one recipient of the data. Class D IP addresses should be used for the multicast scope.

Components of Windows 2000's multicast functionality include

◆ Multicast DHCP (MDHCP)

◆ Multicast forwarding table

◆ Multicast group

◆ Multicast scope

One of the keys to effectively implementing an Active Directory environment is the capability for Windows 2000 workstations using DHCP to be automatically registered in DNS. Three settings can be set for DNS integration:

- ◆ Automatically update DHCP client computer information in DNS. This is enabled by default.

- ◆ Discard forward (name-to-address) lookups when lease expires. This is also enabled by default.

- ◆ Enable updates for DNS client computers that do not support dynamic update.

The capability to register both A- and PTR-type records lets a DHCP server register non-Windows 2000 client computers in DNS. The DHCP server can differentiate between Windows 2000 Professional and other client computers.

The DHCP console is used for managing and monitoring DHCP. It has several features on the Action menu, such as Display Statistics, that will show such items as when the server started. The All Tasks selection allows you to perform the following tasks for your DHCP server:

- ◆ Start

- ◆ Stop

- ◆ Pause

- ◆ Resume

- ◆ Restart

- ◆ Delete

- ◆ Refresh

- ◆ Export List

- ◆ Properties

Counters that can be measured for DHCP include the following:

- ◆ **Packets Received/Sec.** The number of message packets received per second by the DHCP server.

- ◆ **Duplicates Dropped/Sec.** The number of duplicate packets per second dropped by the DHCP server.

- ◆ **Packets Expired/Sec.** The number of packets per second that expire and are dropped by the DHCP server.

- ◆ **Milliseconds per Packet (Avg).** The average time, in milliseconds, that the DHCP server takes to process each packet it receives.

- ◆ **Active Queue Length.** The current length of the internal message queue of the DHCP server. This number represents the number of unprocessed messages received by the server.

- ◆ **Conflict Check Queue Length.** The current length of the conflict check queue for the DHCP server. Before a Windows 2000 DHCP server will issue an address, it checks to see whether any IP address conflicts exist. This queue holds the messages while the DHCP server performs address conflict detection.

- ◆ **Discovers/Sec.** The number of DHCPDiscover messages received per second by the server.

- ◆ **Offers/Sec.** The number of DHCPOffer messages sent per second by the DHCP server to client computers.

◆ **Requests/Sec.** The number of DHCPRequest messages received per second by the DHCP server from client computers. This is the request the client computer sends to request an IP address after it has found a server that can issue addresses.

◆ **Informs/Sec.** The number of DHCPInform messages received per second by the DHCP server.

◆ **Acks/Sec.** The number of DHCPAck messages sent per second by the DHCP server to client computers.

◆ **Nacks/Sec.** The number of DHCPNack acknowledgment messages sent per second by the DHCP server to client computers. This indicates that the server is unable to fulfill the DHCP request.

◆ **Declines/Sec.** The number of DHCPDecline messages received per second by the DHCP server from client computers. This counter indicates that the DHCP client computer has declined the IP address issued by the server.

◆ **Releases/Sec.** The number of DHCPRelease messages received per second by the DHCP server from client computers.

The DHCP console now supports Simple Network Management Protocol (SNMP) and Management Information Bases (MIBs), which allow the DHCP server to report statistics and send alerts to any of a number of management platforms, including HP OpenView, Seagate Nerve Center, and even Novell's ManageWise product. This allows administrators to monitor DHCP information, including the following:

◆ The number of available addresses

◆ The number of used addresses

◆ The number of leases being processed per second

◆ The number of messages and offers processed

◆ The number of requests, acknowledgements, declines, negative status acknowledgment messages (Nacks), and releases received

◆ The total number of scopes and addresses on the server, the number used, and the number available

CONFIGURING, MANAGING, MONITORING, AND TROUBLESHOOTING REMOTE ACCESS IN A WINDOWS 2000 NETWORK INFRASTRUCTURE

In Windows 2000, not only is the Routing and Remote Access Service (which replaces the Remote Access Service that came with Windows NT Server 4) installed automatically with the operating system, it also bundles features that used to be distributed through other services, such as the Windows 2000 virtual private network (VPN) service.

A remote access policy is a set of actions that can be applied to a group of users that meet a specified set of requirements.

When creating a remote access dial-in profile, you have access to the following tabs:

◆ **Dial-in Constraints.** Allows you to configure the restrictions on the dial-in users, including the idle disconnect timer, the maximum length of the session, the time and the day access is permitted, the dial-in number allowed, and the dial-in media allowed.

◆ **IP.** Used to determine the IP Address Assignment Policy and also allows you to apply IP Packet Filters, if necessary.

◆ **Multilink.** Allows you to configure Windows 2000's capability to aggregate multiple analog phone lines connected to multiple modems to provide greater bandwidth.

◆ **Authentication.** Allows you to configure the authentication methods supported by Windows 2000. The protocols include Extensible Authentication Protocol (EAP)-Transport Layer Security Protocol (TLS), challenge handshake authentication protocol (CHAP), Microsoft Challenge Handshake Authentication Protocol (MS-CHAP), Shiva's Password Authentication Protocol (SPAP), and password authentication protocol (PAP).

◆ **Encryption.** Allows you to set the level of encryption required with Routing and Remote Access authentication. You can set it to No Encryption, Basic, Strong, or allow any combination of the three.

◆ **Advanced.** Allows you to add connection attributes to be returned to the remote access server. This is usually used in conjunction with Remote Authentication Dial-In User Service (RADIUS).

Windows 2000 has two main encryption protocols that are used in the VPN:

◆ **Point-to-Point Tunneling Protocol (PPTP).** Developed jointly by Microsoft Corporation, U.S. Robotics, and several remote access vendor companies, it has never been widely accepted by the security community.

◆ **IP Security Protocol (IPSec).** A suite of cryptography-based protection services and security protocols that can provide machine-level authentication as well as data encryption for Layer 2 Tunneling Protocol (L2TP)-based VPN connections. Unlike some other IPSec-based VPNs, Microsoft's implementation uses the L2TP protocol for encrypting the usernames, passwords, and data, whereas IPSec is used to negotiate the secure connection between your computer and its remote tunnel server. Available encryptions for IPSec include Data Encryption Standard (DES) and Triple DES (3DES). These are the encryption protocols available for remote access in Windows 2000. Windows 2000 does use other encryption, such as Kerberos, for logging on to a domain, but it is not applicable to remote access.

Windows 2000 includes the capability of aggregating multiple modem lines to form a single, higher-bandwidth connection to a remote access server. This is known as multilink and is usually to an Internet Service Provider (ISP) connection, but it could also be to another Windows 2000 server. Multilink is configured on the Incoming Connections Properties dialog box beneath Network and Dial-up Connections.

When the remote access server is configured to use DHCP, the Routing and Remote Access server uses the DHCP client component to obtain 10 IP addresses from a DHCP server. This could be on the network or on the same server as the Routing and Remote Access server. The remote access server uses the first IP address obtained from DHCP for the remote access service (RAS) interface, and subsequent addresses are allocated to TCP/IP-based remote access client computers as they connect. IP addresses freed because of remote access client computers disconnecting are reused. When all 10 addresses have been allocated, the process starts again with the DHCP client computer requesting an additional 10 addresses.

To configure Routing and Remote Access for DHCP Integration, open the Routing and Remote Access console within the Routing and Remote Access portion of Administrative Tools.

Monitoring remote access can be done with the following counters in the Performance utility:

◆ **Alignment Errors.** The size of the packet received is different from the size expected.

◆ **Buffer Overrun Errors.** The software is unable to handle the rate that data is being received.

◆ **Bytes Received.** The total amount of bytes received by the service.

◆ **Bytes Received/Sec.** The number of bytes received by the service in a second.

◆ **Bytes Transmitted.** The total amount of bytes transmitted by the service.

◆ **Bytes Transmitted/Sec.** The number of bytes transmitted by the service in a second.

◆ **Cyclical Redundancy Check (CRC) Errors.** A frame received contains erroneous data and the packet did not pass the CRC.

◆ **Frames Received.** The total number of frames received by the service.

◆ **Frames Received/Sec.** The number of frames received by the service per second.

◆ **Frames Transmitted.** The total number of frames transmitted by the service.

◆ **Frames Transmitted/Sec.** The number of frames transmitted by the service per second.

◆ **Percent Compression In.** Tells how well inbound traffic is being compressed.

◆ **Percent Compression Out.** Tells how well outbound traffic is being compressed.

◆ **Errors.** Serial Overrun Errors, Timeout Errors, Total Errors, and Total Errors/Sec. These objects handle all the error information for the Routing and Remote Access Service.

To configure remote access security, open the Routing and Remote Access console, right-click the server and select Properties, and then select the Security tab. By default, the authentication provider is Windows Authentication, but you can also set it for RADIUS authentication.

INSTALLING, CONFIGURING, MANAGING, MONITORING, AND TROUBLESHOOTING NETWORK PROTOCOLS IN A WINDOWS 2000 NETWORK INFRASTRUCTURE

Within Windows 2000, TCP/IP is installed by default. Many features of Windows 2000 are reliant on TCP/IP, which requires a valid IP address, a subnet mask, a default gateway, and a DNS server. This information may be entered manually at each client computer and server or, preferably, through DHCP. DHCP assigns the host an IP address as it's needed by the client computer.

If you're mixing Windows 2000 with an older network basic input output system (NetBIOS), chances are you'll be using the Windows Internet Naming Service (WINS) to resolve "computer" names to IP addresses. You can access the WINS properties through the Advanced tab of TCP/IP Properties dialog box.

When integrating with NetWare, you need to know the network number and frame type that the NetWare servers require. Windows 2000 can detect the frame type currently in use, or you can add the frame type manually. As a general rule, NetWare servers 3.11 and earlier used 802.3 as their frame type, whereas NetWare 3.12 and later use 802.2.

You must also utilize the NWLink protocol to obtain the Internet Packet Exchange/Sequenced Packet Exchange (IPX/SPX) compatibility needed by older NetWare servers (newer can use TCP/IP). NWLink is Microsoft's 32-bit implementation of IPX/SPX. Software such as Gateway Services for NetWare (GSNW) or File and Print Services for NetWare (FPNW) are required, in addition to the protocols, to complete connectivity with NetWare servers and client computers.

Network bindings are a way of ordering network providers, protocols, and connections in the order in which they will most likely be used by the operating system (OS). In short, it allows you to specify which protocol should be referenced, or used, first when attempting to connect to resources. Windows 2000 allows you to bind or unbind protocols to services installed on this computer. You may arrange the desired order of the protocols independently of the services and adapters installed.

In broad terms, a provider is a network client computer that provides access to resources, and a connection is a component that represents how this host will connect to another host: local area network (LAN), WAN, or dial-up.

Address Resolution Protocol (ARP) is the protocol that resolves IP addresses into MAC addresses.

A TCP/IP packet filter is a way to prevent certain types of packets from reaching your Windows 2000 computer. You can set filters for TCP, UDP, or IP numbers. You can create a universal setting for all adapters or configure each adapter individually. Access to IP filtering is on the Options tab, through the Advanced button on the TCP/IP Properties dialog box.

IP packet filtering is not the same, or as secure as, IPSec: IPSec is used to secure packets between two host identifiers (IDs). Encrypting File System (EFS) is not encrypted when transferring the data on a network, and you must use IPSec to encrypt the data on the network, as well. Tunneling is the process of encapsulating packets inside other packets for data integrity, security, and convenience. L2TP uses IPSec if it's available because L2TP uses a UDP-like packet for transmissions. IPSec tunneling is required if your routers or remote hosts cannot accept L2TP.

Proxy servers can act as firewalls to prevent incoming packets from reaching host IDs on a specified network. Security hosts can be implemented to secure logons, authentication, and network security. These security hosts are typically intermediary devices for dial-up client computers.

Kerberos V5 authentication is an industry standard authentication protocol. Through tickets and keys, users are granted rights to the resources. Kerberos is in place on Windows 2000 domains. Kerberos can be configured to interact with MIT-based realms so that client computers from other operating systems may access resources in the Active Directory.

A VPN is an extension of a physical network, using the Internet as the backbone between two segments. VPN technology is founded on PPTP or L2TP. VPNs are a way of connecting networks while, most likely, using the existing structure of the Internet as their backbone. IPSec can be coupled with VPNs to ensure quality and to guarantee delivery of packets.

As a network grows, so does the amount of traffic created. Administrators need to get rid of unneeded protocols and services to reduce traffic.

Administrators must also monitor this traffic through Network Monitor. Network Monitor allows you to capture real-time activity, create filters on protocols types, and save that information to a file. It is important that you create a baseline before passing judgment on what data you are collecting so that you have a historical perspective on performance.

The Network Monitor included with Windows 2000 is not the full Network Monitor. The full Network Monitor is included with SMS. You can add the Network Monitor Driver (actually a protocol) on workstations and servers to be monitored through the short messaging service (SMS) Network Monitor.

INSTALLING, CONFIGURING, MANAGING, MONITORING, AND TROUBLESHOOTING WINS IN A WINDOWS 2000 NETWORK INFRASTRUCTURE

NetBIOS name resolution can be done with LMHOSTS files, or WINS. An LMHOST file is a text file that must be edited manually and copied to every computer on the network.

WINS consists of four elements:

◆ **WINS servers.** When WINS client computers enter the network, they contact a WINS server using a directed message. The client computer registers its name with the WINS server and uses the WINS server to resolve NetBIOS names to IP addresses.

◆ **WINS client computers.** WINS clients use directed point-to-point node (P-node) messages to communicate with WINS servers and are typically configured to use hybrid node (H-node) communication. Windows 2000, Windows NT, Windows 95 and 98, and Windows for Workgroups computers can be WINS client computers.

◆ **Non-WINS client computers.** Older Microsoft network client computers that can't use P-node can still benefit from WINS. Their broadcast messages are intercepted by WINS proxy computers that act as intermediaries between the broadcast node (B-node) client computers and WINS servers. MS-DOS and Windows 3.1 client computers function as non-WINS client computers.

◆ **WINS proxies.** Windows NT, Windows 95 and 98, and Windows for Workgroups client computers can function as WINS proxies. They intercept B-node broadcasts on their local subnet and communicate with a WINS server on behalf of the B-node client computer.

The WINS server should use a static (rather than a dynamic) IP address. If this is not done, all users could lose access to the server if it is issued an address different from what it had been issued by the DHCP server.

The WINS console is a Microsoft Management Console (MMC) snap-in that is used for interacting with the WINS service. Within the WINS console, right-click the server and select Properties to see the following tabs:

◆ **General.** Used to configure the following parameters:

- Statistics

- WINS Database Backup

◆ **Intervals.** Used to set the WINS database records renewal, deletion, and verification intervals. You can set the following intervals:

- Renew Interval

- Extinction Interval

- Extinction Timeout

- Verification Interval

◆ **Database Verification.** Allows you to configure the parameters associated with the WINS database.

◆ **Advanced.** Used to configure a variety of parameters, including

- Logging.

- Burst handling. This can be set to Low, Medium, High, or Custom, which allows you to specify a number of connections.

- Database path.

- Database version number.

- LAN Manager compatibility.

One of the new features of the Windows 2000 WINS server is its capability to maintain a persistent connection with one or more of its replication partners, enabling real-time replication. The different types of replication you can configure for the WINS service are the following:

◆ Pull replication.

◆ Push replication.

◆ Replication partner type. This can be push, pull, or push/pull.

In push replication, your server pushes its database to the replication partner. A push replication is event driven, and the number of database updates determines when the event occurs. In pull replication, your server pulls the database from the replication partner. A pull replication is time based and occurs at the time you have configured. In push/pull replication, database replication can occur using either method.

The majority of WINS troubleshooting issues relate to connectivity. Tools that can assist in troubleshooting include

◆ PING.EXE

◆ IPCONFIG

◆ Task Manager

To get the server statistics, just open WINS console and right-click the server in question. From the Context menu, select Display Server Statistics, and a snapshot of the server statistics will be displayed.

Node types to know for WINS and networking are

◆ **B-node.** Relies exclusively on broadcast messages and is the oldest NetBIOS name resolution mode.

◆ **P-node.** Relies on WINS servers for NetBIOS name resolution. Client computers register themselves with a WINS server when they come on the network. They then contact the WINS server with NetBIOS name resolution requests.

◆ **Modified node (M-node).** A hybrid mode that first attempts to resolve NetBIOS names using the B-node mechanism. If that fails, an attempt is made to use P-node name resolution.

◆ **H-node.** A hybrid mode that favors the use of WINS for NetBIOS name resolution. When a computer needs to resolve a NetBIOS name, it first attempts to use P-node resolution to resolve a name via WINS. Only if WINS resolution fails does the host resort to B-node to resolve the name via broadcasts.

INSTALLING, CONFIGURING, MANAGING, MONITORING, AND TROUBLESHOOTING IP ROUTING IN A WINDOWS 2000 NETWORK INFRASTRUCTURE

Routing is the process of forwarding a packet based on the destination IP address. Routing occurs at a sending TCP/IP host, which is known as host routing, and at an IP router, which is known as router routing.

For the host to send the packet to its destination via the router, it must first determine the address of the router to send the packet to. This can be accomplished via the following:

◆ The default gateway address is determined and then the local ARP cache is queried to identify the physical address to be used to reach the desired router.

◆ An Internet Control Message Protocol (ICMP) redirect message is sent by an IP router to the sending host, informing it of a better route to a destination host. The better route becomes a host route in the routing table.

◆ A TCP/IP host has the capability to listen to the routing protocol traffic used by routers. This is known as eavesdropping or wiretapping. Windows 2000 implements eavesdropping through a feature called silent Routing Information Protocol (RIP).

With router routing, the decision as to which router to forward the packet to is determined by a number of variables about each of the network paths to the destination host, including the number of hops and the cost of each hop. Windows 2000 Advanced Server provides router routing using Routing and Remote Access Service.

Routing tables can be manually configured (static) or created through the use of a dynamic routing protocol. Two dynamic routing protocols that are provided with Windows 2000 are

◆ RIP

◆ Open Shortest Path First (OSPF)

Dynamic routers have the capability to learn from other routers. Having the capability to learn makes dynamic routing fault tolerant. If a router or link goes down, the routers sense the change in the internetwork topology through the expiration of the route information in the routing table. The router can then rebuild its links based on the new network topology and forward the routing information to other routers so that all the routers on the internetwork become aware of the new internetwork topology.

Routing can employ either distance-vector routing or link-state routing technologies. The main differences between the two routing protocols are

◆ What routing information is exchanged

◆ How the information is exchanged

◆ How quickly the internetwork can recover from a downed link or a downed router

Distance-vector routing is the oldest and most common routing algorithm. Distance-vector routers build their routing information tables based on information received from other routers. The routers pass on this information to other routers on each of their attached segments.

Link-state routing protocols exchange information only about the specific routes that have changed. Routers using link-state routing protocols learn about their network environment by "meeting" their neighboring routers. This is done through a "hello" packet. This network information is then sent to each of the neighboring routers using a link-state advertisement. The neighboring routers copy the contents of the packet and forward the link-state advertisement to each attached network, except for the one the link-state advertisement was received on. This is known as *flooding*.

The RIP is a distance-vector protocol that uses hop count as its metric for measuring the number of routers that must be crossed to reach the desired network. RIP is widely used for routing traffic in the global Internet and is an Interior Gateway Protocol (IGP), which means that it performs routing within a single autonomous system. There are two versions of RIP, version 1 and version 2. RIP routers advertise the contents of their routing tables every 30 seconds on all attached networks through an IP subnet and MAC-level broadcast. (RIP v2 routers can be configured to multicast RIP announcements.)

RIP uses a single routing metric (hop count) to measure the distance between the source and a destination network. Each hop in a path from source to destination is assigned a hop count value, which typically is 1. The maximum number of hops in a path is 15; therefore, only 15 routers can be between any two hosts.

OSPF is a link-state routing protocol that functions by sending link-state advertisements (LSAs) to all other routers within the same hierarchical area. OSPF has the following features:

◆ Better convergence than RIP.

◆ OSPF calculated routes that are always loop free.

◆ OSPF sends updates only when the routing changes, rather than sending routing updates periodically. This makes better use of bandwidth.

◆ OSPF allows for logical definition of networks where routers can be divided into areas.

◆ OSPF was designed to advertise the subnet mask with the network. OSPF supports variable-length subnet masks (VLSM), disjointed subnets, and supernetting.

◆ OSPF allows for routing authentication using different methods of password authentication.

◆ Routes outside of the OSPF autonomous system are advertised within the autonomous system so that OSPF routers can calculate the least-cost route to external networks.

Demand-dial routing can be used to allow packets to be routed across a dial-up link. A demand-dial network consists of a calling router and an answering router. Both the calling and receiving routers have Routing and Remote Access Service installed. Several types of connections can be used with the demand-dial router, including

◆ Modem or ISDN connection

◆ Direct serial or direct parallel port connection

Demand-dial security provides a number of security features to ensure that the appropriate calling router is initiating the connection and that the proper answering router is answering the connection:

◆ Remote access permission

◆ Authentication

◆ Encryption

◆ Callback

◆ Caller ID

◆ Remote access account lockout

The route command is primarily used to configure static routes within a network. It can also be used to troubleshoot by listing all the routes that this computer knows about. Summary Table 3 lists common problems and resolutions with RIP, and Summary Table 4 does the same for OSPF:

SUMMARY TABLE 3
RIP ISSUES AND RESOLUTION

Problem	*Solution*
Routing tables have improper routing information within a mixed RIP version 1 and 2 network.	RIP version 2 routers are configured to multicast announcements. Multicast announcements are never received by RIP version 1 routers.
	If you have a mixed environment of RIP version 1 and RIP version 2, ensure that the routers configured with RIP version 2 are using broadcast instead of multicast.
Silent RIP hosts are not receiving routes.	RIP version 2 routers are configured to multicast announcements. Multicast announcements are never received by silent RIP hosts.
	If silent RIP hosts are on a network that is not receiving routes from the local RIP router, verify the version of RIP supported by the silent RIP hosts. If it is the listening service in Windows NT 4 Service Pack 4 or Windows 2000, you must configure the RIP routers for RIP version 1 or RIP version broadcasting.
RIP routers are not being updated properly with valid routes.	You are deploying variable length subnetting, disjointed subnets, or supernetting in a RIP version 1 or mixed RIP version 1 and RIP version 2 environment.
	Do not deploy variable length subnetting, disjointed subnets, or supernetting in a RIP version 1 or mixed RIP version 1 and RIP version 2 environment because it is not supported.
RIP routers are not being updated properly with valid routes.	You are using autostatic RIP and you did not do an initial manual update.
	When you use autostatic RIP on a demand-dial interface, the first time you make a connection, you must manually update routes.
	You must also update routes manually on the router for the corresponding interface. The routes then appear in the IP routing table.
Host or default routes are not being propagated.	RIP by default is not configured to propagate host or default routes. If these need to be propagated, change the default settings on the Advanced tab of the properties of a RIP interface.

SUMMARY TABLE 4
OSPF ISSUES AND RESOLUTION

Problem	*Solution*
OSPF adjacency is not forming between two neighbors.	OSPF is not enabled on the interface. Verify that OSPF is enabled on the interface on the network segment where an adjacency should form. By default, when you add an interface to the OSPF routing protocol, OSPF is disabled for the interface and must be manually enabled.
OSPF adjacency is not forming between two neighbors.	Ping the neighboring router to ensure basic IP and network connectivity. Use the `tracert` command to trace the route to the neighboring router. There should not be any routers between the neighboring routes.
A virtual link is not forming between two areas.	Mismatched configuration of password, hello interval, or dead interval. Verify that the virtual link neighbor routers are configured for the same password, hello interval, and dead interval.
A virtual link is not forming between two areas.	Virtual link neighbors are configured for the incorrect transit area ID. Verify that both virtual link neighbors are configured for the same correct transit area ID.
Routing tables are not being updated with OSPF routes, or improper OSPF routes are present.	Not receiving summarized routes. If you are not receiving summarized OSPF routes for an area, verify that the area border routers (ABRs) for the area are configured with the proper {destination, network mask} pairs summarizing that area's routes.
Routing tables are not being updated with OSPF routes, or improper OSPF routes are present.	All ABRs are not connected to the backbone. Verify that all ABRs are either physically connected to the backbone or logically connected to the backbone by using a virtual link. There should not be back door routers, which are routers that connect two areas without going through the backbone.

INSTALLING, CONFIGURING, AND TROUBLESHOOTING NETWORK ADDRESS TRANSLATION (NAT)

The Internet Connection Sharing (ICS) service provides an automated demand-dial installation process for the following services:

- ◆ NAT
- ◆ DHCP
- ◆ DNS Proxy

These services make ICS a quick and easy solution for a small office looking for a way to connect to the Internet via dial-up. ICS also has features that are not available in the NAT implementation:

- ◆ **H.323 Proxy.** This feature permits users to make and receive Microsoft NetMeeting calls.

- ◆ **Lightweight Directory Access Protocol (LDAP) Proxy.** The capability to proxy LDAP requests allows users to register with an Internet Locater Service (ILS) server as part of a NetMeeting directory.

- ◆ **Directplay Proxy.** This allows users to play Directplay games across the NAT router. This feature is more suited for home use than for a small office, and it is also offered in the Windows 98 version of ICS.

ICS will do the following upon install:

- ICS sets the IP address of the LAN interface to 192.168.0.1, a private IP address. A private IP address is an address that cannot be routed across the Internet. Reserved addresses are specifically set aside for private networks.

- The WAN interface (usually a modem) is set to be a demand-dial router pointed at the ISP.

- A DNS Proxy service is installed to provide DNS services to the office. This service passes client computer DNS requests to the DNS server configured in the ICS server's DHCP settings.

- The AutoDHCP service is installed. This service provides a subset of the services included with a full DHCP installation, but AutoDHCP is configured to issue addresses on the new 198.168.0.0 network.

If you have a larger network than the one ICS can support, you can use the NAT capabilities of Windows 2000. NAT takes an IP address entering on one interface of the Windows 2000 server and translates it to a different address exiting a different (usually the Internet-connected) interface. The following are two reasons for doing this:

- Security

- IP address conservation

If you are planning to use NAT, the easiest way to enable the client computers is through the NAT DHCP service. This will configure the client computers with the correct information to use the NAT gateway when they are assigned their IP address via DHCP. If you are using the NAT DHCP, you will not need the Windows 2000 DHCP service.

A NAT interface defines the connection properties for the NAT. This can be either the private interface, connected to the internal (private) network, or the public interface, connected to the Internet.

Any logging events will be logged in the System Event Log and can be viewed with the Event Viewer.

INSTALLING, CONFIGURING, MANAGING, MONITORING, AND TROUBLESHOOTING CERTIFICATE SERVICES

Windows 2000 includes Certificate Services for securing an intranet and extranets. Digital signatures ensure that data is from the said user and has not been tampered with. Public Key Infrastructure (PKI) is implemented because of the openness of TCP/IP.

PKI has been developed in tandem with TCP/IP as means to offer security for data sent between hosts through the use of encryption. The key to this encryption is the certificate. A digital certificate is the electronic version of your password or employee identification. It proves that you are who you say you are and is used as part of the encryption that makes PKI possible.

Certificates are issued by a Certification Authority (CA) that verifies that the owner of the certificate is who he says he is. The CA is essentially ensuring that the user of the digital identity is a valid, real person, with true credentials.

Contents of a digital certificate:

- The user's name

- The user's public key

◆ Serial number

◆ Expiration date

◆ Information on the certificate itself

◆ Information on the CA that issued the certificate

A Windows 2000 enterprise CA provides certificates for the internal security of an entire organization, whereas an external CA provides security for external security needs. Microsoft provides support for both, and you may mix and match as your business needs see fit.

Requirements of a Windows 2000 enterprise CA:

◆ The CA server may run any Windows 2000 server. Plan for activity, network load, and physical placement of the server for best implementation.

◆ The name of the server should be determined before implementing CA services. The reason is that the CA name is integrated into the certificates it assigns.

◆ The enterprise CA is integrated into the Active Directory.

◆ When you've installed an enterprise CA, a policy module is created. An administrator may edit the policy.

◆ Plan for fault tolerance. Because the CA is crucial for the successful implementation of the PKI, you should plan on a fault-tolerance scheme. In addition, regular secure backups should occur.

Windows 2000 allows you to install a standalone CA. These do not require the interaction of an Active Directory but can use one if it's available.

A standalone CA is useful to issue certificates, digital signatures, support secure email (S/MIME) and SSL

(secure sockets layer) or TLS (transport layer security).

Attributes of a typical standalone CA are the following:

◆ Does not require Active Directory interaction.

◆ Used with extranets.

◆ The standalone CA does not verify the requests for certificates. All requests are set to pending until an administrator approves them.

◆ Users requesting a certificate from a standalone CA must supply all user account information. This is not required within an enterprise CA because the user is recognized from the logon account in the Active Directory.

◆ No certificate templates are used.

◆ Windows 2000 logon credential certificates are not stored on smart cards. Other certificates can be, however.

◆ An administrator must distribute the standalone CA certificate to the trusted root store.

If an Active Directory exists and a standalone CA can access it, additional options are available:

◆ If a domain administrator with write access to the Active Directory installs the standalone CA, the standalone is added to the Trusted Root CA's certificate store. What this means is that if the default action of pending requests is changed, the standalone CA will automatically approve all requests for certificates. In other words, do not change the default action of pending certificate requests on a standalone CA.

◆ If a domain administrator group member of the parent domain (or an administrator with write access to the Active Directory) installs the standalone CA, the standalone CA will publish the certificate and the certificate revocation list to the Active Directory.

Windows 2000 PKI allows for and encourages a dispersed hierarchy of CAs. Building a tree of CAs allows for scalability with other organizations, internal and external resources, and compatibility with third-party CA implementations.

Reasons for creating a CA hierarchy include the following:

◆ **Varying usages.** Certificates can be issued for a number of purposes, such as secure email, SSL, and TSL. Different CAs can be responsible for different areas of security.

◆ **Politics.** Differences of opinion exist throughout the enterprise on how policies are enforced. Different degrees of security are needed, based on the organization.

◆ **Geography.** In a WAN environment, a need may exist for a different CA in each physical location to save on network resources.

◆ **Security.** Position the root authority in a very secure environment with fault-tolerant devices. Subordinate CAs would not require the same amount and type of security as the root.

◆ **Revoking.** Most organizations need to have the ability to revoke individual CAs rather than be forced to revoke an entire enterprise.

You can install a CA in several ways:

◆ **After Windows 2000 has been installed.** Use the Add/Remove Programs applet in Control Panel to add the services to the current installation.

◆ **As part of the Windows 2000 installation.** During the installation of Windows 2000, you can choose from the optional components. After Windows 2000 is installed, you will complete the installation of the service according to your PKI plans.

◆ **Upgrading from Certificate Server 1.0.** When you install Windows 2000 on a server that is running Certificate Server 1.0, the Windows 2000 installation program will automatically upgrade the service.

◆ **Through an unattended installation.** If you are using an unattended installation to install Windows 2000, you can include the installation of a CA through the setup file.

Whichever method you choose to install Certificate Services, you'll be required to supply the following:

◆ **CA type.** What type of CA will this be?

  • **Enterprise Root CA.** The is the root of all CAs in your hierarchy. Typically, there is only one of these per enterprise. Requires Active Directory. Subordinate CAs branch off this server. This is the parent only.

  • **Enterprise Subordinate CA.** A subordinate CA must obtain its certificate from a CA higher in the hierarchy to obtain its certificate. Requires Active Directory. This is the child of another CA. It is possible that this CA could also be a parent to another CA.

- **Standalone Root CA.** A standalone root CA is like an enterprise root CA, except that it does not require Active Directory but can use it if it exists. Often, this CA is offline to protect the validity of the originating certificates and keys.

- **Standalone Subordinate CA.** This CA does not require Active Directory, but may use it if Active Directory is available to it. The subordinate CA must obtain its certificate from another CA. This is the child in the relationship, but it may become a parent if it supplies a certificate to another CA.

◆ **Advanced options.** If you enable Advanced options during the install of your CA, you'll have to provide the following:

- **The cryptographic service provider (CSP).** The CSP generates the public and private keys.

- **Key length.** The longer the key, the more secure the key.

- **Hash algorithm.** It's a computation to produce a hash value of some piece of data. The default is Secure Hash Algorithm (SHA)-1, which is a 160-bit hash value.

◆ **CA name.** The name of the CA. You can use just about any character you want. The name you assign the CA will also be the common name (CN) of the CA's distinguished name in Active Directory. Special characters (non-American Standard Code for Information Interchange (ASCII) and ASCII punctuation) are stripped out in a sanitized name. Also remember that Active Directory is limited to 64 characters before it truncates names.

◆ **Organization.** The name of your organization as it is known throughout its community.

◆ **Organizational unit.** What division does this CA manage?

◆ **Locality.** City.

◆ **State or province.**

◆ **Country.** The X.500 two-character code for your country.

◆ **Location of the database.** By default, it's stored in \systemroot\system32\certlog.

◆ **Shared folder.** You can create a shared folder for certificate authorities information if the CA is not participating in an Active Directory (such as a standalone server).

The next critical piece of information is the methods for mapping certificates to user accounts. This can be done in the following ways:

◆ **User principal name mapping.** Through Active Directory, the user's principal name is matched with the certificate from the enterprise CA. As part of the creation of certification on an enterprise CA, users' principal names are included in the certificate.

◆ **One-to-one mapping.** One-to-one mapping is a single certificate mapped to a single user account.

◆ **Many-to-one mapping.** A bit more rare, but occasionally needed, is many-to-one mapping. Just as it names implies, this option allows you to map many certificates, from different CAs to one individual Windows 2000 account.

After a certificate is issued, it may need to be revoked. The reasons available for revoking a certificate include the following:

◆ Unspecified

◆ Key Compromise

◆ CA Compromise

◆ Affiliation Changed

◆ Superseded

◆ Cessation of Operation

The two important concepts in using encryption keys in conjunction with the EFS are

◆ **Removing the EFS Keys.** This is done to prevent unauthorized users from accessing the data while allowing authorized users the capability to access the data if the user is unavailable.

◆ **Restoring EFS Keys.** You will need to do this if you need to access the data on the system without access to the end user's account information.

The EFS is ideal for laptop users. By encrypting the data on the laptop and then removing the public and private keys, the data is secure should the computer be vandalized or stolen. To access the data, the private key is required. By removing the EFS keys from the laptop, you make it impossible for an intruder to gain access to the data simply by logging on to the laptop. The keys for the data should be stored elsewhere, such as on floppy disks.

This element of the book provides you with some general guidelines for preparing for a certification exam. It is organized into four sections. The first section addresses your learning style and how it affects your preparation for the exam. The second section covers your exam preparation activities and general study tips. This is followed by an extended look at the Microsoft Certification exams, including a number of specific tips that apply to the various Microsoft exam formats and question types. Finally, changes in Microsoft's testing policies, and how these might affect you, are discussed.

LEARNING STYLES

To better understand the nature of preparation for the test, it is important to understand learning as a process. You probably are aware of how you best learn new material. You may find that outlining works best for you, or, as a visual learner, you may need to "see" things. Whatever your learning style, test preparation takes place over time. Obviously, you shouldn't start studying for these exams the night before you take them; it is very important to understand that learning is a developmental process. Understanding it as a process helps you focus on what you know and what you have yet to learn.

Thinking about how you learn should help you recognize that learning takes place when you are able to match new information to old. You have some previous experience with computers and networking. Now you are preparing for this certification exam. Using this book, software, and supplementary materials will not just add incrementally to what you know; as you study, the organization of your knowledge actually restructures as you integrate new information into your existing knowledge base. This will lead you to a more comprehensive understanding of the tasks and concepts

Study and Exam Prep Tips

outlined in the objectives and of computing in general. Again, this happens as a result of a repetitive process rather than a singular event. Keep this model of learning in mind as you prepare for the exam, and you will make better decisions concerning what to study and how much more studying you need to do.

STUDY TIPS

There are many ways to approach studying just as there are many different types of material to study. However, the tips that follow should work well for the type of material covered on the certification exams.

Study Strategies

Although individuals vary in the ways they learn information, some basic principles of learning apply to everyone. You should adopt some study strategies that take advantage of these principles. One of these principles is that learning can be broken into various depths. Recognition (of terms, for example) exemplifies a more surface level of learning in which you rely on a prompt of some sort to elicit recall. Comprehension or understanding (of the concepts behind the terms, for example) represents a deeper level of learning. The ability to analyze a concept and apply your understanding of it in a new way represents a further depth of learning.

Your learning strategy should enable you to know the material at a level or two deeper than mere recognition. This will help you perform well on the exams. You will know the material so thoroughly that you can easily handle the recognition-level types of questions used in multiple-choice testing. You will also be able to apply your knowledge to solve new problems.

Macro and Micro Study Strategies

One strategy that can lead to this deeper learning includes preparing an outline that covers all the objectives and subobjectives for the particular exam you are working on. You should delve a bit further into the material and include a level or two of detail beyond the stated objectives and subobjectives for the exam. Then expand the outline by coming up with a statement of definition or a summary for each point in the outline.

An outline provides two approaches to studying. First, you can study the outline by focusing on the organization of the material. Work your way through the points and sub-points of your outline with the goal of learning how they relate to one another. For example, be sure you understand how each of the main objective areas is similar to and different from another. Then, do the same thing with the subobjectives; be sure you know which subobjectives pertain to each objective area and how they relate to one another.

Next, you can work through the outline, focusing on learning the details. Memorize and understand terms and their definitions, facts, rules and strategies, advantages and disadvantages, and so on. In this pass through the outline, attempt to learn detail rather than the big picture (the organizational information that you worked on in the first pass through the outline).

Research has shown that attempting to assimilate both types of information at the same time seems to interfere with the overall learning process. Separate your studying into these two approaches, and you will perform better on the exam.

Active Study Strategies

The process of writing down and defining objectives, subobjectives, terms, facts, and definitions promotes a more active learning strategy than merely reading the material. In human information-processing terms, writing forces you to engage in more active encoding of the information. Simply reading over it exemplifies more passive processing.

Next, determine whether you can apply the information you have learned by attempting to create examples and scenarios on your own. Think about how or where you could apply the concepts you are learning. Again, write down this information to process the facts and concepts in a more active fashion.

The hands-on nature of the step-by-step tutorials and exercises at the ends of the chapters provide further active learning opportunities that will reinforce concepts as well.

Common-Sense Strategies

Finally, you should also follow common-sense practices when studying. Study when you are alert, reduce or eliminate distractions, and take breaks when you become fatigued.

Pre-Testing Yourself

Pre-testing allows you to assess how well you are learning. One of the most important aspects of learning is what has been called "meta-learning." Meta-learning has to do with realizing when you know something well or when you need to study some more. In other words, you recognize how well or how poorly you have learned the material you are studying.

For most people, this can be difficult to assess objectively on their own. Practice tests are useful in that they reveal more objectively what you have learned and what you have not learned. You should use this information to guide review and further studying. Developmental learning takes place as you cycle through studying, assessing how well you have learned, then reviewing, and then assessing again until you feel you are ready to take the exam.

You may have noticed the practice exam included in this book. Use it as part of the learning process. The *ExamGear, Training Guide Edition* test simulation software included on the CD also provides you with an excellent opportunity to assess your knowledge.

You should set a goal for your pre-testing. A reasonable goal would be to score consistently in the 90-percent range.

See Appendix D, "Using the *ExamGear, Training Guide Edition* Software," for more explanation of the test simulation software.

EXAM PREP TIPS

Having mastered the subject matter, the final preparatory step is to understand how the exam will be presented. Make no mistake: A Microsoft Certified Professional (MCP) exam will challenge both your knowledge and your test-taking skills. This section starts with the basics of exam design, reviews a new type of exam format, and concludes with hints targeted to each of the exam formats.

The MCP Exam

Every MCP exam is released in one of three basic formats. What's being called exam format here is really little more than a combination of the overall exam structure and the presentation method for exam questions.

Understanding the exam formats is key to good preparation because the format determines the number of questions presented, the difficulty of those questions, and the amount of time allowed to complete the exam.

Each exam format uses many of the same types of questions. These types or styles of questions include several types of traditional multiple-choice questions, multiple-rating (or scenario-based) questions, and simulation-based questions. Some exams include other types of questions that ask you to drag and drop objects on the screen, reorder a list, or categorize things. Still other exams ask you to answer these types of questions in response to a case study you have read. It's important that you understand the types of questions you will be asked and the actions required to properly answer them.

The rest of this section addresses the exam formats and then tackles the question types. Understanding the formats and question types will help you feel much more comfortable when you take the exam.

Exam Format

As mentioned above, there are three basic formats for the MCP exams: the traditional fixed-form exam, the adaptive form, and the case study form. As its name implies, the fixed-form exam presents a fixed set of questions during the exam session. The adaptive form, however, uses only a subset of questions drawn from a larger pool during any given exam session. The case study form includes case studies that serve as the basis for answering the various types of questions.

Fixed-Form

A fixed-form computerized exam is based on a fixed set of exam questions. The individual questions are presented in random order during a test session. If you take the same exam more than once, you won't necessarily see the exact same questions. This is because two or three final forms are typically assembled for every fixed-form exam Microsoft releases. These are usually labeled Forms A, B, and C.

The final forms of a fixed-form exam are identical in terms of content coverage, number of questions, and allotted time, but the questions are different. You may notice, however, that some of the same questions appear on, or rather are shared among, different final forms. When questions are shared among multiple final forms of an exam, the percentage of sharing is generally small. Many final forms share no questions, but some older exams may have a 10–15 percent duplication of exam questions on the final exam forms.

Fixed-form exams also have a fixed time limit in which you must complete the exam. The *ExamGear, Training Guide Edition* software on the CD-ROM that accompanies this book provides fixed-form exams.

Finally, the score you achieve on a fixed-form exam, which is always reported for MCP exams on a scale of 0 to 1,000, is based on the number of questions you answer correctly. The passing score is the same for all final forms of a given fixed-form exam.

The typical format for the fixed-form exam is as follows:

◆ 50–60 questions.

◆ 75–90 minute testing time.

◆ Question review is allowed, including the opportunity to change your answers.

Adaptive Form

An adaptive-form exam has the same appearance as a fixed-form exam, but its questions differ in quantity and process of selection. Although the statistics of adaptive testing are fairly complex, the process is concerned with determining your level of skill or ability with the exam subject matter. This ability assessment begins with the presentation of questions of varying levels of difficulty and ascertaining at what difficulty level you can reliably answer them. Finally, the ability assessment determines whether that ability level is above or below the level required to pass that exam.

Examinees at different levels of ability will see quite different sets of questions. Examinees who demonstrate little expertise with the subject matter will continue to be presented with relatively easy questions. Examinees who demonstrate a high level of expertise will be presented progressively more difficult questions. Individuals of both levels of expertise may answer the same number of questions correctly, but because the higher-expertise examinee can correctly answer more difficult questions, he or she will receive a higher score and is more likely to pass the exam.

The typical design for the adaptive form exam is as follows:

◆ 20–25 questions.

◆ 90 minute testing time (although this is likely to be reduced to 45–60 minutes in the near future).

◆ Question review is not allowed, providing no opportunity for you to change your answers.

The Adaptive-Exam Process

Your first adaptive exam will be unlike any other testing experience you have had. In fact, many examinees have difficulty accepting the adaptive testing process because they feel that they were not provided the opportunity to adequately demonstrate their full expertise.

You can take consolation in the fact that adaptive exams are painstakingly put together after months of data gathering and analysis and that adaptive exams are just as valid as fixed-form exams. The rigor introduced through the adaptive testing methodology means that there is nothing arbitrary about the exam items you'll see. It is also a more efficient means of testing, requiring less time to conduct and complete than traditional fixed-form exams.

As you can see in Figure 1, a number of statistical measures drive the adaptive examination process. The measure most immediately relevant to you is the ability estimate. Accompanying this test statistic are the standard error of measurement, the item characteristic curve, and the test information curve.

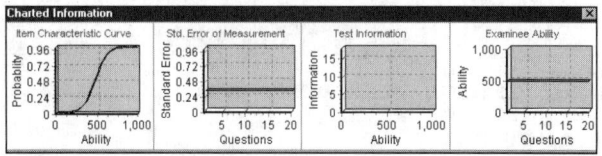

FIGURE 1
Microsoft's adaptive testing demonstration program.

The standard error, which is the key factor in determining when an adaptive exam will terminate, reflects the degree of error in the exam ability estimate. The item characteristic curve reflects the probability of a correct response relative to examinee ability. Finally, the test information statistic provides a measure of the information contained in the set of questions the examinee has answered, again relative to the ability level of the individual examinee.

When you begin an adaptive exam, the standard error has already been assigned a target value below which it must drop for the exam to conclude. This target value reflects a particular level of statistical confidence in the process. The examinee ability is initially set to the mean possible exam score (500 for MCP exams).

As the adaptive exam progresses, questions of varying difficulty are presented. Based on your pattern of responses to these questions, the ability estimate is recalculated. At the same time, the standard error estimate is refined from its first estimated value of one toward the target value. When the standard error reaches its target value, the exam is terminated. Thus, the more consistently you answer questions of the same degree of difficulty, the more quickly the standard error estimate drops, and the fewer questions you will end up seeing during the exam session. This situation is depicted in Figure 2.

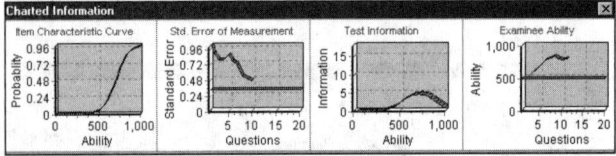

FIGURE 2
The changing statistics in an adaptive exam.

As you might suspect, one good piece of advice for taking an adaptive exam is to treat every exam question as if it were the most important. The adaptive scoring algorithm attempts to discover a pattern of responses that reflects some level of proficiency with the subject matter. Incorrect responses almost guarantee that additional questions must be answered (unless, of course, you get every question wrong). This is because the scoring algorithm must adjust to information that is not consistent with the emerging pattern.

Case Study Form

The case study-based format first appeared with the advent of the 70-100 exam (Solution Architectures). The questions in the case study format are not the independent entities that they are in the fixed and adaptive formats. Instead, questions are tied to a case study, a long scenario-like description of an information technology situation. As the test taker, your job is to extract from the case study the information that needs to be integrated with your understanding of Microsoft technology. The idea is that a case study will provide you with a situation that is more like a "real life" problem situation than the other formats provide.

The case studies are presented as "testlets." These are sections within the exam in which you read the case study, then answer 10 to 15 questions that apply to the case study. When you finish that section, you move onto another testlet with another case study and its associated questions. There may be as many as five of these testlets that compose the overall exam. You will be given more time to complete such an exam because it takes time to read through the cases and analyze them. You may have as much as three hours to complete the exam—and you may need all of it. The case studies are always available through a linking button while you are in a testlet. However, once you leave a testlet, you cannot come back to it.

Figure 3 provides an illustration of part of a case study.

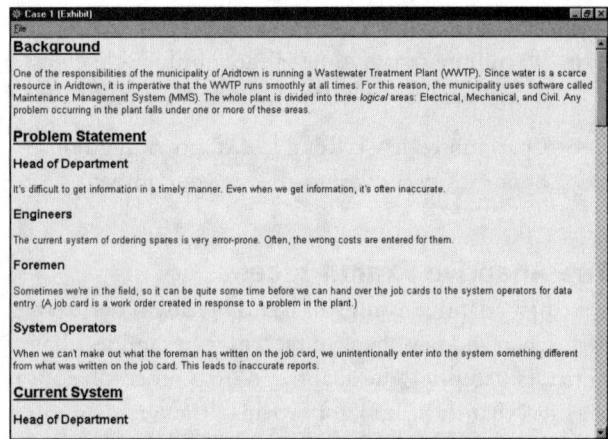

FIGURE 3
An example of a case study.

Question Types

A variety of question types can appear on MCP exams. Examples of many of the various types appear in this book and the *ExamGear, Training Guide Edition* software. We have attempted to cover all the types that were available at the time of this writing. Most of the question types discussed in the following sections can appear in each of the three exam formats.

The typical MCP exam question is based on the idea of measuring skills or the ability to complete tasks. Therefore, most of the questions are written so as to present you with a situation that includes a role (such as a system administrator or technician), a technology environment (100 computers running Windows 98 on a Windows 2000 Server network), and a problem to be solved (the user can connect to services on the LAN, but not the intranet). The answers indicate actions that you might take to solve the problem or create setups or environments that would function correctly from the start. Keep this in mind as you read the questions on the exam. You may encounter some questions that just call for you to regurgitate facts, but these will be relatively few and far between.

In the following sections we will look at the different question types.

Multiple-Choice Questions

Despite the variety of question types that now appear in various MCP exams, the multiple-choice question is still the basic building block of the exams. The multiple-choice question comes in three varieties:

◆ **Regular multiple-choice.** Also referred to as an alphabetic question, it asks you to choose one answer as correct.

◆ **Multiple-answer multiple-choice.** Also referred to as a multi-alphabetic question, this version of a multiple-choice question requires you to choose two or more answers as correct. Typically, you are told precisely the number of correct answers to choose.

◆ **Enhanced multiple-choice.** This is simply a regular or multiple-answer question that includes a graphic or table to which you must refer to answer the question correctly.

Examples of such questions appear at the end of each chapter.

Multiple-Rating Questions

These questions are often referred to as scenario questions. Similar to multiple-choice questions, they offer more extended descriptions of the computing environment and a problem that needs to be solved. Required and desired optional results of the problem-solving are specified, as well as a solution. You are then asked to judge whether the actions taken in the solution are likely to bring about all or part of the required and desired optional results. There is, typically, only one correct answer.

You may be asking yourself, "What is multiple about multiple-rating questions?" The answer is that rather than having multiple answers, the question itself may be repeated in the exam with only minor variations in the required results, optional results, or solution introduced to create "new" questions. Read these different versions very carefully; the differences can be subtle.

Examples of these types of questions appear at the end of the chapters.

Simulation Questions

Simulation-based questions reproduce the look and feel of key Microsoft product features for the purpose of testing. The simulation software used in MCP exams has been designed to look and act, as much as possible, just like the actual product. Consequently, answering simulation questions in an MCP exam entails completing one or more tasks just as if you were using the product itself.

The format of a typical Microsoft simulation question consists of a brief scenario or problem statement, along with one or more tasks that you must complete to solve the problem. An example of a simulation question for MCP exams is shown in the following section.

A Typical Simulation Question

It sounds obvious, but your first step when you encounter a simulation question is to carefully read the question (see Figure 4). Do not go straight to the simulation application! You must assess the problem that's presented and identify the conditions that make up the problem scenario. Note the tasks that must be performed or outcomes that must be achieved to answer the question, and then review any instructions you're given on how to proceed.

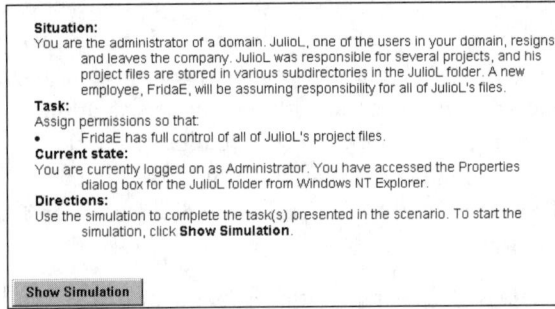

FIGURE 4
A typical MCP exam simulation question with directions.

The next step is to launch the simulator by using the button provided. After clicking the Show Simulation button, you will see a feature of the product, as shown in the dialog box in Figure 5. The simulation application will partially obscure the question text on many test center machines. Feel free to reposition the simulator and to move between the question text screen and

the simulator by using hotkeys or point-and-click navigation, or even by clicking the simulator's launch button again.

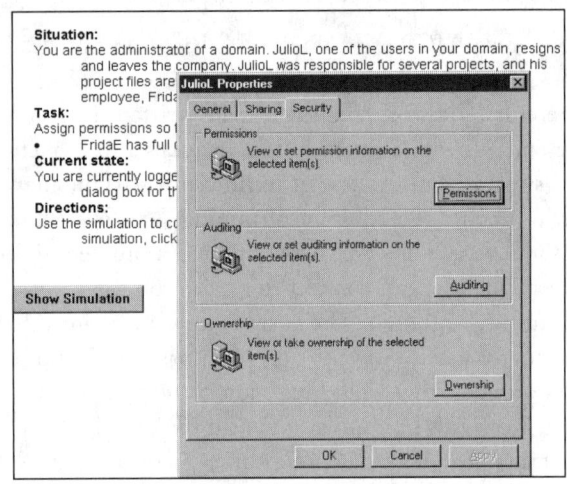

FIGURE 5
Launching the simulation application.

It is important for you to understand that your answer to the simulation question will not be recorded until you move on to the next exam question. This gives you the added capability of closing and reopening the simulation application (using the launch button) on the same question without losing any partial answer you may have made.

The third step is to use the simulator as you would the actual product to solve the problem or perform the defined tasks. Again, the simulation software is designed to function—within reason—just as the product does. But don't expect the simulator to reproduce product behavior perfectly. Most importantly, do not allow yourself to become flustered if the simulator does not look or act exactly like the product.

Figure 6 shows the solution to the example simulation problem.

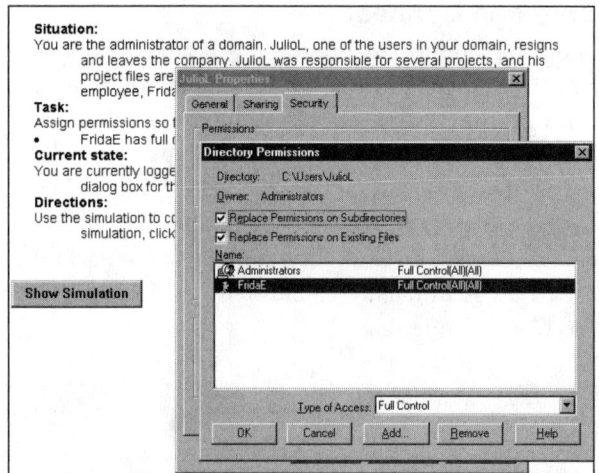

FIGURE 6
The solution to the simulation example.

Two final points will help you tackle simulation questions. First, respond only to what is being asked in the question; do not solve problems that you are not asked to solve. Second, accept what is being asked of you. You may not entirely agree with conditions in the problem statement, the quality of the desired solution, or the sufficiency of defined tasks to adequately solve the problem. Always remember that you are being tested on your ability to solve the problem as it is presented.

The solution to the simulation problem shown in Figure 6 perfectly illustrates both of those points. As you'll recall from the question scenario (refer to Figure 4), you were asked to assign appropriate permissions to a new user, Frida E. You were not instructed to make any other changes in permissions. Thus, if you were to modify or remove the administrator's permissions, this item would be scored wrong on an MCP exam.

Hot Area Question

Hot area questions call for you to click on a graphic or diagram in order to complete some task. You are asked a question that is similar to any other, but rather than clicking an option button or check box next to an answer, you click the relevant item in a screen shot or on a part of a diagram. An example of such an item is shown in Figure 7.

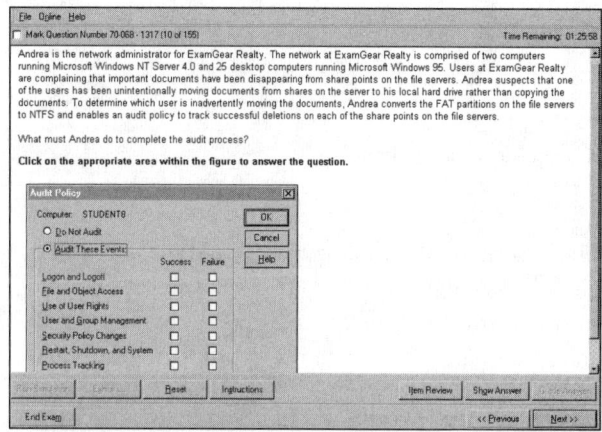

FIGURE 7
A typical hot area question.

Drag and Drop Style Questions

Microsoft has utilized two different types of drag and drop questions in exams. The first is a Select and Place question. The other is a Drop and Connect question. Both are covered in the following sections.

Select and Place

Select and Place questions typically require you to drag and drop labels on images in a diagram so as to correctly label or identify some portion of a network. Figure 8 shows you the actual question portion of a Select and Place item.

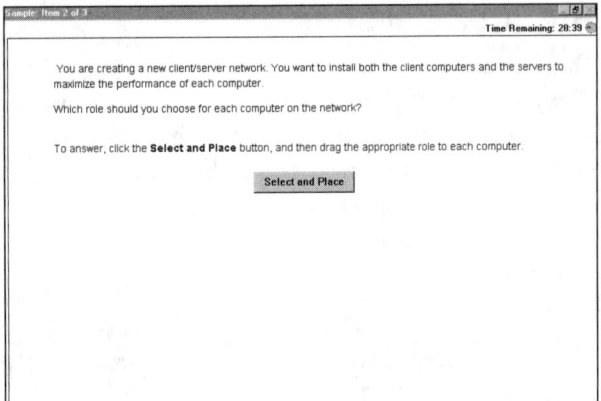

FIGURE 8
A Select and Place question.

Figure 9 shows the window you would see after you chose Select and Place. It contains the actual diagram in which you would select and drag the various server roles and match them with the appropriate computers.

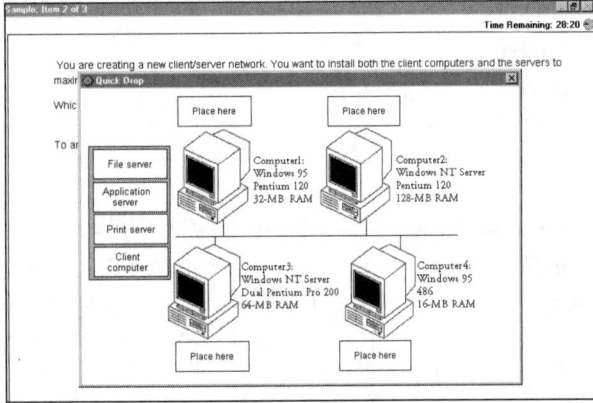

FIGURE 9
The window containing the diagram.

Drop and Connect

Drop and Connect questions provide a different spin on the drag and drop question. The question provides you with the opportunity to create boxes that you can label, as well as connectors of various types with which to link them. In essence, you are creating a model or diagram in order to answer the question. You might have to create a network diagram or a data model for a database system. Figure 10 illustrates the idea of a Drop and Connect question.

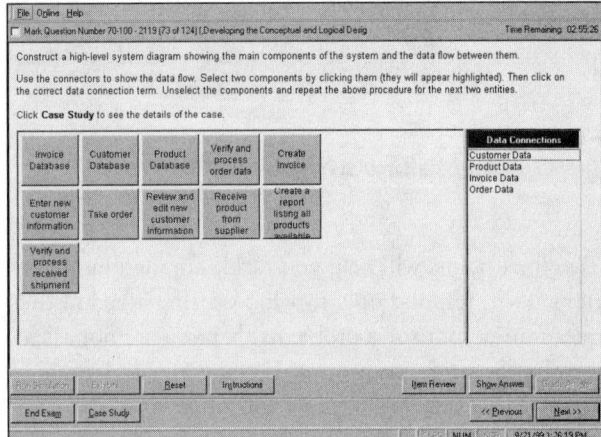

FIGURE 10
A Drop and Connect question.

Ordered List Questions

Ordered list questions simply require you to consider a list of items and place them in the proper order. You select items and then use a button to add them to a new list in the correct order. You have another button that you can use to remove the items in the new list in case you change your mind and want to reorder things. Figure 11 shows an ordered list item.

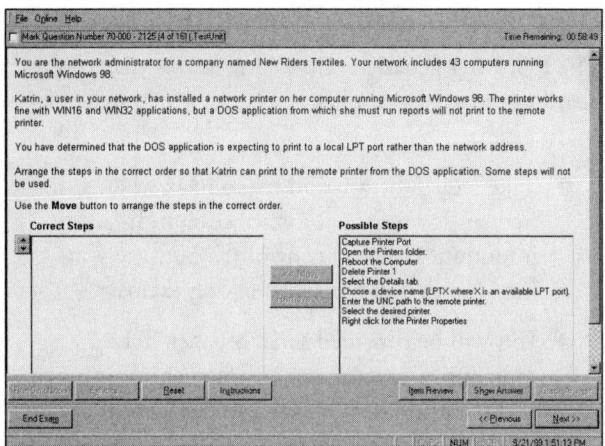

FIGURE 11
An ordered list question.

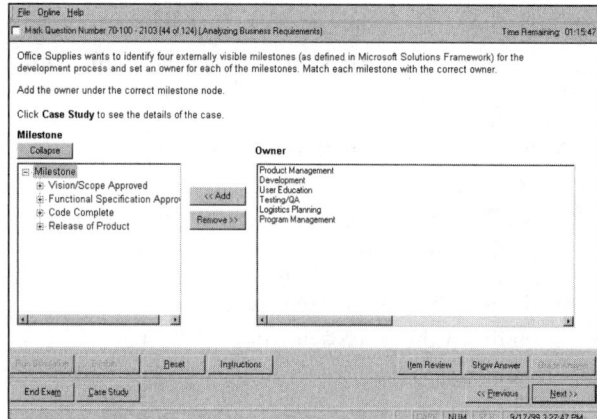

FIGURE 12
A tree question.

Tree Questions

Tree questions require you to think hierarchically and categorically. You are asked to place items from a list into categories that are displayed as nodes in a tree structure. Such questions might ask you to identify parent-child relationships in processes or the structure of keys in a database. You might also be required to show order within the categories, much as you would in an ordered list question. Figure 12 shows a typical tree question.

As you can see, Microsoft is making an effort to utilize question types that go beyond asking you to simply memorize facts. These question types force you to know how to accomplish tasks and understand concepts and relationships. Study so that you can answer these types of questions rather than those that simply ask you to recall facts.

Putting It All Together

Given all these different pieces of information, the task now is to assemble a set of tips that will help you successfully tackle the different types of MCP exams.

More Exam Preparation Tips

Generic exam-preparation advice is always useful. Tips include the following:

◆ Become familiar with the product. Hands-on experience is one of the keys to success on any MCP exam. Review the exercises and the Step by Steps in the book.

◆ Review the current exam-preparation guide on the Microsoft MCP Web site (www.microsoft.com/mcp/examinfo/exams.htm). The documentation Microsoft makes available over the Web identifies the skills every exam is intended to test.

◆ Memorize foundational technical details, but remember that MCP exams are generally heavier on problem solving and application of knowledge than on questions that require only rote memorization.

◆ Take any of the available practice tests. We recommend the one included in this book and the ones you can create using the *ExamGear* software on the CD-ROM. As a supplement to the material bound with this book, try the free practice tests available on the Microsoft MCP Web site.

◆ Look on the Microsoft MCP Web site for samples and demonstration items. These tend to be particularly valuable for one significant reason: They help you become familiar with new testing technologies before you encounter them on MCP exams.

During the Exam Session

The following generic exam-taking advice that you've heard for years also applies when you're taking an MCP exam:

◆ Take a deep breath and try to relax when you first sit down for your exam session. It is very important that you control the pressure you may (naturally) feel when taking exams.

◆ You will be provided scratch paper. Take a moment to write down any factual information and technical details that you committed to short-term memory.

◆ Carefully read all information and instruction screens. These displays have been put together to give you information relevant to the exam you are taking.

◆ Accept the non-disclosure agreement and preliminary survey as part of the examination process. Complete them accurately and quickly move on.

◆ Read the exam questions carefully. Reread each question to identify all relevant detail.

◆ Tackle the questions in the order in which they are presented. Skipping around won't build your confidence; the clock is always counting down (at least in the fixed form exams).

◆ Don't rush, but also don't linger on difficult questions. The questions vary in degree of difficulty. Don't let yourself be flustered by a particularly difficult or wordy question.

Fixed-Form Exams

Building from this basic preparation and test-taking advice, you also need to consider the challenges presented by the different exam designs. Because a fixed-form exam is composed of a fixed, finite set of questions, add these tips to your strategy for taking a fixed-form exam:

◆ Note the time allotted and the number of questions on the exam you are taking. Make a rough calculation of how many minutes you can spend on each question, and use this figure to pace yourself through the exam.

◆ Take advantage of the fact that you can return to and review skipped or previously answered questions. Record the questions you can't answer confidently on the scratch paper provided, noting the relative difficulty of each question. When you reach the end of the exam, return to the more difficult questions.

◆ If you have session time remaining after you complete all the questions (and if you aren't too fatigued!), review your answers. Pay particular attention to questions that seem to have a lot of detail or that require graphics.

◆ As for changing your answers, the general rule of thumb here is *don't*! If you read the question carefully and completely and you felt like you knew the right answer, you probably did. Don't second-guess yourself. If, as you check your answers, one clearly stands out as incorrect, however, of course you should change it. But if you are at all unsure, go with your first impression.

Adaptive Exams

If you are planning to take an adaptive exam, keep these additional tips in mind:

◆ Read and answer every question with great care. When you're reading a question, identify every relevant detail, requirement, or task you must perform and double-check your answer to be sure you have addressed every one of them.

◆ If you cannot answer a question, use the process of elimination to reduce the set of potential answers, and then take your best guess. Stupid mistakes invariably mean that additional questions will be presented.

◆ You cannot review questions and change answers. When you leave a question, whether you've answered it or not, you cannot return to it. Do not skip any question, either; if you do, it's counted as incorrect.

Case Study Exams

This new exam format calls for unique study and exam-taking strategies. When you take this type of exam, remember that you have more time than in a typical exam. Take your time and read the case study thoroughly. Use the scrap paper or whatever medium is provided to you to take notes, diagram processes, and actively seek out the important information. Work through each testlet as if each were an independent exam. Remember, you cannot go back after you have left a testlet. Refer to the case study as often as you need to, but do not use that as a substitute for reading it carefully initially and for taking notes.

FINAL CONSIDERATIONS

Finally, a number of changes in the MCP program will impact how frequently you can repeat an exam and what you will see when you do.

- ◆ Microsoft has instituted a new exam retake policy. The new rule is "two and two, then one and two." That is, you can attempt any exam twice with no restrictions on the time between attempts. But after the second attempt, you must wait two weeks before you can attempt that exam again. After that, you will be required to wait two weeks between subsequent attempts. Plan to pass the exam in two attempts or plan to increase your time horizon for receiving the MCP credential.

- ◆ New questions are being seeded into the MCP exams. After performance data is gathered on new questions, the examiners will replace older questions on all exam forms. This means that the questions appearing on exams will regularly change.

- ◆ Many of the current MCP exams will be republished in adaptive form. Prepare yourself for this significant change in testing; it is entirely likely that this will become the preferred MCP exam format for most exams. The exception to this may be the case study exams because the adaptive approach may not work with that format.

These changes mean that the brute-force strategies for passing MCP exams may soon completely lose their viability. So if you don't pass an exam on the first or second attempt, it is likely that the exam's form will change significantly by the next time you take it. It could be updated from fixed-form to adaptive, or it could have a different set of questions or question types.

Microsoft's intention is not to make the exams more difficult by introducing unwanted change, but to create and maintain valid measures of the technical skills and knowledge associated with the different MCP credentials. Preparing for an MCP exam has always involved not only studying the subject matter, but also planning for the testing experience itself. With the recent changes, this is now more true than ever.

This exam consists of 65 questions reflecting the material you have covered in the chapters. The questions are representative of the types that you should expect to see on the actual exam, but they are not intended to exactly match those on the exam.

Most of the questions do not require you simply to recall facts; they also require deduction on your part to come up with the best answer. Often, you are required to identify the best course of action to take in a given situation. Many of the questions require that you read them carefully and thoroughly before you attempt to answer them. It is strongly suggested that when you take this exam, you treat it just as you would the actual exam at the test center. Time yourself, read carefully, and answer all the questions to the best of your ability.

The answers to all questions appear in the section following the exam. Check your letter answers against those in the answer section, and then read the explanations provided. You may also want to return to the chapters in the book to review material associated with your incorrect answers.

Practice Exam

1. You are the network administrator for Sunshine Networks. You have noticed lately that you are receiving a larger number of Host Unreachable error messages. You believe that your routing tables are not accurate. What should you enable in Routing and Remote Access to prevent routing loops and count-to-infinity problems?

   A. Distance-vector routing

   B. Split horizon

   C. Poison reverse

   D. Topological database

2. You have installed DNS and configured your server as a cache-only server. Where does it store the zone information?

   A. In your %systemroot%\DNS directory.

   B. In your %systemroot%\system32\ DNS directory.

   C. The information is stored in Active Directory.

   D. Cache-only servers do not have any zone information.

3. You are the network administrator for JMS Technologies. You have a network with 100 computers running Windows 2000 Professional, 3 computers running Windows 2000 Server configured with Active Directory, DHCP, and DDNS. When your client computer obtains an IP address from the DHCP server, who registers the computer's hostname with the DNS server?

   A. The client computer

   B. The DHCP server

   C. The WINS server

   D. Active Directory

4. You are the WAN administrator for IVS Technologies. You are trying to decide what routing technology you should be using for your company. You finally decide to go with distance-vector routing. What is one of the major disadvantages of distance-vector routing?

   A. Slow convergence problems

   B. High overhead on your network

   C. Count-to-infinity problem

   D. Can connect to a maximum of only 15 hops

5. You are the network administrator for Long Beach Networks. Your network consists of 100 computers running Windows 95, 125 computers running Windows 98, and 240 computers running Windows 2000 Professional. All computers are located on the same network segment. Lynne, your supervisor, has asked you to automate the process of assigning IP addresses. What do you need to configure?

   A. Install DHCP and configure DNS integration.

   B. Install DHCP and configure a scope.

   C. Install DHCP and configure a superscope.

   D. Install DHCP and configure BOOTP.

6. You are the administrator of a small dental clinic and one of your sales representatives has just left the company. You would like to prevent him from retrieving some secure information. What is the best way of accomplishing this?

   A. Prevent him from gaining access to your certificate server.

   B. Stop the service on your certificate server until his account has been disabled.

   C. Revoke his certificate.

   D. There is nothing you can do until his certificate expires.

7. A small computer-training company has decided to install the DNS services on its network to replace the one currently supplied by its ISP. Your network currently consists of 300 Windows 2000 Professional computers.

   You are hired as a setup consultant to provide a solution for this small training company.

   Required Results:

   Provide an easy way to configure your client computers with the IP address of your DNS server.

   Provide a backup strategy to ensure that your client computers will always have a DNS server available.

   Optional Desired Results:

   Your network must be able to resolve FQDNs to IP addresses.

   Your network must be able to resolve IP addresses to hostnames.

   Update the client computer information in DNS automatically.

   Proposed Solution:

   Install Windows 2000 Advanced Server and configure it with DNS and Active Directory.

   You install and configure a second DNS server. This server will be configured as secondary master to your first DNS server.

   In your MMC DNS applet, you configure a forward lookup zone.

   In your MMC DNS applet, you configure a reverse lookup zone.

   Configure your client computers to use DHCP.

   Your DHCP server has been configured to assign an IP address with a subnet mask, a default gateway, and the IPs of your DNS server.

   Which result(s) does the proposed solution produce?

   A. The proposed solution produces all the required results and all the optional desired results.

   B. The proposed solution produces one of the required results and all the optional desired results.

   C. The proposed solution produces all the required results and one of the optional results.

   D. The proposed solution produces all the required results and two of the optional desired results.

   E. The proposed solution produces none of the required results and none of the optional desired results.

8. You are part of the team of network administrators for SunShine Networks. Your task is to segment your Class C IP address into three subnets. You have been assigned the IP address of 210.115.64.0. You must allow for the number of networks to increase. The maximum number of hosts per subnet will never surpass 14 hosts. What subnet mask would allow you to segment your network and allow for the required growth?

   A. 255.255.255.224

   B. 255.255.255.240

   C. 255.255.255.248

   D. 255.255.255.255

9. You are the senior network administrator for JMS Technologies. Your client complains that the company lost all network connectivity to the network after installing some new services. He also mentions that they might have misconfigured a setting. When you ask what services they installed, he answered that they are not certain.

To try to troubleshoot the server, you type **ipconfig /all** at a command prompt and receive the following. What could be the problem?

IP address	192.168.0.1
Subnet mask	255.255.0.0
Default gateway	192.168.0.1
DNS server	192.168.0.1
WINS server	192.168.0.1

A. Your IP address is the same as the default gateway.

B. They installed ICS by mistake.

C. They installed NAT by mistake.

D. Your DNS server is the same as your default gateway.

10. You are the administrator of a very large multi-national organization. During the process of configuring your network, you have installed a Windows 2000 server and configured NAT on it to secure your network. Your users, however, complain that they cannot play their games across the server. What could be the problem?

A. You need to configure a custom application for inbound access and open the proper ports.

B. You need to configure a custom application for outbound access and open the proper ports.

C. You need to configure a custom application for inbound access and allow the proper IP address.

D. You need to configure a custom application for outbound access and allow the proper IP address.

E. NAT does not support games.

11. You are the network supervisor for CMS Networks. Your network consists of 100 computers running Windows 2000 Professional, four computers running Windows 2000 Server, and two computers running NetWare 5.1 Server. You are trying to configure ICS on your server, but you are not able to install the ICS component. What could explain why you don't have the option to install ICS?

A. Your IP address is not set to 192.168.0.1.

B. You have configured your DNS server.

C. You have not installed your DHCP server.

D. You have not installed your dial-up connection.

12. You are the network administrator for JMS Technologies and you are trying to determine what settings (in addition to an IP address with your DHCP server) can be assigned to client computers running Windows 2000 Professional. Please select all that apply.

A. The IP address of your DNS server

B. The IP address of your DHCP server

C. The IP address of your file server

D. The IP address of your default gateway

E. The IP address of your Active Directory server

13. Your supervisor has just asked you for some advice to configure the new computers that will be arriving next week. He mentions to you that you will be receiving 30 new Compaq computers for the sales department. You will also be receiving 25 new IBM computers for the marketing department. As the network administrator, you are aware that these two departments are on the

same physical network but will require different TCP/IP configurations. What component of Windows 2000 Server would help you in configuring the different settings?

A. DNS services

B. Active Directory

C. DHCP services

D. Active Directory with policies

14. You are the setup technician for a national training center. You are in the process of discussing some network concepts with one of your co-workers and he is having some difficulty understanding the differences between DNS and WINS. If you are trying to explain WINS, what file does WINS replace?

A. LMHOST

B. HOST

C. LMHOST.SAM

D. HOST.DNS

15. You are the senior instructor for a training center, and you are trying to explain some concepts to your students. During the DNS module, you are trying to explain each part of an FQDN. Which identifies the host portion of Carolyne.training.pbsc.com?

A. Carolyne

B. Training

C. Pbsc

D. Com

16. You are the network administrator for IVS Networks. Your clients complain that they cannot connect to www.newriders.com. You go to your DNS server to determine what the problem could

be. What is the logical order that the DNS server will use to resolve FQDN?

A. Root server—cache server

B. Cache server—zone server

C. Zone server—cache server

D. Cache server—root server

17. You are the network administrator for Balzac Petroleum. You need to manually add one record to your DNS server. What type of record do you need to add if you want to add an alias to your DNS server?

A. A record

B. MINFO record

C. CNAME record

D. PTR record

18. You are the senior instructor for a training center. During a discussion with your colleagues about FQDN names, this question was asked: What would you say is the maximum number of characters for a node in an FQDN?

A. 43 characters

B. 63 characters

C. 255 characters

D. 512 characters

19. A small computer-training company has decided to install the DNS services on its network to replace the one currently supplied by its ISP. Your network currently consists of 300 computers running Windows 98 and 40 computers running Windows 2000 Professional.

You are hired as a setup consultant to provide a solution for this small training company.

Required Results:

Provide an easy way to configure your client computers with the IP address of your DNS server.

Provide a backup strategy to ensure that your client's computers will always have a DNS server available.

Optional Desired Results:

Your network must be able to resolve FQDN to IP addresses.

Your network must be able to resolve IP addresses to hostnames.

Update the client's information in DNS automatically.

Proposed Solution:

Install Windows 2000 Advanced Server and configure it with DNS and Active Directory.

You install and configure a second DNS server. This server will be configured as secondary master to your first DNS server.

In your MMC DNS applet, you configure a forward lookup zone.

In your MMC DNS applet, you configure a reverse lookup zone.

Configure your client computers with a static IP, a default gateway, and a subnet mask.

Which result(s) does the proposed solution produce?

A. The proposed solution produces all the required results and all the optional desired results.

B. The proposed solution produces one of the required results and all the optional desired results.

C. The proposed solution produces all the required results and one of the optional results.

D. The proposed solution produces all the required results and none of the optional desired results.

E. The proposed solution produces none of the required results and none of the optional desired results.

20. The Windows 2000 Professional client computer will receive a DHCPNack broadcast message from the DHCP server after which of the following events?

A. Successfully receiving a TCP/IP address from the DHCP server.

B. Unsuccessfully receiving a TCP/IP address from the DHCP server.

C. Receiving a TCP/IP lease offer from the DHCP server.

D. Unsuccessfully receiving a TCP/IP lease offer from the DHCP server.

21. You are the network administrator for Balzac Petroleum. You currently have a supernetted network and would like to simplify the management of your DHCP. What component should you configure in DHCP?

A. Scope

B. Superscope

C. Multicast scope

D. BOOTP scope

22. You are the network administrator for Balzac Petroleum. You have just installed and configured your DHCP server. After the installation, the wizard asked you to activate the scope and you did. Staff from your company are complaining, however, that they are not obtaining any IP addresses. What could be the problem?

A. You did not activate the server.

B. You were not authorized to activate the scope; only administrators can activate the scope.

C. You did not authorize the server.

D. Your scope must be misconfigured.

23. You are the administrator of a very large multinational organization You are getting some error messages from your DHCP server. What counter in Performance console would display the number of DHCPOffer messages sent per second by the DHCP server to a client computer?

   A. Offers/sec

   B. Discover/sec

   C. Ack/sec

   D. DHCPAck/sec

24. You are the network administrator for the ShoeBox Shoe company. The corporation is running a routed network with a centrally located Windows 2000 DHCP server. The server is able to issue addresses to users on the local segment but cannot issue addresses to any of the sites that are across a router. What is the most probable cause of this problem?

   A. The DHCP Forwarder service is not enabled on the DHCP server.

   B. The BOOTP Forwarder service is not enabled on the DHCP server.

   C. The DHCP Forwarder service is not enabled on the routers.

   D. The BOOTP Forwarder service is not enabled on the routers.

25. You are the network administrator for Youppi Bear Networks. You are preparing for an upgrade on your network and you are trying to decide whether you should install NAT or ICS. Isabelle, your supervisor, mentioned that some features of ICS are not included in NAT. What advantages would you consider that are supported by ICS and that are not supported with NAT?

   A. To be able to conduct NetMeeting calls

   B. To be able to play Directplay games

   C. To be able to MAP network drives across the connection

   D. To be able to register with an Internet Locator Service

   E. To be able to print to the other side of the network

26. You are the network supervisor for Balzac Candies. You have just installed and configured NAT on your Windows 2000 server, and you would like to monitor the usage of your server. However, no statistics appear in Event Viewer. What could the problem be?

   A. You have not enabled the counters in Routing and Remote Access console.

   B. You do not use Event Viewer to monitor NAT; you must use Performance Monitor.

   C. There is no counter available for NAT.

   D. You have not enabled the counters in Performance Monitor.

27. You are the administrator of a very large multinational organization. You have started to read about the new functionality of DNS. What is the new type of replication supported in Windows 2000 DNS?

   A. IXFR

   B. AXFR

   C. FRIX

   D. FRAX

28. You are the network administrator for Balzac Petroleum. You need to explain to your colleagues how a digital certificate works. How would you explain it?

   A. Digital certificates use a public key encryption and decryption for security.

   B. Digital certificates use a private key encryption and decryption for security.

   C. Digital certificates use a public/private key encryption and decryption for security.

   D. Digital certificates use EFS for security.

29. You are the network administrator for JMS Technologies. After installing and configuring DNS on your Windows 2000 server, you set up an Active Directory-integrated zone. Where does it store the zone information?

   A. In your %systemroot%\DNS directory.

   B. In your %systemroot%\system32\ DNS directory.

   C. The information is stored in Active Directory.

   D. The information is stored in cache.

30. You have just been promoted and are now in charge of a new task force in your corporation. Your primary mandate is security. You must ensure that information stored on laptops is secure under every possible scenario. What would be the most secure process?

   A. Implement EFS and store the recovery key on a smart card.

   B. Implement NTFS security for local information.

   C. Implement EFS on all local files.

   D. Implement certificate services on your domain.

31. You are the network administrator for Savage Plumbing and Heating. The employees spend a majority of their time surfing the Internet. To speed up the surfing process, you configure a cache-only server. What would you qualify as the most important resource on that server?

   A. The speed and type of the hard drive

   B. The speed of the network adapter card

   C. The processor speed

   D. RAM

32. As a junior network administrator, you are trying to troubleshoot one of your DNS servers. It seems that your computers running Windows 2000 Professional have not registered dynamically with your DNS server. You would like to force these computers to register with DNS. What should you do?

   A. Get the user to reboot the system.

   B. At the command prompt, type `ipconfig /renew`.

   C. At the command prompt, type `ipconfig /registerdns`.

   D. At the command prompt, type `ipconfig /register`.

33. You have a network with 100 computers running Windows 2000 Professional and 3 computers running Windows 2000 Server configured with Active Directory, DHCP, and DDNS. When your client computers obtain an IP address from the DHCP server, who registers the computers' "A" names with the DNS server?

   A. The client computer

   B. The DHCP server

   C. The WINS server

   D. Active Directory

34. You are the network administrator for New Riders Publishing. You are trying to explain DNS and reverse lookup zone to your co-workers. What would you mention that reverse lookup-zone allows users to resolve?

    A. An IP address to a hostname

    B. A hostname to an IP address

    C. A hostname to a MAC

    D. A hostname to an FQDN

35. You are the LAN administrator for the OUI Find-em detective agency. You would like to be able to verify some entries on your DNS server. What utility would you recommend using?

    A. The Properties dialog box of your DNS server in your MMC.

    B. NSLOOKUP at a command prompt.

    C. IPCONFIG at a command prompt.

    D. Event Viewer.

36. You are the network administrator for New Riders Publishing. You want to ensure that you are backward compatible because you have 200 computers running Windows 95 on your network. What service is required to resolve NetBIOS names to IP addresses?

    A. WINS

    B. DNS

    C. DHCP

    D. BOOTP

37. You are the network administrator for New Riders Publishing. You are trying to eliminate broadcast traffic on your network. To help you in this process, you install and configure a WINS server. However, you still have 50 computers that are non-WINS client computers on your network. You would like these computers to be able to use WINS to resolve some static entries in your WINS database. What component must you configure?

    A. BOOTP relay

    B. WINS Proxy

    C. WINS properties to accept non-WINS client computers to query your WINS server

    D. Active Directory

    E. DNS services

38. You are a network administrator for the RollUp YoYo company. You have 200 computers running Windows 2000 Professional. Of those, 30 are laptops that need to be able to dial in to your network at night. You configure and install RRAS on one of your computers running Windows 2000 Advanced Server configured with Active Directory and running in native mode. You have configured a number of policies to secure your server and allow access. The users still complain that they cannot access any information. What could be the problem?

    A. RRAS does not support dial-in.

    B. You have some conflicting policies and the first one applied refuses them access.

    C. You did not enable MS-CHAP.

    D. You did not modify the default dial-in policy.

39. Vincent is the senior technical instructor for a training center, and he is trying to explain to his peers over lunch where the remote access policies of RRAS are stored on the network. Where would he say that they are stored?

    A. Remote access policies are stored in the user properties in Active Directory.

B. Remote access policies are stored in the computer properties in Active Directory.

C. Remote access policies are stored on the root server in Active Directory.

D. Remote access policies are stored individually on every RRAS server.

40. You are the network administrator for JMS Technologies. You are in the process of configuring your DHCP server for your client computers. Where would you configure the node type to H-node if you want your client computers to use the WINS server?

A. In the properties of your WINS server

B. In the properties of your DHCP server

C. In the properties of your DNS server

D. In the policy files in Active Directory

E. In the DHCP scope options.

41. You are the network administrator for the ShoeBox Shoe company and you are trying to eliminate broadcast traffic on your network. What node type configuration will force the client computers to query the WINS server to resolve the IP to a NetBIOS name before it issues a broadcast on your network?

A. The B-node will first query the WINS server.

B. The H-node will first query the WINS server.

C. The P-node will first query the WINS server.

D. The W-node will first query the WINS server.

42. You are the network administrator for the ShoeBox Shoe company. During the process of configuring your WINS server, you would like some information on WINS replication. What setting of WINS server allows for one server to send notification to other WINS partners when a certain amount of changes have occurred?

A. Configure for a push partner on the Advanced tab of your WINS console.

B. Configure for a pull partner on the Advanced tab of your WINS console.

C. Configure for a push partner on the Settings tab of your WINS console.

D. Configure for a pull partner on the Settings tab of your WINS console.

43. As the administrator of a small legal firm, you would like to get certain statistics on your WINS server. You would like to find out the last time it replicated, the last periodic scavenging, and the number of queries it resolved. Where would you go to easily retrieve all this information?

A. By using Performance console

B. In the application log of Event Viewer

C. In the log of Event Viewer

D. By selecting the server statistics on the Action menu of your WINS server icon in MMC

44. You are the network administrator for the Winni House. You have noticed that your network activity has increased today. When using Network Monitor, you notice that all your computers running Windows 2000 are issuing broadcasts. In the Event Viewer log files on your WINS server, you notice error messages reporting that the WINS database is corrupted. You would like to restore your WINS.mdb file that your WINS server created automatically. Where would you find this file?

A. In the %systemroot%\WINS directory.

B. In the %systemroot%\system\WINS directory.

C. In the %systemroot%\system32\WINS directory.

D. By default, the system does not create the file until you select where to back up the file.

45. You are the administrator of a small dental clinic, and you would like to view certain statistics in Performance console of your WINS server. What information would be returned when viewing info on the queries/sec counter?

    A. The rate at which queries are being received

    B. The total number of queries received

    C. The number of successful queries per second

    D. The amount of time it takes on average to resolve a query

46. As the administrator of a small legal firm, you are in the process of converting some IP addresses from decimal to binary. What would be the binary value of 209.168.241.158?

    A. 11010001.10101000.11110001.10011110

    B. 11001001.10101000.11110001.10011110

    C. 11010001.10101000.11101001.10011110

    D. 11010001.10101010.11110001.10011110

47. As the administrator of a big construction company, you are in the process of converting some IP addresses from binary to decimal. What would be the decimal value of 11001100.10101110.00011101.11101010?

    A. 204.176.29.234

    B. 198.174.29.234

    C. 204.174.29.234

    D. 204.174.29.240

48. You are the network administrator for CMS Technologies. You are in the process of configuring your security for your RRAS server. You need to select the protocols that use PPP to provide the original envelope for the data. Select all the correct answers.

    A. PPTP

    B. L2TP

    C. IPSEC

    D. EAP

49. You have just been promoted to the Web designer for a training facility. One of your first duties is to allow your sales agents to retrieve files on your FTP server on your network. Your sales team complains that they cannot connect to the FTP server. What could be the problem?

    A. You need to configure a custom application for inbound access and open the proper ports.

    B. You need to configure a custom application for outbound access and open the proper ports.

    C. You need to configure a custom application for inbound access and allow the proper IP address.

    D. You need to configure a custom application for outbound access and allow the proper IP address.

50. As the administrator of a small legal firm, you are trying to find out additional information from your colleagues about RRAS. During a lunch-and-learn session one day, one of your peers is explaining smart card authentication. What protocol supports smart card authentication?

    A. PPTP

    B. L2TP

    C. IPSEC

    D. EAP

51. You are the network administrator for GasUp Petroleum. All your sales representatives need to dial in to access resources on your network. The problem you are having is that different users need different rights. How can you address this issue?

    A. Create a different remote access policy for the different users.

    B. You will have to configure multiple RRAS servers with different local policies and get the different groups to dial in to their respective servers.

    C. Create local policies with the policy editor.

    D. It cannot be done. All dial-in users will have the same rights.

52. You are the network administrator for IVS Technologies. You are in the process of discussing some network concepts with one of your co-workers, and he is having some difficulty understanding the differences between DNS and WINS. If you are trying to explain DNS, what file does DNS replace?

    A. LMHOST

    B. HOST

    C. LMHOST.SAM

    D. HOST.DNS

53. You are a network administrator for the RollUp YoYo company. Your supervisor has asked you to explain certificate servers to him. He wants to know what an Intermediary CA is. How would you explain an Intermediary CA?

    A. It replaces the root CA in the event of failure.

    B. It is responsible for issuing certificates to the child CA.

    C. It is responsible for issuing certificates to users in your domain.

    D. It is used only to revoke certificates from users.

54. You are a consultant for Champagne Glasses Corporation. You have been asked to simplify the process of configuring TCP/IP on all the client computers. The network consist of 40 computers running Windows 98 and 60 computers running Windows 2000 Professional. What service of Windows 2000 will help you in accomplishing your task?

    A. Install and configure DHCP

    B. Install and configure DNS

    C. Install and configure WINS

    D. Install and configure BOOTP

55. You are the network supervisor for Travel Travel Company. You are trying to determine whether you should implement certificates. Of the following, which are valid reasons for implementing certificates in your environment?

    A. Certificates ensure that incoming and outgoing data has not been compromised.

    B. Certificates ensure that the identity of individuals accessing some secure information is accurate.

    C. Certificates can be issued through Microsoft's Certificate Services.

    D. Certificates can be created only through a third-party vendor, such as VeriSign.

56. You are the network administrator for New Riders Publishing. You want to ensure that your network is backward compatible because you have 125 computers running Windows 95 on

your network. What service is required to resolve hostnames to IP addresses?

A. WINS

B. DNS

C. DHCP

D. BOOTP

57. You are a senior consultant for a local firm and a large local bank has called you for some questions they have about certificates. They would like to know to whom can they assign certificates. Select all the correct answers.

A. Individuals can receive certificates.

B. Organizations can receive certificates.

C. Routers can receive certificates.

D. DNS entries can receive certificates.

58. You are the network administrator for a local nursing home and you have 200 computers running Windows 2000 Professional. Of those, 30 are laptops that need to be able to dial in to your network at night. You configure and install RRAS on one of your computers running Windows 2000 Advanced Server configured with Active Directory and running in native mode. The users still complain that they cannot access any information. What could be the problem?

A. RRAS does not support dial-in.

B. You have some conflicting policies and the first one that they apply refuses them access.

C. You did not enable MS-CHAP.

D. You did not modify the default dial-in policy.

59. You are the network supervisor for JMS Technologies. Your network has 80 computers running Windows 2000 Professional, 8 computers running Windows 2000 servers, 2 computers running NetWare 3.11 servers, and 2 servers running NetWare 4.11. You have installed NWLink and CSNW on all your client computers, but they still cannot connect to the 3.11 servers. What could be the problem?

A. You did not configure NWLink with manual frame type detection.

B. You did not configure NWLink with auto frame type detection.

C. You must install GSNW on all your servers before clients will be able to connect.

D. Your NetWare server needs a patch before Windows 2000 client computers can connect.

60. You are part of the team of network administrators for SunShine Networks. Your task is to segment your Class B IP address in 20 different subnets. You have been assigned the IP address of 145.65.0.0. You must allow for the number of networks to increase. The maximum number of hosts per subnet will never surpass 950 hosts. What subnet mask would enable you to segment your network and allow for the required growth?

A. 255.255.255.252

B. 255.255.0.0

C. 255.255.240.0

D. 255.255.252.0

61. You are the network administrator for Sunshine Networks. You have noticed lately that you are receiving a larger number of Host Unreachable error messages. Also, a number of your hosts do not seem to get routed appropriately. You start Network Monitor to capture network traffic, but you don't seem to be capturing all the network traffic. When you view the capture, you see only the packet sent to and from your own computer. What could be the problem?

   A. You have not installed the network component on all your servers.

   B. Your network adapter is not running in promiscuous mode.

   C. You have not enabled RIP on your network adapter.

   D. You must have installed the wrong network adapter driver for your NIC. Just reinstall the driver and redo the capture.

62. You are the WAN administrator for CMS Technologies. Your network consist of 50 Windows NT 4 servers and 10 Windows 2000 Advanced servers. Some of your NT 4 servers are configured as routers. You have just started to configure some of your Windows 2000 servers as routers, but you are having some problems. Your new routers cannot communicate with your old routers. You confirm that they are both configured to use RIP. What could be the problem?

   A. You have to configure RIP to use broadcast, not multicast.

   B. You will need to install and configure OSPF.

   C. The RIP protocol does not propagate more than 15 hops.

   D. You need to add an entry in your routing tables to point to your old routers.

63. Vinni, the senior MCSE in your company, is explaining to you some of the differences between using PPTP and L2TP to create some VPNs on your network. Select all the correct explanations about PPTP and L2TP.

   A. L2TP requires an IP-based transit internetwork.

   B. L2TP supports header compression.

   C. PPTP supports header compression.

   D. L2TP supports tunnel authentication.

   E. L2TP requires IPSEC for encryption.

64. You are the WAN administrator for JMS Technologies. You are trying to decide what routing technology you should be using for your company. You finally decide to go with distance-vector routing. You are aware that one of the major problems with distance-vector routing is the count to infinity. What are some avoidance mechanisms that could be implemented to prevent any problems? Select the correct answer(s).

   A. Split horizon

   B. Split horizon with poison reverse

   C. Triggered update

   D. Link-state routing

65. You are the network administrator for JMS Technologies. You have just installed the DHCP service through the Control Panel's Add/Remove Programs. You now need to configure your DHCP to support a multicast scope. In the MMC, you right-click the server icon under DHCP. What option should you select to configure your scope?

   A. New scope

   B. New superscope

   C. New IP scope

   D. New multicast scope

ANSWERS TO EXAM QUESTIONS

1. **B.** Split horizon is a mechanism that prevents routing information from being sent back in the direction it was received. For more information, see Chapter 6, "Installing, Configuring, Managing, Monitoring, and Troubleshooting IP Routing in a Windows 2000 Network Infrastructure."

2. **D.** When you configure a DNS server as cache-only, it does not have any zone information. For more information, see Chapter 1, "Installing, Configuring, Managing, Monitoring, and Troubleshooting DNS in a Windows 2000 Network Infrastructure."

3. **B.** Windows 2000 client computers interact directly with the DNS server to update their A resource record. The DHCP server will update the PRT record for Windows 2000 client computers and both the A record and the PTR record for non-Windows 2000 client computers. For more information, see Chapter 1.

4. **C.** A and B could also be good answers, but the best answer is C. One of the major problems with distance-vector routing is the count-to-infinity problem. For more information, see Chapter 6.

5. **C.** B could be a good answer but because you have 465 computers on the same segment, you will need to get two Class C addresses and configure a superscope. For more information, see Chapter 2, "Installing, Configuring, Managing, Monitoring, and Troubleshooting DHCP in a Windows 2000 Network Infrastructure."

6. **C.** If you revoke the sales representative's certificate, he will no longer be able to retrieve information through the Internet. For more information, see Chapter 8, "Installing, Configuring, Managing, Monitoring, and Troubleshooting Certificate Services."

7. **D.** It produces all the required results but only two of the optional results. It does not update the client computer information in DNS automatically. You have not enabled dynamic update. For more information, see Chapter 1.

8. **B.** Because they mention that you will never exceed 14 hosts per subnet, your correct subnet mask should be 255.255.255.240. For more information, see Chapter 5, "Installing, Configuring, Managing, Monitoring, and Troubleshooting WINS in a Windows 2000 Network Infrastructure."

9. **B.** During the process of installing ICS, your server's IP address was changed to 192.168.0.1. Because your IP address was changed from its default, you have lost all connectivity. For more information, see Chapter 7, "Installing, Configuring, and Troubleshooting Network Address Translation (NAT)."

10. **E.** NAT does not support games at this time. For more information, see Chapter 7.

11. **D.** ICS will not install unless you have a Network and Dial-up Connection configured. For more information, see Chapter 7.

12. **A, D.** The DHCP server's primary function is to assign a unique IP address to the requesting client computers. They can also be used to assign the IP address of the DNS server, the default gateway, the WINS server, and many more. For more information, see Chapter 2.

13. **C.**   Configuring vendor-defined classes in DHCP server will allow you to configure different IP settings. For more information, see Chapter 2.

14. **A.**   WINS is used to replace the LMHOST file. For more information, see Chapter 5.

15. **A.**   In the FQDN Carolyne.training.pbsc.com., Carolyne identifies the host part. Training identifies the child domain, pbsc is the domain name, and com is the root domain. For more information, see Chapter 1.

16. **D.**   The logical processing order that the DNS server will use to resolve FQDNs to IP addresses is that it will first verify the local cache. If the DNS cannot resolve the FQDNs from cache, it will then forward the request to the root server. For more information, see Chapter 1.

17. **C.**   The correct record to add to your DNS server when you want to add an alias is a CNAME record. For more information, see Chapter 1.

18. **B.**   The maximum number of characters that you can have in a node is 63. Your FQDN name has a maximum of 255 characters. For more information, see Chapter 1.

19. **E.**   By manually configuring your client computers with static IP with no DNS configuration, you do not obtain any of the desired or optional results. For more information, see Chapter 1.

20. **B.**   The client computer will receive a DHCPNack after unsuccessfully receiving a TCP/IP address from the DHCP server. When the client computer first requests an IP address, it will issue a DHCPDiscover message to find a DHCP server. It will then receive a DHCPOffer from all DHCP servers. For more information, see Chapter 2.

21. **B.**   What you need to configure is a superscope. For more information, see Chapter 2.

22. **C.**   Before a Windows 2000 DHCP server will issue any IP addresses, it needs to be authorized. Only members of the enterprise administration have the right to authorize a DHCP server. For more information, see Chapter 2.

23. **A.**   The performance counter that counts the number of DHCPOffer messages sent per second by the DHCP server to a client computer is the offers/sec. For more information, see Chapter 2.

24. **D.**   Before your IP addresses will cross over your router, you will need to enable The BOOTP Forwarder. For more information, see Chapter 2.

25. **A, B, D.**   ICS has some functionality that is not supported with NAT, including H.323 Proxy, LDAP Proxy, and Directplay Proxy. For more information, see Chapter 7.

26. **A.**   You must enable the counters in Routing and Remote Access. For more information, see Chapter 7.

27. **A.**   Incremental zone transfer (IXFR) is new in Windows 2000. For more information, see Chapter 1.

28. **C.**   Digital certificates use a public/private key encryption and decryption for security. For more information, see Chapter 8.

29. **C.**   When you configure an Active Directory-integrated zone, the information is stored in Active Directory. For more information, see Chapter 1.

30. **A.**   The best way of securing the information on all laptops is by removing the local EFS key and storing it on a smart card. For more information, see Chapter 8.

31. **D.** RAM is the most critical resource on a cache-only server because all the cache entries are stored in RAM. For more information, see Chapter 1.

32. **C.** To get a client computer to register dynamically with a DNS server at the command prompt, type `ipconfig /registerdns`. For more information, see Chapter 1.

33. **A.** Windows 2000 client computers interact directly with the DNS server to update their A resource record. The DHCP server will update the PRT record for Windows 2000 client computers and both the A record and the PTR record for non-Windows 2000 client computers. For more information, see Chapter 1.

34. **A.** A reverse lookup zone allows you to resolve an IP address to a hostname. For more information, see Chapter 1.

35. **B.** NSLOOKUP will allow you to query the DNS server to verify entries. For more information, see Chapter 1.

36. **A.** WINS is required in Windows 2000 to support backward compatibility for Windows 95 client computers to resolve NetBIOS names to IP addresses. For more information, see Chapter 5.

37. **B.** WINS Proxy will enable your non-WINS client computers to query the WINS database. The WINS Proxy will intercept the non-WINS client computers' broadcast and redirect them to the WINS server. For more information, see Chapter 5.

38. **D.** If you did not modify the default dial-in policy, no users will be able to connect. The default policy is permissions = deny access for everyone. For more information, see Chapter 3, "Configuring, Managing, Monitoring, and Troubleshooting Remote Access in a Windows 2000 Network Infrastructure."

39. **D.** Remote access policies are stored individually on every RRAS server. For more information, see Chapter 3.

40. **E.** You should configure the scope options in DHCP if you want your client computers to query the WINS server to resolve NetBIOS names to IP addresses. Configuring the DHCP scope options allows you to dynamically configure your client computers. For more information, see Chapter 5.

41. **B.** The H-node will force the client computers to query the WINS server before it issues a broadcast. For more information, see Chapter 5.

42. **A.** If you want your WINS server to send notification to replication partners that a number of changes have happened on your WINS server, you need to select the Push option on the Advanced tab of the WINS manager. For more information, see Chapter 5.

43. **D.** By selecting the server statistics on the Action menu of your WINS server icon in MMC, you will be able to retrieve many server statistics. For more information, see Chapter 5.

44. **D.** You must select where you want the file to be backed up before it will start the backup process. For more information, see Chapter 5.

45. **A.** The queries/sec counter will return the rate at which queries are being received. For more information, see Chapter 5.

46. **A.** When converting from decimal to binary, 209.168.241.158 is equal to 11010001. 10101000.11110001.10011110. For more information, see Chapter 4, "Installing, Configuring, Managing, Monitoring, and Troubleshooting Network Protocols in a Windows 2000 Network Infrastructure."

47. **C.** When converting from binary to decimal, 11001100.10101110.00011101.11101010 is equal to 204.174.29.234. For more information, see Chapter 4.

48. **A, B.** Both PPTP and L2TP use PPP to provide the original envelope for the data. For more information, see Chapter 3.

49. **A.** Before users on the Internet are able to access servers on your private network, you will need to configure a custom application for inbound access and open the proper ports. For more information, see Chapter 7.

50. **D.** Extensible Authentication Protocol, or EAP, supports smart card authentication. For more information, see Chapter 3.

51. **A.** You will need to create a different remote access policy for the different users. For more information, see Chapter 3.

52. **B.** DNS is used to replace the flat structure HOST file. For more information, see Chapter 1.

53. **B.** An Intermediary CA is responsible for issuing certificates to a child CA. For more information, see Chapter 8.

54. **A.** Windows 2000 DHCP services is the service that automatically assigns IP addresses to client computers. For more information, see Chapter 2.

55. **A, B, C.** Certificates ensure that your incoming and outgoing data has not been compromised. Certificates also ensure that the identity of individuals accessing some secure information is accurate. Certificates can be issued through Microsoft's Certificate Services; it is not limited to VeriSign. For more information, see Chapter 8.

56. **B.** To resolve hostnames to IP addresses, DNS is required. In a pure Windows 2000 environment, DNS will resolve hostnames and NetBIOS names. For more information, see Chapter 1.

57. **A, B, C.** Certificates are issued not only to individuals but also to organizations, businesses, routers, and other entities as a way of controlling and securing data. For more information, see Chapter 8.

58. **B.** You have some conflicting policies and the first one that is applied refuses them access. For more information, see Chapter 3.

59. **A.** You did not configure NWLink with manual frame type detection. NetWare 3.12 servers and earlier use a different frame type than the NetWare 4 servers and later. For more information, see Chapter 4.

60. **D.** By using the first 6 bits of your 3 octets, you will allow up to 1,024 host per network. You are also allowing for your network to be segmented up to 62 subnets. For more information, see Chapter 4.

61. **B.** Before your network adapter intercepts all the packets on the network, it will have to be running in promiscuous mode. For more information, see Chapter 6.

62. **A.** You have to configure RIP to use broadcast, not multicast. For more information, see Chapter 6.

63. **B, D, E.** PPTP requires an IP-based transit network. L2TP requires only that the tunnel media provide packet-oriented. L2TP supports header compression, whereas PPTP does not. L2TP supports tunnel authentication, whereas PPTP does not. PPTP uses encryption; L2TP requires IPSec for encryption. For more information, see Chapter 3.

64. **A, B, C.**   There are many ways to prevent the count-to-infinity problems, including split horizon, split horizon with poison reverse, and triggered update. Link-state routing is another routing technology. For more information, see Chapter 6.

65. **D.**   To configure a new multicast scope, you must select the option New Multicast Scope. For more information, see Chapter 2.

PART

III

Appendixes

A   Glossary

B   Overview of the Certification Process

C   What's on the CD-ROM

D   Using the *ExamGear, Training Guide Edition* Software

Glossary

%SystemRoot%   A universal reference to the directory in which the Windows 2000 system files are installed. Typically, %SystemRoot% is C:\Winnt. If multiple copies of Windows 2000 are installed in a multiboot system, each copy will have its own %SystemRoot% directory.

A

Access Control List (ACL)   A list that contains entries defining the levels of access to an object.

Active Directory Services   The directory services included with Windows 2000 Server. Based on the DNS hierarchy, Active Directory provides a domain-based directory service for organizing all the objects and services in a Windows 2000 network.

Address pool   Available IP addresses within a scope for dynamic assignment by the DHCP server to DHCP clients.

Address reservation   An address reservation is an IP address from a scope that is reserved for a client by its MAC address.

Address Resolution Protocol (ARP)   ARP is the part of the TCP/IP protocol suite that resolves an IP address to a MAC address. The ARP.EXE utility can be used to view the table of resolutions.

Adjacency   A term in routing referring to the record that a router keeps about the state of its connectivity with a neighbor and the attributes of the neighboring router.

Administrative share   A hidden share, created by the Windows 2000 installation process. These shares may not be removed and are identified by a trailing $ in the name; for example, C$, D$. Any share name appended with a $ is a hidden share. Only those shares created at installation are considered administrative shares.

AppleShare   Network client software that comes with Macintosh computers and Apple servers.

AppleTalk   A network protocol developed by Apple Computer.

Area   In an OSPF routing environment, an area is a logical grouping of routers within the OSPF hierarchy.

ARP (Address Resolution Protocol)   The ARP protocol is used to provide address translation from an IP address of a host to the host's physical address on the network. A host wanting to obtain a physical address broadcasts an ARP request onto the TCP/IP network. The host on the network that has the IP address in the request then replies with its physical hardware address.

ARP table   The table of IP to MAC address translations used by a router to identify the physical addresses of devices on a local subnet.

Authentication   The process of verifying a user's identity on a network.

Authoritative   When a DNS name server supports the name database for a domain, it is said to be authoritative for that domain.

AutoDHCP   AutoDHCP is the DHCP service included as part of the Windows 2000 Network Address Translation (NAT) protocol. A subset of the DHCP service, AutoDHCP is used to distribute reserved addresses to NAT users.

B

Backup browser   A computer that stores a copy of the master browser database. Browse clients can browse the domain or workgroup by querying the backup browser for the browse database.

Backup set   A collection of files, folders, or other data that have been backed up to a file or a tape.

Basic disk   A physical hard drive that utilizes the primary partition, extended partition, and logical drive-partitioning architecture.

Basic volume   A logical volume that has been created on a basic disk.

Baseline   Measurement taken on a network to provide comparison data in the event of a problem on the network. A baseline represents the "typical" state of a network at any given time. Future measurements are compared to the baseline.

Binding   The relationship between network adapters, drivers, and protocols in a computer's network communication configuration. For example, the TCP/IP protocol binding connects the protocol to the Network Interface Card (NIC).

BOOTP protocol   Short for Bootstrap Protocol, BOOTP is an Internet protocol that enables a diskless workstation to discover its own IP address from a BOOTP server. This protocol is still used to allow DHCP requests and responses to traverse a routed network.

Border Gateway Protocol (BGP)   An IP routing protocol that enables groups of routers (organized in autonomous systems) to share routing information to create efficient routes. BGP is commonly used by Internet Service Providers (ISPs) as an Internet routing protocol. The protocol is defined in RFC 1771.

Bridge   A bridge works on the physical layer (or Layer 2) of the OSI model to connect two network segments. A bridge listens to traffic on both segments and builds a list of MAC addresses that reside on each. It forwards packets from one segment to the other if the destination system is known. Unlike a router, a bridge will pass all broadcast traffic between segments.

Broadcast node (B-node)   One of the four node types that can be set for NetBIOS name resolution.

Browse client   A computer that doesn't store a copy of the domain or workgroup database and must browse the network by querying the browse database on a backup or master browser.

Browser elections   Part of the Microsoft browser system, browser elections are used to decide which system will be the master browser on a network segment. When an election is called, all systems capable of being the master browser respond after a set time. The system that responds first wins the election and becomes the master browser. It will remain the master browser until circumstances require another election.

Browser service   In Windows NT, the browser service handles your computer's role in the Microsoft browser system.

Built-in groups   The groups that come predefined by Windows 2000 Server.

C

Cache file   In a DNS implementation, the cache file is the file that contains the address of servers higher in the DNS hierarchy. The cache file that installs as part of the Windows 2000 DNS server contains the Internet's root-level servers.

Caching   A high-speed access mechanism in which routes, addresses, or DNS resolutions are stored in memory to speed further requests for the information.

Caching-only server   A DNS server that does not have authority for any zone. It doesn't provide authoritative answers for other DNS servers, but responds with the information in its cache.

Callback   A feature of the Routing and Remote Access service. Callback allows the Routing and Remote Access service to call a user back by initiating a new connection after the user's initial modem connection. Used mostly for security reasons, callback can also be used to minimize user long-distance charges.

Canonical name (CNAME) record   A CNAME record in a DNS zone file that acts as an alias for another entry in the DNS zone. This allows a single server to be mapped to multiple names.

Certificate Authority   A service that verifies that the owner of the certificate is who he says he is.

Certificate services   Software that provides authentication support.

Certificate   A credential used to authenticate the origin, identity, and purpose of the public half of a public/private key pair. A certificate ensures that the data sent and received is kept secure.

Chart view   One of the views in the Performance Monitor. The Chart view displays a graphical representation of either real-time or logged data.

Child domain   A Windows 2000 Server domain that exists directly beneath a parent domain in a tree hierarchy.

Class A network   The largest of the classes of IP networks. There are 126 Class A networks, each capable of addressing up to 16,777,214 hosts.

Class B network   The second-largest class of IP networks. There are 16,384 Class B networks, each capable of addressing up to 65,534 hosts.

Class C network   The smallest class of IP networks. There are 2,097,152 Class C networks, each capable of addressing up to 254 hosts.

Client   A computer that accesses resources that are shared on a network, or the software component of a computer that lets the computer access resources shared on a network.

Cluster   A technology that allows for multiple servers to provide fail-over of services.

Convergence   Usually referred to in conjunction with the RIP, OSPF, or BGP TCP/IP routing protocols. Convergence is a state in which all the routers in a network are aware of all available routes.

Counter   With respect to the Performance utility, a counter represents the metrics associated with a specific object.

Cryptography   A process that defines a secure method for transmitting data using encryption algorithms.

D

Default gateway   The configured router on a Microsoft TCP/IP-enabled system. If a packet is bound for a remote network but no route is specified, the packet will be sent to this address. Also known as the default router.

Default router   Also known as the default gateway. When a host needs to transmit a packet to a destination not on the local network, it sends the packet to a default router, which is then responsible for routing the packet to its destination network.

DHCP client   Any computer that has DHCP settings enabled and is requesting addresses from a DHCP server.

DHCP server   Any computer running the Windows 2000 DHCP service.

DHCPAck   An acknowledgment from a DHCP server to a DHCP client indicating that the request for a lease (or renewal) was successful.

DHCPDiscover   A message sent from a DHCP client to the network broadcast address. This is the beginning of the lease process, which causes any appropriately configured DHCP server to offer a lease.

DHCPNAck   A negative acknowledgment from a DHCP server to a DHCP client indicating that the request for a lease (or renewal) was not successful.

DHCPOffer   A message from the DHCP server to the client that has sent a discover message indicating an address that is available.

DHCPRequest   A message sent from a DHCP client to the server requesting an offer or renewing an IP address lease.

Dial-Up Networking   The part of a Microsoft operating system (Windows 2000, Windows NT, Windows 9x) used to dial remote servers to gain access to a network.

Directplay proxy   A proxy service included with the Windows 2000 Internet Connection Sharing (ICS) service to allow for the use of the Directplay protocol in conjunction with NAT. Directplay is protocol typically used in writing multiuser games.

Disk drives, duplexing   A configuration of mirrored disk drives in which each disk drive is serviced by a separate drive adapter. This arrangement lets one drive of the pair continue functioning if there is a failure in a disk drive adapter.

Disk drives, mirroring   A configuration of two disk drives in which both drives store the same data. A mirrored disk drive set can continue to function when one of the disk drives malfunctions.

Disk drives, stripe set with parity   A stripe set in which one record in each set contains parity data. The parity data can be used to recover data if any one drive in the stripe set fails. A stripe set with parity can continue to function despite the failure of a single disk drive.

Disk drives, stripe set   A configuration of three or more disk drives in which data is written in blocks sequentially to each drive. Stripe sets have better storage and retrieval times than single hard disks with comparable specifications, but they also are more subject to hardware failure.

Disk quota   The amount of space allocated by an administrator to a user or group of users.

Distance vector   A routing algorithm used to calculate the best path in an OSPF environment.

Distributed file system (Dfs)   A service used to present a single directory tree of file shares that can be located on multiple machines and as multiple shares.

DNS client   Any host that utilizes a DNS server for name resolution services.

DNS server   A server running the Domain Name Service to provide name and address resolution services in a TCP/IP environment.

Domain Name Service (DNS)   Service for dynamically providing name and address resolution services in a TCP/IP environment.

Domain local groups   A group object that may include users or groups from only the local domain.

Domain master browser   A browser on Microsoft TCP/IP networks that collects service announcements from all servers in a domain and creates a master browser database for the domain. Master browsers on other subnets can obtain the domain master browser database for use by browse clients on the local subnets.

Domain   A container in the DNS name hierarchy. Also the network organizational unit for Windows NT networks.

Duplexing   See disk drives, duplexing.

Dynamic DNS (DDNS)   A new addition to Microsoft's DNS implementation, Dynamic DNS is a process in which a workstation's name and address are entered into the DNS table when an IP address is obtained through DHCP.

Dynamic Host Configuration Protocol (DHCP) A standards-based method of automatically assigning and configuring IP addresses for DHCP clients.

Dynamic Routing   Provides an automatic mechanism for routers to learn available routes. This is done using a routing protocol such as RIP, OSPF, or BGP.

Dynamic volume   A volume that can be created, extended, or deleted without requiring a reboot of this system. This type of volume is new to Windows 2000.

E

Encrypting File System (EFS)   The public key-based service that provides file-system encryption for Windows 2000 servers.

Encryption   A mechanism for securing data, encryption takes data and translates it into a secret code, which can be read only with the correct key to translate the secret code back to the original data.

Enterprise Root Authority   The first Certification Authority (CA) in a branch of CAs. It is responsible for assigning certificates to intermediary CAs and other subordinate CAs.

Ethernet   A network standard that uses Carrier Sense Multi-Access with Collision Detection (CSMA/CD) on a bus topology. Ethernet currently runs at 10Mbps, 100Mbps and 1Gbps.

Exclusion   Indicates the process where IP addresses and address ranges are removed (excluded) from a DHCP scope.

Extended partition   A partition that can be configured with one or more logical drives. MS-DOS supports extended partitions as the means of configuring more than one volume on a hard disk.

Exterior Gateway Protocol (EGP)   The original exterior protocol, EGP is used to exchange routing information between networks that do not share a common administration.

Extinction   The Windows Internet Naming Service (WINS) process used to remove released WINS database entries from the database.

F

Fail-over   A technology that monitors the "heartbeat" of a server and automatically transfers failing services to another server.

FAT (file allocation table)   A list maintained by some operating systems to keep track of file storage on disk.

FAT32   An advanced implementation of FAT that uses smaller clusters.

File Transfer Protocol (FTP)   A standard TPC/IP protocol and utility that uses ports 20 and 21 to transfer files between hosts. User authentication information is sent as clear text.

Forest   A structure created by domains in more than one Active Directory tree, that share the same domain configuration but do not share the same DNS namespace.

Forward lookup   In DNS, a forward lookup is a name to IP-address resolution.

Forwarder   A caching-only DNS server that has been configured to send name resolution requests to another DNS server.

Frame   One term for a basic unit of network communication, consisting of a message and the information required for delivery. Also referred to as a packet.

Frame type   Defines the makeup of a data packet.

Full backup   Copying the entire contents of a computer's hard drive(s) to a media format, such as tape, CD-ROM, or to another disk.

Fully qualified domain name (FQDN)   The complete DNS name of a host, including the hostname and all domains that connect the host to the root domain. Typically expressed without a trailing period, with the root domain assumed.

Fully qualified name   The name of a container or data object in a hierarchy, consisting of the object's name and the names of all containers that connect the object to the root container.

G

Global catalog   A partial replica of every partition in an Active Directory that is used to speed searching.

Global group   A group object that includes only users or groups from their local domain; however, they can also be defined to access resources outside of their local domain.

Global options   In the context of DHCP, global options will be sent to all systems leasing an address regardless of the scope from which they lease. These include things such as the DNS and WINS server addresses.

Group policy   Used to define user and computer configurations for groups in a Windows 2000 network environment.

H

H.323 Proxy   A standard used to allow videoconferencing applications to interoperate.

Hardware Compatibility List (HCL)   Microsoft's published list of hardware that has passed testing on Windows 2000.

Hierarchy   A database structure based on the principle of categories and subcategories, typically represented in the form of an inverted tree. Each hierarchy has exactly one master category, typically called the root, and all other categories are subcategories of the root category. Categories can contain subcategories as well as data.

Hive   Registry data is stored in six or more sets of files, called hives. Each hive consists of two files: a data file and a log file.

Hop   A common metric used with routing protocols, in which one hop is counted for each network that a message traverses on a route.

Host record   The most common record in a DNS zone file (also known as an "A" or "Alias" record). It allows a host's DNS name to be resolved to an IP address.

Host   A device that is attached to a TCP/IP network.

Host ID   The portion of an IP address that uniquely identifies a host on its local TCP/IP network.

HOSTS.TXT, Hosts file   A static database file used to resolve names on TCP/IP networks.

Hybrid node (H-node)   One of four node types that can be set for NetBIOS name resolution.

I

Instance   After selecting a counter in the Performance utility, all instances (occurrences) of the object are shown so that you can choose which one you want to monitor. For example, a server with two CPUs would show two instances—one for each processor.

Integrated Services Digital Network (ISDN)   ISDN is a type of communications line that provides higher-speed access to a network. Special equipment is required on both ends of the line to acquire higher speed.

Intellimirror   A set of technologies included in Windows 2000 to allow a user's desktop configuration to follow that user to any machine on the network.

Interface   Something that connects two separate entities. These can be hardware devices, software applications, or even a user and an application.

Interior Gateway Protocol (IGP)   Used to pass routing information for routing networks that are under a common network administration.

Intermediate CA   A CA that assigns certificates to subordinate CAs only. The subordinate CAs do not request a certificate from the root CA.

Internal network number   On IPX networks, each server must have an internal network number and an eight-digit hexadecimal number used to deliver data to the correct process within the server.

Internet Connection Sharing (ICS)   A Windows 2000 service used to allow a small office to share a dial-up Internet connection easily and securely.

Internet Control Message Protocol (ICMP)   A protocol in the TCP/IP suite of protocols used for testing connectivity.

Internet Explorer   A browser from Microsoft that is used to view Web pages.

Internet Group Management Protocol (IGMP)   One of the core protocols in the TCP/IP suite. It is a routing protocol used as part of multicasting.

Internet Information Server (IIS)   Microsoft's Internet-hosting software.

Internet Protocol (IP)   The portion of the TCP/IP protocol suite used to provide IP packet routing.

Internet Protocol Configuration (IPCONFIG)   A Windows 2000/Windows NT utility that can be used to view the configuration details for the hosts TCP/IP. IPCONFIG can also be used to release or renew an address leased from a DHCP server.

Internet Protocol Security (IPSec)   The standard IP-based VPN protocol used to provide secure communications across a public network.

Internet Service Provider (ISP)   A vendor that provides network connectivity to the Internet as well as support services such as name, news, and electronic mail.

Internet   The worldwide network that has evolved out of the ARPANET developed by the United States Department of Defense.

Internetwork   An extended network consisting of discrete networks that communicate through routers A "network of networks." Also called an Internet.

IP address   The 32-bit binary address used to identify a TCP/IP host's network and host ID.

IP address conservation   The act of configuring your network in conjunction with DHCP to use the least amount of IP addresses possible.

Iterative query   A DNS query sent from a DNS server to one or more DNS servers in search of the DNS server that is authoritative for the name being sought.

J, K

Kerberos   An identity-based security protocol based on Internet security standards used by Windows 2000 to authenticate users.

L

Layer 2 Tunneling Protocol (L2TP)   A VPN protocol created by combining the PPTP and L2F tunneling protocols. Used as the transport protocol in the Windows 2000 VPN service in conjunction with IPSec.

LAN Manager HOSTS file (LMHOSTS)   The LMHOSTS file is modeled after the TCP/IP HOSTS file and is used to provide a static NetBIOS name to IP address resolution in a Windows environment. The HOST file was originally used for name resolution in a TCP/IP network environment. As the HOSTS file was replaced by DNS, the LMHOSTS file was replaced by WINS.

Leaf   The end object in a hierarchical tree structure.

Lease duration   A DHCP lease duration is the length of time the DHCP client is authorized to use the leased address. The client will start trying to renew the address at 50 percent of the lease duration.

Lease   The length of time a client computer can use a dynamically assigned IP address.

Lightweight Directory Access Protocol (LDAP)   A lightweight version of the X.500 directory standard used as the primary access protocol for Active Directory.

Link state   Used by dynamic routing protocols to test the condition of a connection (link) between routers. OSPF is a Link state protocol.

Log view   A view within the Performance utility that allows you to log performance data about your system to a file.

Logical drive   A portion of an extended partition that can be formatted as a volume.

M

Mail Exchange (MX) record   A record in the DNS zone file that indicates which host in your network will receive mail.

Management Information Base (MIB)   Organizes a set of manageable objects for an installed service or device. MIBs are used in conjunction with the SNMP protocol.

Many-to-one mapping   Many certificates mapped to one user account.

Master browser   A computer that collects service announcements from servers and constructs a browse list. Backup browsers periodically contact the master browser to obtain an updated copy of the master browser database.

Media Access Control (MAC)   Part of the Data Link layer from the OSI model. The physical address of an NIC is called a MAC address.

Medium   The vehicle that carries data between a server and a client. Network media include copper cable, optical fiber, microwaves, and light pulses.

Metric   A number that assigns a preference to a route within routing protocols. The route with the lowest metric is the preferred route.

Microsoft Management Console (MMC)   A framework used for hosting administrative tools.

Mirroring   See disk drives, mirroring.

Mixed mode   The default mode that Windows 2000 operates in, used to support both Windows 2000 computers and pre-Windows 2000 computers.

Mixed node (M-node)   One of the four node types that can be set for NetBIOS name resolution.

Modem (Modulating/demodulating device) Hardware device used to convert digital signals to analog, and vice versa. This allows digital communications to occur over regular (analog) phone lines.

Multicast scope   A range of IP multicast addresses in the range of 239.0.0.0 to 239.254.255.255. Multicast addresses in this range can be prevented from propagating in either direction (send or receive) through the use of scope-based multicast boundaries.

Multicasting   A method of sending a series of packets to a group of computers instead of to a single computer or all computers on a network. IGMP support is required to use multicasting.

Multilink   A capability included in Windows 2000 that allows the aggregating of multiple modem connections from a Windows 2000 host to a dial-up network.

N

Name registration   The act of registering a host's NetBIOS name on the network. Name registration occurs when a system starts, when a service starts, or when a user logs on. Registrations can be sent as a broadcast on the local network or to a WINS server, where the name and IP address are added to the database.

Name release   An event that occurs when a system notifies other systems (such as the master browser or a WINS server) that a system is shutting down.

Name renewal   A transmission sent to a WINS server requesting a renewal of the host's WINS database entry.

Name resolution   The process of determining the network address associated with a computer name.

Native mode   The mode Windows 2000 operates in when supporting Windows 2000 computers only. This mode supports the additional functionality of multi-master replication and nested groups and does not support the capability to replicate with Windows NT 4.0 domain controllers.

NetBIOS name cache   A list of system NetBIOS names that a host has resolved or that have been pre-loaded from the LMHOSTS file.

NetBIOS name   The computer name for NetBIOS networking. This name can be 16 characters long: 15 provide the hostname, and the 16th represents the service registering the name.

NetBIOS node type   The node type determines the order of name resolution for NetBIOS names. There are four types: B-node, P-node, M-node, and H-node.

NetBIOS over TCP/IP (NBT or NetBT)   The name given to the process of running NetBIOS network services over TCP/IP.

NetBIOS over TCP/IP Statistics (NBTSTAT) utility This utility allows you to verify the current connections over the NBT protocol. It also allows you to check and load the NetBIOS name cache.

Network Address Translation (NAT)   An Internet standard that enables a Windows 2000 Server to use one set of IP addresses on the internal network and a different set of IP addresses on the external network. This can be done to hide the internal addresses or to allow unregistered addresses to be used on the internal network, whereas registered addresses are used externally.

Network Basic Input/Output System (NetBIOS)
An Application layer networking protocol that works at the Application, Presentation, and Session layers of the OSI model. Legacy Microsoft networking used NetBIOS as the default Application layer protocol.

Network binding See binding.

Network ID The portion of an IP address that identifies the network to which a host is attached.

Network monitor An application included with Windows 2000 that allows you to monitor the packets sent to and from your Windows 2000 host.

Network number On IPX networks, the network number is an eight-digit hexadecimal number that uniquely identifies each network on an Internetwork.

New Technology File System (NTFS) Advanced file system used in Windows 2000 to offer advanced security features.

Node A device that communicates on the network and is identified by a unique address. In hierarchies, a node is a container that contains other containers and data.

Null modem A cable that lets computers communicate through serial ports by simulating a modem connection.

NWLink Protocol written to allow Windows operating systems to communicate using the IPX protocol.

O

Octet Commonly used to refer to groups of eight bits in network addresses, such as IP addresses. A 32-bit IP address consists of four octets.

One-to-one mapping A single certificate mapped to a single user account.

Open Shortest Path First (OSPF) A routing protocol that allows routers to share their routing information, making them dynamic routers.

P

Packet Internet Groper Utility (PING) A utility used to troubleshoot TCP/IP problems. PING sends a packet with data asking the remote system to echo the packet.

Paging file A temporary file used to support virtual memory.

Paging The process of swapping data between RAM and disk-based virtual memory.

Parent domain The highest domain structure in a Windows 2000 Server domain tree hierarchy.

Partition A physical subdivision of a disk drive that can be formatted with a file system.

Pointer record (PTR) In DNS, a pointer record is a host entry used in a reverse zone file to allow IP address-to-fully qualified domain name resolution.

Point-to-Point node (P-node) One of the four node types that can be set for NetBIOS name resolution.

Point-to-Point Protocol (PPP) A serial-line protocol that replaces the frame types found on networks when communicating over a serial line. It defines how the data is physically transmitted.

Port, hardware A hardware component that lets a computer communicate with other devices. Examples are printer ports, serial ports, and network ports.

Port, TCP A software address that lets the TCP/IP protocols deliver messages to the correct process on a computer. Each process running on a TCP/IP computer must be associated with a unique combination of an

IP address and a port number. The combination of an IP address and a port number is called a socket.

Point-to-Point Tunneling Protocol (PPTP) A protocol used by Microsoft and others to create a virtual private network.

Primary DNS server The name server that contains the master copy of a zone file.

Primary master See Primary DNS server.

Primary partition A partition that can be used to boot an operating system.

Primary zone A DNS zone that contains the master copies of resource records for a domain.

Print server A computer configured to share its printer through the network. Windows 2000 computers become print servers when their printers are shared.

Private IP address An IP address range reserved for private (non-Internet connected) networks. There are private address ranges in the Class A, Class B, and Class C address blocks.

Profile, local A user profile stored on the user's workstation.

Profile, locally cached See profile, local.

Profile, mandatory A user profile that can be accessed from any workstation on a network. Users can't save changes made to a mandatory profile.

Profile, roaming A personal user profile that can be accessed from any workstation on a network. Users can change settings in roaming profiles.

Profile See user profile.

Protocol A standard set of rules for communicating between computers.

Provider connections A provider is a component that allows you to connect to network resources. A

connection is either a network connection, local or remote, or a DUN (Dial-Up Networking) connection.

Proxy service Sits between a client application, such as a Web browser, and the destination server. It intercepts all requests to the destination to see if it can fulfill the requests itself. If not, it forwards the request to the real server. Proxy services frequently contain caching capabilities.

Public Switched Telephone Network (PSTN) The public telephone network.

Pull replication The act of replicating a copy of the WINS database from a WINS replication partner.

Push replication The act of replicating a copy of the WINS database to a WINS replication partner.

Q

Quality of Service (QoS) A set of standards used to ensure a specified quality for data transmissions across a network.

R

Record types The different types of entries that can be created in a DNS table.

Recursive query A DNS query used to request an authoritative answer or an answer indicating that there is no resolution for a DNS lookup.

Registered IP address Any block of addresses registered with the Internet Assigned Numbers Authority.

Registry key A container for data in the Registry data hierarchy.

Remote Access Service (RAS) A feature built in to Windows NT that enables users to log in to an NT-based LAN using a modem. Replaced by the Routing and Remote Access Service in Windows 2000.

Repeater A physical device that takes a signal from one interface and retransmits it to another. This allows a network segment to be extended beyond the normal distances dictated by the limits of the topology.

Replication partner A server in a WINS architecture that sends or receives a copy of the WINS database from another WINS server.

Reservation A permanent address lease assignment from the DHCP server to a specified client.

Resource record A data record in a DNS zone. For example, an address resource record is the data record that describes the address-to-name relationship for a host. Many types of resource records are available.

Reverse lookup In DNS, an IP-address to name resolution.

Revocation list A published list of certificates that have been revoked.

Revoked certificate A certificate that is no longer valid because the validity of the certificate was discontinued.

Request for Comment (RFC) Used to make notes about the Internet and Internet technologies.

Root In a hierarchy, the container that holds all other containers.

Router A system or device that forwards or drops packets between networks, based on the entries in its routing table.

Routing and Remote Access (RRAS) The Windows 2000 Server Routing and Remote Access allows for remote connection to the server.

Routing Information Protocol (RIP) A protocol used by dynamic routers to share their routing tables. Similar to OSPF and BGP protocols, RIP is an older, less-efficient routing protocol.

Routing protocol Used by dynamic routers to share their routing tables with other routers.

Routing Table (ROUTE) utility The Windows ROUTE utility allows you to view and modify the routing table on a Windows computer.

Routing table Each TCP/IP host maintains a routing table that describes routing decisions the host can make. Minimum entries in the routing table include routes to each local network and a default route.

S

Scope The full, consecutive range of possible IP addresses for a network.

Secondary DNS server Provides name resolution for a zone, but cannot be used to modify the zone. It contains a read-only copy of the zone file.

Secondary master See Secondary DNS server.

Secondary zone A DNS zone that obtains copies of the resource records for a domain through a zone transfer from a primary zone.

Security Access Manager (SAM) The component of Windows 2000 that manages the security database and all security functions.

Security ID (SID) An alphanumeric code used internally by Windows 2000 to identify computers, users, and other objects described in the SAM database.

Serial Line Internet Protocol (SLIP) A line protocol for serial communications that replaces the frames on a physical network. The SLIP protocol can only transfer TCP/IP packets and provides only limited security.

Server mirroring   Real-time replication of a server's data to another server.

Server   A computer that shares resources on a network.

Simple Network Management Protocol (SNMP)   Used by a management station to read information from agents.

Site   On an Internet server such as a World Wide Web server, a site is a logical server. Each site must be defined by a unique combination of properties. For example, each Web site running on a given computer must be defined by a unique combination of an IP address and a TCP port.

Snap-in   A tool that you can add to a Microsoft Management Console.

Socket   The unique combination of an IP address and a TCP port number that identifies a particular process running on a particular TCP/IP computer.

Spanned volume   A volume of disk space that resides on more than one physical disk.

Special permissions   Highly granular type of NTFS permissions that can be assigned to user or group objects.

Split horizon   The split horizon mechanism used with the RIP protocol to prevent routing loops. Split horizon blocks information about routes from being advertised by a router out any interface from which that information originated.

Split horizon with poison reverse   Whereas standard split horizon blocks routes from being advertised by a router out any interface from which that information originated, split horizon with poison reverse broadcasts the routes with an infinite routing metric.

Standalone Certification Authorities   Do not require Active Directory. Certificate requests are set to pending until an Administrator approves the request.

Standard permissions   A group of six NTFS permissions that can be assigned to user or group objects.

Start of Authority (SOA)   In a DNS zone file, used to provide the zone parameters to all the DNS servers for the zone. The SOA record also provides the name of the primary server and the person in charge of the domain.

Static route   An item in a routing table that is entered manually and that doesn't change based on information received from a routing protocol.

Stripe set with parity   See disk drives, stripe set with parity.

Stripe set   See disk drives, stripe set.

Subdomain   A DNS domain located directly beneath another DNS domain in the DNS hierarchy.

Subnet   A subdivision of a TCP/IP Internetwork that communicates with other subnets through routers.

Subnet mask   In TCP/IP, a subnet mask is a mask used to determine what subnet an IP address belongs to. The subnet mask enables a host or a router to determine which portion of an IP address is the net ID, and which is the host ID. The host can then use this information to determine whether to send a packet to a host on the local network or to a router.

Suffix   A domain suffix indicates the root domain. For example, COM is a domain suffix.

Supernetted network   A network that has multiple network addresses or subnets running on the same segment.

Superscope   A grouping of scopes that are used to support multinetted IP subnets on the same physical network.

T

TCP port   See port, TCP.

Terminal Emulation (Telnet)   This protocol/utility is part of the TCP/IP suite and is used to provide a terminal window to another station on the network. This is generally used in conjunction with UNIX hosts.

Token ring   A networking technology comparable to Ethernet, in which a token is used to determine who can send traffic onto the network. The data circulates through the ring until the system that it is intended for receives it and marks the token with an acknowledgement. The token then circles back to the sending system, which releases the token to the other stations on the ring.

Top-Level Domain (TLD)   The suffix attached to Internet domain names. There are a limited number of predefined suffixes, and each one represents a top-level domain.

Trace Router (TRACERT) utility   Traces the route that packets travel between the local host and the destination host and displays it to the screen.

Transmission Control Protocol/Internet Protocol (TCP/IP)   The suite of communications protocols used to connect hosts on the Internet.

TCP/IP filter   Used to prevent certain addresses or protocols from traversing a router.

Tree   A logical group of Windows 2000 Server domains that share a common schema.

Trusted domain   A domain that allows another domain to share its security database.

Trusting domain   A domain that assigns user permissions based on user account and group memberships in another domain that it trusts.

Tunneling   Used to provide a secure connection to a private network across a public one. It works by encapsulating a network protocol within packets carried by the second network.

Twisted pair   Cable in which pairs of wires are twisted to reduce sensitivity to electronic noise.

U

Unicast addresses   TCP/IP addresses used for host-to-host communications. Unicast addresses are the most commonly used types of TCP/IP addresses.

Universal group   A group object that may include any users or groups that are within the same tree or forest.

Universal Naming Convention (UNC)   Naming convention used for defining a resource on a Windows 2000 Server network.

User Datagram Protocol (UDP)   A connectionless protocol that is part of the TCP/IP suite. UDP is frequently used in broadcasts.

UserPrincipalName (UPN) mapping   Mapping a certificate to a user's principal name in Active Directory.

User profile   A database that stores a user's personal computer settings so that the settings are available each time the user logs on.

V

Validity period   The length of time the certificate is considered valid.

Variable Length Subnet Mask (VLSM)   A subnet mask that is used either to split a large network into smaller pieces (subnetting) or combine smaller networks into a larger one (supernetting).

Virtual memory   A technique for simulating RAM by swapping memory contents between RAM and disk-based files.

Volume   A portion of one or more disk drives that can be formatted as a single storage unit. Volumes are usually identified by a drive letter from A through Z.

Virtual private network (VPN)   A mechanism for providing secure, private communications utilizing a public network (such as the Internet) as the transport method. VPNs use a combination of encryption and authentication technologies to ensure data integrity and security.

W

Web server   On IIS, a single computer can run one instance of the World Wide Web Server service, and it functions as one Web server.

Web site   A Web server can support multiple Web sites. Each Web site must be identified by a unique combination of an IP address and a port number.

Windows Internet Naming Service (WINS)   A service that runs on a Windows 2000 Server to provide NetBIOS name resolution. When you use WINS, name resolution is done using directed transmissions, resulting in a reduction in broadcast traffic and the capability to find systems on different subnets. WINS replaces the LMHOSTS file in a fashion similar to the way DNS replaced the HOSTS file.

WINS replication   WINS servers use WINS replication to copy its database of names with other WINS servers.

X

xDSL   Refers collectively to all types of digital subscriber lines (DSL). DSL technologies use sophisticated modulation schemes to pack data onto copper wires and are the main competitor to cable modems for providing high-speed Internet access to the home user.

Y, Z

Zone transfer   The process of copying DNS resource records from a primary zone to a secondary zone.

Zone   A domain for which a Microsoft DNS server is authoritative.

Overview of the Certification Process

You must pass rigorous certification exams to become a Microsoft Certified Professional. These closed-book exams provide a valid and reliable measure of your technical proficiency and expertise. Developed in consultation with computer industry professionals who have experience with Microsoft products in the workplace, the exams are conducted by two independent organizations. Virtual University Enterprises (VUE) testing centers offer exams at more than 2,700 locations in 128 countries. Prometric offers the exams at more than 2,000 authorized Prometric Testing Centers around the world as well.

To schedule an exam, call Sylvan Prometric Testing Centers at 800-755-EXAM (3926) (or register online at http://www.2test.com/register) or VUE at 888-837-8734 (or register online at http://www.vue.com/ms/msexam.html). At the time of this writing, Microsoft offered eight types of certification, each based on a specific area of expertise. Please check the Microsoft Certified Professional Web site for the most up-to-date information (www.microsoft.com/mcp/).

TYPES OF CERTIFICATION

◆ **Microsoft Certified Professional (MCP).** Persons with this credential are qualified to support at least one Microsoft product. Candidates can take elective exams to develop areas of specialization. MCP is the base level of expertise.

◆ **Microsoft Certified Professional+Internet (MCP+Internet).** Persons with this credential are qualified to plan security, install and configure server products, manage server resources, extend service to run CGI scripts or ISAPI scripts, monitor and analyze performance, and troubleshoot problems. Expertise is similar to that of an MCP but with a focus on the Internet.

◆ **Microsoft Certified Professional+Site Building (MCP+Site Building).** Persons with this credential are qualified to plan, build, maintain, and manage Web sites using Microsoft technologies and products. The credential is appropriate for people who manage sophisticated, interactive Web sites that include database connectivity, multimedia, and searchable content.

◆ **Microsoft Certified Database Administrator (MCDBA).** Qualified individuals can derive physical database designs, develop logical data models, create physical databases, create data services by using Transact-SQL, manage and maintain databases, configure and manage security, monitor and optimize databases, and install and configure Microsoft SQL Server.

◆ **Microsoft Certified Systems Engineer (MCSE).** These individuals are qualified to analyze the business requirements for a system architecture; design solutions; deploy, install, and configure architecture components; and troubleshoot system problems.

◆ **Microsoft Certified Systems Engineer+Internet (MCSE+Internet).** Persons with this credential are qualified in the core MCSE areas and also are qualified to enhance, deploy, and manage sophisticated intranet and Internet solutions that include a browser, proxy server, host servers, database, and messaging and commerce components. An MCSE+Internet-certified professional is able to manage and analyze Web sites.

◆ **Microsoft Certified Solution Developer (MCSD).** These individuals are qualified to design and develop custom business solutions by using Microsoft development tools, technologies, and platforms. The new track includes certification exams that test the user's ability to build Web-based, distributed, and commerce applications by using Microsoft products such as Microsoft SQL Server, Microsoft Visual Studio, and Microsoft Component Services.

◆ **Microsoft Certified Trainer (MCT).** Persons with this credential are instructionally and technically qualified by Microsoft to deliver Microsoft Education Courses at Microsoft-authorized sites. An MCT must be employed by a Microsoft Solution Provider Authorized Technical Education Center or a Microsoft Authorized Academic Training site.

NOTE | For up-to-date information about each type of certification, visit the Microsoft Training and Certification Web site at http://www.microsoft.com/mcp. You can also contact Microsoft through the following sources:

- Microsoft Certified Professional Program: 800-636-7544

- mcp@msource.com

- Microsoft Online Institute (MOLI): 800-449-9333

CERTIFICATION REQUIREMENTS

The following sections describe the requirements for the various types of Microsoft certifications.

NOTE | An asterisk following an exam in any of the following lists means that it is slated for retirement.

How to Become a Microsoft Certified Professional

To become certified as an MCP, you need only pass any Microsoft exam (with the exceptions of Networking Essentials, #70-058* and Microsoft Windows 2000 Accelerated Exam for MCPs Certified on Microsoft Windows NT 4.0, #70-240).

How to Become a Microsoft Certified Professional+Internet

To become an MCP specializing in Internet technology, you must pass the following exams:

◆ Internetworking with Microsoft TCP/IP on Microsoft Windows NT 4.0, #70-059*

◆ Implementing and Supporting Microsoft Windows NT Server 4.0, #70-067*

◆ Implementing and Supporting Microsoft Internet Information Server 3.0 and Microsoft Index Server 1.1, #70-077*

 OR Implementing and Supporting Microsoft Internet Information Server 4.0, #70-087*

How to Become a Microsoft Certified Professional+Site Building

To be certified as an MCP+Site Building, you need to pass two of the following exams:

◆ Designing and Implementing Web Sites with Microsoft FrontPage 98, #70-055

◆ Designing and Implementing Commerce Solutions with Microsoft Site Server 3.0, Commerce Edition, #70-057

◆ Designing and Implementing Web Solutions with Microsoft Visual InterDev 6.0, #70-152

How to Become a Microsoft Certified Database Administrator

There are two MCDBA tracks, one tied to Windows 2000, the other based on Windows NT 4.0.

Windows 2000 Track

To become an MCDBA in the Windows 2000 track, you must pass three core exams and one elective exam.

Core Exams

The core exams required to become an MCDBA in the Windows 2000 track are as follows:

◆ Installing, Configuring, and Administering Microsoft Windows 2000 Server, #70-215

 OR Microsoft Windows 2000 Accelerated Exam for MCPs Certified on Microsoft Windows NT 4.0, #70-240 (only for those who have passed exams #70-067*, #70-068*, and #70-073*)

◆ Administering Microsoft SQL Server 7.0, #70-028

◆ Designing and Implementing Databases with Microsoft SQL Server 7.0, #70-029

Elective Exams

You must also pass one elective exam from the following list:

◆ Implementing and Administering a Microsoft Windows 2000 Network Infrastructure, #70-216 (only for those who have *not* already passed #70-067*, #70-068*, and #70-073*)

OR Microsoft Windows 2000 Accelerated Exam for MCPs Certified on Microsoft Windows NT 4.0, #70-240 (only for those who have passed exams #70-067*, #70-068*, and #70-073*)

◆ Designing and Implementing Distributed Applications with Microsoft Visual C++ 6.0, #70-015

◆ Designing and Implementing Data Warehouses with Microsoft SQL Server 7.0 and Microsoft Decision Support Services 1.0, #70-019

◆ Implementing and Supporting Microsoft Internet Information Server 4.0, #70-087*

◆ Designing and Implementing Distributed Applications with Microsoft Visual FoxPro 6.0, #70-155

◆ Designing and Implementing Distributed Applications with Microsoft Visual Basic 6.0, #70-175

Windows NT 4.0 Track

To become an MCDBA in the Windows NT 4.0 track, you must pass four core exams and one elective exam.

Core Exams

The core exams required to become an MCDBA in the Windows NT 4.0 track are as follows:

◆ Administering Microsoft SQL Server 7.0, #70-028

◆ Designing and Implementing Databases with Microsoft SQL Server 7.0, #70-029

◆ Implementing and Supporting Microsoft Windows NT Server 4.0, #70-067*

◆ Implementing and Supporting Microsoft Windows NT Server 4.0 in the Enterprise, #70-068*

Elective Exams

You must also pass one elective exam from the following list:

◆ Designing and Implementing Distributed Applications with Microsoft Visual C++ 6.0, #70-015

◆ Designing and Implementing Data Warehouses with Microsoft SQL Server 7.0 and Microsoft Decision Support Services 1.0, #70-019

◆ Internetworking with Microsoft TCP/IP on Microsoft Windows NT 4.0, #70-059*

◆ Implementing and Supporting Microsoft Internet Information Server 4.0, #70-087*

◆ Designing and Implementing Distributed Applications with Microsoft Visual FoxPro 6.0, #70-155

◆ Designing and Implementing Distributed Applications with Microsoft Visual Basic 6.0, #70-175

How to Become a Microsoft Certified Systems Engineer

You must pass operating system exams and two elective exams to become an MCSE. The MCSE certification path is divided into two tracks: Windows 2000 and Windows NT 4.0.

The following lists show the core requirements for the Windows 2000 and Windows NT 4.0 tracks and the electives.

Windows 2000 Track

The Windows 2000 track requires you to pass five core exams (or an accelerated exam and another core exam). You must also pass two elective exams.

Core Exams

The Windows 2000 track core requirements for MCSE certification include the following for those who have *not* passed #70-067, #70-068, and #70-073:

◆ Installing, Configuring, and Administering Microsoft Windows 2000 Professional, #70-210

◆ Installing, Configuring, and Administering Microsoft Windows 2000 Server, #70-215

◆ Implementing and Administering a Microsoft Windows 2000 Network Infrastructure, #70-216

◆ Implementing and Administering a Microsoft Windows 2000 Directory Services Infrastructure, #70-217

The Windows 2000 Track core requirements for MCSE certification include the following for those who have passed #70-067*, #70-068*, and #70-073*:

◆ Microsoft Windows 2000 Accelerated Exam for MCPs Certified on Microsoft Windows NT 4.0, #70-240

All candidates must pass one of these three additional core exams:

◆ Designing a Microsoft Windows 2000 Directory Services Infrastructure, #70-219

  OR Designing Security for a Microsoft Windows 2000 Network, #70-220

  OR Designing a Microsoft Windows 2000 Infrastructure, #70-221

Elective Exams

Any MCSE elective exams that are current (not slated for retirement) when the Windows 2000 core exams are released can be used to fulfill the requirement of two elective exams. In addition, core exams #70-219,

#70-220, and #70-221 can be used as elective exams, as long as they are not already being used to fulfill the "additional core exams" requirement outlined previously. Exam #70-222 (Upgrading from Microsoft Windows NT 4.0 to Microsoft Windows 2000), can also be used to fulfill this requirement. Finally, selected third-party certifications that focus on interoperability may count for this requirement. Watch the Microsoft MCP Web site (www.microsoft.com/mcp) for more information on these third-party certifications.

Windows NT 4.0 Track

The Windows NT 4.0 track is also organized around core and elective exams.

Core Exams

The four Windows NT 4.0 track core requirements for MCSE certification are as follows:

◆ Implementing and Supporting Microsoft Windows NT Server 4.0, #70-067*

◆ Implementing and Supporting Microsoft Windows NT Server 4.0 in the Enterprise, #70-068*

◆ Microsoft Windows 3.1, #70-030*

  OR Microsoft Windows for Workgroups 3.11, #70-048*

  OR Implementing and Supporting Microsoft Windows 95, #70-064*

  OR Implementing and Supporting Microsoft Windows NT Workstation 4.0, #70-073*

  OR Implementing and Supporting Microsoft Windows 98, #70-098

◆ Networking Essentials, #70-058*

Elective Exams

For the Windows NT 4.0 track, you must pass two of the following elective exams for MCSE certification:

◆ Implementing and Supporting Microsoft SNA Server 3.0, #70-013

   OR Implementing and Supporting Microsoft SNA Server 4.0, #70-085

◆ Implementing and Supporting Microsoft Systems Management Server 1.2, #70-018

   OR Implementing and Supporting Microsoft Systems Management Server 2.0, #70-086

◆ Designing and Implementing Data Warehouse with Microsoft SQL Server 7.0, #70-019

◆ Microsoft SQL Server 4.2 Database Implementation, #70-021*

   OR Implementing a Database Design on Microsoft SQL Server 6.5, #70-027

   OR Implementing a Database Design on Microsoft SQL Server 7.0, #70-029

◆ Microsoft SQL Server 4.2 Database Administration for Microsoft Windows NT, #70-022*

   OR System Administration for Microsoft SQL Server 6.5 (or 6.0), #70-026

   OR System Administration for Microsoft SQL Server 7.0, #70-028

◆ Microsoft Mail for PC Networks 3.2-Enterprise, #70-037*

◆ Internetworking with Microsoft TCP/IP on Microsoft Windows NT (3.5–3.51), #70-053*

   OR Internetworking with Microsoft TCP/IP on Microsoft Windows NT 4.0, #70-059*

◆ Implementing and Supporting Web Sites Using Microsoft Site Server 3.0, #70-056

◆ Implementing and Supporting Microsoft Exchange Server 4.0, #70-075*

   OR Implementing and Supporting Microsoft Exchange Server 5.0, #70-076

   OR Implementing and Supporting Microsoft Exchange Server 5.5, #70-081

◆ Implementing and Supporting Microsoft Internet Information Server 3.0 and Microsoft Index Server 1.1, #70-077*

   OR Implementing and Supporting Microsoft Internet Information Server 4.0, #70-087*

◆ Implementing and Supporting Microsoft Proxy Server 1.0, #70-078

   OR Implementing and Supporting Microsoft Proxy Server 2.0, #70-088

◆ Implementing and Supporting Microsoft Internet Explorer 4.0 by Using the Internet Explorer Resource Kit, #70-079

   OR Implementing and Supporting Microsoft Internet Explorer 5.0 by Using the Internet Explorer Resource Kit, #70-080

◆ Designing a Microsoft Windows 2000 Directory Services Infrastructure, #70-219

◆ Designing Security for a Microsoft Windows 2000 Network, #70-220

◆ Designing a Microsoft Windows 2000 Infrastructure, #70-221

◆ Upgrading from Microsoft Windows NT 4.0 to Microsoft Windows 2000, #70-222

How to Become a Microsoft Certified Systems Engineer+Internet

You must pass seven operating system exams and two elective exams to become an MCSE specializing in Internet technology.

Core Exams

The following seven core exams are required for MCSE+Internet certification:

◆ Networking Essentials, #70-058*

◆ Internetworking with Microsoft TCP/IP on Microsoft Windows NT 4.0, #70-059*

◆ Implementing and Supporting Microsoft Windows 95, #70-064*

   OR Implementing and Supporting Microsoft Windows NT Workstation 4.0, #70-073*

   OR Implementing and Supporting Microsoft Windows 98, #70-098

◆ Implementing and Supporting Microsoft Windows NT Server 4.0, #70-067*

◆ Implementing and Supporting Microsoft Windows NT Server 4.0 in the Enterprise, #70-068*

◆ Implementing and Supporting Microsoft Internet Information Server 3.0 and Microsoft Index Server 1.1, #70-077*

   OR Implementing and Supporting Microsoft Internet Information Server 4.0, #70-087*

◆ Implementing and Supporting Microsoft Internet Explorer 4.0 by Using the Internet Explorer Resource Kit, #70-079

OR Implementing and Supporting Microsoft Internet Explorer 5.0 by Using the Internet Explorer Resource Kit, #70-080

Elective Exams

You must also pass two of the following elective exams for MCSE+Internet certification:

◆ System Administration for Microsoft SQL Server 6.5, #70-026

   OR Administering Microsoft SQL Server 7.0, #70-028

◆ Implementing a Database Design on Microsoft SQL Server 6.5, #70-027

   OR Designing and Implementing Databases with Microsoft SQL Server 7.0, #70-029

◆ Implementing and Supporting Web Sites Using Microsoft Site Server 3.0, # 70-056

◆ Implementing and Supporting Microsoft Exchange Server 5.0, #70-076

   OR Implementing and Supporting Microsoft Exchange Server 5.5, #70-081

◆ Implementing and Supporting Microsoft Proxy Server 1.0, #70-078

   OR Implementing and Supporting Microsoft Proxy Server 2.0, #70-088

◆ Implementing and Supporting Microsoft SNA Server 4.0, #70-085

How to Become a Microsoft Certified Solution Developer

The MCSD certification has undergone substantial revision. Listed below are the requirements for the new track (available fourth quarter 1998) as well as the old.

New Track

For the new track, you must pass three core exams and one elective exam.

Core Exams

The core exams are as follows. You must pass one exam in each of the following groups:

Desktop Applications Development (one required)

◆ Designing and Implementing Desktop Applications with Microsoft Visual C++ 6.0, #70-016

   OR Designing and Implementing Desktop Applications with Microsoft Visual FoxPro 6.0, #70-156

   OR Designing and Implementing Desktop Applications with Microsoft Visual Basic 6.0, #70-176

Distributed Applications Development (one required)

◆ Designing and Implementing Distributed Applications with Microsoft Visual C++ 6.0, #70-015

   OR Designing and Implementing Distributed Applications with Microsoft Visual FoxPro 6.0, #70-155

   OR Designing and Implementing Distributed Applications with Microsoft Visual Basic 6.0, #70-175

Solution Architecture (required)

◆ Analyzing Requirements and Defining Solution Architectures, #70-100

Elective Exam

You must pass one of the following elective exams:

◆ Designing and Implementing Distributed Applications with Microsoft Visual C++ 6.0, #70-015

◆ Designing and Implementing Desktop Applications with Microsoft Visual C++ 6.0, #70-016

◆ Designing and Implementing Data Warehouses with Microsoft SQL Server 7.0, #70-019

◆ Developing Applications with C++ Using the Microsoft Foundation Class Library, #70-024

◆ Implementing OLE in Microsoft Foundation Class Applications, #70-025

◆ Implementing a Database Design on Microsoft SQL Server 6.5, #70-027

◆ Implementing a Database Design on Microsoft SQL Server 7.0, #70-029

◆ Designing and Implementing Web Sites with Microsoft FrontPage 98, #70-055

◆ Designing and Implementing Commerce Solutions with Microsoft Site Server 3.0, Commerce Edition, #70-057

◆ Programming with Microsoft Visual Basic 4.0, #70-065*

◆ Application Development with Microsoft Access for Windows 95 and the Microsoft Access Developer's Toolkit, #70-069

◆ Designing and Implementing Solutions with Microsoft Office 2000 and Microsoft Visual Basic for Applications, #70-091

◆ Designing and Implementing Database Applications with Microsoft Access 2000, #70-097

◆ Designing and Implementing Collaborative Solutions with Microsoft Outlook 2000 and Microsoft Exchange Server 5.5, #70-105

◆ Designing and Implementing Web Solutions with Microsoft Visual InterDev 6.0, #70-152

◆ Designing and Implementing Distributed Applications with Microsoft Visual FoxPro 6.0, #70-155

◆ Designing and Implementing Desktop Applications with Microsoft Visual FoxPro 6.0, #70-156

◆ Developing Applications with Microsoft Visual Basic 5.0, #70-165

◆ Designing and Implementing Distributed Applications with Microsoft Visual Basic 6.0, #70-175

◆ Designing and Implementing Desktop Applications with Microsoft Visual Basic 6.0, #70-176

Old Track

For the old track, you must pass two core technology exams and two elective exams for MCSD certification. The following lists show the required technology exams and elective exams needed for MCSD certification.

Core Exams

You must pass the following two core technology exams to qualify for MCSD certification:

◆ Microsoft Windows Architecture I, #70-160*

◆ Microsoft Windows Architecture II, #70-161*

Elective Exams

You must also pass two of the following elective exams to become an MSCD:

◆ Designing and Implementing Distributed Applications with Microsoft Visual C++ 6.0, #70-015

◆ Designing and Implementing Desktop Applications with Microsoft Visual C++ 6.0, #70-016

◆ Designing and Implementing Data Warehouses with Microsoft SQL Server 7.0, #70-019

◆ Microsoft SQL Server 4.2 Database Implementation, #70-021*

   OR Implementing a Database Design on Microsoft SQL Server 6.5, #70-027

   OR Implementing a Database Design on Microsoft SQL Server 7.0, #70-029

◆ Developing Applications with C++ Using the Microsoft Foundation Class Library, #70-024

◆ Implementing OLE in Microsoft Foundation Class Applications, #70-025

◆ Programming with Microsoft Visual Basic 4.0, #70-065

   OR Developing Applications with Microsoft Visual Basic 5.0, #70-165

   OR Designing and Implementing Distributed Applications with Microsoft Visual Basic 6.0, #70-175

◆ Designing and Implementing Desktop Applications with Microsoft Visual Basic 6.0, #70-176

◆ Microsoft Access 2.0 for Windows-Application Development, #70-051*

   OR Microsoft Access for Windows 95 and the Microsoft Access Development Toolkit, #70-069

   OR Designing and Implementing Database Applications with Microsoft Access 2000, #70-097

◆ Developing Applications with Microsoft Excel 5.0 Using Visual Basic for Applications, #70-052*

◆ Programming in Microsoft Visual FoxPro 3.0 for Windows, #70-054*

   OR Designing and Implementing Distributed Applications with Microsoft Visual FoxPro 6.0, #70-155

   OR Designing and Implementing Desktop Applications with Microsoft Visual FoxPro 6.0, #70-156

◆ Designing and Implementing Web Sites with Microsoft FrontPage 98, #70-055

◆ Designing and Implementing Commerce Solutions with Microsoft Site Server 3.0, Commerce Edition, #70-057

◆ Designing and Implementing Solutions with Microsoft Office (code-named Office 9) and Microsoft Visual Basic for Applications, #70-091

◆ Designing and Implementing Collaborative Solutions with Microsoft Outlook 2000 and Microsoft Exchange Server 5.5, #70-105

◆ Designing and Implementing Web Solutions with Microsoft Visual InterDev 6.0, #70-152

Becoming a Microsoft Certified Trainer

To fully understand the requirements and process for becoming an MCT, you need to obtain the Microsoft Certified Trainer Guide document from the following WWW site:

    http://www.microsoft.com/mcp/certstep/mct.htm

At this site, you can read the document as a Web page or display and download it as a Word file. The MCT Guide explains the process for becoming an MCT. The general steps for the MCT certification are as follows:

1. Complete and mail a Microsoft Certified Trainer application to Microsoft. You must include proof of your skills for presenting instructional material. The options for doing so are described in the MCT Guide.

2. Obtain and study the Microsoft Trainer Kit for the Microsoft Official Curricula (MOC) courses for which you want to be certified. Microsoft Trainer Kits can be ordered by calling 800-688-0496 in North America. Those of you in other regions should review the MCT Guide for information on how to order a Trainer Kit.

3. Take and pass any required prerequisite MCP exam(s) to measure your current technical knowledge.

4. Prepare to teach a MOC course. Begin by attending the MOC course for which you want to be certified. This is required so that you understand how the course is structured, how labs are completed, and how the course flows.

5. Pass any additional exam requirement(s) to measure any additional product knowledge that pertains to the course.

6. Submit your course preparation checklist to Microsoft so that your additional accreditation may be processed and reflect on your transcript.

> **WARNING**
>
> You should consider the preceding steps a general overview of the MCT certification process. The precise steps that you need to take are described in detail on the Web site mentioned earlier. Do not misinterpret the preceding steps as the exact process you must undergo.

If you are interested in becoming an MCT, you can obtain more information by visiting the Microsoft Certified Training WWW site at `http://www.microsoft.com/train_cert/mct/` or by calling 800-688-0496.

What's on the CD-ROM

This appendix is a brief rundown of what you'll find on the CD-ROM that comes with this book. For a more detailed description of the newly developed *ExamGear, Training Guide Edition* exam simulation software, see Appendix D, "Using the *ExamGear, Training Guide Edition* Software." All items on the CD-ROM are easily accessible from the simple interface. In addition to *ExamGear, Training Guide Edition*, the CD-ROM includes the electronic version of the book in Portable Document Format (PDF), several utility and application programs, and a complete listing of the test objectives and where they are covered within the book.

EXAMGEAR, TRAINING GUIDE EDITION

ExamGear is an exam environment developed exclusively for New Riders Publishing. It is, we believe, the best exam software available. In addition to providing a means of evaluating your knowledge of the *Training Guide* material, *ExamGear, Training Guide Edition* features several innovations that help you to improve your mastery of the subject matter.

For example, the practice tests allow you to check your score by exam area or category to determine which topics you need to study more. In another mode, *ExamGear, Training Guide Edition* allows you to obtain immediate feedback on your responses in the form of explanations for the correct and incorrect answers.

Although *ExamGear, Training Guide Edition* exhibits most of the full functionality of the retail version of *ExamGear*, including the exam format and question types, this special version is written to the Training Guide content. It is designed to aid you in assessing how well you understand the Training Guide material and enable you to experience most of the question formats you will see on the actual exam. It is not as complete a simulation of the exam as the full *ExamGear* retail product. It also does not include some of the features of the full retail product, such as access to the mentored discussion groups. However, it serves as an excellent method for assessing your knowledge of the Training Guide content and gives you the experience of taking an electronic exam.

Again, for a more complete description of *ExamGear, Training Guide Edition* features, see Appendix D.

EXCLUSIVE ELECTRONIC VERSION OF TEXT

The CD-ROM also contains the electronic PDF version of this book. The electronic version comes complete with all figures as they appear in the book. You will find that the search capabilities of the reader come in handy for study and review purposes.

COPYRIGHT INFORMATION AND DISCLAIMER

New Riders Publishing's *ExamGear* test simulator:
Copyright ©2000 by New Riders Publishing. All rights reserved. Made in U.S.A.

Using the *ExamGear, Training Guide Edition* Software

This training guide includes a special version of *ExamGear*—a revolutionary new test engine that is designed to give you the best in certification exam preparation. *ExamGear* offers sample and practice exams for many of today's most in-demand technical certifications. This special Training Guide edition is included with this book as a tool to utilize in assessing your knowledge of the Training Guide material while also providing you with the experience of taking an electronic exam.

In the rest of this appendix, we describe in detail what *ExamGear, Training Guide Edition* is, how it works, and what it can do to help you prepare for the exam. Note that although the Training Guide edition includes nearly all the test simulation functions of the complete, retail version, the questions focus on the Training Guide content rather than on simulating the actual Microsoft exam. Also, this version does not offer the same degree of online support that the full product does.

EXAM SIMULATION

One of the main functions of *ExamGear, Training Guide Edition* is exam simulation. To prepare you to take the actual vendor certification exam, the Training Guide edition of this test engine is designed to offer the most effective exam simulation available.

Question Quality

The questions provided in the *ExamGear, Training Guide Edition* simulations are written to high standards of technical accuracy. The questions tap the content of the Training Guide chapters and help you review and assess your knowledge before you take the actual exam.

Interface Design

The *ExamGear, Training Guide Edition* exam simulation interface provides you with the experience of taking an electronic exam. This enables you to effectively prepare for taking the actual exam by making the test experience a familiar one. Using this test simulation can help eliminate the sense of surprise or anxiety that you might experience in the testing center, because you will already be acquainted with computerized testing.

STUDY TOOLS

ExamGear provides you with several learning tools to help prepare you for the actual certification exam.

Effective Learning Environment

The *ExamGear, Training Guide Edition* interface provides a learning environment that not only tests you through the computer, but also teaches the material you need to know to pass the certification exam. Each question comes with a detailed explanation of the correct answer and provides reasons why the other options were incorrect. This information helps to reinforce the knowledge you have already and also provides practical information you can use on the job.

Automatic Progress Tracking

ExamGear, Training Guide Edition automatically tracks your progress as you work through the test questions. From the Item Review tab (discussed in detail later in this appendix), you can see at a glance how well you are scoring by objective, by unit, or on a question-by-question basis (see Figure D.1). You can also configure *ExamGear* to drill you on the skills you need to work on most.

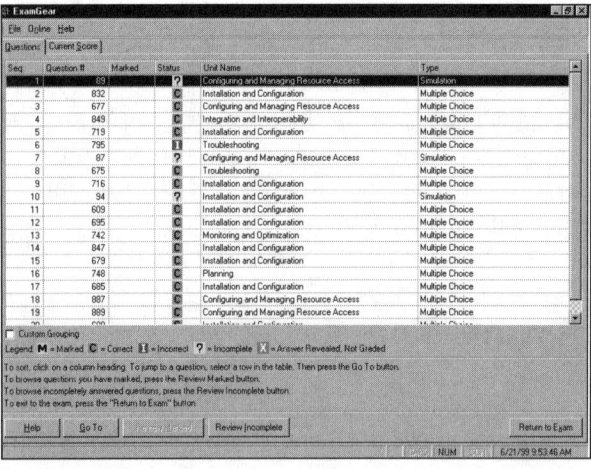

FIGURE D.1
Item review.

How *ExamGear, Training Guide Edition* Works

ExamGear comprises two main elements: the interface and the database. The *interface* is the part of the program that you use to study and to run practice tests. The *database* stores all the question-and-answer data.

Interface

The *ExamGear, Training Guide Edition* interface is designed to be easy to use and provides the most effective study method available. The interface enables you to select from among the following modes:

◆ **Study Mode.** In this mode, you can select the number of questions you want to see and the time you want to allow for the test. You can select questions from all the chapters or from specific chapters. This enables you to reinforce your knowledge in a specific area or strengthen your knowledge in areas pertaining to a specific objective. During the exam, you can display the correct answer to each question along with an explanation of why it is correct.

◆ **Practice Exam.** In this mode, you take an exam that is designed to simulate the actual certification exam. Questions are selected from all test-objective groups. The number of questions selected and the time allowed are set to match those parameters of the actual certification exam.

◆ **Adaptive Exam.** In this mode, you take an exam simulation using the adaptive testing technique. Questions are taken from all test-objective groups. The questions are presented in a way that ensures your mastery of all the test objectives. After you have a passing score or if you reach a point where it is statistically impossible for you to pass, the exam is ended. This method provides a rapid assessment of your readiness for the actual exam.

Database

The *ExamGear, Training Guide Edition* database stores a group of test questions along with answers and explanations. At least three databases are included for each Training Guide edition product. One includes the questions from the ends of the chapters. Another includes the questions from the Practice Exam. The third is a database of new questions that have not appeared in the book. Additional exam databases may also be available for purchase online and are simple to download. Look ahead to the section "Obtaining Updates" in this appendix to find out how to download and activate additional databases.

INSTALLING AND REGISTERING EXAMGEAR, TRAINING GUIDE EDITION

This section provides instructions for *ExamGear, Training Guide Edition* installation and describes the process and benefits of registering your Training Guide edition product.

Requirements

ExamGear requires a computer with the following:

◆ Microsoft Windows 95, Windows 98, Windows NT 4.0, or Windows 2000.

A Pentium or later processor is recommended.

◆ Microsoft's Internet Explorer 4.01 or later version.

Internet Explorer 4.01 (or a later version) must be installed. (Even if you use a different browser, you still need to have Internet Explorer 4.01 or later installed.)

◆ A minimum of 16MB of RAM.

As with any Windows application, the more memory, the better your performance.

◆ A connection to the Internet.

An Internet connection is not required for the software to work, but it is required for online registration, product updates, downloading bonus question sets, and for unlocking other exams. These processes are described in more detail later.

Installing *ExamGear, Training Guide Edition*

Install *ExamGear, Training Guide Edition* by running the setup program that you found on the *ExamGear, Training Guide Edition* CD. Follow these instructions to install the Training Guide edition on your computer:

1. Insert the CD in your CD-ROM drive. The Autorun feature of Windows should launch the software. If you have Autorun disabled, click Start, and choose Run. Go to the root directory of the CD and choose START.EXE. Click Open and OK.

2. Click the button in the circle, and you see the welcome screen. From here you can install *ExamGear*. Click the ExamGear button to begin installation.

3. The Installation Wizard appears onscreen and prompts you with instructions to complete the installation. Select a directory on which to install *ExamGear, Training Guide Edition* (the Installation Wizard defaults to `C:\Program Files\ExamGear`).

4. The Installation Wizard copies the *ExamGear, Training Guide Edition* files to your hard drive, adds ExamGear, Training Guide Edition to your Program menu, adds values to your Registry, and installs test engine's DLLs to the appropriate system folders. To ensure that the process was successful, the Setup program finishes by running *ExamGear, Training Guide Edition.*

5. The Installation Wizard logs the installation process and stores this information in a file named `INSTALL.LOG`. This log file is used by the uninstall process in the event that you choose to remove *ExamGear, Training Guide Edition* from your computer. Because the *ExamGear* installation adds Registry keys and DLL files to your computer, it is important to uninstall the program appropriately (see the section "Removing *ExamGear, Training Guide Edition* from Your Computer").

Registering *ExamGear, Training Guide Edition*

The Product Registration Wizard appears when *ExamGear, Training Guide Edition* is started for the first time, and *ExamGear* checks at startup to see whether you are registered. If you are not registered, the main menu is hidden, and a Product Registration Wizard appears. Remember that your computer must have an Internet connection to complete the Product Registration Wizard.

The first page of the Product Registration Wizard details the benefits of registration; however, you can always elect not to register. The Show This Message at Startup Until I Register option enables you to decide whether the registration screen should appear every time *ExamGear, Training Guide Edition* is started. If you click the Cancel button, you return to the main menu. You can register at any time by selecting Online, Registration from the main menu.

The registration process is composed of a simple form for entering your personal information, including your name and address. You are asked for your level of experience with the product you are testing on and whether you purchased *ExamGear, Training Guide Edition* from a retail store or over the Internet. The information will be used by our software designers and marketing department to provide us with feedback about the usability and usefulness of this product. It takes only a few seconds to fill out and transmit the registration data. A confirmation dialog box appears when registration is complete.

After you have registered and transmitted this information to New Riders, the registration option is removed from the pull-down menus.

Registration Benefits

Remember that registration allows you access to download updates from our FTP site using *ExamGear, Training Guide Edition* (see the later section "Obtaining Updates").

Removing *ExamGear, Training Guide Edition* from Your Computer

In the event that you elect to remove the *ExamGear, Training Guide Edition* product from your computer, an uninstall process has been included to ensure that it is removed from your system safely and completely. Follow these instructions to remove *ExamGear* from your computer:

1. Click Start, Settings, Control Panel.

2. Double-click the Add/Remove Programs icon.

3. You are presented with a list of software that is installed on your computer. Select ExamGear, Training Guide Edition from the list and click the Add/Remove button. The *ExamGear, Training Guide Edition* software is then removed from your computer.

It is important that the INSTALL.LOG file be present in the directory where you have installed *ExamGear, Training Guide Edition* should you ever choose to uninstall the product. Do not delete this file. The INSTALL.LOG file is used by the uninstall process to safely remove the files and Registry settings that were added to your computer by the installation process.

USING *EXAMGEAR, TRAINING GUIDE EDITION*

ExamGear is designed to be user friendly and very intuitive, eliminating the need for you to learn some confusing piece of software just to practice answering questions. Because the software has a smooth learning curve, your time is maximized because you start practicing almost immediately.

General Description of How the Software Works

ExamGear has three modes of operation: Study Mode, Practice Exam, and Adaptive Exam (see Figure D.2). All three sections have the same easy-to-use interface. Using Study Mode, you can hone your knowledge as well as your test-taking abilities through the use of the Show Answers option. While you are taking the test, you can expose the answers along with a brief description of why the given answers are right or wrong. This gives you the ability to better understand the material presented.

The Practice Exam section has many of the same options as Study Mode, but you cannot reveal the answers. This way, you have a more traditional testing environment with which to practice.

The Adaptive Exam questions continuously monitor your expertise in each tested topic area. If you reach a point at which you either pass or fail, the software ends the examination. As in the Practice Exam, you cannot reveal the answers.

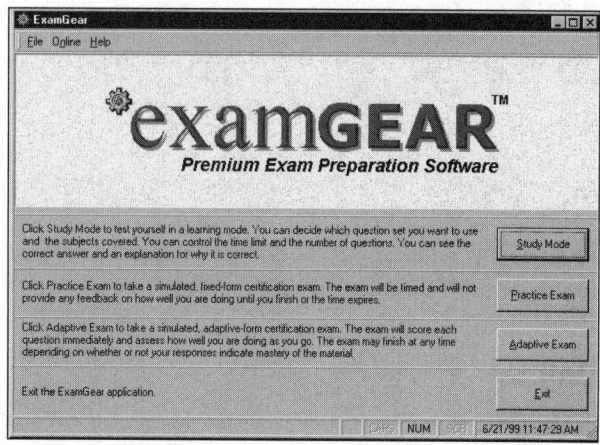

FIGURE D.2
The opening screen offers three testing modes.

Menu Options

The *ExamGear, Training Guide Edition* interface has an easy-to-use menu that provides the following options:

Menu	Command	Description
File	Print	Prints the current screen.
	Print Setup	Allows you to select the printer.
	Exit ExamGear	Exits the program.
Online	Registration	Starts the Registration Wizard and allows you to register online. This menu option is removed after you have successfully registered the product.
	Check for Product Updates	Downloads product catalog for Web-based updates.
	Web Browser	Opens the Web browser. It appears like this on the main menu, but more options appear after the browser is opened.
Help	Contents	Opens *ExamGear, Training Guide Edition's* help file.
	About	Displays information about *ExamGear, Training Guide Edition*, including serial number, registered owner, and so on.

File

The File menu allows you to exit the program and configure print options.

Online

In the Online menu, you can register *ExamGear, Training Guide Edition*, check for product updates (update the *ExamGear* executable as well as check for free, updated question sets), and surf Web pages. The Online menu is always available, except when you are taking a test.

Registration

Registration is free and allows you access updates. Registration is the first task that *ExamGear, Training Guide Edition* asks you to perform. You will not have access to the free product updates if you do not register.

Check for Product Updates

This option takes you to *ExamGear, Training Guide Edition's* Web site, where you can update the software. Registration is required for this option to be available. You must also be connected to the Internet to use this option. The *ExamGear* Web site lists the options that have been made available since your version of *ExamGear* was installed on your computer.

Web Browser

This option provides a convenient way to start your Web browser and connect to the New Riders Web site while you are working in *ExamGear, Training Guide Edition*. Click the Exit button to leave the Web browser and return to the *ExamGear* interface.

Help

As it suggests, this menu option gives you access to *ExamGear's* help system. It also provides important information like your serial number, software version, and so on.

Starting a Study Mode Session

Study Mode enables you to control the test in ways that actual certification exams do not allow:

◆ You can set your own time limits.

◆ You can concentrate on selected skill areas (units).

◆ You can reveal answers or have each response graded immediately with feedback.

◆ You can restrict the questions you see again to those missed or those answered correctly a given number of times.

◆ You can control the order in which questions are presented (random order or in order by skill area/unit).

To begin testing in Study Mode, click the Study Mode button from the main Interface screen. You are presented with the Study Mode configuration page (see Figure D.3).

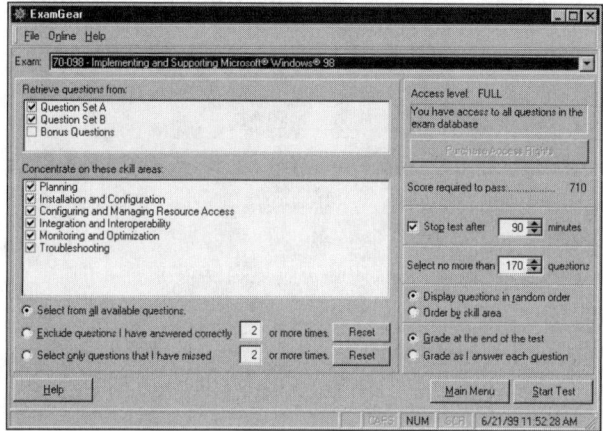

FIGURE D.3
The Study Mode configuration page.

At the top of the Study Mode configuration screen, you see the Exam drop-down list. This list shows the activated exam that you have purchased with your *ExamGear, Training Guide Edition* product, as well as any other exams you may have downloaded or any Preview exams that were shipped with your version of *ExamGear*. Select the exam with which you want to practice from the drop-down list.

Below the Exam drop-down list, you see the questions that are available for the selected exam. Each exam has at least one question set. You can select the individual

question set or any combination of the question sets if there is more than one available for the selected exam.

Below the Question Set list is a list of skill areas or chapter on which you can concentrate. These skill areas or chapters reflect the units of exam objectives defined by Microsoft for the exam. Within each skill area you will find several exam objectives. You can select a single skill area or chapter to focus on, or you can select any combination of the available skill areas/chapters to customize the exam to your individual needs.

In addition to specifying which question sets and skill areas you want to test yourself on, you can also define which questions are included in the test based on your previous progress working with the test. *ExamGear, Training Guide Edition* automatically tracks your progress with the available questions. When configuring the Study Mode options, you can opt to view all the questions available within the question sets and skill areas you have selected, or you can limit the questions presented. Choose from the following options:

◆ **Select from All Available Questions.** This option causes *ExamGear, Training Guide Edition* to present all available questions from the selected question sets and skill areas.

◆ **Exclude Questions I Have Answered Correctly *X* or More Times.** *ExamGear* offers you the option to exclude questions that you have previously answered correctly. You can specify how many times you want to answer a question correctly before *ExamGear* considers you to have mastered it (the default is two times).

◆ **Select Only Questions That I Have Missed *X* or More Times.** This option configures *ExamGear, Training Guide Edition* to drill you only on questions that you have missed repeatedly. You may specify how many times you must miss a question before *ExamGear* determines that you have not mastered it (the default is two times).

At any time, you can reset *ExamGear, Training Guide Edition*'s tracking information by clicking the Reset button for the feature you want to clear.

At the top-right side of the Study Mode configuration sheet, you can see your access level to the question sets for the selected exam. Access levels are either Full or Preview. For a detailed explanation of each of these access levels, see the section "Obtaining Updates" in this appendix.

Under your access level, you see the score required to pass the selected exam. Below the required score, you can select whether the test will be timed and how much time will be allowed to complete the exam. Select the Stop Test After 90 Minutes check box to set a time limit for the exam. Enter the number of minutes you want to allow for the test (the default is 90 minutes). Deselecting this check box allows you to take an exam with no time limit.

You can also configure the number of questions included in the exam. The default number of questions changes with the specific exam you have selected. Enter the number of questions you want to include in the exam in the Select No More than *X* Questions option.

You can configure the order in which *ExamGear, Training Guide Edition* presents the exam questions. Select from the following options:

◆ **Display Questions in Random Order.** This option is the default option. When selected, it causes *ExamGear, Training Guide Edition* to present the questions in random order throughout the exam.

◆ **Order by Skill Area.** This option causes *ExamGear* to group the questions presented in the exam by skill area. All questions for each selected skill area are presented in succession. The test progresses from one selected skill area to the next, until all the questions from each selected skill area have been presented.

ExamGear offers two options for scoring your exams. Select one of the following options:

◆ **Grade at the End of the Test.** This option configures *ExamGear, Training Guide Edition* to score your test after you have been presented with all the selected exam questions. You can reveal correct answers to a question, but if you do, that question is not scored.

◆ **Grade as I Answer Each Question.** This option configures *ExamGear* to grade each question as you answer it, providing you with instant feedback as you take the test. All questions are scored unless you click the Show Answer button before completing the question.

You can return to the *ExamGear, Training Guide Edition* main startup screen from the Study Mode configuration screen by clicking the Main Menu button. If you need assistance configuring the Study Mode exam options, click the Help button for configuration instructions.

When you have finished configuring all the exam options, click the Start Test button to begin the exam.

Starting Practice Exams and Adaptive Exams

This section describes practice exams and adaptive exams, defines the differences between these exam options and the Study Mode option, and provides instructions for starting them.

Differences Between the Practice and Adaptive Exams and Study Modes

Question screens in the practice and adaptive exams are identical to those found in Study Mode, except that the

Show Answer, Grade Answer, and Item Review buttons are not available while you are in the process of taking a practice or adaptive exam. The Practice Exam provides you with a report screen at the end of the exam. The Adaptive Exam gives you a brief message indicating whether you've passed or failed the exam.

When taking a practice exam, the Item Review screen is not available until you have answered all the questions. This is consistent with the behavior of most vendors' current certification exams. In Study Mode, Item Review is available at any time.

When the exam timer expires, or if you click the End Exam button, the Examination Score Report screen comes up.

Starting an Exam

From the *ExamGear, Training Guide Edition* main menu screen, select the type of exam you want to run. Click the Practice Exam or Adaptive Exam button to begin the corresponding exam type.

What Is an Adaptive Exam?

To make the certification testing process more efficient and valid and therefore make the certification itself more valuable, some vendors in the industry are using a testing technique called *adaptive testing*. In an adaptive exam, the exam "adapts" to your abilities by varying the difficulty level of the questions presented to you.

The first question in an adaptive exam is typically an easy one. If you answer it correctly, you are presented with a slightly more difficult question. If you answer that question correctly, the next question you see is even more difficult. If you answer the question incorrectly, however, the exam "adapts" to your skill level by presenting you with another question of equal or lesser difficulty on the same subject. If you answer that question correctly, the test begins to increase the difficulty level again. You must correctly answer several questions at a predetermined difficulty level to pass the exam. After you have done this successfully, the exam is ended and scored. If you do not reach the required level of difficulty within a predetermined time (typically 30 minutes) the exam is ended and scored.

Why Do Vendors Use Adaptive Exams?

Many vendors who offer technical certifications have adopted the adaptive testing technique. They have found that it is an effective way to measure a candidate's mastery of the test material in as little time as necessary. This reduces the scheduling demands on the test taker and allows the testing center to offer more tests per test station than they could with longer, more traditional exams. In addition, test security is greater, and this increases the validity of the exam process.

Studying for Adaptive Exams

Studying for adaptive exams is no different from studying for traditional exams. You should make sure that you have thoroughly covered all the material for each of the test objectives specified by the certification exam vendor. As with any other exam, when you take an adaptive exam, either you know the material or you don't. If you are well prepared, you will be able to pass the exam. *ExamGear, Training Guide Edition* allows you to familiarize yourself with the adaptive exam testing technique. This will help eliminate any anxiety you might experience from this testing technique and allow you to focus on learning the actual exam material.

ExamGear's Adaptive Exam

The method used to score the adaptive exam requires a large pool of questions. For this reason, you cannot use this exam in Preview mode. The adaptive exam is presented in much the same way as the practice exam. When you click the Start Test button, you begin answering questions. The adaptive exam does not allow item review, and it does not allow you to mark questions to skip and answer later. You must answer each question when it is presented.

Assumptions

This section describes the assumptions made when designing the behavior of the *ExamGear, Training Guide Edition* adaptive exam.

◆ You fail the test if you fail any chapter or unit, earn a failing overall score, or reach a threshold at which it is statistically impossible for you to pass the exam.

◆ You can fail or pass a test without cycling through all the questions.

◆ The overall score for the adaptive exam is Pass or Fail. However, to evaluate user responses dynamically, percentage scores are recorded for units and the overall score.

Algorithm Assumptions

This section describes the assumptions used in designing the *ExamGear, Training Guide Edition* Adaptive Exam scoring algorithm.

Unit Scores

You fail a unit (and the exam) if any unit score falls below 66%.

Overall Scores

To pass the exam, you must pass all units and achieve an overall score of 86% or higher.

You fail if the overall score percentage is less than or equal to 85% or if any unit score is less than 66%.

Inconclusive Scores

If your overall score is between 67 and 85%, it is considered to be *inconclusive*. Additional questions will be asked until you pass or fail or until it becomes statistically impossible to pass without asking more than the maximum number of questions allowed.

Question Types and How to Answer Them

Because certification exams from different vendors vary, you will face many types of questions on any given exam. *ExamGear, Training Guide Edition* presents you with different question types to allow you to become familiar with the various ways an actual exam may test your knowledge. The Solution Architectures exam, in particular, offers a unique exam format and utilizes question types other than multiple choice. This version of *ExamGear* includes cases—extensive problem descriptions running several pages in length, followed by a number of questions specific to that case. Microsoft refers to these case/question collections as *testlets*. This version of *ExamGear, Training Guide Edition* also includes regular questions that are not attached to a case study. We include these question types to make taking the actual exam easier because you will already be familiar with the steps required to answer each question type. This section describes each of the question types presented by *ExamGear* and provides instructions for answering each type.

Multiple Choice

Most of the questions you see on a certification exam are multiple choice (see Figure D.4). This question type asks you to select an answer from the list provided. Sometimes you must select only one answer, often indicated by answers preceded by option buttons (round selection buttons). At other times, multiple correct answers are possible, indicated by check boxes preceding the possible answer combinations.

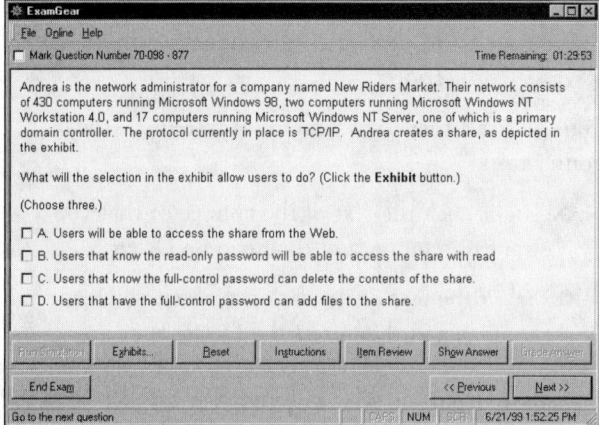

FIGURE D.4
A typical multiple-choice question.

You can use three methods to select an answer:

◆ Click the option button or check box next to the answer. If more than one correct answer to a question is possible, the answers will have check boxes next to them. If only one correct answer to a question is possible, each answer will have an option button next to it. *ExamGear, Training Guide Edition* prompts you with the number of answers you must select.

◆ Click the text of the answer.

◆ Press the alphabetic key that corresponds to the answer.

You can use any one of three methods to clear an option button:

◆ Click another option button.

◆ Click the text of another answer.

◆ Press the alphabetic key that corresponds to another answer.

You can use any one of three methods to clear a check box:

◆ Click the check box next to the selected answer.

◆ Click the text of the selected answer.

◆ Press the alphabetic key that corresponds to the selected answer.

To clear all answers, click the Reset button.

Remember that some of the questions have multiple answers that are correct. Do not let this throw you off. The *multiple correct* questions do not have one answer that is more correct than another. In the *single correct* format, only one answer is correct. *ExamGear, Training Guide Edition* prompts you with the number of answers you must select.

Drag and Drop

One form of drag and drop question is called a *drop and connect* question. These questions present you with a number of objects and connectors. The question prompts you to create relationships between the objects by using the connectors. The gray squares on the left side of the question window are the objects you can select. The connectors are listed on the right side of the question window in the Connectors box. An example is shown in Figure D.5.

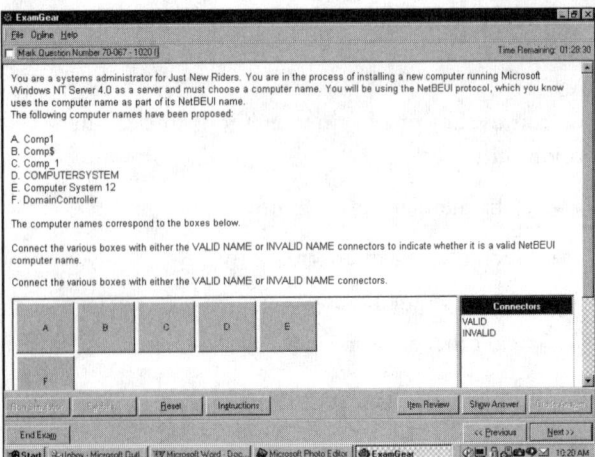

FIGURE D.5
A typical drop and connect question.

To select an object, click it with the mouse. When an object is selected, it changes color from a gray box to a white box. To drag an object, select it by clicking it with the left mouse button and holding the left mouse button down. You can move (or drag) the object to another area on the screen by moving the mouse while holding the left mouse button down.

To create a relationship between two objects, take the following actions:

1. Select an object and drag it to an available area on the screen.

2. Select another object and drag it to a location near where you dragged the first object.

3. Select the connector that you want to place between the two objects. The relationship should now appear complete. Note that to create a relationship, you must have two objects selected. If you try to select a connector without first selecting two objects, you are presented with an error message like that illustrated in Figure D.6.

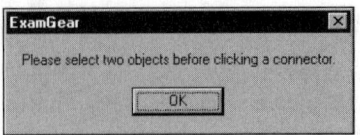

FIGURE D.6
The error message.

Initially, the direction of the relationship established by the connector is from the first object selected to the second object selected. To change the direction of the connector, right-click the connector and choose Reverse Connection.

You can use either of two methods to remove the connector:

◆ Right-click the text of the connector that you want to remove, and then choose Delete.

◆ Select the text of the connector that you want to remove, and then press the Delete key.

To remove from the screen all the relationships you have created, click the Reset button.

Keep in mind that connectors can be used multiple times. If you move connected objects, it will not change the relationship between the objects; to remove the relationship between objects, you must remove the connector that joins them. When *ExamGear, Training Guide Edition* scores a drag-and-drop question, only objects with connectors to other objects are scored.

Another form of drag and drop question is called the *select and place* question. Instead of creating a diagram as you do with the drop and connect question, you are asked a question about a diagram. You then drag and drop labels onto the diagram in order to correctly answer the question.

Ordered-Questions List

In the *ordered-list* question type (see Figure D.7), you are presented with a number of items and are asked to perform two tasks:

1. Build an answer list from items on the list of choices.

2. Put the items in a particular order.

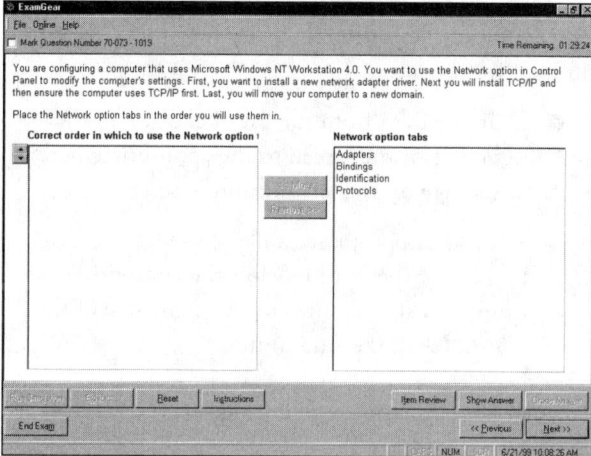

FIGURE D.7
A typical ordered-list question.

You can use any one of the following three methods to add an item to the answer list:

◆ Drag the item from the list of choices on the right side of the screen to the answer list on the left side of the screen.

◆ From the available items on the right side of the screen, double-click the item you want to add.

◆ From the available items on the right side of the screen, select the item you want to add; then click the Move button.

To remove an item from the answer list, you can use any one of the following four methods:

◆ Drag the item you want to remove from the answer list on the left side of the screen back to the list of choices on the right side of the screen.

◆ On the left side of the screen, double-click the item you want to remove from the answer list.

◆ On the left side of the screen, select the item you want to remove from the answer list, and then click the Remove button.

◆ On the left side of the screen, select the item you want to remove from the answer list, and then press the Delete key.

To remove all items from the answer list, click the Reset button.

If you need to change the order of the items in the answer list, you can do so using either of the following two methods:

◆ Drag each item to the appropriate location in the answer list.

◆ In the answer list, select the item that you want to move, and then click the up or down arrow button to move the item.

Keep in mind that items in the list can be selected twice. You may find that an ordered-list question will ask you to list in the correct order the steps required to perform a certain task. Certain steps may need to be performed more than once during the process. Don't think that after you have selected a list item, it is no longer available. If you need to select a list item more than once, you can simply select that item at each appropriate place as you construct your list.

Ordered Tree

The *ordered-tree* question type (see Figure D.8) presents you with a number of items and prompts you to create a tree structure from those items. The tree structure includes two or three levels of nodes.

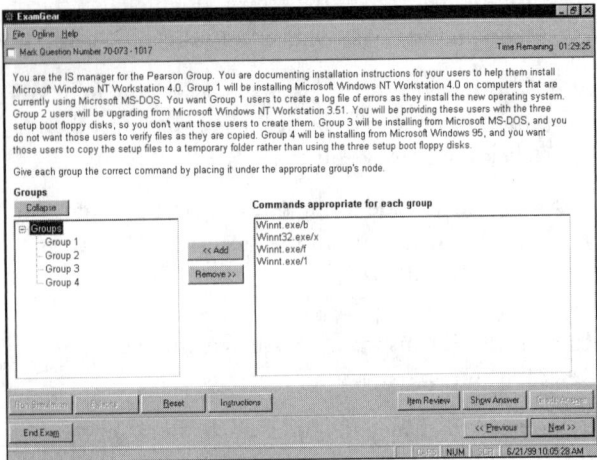

FIGURE D.8
A typical ordered-tree question.

An item in the list of choices can be added only to the appropriate node level. If you attempt to add one of the list choices to an inappropriate node level, you are presented with the error message shown in Figure D.9

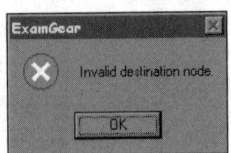

FIGURE D.9
The Invalid Destination Node error message.

Like the ordered-list question, realize that any item in the list can be selected twice. If you need to select a list item more than once, you can simply select that item for the appropriate node as you construct your tree.

Also realize that not every tree question actually requires order to the lists under each node. Think of them as simply tree questions rather than ordered-tree questions. Such questions are just asking you to categorize hierarchically. Order is not an issue.

You can use either of the following two methods to add an item to the tree:

◆ Drag the item from the list of choices on the right side of the screen to the appropriate node of the tree on the left side of the screen.

◆ Select the appropriate node of the tree on the left side of the screen. Select the appropriate item from the list of choices on the right side of the screen. Click the Add button.

You can use either of the following two methods to remove an item from the tree:

◆ Drag an item from the tree to the list of choices.

◆ Select the item and click the Remove button.

To remove from the tree structure all the items you have added, click the Reset button.

Simulations

Simulation questions (see Figure D.10) require you to actually perform a task.

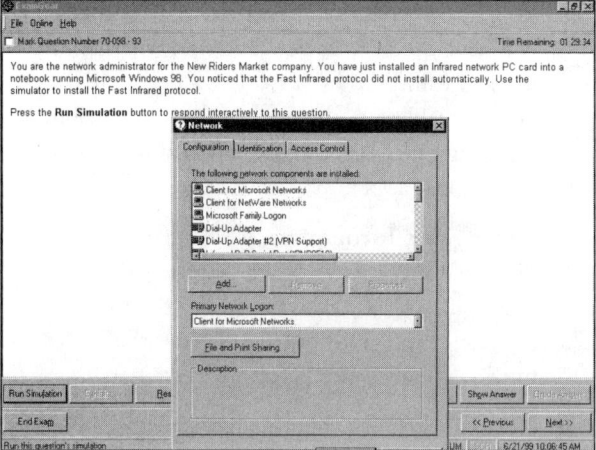

FIGURE D.10
A typical simulation question.

The main screen describes a situation and prompts you to provide a solution. When you are ready to proceed, you click the Run Simulation button in the lower-left corner. A screen or window appears on which you perform the solution. This window simulates the actual software that you would use to perform the required task in the real world. When a task requires several steps to complete, the simulator displays all the necessary screens to allow you to complete the task. When you have provided your answer by completing all the steps necessary to perform the required task, you can click the OK button to proceed to the next question.

You can return to any simulation to modify your answer. Your actions in the simulation are recorded, and the simulation appears exactly as you left it.

Simulation questions can be reset to their original state by clicking the Reset button.

Hot Spot Questions

Hot spot questions (see Figure D.11) ask you to correctly identify an item by clicking an area of the graphic or diagram displayed. To respond to the question, position the mouse cursor over a graphic. Then press the right mouse button to indicate your selection. To select another area on the graphic, you do not need to deselect the first one. Just click another region in the image.

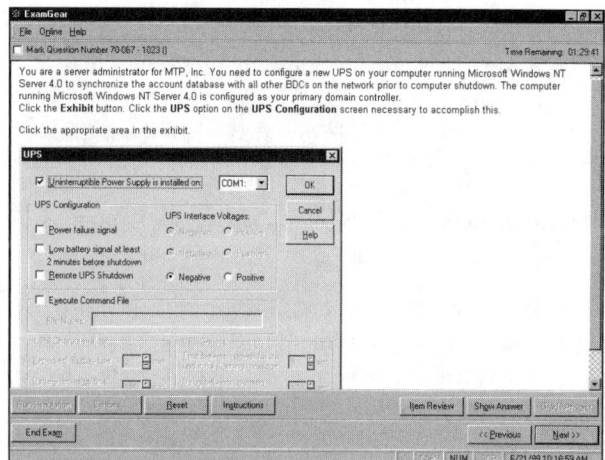

FIGURE D.11
A typical hot spot question.

Standard *ExamGear, Training Guide Edition* Options

Regardless of question type, a consistent set of clickable buttons enables you to navigate and interact with questions. The following list describes the function of each of the buttons you may see. Depending on the question type, some of the buttons will be grayed out and will be inaccessible. Buttons that are appropriate to the question type are active.

◆ **Run Simulation.** This button is enabled if the question supports a simulation. Clicking this button begins the simulation process.

◆ **Exhibits.** This button is enabled if exhibits are provided to support the question. An *exhibit* is an image, video, sound, or text file that provides supplemental information needed to answer the question. If a question has more than one exhibit, a dialog box appears, listing exhibits by name. If only one exhibit exists, the file is opened immediately when you click the Exhibits button.

◆ **Reset.** This button clears any selections you have made and returns the question window to the state in which it appeared when it was first displayed.

◆ **Instructions.** This button displays instructions for interacting with the current question type.

◆ **Item Review.** This button leaves the question window and opens the Item Review screen. For a detailed explanation of the Item Review screen, see the "Item Review" section later in this appendix.

◆ **Show Answer.** This option displays the correct answer with an explanation of why it is correct. If you choose this option, the current question will not be scored.

◆ **Grade Answer.** If Grade at the End of the Test is selected as a configuration option, this button is disabled. It is enabled when Grade as I Answer Each Question is selected as a configuration option. Clicking this button grades the current question immediately. An explanation of the correct answer is provided, just as if the Show Answer button were pressed. The question is graded, however.

◆ **End Exam.** This button ends the exam and displays the Examination Score Report screen.

◆ **<< Previous.** This button displays the previous question on the exam.

◆ **Next >>.** This button displays the next question on the exam.

◆ **<< Previous Marked.** This button is displayed if you have opted to review questions that you have marked using the Item Review screen. This button displays the previous marked question. Marking questions is discussed in more detail later in this appendix.

◆ **<< Previous Incomplete.** This button is displayed if you have opted to review questions that you have not answered using the Item Review screen. This button displays the previous unanswered question.

◆ **Next Marked >>.** This button is displayed if you have opted to review questions that you have marked using the Item Review screen. This button displays the next marked question. Marking questions is discussed in more detail later in this appendix.

◆ **Next Incomplete>>.** This button is displayed if you have opted to review questions, using the Item Review screen, that you have not answered. This button displays the next unanswered question.

Mark Question and Time Remaining

ExamGear provides you with two methods to aid in dealing with the time limit of the testing process. If you find that you need to skip a question or if you want to check the time remaining to complete the test, use one of the options discussed in the following sections.

Mark Question

Check this box to mark a question so that you can return to it later using the Item Review feature. The adaptive exam does not allow questions to be marked because it does not support item review.

Time Remaining

If the test is timed, the Time Remaining indicator is enabled. It counts down minutes remaining to complete the test. The adaptive exam does not offer this feature because it is not timed.

Item Review

The Item Review screen allows you to jump to any question. *ExamGear, Training Guide Edition* considers an *incomplete* question to be any unanswered question or any multiple-choice question for which the total number of required responses has not been selected. For example, if the question prompts for three answers and you selected only A and C, *ExamGear* considers the question to be incomplete.

The Item Review screen enables you to review the exam questions in different ways. You can enter one of two *browse sequences* (series of similar records): Browse Marked Questions or Browse Incomplete Questions. You can also create a custom grouping of the exam questions for review based on a number of criteria.

When using Item Review, if Show Answer was selected for a question while you were taking the exam, the question is grayed out in item review. The question can be answered again if you use the Reset button to reset the question status.

The Item Review screen contains two tabs. The Questions tab lists questions and question information in columns. The Current Score tab provides your exam score information, presented as a percentage for each unit and as a bar graph for your overall score.

The Item Review Questions Tab

The Questions tab on the Item Review screen (see Figure D.12) presents the exam questions and question information in a table. You can select any row you want by clicking in the grid. The Go To button is enabled whenever a row is selected. Clicking the Go To button displays the question on the selected row. You can also display a question by double-clicking that row.

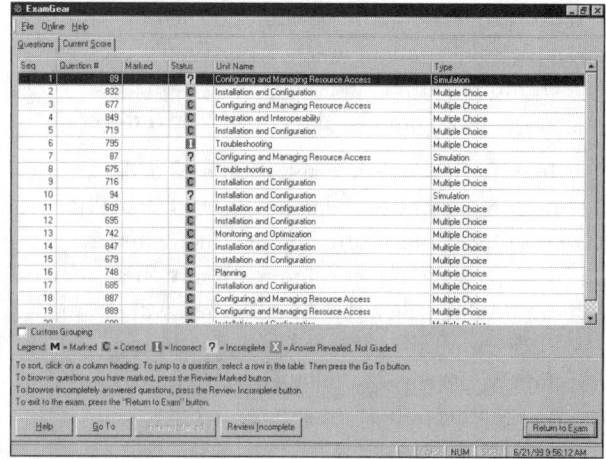

FIGURE D.12
The Questions tab on the Item Review screen.

Columns

The Questions tab contains the following six columns of information:

◆ **Seq.** Indicates the sequence number of the question as it was displayed in the exam.

◆ **Question Number.** Displays the question's identification number for easy reference.

◆ **Marked.** Indicates a question that you have marked using the Mark Question check box.

◆ **Status.** The status can be M for Marked, ? for Incomplete, C for Correct, I for Incorrect, or X for Answer Shown.

- ◆ **Unit Name.** The unit associated with each question.

- ◆ **Type.** The question type, which can be Multiple Choice, Drag and Drop, Simulation, Hot Spot, Ordered List, or Ordered Tree.

To resize a column, place the mouse pointer over the vertical line between column headings. When the mouse pointer changes to a set of right and left arrows, you can drag the column border to the left or right to make the column more or less wide. Simply click with the left mouse button and hold that button down while you move the column border in the desired direction.

The Item Review screen enables you to sort the questions on any of the column headings. Initially, the list of questions is sorted in descending order on the sequence number column. To sort on a different column heading, click that heading. You will see an arrow appear on the column heading indicating the direction of the sort (ascending or descending). To change the direction of the sort, click the column heading again.

The Item Review screen also allows you to create a *custom grouping*. This feature enables you to sort the questions based on any combination of criteria you prefer. For instance, you might want to review the question items sorted first by whether they were marked, then by the unit name, then by sequence number. The Custom Grouping feature allows you to do this. Start by checking the Custom Grouping check box (see Figure D.13). When you do so, the entire questions table shifts down a bit onscreen, and a message appears at the top of the table that reads `Drag a column header here to group by that column`.

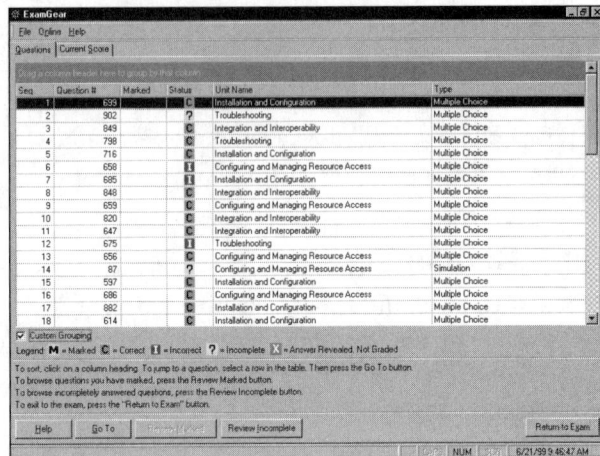

FIGURE D.13
The Custom Grouping check box allows you to create your own question sort order.

Simply click the column heading you want with the left mouse button, hold that button down, and move the mouse into the area directly above the questions table (the custom grouping area). Release the left mouse button to drop the column heading into the custom grouping area. To accomplish the custom grouping previously described, first check the Custom Grouping check box. Then drag the Marked column heading into the custom grouping area above the question table. Next, drag the Unit Name column heading into the custom grouping area. You will see the two column headings joined together by a line that indicates the order of the custom grouping. Finally, drag the Seq column heading into the custom grouping area. This heading will be joined to the Unit Name heading by another line indicating the direction of the custom grouping.

Notice that each column heading in the custom grouping area has an arrow indicating the direction in which items are sorted under that column heading. You can reverse the direction of the sort on an individual column-heading basis using these arrows. Click the column heading in the custom grouping area to change the direction of the sort for that column heading only. For example, using the custom grouping created previously, you can display the question list sorted first in descending order by whether the question was marked, in descending order by unit name, and then in ascending order by sequence number.

The custom grouping feature of the Item Review screen gives you enormous flexibility in how you choose to review the exam questions. To remove a custom grouping and return the Item Review display to its default setting (sorted in descending order by sequence number), simply uncheck the Custom Grouping check box.

The Current Score Tab

The Current Score tab of the Item Review screen (see Figure D.14) provides a real-time snapshot of your score. The top half of the screen is an expandable grid. When the grid is collapsed, scores are displayed for each unit. Units can be expanded to show percentage scores for objectives and subobjectives. Information about your exam progress is presented in the following columns:

◆ **Unit Name.** This column shows the unit name for each objective group.

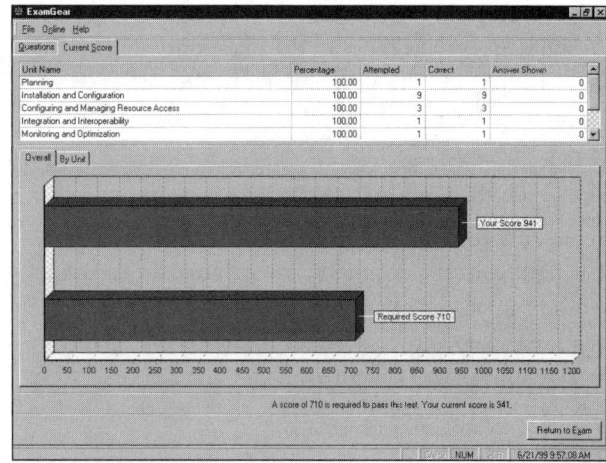

FIGURE D.14
The Current Score tab on the item review screen.

◆ **Percentage.** This column shows the percentage of questions for each objective group that you answered correctly.

◆ **Attempted.** This column lists the number of questions you answered either completely or partially for each objective group.

◆ **Correct.** This column lists the actual number of questions you answered correctly for each objective group.

◆ **Answer Shown.** This column lists the number of questions for each objective group that you chose to display the answer to using the Show Answer button.

The columns in the scoring table are resized and sorted in the same way as those in the questions table on the Item Review Questions tab. Refer to the earlier section "The Item Review Questions Tab" for more details.

A graphical overview of the score is presented below the grid. The graph depicts two red bars: The top bar represents your current exam score, and the bottom bar represents the required passing score. To the right of the bars in the graph is a legend that lists the required score and your score. Below the bar graph is a statement that describes the required passing score and your current score.

In addition, the information can be presented on an overall basis or by exam unit. The Overall tab shows the overall score. The By Unit tab shows the score by unit.

Clicking the End Exam button terminates the exam and passes control to the Examination Score Report screen.

The Return to Exam button returns to the exam at the question from which the Item Review button was clicked.

Review Marked Items

The Item Review screen allows you to enter a browse sequence for marked questions. When you click the Review Marked button, questions that you have previously marked using the Mark Question check box are presented for your review. While browsing the marked questions, you will see the following changes to the buttons available:

◆ The caption of the Next button becomes Next Marked.

◆ The caption of the Previous button becomes Previous Marked.

Review Incomplete

The Item Review screen allows you to enter a browse sequence for incomplete questions. When you click the Review Incomplete button, the questions you did not answer or did not completely answer are displayed for your review. While browsing the incomplete questions, you will see the following changes to the buttons:

◆ The caption of the Next button becomes Next Incomplete.

◆ The caption of the Previous button becomes Previous Incomplete.

Examination Score Report Screen

The Examination Score Report screen (see Figure D.15) appears when the Study Mode, Practice Exam, or Adaptive Exam ends—as the result of timer expiration, completion of all questions, or your decision to terminate early.

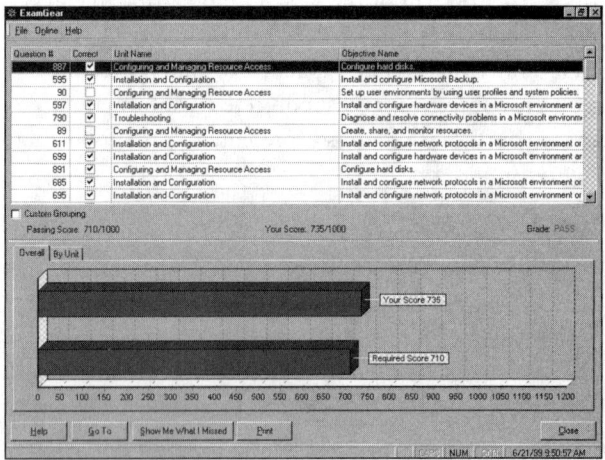

FIGURE D.15
The Examination Score Report screen.

This screen provides you with a graphical display of your test score, along with a tabular breakdown of scores by unit. The graphical display at the top of the screen compares your overall score with the score required to pass the exam. Buttons below the graphical display allow you to open the Show Me What I Missed browse sequence, print the screen, or return to the main menu.

Show Me What I Missed Browse Sequence

The Show Me What I Missed browse sequence is invoked by clicking the Show Me What I Missed button from the Examination Score Report or from the configuration screen of an adaptive exam.

Note that the window caption is modified to indicate that you are in the Show Me What I Missed browse sequence mode. Question IDs and position within the browse sequence appear at the top of the screen, in place of the Mark Question and Time Remaining indicators. Main window contents vary, depending on the question type. The following list describes the buttons available within the Show Me What I Missed browse sequence and the functions they perform:

- ◆ **Return to Score Report.** Returns control to the Examination Score Report screen. In the case of an adaptive exam, this button's caption is Exit, and control returns to the adaptive exam configuration screen.

- ◆ **Run Simulation.** Opens a simulation in Grade mode, causing the simulation to open displaying your response and the correct answer. If the current question does not offer a simulation, this button is disabled.

- ◆ **Exhibits.** Opens the Exhibits window. This button is enabled if one or more exhibits are available for the question.

- ◆ **Instructions.** Shows how to answer the current question type.

- ◆ **Print.** Prints the current screen.

- ◆ **Previous or Next.** Displays missed questions.

Checking the Web Site

To check the New Riders Home Page or the *ExamGear, Training Guide Edition* Home Page for updates or other product information, choose the desired Web site from the Web Sites option of the Online menu. You must be connected to the Internet to reach these Web sites. When you select a Web site, the Internet Explorer browser opens inside the *ExamGear, Training Guide Edition* window and displays the Web site.

OBTAINING UPDATES

The procedures for obtaining updates are outlined in this section.

The Catalog Web Site for Updates

Selecting the Check for Product Updates option from the Online menu shows you the full range of products you can either download for free or purchase. You can download additional items only if you have registered the software.

Product Updates Dialog Box

This dialog box appears when you select Check for Product Updates from the Online menu. *ExamGear, Training Guide Edition* checks for product updates from the New Riders Internet site and displays a list of products available for download. Some items, such as *ExamGear* program updates or bonus question sets for exam databases you have activated, are available for download free of charge.

Types of Updates

Several types of updates may be available for download, including various free updates and additional items available for purchase.

Free Program Updates

Free program updates include changes to the *ExamGear, Training Guide Edition* executables and runtime libraries (DLLs). When any of these items are downloaded, *ExamGear* automatically installs the upgrades. *ExamGear, Training Guide Edition* will be reopened after the installation is complete.

Free Database Updates

Free database updates include updates to the exam or exams that you have registered. Exam updates are contained in compressed, encrypted files and include exam databases, simulations, and exhibits. *ExamGear, Training Guide Edition* automatically decompresses these files to their proper location and updates the *ExamGear* software to record version changes and import new question sets.

CONTACTING NEW RIDERS PUBLISHING

At New Riders, we strive to meet and exceed the needs of our customers. We have developed *ExamGear, Training Guide Edition* to surpass the demands and expectations of network professionals seeking technical certifications, and we think it shows. What do you think?

If you need to contact New Riders regarding any aspect of the *ExamGear, Training Guide Edition* product line, feel free to do so. We look forward to hearing from you. Contact us at the following address or phone number:

New Riders Publishing
201 West 103 Street
Indianapolis, IN 46290
800-545-5914

You can also reach us on the World Wide Web:

http://www.newriders.com

Technical Support

Technical support is available at the following phone number during the hours specified:

317-581-3833

Monday through Friday, 10:00 a.m.–3:00 p.m. Central Standard Time.

Customer Service

If you have a damaged product and need a replacement or refund, please call the following phone number:

800-858-7674

Product Updates

Product updates can be obtained by choosing *ExamGear, Training Guide Edition*'s Online pull-down menu and selecting Products Updates. You'll be taken to a private Web site with full details.

Product Suggestions and Comments

We value your input! Please email your suggestions and comments to the following address:

    `certification@mcp.com`

LICENSE AGREEMENT

YOU SHOULD CAREFULLY READ THE FOLLOWING TERMS AND CONDITIONS BEFORE BREAKING THE SEAL ON THE PACKAGE. AMONG OTHER THINGS, THIS AGREEMENT LICENSES THE ENCLOSED SOFTWARE TO YOU AND CONTAINS WARRANTY AND LIABILITY DISCLAIMERS. BY BREAKING THE SEAL ON THE PACKAGE, YOU ARE ACCEPTING AND AGREEING TO THE TERMS AND CONDITIONS OF THIS AGREEMENT. IF YOU DO NOT AGREE TO THE TERMS OF THIS AGREEMENT, DO NOT BREAK THE SEAL. YOU SHOULD PROMPTLY RETURN THE PACKAGE UNOPENED.

LICENSE

Subject to the provisions contained herein, New Riders Publishing (NRP) hereby grants to you a nonexclusive, nontransferable license to use the object-code version of the computer software product (Software) contained in the package on a single computer of the type identified on the package.

SOFTWARE AND DOCUMENTATION

NRP shall furnish the Software to you on media in machine-readable object-code form and may also provide the standard documentation (Documentation) containing instructions for operation and use of the Software.

LICENSE TERM AND CHARGES

The term of this license commences upon delivery of the Software to you and is perpetual unless earlier terminated upon default or as otherwise set forth herein.

TITLE

Title, ownership right, and intellectual property rights in and to the Software and Documentation shall remain in NRP and/or in suppliers to NRP of programs contained in the Software. The Software is provided for your own internal use under this license. This license does not include the right to sublicense and is personal to you and therefore may not be assigned (by operation of law or otherwise) or transferred without the prior written consent of NRP. You acknowledge that the Software in source code form remains a confidential trade secret of NRP and/or its suppliers and therefore you agree not to attempt to decipher or decompile, modify, disassemble, reverse engineer, or prepare derivative works of the Software or develop source code for the Software or knowingly allow others to do so. Further, you may not copy the Documentation or other written materials accompanying the Software.

UPDATES

This license does not grant you any right, license, or interest in and to any improvements, modifications, enhancements, or updates to the Software and Documentation. Updates, if available, may be obtained by you at NRP's then-current standard pricing, terms, and conditions.

LIMITED WARRANTY AND DISCLAIMER

NRP warrants that the media containing the Software, if provided by NRP, is free from defects in material and workmanship under normal use for a period of sixty (60) days from the date you purchased a license to it.

THIS IS A LIMITED WARRANTY AND IT IS THE ONLY WARRANTY MADE BY NRP. THE SOFTWARE IS PROVIDED "AS IS" AND NRP SPECIFICALLY DISCLAIMS ALL WARRANTIES OF ANY KIND, EITHER EXPRESS OR IMPLIED, INCLUDING, BUT NOT LIMITED TO, THE IMPLIED WARRANTY OF MERCHANTABILITY AND FITNESS FOR A PARTICULAR PURPOSE. FURTHER, COMPANY DOES NOT WARRANT, GUARANTEE, OR MAKE ANY REPRESENTA-TIONS REGARDING THE USE, OR THE RESULTS OF THE USE, OF THE SOFTWARE IN TERMS OR CORRECTNESS, ACCURACY, RELIABILITY, CURRENTNESS, OR OTHERWISE AND DOES NOT WARRANT THAT THE OPERATION OF ANY SOFTWARE WILL BE UNINTERRUPTED OR ERROR FREE. NRP EXPRESSLY DISCLAIMS ANY WARRANTIES NOT STATED HEREIN. NO ORAL OR WRITTEN INFORMATION OR ADVICE GIVEN BY NRP, OR ANY NRP DEALER, AGENT, EMPLOYEE, OR OTHERS SHALL CREATE,

MODIFY, OR EXTEND A WARRANTY OR IN ANY WAY INCREASE THE SCOPE OF THE FOREGOING WARRANTY, AND NEITHER SUBLICENSEE OR PURCHASER MAY RELY ON ANY SUCH INFORMATION OR ADVICE. If the media is subjected to accident, abuse, or improper use, or if you violate the terms of this Agreement, then this warranty shall immediately be terminated. This warranty shall not apply if the Software is used on or in conjunction with hardware or programs other than the unmodified version of hardware and programs with which the Software was designed to be used as described in the Documentation.

LIMITATION OF LIABILITY

Your sole and exclusive remedies for any damage or loss in any way connected with the Software are set forth below.

UNDER NO CIRCUMSTANCES AND UNDER NO LEGAL THEORY, TORT, CONTRACT, OR OTHERWISE, SHALL NRP BE LIABLE TO YOU OR ANY OTHER PERSON FOR ANY INDIRECT, SPECIAL, INCIDENTAL, OR CONSEQUENTIAL DAMAGES OF ANY CHARACTER INCLUDING, WITHOUT LIMITATION, DAMAGES FOR LOSS OF GOODWILL, LOSS OF PROFIT, WORK STOPPAGE, COMPUTER FAILURE OR MALFUNCTION, OR ANY AND ALL OTHER COMMERCIAL DAMAGES OR LOSSES, OR FOR ANY OTHER DAMAGES EVEN IF NRP SHALL HAVE BEEN INFORMED OF THE POSSIBILITY OF SUCH DAMAGES, OR FOR ANY CLAIM BY ANOTHER PARTY. NRP'S THIRD-PARTY PROGRAM SUPPLIERS MAKE NO WARRANTY, AND HAVE NO LIABILITY WHATSOEVER, TO YOU. NRP's sole and exclusive obligation and liability and your exclusive remedy shall be: upon NRP's election, (i) the replacement of our defective media; or (ii) the repair or correction of your defective media if NRP is able, so that it will conform to the above warranty; or (iii) if NRP is unable to replace or repair, you may terminate this license by returning the Software. Only if you inform NRP of your problem during the applicable warranty period will NRP be obligated to honor this warranty. SOME STATES OR JURISDICTIONS DO NOT ALLOW THE EXCLUSION OF IMPLIED WARRANTIES OR LIMITATION OR EXCLUSION OF CONSE-QUENTIAL DAMAGES, SO THE ABOVE LIMITATIONS OR EXCLUSIONS MAY NOT APPLY TO YOU. THIS WARRANTY GIVES YOU SPECIFIC LEGAL RIGHTS AND YOU MAY ALSO HAVE OTHER RIGHTS WHICH VARY BY STATE OR JURISDICTION.

MISCELLANEOUS

If any provision of the Agreement is held to be ineffective, unenforceable, or illegal under certain circumstances for any reason, such decision shall not affect the validity or enforceability (i) of such provision under other circumstances or (ii) of the remaining provisions hereof under all circumstances, and such provision shall be reformed to and only to the extent necessary to make it effective, enforceable, and legal under such circumstances. All headings are solely for convenience and shall not be considered in interpreting this Agreement. This Agreement shall be governed by and construed under New York law as such law applies to agreements between New York residents entered into and to be performed entirely within New York, except as required by U.S. Government rules and regulations to be governed by Federal law.

YOU ACKNOWLEDGE THAT YOU HAVE READ THIS AGREEMENT, UNDERSTAND IT, AND AGREE TO BE BOUND BY ITS TERMS AND CONDITIONS. YOU FURTHER AGREE THAT IT IS THE COMPLETE AND EXCLUSIVE STATE-MENT OF THE AGREEMENT BETWEEN US THAT SUPERSEDES ANY PROPOSAL OR PRIOR AGREEMENT, ORAL OR WRITTEN, AND ANY OTHER COMMUNICATIONS BETWEEN US RELATING TO THE SUBJECT MATTER OF THIS AGREEMENT.

U.S. GOVERNMENT RESTRICTED RIGHTS

Use, duplication, or disclosure by the Government is subject to restrictions set forth in subparagraphs (a) through (d) of the Commercial Computer-Restricted Rights clause at FAR 52.227-19 when applicable, or in subparagraph (c) (1) (ii) of the Rights in Technical Data and Computer Software clause at DFARS 252.227-7013, and in similar clauses in the NASA FAR Supplement.

Index

A

acks/sec (DHCP statistic), 110
Action menu (DHCP manager)
    All Tasks command, 105
    Delete command, 106
    Display Statistics command, 104
    Export List command, 106
    Properties command, 106
    Reconcile All Scopes command, 105
    Refresh command, 106
    Unauthorize command, 105
actions, DNS console, 56-57
Activate Scope dialog box, 96
Active Directory, 97-98
authorizing, 97-98
    DNS modifications, 46-47
    user principal name mapping, 404
Active Directory-integrated storage (zones), 35
active queue length, monitoring (DHCP), 109
active study strategies, 452
adaptive exams
    described, 454-455
    process, 455-456
    tips, 463
Add Exclusions dialog box, 93–94
Add Standalone Snap-In dialog box, 400
Add/Remove applet, WINS installation, 249-250
Add/Remove Programs dialog box, 32
Add/Remove Snap-In dialog box, 217
adding
    areas to autonomous system, 316
    Certificates snap-in to MMC, 399
    counters to System Monitor, 269
    custom applications to ICS, 358
    DNS table entries, 55-56
    IP addresses, 190
    Network Monitor, 204-205
    NWLink, 192-193
    RIP, 294-295
    snap-ins to MMC, 35, 250-251
    TCP/IP, 187, 189
Address Assignment tab (Routing and Remote Access Window), 365
addresses
    classes, 301
    resolution, 287
    translation
        DNS names, 366
        internal addresses, 361
        NAT, 362
adjacencies, 319-320
administrative tools
    Performance console, 154
    WINS manager
        Advanced tab, 254
        Database Verification tab, 253
        General tab, 252
        Intervals tab, 252
        properties, configuring, 252
Advanced Settings dialog box, 195
Advanced tab
    DHCP manager, 107-108
    TCP/IP Properties dialog box, 191
    WINS manager, 254
Advanced TCP/IP Settings dialog box, 198
    DNS client computer configuration, 45

advertisements
  link-state, 299, 443
  LSAs, 309
aggregating connections, 151
AH (Authentication Header), 212–213
aliases, FQDNs, 50
All Tasks command (Action menu),
  DHCP manager, 105
allocating IP addresses (DHCP), 151
anti-replay, ESP, 214
APIs, MADCAP, 91
applets, Add/Remove, 249-250
applications
  Configure Your Server, 83
  DHCP manager
    Advanced tab, 107-108
    Properties tab, 106
    Server Statistics screen, 104-105
  DNS console
    actions, 56-57
    testing DNS service, 53
  Network Monitor, 440
    installing, 204-205
    panes, 207
  predefined port numbers, 360
  Web browsers, testing DNS services, 54
  WINS manager, 265-267
Applications tab (Connection Properties dialog box), 358
areas, 312
  backbone, 312-314
  creating, 316
  routing, 315
  stub areas, 318
ARPA (Advanced Research Projects Agency), 179
ASBR (autonomous system border routing), 317–318
assigning IP addresses, 190
    DHCP, 433-434
attacks, replay, 214
attributes (remote access policies), selecting, 141
authentication, 200
  AH, 212–213
  EAP, configuring, 158
  Kerberos V5, 439
    domain controllers, 201
    interoperability, 202

  logon process, 201
  PAP, configuring, 159
  PPP, demand-dial routing, 329-330
  RADIUS, 147
  SPAP, configuring, 159
Authentication Data field
  AH, 213
  ESP, 214
AutoDHCP service, 357
automatic backup (WINS database), configuring, 252
automating BOOTP functionality, 82
autonomous systems, 301
  areas, 312, 315
  backbone, 312-314
autostatic updates, 327
availability (routers), 293
avoiding count-to-infinity, 297
AXFR counters, 61

B

B-nodes, 246, 262-263, 441
Back Up Database option (WINS manager), 266
backbone (OSPF), 312-313
backing up WINS database, 252
backup designated routers, 319
backward compatibility, WINS , 244, 262
BAP (Bandwidth Allocation Protocol), 146, 151
baselines, 209
best-effort delivery, 196-197
binary, converting to decimal, 183
bindings, 194-195, 439
BOOTP, 82
  DHCP server, configuring, 106
  Forwarder, 80
bottlenecks, VPNs, 150
broadcasting
  B-nodes, 246
  NetBIOS, 245
browsers (Web), testing DNS services, 54
brute force attacks, 397
bundled features (RAS), 132
burst handling, WINS database, 254

C

CA Certificate Request dialog box, 394
CA Identifying Information dialog box, 393
Caching Memory counter, 60
caching-only servers (DNS), 42-43, 432
calculating
    hops, 297
    SPF, 312
callback, 330
    options, 138
caller ID, 330
captures, 206, 333-334
    creating, 207-208
    filtering, 209
    interpreting, 209
CAs (Certification Authorities), 384, 446
    advanced options, 449
    certificates
        checking pending requests, 401-402
        CRL, 407-408
        mapping to user accounts, 403-404
        processing requests, 401
        renewing, 397-398
        revoking, 406-407
        viewing, 405
    enterprise root CAs, 448
    enterprise subordinate CAs, 448
    installing, 386-389, 448-450
        requirements, 390-391
    Intermediate, 398
    mapping to user accounts, 450
    parent-child relationship, 389
    renewing, 388
    requirements, 447
    Root CA, 388, 397
    standalone root CAs, 385-386, 449
        attributes, 447
        installing , 394
    standalone subordinate CAs , 391-394, 449
    Windows 2000 Certification Authority, 384-385
case studies
    exams
        format, 456
        tips, 463

    implementing DHCP, 114-116
    NAT configuration, 270, 369-370
    remote access, implementing in complex environments,
      161-162
    Rockwell Financial Services, 413-414
    small office with dedicated connections, 339-340
CC (DNS domain), 21
central IAS policies, 136
Certificate Import Wizard dialog box, 411
Certificate Server 1.0, upgrading, 394
Certificate Services, 446
certificates, 383, 446
    CAs, 384
        installing, 386-388
        Standalone CAs, 385-386
        Windows 2000 Certification Authority, 384-385
    CRL, 407-408
    mapping to user accounts, 403–404
    pending requests, checking, 401-402
    processing requests, 401
    renewing, 398
    requesting, 399
        Windows 2000 Certificates Services Web page, 400
    revoking, 406-407
    validity period, 388
    viewing, 405
Certificates snap-in, 399
Certification Authority. *See* CAs
certification process. *See also* exams
    exams, scheduling, 503
    requirements
        Microsoft Certified Database Administrator
            (MCDBA), 505-506
        Microsoft Certified Professional (MCP), 504
        Microsoft Certified Professional + Internet
            (MCP + Internet), 505
        Microsoft Certified Professional + Site Building
            (MCP + Site Building), 505
        Microsoft Certified Solution Developer (MCSD),
            509-512
        Microsoft Certified Systems Engineer (MCSE),
            506-508
        Microsoft Certified Systems Engineer + Internet
            (MCSE+ Internet), 509
        Microsoft Certified Trainer (MCT), 512-513

sources for information on, 504

types of certification

Microsoft Certified Database Administrator
(MCDBA), 504

Microsoft Certified Professional (MCP), 503

Microsoft Certified Professional + Internet (MCP+
Internet), 503

Microsoft Certified Professional + Site Building
(MCP + Site Building), 503

Microsoft Certified Solution Developer
(MCSD), 504

Microsoft Certified Systems Engineer (MCSE), 504

Microsoft Certified Systems Engineer + Internet
(MCSE +Internet), 504

Microsoft Certified Trainer (MCT), 504

CHAP (Challenge Handshake Authentication
Protocol), 158

characteristics

Standalone CAs, 385

Windows 2000 Certification Authority, 385

checking pending certificate requests, 401-402

class D IP addresses, multicast scopes, 91

class-based internetworks, RIP version 1, 305

classes, 183-184

IP addresses, 301

variable length subnet masks, 185–186

clearing DNS server cache, 58

client computers

DNS

advanced TCP/IP configuration, 45

configuring, 44

NAT, enabling, 446

WINS, 246

Client Services for NetWare. *See* CSNW

clients

DHCP, 83

NAT, enabling, 365

WINS, troubleshooting, 259

CNAMEs, 50

COM (DNS domain), 20

commands

DHCP manager, Action menu

All Tasks, 105

Delete, 106

Display Statistics, 104

Export List, 106

Properties, 106

Reconcile All Scopes, 105

Refresh, 106

Unauthorize Scopes, 105

NSLOOKUP, 51

ROUTE

destination parameter, 332

gateway parameter, 332

metric parameter, 332

syntax, 331

common-sense study strategies, 453

communication, directed messages, 262

comparing

ICS and NAT, 356

L2TP

and IPSec, 215-216

and PPTP, 149, 202

link-state and distance-vector routing, 295

MS-CHAP and MS-CHAP v2, 158

tunnel mode and transport mode, 211

compatibility. *See also* backward compatibility

Completing the Configure DNS Server Wizard
dialog box, 40

Completing the Network Connection dialog box, 139

Completing the Windows Components Wizard
dialog box, 85

Configure Devices dialog box, 150

configuring

bindings, providers, 195

DDNS, 47

DHCP, 111

advanced options, 107-108

objectives, 77

scope gateway addresses, 97

server, 106

DNS

caching-only servers, 42-43

client computer, 44-45

delegated zones, 54-55

DHCP clients, 102-104

performance monitoring, 62-63

record scavenging, 57-58

reverse lookup zones, 41-42

root name server, 33

server properties, 58-60

Standard Primary Forward Lookup zones, 39-40

zones, 34-38

Event Logging, 363
IPSec
    policies, 216-218
    remote access logging, 228
    transport mode, 222
multilink, 151
NAT, 363
    case study, 270, 369-370
    DHCP, 365
    DNS, 365
    interfaces, 354, 366-368
    properties, 353
    timeout values, 364
NetBIOS, 261
Netowork Monitor, captures, 207-208
network bindings, 194-195
NWLink, 193-194
OSPF, 309, 311
private network servers, 359
remote access, 132
    authentication protocols, 158-159
    encryption protocols, 159-160
    inbound connections, 136-139
    profiles, 143-146
    remote users, 135-136
    security, 156-157, 438
RIP, 303–305
RIP Version 2, 306
RRAS, DHCP integration, 152
servers, Internet access, 359
static routes, 331-332
TCP/IP
    DHCP, 189-190
    packet filtering, 197-199
    WINS, 191
virtual links, 315
VPNs, 147, 149-150
WINS, 250–252
    performance monitoring, 268-269
    replication, 254-255, 257
WINS Manager
    Advanced tab, 254
    Database Verification tab, 253
    General tab, 252
    Intervals tab, 252

conflicts (DHCP)
    check queue length, monitoring, 109–110
    conflict detection, enabling, 111
Connection Properties dialog box, 358
    Applications tab, 358
    Services tab, 359
connections
    aggregating, 151
    data link protocols, 134
    demand-dial routing, 443
        establishing, 324
        one-way, 325
        persistent, 325-326
        two-way, 325
    IPSec, monitoring, 226
    network bindings, configuring, 194-195
    providers, 194
    remote access
        authentication protocols, configuring, 158-159
        encryption protocols, configuring, 159-160
        implementing in complex environments, 161-162
        managing, 152
        monitoring, 154-155
        policies, 136, 139-142
        profiles, configuring, 143-146
        security, configuring, 156-157
    VPNs, 202, 211
    WINS, troubleshooting, 259
conserving IP addresses, 89, 362
Control Panel, DHCP installation, 87
convergence, 296
    count-to-infinity, 296
    split horizon, 297
    triggered updates, 298
converting
    binary to decimal, 183
    dotted decimal notation to binary, 181–183
count-to-infinity, 296
counters (performance)
    DHCP, 435-436
    DNS, 60, 433
    identifying, 61
    RAS object, 152-153
    remote access, 438
    WINS object, 267-268

creating
  areas, 316
  delegated zones, 54-55
  DHCP scopes, 91-96
  dial-up connections, 136-139
  IP packet filters, 197-199
  IPSec policies, 216-218
  multicast scopes, 100-101
  network captures, 207-208
  remote access
    policies, 139-143
    profiles, 436-437
  resource records, 55-56
  reverse lookup zones, 41-42
  Standard Primary Forward Lookup zones, 39-40
  superscopes, 99-100
criteria, establishing multilink connecions, 151
CRL (certificate revocation list), 406-408
Crocker, Steve, 80
Croft, Bill, 82
CSNW (Client Services for NetWare), 193
custom applications, adding to ICS, 358
customer service, *ExamGear, Training Guide Edition*
  software, 538
customizing IPSec, 220, 224-225

D

data link protocols, 134
data security, 199
Data Storage Location dialog box, 393
Database Node Memory counter, 60
Database Verification tab, WINS manager, 253
databases
  CA, importing, 395, 397
  DNS
    record types, 26
    SOA records, 33
  exchange process, 320
  link-state, 309
  routing table, lookup process, 292
  scopes, 189
  topological, 312

WINS
  backing up, 252
  intervals, configuring, 252
  replication, configuring, 247, 254-255, 257, 441
Dynamic DNS, 47, 432
declines/sec (DHCP statistic), 110
default gateway address, 187, 442
Default Response Rule Authentication Method
  dialog box, 219
Delegated Domain Name dialog box, 54
delegating
  CA issuance, 398
  domains, 432
  zones, 54-55
Delete command (Action menu), DHCP manager, 106
demand-dial routing, 443
  autostatic updates, 327
  callback, 330
  connections
    establishing, 324
    one-way, 325
    persistent, 325-326
    two-way, 325
  enabling, 321-322
  security, 328, 443
    PPP authentication protocols, 329
    remote access account lockout, 330
  static routes, 327
  tunneling, 324
designated routers, 318-319
designing
  remote access policies, 143
  networks, traffic considerations, 204
destination parameter (ROUTE command), 332
destination unreachable packets, 287
devices
  node types, 262-264
  routers, 180
  security hosts, 200
DHCP (Dynamic Host Configuration Protocol), 80-81,
  151, 433
  Active Directory, 97-98
  AutoDHCP service, 357
  clients, 83
  configuring, 152, 190, 435-436
  DNS integration, 102-104, 435

implementing, case study, 114-116
installing, 83–87
IP addresses, 79
    obtaining, 433-434
leases, extending, 97
manager application, Server Statistics screen, 104-105
managing, 104-113
multicasting, 90, 100-101
NAT configuration, 365
objectives, 77
performance, configuring, 111
scopes, 88, 434
    creating on servers, 91-96
statistics, 109, 111
superscopes, 88-89, 99-100, 434
unregistered addresses, 433
user classes, 105
vendor classes, 105
DHCP Manager
Action menu
    All Tasks command, 105
    Delete command, 106
    Display Statistics command, 104
    Export List command, 106
    Properties command, 106
    Reconcile All Scopes command, 105
    Refresh command, 106
    Unauthorize command, 105
Advanced tab, 107-108
General tab, 106
dial-in connections
inbound, 135–139
media, selecting, 144
multilink, 437
remote access profiles, configuring, 143-146
dialog boxes
Activate Scope, 96
Add Exclusion, 93-94
Add Standalone Snap-In, 400
Add/Remove Program, 32
Add/Remove Snap-In, 217
Advanced Settings, 195
Advanced TCP/IP Settings, 45, 198
CA Certificate Request, 394
CA Identifying Information, 393
Completing the Configure DNS Server
    Wizard, 40

Completing the Network Connection, 139
Completing the Windows Components Wizard, 85
Configure Devices, 150
Connection Properties, 358
    Applications tab, 358
    Services tab, 359
Data Storage Location, 393
Default Response Rule Authentication Method, 219
Delegated Domain Name, 54
DNS Suffix and NetBIOS Computer Name, 46
Edit Dial-In Profile, 143
Incoming Connections Properties, 151
IP Filter List, 223
IP Security Policy Wizard, 219
Lease Duration, 94
Local Area Connection Properties, 44, 249
Local Area Connection Status, 188, 190
Local File Properties, 227
Management and Monitoring Tools, 205
Network Connection Type, 137
Network Connections, 139
Networking Components, 138
Networking Services, 31
New Replication Partner, 255
New Resource Record, 43
Policy Properties, 144
Properties, 106-107
Public and Private Key Pair, 393
Renew CA Certificate, 398
Request for Secure Communication, 218
Security Policy Properties, 219
Server Aging/Scavenging Properties, 57
System Properties, 46
TCP/IP Properties, Advanced tab, 191
Windows Components, 84-85, 248, 250
Windows Optional Networking, 87
Zone File, 42
Zone Type, 36, 41
dictionary attacks, 330
digital certificates, 383
digital signatures, 446
directed messages, 262
directories, remote access policies, storage, 136
Directplay Proxy, 356, 445
disabling
logging, 364
recursive queries, 58

discoveries/sec (DHCP statistic), 109
disjointed subnets, 306, 309
Display Server Statistics option (WINS manager), 265
displaying
    certificates, 405
    logging events, 364
    scope information, 88
    VPN connection statistics, 156
distance-vector routing protocols, 296, 442-443
    comparing to link-state, 295
    convergence, 296
    count-to-infinity, 296
    disadvantages, 298
    hops, calculating, 297
    RIP, 443
        configuring, 303, 305
        hop count, 308
        troubleshooting, 336-337
        updates, 307
    RIP Version 2, configuring, 306
distribution points (CRL), 408
DNS (Domain Name Service), 429
    actions, 56-57
    caching-only servers, 432
        configuring, 42-43
    client computer, 44-45
    configuring, 191
    counters, 433
    database, TTL, 34
    delegated zones, creating, 54-55
    DHCP clients, configuring, 102-104
    DHCP workstations, registering, 435
    domains, 18
        delegating, 432
        forwarders, 58
        registering, 22
    dynamic updates. *See* DDNS
    FQDNs, 19, 430
        aliases, 50
        restrictions, 431
    history of, 16-17
    ICS, 357
    installing, 29, 31-32
    leaves, 19
    name resolution, 23-24, 430
        reverse lookup, 430
        testing, 432

namespace architecture, 18
naming conventions, 28
NAT configuration, 365
NetBIOS names, support for, 28
netmask ordering, 59
nodes, 19
performance monitoring, 62-63
primary master servers, 22, 430
record types, 26, 430-431
registration, forcing, 432
resource record, creating manually, 55-56
reverse lookups, 25
    zones, creating, 41-42
root servers, 24
    configuring, 33
    domains, 20
round robin, 59
secondary master servers, 22, 430
servers
    managing, 56-58
    monitoring, 60
SOA record, 33
Standard Primary Forward Lookup zones, creating, 39-40
table entries, scavenging, 57-58
testing
    DNS console, 53
    NSLOOKUP.EXE, 50-53
    PING, 49-50
    Web browsers, 54
tree structure, 19, 430
zones, 19, 22, 430
    configuring, 34-38
    dynamic updates, 432
    storage, 35
DNS console. *See* MMC
DNS Suffix and NetBIOS Computer Name dialog box, 46
documentation, RFCs, 80
DOD (Department of Defense), ARPAnet, 179
domain controllers, 201
domains
    delegating, 54-55, 432
    DNS, 18
        name resolution, 23-24
        record types, 26
        reverse lookups, 25

forwarders, 58
registering, 22
zones, 22
dotted decimal notation, converting to binary, 181–183
drag and drop style questions, 459-460
duplicate scopes, troubleshooting, 96-97
duplicates dropped/sec (DHCP statistic), 108
dynamic address assignment (DHCP), 80-81
dynamic membership, 90
dynamic routing protocols, 292, 442
fault tolerance, 293
on-demand connections, 326
RIP, adding, 294-295
Dynamic Update counter, 60
dynamic updating (DNS), 49, 102-104, 432
dynamically addressed servers, WINS installation, 249

E

EAP (Extensible Authentication Protocol), 158
EAP-TLS (Extensible Authentication Protocol-Transport Layer Security), 329
eavesdropping, 442
enabling, 288-289
silent RIP, 304
Edit Dial-In Profile dialog box, 143
editing IPSec policy rules, 220, 222
EDU (DNS domain), 20
EFS (Encrypting File System) keys, 408, 450
exporting, 409-411
restoring, 411-412
elections, designated routers, 319
email, spamming, 25
enabling
autonomous system border routing, 317-318
conflict detection, 111
encryption
EFS, 408
keys, exporting, 409-411
keys, restoring, 411-412
IPSec, 439
PKI, 382–386
protocols, configuring, 159-160
PPTP, comparing to L2TP, 149
encryption protocols, 148, 202, 437

end-to-end security models, 210
Enterprise Root CAs, 448
Enterprise Subordinate CAs, 448
errors, logging, 363
ESP
anti-replay, 214
trailer fields, 214
establishing
demand-dial connections, 324
multilink connections, 151
Ethernet, 179
Event Logging, configuring, 363
events, displaying, 364
exam prep tips, 453-454
adaptive exams, 463
case study exams, 463
exam session, 462
fixed-form exams, 463
format of exam, 454
adaptive exam, 454-456
case study format, 456
fixed-form exam, 454
list of, 462
question types, 456-457
drag and drop style questions, 459-460
hot area questions, 459
multiple-choice questions, 457
multiple-rating questions, 457
ordered list questions, 460
simulation questions, 457-459
tree questions, 461
retaking exams, 464
scheduling, 503
See also study tips
ExamGear, Training Guide Edition software
adaptive exam mode, 518, 524-526
adaptive exams described, 525
inconclusive scores, 526
overall scores, 526
starting, 525
studying, 525
unit scores, 526
vendors, use of adaptive exams, 525
buttons available, 531-532
customer service, 538
database, 519
described, 517, 521

drag and drop questions, 527-528
exam simulation, 517
Examination Score Report screen, 536
File menu, 522
help, 522
hot spot questions, 531
installation, 519
    process, 519-520
    registration, 520
    requirements, 519
interface, 518
    adaptive exam mode, 518
    practice exam mode, 518
    study mode, 518
interface design, 517
Item Review screen, 533
    Current Score tab, 535-536
    Questions tab, 533-535
    Review Incomplete button, 536
    Review Marked button, 536
learning environment, 518
license agreement, 539-541
mark question option, 533
menu options, 522
    File menu, 522
    help, 522
    Online menu, 522
    product updates, 522
    registration, 522
    Web browser, 522
multiple choice questions, 527
New Riders Publishing, contacting, 538
Online menu, 522
ordered list questions, 529
ordered tree questions, 530
practice exam mode, 518, 524-525
product updates, 522, 538
progress tracking, 518
question types, 526
    drag and drop, 527-528
    hot spot questions, 531
    multiple choice, 527
    ordered list, 529
    ordered tree, 530
    simulations, 531

registration, 520, 522
removing, 520-521
simulation questions, 531
study mode, 518, 522-524
study tools, 517
    learning environment, 518
    progress tracking, 518
suggestions and comments about, 539
technical support, 538
Time Remaining indicator, 533
updates, 537
    Check for Product Updates option, 537
    free database updates, 538
    free program updates, 538
    Product Updates dialog box, 537
Web browser, 522
Web site, 537
excluding
    addresses from DHCP client pool, 94
    routers from DHCP scopes, 97
expiration time, DNS records, 34
expired certificates, renewing, 388, 397-398
**Export List command (Action menu),
  DHCP manager, 106**
exporting EFS keys, 409-411
extending DHCP leases, 97
external routes, autonomous system border routing, 317
extinction interval (WINS database), 253
extinction timeout (WINS database), 253
extranets, one-to-one certificate mapping, 404

F

fault tolerance, dynamic routing, 293
features, Routing and Remote Access Service, 133
fields
    AH (Authentication Header), 213
    ESP trailers, 214
File and Print Services for NetWare. *See* **FPNW**
file systems, hierarchical structure, 19
files, LMHOSTS, 246, 440
filtering
    captures, 209
    IPSec tunnel mode configuration, 224-225
    packets, 197-199

firewalls, proxy servers, 200
first-level domains, 20
fixed-form exams, 454, 463
flat routing architecture, 301
flooding, 299, 443
forcing registration, 432
format, SOA records, 33
forward lookup
    DNS, 23-24
    Standard Primary Forward Lookup zones,
        creating, 39-40
    zones, 36
forwarders, 58
forwarding
    DHCPDiscover messages, 80
    IP multicast traffic, 90
FPNW (File and Print Services for NetWare), 193
FQDNs (fully qualified domain names), 19, 430
    alias, 50
    option 81, 48
    restrictions, 431
frames, 334
fully qualified domain names. *See* FQDNs

G

gateway addresses (DHCP scopes)
    configuring, 97
    ROUTE command parameter, 332
Gateway Services for NetWare. *See* GSNW
General tab
    DHCP manager, 106
    Routing and Remote Access Window, 363
    WINS manager, 252
Gilmore, John, 82
global replication properties (WINS), 257-258
GOV (DNS domain), 21
Graph Pane (Network Monitor), 207
group policies, 136
GSNW (Gateway Services for NetWare), 193

H

H-nodes, 442
H.323 Proxy, 356, 445
hashing algorithms, AH, 212
headers, ESP, 214
hello packets, 299, 443
    backup designated routers, electing, 319
hierarchical internetworks, 302
hierarchies
    CA, planning, 387-388
    DNS, 18–20
    file systems, 19
    OSPF, 312–313
history
    of DNS, 16-17
    of TCP/IP, 178
hop counts, 308
    calculating, 297
    RIP, 443
host routing, 286, 442
    destination unreachable packets, 287
    eavesdropping, 288-289
hosts, security hosts, 200
HOSTS files, 429
hot area questions, 459
hybrid nodes, 262-263

I

IAHC (Internet Ad Hoc Committee), TLDs, 21-22
IANA (Internet Assigned Numbers Authority), 80
    port numbers, selecting, 360
IAS (Internet Authentication Services), 136
ICMP (Internet Control Messaging Protocol), redirect
    messages, 288, 442
ICS (Internet Connection Sharing), 353, 445
    comparing to NAT, 356
    custom applications, adding, 358
    Directplay proxy, 356
    DNS services, 357
    H.323 Proxy, 356
    installing, 356-359
    LDAP Proxy, 356

ICV (Integrity Check Value), 213-214
identifying
    counters, 61
    NetBIOS node types, 264
IETF (Internet Engineering Task Force), 79
    drafts, dynamic DNS updates, 103
    RFCs, exam questions, 80
IGP (Interior Gateway Protocol), 443
illegal subnets, 186
implementing
    DHCP, case study, 114-116
    remote access in complex environments, case study, 161-162
importing old CA database, 395, 397
inbound access, server configuration, 359
inbound applications, adding to NAT, 364
inbound dial-in connections, configuring, 135–139
Incoming Connections Properties dialog box, 151
informs/sec (DHCP statistic), 110
installing
    CAs, 386–389, 448-450
        hierarchies, planning, 387-388
        PKI, planning, 387
        requirements, 390-391
        Standalone Root CA, 394
        Subordinate CAs, 391-394
    DHCP, 83–85
        with Control Panel, 87
    DNS, 29-32
    ExamGear, Training Guide Edition software, 519
        process, 519-520
        registration, 520
        requirements, 519
    ICS, 356-359
    IP routing protocols, objectives, 283
    NAT, 361-362
    Network Monitor, 204-205
    Network Monitor Driver, 206
    NWLink, 192-193
    OSPF, 309–311
    RIP, 294-295
    RRAS, 290-291
    TCP/IP, 187–189
    WINS, 247-250
integrating DHCP in DNS environment, 102-103
inter-area routing, 315

interactive mode, NSLOOKUP, 52
interfaces, NAT, configuring, 354, 366-368
interior routing protocols, 301
Intermediate CAs, 398
internal addresses, NAT translation process, 361
Internet
    address classes, 301
    RFCs, 17, 80
    routing, scalability, 301
Internet Connection Sharing. See ICS
Internet Security Assocation and Key Management Protocol. See ISAKMP
InterNIC. See Network Solutions
interoperability, Kerberos V5, 202
interpreting network captures, 209
Intervals tab (WINS manager), 252
intra-area routing, 315
inverted tree, 19, 430
IP addresses, 79, 179
    adding to subnets, 190
    allocating, 151
    binary, converting to decimal notation, 183
    class D, 91
    classes, 183-184
    conservation, 362
    default gateway, 187
    DHCP, 80-81
        assigning, 433-434
    domain name resolution (DNS), 23-25
    dotted decimal notation, converting to binary, 181–183
    manual configuration, 190
    multicasting, 89
        forwarding table, 90
        groups, joining/leaving, 91
        MADCAP, 90
        scopes, creating, 100-101
    name resolution, WINS, 244
    NAT translation, 362
    packet filters, creating, 197-199
    private addresses, 356
    routing protocols, objectives, 283
    scopes, 88–90, 189, 434
    subnets, 184–186
    supernetting, 89
    superscopes, 88-89, 99–100

unregistered, 80
variable length subnet masks, 185–186
IP Filter List dialog box, 223
IP Security Policy Wizard dialog box, 219
IPConfig utility, 260
reregistering name-to-IP address mappings, 49
IPSec (IP Security Protocol), 148, 199, 210, 437–439
AH (Authentication Header), 212–213
comparing to L2TP, 215-216
customizing, 220
ESP, trailer fields, 214
features, 211-212
ISAKMP/Oakley, 215
monitoring, 226
objectives, 176
policies
configuring, 216-218
rules, editing, 220–222
remote access logging, configuring, 228
transport mode, configuring, 222
tunnel mode, configuring, 222, 224-225
IPX (Internetwork Packet eXchange),
NWLink protocol, 245
ISAKMP (Internet Security Association and Key
Management Protocol), 212
Oakley, 215
issued certificates
CRL, 407-408
revoking, 406-407
iterative queries, 53
IXFR counters, 60-61

J-K

joining multicast groups, 91

Kerberos V5, 201
authentication, 439
domain controllers, 201
interoperability, 202
logon process, 201
keys
digital certificates, 383
EFS, 408
exporting, 409-411
restoring, 411-412

L

L2TP (Layer-2 Tunneling Protocol), 211, 437–439
comparing to IPSec, 215-216
comparing to PPTP, 149, 202
LANs, 179
LDAP (Lightweight Directory Access Protocol), 445
LDAP Proxy, 356
leaves, 19
learning styles, 451-452
Lease Duration dialog box, 94
leases, extending, 97
leaving multicast groups, 91
legacy servers, WINS, objectives, 241-242
Length field (AH), 213
limitations of FQDNs, 431
link-state routing protocols, 299, 442-443
comparing to distance-vector, 295
flooding, 300
OSPF, 309, 443
adjacencies, 320
areas, 312
autonomous system border routing, 317
backbone, 312-313
configuring, 309–311
designated routers, 318-319
inter-area routing, 315
intra-area routing, 315
neighbors, 318
troubleshooting, 445
RIP, troubleshooting, 338-339
listening. *See* eavesdropping
LMHOSTS file, 246, 440
Local Area Connection Properties dialog box, 44, 249
Local Area Connection Status dialog box, 188–190
Local File Properties dialog box, 227
local IAS policies, 136
Local Security Policy console, 218
logging
DHCP server, 106
disabling, 364
IPSec parameters, configuring, 228
NAT, 363
WINS, 254
logon process, 201

lookup
    process (DNS), 23-24, 292
    zones
        delegated, creating, 54-55
        dynamic updates, configuring, 47
        reverse lookup, 25, 41–42
        Standard Primary Forward Lookup, creating, 39-40
LSAs (link-state advertisements), 309, 443
    topological database, 312

M

M-nodes, 262
MAC (Message Authentication Code), 214
MAC (Media Access Control) addresses, 179
macro/micro study strategies, 452
MADCAP (Multicast Dynamic Client Allocation
    Protocol), 90
Management and Monitoring Tools dialog box, 205
managing
    DHCP, 104-109, 111-113
        objectives, 77
        user classes, 105
        vendor classes, 105
    DNS servers, 56-58
    IP routing protocols, 335
        Network Monitor, 333-334
        objectives, 283
    remote access, 152
    WINS, 265
        objectives, 242
manual IP address configuration, 190
mapping
    certificates to user accounts, 403–404, 450
    NAT interfaces, 368
MCDBA. See Microsoft Certified Database
    Administrator
MCP + Internet. See Microsoft Certified Professional +
    Internet
MCP + Site Building. See Microsoft Certified
    Professional + Site Building
MCP. See Microsoft Certified Professional (MCP)
MCSD. See Microsoft Certified Solution Developer
MCSE + Internet. See Microsoft Certified Systems
    Engineer + Internet

MCSE. See Microsoft Certified Systems Engineer
MCT. See Microsoft Certified Trainer
media, selecting dial-in connections, 144
messages
    broadcasts, 245
    DHCPDiscover, 80
    directed, 262
    multicasting, 258, 434
    P-node, 246
metric parameter (ROUTE command), 332
metrics
    remote access, monitoring, 154-155
    RIP, 308, 443
MIBs (management information bases), 112-113
micro/macro study strategies, 452
Microsoft
    MS-CHAP, 158
    NetBEUI, 244
    NetBIOS
        configuring, 261
        LMHOSTS file, 246
    NWLink protocol, 245
Microsoft Certified Database Administrator
    (MCDBA), 504–506
Microsoft Certified Professional (MCP), 503–504
Microsoft Certified Professional + Internet
    (MCP + Internet), 503
Microsoft Certified Professional + Internet
    (MCP+ Internet), certification requirements, 505
Microsoft Certified Professional + Site Building
    (MCP + Site Building), 503–505
Microsoft Certified Solution Developer (MCSD), 504,
    509–512
Microsoft Certified Systems Engineer (MCSE), 504,
    506–508
Microsoft Certified Systems Engineer + Internet
    (MCSE + Internet), 504, 509
Microsoft Certified Trainer (MCT), 504, 512–513
milliseconds/packet (DHCP statistic), 109
MMC (Microsoft Management Console)
    DNS console, actions, 56-57
    snap-ins
        adding, 35
        Certificates snap-in, 399
        Routing and Remote Access, 136
        selecting, 250-251
        WINS management, 247

mobile users, configuring remote access, 135-136

Mockapetris, Paul, 17

modems, aggregating connections, 151

modes, NSLOOKUP, 52

monitoring
    certificate expiration dates, 398
    DHCP, 104-109, 111-113
        objectives, 77
        statistics, 109–111
    DNS, 60
        counters, 433
        servers, 56
    IPSec, 226
    network traffic, 203
    port status, 156
    remote access, 152-155
        counters, 438
    routing protocols, 335
    traffic, 440
    WINS performance
        configuring, 268-269
        counters, 267-268

MS-CHAP (Microsoft CHAP), 158

Multicast Dynamic Client Allocation Protocol.
    See MADCAP

multicasting, 89, 258, 434
    MADCAP, 90
    scopes, 90–91, 100-101

multilink connections, 437
    establishing, 151

multinetting. *See* supernetting

multipath networks
    routing, 301
    split horizon, 298

multiple rating questions, 457

multiple-choice questions, 457

N

nacks/sec (DHCP statistic), 110

name resolution
    DNS, 23-24, 430
        domains, 18
        history of, 16-17
        registering domain names, 22
        reverse lookup, 430
        testing, 432
        zones, 19, 22
        See also reverse lookups
    HOSTS files, 429
    NetBIOS, 440
        configuring, 261
        LMHOSTS file, 246
        node types, 262-264
    WINS, 244, 263
        client setup, troubleshooting, 259
        configuring, 250, 252
        counters, 267-268
        database replication, 247
        managing, 265
        objectives, 241-242
        proxies, 264
        registration, 264
        troubleshooting, 259

Name Resolution Tab (Routing and Remote Access Window), 365-366

name servers (DNS), 429

namespace (DNS)
    architecture, 18
    configuring, 34-38

naming conventions
    DNS, 28
    reverse lookups, 26

NAT (Network Address Translation)
    client computers, enabling, 365, 446
    comparing to ICS, 356
    configuring, 363
        case study, 270, 369-370
    DHCP, configuring, 365
    DNS, configuring, 365
    ICS, Directplay proxy, 356
    inbound applications, adding, 364
    installing, 361-362
    interfaces
        configuring, 354, 366-368
        mappings, 368
    logging, 363
    objectives, 353–355
    properties, 353
    timeout values, configuring, 364
    translation process, 361

Nbstat Memory counter, 61
neighbors, 318
    adjacencies, 319-320
NET (DNS domain), 21
NetBEUI, 244
NetBIOS
    broadcasting, 245
    configuring, 261
    LMHOSTS file, 246
    name resolution, 440
    node types, 262-264
    WINS, objectives, 242
netmask ordering, 59
NetWare, NWLink protocol, 245
Network Connection dialog box, 139
Network Connection Type dialog box, 137
network management protocols, SNMP, 112-113
Network Monitor, 333-334, 440
    captures
        creating, 207-208
        interpreting, 209
    installing, 204-205
    panes, 207
Network Monitor Driver, 205–206
Network Solutions, 22
Networking Components dialog box, 138
Networking Services dialog box, 31
networks
    baselines, 209
    bindings, 439
        configuring, 194-195
        providers, 194
    classes, 184
    data security, 199
    demand-dial, 443
    designing, traffic considerations, 204
    providers, 194–195
    security hosts, 200
    VPNs, 439
new host records, creating, 55
New Replication Partner dialog box, 255
New Resource Record dialog box, 43
New Riders Publishing, 538
New Zone Wizard, 41
Next Header field (AH), 213

nodes, 19, 262–263, 430
    identifying, 264
    WINS, 441
non-WINS client computers, 246
noninteractive mode, NSLOOKUP, 52
Notify Received/Sent counter, 61
NSLOOKUP.EXE
    DNS, testing, 50-53
    modes, 52
NWLink, 178, 245, 439
    configuring, 193-194
    CSNW, 193
    installing, 192-193

O

Oakley key generation protocol, ISAKMP/Oakley, 215
objectives
    DHCP, 77
    IP routing protocols, 283
    IPSec, 176
    NAT, 353, 355
    remote access, 129
    security, 130
    WINS, 241
        managing, 242
        NetBIOS, 242
        replication, 241
object counters, RAS, 152-153
octets, 181
    converting to binary, 182-183
offers/sec (DHCP statistic), 109
one-way connections, demand-dial routing, 325
option 81, 48
options
    DNS client computers, advanced TCP/IP, 45
    WINS manager, 265-267
ordered list questions, 460
ORG (DNS domain), 20
OSPF (Open Shortest Path First), 309, 443
    adjacencies, 320
    areas, 312
        creating, 316
        stub areas, 318

autonomous system border routing, 317
backbone, 312-313
backup designated routers, 319
configuring, 309–311
designated routers, 318-319
inter-area routing, 315
intra-area routing, 315
neighbors, 318–319
Router Priority, 319
troubleshooting, 338-339, 445
owner servers, 253

P

P-nodes, 246, 262, 441
packets
AH (Authentication Header), 212–213
best-effort delivery, 196-197
captures, 206
creating, 207-208
interpreting, 209
destination unreachable, 287
ESP, trailer fields, 214
filters, 439
creating, 197-199
TCP ports, 196
hello, 299, 443
routing, 180, 286, 442
default gateway, 187
lookup process, 292
tunneling, 439
packets expired/sec (DHCP statistic, 108
packets received/sec (DHCP statistic), 108
panes (Network Monitor), 207
PAP (Password Authentication Protocol), 159
parent-child relationship, CAs, 389
partners (WINS replication), specifying, 255-257
pausing DHCP service, 106
pending requests (certificates), checking, 401-402
performance
baselines, 209
counters
identifying, 61
RAS object, 152-153

DHCP
configuring, 111
counters, 435-436
monitoring, 111-113
DNS, monitoring, 62-63
remote access
counters, 438
monitoring, 154-155
traffic monitoring, 203
VPNs, 150
WINS counters, 267-268
persistent connections, demand-dial routing, 325-326
PING, 259
DNS, testing, 49-50
switches, 50
syntax, 49
PKI (Public Key Infrastructure), 382
CAs, 384
advanced options, 449
certificates, renewing, 397-398
checking pending requests, 401-402
installing, 386-394, 448-450
Intermediate, 398
parent-child relationship, 389
processing certificate requests, 401
renewing, 388
requirements, 447
standalone, 385-386, 447
Windows 2000 Certification Authority, 384-385
digital certificates, 383, 446
validity period, 388
place value system, converting binary to decimal notation, 183
planning CA hierarchies, 387-388
policies
IAS, 136
IPSec
configuring, 216-218
rules, editing, 220, 222
remote access, 136
creating, 139–143, 436-437
Policy Properties dialog box, 144
Poor Man's Load Balancing, 59

ports
IPSec, monitoring, 226
predefined numbers, 360
status, checking, 156
TCP, 196
UDP, 196-197
PPP (point-to-point protocol), 134
demand-dial security, 329-330
PPTP (Point-to-Point Tunneling Protocol), 148–149, 202, 437
pre-testing (study tips), 453
predefined port numbers, 360
prerequisites, establishing multilink connections, 151
primary master server (DNS), 22, 430
print providers, 194
private interfaces, NAT configuration, 366-368
private IP addresses, 356
RFC 1597, 362
private networks
servers, configuring, 359
VPNs
configuring, 147-150
performance, 150
security protocols, 148, 202
processing requests for CAs, 401
profiles (remote access), configuring, 143-146
programs, WINS manager. *See also* applications
Advanced tab, 254
Database Verification tab, 253
General tab, 252
Intervals tab, 252
properties, configuring, 252
properties
DNS servers, configuring, 58-60
NAT, 353, 363
WINS
configuring, 252
global replication, 257-258
WINS manager
Advanced tab, 254
configuring, 252
Database Verification tab, 253
General tab, 252
Intervals tab, 252
Properties command (Action menu), DHCP manager, 106

Properties dialog box, 106-107
protocols
authentication, EAP, 158
BOOTP, 82
data link, 134
encryption, 148, 202
packet filters, creating, 197-199
security, network data, 199
providers, 194–195, 439
proxy servers, 200, 439
WINS, 264
PTR records (DNS), updating, 102-103
Public and Private Key Pair dialog box, 393
public interfaces, NAT
configuring, 366-367
registered addresses, 368
Public Key Infrastructure. *See* PKI
pull replication, 255, 257, 441
Pure IPSec Tunnel Mode, 210
push replication, 255, 257, 441

Q–R

questions. *See* exam prep tips, question types

RADIUS (Remote Authentication Dial-in User Service), 147
RAS (remote access service), 132
bundled features, 132
objects counters, 152-153
upgrades, 132
reachability, 293
Reconcile All Scopes command (Action menu), DHCP manager, 105
Record Flow Memory counter, 61
records
resource, registration, 48
DNS database, 26, 430-431
creating, 55-56
serial number, 33
SOA, 33
TTL, 34
scavenging, 57-58
recovery keys (EFS), 408
exporting, 409-411
restoring, 411-412

recursive queries, 53
  counters, 61
  disabling, 58
redirect messages (ICMP), 288, 442
redundancy, demand-dial routing, 321-322
Refresh command (Action menu), DHCP manager, 106
refresh time, DNS records, 33
registered addresses, 361
  configuring for public interfaces (NAT), 368
registration
  DHCP workstations in DNS, 435
  domain names, 22
  forcing, 432
  WINS, 264
releases/sec (DHCP statistic), 111
remote access, 129
  account lockout, 330
  configuring, 132
  counters, 438
  implementing in complex environments, case study, 161-162
  inbound dial-in connections, configuring, 136-139
  managing, 152
  mobile users, 135-136
  monitoring, 154-155
  multilink, 437
  objectives, 129
  policies, 136
    attributes, selecting, 141
    creating, 139-143, 436-437
  profiles, configuring, 143-146
  security, configuring, 156-157, 438
    authentication protocols, 158-159
    encryption protocols, 159-160
    IPSec, logging, 228
  VPNs, 202
    performance, 150
removing EFS keys, 409-411
Renew CA Certificate dialog box, 398
renew interval (WINS database), 253
renewing
  CAs, 388
  certificates, 397-398
  expired certificates, 398
replaying, 214

replication, WINS database, 247, 441
  configuring, 254-255, 257
  objectives, 241
  partners, specifying, 255-257
requesting certificates, Windows 2000 Certificates Services Web page, 399–400
Requests for Secure Communication dialog box, 218
requests/sec (DHCP statistic), 110
requirements
  CA installation, 390-391, 447
  certification. *See* certification process, requirements
  establishing multilink connections, 151
  NWLink installation, 192
  TCP/IP installation, 187
researching domain names, 22
resolving
  IP addresses to host name, 287
  names to IP addresses, 23-24
  See also reverse lookups
resource records
  creating manually, 55-56
  new host, creating, 55
  scavenging, 57-58
  updating, 102-103
restarting DHCP service, 106
Restore the Database option (WINS manager), 266
restoring EFS keys, 411-412
restrictions
  DNS names, 28
  FQDNs, 431
  variable length subnet masks, 186
resuming DHCP service, 106
retaking exams, 464
retry time (DNS records), 33
reverse lookup, 25, 430
  zones, 37, 41-42
revoking certificates, 406-407
RFC 1597, private addressing, 362
RFC 2136, DDNS, 48
RFCs (requests for comments), 17
  exam questions, 80
RIP (Routing Information Protocol), 443
  configuring, 303–305
  hop counts, 308, 443
  installing, 294-295
  stability, 308

troubleshooting, 336-337, 444
updates, 307
RIP Version 2, configuring, 306
Root CAs, 388
renewing, 398
security, 397
root domains, 20
root servers (DNS), 24
configuring, 33
round robin DNS, 59
ROUTE command
destination parameter, 332
gateway parameter, 332
metric parameter, 332
syntax, 331
route-aging algorithm, 296
Router Priority (OSPF), 319
routing, 180, 286, 442
autonomous system border routing, 317-318
availability, 293
default gateway address, 187, 442
demand-dial, 443
autostatic updates, 327
callback, 330
enabling, 321-322
one-way, 325
persistent connections, 325–326
security, 328-330, 443
static routes, 327
tunneling, 324
two-way, 325
dynamic, fault tolerance, 293
eavesdropping, 442
excluding from DHCP scopes, 97
flat architecture, 301
host routing, 287
destination unreachable packets, 287
eavesdropping, 288-289
multipath networks, 301
router routing, 289
routing tables, 442
lookup process, 292
scalability, 301
single-path networks, 300
static routing, 292
subnet masks, 184
Routing and Remote Access Services. *See* **RRAS**

Routing and Remote Access snap-in, 136
Routing and Remote Access Window
Address Assignment Tab, 365
General Tab, 363
Name Resolution Tab, 365-366
Translation Tab, 364
routing protocols
comparing, 295
distance-vector
convergence, 296
count-to-infinity, 296
disadvantages, 298
hops, calculating, 297
RIP, 303-308, 443
RIP Version 2, 306
dynamic, 292
link-state, 299-300
OSPF, 309-313, 443
managing, 335
NAT, 363
on-demand connections, 326
RIP, installing, 294-295
silent RIP, 442
static routes, configuring, 331-332
routing tables
lookup process, 292
multipath networks, 301
triggered updates, 298
RRAS (Routing and Remote Access Services), 133
enabling, 290-291
areas (OSPF), creating, 316
demand-dial-routing, enabling, 321-322
DHCP integration, configuring, 152
required tasks, 335
RIP, configuring, 303–305
RIP Version 2, configuring, 306
virtual links, configuring, 315
rules, editing IPSec policies, 220–222

S

SAP (Service Advertising Protocol), 194
SAs (security associations), 211
scalability, Internet routing, 301
Scavenge Database option (WINS manager), 265
scavenging WINS database records, 57-58

scenarios, ICS service, 356
scheduling exams, 503
scopes, 88, 189, 434
    creating, 91-96
    DHCP, gateway addresses
    configuring, 97
    duplicate, troubleshooting, 96-97
    multicast, 90
        class D IP addresses, 91
        creating, 100-101
    superscopes, 434
        creating, 99-100
secondary master server (DNS), 22, 430
secure update counters, 61
security
    authentication protocols
        EAP, 158
        RADIUS, 147
    CAs, 384
        CRL, 407-408
        installing, 386-394
        renewing, 388
        Standalone CAs, 385-386
        Windows 2000 Certification Authority, 384-385
    certificates
        revoking, 406-407
        viewing, 405
    demand-dial routing, 328-329, 443
        callback, 330
        caller ID, 330
        PPP authentication protocols, 329-330
        remote access account lockout, 330
    digital certificates, 383
    EFS (Encrypting File System), 408
        keys, exporting, 409-411
        keys, restoring, 411-412
    encryption protocols, 148, 202, 437
    end-to-end models, 210
    IPSec, 199, 210
        AH, 212-213
        comparing to L2TP, 215-216
        customizing, 220
        features, 211-212
        ISAKMP/Oakley, 215
        monitoring, 226
        policies, 216-218
        tunnel mode, 222-225

    Kerberos V5, 201, 439
        domain controllers, 201
        interoperability, 202
        logon process, 201
    network data, 199
    objectives, 130
    proxy servers, 200
        firewalls, 439
    remote access
        authentication protocols, configuring, 158-159
        callback options, 138
        configuring, 156-157, 438
        encryption protocols, configuring, 159-160
    replay attacks, 214
    VPN connections, 211
security hosts, 200
Security Policy Properties dialog box, 219
selecting
    attributes for remote access policies, 141
    counters, WINS object, 268-269
    demand-dial connections, 326
    media for dial-in connections, 144
    port numbers, 360
    snap-ins for services, 250-251
Sequence Number, 214
serial number (DNS database records), 33
Server Aging/Scavenging Properties dialog box, 57
Server Statistics screen (DHCP manager), 104-105
servers
    caching-only (DNS), 432
    Certificate Server 1.0, upgrading, 394
    DHCP
        authorizing in Active Directory, 97-98
        configuring, 106
        conflict detection, 111
        installing, 83–87
        managing, 104-113
        scopes, creating, 91-96
    DNS
        cache, clearing, 58
        caching-only, configuring, 42-43
        managing, 56-58
        monitoring, 60
        name resolution process, 23-24
        performance monitoring, 62-63
        primary master, 22
        properties, configuring, 58-60

reverse lookups, 25
root servers, 24, 33
secondary master, 22
TTL, 34
dynamic addresses, WINS installation, 249
Internet access, configuring, 359
owner servers, 253
private networks, configuring, 359
WINS, 246
managing, 265
proxies, 264
replication partner, specifying, 255-257
statistics, obtaining, 441
troubleshooting, 261
services
DHCP
pausing, 106
resuming, 106
starting, 105
stopping, 106
DNS
client computer, configuring, 44-45
delegated zones, creating, 54-55
installing, 29-32
server management, 56-58
testing, 49-53
ICS
adding custom applications, 358
Directplay proxy, 356
DNS, 357
H.323 Proxy, 356
installing, 356-359
LDAP Proxy, 356
snap-ins, selecting, 250-251
WINS
automatic database backups, 252
client setup, troubleshooting, 259
configuring, 250, 252
counters, 267-268
installing, 247-250
managing, 265
name resolution, 263
node types, 262-264
replication, 255–257
troubleshooting, 259
Services tab (Connection Properties dialog box), 359
Sessions Stats pane (Network Monitor), 207

SHA (Secure Hash Algorithm), 213
Shiva Password Authentication Protocol. *See* SPAP
silent RIP, 442
enabling, 288-289, 304
simple queries, 53
simulation questions, 457-459
single-path networks, 300
split horizon, 297
sites (Web), Network Solutions, 22
SLIP (serial line interface protocol), 134
smart cards, 384, 387
snap-ins (MMC)
adding to MMC, 35
Certificates snap-in, revoking issued certificates, 406-407
Certificates snap-in, 399
DNS console, actions, 56-57
Routing and Remote Access, 136
WINS management, 247
SNMP (Simple Network Management Protocol), 112-113
SOA (Start of Authority) record, 33
spamming, 25
SPAP (Shiva Password Authentication Protocol), 159
specifying WINS replication partner, 255-257
SPF (Shortest Path First) algorithm, 309
calculating, 312
SPI (Security Parameters Index), 214
split horizon, 297–298
SPX (Sequence Packet Exchange), NWLink protocol, 245
stability, RIP, 308
Standalone CAs, 385-386
attributes, 447
certificates, requesting, 400
installing, 394
root CAs, 449
subordinate CAs, 449
Standard Primary Forward Lookup zones, creating, 39-40
standard storage, 35
standardization, dynamic DNS updates, 103
Start Pull Replication option (WINS manager), 266
Start Push Replication option (WINS manager), 266
starting
Certificates snap-in, 399
DHCP service, 105

static routing, 292, 327

configuring, 331-332

Station Stats pane (Network Monitor), 207

statistics

DHCP server, 109–111

configuring, 106

DNS server, performance monitoring, 62-63

ports, monitoring, 156

stopping DHCP service, 106

storing

remote access policies, 136

zones, 35

stub areas, 318

study strategies

active study strategies, 452

common-sense strategies, 453

described, 452

learning styles, 451-452

macro/micro strategies, 452

pre-testing, 453

WINS, 243

See also exam prep tips

subnets, 309

disjointed, 306

illegal, 186

IP addresses, adding, 190

masks, 184

scopes, 88, 189

superscopes, creating, 99-100

VLSMs, 185

Subordinate CAs, installing, 391-394

supernetting, 88–89, 309

RIP, 306

superscopes, 88-89, 434

creating, 99-100

multicast, creating, 100-101

switches, PING utility, 50

synchronizing adjacencies, 320

syntax

PING command, 49, 259

ROUTE command, 331

System Monitor, 269

System Properties, DNS configuration, 44–47

System Properties dialog box, 46

T

table entries (DNS)

creating, 55-56

scavenging, 57-58

Task Manager (WINS Manager)

Tasks option, 266

troubleshooting, 261

TCP (Transport Control Protocol), ports, 196

TCP/IP, 178, 438

connectivity, troubleshooting, 259

DHCP, configuring, 189-190

DNS

client computers, 45

configuring, 191

history, 178

installing, 187–189

IP addresses, 79, 181

allocating, 151

classes, 183-184

default gateway, 187

DHCP, 80-81

dotted decimal notation, 181

manual configuration, 190

multicasting, 89

scopes, 88

subnets, 184

superscopes, 88-89

IP addressing, variable length subnet masks, 185

MAC addresses, 179

packet filters, 439

creating, 197-199

replay attacks, 214

WINS, configuring, 191

See also IP addresses

TCP/IP Properties dialog box, Advanced tab, 191

TCP/UDP counter, 61

technical support, ExamGear, 538

testing

DNS

console application, 53

name resolution, 432

NSLOOKUP.EXE, 50-53

PING, 49-50

Web browsers, 54

TCP/IP connectivity, 259

time to live. *See* TTL

Timeout Errors counter (RAS object), 153

timeout values, NAT configuration, 364

TLDs (top-level domains), 19-22, 430

tools, Network Monitor, 333-334

   See also applications

topological databases, 312

   synchronizing adjacencies, 320

Total Errors counter (RAS object), 153

Total Errors/Sec counter (RAS object), 153

Total Stats pane (Network Monitor), 207

totals counters, 61

traffic

   captures, 206, 333-334

      creating, 207-208

      filtering, 209

      interpreting, 209

   frames, 334

   monitoring, 203, 440

   VPNs, bottlenecks,150

trailers, ESP fields, 214

transit areas, 314

translating

   DNS names, 366

   internal addresses, 361

   IP addresses, NAT, 362

   See also NAT

Translation Tab, Routing and Remote Access Window, 364

transport mode, 210

   IPSec configuration, 222

tree questions, 461

tree structure, 19

   nodes, 430

   See also hierarchies

triggered updates, 298

troubleshooting

   count-to-infinity, 297

   DNS

      console, 53

      NSLOOKUP.EXE, 50-53

      PING, 49-50

      Web browsers, 54

   duplicate scopes, 96-97

   IP routing protocols, objectives, 283

   OSPF, 338-339, 445

remote access, 132

RIP, 336-337, 444

WINS, 259

   client configuration, 259

   servers, 261

TTL (time to live), 34

tunneling, 210, 324, 439

   IPSec configuration, 222-225

   L2TP, comparing to IPSec, 215-216

two-way connections, demand-dial routing, 325

U

UDP (Unreliable Datagram Protocol), best-effort delivery, 196-197

Unauthorize command (Action menu), DHCP manager, 105

UNIX

   Kerberos V5, 202

   TCP/IP development, 179

unregistered addresses, 80, 433

updates

   count-to-infinity, 296

   DNS, DHCP configuration, 102-104

   dynamic, 49

   hello packets, 299

   RIP, 307

   routing, 296

   triggered, 298

upgrades

   RAS, 132

   Certificate Server 1.0, 394

user accounts

   certificates, mapping to, 403–404

   dial-up permissions, granting, 328

   remote access, granting, 136

user classes, 105

UTF-8, 28

utilities

   Configure Your Server, 83

   DNS console, 53

   IPConfig, 260

      reregistering name-to-IP address mappings, 49

   Network Monitor, 333-334

   NSLOOKUP.EXE, testing DNS, 50-53

PING, 259
> switches, 50
> testing DNS, 49-50
> System Monitor, 269
> WINS manager, 247, 265-267
utilization, Internet addresses, 301

V

validity period (certificates), 388
variable length subnet masks, 185–186
vendor classes, 105
verification interval, WINS database, 253
Verify Database Consistency option
  (WINS manager), 265
Verify Version ID Consistency option
  (WINS manager), 265
VeriSign, Inc., 384
versions
> RIP, 303
> WINS database, configuring, 254
viewing
> certificates, 405
> scope information, 88
> VPN connection statistics, 156
virtual links, 314–315
virtual private networks (VPNs), 202, 439
> configuring, 147, 149-150
> connections, security, 211
> encryption protocols, 148, 202
> performance, 150
> tunnel mode, configuring, 222, 224-225

W

WANs, 180
warnings, logging, 363
Web browsers, testing DNS, 54
Web pages, Windows 2000 Certificates Services, 400
Web sites
> dynamic DNS updates, standardization, 103
> *ExamGear, Training Guide Edition* software, 537
> Network Solutions, 22
> RFC listing, 80

Windows 2000
> callback options, 138
> WINS, backward compatibility, 244
Windows 2000 Certificate Services Web page, 400
Windows 2000 Certification Authority, 384-385
Windows 2000 DNS Server service,
  installing, 29-32
Windows 2000 Server, installing, 83
Windows 2000 certification track
> core exams
>> Microsoft Certified Database Administrator
>>> (MCDBA), 505
>> Microsoft Certified Systems Engineer (MCSE),
>>> 506-507
> elective exams
>> Microsoft Certified Database Administrator
>>> (MCDBA) certification requirements, 505-506
>> Microsoft Certified Systems Engineer (MCSE), 507
Windows Components dialog box, 84-85, 248, 250
Windows Components wizard, 85
Windows NT 4.0 certification track
> core exams
>> Microsoft Certified Database Administrator
>>> (MCDBA), 506
>> Microsoft Certified Systems Engineer (MCSE), 507
> elective exams
>> Microsoft Certified Database Administrator
>>> (MCDBA), 506
>> Microsoft Certified Systems Engineer (MCSE), 508
Windows Optional Networking Components
  dialog box, 87
Windows-Groups attribute (remote access policies), 141
WINS (Windows Internet Naming Service), 244
> backward compatibility, 262
> client configuration, troubleshooting, 259
> components, 440
> configuring, 191, 250–252
> counters, 61
> database
>> backing up, 252
>> replication, 247, 255, 441
> installing, 247-250
> management snap-in, 247
> managing, 265
>> objectives, 242
> name resolution, 263
> necessity of, 244

NetBIOS, objectives, 242

node types, 262-264, 441

objectives, 241

performance

    counters, 267-268

    monitoring, 268-269

proxies, 247, 264

registration, 264

replication

    configuring, 254-255, 257

    objectives, 241

server

    statistics, obtaining, 441

    statistics, verifying, 261

study strategies, 243

troubleshooting, 259–261

WINS Manager, Properties

Advanced tab, 254

configuring, 252

Database Verification tab, 253

General tab, 252

Intervals tab, 252

wiretapping, 288, 442

Wizards

Configure Your Server application, 83

New Zone, 41

Windows Components, 85

X–Z

Zeltserman, David, 113

Zone File dialog box, 42

Zone Type dialog box, 36, 41

zones (DNS), 19, 430

configuring, 34-38

delegated, creating, 54-55

DNS, 22

dynamic updates, 49, 432

    configuring, 47

forward lookup, 36

reverse lookup, 25, 37

    creating, 41-42

Standard Primary Forward Lookups, creating, 39-40

storage, 35

transfer counters, 61

Additional Tools for Certification Preparation

Taking the author-driven, no-nonsense approach that we pioneered with our *Landmark* books, New Riders proudly offers something unique for Windows 2000 administrators—an interesting and discriminating book on Windows 2000 Server, written by someone in the trenches who can anticipate your situation and provide answers you can trust.

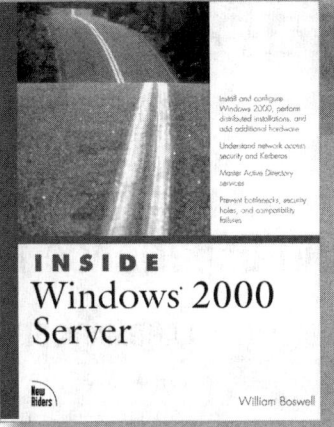

INSIDE
Windows 2000 Server

William Boswell

ISBN: 1–56205–929–7

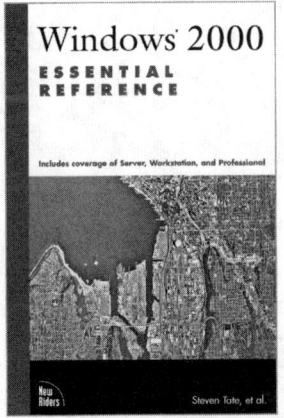

Windows 2000
ESSENTIAL REFERENCE

Includes coverage of Server, Workstation, and Professional

Steven Tate, et al.

Architected to be the most navigable, useful, and value-packed reference for Windows 2000, this book uses a creative "telescoping" design that you can adapt to your style of learning. It's a concise, focused, and quick reference for Windows 2000, providing the kind of practical advice, tips, procedures, and additional resources that every administrator will need.

ISBN: 0–7357–0869–X

Understanding the Network is just one of several new titles from New Riders' acclaimed *Landmark Series*. This book addresses the audience in practical terminology, and describes the most essential information and tools required to build high-availability networks in a step-by-step implementation format. Each chapter could be read as a stand-alone, but the book builds progressively toward a summary of the essential concepts needed to put together a wide area network.

Understanding the Network
A Practical Guide to Internetworking

Michael J. Martin

ISBN: 0–7357–0977–7

New Riders
Windows 2000 Resources

Advice and Experience for the Windows 2000 Networker

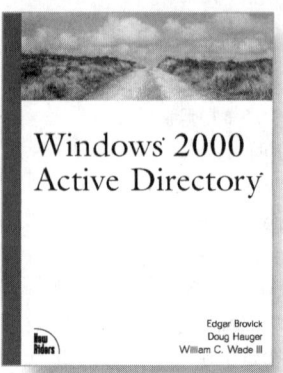

LANDMARK SERIES

We know how important it is to have access to detailed, solution-oriented information on core technologies. *Landmark* books contain the essential information you need to solve technical problems. Written by experts and subjected to rigorous peer and technical reviews, our *Landmark* books are hard-core resources for practitioners like you.

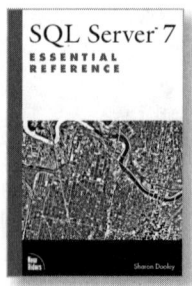

ESSENTIAL REFERENCE SERIES

The *Essential Reference* series from New Riders provides answers when you know what you want to do but need to know how to do it. Each title skips extraneous material and assumes a strong base of knowledge. These are indispensable books for the practitioner who wants to find specific features of a technology quickly and efficiently. Avoiding fluff and basic material, these books present solutions in an innovative, clean format—and at a great value.

CIRCLE SERIES

The *Circle Series* is a set of reference guides that meet the needs of the growing community of advanced, technical-level networkers who must architect, develop, and administer Windows NT/2000 systems. These books provide network designers and programmers with detailed, proven solutions to their problems.

The Road to MCSE Windows 2000

The new Microsoft Windows 2000 track is designed for information technology professionals working in a typically complex computing environment of medium to large organizations. A Windows 2000 MCSE candidate should have at least one year of experience implementing and administering a network operating system.

MCSEs in the Windows 2000 track are required to pass **five core exams and two elective exams** that provide a valid and reliable measure of technical proficiency and expertise.

See below for the exam information and the relevant New Riders title that covers that exam.

Core Exams

New MCSE Candidates (Who Have Not Already Passed Windows NT 4.0 Exams) Must Take All 4 of the Following Core Exams:

Exam 70-210: Installing, Configuring and Administering Microsoft® Windows® 2000 Professional

Exam 70-215: Installing, Configuring and Administering Microsoft Windows 2000 Server

Exam 70-216: Implementing and Administering a Microsoft Windows 2000 Network Infrastructure

Exam 70-217: Implementing and Administering a Microsoft Windows 2000 Directory Services Infrastructure

ISBN 0-7357-0965-3

ISBN 0-7357-0968-8

ISBN 0-7357-0966-1

ISBN 0-7357-0976-9

or

MCPs Who Have Passed 3 Windows NT 4.0 Exams (Exams 70-067, 70-068, and 70-073) Instead of the 4 Core Exams at Left, May Take:

Exam 70-240: Microsoft Windows 2000 Accelerated Exam for MCPs Certified on Microsoft Windows NT 4.0.

(This accelerated, intensive exam, which will be available until December 31, 2001, covers the core competencies of exams 70-210, 70-215, 70-216, and 70-217.)

ISBN 0-7357-0979-3

MCSE Training Guide: Core Exams (Bundle)

ISBN 0-7357-0988-2

PLUS - All Candidates - 1 of the Following Core Elective Exams Required:

*Exam 70-219: Designing a Microsoft Windows 2000 Directory Services Infrastructure

*Exam 70-220: Designing Security for a Microsoft Windows 2000 Network

*Exam 70-221: Designing a Microsoft Windows 2000 Network Infrastructure

ISBN 0-7357-0983-1

ISBN 0-7357-0984-X

ISBN 0-7357-0982-3

PLUS - All Candidates - 2 of the Following Elective Exams Required:

Any current MCSE electives (visit www.microsoft.com for a list of current electives)

(Selected third-party certifications that focus on interoperability will be accepted as an alternative to one elective exam. Please watch for more information on the third-party certifications that will be acceptable.)

*Exam 70-219: Designing a Microsoft Windows 2000 Directory Services Infrastructure

*Exam 70-220: Designing Security for a Microsoft Windows 2000 Network

*Exam 70-221: Designing a Microsoft Windows 2000 Network Infrastructure

Exam 70-222: Upgrading from Microsoft Windows NT 4.0 to Microsoft Windows 2000

ISBN 0-7357-0983-1   ISBN 0-7357-0984-X   ISBN 0-7357-0982-3

*Core exams that can also be used as elective exams may only be counted once toward a certification; that is, if a candidate receives credit for an exam as a core in one track, that candidate will not receive credit for that same exam as an elective in that same track.

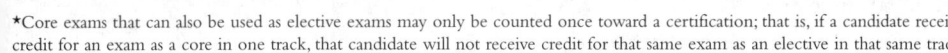

New Riders

WWW.NEWRIDERS.COM

New Riders — Books for Networking Professionals

Windows NT/2000 Titles

Windows 2000 TCP/IP
By Karanjit Siyan, Ph.D.
2nd Edition
700 pages, $34.99
ISBN: 0-7357-0992-0

Windows 2000 TCP/IP cuts through the complexities and provides the most informative and complex reference book on Windows 2000-based TCP/IP topics. The book is a tutorial-reference hybrid, focusing on how Microsoft TCP/IP works, using hands-on tutorials and practical examples. Concepts essential to TCP/IP administration are explained thoroughly, and are then related to the practical use of Microsoft TCP/IP in a serious networking environment.

Windows 2000 DNS
By Roger Abell, Herman Knief, Andrew Daniels, and Jeffrey Graham
2nd Edition
450 pages, $39.99
ISBN: 0-7357-0973-4

The Domain Name System is a directory of registered computer names and IP addresses that can be instantly located. Without proper design and administration of DNS, computers wouldn't be able to locate each other on the network, and applications like email and Web browsing wouldn't be feasible. Administrators need this information to make their networks work. *Windows 2000 DNS* provides a technical overview of DNS and WINS, and how to design and administer them for optimal performance in a Windows 2000 environment.

Windows 2000 Server Professional Reference
By Karanjit Siyan, Ph.D.
3rd Edition
1800 pages, $75.00
ISBN: 0-7357-0952-1

Windows 2000 Server Professional Reference is the benchmark of references available for Windows 2000. Although other titles take you through the setup and implementation phase of the product, no other book provides the user with detailed answers to day-to-day administration problems and tasks. Real-world implementations are key to help administrators discover the most viable solutions for their particular environments. Solid content shows administrators how to manage, troubleshoot, and fix problems that are specific to heterogeneous Windows networks, as well as Internet features and functionality.

Windows 2000 Professional

By Jerry Honeycutt
350 pages, $34.99 US
ISBN: 0-7357-0950-5

Windows 2000 Professional explores the power available to the Windows workstation user on the corporate network and Internet. The book is aimed directly at the power user who values the security, stability, and networking capabilities of NT alongside the ease and familiarity of the Windows 95/98 user interface. This book covers both user and administration topics, with a dose of networking content added for connectivity.

Windows NT Power Toolkit

By Stu Sjouwerman and Ed Tittel
1st Edition
800 pages, $49.99
ISBN: 0-7357-0922-X

This book covers the analysis, tuning, optimization, automation, enhancement, maintenance, and troubleshooting of Windows NT Server 4.0 and Windows NT Workstation 4.0. In most cases, the two operating systems overlap completely. Where the two systems diverge, each platform is covered separately. This advanced title comprises a task-oriented treatment of the Windows NT 4.0 environment. By concentrating on the use of operating system tools and utilities, resource kit elements, and selected third-party tuning, analysis, optimization, and productivity tools, this book will show you how to carry out everyday and advanced tasks.

Windows 2000 User Management

By Lori Sanders
300 pages, $34.99
ISBN: 1-56205-886-X

With the dawn of Windows 2000, it has become even more difficult to draw a clear line between managing the user and managing the user's environment and desktop. This book, written by a noted trainer and consultant, provides comprehensive, practical advice to managing users and their desktop environments with Windows 2000.

Windows 2000 Deployment & Desktop Management

By Jeffrey A. Ferris, MCSE
1st Edition
400 pages, $34.99
ISBN: 0-7357-0975-0

More than a simple overview of new features and tools, *Windows 2000 Deployment & Desktop Management* is a thorough reference to deploying Windows 2000 Professional to corporate workstations. Incorporating real-world advice and detailed excercises, this book is a one-stop resource for any system administrator, integrator, engineer, or other IT professional.

Planning for Windows 2000

By Eric K. Cone, Jon Boggs, and Sergio Perez
1st Edition
400 pages, $29.99
ISBN: 0-7357-0048-6

Windows 2000 is poised to be one of the largest and most important software releases of the next decade, and you are charged with planning, testing, and deploying it in your enterprise. Are you ready? With this book, you will be. *Planning for Windows 2000* lets you know what the upgrade hurdles will be, informs you of how to clear them, guides you through effective Active Directory design, and presents you with detailed rollout procedures. Eric K. Cone, Jon Boggs, and Sergio Perez give you the benefit of their extensive experiences as Windows 2000 Rapid Deployment Program members by sharing problems and solutions they've encountered on the job.

SQL Server System Administration

By Sean Baird, Chris Miller, et al.
1st Edition
352 pages, $29.99
ISBN: 1-56205-955-6

How often does your SQL Server go down during the day when everyone wants to access the data? Do you spend most of your time being a "report monkey" for your coworkers and bosses? *SQL Server System Administration* helps you keep data consistently available to your users. This book omits introductory information. The authors don't spend time explaining queries and how they work. Instead, they focus on the information you can't get anywhere else, like how to choose the correct replication topology and achieve high availability of information.

Inside Windows 2000 Server

By William Boswell
2nd Edition
1533 pages, $49.99
ISBN: 1-56205-929-7

Finally, a totally new edition of New Riders' best-selling *Inside Windows NT Server 4.* Taking the author-driven, no-nonsense approach pioneered with the *Landmark* books, New Riders proudly offers something unique for Windows 2000 administrators—an interesting, discriminating book on Windows 2000 Server written by someone who can anticipate your situation and give you workarounds that won't leave a system unstable or sluggish.

Internet Information Services Administration
By Kelli Adam
1st Edition,
200 pages, $29.99
ISBN: 0-7357-0022-2

Are the new Internet technologies in Internet Information Services giving you headaches? Does protecting security on the Web take up all of your time? Then this is the book for you. With hands-on configuration training, advanced study of the new protocols, the most recent version of IIS, and detailed instructions on authenticating users with the new Certificate Server and implementing and managing the new e-commerce features, *Internet Information Services Administration* gives you the real-life solutions you need. This definitive resource prepares you for upgrading to Windows 2000 by giving you detailed advice on working with Microsoft Management Console, which was first used by IIS.

SMS 2 Administration
By Michael Lubanski and Darshan Doshi
1st Edition
350 pages, $39.99
ISBN: 0-7357-0082-6

Microsoft's new version of its Systems Management Server (SMS) is starting to turn heads. Although complex, it allows administrators to lower their total cost of ownership and more efficiently manage clients, applications, and support operations. If your organization is using or implementing SMS, you'll need some expert advice. Michael Lubanski and Darshan Doshi can help you get the most bang for your buck with insight, expert tips, and real-world examples. Michael and Darshan are consultants specializing in SMS and have worked with Microsoft on one of the most complex SMS rollouts in the world, involving 32 countries, 15 languages, and thousands of clients.

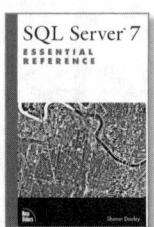

SQL Server 7 Essential Reference
By Sharon Dooley
1st Edition
500 pages, $35.00 US
ISBN: 0-7357-0864-9

SQL Server 7 Essential Reference is a comprehensive reference of advanced how-tos and techniques for SQL Server 7 administrators. This book provides solid grounding in fundamental SQL Server 7 administrative tasks to help you tame your SQL Server environment. With coverage ranging from installation, monitoring, troubleshooting security, and backup and recovery plans, this book breaks down SQL Server into its key conceptual areas and functions. This easy-to-use reference is a must-have for any SQL Server administrator.

Lotus Notes and Domino Titles

Domino System Administration
By Rob Kirkland, CLP, CLI
1st Edition
850 pages, $49.99
ISBN: 1-56205-948-3

Your boss has just announced that you will be upgrading to the newest version of Notes and Domino when it ships. How are you supposed to get this new system installed, configured, and rolled out to all of your end users? You understand how Lotus Notes works—you've been administering it for years. What you need is a concise, practical explanation of the new features and how to make some of the advanced stuff work smoothly by someone like you, who has worked with the product for years and understands what you need to know. *Domino System Administration* is the answer—the first book on Domino that attacks the technology at the professional level with practical, hands-on assistance to get Domino running in your organization.

Networking Titles

Network Intrusion Detection: An Analyst's Handbook
By Stephen Northcutt
1st Edition
267 pages, $39.99
ISBN: 0-7357-0868-1

Get answers and solutions from someone who has been in the trenches. The author, Stephen Northcutt, original developer of the Shadow intrusion detection system and former director of the United States Navy's Information System Security Office at the Naval Security Warfare Center, gives his expertise to intrusion detection specialists, security analysts, and consultants responsible for setting up and maintaining an effective defense against network security attacks.

Understanding Data Communications, Sixth Edition
By Gilbert Held
Sixth Edition
600 pages, $39.99
ISBN: 0-7357-0036-2

Updated from the highly successful fifth edition, this book explains how data communications systems and their various hardware and software components work. More than an entry-level book, it approaches the material in textbook format, addressing the complex issues involved in internetworking today. A great reference book for the experienced networking professional that is written by the noted networking authority, Gilbert Held.

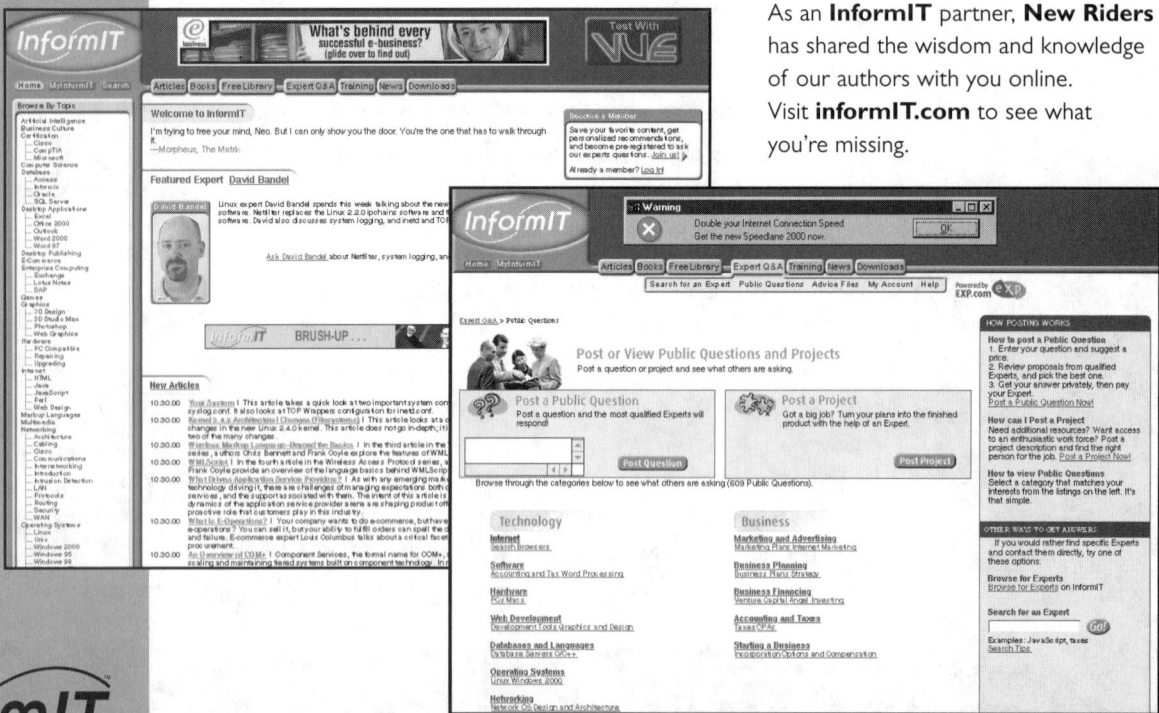

Other Books By New Riders

MICROSOFT TECHNOLOGIES

ADMINISTRATION

Inside Windows 2000 Server
1-56205-929-7 • $49.99 US / $74.95 CAN

Windows Windows 2000 Essential Reference
0-7357-0869-X • $35.00 US / $52.95 CAN

Windows 2000 Active Directory
0-7357-0870-3 • $29.99 US / $44.95 CAN

Windows 2000 Routing and Remote Access Service
0-7357-0951-3 • $34.99 US / $52.95 CAN

Windows 2000 Deployment & Desktop Management
0-7357-0975-0 • $34.99 US / $52.95 CAN

Windows 2000 DNS
0-7357-0973-4 • $39.99 US / $59.95 CAN

Windows 2000 User Management
1-56205-886-X • $34.99 US / $52.95 CAN

Windows 2000 Professional
0-7357-0950-5 • $34.99 US / $52.95 CAN

Planning for Windows 2000
0-7357-0048-6 • $29.99 US / $44.95 CAN

Windows 2000 Server Professional Reference
0-7357-0952-1 • $75.00 US / $111.95 CAN

Windows 2000 Security
0-7357-0991-2 • $39.99 US / $59.95 CAN

Windows 2000 TCP/IP
0-7357-0992-0 • $39.99 US / $59.95 CAN

Windows NT/2000 Network Security
1-57870-253-4 • $45.00 US / $67.95 CAN

Windows NT/2000 Thin Client Solutions
1-57870-239-9 • $45.00 US / $67.95 CAN

Windows 2000 Virtual Private Networking
1-57870-246-1 • $45.00 US / $67.95 CAN

Windows 2000 Active Directory Design & Deployment
1-57870-242-9 • $45.00 US / $67.95 CAN

Windows 2000 and Mainframe Integration
1-57870-200-3 • $40.00 US / $59.95 CAN

Windows 2000 Server: Planning and Migration
1-57870-023-X • $40.00 US / $59.95 CAN

Windows 2000 Quality of Service
1-57870-115-5 • $45.00 US / $67.95 CAN

Windows NT Power Toolkit
0-7357-0922-X • $49.99 US / $74.95 CAN

Windows NT Terminal Server and Citrix MetaFrame
1-56205-944-0 • $29.99 US / $44.95 CAN

Windows NT Performance: Monitoring, Benchmarking, and Tuning
1-56205-942-4 • $29.99 US / $44.95 CAN

Windows NT Registry: A Settings Reference
1-56205-941-6 • $29.99 US / $44.95 CAN

Windows NT Domain Architecture
1-57870-112-0 • $38.00 US / $56.95 CAN

SYSTEMS PROGRAMMING

Windows NT/2000 Native API Reference
1-57870-199-6 • $50.00 US / $74.95 CAN

Windows NT Device Driver Development
1-57870-058-2 • $50.00 US / $74.95 CAN

DCE/RPC over SMB: Samba and Windows NT Domain Internals
1-57870-150-3 • $45.00 US / $67.95 CAN

WEB PROGRAMMING

Real World Web Code: Techniques for Structured ASP Programming
0-7357-1033-3 • $39.99 US / $59.95 CAN • Available March 2001

Exchange & Outlook: Constructing Collaborative Solutions
1-57870-252-6 • $40.00 US / $59.95 CAN

APPLICATION PROGRAMMING

Delphi COM Programming
1-57870-221-6 • $45.00 US / $67.95 CAN

Windows NT Applications: Measuring and Optimizing Performance
1-57870-176-7 • $40.00 US / $59.95 CAN

Applying COM+
0-7357-0978-5 • $49.99 US / $74.95 CAN

SCRIPTING

Windows Script Host
1-57870-139-2 • $35.00 US / $52.95 CAN

Windows NT Shell Scripting
1-57870-047-7 • $32.00 US / $45.95 CAN

Windows NT Win32 Perl Programming: The Standard Extensions
1-57870-067-1 • $40.00 US / $59.95 CAN

Windows NT/2000 ADSI Scripting for System Administration
1-57870-219-4 • $45.00 US / $67.95 CAN

Windows NT Automated Deployment and Customization
1-57870-045-0 • $32.00 US / $45.95 CAN

Win32 Perl Scripting: The Administrator's Handbook
1-57870-215-1 • $35.00 US / $52.95 CAN

BACK OFFICE

SMS 2 Administration
0-7357-0082-6 • $39.99 US / $59.95 CAN

Internet Information Services Administration
0-7357-0022-2 • $29.99 US / $44.95 CAN

SQL Server System Administration
1-56205-955-6 • $29.99 US / $44.95 CAN

SQL Server 7 Essential Reference
0-7357-0864-9 • $35.00 US / $52.95 CAN

Inside Exchange 2000 Server
0-7357-1027-9 • $49.99 US / $74.95 CAN

WEB DESIGN & DEVELOPMENT

OPEN SOURCE

MySQL
0-7357-0921-1 • $49.99 US / $74.95 CAN

Web Application Development with PHP 4.0
0-7357-0997-1 • $39.99 US / $59.95 CAN

PHP Functions Essential Reference
0-7357-0970-X • $35.00 US / $52.95 CAN
• Available September 2001

Python Essential Reference
0-7357-0901-7 • $34.95 US / $52.95 CAN

Qt: The Official Documentation
1-57870-209-7 • $50.00 US / $74.95 CAN

Berkeley DB
0-7357-1064-3 • $39.99 US / $59.95 CAN
• Available June 2001

GNU Autoconf, Automake, and Libtool
1-57870-190-2 • $40.00 US / $59.95 CAN

CREATIVE MEDIA

Designing Web Usability
1-56205-810-X • $45.00 US / $67.95 CAN

Designing Web Graphics.3
1-56205-949-1 • $55.00 US / $81.95 CAN

Flash 4 Magic
0-7357-0896-7 • $45.00 US / $67.95 CAN

<creative.html design>
1-56205-704-9 • $39.99 US / $59.95 CAN

Creating Killer Web Sites, Second Edition
1-56830-433-1 • $49.99 US / $74.95 CAN

Secrets of Successful Web Sites
1-56830-382-3 • $49.99 US / $74.95 CAN

XML

Inside XML
0-7357-1020-1 • $49.99 US / $74.95 CAN

XHTML
0-7357-1034-1 • $39.99 US / $59.95 CAN

Inside XSLT
0-7357-1136-4 • $49.99 US / $74.95 CAN
• Available July 2001

LINUX/UNIX ADMINISTRATION

Networking Linux: A Practical Guide to TCP/IP
0-7357-1031-7 • $39.99 US / $59.95 CAN
• Available February 2001

Inside Linux
0-7357-0940-8 • $39.99 US / $59.95 CAN

Vi iMproved (VIM)
0-7357-1001-5 • $49.99 US / $74.95 CAN

Linux System Administration
1-56205-934-3 • $29.99 US / $44.95 CAN

Linux Firewalls
0-7357-0900-9 • $39.99 US / $59.95 CAN

Linux Essential Reference
0-7357-0852-5 • $24.95 US / $37.95 CAN

UnixWare 7 System Administration
1-57870-080-9 • $40.00 US / $59.99 CAN

DEVELOPMENT

Developing Linux Applications with GTK+ and GDK
0-7357-0021-4 • $34.99 US / $52.95 CAN

GTK+/Gnome Application Development
0-7357-0078-8 • $39.99 US / $59.95 CAN

KDE Application Development
1-57870-201-1 • $39.99 US / $59.95 CAN

GIMP

Grokking the GIMP
0-7357-0924-6 • $39.99 US / $59.95 CAN

GIMP Essential Reference
0-7357-0911-4 • $24.95 US / $37.95 CAN

SOLARIS

Solaris Advanced System Administrator's Guide, Second Edition
1-57870-039-6 • $39.99 US / $59.95 CAN

Solaris System Administrator's Guide, Second Edition
1-57870-040-X • $34.99 US / $52.95 CAN

Solaris Essential Reference
0-7357-0023-0 • $24.95 US / $37.95 CAN

Solaris System Management
0-7357-1018-X • $39.99 US / $59.95 CAN

Solaris 8 Essential Reference
0-7357-1007-4 • $34.99 US / $52.95 CAN

NETWORKING

STANDARDS & PROTOCOLS

Differentiated Services for the Internet
1-57870-132-5 • $50.00 US / $74.95 CAN

Cisco Router Configuration & Troubleshooting, Second Edition
0-7357-0999-8 • $34.99 US / $52.95 CAN

Understanding Directory Services
0-7357-0910-6 • $39.99 US / $59.95 CAN

Understanding the Network: A Practical Guide to Internetworking
0-7357-0977-7 • $39.99 US / $59.95 CAN

Understanding Data Communications, Sixth Edition
0-7357-0036-2 • $39.99 US / $59.95 CAN

LDAP: Programming Directory Enabled Applications
1-57870-000-0 • $44.99 US / $67.95 CAN

Gigabit Ethernet Networking
1-57870-062-0 • $50.00 US / $74.95 CAN

Supporting Service Level Agreements on IP Networks
1-57870-146-5 • $50.00 US / $74.95 CAN

Directory Enabled Networks
1-57870-140-6 • $50.00 US / $74.95 CAN

Policy-Based Networking: Architecture and Algorithms
1-57870-226-7 • $50.00 US / $74.95 CAN

Networking Quality of Service and Windows Operating Systems
1-57870-206-2 • $50.00 US / $74.95 CAN

Policy-Based Management
1-57870-225-9 • $55.00 US / $81.95 CAN

Quality of Service on IP Networks
1-57870-189-9 • $50.00 US / $74.95 CAN

Designing Addressing Architectures for Routing and Switching
1-57870-059-0 • $45.00 US / $69.95 CAN

Understanding & Deploying LDAP Directory Services
1-57870-070-1 • $50.00 US / $74.95 CAN

Switched, Fast and Gigabit Ethernet, Third Edition
1-57870-073-6 • $50.00 US / $74.95 CAN

Wireless LANs: Implementing Interoperable Networks
1-57870-081-7 • $40.00 US / $59.95 CAN
Local Area High Speed Networks
1-57870-113-9 • $50.00 US / $74.95 CAN
Wide Area High Speed Networks
1-57870-114-7 • $50.00 US / $74.95 CAN
The DHCP Handbook
1-57870-137-6 • $55.00 US / $81.95 CAN
Designing Routing and Switching Architectures for Enterprise Networks
1-57870-060-4 • $55.00 US / $81.95 CAN
Network Performance Baselining
1-57870-240-2 • $50.00 US / $74.95 CAN
Economics of Electronic Commerce
1-57870-014-0 • $49.99 US / $74.95 CAN

SECURITY

Intrusion Detection
1-57870-185-6 • $50.00 US / $74.95 CAN
Understanding Public-Key Infrastructure
1-57870-166-X • $50.00 US / $74.95 CAN
Network Intrusion Detection: An Analyst's Handbook, 2E
0-7357-1008-2 • $45.00 US / $67.95 CAN
Linux Firewalls
0-7357-0900-9 • $39.99 US / $59.95 CAN
Intrusion Signatures and Analysis
0-7357-1063-5 • $39.99 US / $59.95 CAN
Hackers Beware
0-7357-1009-0 • $45.00 US / $67.95 CAN
• Available August 2001

LOTUS NOTES/DOMINO

Domino System Administration
1-56205-948-3 • $49.99 US / $74.95 CAN
Lotus Notes & Domino Essential Reference
0-7357-0007-9 • $45.00 US / $67.95 CAN

PROFESSIONAL CERTIFICATION

TRAINING GUIDES

A+ Certification Training Guide, 3rd Ed.
0-7357-1088-0 • $59.99 US / $89.95 CAN
MCSE Training Guide: Networking Essentials, 2nd Ed.
1-56205-919-X • $49.99 US / $74.95 CAN
MCSE Training Guide: Windows NT Server 4, 2nd Ed.
1-56205-916-5 • $49.99 US / $74.95 CAN
MCSE Training Guide: Windows NT Workstation 4, 2nd Ed.
1-56205-918-1 • $49.99 US / $74.95 CAN
MCSE Training Guide: Windows NT Server 4 Enterprise, 2nd Ed.
1-56205-917-3 • $49.99 US / $74.95 CAN
MCSE Training Guide: Core Exams Bundle, 2nd Ed.
1-56205-926-2 • $149.99 US / $223.95 CAN
MCSE Training Guide: TCP/IP, 2nd Ed.
1-56205-920-3 • $49.99 US / $74.95 CAN
MCSE Training Guide: IIS 4, 2nd Ed.
0-7357-0865-7 • $49.99 US / $74.95 CAN
MCSE Training Guide: SQL Server 7 Administration
0-7357-0003-6 • $49.99 US / $74.95 CAN
MCSE Training Guide: SQL Server 7 Database Design
0-7357-0004-4 • $49.99 US / $74.95 CAN
MCSD Training Guide: Visual Basic 6 Exams
0-7357-0002-8 • $69.99 US / $104.95 CAN
MCSD Training Guide: Solution Architectures
0-7357-0026-5 • $49.99 US / $74.95 CAN
MCSD Training Guide: 4-in-1 Bundle
0-7357-0912-2 • $149.99 US / $223.95 CAN
A+ Certification Training Guide, Second Edition
0-7357-0907-6 • $49.99 US / $74.95 CAN
Network+ Certification Guide
0-7357-0077-X • $49.99 US / $74.95 CAN
Solaris 2.6 Administrator Certification Training Guide, Part I
1-57870-085-X • $40.00 US / $59.95 CAN

Solaris 2.6 Administrator Certification Training Guide, Part II
1-57870-086-8 • $40.00 US / $59.95 CAN
Solaris 7 Administrator Certification Training Guide, Part I and II
1-57870-249-6 • $49.99 US / $74.95 CAN
MCSE Training Guide: Windows 2000 Professional
0-7357-0965-3 • $49.99 US / $74.95 CAN
MCSE Training Guide: Windows 2000 Server
0-7357-0968-8 • $49.99 US / $74.95 CAN
MCSE Training Guide: Windows 2000 Network Infrastructure
0-7357-0966-1 • $49.99 US / $74.95 CAN
MCSE Training Guide: Windows 2000 Network Security Design
0-73570-984X • $49.99 US / $74.95 CAN
MCSE Training Guide: Windows 2000 Network Infrastructure Design
0-73570-982-3 • $49.99 US / $74.95 CAN
MCSE Training Guide: Windows 2000 Directory Svcs. Infrastructure
0-7357-0976-9 • $49.99 US / $74.95 CAN
MCSE Training Guide: Windows 2000 Directory Services Design
0-7357-0983-1 • $49.99 US / $74.95 CAN
MCSE Training Guide: Windows 2000 Accelerated Exam
0-7357-0979-3 • $69.99 US / $104.95 CAN
MCSE Training Guide: Windows 2000 Core Exams Bundle
0-7357-0988-2 • $149.99 US / $223.95 CAN

FAST TRACKS

CLP Fast Track: Lotus Notes/Domino 5 Application Development
0-73570-877-0 • $39.99 US / $59.95 CAN
CLP Fast Track: Lotus Notes/Domino 5 System Administration
0-7357-0878-9 • $39.99 US / $59.95 CAN
Network+ Fast Track
0-7357-0904-1 • $29.99 US / $44.95 CAN
A+ Fast Track
0-7357-0028-1 • $34.99 US / $52.95 CAN
MCSD Fast Track: Visual Basic 6, Exam #70-175
0-7357-0019-2 • $19.99 US / $29.95 CAN
MCSD FastTrack: Visual Basic 6, Exam #70-175
0-7357-0018-4 • $19.99 US / $29.95 CAN

SOFTWARE ARCHITECTURE & ENGINEERING

Designing for the User with OVID
1-57870-101-5 • $40.00 US / $59.95 CAN
Designing Flexible Object-Oriented Systems with UML
1-57870-098-1 • $40.00 US / $59.95 CAN
Constructing Superior Software
1-57870-147-3 • $40.00 US / $59.95 CAN
A UML Pattern Language
1-57870-118-X • $45.00 US / $67.95 CAN

■ TEST YOUR "IT" SKILLS

Play the Game!

WIN PRIZES & GET ON THE LIST ■

So you've read a book or two, worn out a couple of practice test disks, and memorized lots of stuff...now you think you're ready for the IT Certification test. Wait a minute!

Go to our games website.
www.eitgames.com is for IT certification* candidates.
Game questions derived from New Riders MCSE Training Guides

Play free demo game.
Gauge your skill level and challenge yourself.

Win great merchandise.
Test vouchers, reference books, software, etc.

Get on our Top Performers list.
Our Top Performers list is one handy place for job recruiters to find the most knowledgeable IT people.

eITgames®
www.eitgames.com

THE OFFICIAL IT CERTIFICATION TEST GAMES SITE

*MCSE A+ NETWORK+ i-NET+ CCNA

New Riders

www.newriders.com

HOW TO CONTACT US

IF YOU NEED THE LATEST UPDATES ON A TITLE THAT YOU'VE PURCHASED:

1) Visit our Web site at www.newriders.com.

2) Enter the book ISBN number, which is located on the back cover in the bottom right-hand corner, in the site search box on the left navigation bar.

3) Select your book title from the list of search results. On the book page, you'll find available updates and downloads for your title.

IF YOU ARE HAVING TECHNICAL PROBLEMS WITH THE BOOK OR THE CD THAT IS INCLUDED:

1) Check the book's information page on our Web site according to the instructions listed above, or

2) Email us at userservices@macmillanusa.com, or

3) Fax us at 317-581-4663 ATTN: Tech Support.

IF YOU HAVE COMMENTS ABOUT ANY OF OUR CERTIFICATION PRODUCTS THAT ARE NON-SUPPORT RELATED:

1) Email us at nrfeedback@newriders.com, or

2) Write to us at New Riders, 201 W. 103rd St., Indianapolis, IN 46290-1097, or

3) Fax us at 317-581-4663.

IF YOU ARE OUTSIDE THE UNITED STATES AND NEED TO FIND A DISTRIBUTOR IN YOUR AREA:

Please contact our international department at international@mcp.com.

IF YOU ARE INTERESTED IN BEING AN AUTHOR OR TECHNICAL REVIEWER:

Email us at opportunities@newriders.com. Include your name, email address, phone number, and area of technical expertise.

IF YOU WISH TO PREVIEW ANY OF OUR CERTIFICATION BOOKS FOR CLASSROOM USE:

Email us at nrmedia@newriders.com. Your message should include your name, title, training company or school, department, address, phone number, office days/hours, text in use, and enrollment. Send these details along with your request for desk/examination copies and/or additional information.

IF YOU ARE A MEMBER OF THE PRESS AND WOULD LIKE TO REVIEW ONE OF OUR BOOKS:

Email us at nrmedia@newriders.com. Your message should include your name, title, publication or website you work for, mailing address, and email address.

To better serve you, we would like your opinion on the content and quality of this book. Please complete this card and mail it to us or fax it to 317-581-4663.

Name _____

Address _____

City _____ State _____ Zip _____

Phone _____ Email Address _____

Occupation _____

Which certification exams have you already passed? _____

_____

_____

_____

Which certification exams do you plan to take? _____

_____

_____

_____

What influenced your purchase of this book?

❑ Recommendation   ❑ Cover Design
❑ Table of Contents   ❑ Index
❑ Magazine Review   ❑ Advertisement
❑ Reputation of New Riders   ❑ Author Name

How would you rate the contents of this book?

❑ Excellent   ❑ Very Good
❑ Good   ❑ Fair
❑ Below Average   ❑ Poor

What other types of certification products will you buy/have you bought to help you prepare for the exam?

❑ Quick reference books   ❑ Testing software
❑ Study guides   ❑ Other

What do you like most about this book? Check all that apply.

❑ Content   ❑ Writing Style
❑ Accuracy   ❑ Examples
❑ Listings   ❑ Design
❑ Index   ❑ Page Count
❑ Price   ❑ Illustrations

What do you like least about this book? Check all that apply.

❑ Content   ❑ Writing Style
❑ Accuracy   ❑ Examples
❑ Listings   ❑ Design
❑ Index   ❑ Page Count
❑ Price   ❑ Illustrations

What would be a useful follow-up book to this one for you? _____

Where did you purchase this book? _____

Can you name a similar book that you like better than this one, or one that is as good? Why? _____

_____

_____

How many New Riders books do you own? _____

What are your favorite certification or general computer book titles? _____

_____

What other titles would you like to see us develop? _____

_____

Any comments for us? _____

_____

_____

Fold here and tape to mail

- -

New Riders Publishing
201 W. 103rd St.
Indianapolis, IN 46290

By opening this package, you are bound by the following agreement:

Some of the software included with this product may be copyrighted, in which case all rights are reserved by the respective copyright holder. You are licensed to use software copyrighted by the publisher and its licensors on a single computer. You may copy and/or modify the software as needed to facilitate your use of it on a single computer. Making copies of the software for any other purpose is a violation of the United States copyright laws.

This software is sold "as is" without warranty of any kind, either expressed or implied, including, but not limited to, the implied warranties of merchantability and fitness for a particular purpose. Neither the publisher nor its dealers or distributors assume any liability for any alleged or actual damages arising from the use of this program. (Some states do not allow for the exclusion of implied warranties, so the exclusion may not apply to you.)